THE HABSBURG MONARCHY

The Habsburg Monarchy
From Enlightenment to Eclipse

ROBIN OKEY

First published in 2002 by PALGRAVE MACMILLAN™
175 Fifth Avenue, New York, N.Y. 10010 and
Houndmills, Basingstoke, Hampshire, England RG21 6XS.
Companies and representatives throughout the world.

PALGRAVE MACMILLAN is the global academic imprint of the
Palgrave Macmillan division of St. Martin's Press, LLC and of
Palgrave Macmillan Ltd. Macmillan® is a registered trademark in
the United States, United Kingdom and other countries. Palgrave is
a registered trademark in the European Union and other countries.

ISBN 0–312–23375–2 (hardback) ISBN 1–4039–39654–5
(paperback)

Library of Congress Cataloging-in-Publication Data
Okey, Robin.
The Habsburg monarchy: from enlightenment to eclipse / Robin
Okey

   p.   cm.
  Includes bibliographical references and index.
  ISBN 0–312–23375–2
  1. Habsburg, House of. 2. Austria—History—1519–1740.
3. Austria—History—1789–1900. 4. Nationalism—Austria.
5. Austria—Ethnic Relations. I. Title.

DB363.3H3 o44 2000
943.6'03—dc21   00–039007

First edition 2000 by St. Martin's Press, Scholarly and Reference
Division
175 Fifth Avenue, New York N.Y. 10010

A catalogue record for this book is available from the British
Library.

First Palgrave Macmillan edition, October 2002.
10 9 8 7 6 5 4 3 2 1

Printed in the United States of America.

Contents

Foreword

The Habsburg Monarchy for centuries loomed too large on the map of Europe to have been wholly neglected by historians after its fall in 1918. Events since 1989 have redirected attention to many of the lands it once incorporated and given prominence to the nationality issues for which it became notorious in its latter years. Nonetheless the sum of general works on the Monarchy in major languages remains small compared to those appearing every year on other Great Powers, despite the intensification of detailed research both in the United States, home of the *Austrian History Yearbook*, as well as in Austria and Hungary in particular of the old empire's Succession States. It is hoped that there will be a place, therefore, for a survey of the Monarchy from the later eighteenth century that takes account of advances in Habsburg studies since the publication of C.A. Macartney's magisterial *The Habsburg Empire* in 1968.

The two things best known about the empire, its dynastic character and its multi-national complexity, have both militated against its fuller study. At the popular level Habsburg history moves little outside the dynasty's wide-ranging cast of characters; in more academic concerns preoccupation with nationality questions has divided the field into a host of separate historiographies, cut off from each other by barriers of language and sometimes prejudice. In each case, the tendency to view the Monarchy as an exotic anomaly underplays the extent to which it experienced the same processes as most other European lands in the same period: urbanisation, embourgeoisement and proletarianisation; mass education and the growth of communications; the transition from absolutism to constitutionalism, and from religious prescription to competing secular and clerical norms. The social 'modernisation' of the Monarchy is the third great theme of its history in the generations before 1914. Yet far from diminishing the traditional themes of dynastic power and national confrontation, it heightens their interest by presenting them in the full context to which they belonged.

In particular, modern historiography has led the focus away from tendentious stress on the Monarchy in its final phase as 'prison of the peoples', or betrayed League of Nations before its time, to longer-term processes. More awareness of social cleavages in the Monarchy and of the extent to which they overlapped with ethnic ones has tended to reinforce, if less harshly, the view of Oscar Jászi's pioneering *The Dissolution of the Habsburg Monarchy* (1929) that the balance of forces was shifting against the Monarchy's chances of survival, irrespective of the First World War which brought its doom. The collapse of multi-national states in eastern Europe since 1989 and their difficulties elsewhere point in the same direction. But the continued salience of the problem of multi-national community only makes the Habsburg Empire more interesting as the classic field for study of its pathology. How did social and ethnic factors come to interact there? Did growing concern for social issues tend to marginalise nationality disputes, or exacerbate them? Was nationalism a 'zero-sum game', in the sense of permitting only winners or losers, or were compromises reached which were acceptable to more than one side? Behind these questions is a broader one still. What are the most important elements in the maintenance of a multi-national polity? Is it the role of rational values of common citizenship and tolerance, such as the Habsburg Josephinist tradition championed – and its heirs in rationalism like the socialists thought could be further developed? Or emotive factors like dynastic loyalty and commonalities of culture and habit? Or again, the backbone of power and hierarchy, which the dynasty long represented and which the British historian Lord Acton saw in the leading role of a dominant nation, the Monarchy's Germans?

Of course, the great bulk of the Habsburg Monarchy's subjects never pondered these portentous questions, and the historian's main task is to follow them and try to recreate, however inadequately, the framework within which they lived their lives. To make this attempt is to encounter a distinctive ambience, which came to be marked by an intriguing mix of conservative and liberal values and a style in varying degrees both authoritarian and benign, which have left their imprint in the memory of peoples often little blessed thereafter. Perhaps the broadest way to formulate the problem of the later Habsburg monarchy is to ask whether its conservative–liberal accommodation to nineteenth-century 'modernity' was inextricably rooted in its hierarchical past, or whether it contained the seeds of further evolution into a democratic age.

The book's starting point, as given in its sub-title, is not quite self-explanatory. In 1765 Joseph II became Holy Roman Emperor and joint ruler of the Habsburg lands with his mother Maria Theresa.

To begin a more detailed account here, while giving the substance of the earlier Theresan reforms, seemed on balance better than to delay it till 1780, treating the great empress merely as background, or to take it right back to her accession in 1740.

Modern survey works are expected to provide more coverage of events than a generation ago, while not abandoning the social and economic perspectives then expected. To meet these requirements and to provide a sense of development in a polity whose experience in its last decades was one of gradually mounting crisis, each chapter in the second half of the book combines both thematic and narrative sections, the latter carrying the story forward. As satisfactory treatment of these three themes – political, economic and social – already makes for a long book, other topics, such as cultural and intellectual history, regretfully receive limited attention. Unavoidably, Austro-Germans, Magyars and Czechs are more fully treated than the other peoples of the Monarchy though an attempt has been made to keep them in view as much as possible. In the political sphere, military and diplomatic matters do not figure as prominently as often elsewhere, but this reflects no wish to challenge their great importance for the Monarchy. Since, however, many existing surveys give them more space than they do socio-economic or domestic political issues, this volume's contribution can be to redress the balance somewhat in terms of detail, while providing, it is hoped, a clear picture of the salient military and foreign political themes. More than one kind of history of the Monarchy can be written. If it is still objected – rightly – that these themes of 'high policy' preoccupied dynastic circles and that their realm's fate was particularly dependent on the balance of European politics, it is fair to note that they passed the great bulk of the empire's subjects by, including the nationalist politicians who increasingly limited the elite's real freedom of movement. The Monarchy's capacity for international action was notoriously constrained by its domestic ills. Ultimately it is its unusual domestic structure and experience, including of course their international repercussions, which ground its claim for general study.

No book on such a topic can lay claim to comprehensive coverage. Some freshness was attempted for this one in that it is based not just on English and German material but also on fairly wide reading in Magyar, Serbo-Croat and (largely recent works) Czech, with sparser reading of Polish, Slovene and Slovak. Since so many conventional facts could be adduced about the complex Habsburg realm, and

most to be fully accurate would require heavy qualification, it is
hoped that the preference sometimes for illustration and quotation
as aids to understanding will be forgiven. In slight modification of a
one-time convention whereby survey works were not footnoted,
references are provided for direct quotations or to confirm a few particularly piquant cases or specific historical points. Where historians'
general arguments are mentioned, the works concerned are identified in the relevant chapter bibliographies. Variant forms of place-
names are often given on initial mention, thereafter, mainly the
form used in modern atlases, except where English historical usage
still diverges for major towns: thus Reichenberg for Liberec, Lvov
for L'viv.

As someone ill-adapted to a networking age, I have known specialists in the field mainly through their works. I should like, though, to
express my thanks to a number of scholars who have helped me in
connection with it or in other ways: Professor Robert Evans of
Oxford for saving me from many errors, Professor László Péter of
London, University Professor Gerald Stourzh and Dr Peter Urbanitsch of Vienna, Professor Jan Havránek of Prague, Professor Mirjana Gross of Zagreb, Professor Dušan Kovač of Bratislava, Professor
Peter Vodopivec of Ljubljana, and also my colleagues at Warwick,
Professor Colin Jones and Dr Iain Smith.

ROBIN OKEY

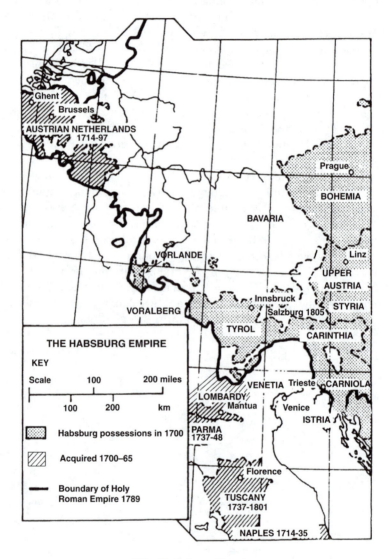

The Habsburg Empire

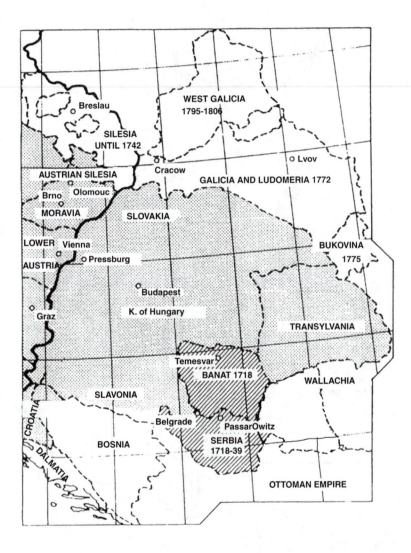

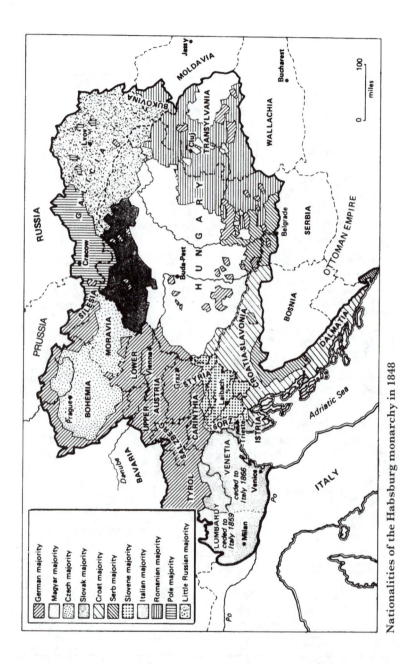

Nationalities of the Habsburg monarchy in 1848

Part I
Dynastic Empire, *c.* 1765–1867

1 Foundations

In 1782, when B.F. Hermann published his *Sketch of the Physical Constitution of the Austrian States*, most of the lands he discussed had been under a common ruler for two and a half centuries. Yet as his title showed they had still not acquired an official collective name. Telltale nomenclature betrays the problem which was henceforth to dog the empire increasingly to the end of its days: its origin as a dynastic rather than ethnic union in a continent of emerging nationalisms. Even in the eighteenth century, when none expected ethnic and political boundaries to coincide, the Habsburg lands stood out for the number of self-conscious national traditions they encompassed. But what lends this problem its peculiar interest is not so much that it remained ultimately unsolved as that elements of identity became as strong as they did. When Hermann wrote, an attempt was being made to create a new cohesion in the Habsburg Empire, an attempt which, for all its failings, helped ensure that in the second half of the empire's life its subjects were linked in many more ways than by loyalty to a family. The later Monarchy's bureaucratic traditions – cumbersome but relatively fair and efficient; the German cultural orientation of its educated classes; the conjunction of manufacturing and agrarian zones and of a semi-official Catholic Church and tolerated religious minorities: all this goes back to the reform period of the second half of the eighteenth century. In this sense these years saw the foundation of the Monarchy as it is still remembered vividly in much of the region today. Much as the reforms owed to monarchical initiative, they also reflected the impact on the Habsburg lands of broader central European, indeed, European developments. It is the interplay between its own complex structures and such wider influences in making and unmaking a multi-national polity which gives the Habsburg Monarchy its distinctive place in modern European history, and which will be the subject of this book.

Government and Elites

The dynasty's rise to prominence began when Rudolf of Habsburg, of a family owning lands in southern Germany and Alsace, seized the

Alpine duchies of Austria and Styria from the Bohemian king Otakar in 1278. Originating as the 'Eastern march' of Charlemagne's Christian empire and long ruled by the Babenbergs from the still older Roman frontier fortress of Vindobona (Vienna), Austria became the nucleus from which, over the next couple of centuries, Rudolf's descendants extended their control westwards to the Tyrol and Vorarlberg, and south-west through the German–Slav borderlands of Carinthia and Carnolia to the Italian Adriatic port of Trieste and the county of Gorizia. From 1445 till 1792 the head of the family was regularly elected Holy Roman Emperor. Achievement as this was, the real break-through came in 1519–26 when, as a result of previous marriage compacts, two grandsons of the Emperor Maximilian, Charles and Ferdinand, inherited respectively the thrones of Spain, and of Hungary and Bohemia. The kingdom of Hungary was in union with that of Croatia, and with Bohemia went the provinces of Moravia and Silesia, collectively known as the Czech lands. Though the territories of the eastern and western inheritances were kept separate, Habsburgs in the sixteenth century emerged predominant in the new world and the old.

Marriage compacts were a regular feature of late medieval politics and frequently resulted in temporary unions of crowns. What gave the Habsburg accession in Hungary and Bohemia unusual permanence was the combination of the Turkish threat and the Counter-Reformation. Ferdinand became king of these two countries because in 1526 his predecessor, Louis, had died childless on the battlefield of Mohács against the Turks. Where nation-states – Bulgaria, Serbia, then Hungary – had failed, the Habsburgs became the supranational defenders of Christianity against Islam. They also became the bulwark of Catholicism against the Protestant-dominated noble estates and towns of east-central Europe. The suppression of Protestantism thus aided them in a movement towards absolutism similar to that gathering strength almost throughout early modern Europe.

Bohemia was the crucial case here. The routing of Bohemian Protestant rebels at the Battle of the White Mountain outside Prague in 1620 led to Habsburg assumption of key rights of the Bohemian Diet over legislation, citizenship and appointments, and – through expropriation or exile – accelerated the displacement of a broad-based native middle nobility by a small aristocracy, exclusively Catholic and largely non-Czech. While other factors than Habsburg vengeance also played their part, by *c.*1770 Bohemian knightly families had revenues amounting to no more than 4% of those of the

nobility as a whole, instead of a half two centuries before. The proscription of Protestantism was accompanied by the re-endowment
of the Catholic Church, a massive programme of church building and the promotion of the cult of the fourteenth-century Bohemian saint Jan of Nepomuk to implant notions of *Bohemia Sacra* − a
Counter-Reformation patriotism − in an initially sullen population.
The fact that Jan of Nepomuk held the dedication of more than half
the statues erected in the German-speaking diocese of Vienna in the
twenty years since his tongue was discovered 'incorrupt' in 1717
shows how the flamboyant symbols and practices of Baroque Catholicism were meant to serve as a binding link between all Habsburg
lands and peoples. Up to 150,000 people attended the annual pil-
grimages to the Styrian miracle site of Maria Zell in the eighteenth
century, where the nonagenarian Empress Zita, last surviving Habsburg sovereign, paid homage in 1985 after a lifetime's exile. By this
time restored Catholicism and a German-speaking aristocracy so
linked the provinces of the Bohemian Crown with the Habsburgs'
original Alpine possessions that both areas were equally deemed to
be part of the dynasty's 'Hereditary Lands'.

In Hungary too the Counter-Reformation played an important
role in the establishment of Habsburg power. Yet here the situation
was more complex. For a century and a half the Turks held the bulk
of central Hungary, while to the east the province of Transylvania
was an autonomous state ruled by a line of Hungarian Protestant
princes. Both before and after the liberation of nearly all Hungary
from the Turks by 1699 there were lengthy wars between the Habsburgs and native opponents, such that the final peace of Szatmár
(1711) bore something of a compromise character. The native
upper class survived to a much greater degree than in the Czech
lands and at least a quarter of the total population of Hungary
remained Protestant, including a Calvinist majority among Magyar
speakers east of the river Tisza; the less numerous Lutherans of north
Hungary were mainly German or Slovak. Habsburg sovereigns were
still obliged to take an oath to uphold Hungary's rights. The Hungarian Diet and the locally self-governing county units retained significant powers. While the Renewed Ordinance of 1627 made
German, mother tongue of the Habsburgs, equal with Czech in the
administration of Bohemia, polyglot Hungary retained Latin as its
official language.

The common distinction between an absolutist Austria and Bohemia and a constitutional Hungary can, however, be overdrawn.

In an age of poor communications and low literacy, monarchical absolutism ran up against limitations even in the Austro-Bohemian lands, whose Diets till the mid-eighteenth century kept a substantial administrative role and a real right to grant direct taxation – the so-called *contributio* for military purposes. Dynastic authority at this level rested on a convergence of its interests with those of provincial magnate elites, expressed in provincial officials' dual responsibility to Diet and sovereign. On the other hand, Hungary's freedoms had narrow limits. Like the rest of the Monarchy in certain fields she was effectively subject to central monarchical institutions, though Hungarian participation in them was usually slight: the Hofkriegsrat (War Council) for military affairs, the State Chancellery, detached from the Austrian General Chancellery in 1742, for foreign policy, the Hofkammer (Court Chamber) which dominated the Hungarian Kammer, for the administration of Crown estates, customs and excise, monopolies and other regalian (royal) economic prerogatives. From 1527 a variously named Privy Council or Privy Conference oversaw problems of the Monarchy as a whole. Moreover, Hungarian constitutionalism, a perhaps anachronistic term, remained undeveloped. Political rights of any kind were confined to the noble class. The Hungarian Diet retained legislative powers – granting the government the right to hold a standing army in Hungary in 1715 – but was rarely summoned in the eighteenth century and barely challenged the Crown's assumption of responsibility for religious matters, or for expanding policy fields like education or welfare, not central to traditional noble concerns. Since Hungarian law also assured the monarch a wide prerogative in matters of appointment, ennoblement and regalian rights, the Lieutenancy Council set up in Pressburg (modern Bratislava) in 1723, responsible to a Hungarian Chancellery in Vienna, developed a considerable role in Hungarian life. Transylvania remained apart, with its own Diet and Chancellor, and the 'Military Frontier' built up since the sixteenth century as bulwark along the Turkish border was directly administered by the Hofkriegsrat. In these circumstances Hungarian constitutionalism took on a beleagered guise, amounting to the enunciation of principles – like regular Diets – rather than their enforcement and deriving its real strength from the stubborn caste spirit of the nobles who ran the most distinctively Hungarian institutions, the courts and the counties.

Yet the distinction between Hungary and Bohemia under Habsburg rule retains its importance. Though the Hungarian great magnates also became, with rare exceptions, an exclusively Catholic body, incomers remained a minority in their ranks. Above all, a large and often Protestant gentry class remained, for all the restrictions reiterated in 1731 on Protestants' freedom of worship and public role. Hungary and Bohemia's relations to the dynasty showed early the pattern of asymmetry which was to culminate in the Austro-Hungarian 'Dualism' of 1867–1918.

Till the end of the seventeenth century, the Turkish occupation of central Hungary, the seniority of the Spanish Habsburgs and the role of the leading German Habsburg as head of the amorphous but still prestigious 'Holy Roman Empire of the German Nation' tended to obscure the identity of the latter's dynastic lands as an empire in its own right. The extinction of the Spanish line of the family in 1700 and increasing enfeeblement of Turkey and the Holy Roman Empire changed this situation and increased the saliency of the 'Austrian Monarchy', though till 1804 the imperial style of its rulers continued to derive from the ancient title of Charlemagne. Charles VI's 'Pragmatic Sanction' of 1713, eventually adopted by the Estates of all his dynastic lands, took them a step nearer to common statehood, for as well as asserting the undivided inheritance of these lands in the Habsburg line, both male and female, it also proclaimed the obligation of common defence. The Pragmatic Sanction was designed to ensure the succession to a sovereign who had at that time no heirs and later a daughter – Maria Theresa – rather than a son. In the formal sense it failed because on Charles VI's death in 1740 Bavarian claims precipitated the War of Austrian Succession (1740–48), begun by Frederick II of Prussia's seizure of Silesia. To the traditional Habsburg enmity with Bourbon France, theme of the previous wars of the Spanish succession (1700–13), was now added a feud with upstart Prussian Hohenzollerns. But the famous rallying of the 1741 Hungarian noble Diet to their young queen's cause showed that a viable polity had nonetheless come into existence. Linked by ties of loyalty and self-interest, dynasty, magnates and Catholic hierarchy stood at the apex of what has been called a *höfische Gesellschaft* or court-orientated society, whose leading positions in Church and state were held by members of the magnate elite, largely created by the Habsburgs themselves. At this august level, at least, the Austrian Monarchy had acquired its own *esprit de corps*, if a fragile one, for many Bohemian and Upper Austrian nobles cooperated with the temporary Franco-Bavarian occupiers.

Thus eight aristocratic families monopolised the post of Royal Commissioner to the Bohemian Diets of 1627–98. In 1756 nine Hungarian bishops held between them twelve high sheriffships of Hungarian counties. Membership of most Austrian cathedral chapters required sixteen quarters of nobility. The most noteworthy overlap was at the top: as Apostolic King of Hungary the Habsburg emperor had the right to a veto in the Papal electoral conclave, exercised as late as 1903 through the Archbishop of Cracow. This union of throne, altar and noble seat was lubricated by wealth. The eighteenth-century Monarchy retained a system of 'hereditary subjection' (*Erbuntertänigkeit*) of feudal origin, whereby, excepting mainly the free peasants of the Tyrol and certain historically rooted free communities in Hungary, the great bulk of the land was held by the privileged orders. This land was categorised either as *dominical* (in Hungary, *allodial*), cultivated as the lord's demesne or let out on temporary terms to cottars, or as *rustical* (Hungary: *urbarial*), on which peasants had rights to the fruits of their labour on performance of a complex set of obligations. Wherever in the early modern period nobles turned towards the *Gutsherrschaft* system of direct demesne farming of their estates there had been pressure to expand dominical land at the peasants' expense; thus in late eighteenth-century Bohemia about two-fifths of land was dominical and in Hungary the lion's share, though the percentages were somewhat inflated by nobles' near monopoly of forest as opposed to arable. Peasant obligations, infinitely varied in detail, followed a roughly common pattern, including dues in cash and kind, services like carting and unpaid labour on the lords' demesne (the notorious *robota*), and the requirement to purchase the lord's wine or beer and use his mill. When an individual magnate might have 35,000 homes on his estates, as Prince Miklós Esterházy had on the three-fifths of Hungary for which figures exist in the survey of 1784–87, the resultant income could be huge – 700,000 florins a year (about £70,000) in this case, probably exceeded by the heads of the Schwarzenberg and Lobkowitz families. The ten wealthiest magnates of Bohemia around 1770 held property with a declared capital value of 71 million florins, by contrast to the five million florins capital of the thirty biggest merchants of flourishing Trieste in 1767. Clerical wealth was almost equally striking. The clergy's share of dominical revenues at this time varied from just over a sixth in once Protestant Bohemia to two-fifths in Upper and Lower Austria – and while the Archbishop of Esztergom had an income of 360,000 florins a year no

Hungarian town's annual revenue exceeded a hundred thousand until the 1790s.

To be sure, this wealth was often a condition for the public role magnates and clerics played in a society still bureaucratically under-developed. Prince Lichtenstein spent ten million florins of his own fortune overhauling Maria Theresa's artillery. The Esterházys and Pálffys maintained army regiments at their own expense. Great estates provided the work-forces and resources for the first manufac-turing ventures of Austrian mercantilism. The Hungarian National Theatre began with a troupe of actors who, like Haydn, had been in Esterházy employ, while its painted scenery came from the estate theatre of the Batthyánys. In Bohemia the theatre company of the Schwarzenberg castle at Krumlov played a not dissimilar role. With its 4268 tallow candles the illuminations of the most spectacular of Esterházy pageants in 1784 exceeded the 3445 oil lamps, six steps apart, which made Vienna the first regularly lit city in Europe, let alone the 300 lights introduced into Pest in 1790. But it was the dynasty which set the tone. No aristocrat could match the 300,000 volumes of the Court Library, available to the public before 12 a.m., or Schönbrunn palace's menagerie and botanical gardens, likewise opened up in 1752–53, or the great scientific expeditions dispatched by Habsburg rulers from 1755, which laid the foundations for the Austrian national museums of natural history and ethnography. A society moving towards 'modern' cultural concerns was still rooted in ancient institutions.

There was some place, too, for the towns in this picture, weak though they were. In the seventeenth and first half of the eighteenth centuries most urban populations failed to keep pace with overall demographic advance, as east-central European cities were detached from the trade route patterns of the Age of Discovery, nobles arro-gated to themselves control of the lucrative corn trade to the West and burgher homes within the walls yielded to noble town houses, monasteries and convents. Vienna, with 200,000 inhabitants and Prague with over 70,000 in 1780 were the only substantial cities in the Austro-Slav lands, while in Hungary Pressburg alone, at 30,000, was built largely in stone. Most town-dwellers, moreover, were not 'burghers' endowed with citizenship rights; the majority were pri-marily engaged in agriculture, particularly in the so-called village towns of the Hungarian plain, where peasants and others had come together for security in the troubled Turkish period. The Royal Free Towns which enjoyed charter status and burgher self-government were a small minority of urban settlements alongside the often more enterprising 'noble towns' on seigneurial land – which sometimes purchased themselves a precarious autonomy – and the yet humbler 'market-places' (*Marktflecken*), mere overgrown villages with rights of market. Thus while Hungary had some 700 market settlements and one-fifth of its people lived in agglomerations of more than two thousand, only 5% inhabited the forty or so Royal Free Towns and less than 2% were house owners or established artisans in these. The Austro-Bohemian lands showed a similar, if somewhat denser pattern, with 72 larger towns, 377 smaller ones and 888 market-places recorded in 1762.

Yet the absorption of this small-scale urban world into the nexus of Habsburg power did not mean total insignificance. Towns were the centres of administration, education and culture. The elegant public buildings of this period remain the best testimony to a common past from Slovak Bratislava to Croatian Zagreb and Transylvanian Cluj (Kolozsvár). Baroque devotional life was at its most intense in the towns, not the under-resourced countryside; Vienna had 103 lay confraternities in 1780. Here too were the agencies of charity, the hospices, chantries and dispensaries of the traditional order and the earliest hospitals, asylums, orphanages and foundling homes of modern type. While education at village level remained primitive and for the majority non-existent, the towns boasted a relatively developed network of secondary schools, usually Jesuit or Piarist but in Hungary also Lutheran and Calvinist, whose non-privileged graduates, inured by study to strict discipline and thankful for any security in a hard world, provided their betters with the administrative and clerical duties the court-orientated society required. Mid-eighteenth-century Hungary, where at most a quarter of children had any primary education, had some 130 secondary schools of various kinds.

Another role of the towns was to aid the dissemination of German as the means of communication between the Monarchy's interlocking elites. Medieval German settlements in the Czech lands, Slovakia and Transylvania were supplemented by fresh movements of German speakers into the towns of inner Bohemia-Moravia, particularly Prague, from the late seventeenth century and into depopulated Hungary after the Turkish withdrawal. The Germanising process in the towns no doubt assisted the growing fashion for German in the upper classes. In the 1720s the Esterházy children began to be educated in German rather than their native Hungarian. By the 1780s the Hungarian Chief Justice Ürményi was reportedly incompetent in his national tongue. Already by mid-century the bulk of the Bohemian upper middle classes and almost the entire aristocracy, including the minority of Czech descent, had made German their first language.

The linguistic trend was undoubtedly linked with shifts in social consciousness in elite circles of the consolidating Monarchy, though these were neither abrupt nor uniform. While Count Harrach, the last Bohemian Chancellor, retired to his office and wept after proclaiming his Chancellery abolished on Maria Theresa's orders in 1749, Prince Kaunitz, the Empress's greatest minister and himself of Moravian Czech descent, failed to understand how people could put their 'regional' loyalties before the interests of the 'state'. The Habsburg achievement was to foster this latter sense of a wider allegiance among large sections of the Monarchy's upper classes. It might be an allegiance more narrowly dynastic than Kaunitz's, like that of the Schwarzenberg who, shot in a hunting accident by Charles VI, exclaimed before dying, 'It was ever my duty to give my life for my sovereign'.[1] It might not be wholly reliable, as in temporary defections of 1741. But this is outweighed by the loyalty in the crisis of the previously restless Hungarian nobility. The overall tendency was plain.

This was further shown in the fact that no Bohemian nobles were executed or dispossessed after 1741, unlike the Croatian frondeurs Frankopan and Zrinski seventy years earlier. A civilising of manners was taking place which was a feature of the eighteenth century. The dynasty's trump-card was that this trend, hailed by contemporaries, was associated with the assertion of monarchical authority and an abatement of particularism and 'feudalism'. The Viennese university professor Justi, commenting in 1764 on the decline in 'upheavals' in contemporary society, ascribed it to the growth of standing armies[2] – one of the main features of absolutist rule. In becoming more regular and less arbitrary, power was also becoming more centralised. This process might arouse the nostalgia of a Harrach, but the complementarity of interests of monarch and aristocracy had become too great for the exponents of creeping absolutism to fear an effective traditionalist backlash. Besides, their actions could usually be justified in terms of a royal prerogative acknowledged in feudal precept, only now more vigorously exercised. One development, minor in itself, reveals the underlying process at work. In 1749 the *Ritterakademie* founded by the Lower Austrian Provincial Diet passed under central government control. Such academies had been founded to train nobles for employment, but as the chief source of noble employment was now the expanding state administration the need for independence no longer seemed so pressing. In an age of increasing interdependence of government and elites, the government held the cards. By the reign of Maria Theresa the main challenge it faced was not from mutinous Hungarians or Bohemians, but from a politically more integrated Prussia, hoping to find in the still diffusely organised Monarchy easy game for its ambitions.

Lands and Peoples

Frederick the Great's bold seizure of Austrian Silesia in 1740 reflected awareness of the shallow base of Habsburg power. Only a few hundred aristocratic families comprised the multi-cultural elite through which the dynasty habitually worked. Beneath it were the thousands of gentry, tens of thousands of petty nobles and burghers, hundreds of thousands of artisans and urban workers, and at the bottom millions of peasants whose traditions still owed little or nothing to Habsburg rule. Here loyalties went to the assorted kingdoms, principalities, archduchies, duchies, counties and other entities subject to the Pragmatic Sanction, which jealously guarded their separate legal codes, their historic tribunals, even their own tariffs.

Central government in such a context could hardly be a matter of fine tuning, especially when the knowledge available in educated circles remained disconcertingly imprecise. 'Some writers will have the number of towns in Moravia at 500 and the villages at 15,000', mused the famous traveller Keysler, though adding tartly that this and another estimate of 33,559 were exaggerations.[3] Confidential statistical information increasingly compiled by government from the 1750s shows that the authorities hopelessly underestimated the population of Hungary until the census of 1787. Nor did the profusion of weights and measures help. The 'geometric' German mile, Keysler noted, numbered 15 to a degree of longitude (about four English miles) but as 'computed' it was often five to six English miles; the Bohemian mile, fixed by King Otakar in 1268, was a third shorter at only 4755 geometric paces!

The bureaucratic and statistical incoherence of pre-modern society was compounded by the Habsburg lands' emphatically multi-national structure. Excepting far-flung possessions in the

Austrian Netherlands, roughly, modern Belgium, and the duchies of Milan and Mantua in Lombardy (all acquired in 1714–15) and the scattered *Vorlande* (including Freiburg) in south-west Germany, the core of the Monarchy still contained a dozen nationalities, albeit in a relatively compact territory (by 1780) of over 230,000 sqare miles, 90% of which was drained by the Danube. The population in this area was then approaching 22 million (the Hungarian lands contributing some 45%, the Czech and Alpine lands 40%, Galicia and the Bukovina 15%) with another 2.4 million in Belgium and 1.5 million in north Italy. Vienna, sited where the Danube rounds the Alpine outliers of the Vienna Woods and moves south, east and south through the Hungarian plain (the *Alföld*)was thus only 134 miles from Budapest and 40 miles from Bratislava, Hungary's medieval and early modern capitals respectively. Prague lay 180 miles to the north-west. This made Vienna the hub of a wheel whose three chief spokes since 1526 had been German, Magyar and Czech, making up in turn approximately a quarter, a fifth and a sixth of the population of the central lands.

Of these three major groups it was the German speakers on whom the dynasty could most naturally rely. Divided between the Alpine and Czech lands, and scattered through Hungary and Transylvania, they had never acquired a collective identity to match their historic loyalties to province, dynasty and, where relevant, Holy Roman Empire. If the statistician Joseph Rohrer's exclamation 'To the mountains, my friends!' and the vivid description of the Semmering pass in his work of 1804 on 'the western provinces of the Austrian state' suggest the beginnings of an Austrian self-perception in modern terms, he still expected his readers' response to be a mutter about avalanches.[4]

In fact, the two and a quarter million inhabitants of the lands of present-day Austria, as of 1754, had the least fraught relations with the dynasty, partly through the relatively peaceful course of the Counter-Reformation there, though Protestant remnants could still be expelled in the 1750s. The lesser nobles once associated with Protestantism, too, had lost ground, as in Bohemia, but less drastically. The noble *latifundia* associated with the shift to the *Gutsherrschaft* system of arable-based demesne farming remained rare, only 9% of noble revenues coming from the demesne in Lower Austria in 1754, as opposed to 38% in Bohemia. The role of the unpopular feudal *robota* was correspondingly restricted, with quite high formal labour requirements of two to four days a week (much lower in

Upper Austria) being extensively commuted to money payments. Indeed, Austrian nobles' income from their peasants came mainly in cash, through commutations, fines imposed in 'patrimonial' or noble courts, taxes on documents needed by peasants, charges for transfer and inheritance of peasant plots, and the sale of noble beer and wine. Onerous as these exactions were – a reflection of the fact that noble estates formed the basic units of local government – the importance of cash commutation and of written documents suggests a peasant community living some way above subsistence level, at least for its better-off members. By the eighteenth century population growth had made for a quite sharply differentiated rural society, where income was regularly supplemented by domestic industry, carting or other ways. The holders of 'full plots' on whom the labour services mentioned above were due had become relatively few and the term peasant (*Bauer*) was conventionally applied to those who held a quarter-plot or more, with services scaled down proportionately. The majority of the rural community already fell into the ranks of cottars (*Kleinhaüsler*), various grades of *Innleute* (sub-letters on *Bauer* land or *Bauer* family dependants) and finally *Gesinde* or domestic servants. By the late eighteenth century the single common room of the traditional house had become the servants' quarters, with the *Bauer*'s private parlour alongside. As the village community lost its old self-regulative functions, so he in his homestead assumed a paternalist role in keeping with the mores of the court-orientated society. In the Salzburg Pinzgau district at the end of the century peasant households might have ten to fifteen servants apiece.

Nonetheless, with the exception of the wine-growing peasantry in the vicinity of Vienna, with their stone houses, even their morning coffee, the peasant lifestyle remained much simpler than the urban. Rye bread with curds, washed down with water, was more common than the wheaten bread, wine, beer and regular meat of the cities; rural meat consumption in 1800 was a third that of Vienna. Spoons were used, personally marked for individual use, though not yet forks or plates. But Austrian peasants did not lack confidence. 'Look, my dear Empress,' young Peter Prosch began a begging letter to Maria Theresa, 'I am a poor lad without mother and father, lodging here at my sister's ... and one night I dreamed of you since I have heard what a good monarch you are.'[5] Simon Hollnmeister (1737–1823) made some twenty trips to Vienna on behalf of his village community. Whatever lay behind his claim to his fellow peasants that he had often sat by the stove talking to the Emperor of 'this and that' as the Empress served them cold meats,[6] it could only have been made in a society where paternalism was a reality.

Self-confidence seems all the more to have been a trait of the Viennese, noted for their much remarked pride in the capital status of their bustling city, with its gates open day and night, its five and a half thousand resident foreigners and its house-maids who wore bespoke clothes. A quarter of the inhabitants of the inner city were in some way or other in the employ of the court. But the superiority syndrome went further than the capital. A Styrian German, wrote a contemporary, would be ashamed to go barefooted or booted rather than shoed, as did the 'Wends' (Slovenes) from the south of the province. Bartenstein, one of Maria Theresa's ministers, commented on the energy of the German townspeople of Bohemia and the very different spirit of their Czech neighbours. The widespread role of German speakers as the landowning and bourgeois class in Slav areas obviously influenced such perspectives, but of whatever class the German-speaking population of the Monarchy saw themselves as a cut above the rest.

The comparison was usually made with the Slavs, most sharply with the Czechs. German-language accounts of eighteenth-century Bohemia convey a sense of impotent alienation on the part of a Czech under-class not dissimilar to pictures of the Gaelic-speaking peasantry of Ireland in the same period. These sturdy workers, good soldier material, wrote one observer in 1757, had the potential talent for profitable employment, but the serfdom under which they groaned had made them fearful and impoverished, 'savage and vengeful'. Another in 1794 noted the Czechs' 'blind obedience and cringing denial of the feeling of human dignity'.[7] It was the graphically named *Stockböhmen* or monoglot Czech speakers who were the particular object of these remarks, as opposed to the 'utraquists' or bilingual Bohemians of Czech mother tongue, and the German speakers of the towns and the mountain rim enclosing the gently undulating inner Bohemian plateau. Germans were over a third of the total population. Equating the Bohemian Germans with Irish Protestants and the utraquists with the eighteenth-century Irish Catholic urban middle class enables the Irish parallel to be drawn still further. In each case defeat of the native elites in the early modern period had taken on the appearance of an irreparable historical reverse, reducing the leaderless masses into hewers of wood and drawers of water. Little more than a century after the Czech Diet of 1615 had made Czech the sole official language of the realm, it had been virtually discarded by the upper class. When in the 1770s the Rosenmüller family sold the concession for the newspaper *Český postillon*, founded in 1719 in a vain attempt to get the Bohemian elite to read the provincial news in Czech, the new concessionaire could raise only nine subscribers.

But though enforced Counter-Reformation had deprived the Czechs, a mainly Protestant people before 1620, of their religion, at least it had put them on the same level as their Austrian Catholic conquerors according to a key criterion of the age. The utraquists of Czech background were therefore less marginal than the English-speaking Catholics of Ireland in the public administration of their country, which, besides, still derived in many ways from the old Czech state and even gave the Czech language a certain ceremonial precedence, rather like French in the Jersey States today. The bilingualism of the utraquists, a largely educated urban group, had a two-fold significance. It encouraged Germans to believe that Bohemia was, in all essentials, a German province, or at least in transition to becoming so, while ensuring a residue of Czech sentiment beyond the village level, and a modest infrastrucure for a Czech world largely beyond German gaze, in terms of pastoral care and primary education in the mother tongue. The role of the utraquists was thus to soften socio-ethnic antitheses in Bohemia as compared to Ireland. Its people, incidentally, had a reputation as the most musical in central Europe, instrumental music teaching being common even in elementary schools: music would retain a prominent place in the Monarchy's life till its end.

Yet the screwing up of *robota* obligations and the noble appropriation of peasant rustical land in the early modern period created tensions in Bohemia not alleviated by ineffective royal patents of 1680, 1717 and 1738. For all some historians' querying of the term serfdom in the Habsburg context, particularly in its German form *Leibeigenschaft*, with its implication of peasant chattel status – Habsburg peasants unlike Tsarist ones could not be sold without their land – peasants' rights, like that to court action, depended in practice on the cooperation of noble-dominated authorities. Moreover, they were subjected in Bohemia, Hungary and Poland to intimidatory corporal punishment to a degree unknown in the Austro-German lands. It is thus not surprising that travellers of the Enlightenment stressed the social roots of the resentments of the *Stockböhmen*. Some recent Irish historiography suggests, however, that continuing ethnic alienation may play a compounding role in such cases. The picture is not clear-cut. In time the Habsburgs undoubtedly won the acceptance, even loyalty, most people usually accord their rulers; the richest vein of surviving Czech popular ballads centre round soldiering for Maria Theresa in the Seven Years War (1757–63). Nervous contemporaries exaggerated the links of underground chiliastic sentiment among the poor to memories of the proto-Protestant martyr Jan Hus, burnt at the stake in 1415. But Baron Riesbeck's observation in 1787 of 'a secret hatred to the Germans' arising from 'a kind of national pride' matches Count Hartig in 1850 on the 'secret hatred of the Czechs against the Germans which has never been extinguished' too closely not to suggest some persistence of popular ethnic sentiment.[8] Eighteenth-century travellers noted Czechs' reluctance to speak German to strangers even when they knew the language. Bohemia was not natural Habsburg territory in the way that German-speaking Austria was.

Was this true of Austria's other non-German lands? While it should not be overlooked, the ethnic sentiment of the time was unlike modern nationalism. Peasant identity was a diffuse mix of religious, linguistic, social and regional factors. 'National consciousness' with a coherent political thrust existed for the most part only where 'historic nations', i.e. nations which had had a state of their own, retained a privileged elite, as in Hungary. It was memories of Bohemian independence, in fair measure, which gave Bohemian Slavs their particular identity. Even the Czech speakers of Moravia, whom contemporaries dauntingly divided into Bohemian Moravians, Hannakites, Moravian Slovaks and Moravian Wallachs (or mountain Slovaks!), could not simply be equated in feeling with their Bohemian neighbours as part of a single Czech nation. For one thing, they lived more interspersed with the Moravian German minority and relationships between the two language groups were warmer than in Bohemia.

The 900,000 Slovenes living athwart the route from Vienna to the Adriatic were an unambiguously 'non-historic' people, criss-crossed by regional and dialect differences in their Alpine homeland, the size of Wales. Over the thousand years that they had lived under Austro-German rule their territory had contracted leaving a Slovene majority only in the province of Carniola with its capital Laibach (modern Ljubljana) and minorities abutting Germans in Styria and Carinthia, and Italians in Gorizia and Trieste. The Slovene language, similar to Serbo-Croat, had flowered in written form only during the short-lived Slovene Reformation, though a trickle of pastoral and polemical publications continued in Counter-Reformation times. Marko Pohlin's *Carniolan Grammar*, published in German in 1768, albeit resentful of neglect of the native tongue, showed in its title how little a collective Slovene identity had yet emerged – the term had first been used in a roughly modern sense eighteen years before. Only 3% of Carniolan children attended school in 1780. The tiny Slovene people, still 93% peasant *c.* 1800 and with no historic axe to grind, for long posed no questions for Habsburg power.

It was otherwise with the Poles of Galicia, who entered the Habsburg orbit only in 1772, on the first partition of Poland by Austria, Prussia and Russia. The Poles were a historic nation *par excellence*, or rather some of them, for the identification of the nobility with the Polish state at the expense of the non-privileged classes had so weakened the body politic that Galicia presented late eighteenth-century Austria more with practical administrative than with national problems. The Galician nobility, some 141,000 strong in a population of 2.3 million in 1773, and divided into great magnates and numerous lesser gentry, appeared to contemporaries to be even ethnically distinct from the Polish-speaking peasantry; these, the so-called Mazurians, were described in similar terms to the *Stockböhmen*. Polish landlords dominated not only the Mazurians in west Galicia but also the Ruthenian majority in the east of the province, whose language was closer to Russian than to Polish. East Galicia is the modern West Ukraine, the cutting edge of contemporary Ukrainian nationalism. Its eighteenth-century inhabitants, however, lacked this overriding identity. Divided by observers into plain-dwelling 'Red Ruthenians' and mountain 'Pokutians', they shared only the Uniate or Greek Catholic Church, with its Orthodox-style liturgy and married clergy, yet loyalty to Rome. It had been introduced by their Polish masters to distance this originally Orthodox people from Tsarist Russia. All but half a dozen Galician towns were subject to noble as well as king, though the average lesser noble lived in a cottage. A large Jewish population subsisted in the interstices of a generally harsh feudal regime. Elsewhere Jews, who were to play so big a role in the Monarchy's later history, were still few, perhaps 30,000 to 40,000 each in Bohemia and Hungary in mid-century, the latter largely rural and increasing rapidly, partly through immigration of the former, who suffered restrictions even on their freedom to marry; Vienna's 550 Jews in 1777 already included wealthy banking families like the Eskeles and Arnsteins. Thus in its 175,000 Jews (*c.* 1773) Galicia showed again that it was separated from German Austria or

even Slavic Bohemia by more than the mountain barrier of the Carpathians. Abutting Galicia on the east, Bukovina, a small province
ceded Austria by Turkey in 1774–75, contained Ruthenians, Romanians and Jews.

Hungary, however, remained the most bafflingly diverse and politically problematic of Habsburg lands. In the words of the British
envoy in 1774, it was 'so unlike the countries that surround it, that in
two days' journey from hence [i.e. Vienna], I thought myself already
removed to the other side of the terraqueous globe', among 'hordes'
who had, he declared, originated from as far apart as the Chinese
Wall and the White Sea, Saxony and Rome, without finding over
the centuries 'sufficient reason for . . . moulding down their opposite
peculiarities into one uniform national character'.[9] The Magyars,
however, a people of non-Indo-European linguistic origin who had
entered the Danube basin in the late ninth century, provided the
cement which till 1918 united the central Hungarian plain and encircling mountains in the 'lands of the Crown of St. Stephen', so-called
after the first Hungarian ruler to be crowned king, in AD 1000. Probably a majority in these lands in the Middle Ages, the Magyars were
reduced by Turkish invasion, non-Magyar encroachment and Habsburg resettlement policies to perhaps 40% in the later eighteenth
century. Yet the Magyar character of the state was preserved by
restriction on participation in the *natio* or political nation to the nobility alone, overwhelmingly of Magyar or assimilated Magyar stock.

Of course, the 160 or so great magnates on whom Habsburg power
could especially rely – there were a further thirty in Transylvania –
held a disproportionate share of the land. West of the Danube 47% of
peasant land in 1767 was in the hands of just 28 lords. But ultimately
it was the more numerous *bene possessionati* or middle nobility who ran
the county administrations with their rumbustious triennial elections
and competed to be county deputy sheriff, the real county executive
officer rather than the high sheriffs appointed by the Crown. Moreover, Calvinism was strongly represented in the middle nobility,
many of whom saw it as the 'Magyar faith' which the Habsburgs
had failed to crush. Cut off from the highest levels of wealth and
power, Hungarian Protestants zealously defended their remaining
institutions, like the great Calvinist colleges of Debrecen and Sáros-
patak and the Lutheran *lycées* of north Hungary, as well as their links
with their co-religionists abroad. The linguistic reformer Ferenc
Kazinczy (1759–1831) has left an affectionate portrait of his Calvinist grandfather, a long-serving county court judge. His life in an

unpretentious house of adobe and thatch revolved around morning prayers, visits to his well-stocked barn, wine-cellars and stables, before settling down in front of the house to chat with passers-by and read pious works or German papers brought him from students abroad.[10] The 'liberties' such men defended from Habsburg absolutism were nobles' sole right to public office and their exemption from taxation and military conscription – except for the feudal levy or *insurrectio* which nobles voluntarily took upon themselves, as on Maria Theresa's behalf in 1741. For Protestant nobles, though, embattled religious freedoms were also at stake, and an element of wider solidarity with the non-noble lineages of pastors and college teachers who provided the majority of Protestant students abroad – seven hundred permits for such study were granted for one sixteen-year period in the later eighteenth century. The proliferation of small nobles, more numerous in many areas than parliamentary voters in pre-1832 Britain, also lent the anti-Habsburg *fronde* its populist allure. Perhaps three-quarters of all nobles belonged to the petty nobility: whether on the fringes of middle noble status (social historians see the transition occuring between owners of 100 to 300 yokes of land or 143 to 429 acres); joint-holding squireens; impoverished small-holders; or the *armalistae* who had been ennobled without land and often offered their services to their landed brethen.

Naturally, the peasants of Hungary fully reflected the country's ethnic diversity. Slovaks and Ruthenes predominated in the Carpathians to the north and north-east; Romanians, with Lutheran Saxons, in Transylvania; Serbs and German Catholic Swabians in the southern plains. But Magyars and non-Magyars shared a common backwardness. Except in parts of Transdanubia to the west and in German areas agriculture was at the two-field or even slash-and-burn stage of development. Peasants built their own homes and made their own clothes and furniture. The round form of the Finno-Ugrian house of the Magyars' ancestors was still reflected in shepherds' huts. Backwardness made for stronger traditions of village community than in Austria. While in general pressures on peasants were on the increase – Transylvanian taxes rose four to ten times in the eighteenth century – local research has also shown interesting evidence of resilience. Nobles did not always succeed in usurping the appointment of village headman, Esterházy estate villagers kept the right to dispose of their plots and some noble jurists accorded peasants virtual property rights to their vineyards and to land they had cleared themselves. The extended communal family existed, with variants, among Magyars and non-Magyars, though it flourished best in its south Slav *zadruga* form. The immensely prolific folk poetry and song that was to yield scores of thousands of examples in the Romantic age likewise revealed both particular and universal traits. Alongside the Finno-Ugrian motifs scholars have traced in Magyar peasant lore were themes found in many lands: the girl who dances herself to death, the soldier who wishes his cloth-wrapped heart to be sent to his loved one, the Bluebeard who locks maidens away in a secret room in a castle . . . The fifteenth-century Hungarian king Matthias Corvinus became a folk hero in Slovak and Slovene popular culture, and it was to his memory that the Serbo-Croat speakers of the Military Frontier appealed in their rising of 1755. Peasant life showed an eclectic profundity alien both to Enlightened reason and the later categories of nationalism.

Yet not all non-Magyars in Hungary were merely peasant, 'non-historic' peoples. The Croats of the south-west had retained elements of autonomy since accepting a common king with the Magyars in 1102. Though Croatian society had developed along Hungarian lines, with a noble constitution and county administration, Croatia had its own governor, the Ban, and Diet, the Sabor, which had negotiated separately with Vienna in 1527 and over the Pragmatic Sanction in 1712. This was not enough, however, to prevent the truncating of the Croatian lands. The three counties of Slavonia after their liberation from the Turks had entered into a somewhat closer association with Hungary than the three counties of Croatia proper and had a class of large landholders as likely to speak German or Magyar as Croatian. The Civil Croatia and Civil Slavonia so constituted were, moreover, separated by part of the Military Frontier. The third part of the 'Triune Kingdom' of Croatia–Slavonia–Dalmatia as conceived by Croatian patriots, Dalmatia, had been ruled by Venice since the fourteenth century. The sense of Croatia's weakness and fragmentation but also of its merits as ancient Roman Illyria and forepost of Christian struggles against the Turks had inspired two different proto-nationalist responses at the end of the seventeenth century: one in the Panslav theories of Juraj Križanić of the greatness of the Slav race of which Croats were part, the other in Ritter-Vitezović's glorification of the alleged historic rights of the Croatian state. But mid-eighteenth-century Croatia was a society in slumber. Of the 65 works published between 1713 and 1750 in Zagreb, two-thirds were devotional and many of the rest were textbooks for the local Jesuit academy.

These splits between various foreign hegemonies, proud past and stunted present, Panslav and state right ideologies – though Vitezović in a sense linked the two – have contributed to the tension in modern Croatian history between aspiration and reality. To them must be added the divide between town and country. While the little towns of Civil Croatia were part and parcel of the Austrian Baroque, as the Dalmatian ports were of the Italian Renaissance, inner Dalmatia and the Military Frontier were home, in contemporary parlance, to some of the 'rudest' of the Slav peoples, whose lifestyle had acquired European notoriety from the Italian Alberto Fortis's work on the 'Morlaks' of Dalmatia, published in 1774. From their diet of coagulated milk, barley cakes and 'succulent herbs' to their smoky, insect-infested huts shared with cattle, and the mournful, monotonous songs with which they occupied their 'artless minds', Fortis's Slavs were the very image of patriarchal simplicity.[11] The other side of the coin was the notorious ferocity of the peasant soldiers of the Military Frontier, making up a quarter of the Habsburg forces in the Seven Years' War – and degraded by Austrian discipline, according to one later account (1787), from being 'open-hearted, hospitable, frank ... like all the children of nature' into 'a band of treacherous, tricking, cowardly robbers'.[12] Few peoples of their relatively small size have had such a complex history and social structure as the Croats.

The Military Frontiersmen held their plots as free peasants in return for army service when required. Actually, nearly a half of them were of Serb or Orthodox stock who had entered Catholic Croatia in flight from Ottoman rule in the Balkans. The largest migration, led by the Serbian Patriarch of Peć in 1690, had won from the Habsburg emperor the so-called Leopoldine Privileges, allowing Serbs religious toleration under their own elective church hierarchy in southern Hungary and Croatia. Here developed in the eighteenth century the most vigorous Serbian society since the fall of medieval Serbia to the Turks, focused around the growing mercantile centre of Novi Sad and the Orthodox metropolitan see of Karlowitz (Sremski Karlovci), with its wealthy monasteries. Serbian life was not without its problems: in the struggles of the settlers against Magyar feudal pressures and Catholic efforts to make them Uniates, above all in the battle to preserve the Privileges as a kind of national constitutional charter against Habsburg attempts to make the Karlowitz metropolitans their nominees and agents in the Serb community. The Privileges thus took the place of the 'historic rights' which all groups who claimed them sought to defend against incursions by the central power.

Slovaks were more numerous in the Monarchy than either Serbs or Croats – some 1,200,000 strong in 1804 as against 1,480,000 for the other two peoples combined. But they were a classic case of a 'non-historic' community. Even the capital of the ninth-century Great Moravian Empire to which Slovaks now lay claim has never been located, and not long afterwards they had fallen under Hungarian rule. To the eighteenth century they appeared a submissive peasant people of upland valleys, sharing their market and mining towns with dominant Magyar and German elements. There is some evidence, however, that the proportion of Slovak-speaking master craftsmen and lesser gentry grew during the century. The Lutheran minority, about one-sixth of the whole, cherished links with once Protestant Bohemia, whose language, very close to their own, they used as their literary medium. Yet Slovaks' primary identity as 'Hungarian Slavs' was bound up with the Hungarian kingdom of which they had so long been part. The great polymath Matthias Bel (1684–1749) expressed this identity well when he described himself as a Slav by mother tongue, a Hungarian by nationality and a German by education.

At the bottom of the pile were the Ruthenians of north-east Hungary and the Romanians of Transylvania. The only intelligentsia they possessed was the hierarchy of the Uniate Church introduced at the end of the seventeenth century, their only significant institutions the Uniate seminary and schools established from the 1730s in the little Transylvanian town of Blaj. For the Austrian army officer Demian in 1804, 'the whole external appearance of the Wallachs', as he called the Romanians:

> betrays the inclination to intemperance of every kind. The low, prematurely wrinkled forehead, the brown unkempt hair hanging over the eyes, the thick bushy eyebrows and small rolling eyes, the lean faces overgrown by beard and moustache and the bony bodies fully reflect the wild spirit that animates them.[13]

Yet ironically the ugly name Wallach (cognate with Welsh) was originally used by German speakers to connote aliens they associated with the Roman empire, and in 1774 the Uniate priest Samuel Clajn elaborated the theory of the continuity of Romanian settlement in their present lands from the time of the Roman province of Dacia (AD 107–270). Whatever the truth – and Hungarian historians see evidence of a Romanian presence only from the twelth century – by the eighteenth century Romanians were a majority both in this province and the adjacent parts of Hungary. They remained, however, excluded from the power-sharing Transylvanian pact of 1437 between Magyars, Magyar-speaking Szeklers and German Saxons. The remoteness of the 'Wallachs' from the predominant power is illustrated by the failure of the government-sponsored Uniate Church to wean most of these predominantly upland herdsmen away from their Orthodox traditions, a failure recognised when Maria Theresa appointed a Transylvanian Orthodox bishop in 1761. His subordination to the Serb-controlled see of Karlowitz was in the spirit of an empire where everything, including ethnicity, was ranked hierarchically.

There were two Habsburg territories in the eighteenth century which could not easily be classified in terms of the core Monarchy's feudal code. Lombardy and the Austrian Netherlands were detached socially and politically as well as geographically from east-central Europe. With their large towns, powerful patriciates, prestigious French and Italian speech – and in the Belgian case provincial estates and charters of liberty like the Brabant *joyeuse entrée* – they were on the whole loyal to a distantly benign authority which saw them as a source of loans and taxes, but was content to step these up by Belgian piecemeal measures or the more ambitious Lombard land tax reform. Completed in 1760, it is considered a major achievement of eighteenth-century statecraft.

The Monarchy just described was one which defies much modern conventional wisdom about pre-industrial 'traditional' society. Contemporary accounts reveal a world little less febrile than our own. Thousands of Czech artisans scoured western Europe, Slovaks hawked their goods all over Hungary, 30% of rural Austrians – mainly the poor – changed home annually, Romanians swarmed back and forth between Transylvania and Wallachia-Moldavia, Serbs migrated in their tens of thousands from the Monarchy to the Ukraine. Ethnicity, far from taking the back seat certain theories lead us to expect, was a matter of frequent and blatant generalisation, often as a tool of social explanation, whether in the fifty years by which Bohemian Slavs were held to be behind Bohemian Germans or the centuries seen between the Romanians and their neighbours. Modern readers attuned to see the very stuff of crisis in ethno-cultural differentials will readily deduce – correctly with hindsight – the fragility of any authority operating in this treacherous terrain.

This was not the perspective of eighteenth-century writers, largely, of course, from dominant groups, because their experience to that point told them differently. For contemporary commentators the fact that very diverse populations lived under the rule of tiny elites bred not apprehension but confidence. If authority had successfully maintained itself so far in these circumstances, what could it not do when reinforced by the new administrative mechanisms, technology and information of an age of unprecedented intellectual activity? The eighteenth century was a high noon of governmental optimism because advancing civilisation was consolidating the elites without yet consolidating the masses. Whether it was a matter of Irish Protestants or the German Baltic barons, Swedish speakers in Helsinki or German speakers in Prague, the various 'ascendancies' followed a natural tendency of human nature and envisaged more of the same. Conscious of the vast human toil taking place beneath them and growingly aware that it could be more efficiently directed; intellectually better informed and psychologically more secure, they felt increasingly able to engage in the constructive as well as the repressive deployment of power. Judged by the standards of a later age the eighteenth century was still far from law-abiding. Maria Theresa's reign was peppered by peasant outbursts. But what is significant about these events is that they were no longer seen as inevitable hazards of government or fruits of original sin, but as evidence of defects in the social order which could and should be put right. The extreme diversity and decentralisation of the Habsburg Monarchy became part of the syndrome of backwardness which had to be addressed if the Monarchy was to remain competitive in a changing continent. The case for Enlightened absolutism came to seem overwhelming.

Towards an Austrian Enlightenment?

Two factors thus underlie the Austrian reform movement of the eighteenth century, associated with the reigns of Maria Theresa (1740–80) and Joseph II (1780–90). One was the need to remedy the weaknesses shown in the War of Austrian Succession (1740–48), through an overhaul of the Monarchy's army and finances in anticipation of renewed conflict. Such conflict was all the more likely because the balance of power aimed at in contemporary international politics was continually threatened by the decline of Poland and Turkey, potential candidates for partition. The other spur to reform was the European Enlightenment: growing secularisation of outlook, increasing confidence in reason as the arbiter of human problems, finally the development of a government-friendly central European variant of these potentially very radical western ideas. All this provided the psychological background and the intellectual basis for change.

These twin factors, the pragmatic and the ideological, have often been set against each other in attempts to explain the reforms. Were they not designed to strengthen the state rather than satisfy enlightened consciences? True, for Maria Theresa overwhelmingly so, but the antithesis seems too sharp. The question is not whether rulers wish to strengthen their states – naturally, they do – but what means they think will have this effect. Nor does one have to prove that politicians followed exactly the blue-print of a *philosophe* to demonstrate intellectual influence. It is more a matter of the assumptions behind a policy and the framework of reference within which it is formulated. This is the context in which the case for an Austrian Enlightened absolutism should be probed.

The transmission of ideas is usually indirect. The west European Enlightenment, with its democratic Rousseau and its atheist d'Holbach could not be transposed lock, stock and barrel to Austria, which had, besides, its own reform tradition, the 'cameralist' advocacy from the late seventeenth century of state-sponsored economic development. Even the north German version of Christian Wolff (1679–1754), which transformed the monarch from feudal *primus inter pares* to sovereign agent of the common good, obliging him only to observe the rule of law, was partly tainted by its Protestant origins. True, from the 1730s Austrian nobles were abandoning the Jesuit colleges for education in German Protestant universities. By the 1760s the influence of the Saxon and Prussian Enlightenment was very strong in nearby Bohemia. The Catholic historian Maass has stressed the role of neo-Protestant rationalism in weakening the Counter-Reformation legacy which had been the ideological cement of early modern Austria. But also at work here were traditions native to Catholicism itself, which paralleled certain Protestant or rationalist motifs: Austrian Gallicanism, or the pursuit of an Erastian state Church by Austrian rulers; Febronianism, a movement in German Catholicism for conciliar rather than Papal government of the Church and, most interesting, Jansenism, a tendency officially condemned by Rome but which continued to influence forms of spirituality in much of Catholic Europe.

Jansenism was an austere creed with Calvinist overtones, reliant on Grace rather than the flamboyant external devotions of Baroque piety, on plain Sunday worship rather than saints' days and processions. It reached Austria partly from the Low Countries and partly from Italy, the Jansenist-inclined Italian priest Muratori's *True Devotion* being published eight times in Vienna between 1752 and 1795. Archbishop Trautson of Vienna (1750–57) echoed Muratori when he lamented that priests talked more to their flock of the rosary than of Jesus Christ. His successor, Migazzi, wrote the foreword to the 1762 edition of *True Devotion*. A third of Austrian bishops had Jansenist sympathies in the 1760s, as did Maria Theresa's influential doctor Gerhard van Swieten. The Jansenists' main critics, the Jesuit order, were in eclipse, with their Piarist rivals in the educational field leading a movement for stress on the mother tongue, modern languages and the natural sciences in the schools. It is in the fusion of a reconceived piety and up-to-date intellectual motifs, drawn in part from Protestant models, that an Austrian Catholic Enlightenment may be seen emerging in the 1760s, championed by men like the charismatic Karl Heinrich Seibt, Professor of Philosophy at the University of Prague. Seibt's inaugural lecture on 'The Influence of Education on the Happiness of the State' set forth the goal of an Austria catching up and outstrippping her Protestant neighbours under the impact of an intellectually open, recharged Catholicism. The sense of the need for a new broom was enhanced by reformers' disquiet at what they felt to be the excesses of Counter-Reformation religion, including such sensitive issues as the enforced reconversion of Bohemia. The psychological parallel is, perhaps, with the reform communism of the early, heady days of Soviet *perestroika*.

In its hostility to inherited forms of religion Reform Catholicism, as it has been called, could imply a critique also of old feudal norms, a dawning individualism. Muratori criticised the proliferation of saints' days because they prevented workers from earning an honest penny. Values were being reshaped, as the Habsburg Monarchy participated in the beginnings of a European demographic upsurge and an economic expansion which has yet to be reversed. The upsurge in the population of the Hungarian lands from some four million in 1720 to nine and a half million in 1787, and trebling of Bohemia's population to 2.6 million between 1648 and 1771, may be explained in large part by recovery from war and devastation, the smaller advance in the Alpine provinces more tentatively by agricultural prosperity in the first half of the century.

Whatever the cause the result was the swelling of the percentage of cottars, small-holders, labourers and also of the outright destitute over the century. In 1727 a twelfth of the people of Upper Austria were recorded as beggars. Though what evidence exists shows that eighteenth-century beggars were disproportionately elderly and female, it was the growth in the able-bodied poor which caused alarm and linked poverty with delinquency in contemporary minds. A Chancellery proposal of 1770 for houses of correction in the Moravian capital Brünn (modern Brno) destined it for criminal delinquents, rebels, serfs, beggars, vagabonds and the mad and infirm – an interesting association of ideas.[14] From mid-century the Monarchy saw a rapid development of government-sponsored work-houses, orphanages, foundling hospitals, spinning schools and 'houses of care', showing both concern to maintain social discipline and a tacit recognition that the welfare role hitherto exercised by the Church was passing to the state. Respect for earlier forms of paternalism was weakening. The otherwise conservative Upper Austrian Baron Hellenbach in 1742 accused nobles who supported begging of thinking only of the revenue they gained from beggars' over-indulgence in noble-owned taverns, and of the fines they could impose for the subsequent mayhem. While the Moravian authorities in 1685 had banned water-powered looms because of the unemployment they caused, in 1751 their commercial organ declared one rich man to be worth more to the state than ten paupers.[15]

Some recent historians, aware of the social context of Enlightened absolutist policies, have seen them as the response of fearful rulers to mounting pressures from below, a kind of Foucaultesque exercise in social control. This oversimplifies what was happening. Alongside the undoubted desire of eighteenth-century rulers to maintain social discipline there was also a novel confidence in the problem-solving power of the new institutional forms that were being copied across Europe. Moreover, if what has been said above is correct, the path of reform had been smoothed in part at least by the weakening of communitarian, externalised forms of piety in favour of a greater stress on rational religion and the inner sense of individual responsibility. English Methodism and German Pietism provide certain parallels here.

Perhaps such attitudes can be related to what Sandgruber, the historian of Austrian consumerism, believes to be the paradox of the eighteenth century: that consumption was increasing though real wages did not rise. People seem to have been working harder.

Bemusingly long as the traditional artisan day was, allowance must be made for the numerous religious festivals, reduction of which in 1771 led indignant Viennese workers to institutionalise 'Blue Monday' or the long week-end. By contrast, the new state institutions and 'manufactories' ran a strict and formidable regime – a 5 a.m. rise in the Wiener Neustadt military academy, founded in 1752, up to 16 hours a day for textile manufactory workers. Harder work may have meant more labour was needed to make both ends meet, but also that rewards and work opportunities were available for extra effort, as consumer evidence implies. In fact, the Habsburg economy was growing and certain of its features, like the expansion of domestic industry in the countryside, fit all the above suppositions. Economic growth was more a matter of better organisation and transport than of technical innovation. Non-agrarian wealth remained preponderantly mercantile rather than industrial and manufacture was mainly a matter of noble not bourgeois initiative. The eighteenth century still saw more plans for infrastructural development on paper – particularly of canals – than were put into effect. But significant things were done. Extending the navigability of the river Sava so that Banat grain could reach the Adriatic and opening the Danube to the Black Sea (the first Danube shipping ordinance was issued in 1770) helped quintuple Hungarian wheat exports and almost sextuple its wool exports between 1748 and 1782. Croatia's 48 fairs became 187 in the second half of the century. The role of Balkan Orthodox merchants in Hungary and in Trieste, extending their commercial networks via the great grain markets of Pest to Vienna and beyond, was paralled by the French, Italian and German merchants of Vienna, whose monopoly of the wholesale trade came increasingly to be shared with native Austrians. This development of inter-regional trade helped stimulate proto-industrialisation and population growth in the German Austrian provinces and particularly in the infertile mountain rim of German-speaking Bohemia, with its long-standing traditions of domestic industry in textiles.

Initiatives were also being taken in agriculture, though only by the big estates. The first Austrian provincial agricultural associations were founded in the 1760s. Trained estate officials began to propagate west European notions of root crops, systematic manuring and breed improvement; on the Schwarzenberg estate, manager Petr Světecký broached the question of dividing the lord's demesne among his tenantry, under the influence of French *physiocratic* ideas of the benefits of a prosperous peasantry. Likewise, from the middle of the century a professionalisation of Hungarian estate management can be seen. The result in Hungary was the reversal of the previous pattern of higher peasant rather than noble productivity, with noble estates overseeing the gradual transition from stock-rearing to arable, if not yet displacing the primacy of cattle and wine (a largely peasant product) in Hungarian exports.

Much of the expertise on which these methods drew stemmed from bourgeois scholarship. In Prague, a private Learned Society grouped a remarkably talented bunch of mathematicians, statisticians, botanists and geologists, while early travelogues of Hungary were largely written by geologists on terrain. The role of the sciences as adjuncts of economic development was reflected in the foundation of new university chairs and in the advance of engineering studies. The 24 engineering students in Prague University in 1767 became 200 by 1780 and a thousand by the end of the century. A secular-minded bourgeois intelligentsia was emerging in Vienna and Prague which developed literary as well as scientific interests. Johann Trattner, Vienna's leading publisher, was the first man of bourgeois origin to build on the grand scale in the city. The works in which he specialised were those of the German Enlightenment, fostering notions of the 'simplicity' and 'naturalness' of German bourgeois culture by contrast to the 'artificiality' of aristocratic French or Italian tastes.

Reform Catholicism, economic expansion and the emergence of bourgeois culture were separate but not unrelated aspects of a society in transition, which shared certain features with European, more particularly, central European ideas. Some character sketches will illustrate the nature and scope of what may, then, be called the Austrian Enlightenment.

Prince Wenzel Anton von Kaunitz (1711–94), Maria Theresa's State Chancellor from 1752 – effectively her foreign minister – was a member of a Germanised Moravian noble family. A self-proclaimed *philosophe* and exemplar of the Enlightenment's love of rational system, whose very foibles were enlightened – he kept windows permanently shut for fear of germs – his liberalism nonetheless stopped short of the idea of the career open to talent: 'a nation can be great if education corresponding to each class of citizens offers youth a healthy and clear idea of its obligations', as he once remarked.[16] Kaunitz engineered the 'Diplomatic Revolution' of 1756 by which Habsburg Austria ended its long feud with Bourbon France and concentrated its fire on crushing the Prussia of Frederick the Great, though failure here confirmed him in the view that the true strength of a state lay in internal prosperity and the gradual removal of 'prejudices'. This was the man who once received the Pope in his dressing-gown and shook the hand outstretched for him to kiss. A grand seigneur who was as at home in French as in German and had sixteen courses served for dinner, though personally abstemious, Kaunitz showed how new thinking could penetrate to the heart of the Habsburg state but in necessarily circumscribed form.

While great nobles continued to occupy the highest offices of state, the theoretical underpinning of their reforms was usually provided by men of bourgeois origin. Men like the Vienna University law professors Martini, Riegger and Justi, advocates of ideas of 'Natural Law' based, it was believed, on universally applicable principles, were public figures, active as members of government commissions, authors of textbooks and memoranda and tutors of the nobility. The career of the Professor of Politics at Vienna, Joseph von Sonnenfels (1732–1817), son of a Jewish rabbi who had converted to Catholicism, shows both the range and the limitations of a reform movement allied to an absolutist state. Sonnenfels's adaptation of Rousseauist terms like 'social contract' and 'civil society' to mean the individual's duty to submit his will to the common good was pure enlightened despotism. But his insistence that the state existed to seek 'the best' for its people implied a right to popular self-fulfilment which struck a different note, while his elevation of subjects to the status of 'citizens' (*Bürger*) subtly altered the nature of nobility. Though nobles' leading role was not questioned, they functioned implicitly for Sonnenfels as an interest group in 'civil society' whose privileges needed to be justified through their mastery of enlightened principles of government. In fact, Sonnenfels tended to take the bourgeois values of the German Enlightenment as the standard for a civil society. In his work as a theatrical censor he opposed both the Viennese tradition of low-life comedy and the French dramas favoured by the upper classes. In this he was true to the growing earnestness of the age.

Also a government employee, Ignaz Born (1742–91) is a striking representative of contemporary scientific advances. Born was a Transylvanian Saxon, educated in Vienna and Prague, who entered the state mining administration and became a geologist, mineralogist and chemist of international repute, an early advocate of the volcanic theory of mountain origin and of the significance of fossils for the study of climate in the past. Dismissing as myth the Biblical story of the flood, which a Jesuit academic rival sought to prove, and supporting Bohemian historians who were similarly demythologising Czech origins, Born was the prime mover in the foundation of the Learned Society in Prague around 1773, ancestor of the Czech Academy of Sciences; if Iceland and Siberia had been subjected to scholarly enquiry, he complained, then why not Austria?[17] Born left Prague to become head of the imperial natural history collections and a leading Viennese Freemason. He lives on as the model for Sarastro in Mozart's *Magic Flute*.

In Kaunitz, by descent a Germanised Slav, Sonnenfels, of Prussian Jewish stock, and the Transylvanian Saxon Born, active in Prague and Vienna, we see how by the last third of the eighteenth century the Habsburg Monarchy had acquired a dominant 'high culture', German in speech though varied in origin and united in the desire to emulate or adapt the experience of its more advanced neighbours. But it was confined very largely to the aristocracy and upper bourgeoisie. The bulk of the Hungarian nobility remained untouched. There was little intellectual friskiness in the 1764 Hungarian Diet's condemnation of a pro-absolutist treatise as being contaminated with the Jansenist heresy, the 'liberal' principles of Grotius, the 'sacrilegious' errors of Luther and the 'godless' doctrines of Machiavelli and Hobbes. Nor were the beleaguered leaders of the Protestant minority, clinging to a narrow religious orthodoxy, the natural allies of new thinking, as the innovative Debrecen college mathematician Hatvani found in a career of uneasy trimming with his superiors. In Croatia Count Oršić's diary in the 1770s expressed the nobility's nostalgia for rustic paternalism and resentment of the first bourgeois lawyers appearing in their midst. In Vienna itself supercilious Protestant observers like the Englishman Wraxall and the Prussian Nicolai mocked the superstition and shallowness of Austrian high society.

But should such outsiders be allowed the last word? In its own terms the Monarchy in the later eighteenth century showed certain novel traits, with some evidence of their penetration even beyond elite circles. The Czech peasant judge and diarist Vavák did not drink, derived a basic Christianity from his Bible reading, wrote a Czech-language agricultural handbook and dedicated himself, in short, to state service and improvement with exemplary seriousness. The two parts of the very popular *Satire* (1762–79) of the Croatian Military Frontier officer Matija Antun Reljković lambasted the 'prejudices and bad customs' of his countrymen and extolled the glass windows, state-built roads and government-recommended beekeeping and silk-worm techniques that passed for modernity in his world. Among the Serbs Zaharije Orfelin and Dositej Obradović challenged monkish obscurantism in a language reflecting common speech rather than the Russianate jargon of earlier writers. What should not be lost sight of is that Habsburg subjects were becoming more used to the concept of a regulating, provident state. The reports of Count Pergen, first Austrian Governor of Galicia, are a sustained diatribe against arrogant, exploitative nobles, lazy, ignorant priests, unsanitary towns without trained midwives and regulated apothecaries, and much nore.

Is this evidence of an Austrian Enlightenment? Sceptics would say that Pergen was a pragmatic politician who was to show the unenlightened face of absolutism as Joseph II's minister of police. There is another way of looking at it. Is it not significant that the pragmatic Pergen's assumptions about his targets, whether nobles, priests or public provision, mirrored those of 'enlightened' discourse? His reports show how far by the 1770s Austrian absolutism had taken on an enlightened tinge. The foundations of modern Habsburg policy, with its curious mix of authoritarianism and benevolence, were already being laid.

The Maria Theresan Reforms

This is the background to the reform movement which gained speed on the conclusion of the War of Austrian Succession in 1748. The immediate motives were wholly practical. The fissiparous tendencies visible at the start of Maria Theresa's reign needed to be checked and parlous state finances strengthened for future struggles, which duly followed in the Seven Years' War of 1756–63. The architect of the first bout of reform in 1748–49, the cameralist-influenced Count F.W. Haugwitz, was no more interested in the *philosophes* than the Empress. She herself was a clear-headed, strong-minded woman, less concerned with speculative ideas than her faith, her authority and the sixteen children she had with her husband Francis Stephen, a sportsman with an entrepreneurial streak who left the politics to his wife. As well as raising the level of the *contributio* to support a standing army of 108,000 men in the Hereditary Lands, Haugwitz got the Diets to grant it every ten years instead of annually, merged the affairs of these lands under a common Directory and set up provincial executives responsible to Vienna, not the Diets. A Supreme Court in Vienna followed in 1751, whose work on unifying legal codes further threatened provincial distinctiveness. For that reason a rearguard action delayed the publication of the first definitive section of the pan-Austrian Civil Code till 1786, while the interim Theresan penal code of 1766 contained many traditional features, including provision for torture and crimes of blasphemy and sorcery. Indeed, provincial sentiment brought back some old estate offices in a splitting up of the cumbersome Directory in 1760–62, though the key provincial demand for the restoration of the Bohemian Chancellery, abolished by Haugwitz, was refused. The guiding spirit of government was now the ostentatiously enlightened Kaunitz, prime mover behind the State Council (*Staatsrat*) set up in 1761 with an advisory brief for the Monarchy as a whole. The downgrading of the provinces was thus confirmed, though Diet standing committees retained a certain importance as conduits of provincial credit to a hard-pressed centre, and detailed legislation was still enacted separately in individual provinces, with local circumstances taken into account.

At first this invigorated government was chiefly concerned to prevent nobles from weakening their peasants' tax-paying capacity. The extension elsewhere of the Bohemian system of appointed officials at district (*Kreis*) level gave Vienna the means to check noble appropriation of peasant land, since though noble land was taxed from 1748 it was so at a lower rate. Even before Kaunitz, however, measures in other fields were less overtly utilitarian. The simplification of church mourning ritual, the banning of trumpets in church processions, the attack on Jesuit dominance in the universities from 1749, the increasingly liberal policies followed by the Court Censorship Commission set up in 1752 all spoke to the rejection of Baroque tradition. It was the Censorship Commission's chairman, the Jansenist doctor Gerhard van Swieten, who examined and absolved an alleged Croatian witch whose sentence Maria Theresa queried in 1758, with the words that other countries did not persecute witches and trials against them were trials against herself.

By the second half of the reign peasant protection took on a more comprehensive character. The state began to intervene directly in the landlord–serf relationship and to adopt the physiocratic standpoint that a prosperous peasantry should be a prime concern of government. Though this reflected awareness that financing future wars would have to rely less on foreign mercenaries and English subsidies, the leading government specialist on peasant matters in the 1760s, Franz Anton von Blanc, actually argued in terms of Natural Law that peasants' right to subsistence came before their obligations to lord and state. Maria Theresa's motives were more mixed. She would not, she once said, risk eternal damnation by being deterred from just policies by a few selfish nobles; but she also believed in a hierarchical society and distrusted peasants for their periodic recalcitrance. The outcome was a see-saw in government–noble relations in which peasant upheavals were regularly turned against obstructive Diets and made the occasion for reforming government intervention, whether in the Patents of Slavonia in 1758, Hungary in 1767, Bohemia in 1775 or Silesia in 1778. Such Patents codified the levels of *robota* which nobles could demand, while other measures chipped away at their rights of preemption of peasant produce, limited the various inheritance charges they could impose and broadened peasants' security of tenure. Most innovative of all, the so-called Raab system introduced on Crown estates in Bohemia from 1775 abolished *robota* altogether and distributed the demesne among rent-paying tenants. It pointed to a post-feudal organisation of the land, along English lines.

The peasant majority was to be educated so that it might learn its responsibilities. The principle of general education was declared in Austria in 1774 and in Hungary in 1777. Schools were to be graded, with one- or two-class schools in villages and small towns, three-class 'main schools' in larger towns and four-class 'normal schools' with teacher training facilities in provincial centres. It was a characteristic of the Austrian Enlightenment to concentrate on primary education for the masses as opposed to the Latin schools for the higher classes. For practical reasons, however, clergy continued to play a leading role in the new educational initiatives though the guiding spirits were men of Reform Catholic stamp, like the author of the 1774 education scheme, Abbot Johann Ignaz Felbiger, bringing Protestant Pietist influences from his native Silesia.

Traditionally minded clerics found the atmosphere more hostile, particularly after the creation of an Ecclesiastical Department in the United Court Chancellery (the main successor body to Haugwitz's Directory) in 1769. Its head, the ennobled bourgeois F.J. Heinke, supported the Erastian policies Kaunitz had already been pursuing in the Duchy of Milan. Both men viewed the Church as an association, albeit the highest, in the state and thus subject to state supervision in all but purely spiritual matters, which they defined quite narrowly. Thus both claimed that many features of church life post-dated the pristine model of early Christianity, like monasticism, 'this reckless contrivance against all the rights of nature', as Heinke put it.[18] While the Pope grudgingly accepted the reduction of the

number of saints' days (1771) and himself dissolved the Jesuit order
in 1773, the restrictions on entering the monastic life and the state
appropriation of the property of Jesuits and of religious brotherhoods
were imposed unilaterally. State interests here led the pious Maria
Theresa to align herself with 'enlightened' positions. But as Catholic
and sovereign she rejected religious pluralism. At the end of her reign
she rejected the strong pleas of Kaunitz and Joseph to grant open toleration to crypto-Protestant communities in Moravia.

Ideological considerations apart, the Church's resources would
have exposed it to pressures from a needy government – though a
modern estimate of Jesuit annual income sets it at only a million florins. Maria Theresa shared the view that the Church's wealth was not
being put to the best public good. Better economic management as a
source of indirect taxation was a potent theme at a time when the
share of direct taxation in spiralling state budgets was falling sharply
despite Haugwitz's pressure tactics, which Kaunitz criticised.
Charles VI under cameralist influence had built roads and 'manufactories'. Energising progress came, though, under his daughter, with
new commercial councils at central and provincial level, the former
successively revamped from 1746, tariff unification of most of the
Austro-Bohemian lands (1775), institutions like the Mining Academy at Schemnitz (Banská Štiavnica) in northern Hungary and government sponsorship of a Trieste that trebled in size. Progress seems
to have come mainly after 1770 when the state turned from direct
subsidy or monopoly to more indirect benefits in terms of tax relief,
grants of sites and favourable access to labour and raw materials,
which did more to stimulate as yet slender entrepreneurial talent.
But the trend to the bourgeois professional over the reign is unmistakable in the ranks of central government itself – though such employment usually brought ennoblement. There were eight counts among
the 24 members of the Directory in 1754 and only one in the fifteen
members of the United Court Chancellery in 1775.

Symptomatic of government's growing coherence were military
innovations, which gave the army its famous black–gold colours
(1745), standardised its uniforms (1750), introduced conscription
districts (1770), raised young lieutenants' pay and restricted the
rights of high-born regimental patrons over corporal punishment
and promotions. A pension fund was also established for invalid officers. The prohibition of duelling, however, remained a dead letter;
no doubt the unification of the officer corps brought about by ennobling its commoner members entailed more traditional values.

Although some innovations were weakly rooted (like the general staff introduced in 1758) and they hardly touched the harsh lot of the common soldier, the army which became so closely associated with the dynasty in its subjects' consciousness was taking shape.

Embourgeoisement, commercial policy and a well-funded army, like much else, ran up against one strong barrier. It was Hungary, though even there expanding technical services of government led to 430 ennoblements over the reign. While certain central policies – in education, for example – were loyally implemented in Hungary, the most important, like the ending of noble immunity from taxation, were not. Austrian opinion was sharp. Vienna's resentment was focused on the Hungarian *contributio*, limited by noble tax exemption to less than half that of the Bohemian lands alone in 1749, though royal cameral revenues and army provisioning profits from Hungary partly made up for the relative Hungarian short-fall. The key to inconsistencies in Hungary's relations with the rest of the Monarchy in these years probably lies in the Empress's own attitudes, which combined a fund of goodwill, based on Hungarian loyalty against Prussia in 1741, with the strong sense of her own authority that she showed also towards the Church. Thus while restoring large areas detached from Hungary's southern flank during the time of Turkish threat, Maria Theresa summoned only three Hungarian Diets in forty years. After the last of these had declined cooperation she imposed her own Urbarium or Patent of 1767, limiting *robota* for a full peasant with a plough team to a day a week and extending the right of appeal to the royal courts held by Austrian peasants to Hungary. Perhaps the most notorious example of the colonial relationship of which Hungarian historians have complained was the subordination of Hungary's economic interests in the tariff arrangements of 1775, which placed heavy duties on Hungarian exports outside the Monarchy and discriminated in favour of Austrian products within. No attempt was made to develop Hungarian manufactures. Between 1760 and 1790 86% of Hungary's commerce was with her wealthier Austrian neighbour.

The Hungarian case shows best that Maria Theresa did not pursue the will-o'-the-wisp of the unitary state. Despite the administrative 'revolution' of 1748–49, administrative structures remained forbiddingly complex. Government performed unevenly. In some spheres – the numbering of all houses for military recruiting (1770), effective border quarantine procedures (1773), the regulation of local food prices – it could be surprisingly efficient; a request of 17 November 1773 from the butchers of Eperjes (Prešov) in north-east Hungary for a meadow for a cattle reserve was answered by 6 December after being processed at several levels up to the Empress herself.[19] But all attempts to avert the Bohemian famine of 1771–72 failed dismally. The overall objective of the reforms, to restore the state without state bankruptcy, was hardly reached. Though the Monarchy put 250,000 troops of a retrained army into the field by 1760, its leaders' cautious tactics and the fall-off of allied support allowed Frederick to end the Seven Years' War in possession of all but a strip of Silesia. Though regular revenues rose from 20 million florins to 50 million over the reign, the cost of the abortive Austro-Prussian War over the Bavarian succession in 1778–79, in which hardly any fighting occurred, was nearly 65 million. Over 40% of the peace-time budget went on the army and a further quarter on interest on the state debt. Less than 1% apiece went on education, trade support and civic public works. The failure to acquire Bavaria or reacquire largely German-speaking Silesia assumes significance against Austrian Germans' nineteenth-century inability to match their cultural and economic power with democratic weight of numbers. The Monarchy's Slavic element was reinforced by its participation in the first partition of Poland, agreed between Austria, Prussia and Russia in 1772. Characteristically, the pious, practical Maria Theresa thought the partition immoral but was unwilling to be left out.

Mixed as it is, this record does not seem quite to justify the view that Maria Theresa is more appropriately viewed as an 'active feudal ruler'[20] than against her Enlightenment context. This chapter has sought to show that a decline in support for feudal values and institutions aided acceptance of the claims of monarchical absolutism in the Habsburg lands. In exercising these claims Maria Theresa drew on many advisers of enlightened persuasion, whose sometimes quite radical schemes benefited from government's freedom from public control. Her reign marked a transition from the court-orientated society of the Austrian Baroque, with its union of throne, altar and aristocracy, to the post-feudal vision of her son. Like all times of transition it had its share of compromises and unresolved tensions: between the Empress, Kaunitz and Joseph, between a common Monarchy and Hungarian autonomy, between serfdom and citizenship and a state religion and freedom of conscience. The foundations of a new Austria were being laid, but with many ambiguities and limitations. To no-one were these more irksome than to Maria Theresa's

co-ruler, son and heir – Joseph himself – with whose brief and turbulent reign the long dénouement of modern Habsburg history may
be said to begin.

2 Joseph II and his Legacy

Few men have taken up the reins of government amid such expectations as Joseph II. The German epic poet Klopstock had dedicated his *Hermannsschlacht* to him in 1769 and hailed him as the Charlemagne of learning. The philosopher Herder had called on him to give a German fatherland to those who yearned for it. Even Frederick of Prussia, no friend of the Habsburgs, spoke of the beginning of a new order.

The object of these attentions was born in 1741 and educated by a variety of private tutors, from his worthy director of studies Count Bartenstein, who prepared the boy six thousand pages of notes on medieval Austrian history, to spokesmen of moderate Enlightenment like Riegger and Blanc. From them Joseph would have acquired certain Enlightenment ideas but nothing incompatible with notions of a conscientious absolutism and an unostentatious faith. The vehemence of his attacks on the Monarchy's governing institutions, particularly the nobility, in early memoranda of 1761 and 1765 was therefore as much the response of a quick intelligence and vigorous temperament to Austria's problems as a matter of book learning. 'We inherit from our parents at birth only animal life', he wrote after being proclaimed joint ruler with his mother on his father's death in 1765.[1] But his new position gave him little chance to put his views into practice. Maria Theresa declared only her son and not herself joint ruler, retaining her own sovereign powers in full. Even in the military affairs ostensibly entrusted to Joseph she continued a secret correspondence with officials behind his back and on the important issue of administrative reform he failed to move her. Joseph's own description of his mother's attitude to him as a petulant kind of loving accurately reflects their often fraught relationship in these years.

Thwarted reforming energies found expression in fields still open, whether simplifying court ceremonial, using his father's fortune to reduce state debts or the dramatic journeys to all parts of his domains which bespoke his thirst to play a public role. Between 1765 and his death Joseph II spent a third of his time on the move. While these expeditions were not always the simple, spartan affairs legend has made them – thirteen vehicles accompanied Joseph on his journey to the Banat in 1768 – the Emperor on horseback quizzing all and sundry, the humble accommodation en route and the bag in which wayside peasants could slip petitions were all real enough. Contemporaries were right to conclude that this unusual monarch was in broad sympathy with key themes of the Enlightenment. He believed that all human beings regardless of status should be treated as rational beings with a right to happiness, that liberalisation in matters of conscience and the press was a means to this end and that feudal and clerical elements would resist such reforms. He was also, however, a convinced absolutist who did not doubt that the welfare of the parts depended on the welfare of the whole, and that only the monarch and his close advisers were in a position to judge what that might be. The man who succeeded Maria Theresa in November 1780 was a strange mixture of benefactor and martinet.

Yet at the start of his brief reign Joseph wrote to his brother Leopold that he intended to go slowly at first. The initial need was to enthuse the administration with his own commitment to the service of the state. One early measure introduced the Prussian system of annual reports on officials' performance by their superiors; another granted them automatic pension rights. Material gain was not, however, to be the primary incentive. In a famous circular of 1783 Joseph wrote that Austria needed men able to renounce all life's pleasures for the sake of the public weal. The demanding ruler who had once given the Governor of Bohemia two days' notice of a major visit issued lists of hundreds of points which *Kreis* commissioners were to cover in their inspections, from the presence of superstitions and roving jugglers to the treatment of disabled children and 'unfortunate girls'. Meanwhile, the structure of government was streamlined. In the non-Hungarian lands the number of provincial governments was reduced to six, each with its Appellate Court, the Diets lost their standing committees and municipal autonomy was much curtailed. Yet at the central level Joseph chose to hector the many noble officials rather than replace them, perhaps because of the lack of alternatives, but giving the impression, as one of them, Count Zinzendorf, wrote in his diary, that he alone loved the country and knew the truth, while all his civil servants were rogues or fools.

Brusque and tactless as he was, in almost every sphere Joseph initially continued along roads his mother had travelled. Peasant reform is the most prominent example. Two Patents of autumn 1781 forbade nobles to fine or physically punish their peasants and abolished noble control over peasant marriage, movement and choice of occupation. This 'abolition of serfdom', a term used in the November Patent itself, was, however, less dramatic than it sounded. Only personal serfdom was annulled, not the economic obligations of *robota* labour service. The Alpine provinces claimed that their peasants had never been serfs (*Leibeigene*) anyway, but *Erbuntertane* (hereditarily subject) with already guaranteed freedom of marriage. Moreover, the Styrian and Galician versions of the Patent granted freedom of movement only to peasants who found a replacement to work their plot. Peasants liable to military conscription still required permission from the state authorities to travel. In the Monarchy's more backward lands, however, there could be no doubt about the innovative impact of the reforms, which helps explain the caution in delaying a corresponding patent for Hungary till 1785.

The 1781 Patents are best seen as steps in a pro-peasant policy begun in the 1750s, whose ultimate effect was to enhance peasants' personal status and security of tenure and to integrate landlords' patrimonial jurisdiction into a developing network of local administration. Thus requirements for legal training for patrimonial officials led to the amalgamation of many patrimonial courts. The Josephinist vision of the future on the land was that already implemented on a small scale for Maria Theresa by her adviser Raab: the replacement of the *robota* system by the division of landed estates (including the demesne) among rent-paying tenants. In 1783 Joseph ordered the extension of Raab's scheme to all cameral estates in Bohemia and Moravia. The ultimate implication of this policy was the emergence of a legally homogenous peasantry in place of the old distinctions between dominical and rustical peasants, 'bought-in' and less secure 'non-bought-in' tenures and the like. It pointed to new principles of social organisation, as did the extension of official supervision to private forests in 1784, anticipating commercial forestry's importance to the Alpine noble economy of the next century. But systemic changes are always easier to see in hindsight, and Joseph left his noble commissioners free to implement the Raab reform in a fairly conservative and pro-landlord spirit.

Indeed, there were important points of detail on which the Josephinist agrarian regime was uncertain or ineffective. Should a peasant's plot be divided among all his children, in line with theories linking demographic and economic growth, or should primogeniture be favoured, because land-holding peasants were exempt from military service? The 1786 Civil Code affirmed the first alternative but an edict of 1787 inclined to primogeniture. Should the village common lands be divided up? Repeated Josephinian edicts were in favour of this, following the original ordinance of 1768, but their reiteration suggests the prescription was largely ignored.

In religious matters, too, Joseph capitalised on an existing momentum for change. The toleration granted in 1781 had been strongly urged by Kaunitz on Maria Theresa. It applied only to specified denominations and did not permit non-Catholic places of worship to have bells or a prominent site. Prospective converts to Protestantism could only apply singly, not *en masse*, and had to submit to a course of instruction by a Catholic priest before confirming their intent. The newly formed Protestant consistories were supervised by Catholics and Catholic priests retained the right to fees from Protestant baptisms and marriages. Much of this testified to a fear of widespread underground Protestantism which was hardly borne out in the event; by 1785 some 151,000 had registered as Protestants in the non-Hungarian lands. Within its limitations, however, the reform was carried out with all Joseph's principled thoroughness. The Governor of Bohemia lost his post because of his obstructive attitude and a Protestant was appointed head of the Vienna teachers' training college. Too much has been made of Joseph's practical motives in introducing toleration to encourage non-Catholic businessmen. His mother had already felt free to ennoble a Swiss Calvinist banker, Johann Fries. But whereas, with individual exceptions, she espoused religious uniformity as a key interest of the state – 'I speak politically, not as a Christian' – Joseph already had a different vision of the state interest, in which a confessionally even-handed polity asked only for civic loyalty from its citizens and was strengthened by the gratitude of religious minorities. In this essentially modern concept faith became a matter between man and God in which the state need not intervene.

This approach underlay Joseph's policy to the Jews, responsive though it was initially to the Court Chancellery's cautious instincts. The Patent of 1782 repealed dress restrictions on Jews and widened the range of professions they could follow, but did not imply a willingness to see an increase in the number and size of Jewish urban settlements. Nor did it apply to the Monarchy's most Jewish province, Galicia. There decrees of 1785 and 1789 went further, abolishing the Jewish Directory or separate administration which Maria Theresa had hoped would keep Jews and Christians apart and requiring Jews to perform military service (initially in the transport corps); henceforth they could marry only on proof that they had attended a German school to lose what Joseph called their 'repellent Jewish characteristics'.[2] For many Jews this was the unacceptable face of integration.

Traditional Catholics had most cause for resentment. Direct contact of Austrian bishops with the Curia was prohibited, as was the publication of Papal acts without permission. Some 530 out of 1188 monasteries in the Austro-Slav lands, and a further 117 in Hungary, were dissolved and their property of 60 million florins taken over by the state on the grounds that they were merely 'contemplative' institutions lacking educational or welfare functions. Their libraries were distributed to teaching bodies or pulped; their raiment ended up in a depot in Vienna. The expropriation of monasteries in the eighteenth century was the equivalent for would-be progressives of the nationalisation of private enterprise in the twentieth, justified by the argument that their wealth resulted from past gifts made for public cultural and religious purposes, and had in this sense always been national. Accordingly, resources taken over by the state were used to form a Religious Fund from which about 1700 new parishes were created, as well as numerous welfare institutions. In Vienna the lying-in hospital for expectant mothers, the Deaf and Dumb Institute, and the vast General Hospital, with its two thousand beds, date from this time. Moreover, the expanded clergy were to be trained in six newly instituted 'General Seminaries', rather than in monastic centres or the diocesan seminars favoured by the Council of Trent. The Marriage Patent of 1783 treated marriage essentially as a civil contract.

Yet that these changes were not just the diktat of an unsympathetic state can be seen from the readiness with which scholarly Reform Catholics participated in them, like the father of Czech studies, Josef Dobrovský, who headed the General Seminary in Moravia, or Abbot Rautenstrauch, who took on the overhaul of theological studies. The cataloguing of confiscated monastic books was carried out by a Josephinist-minded priest who believed 'superstitious and childish things' were best destroyed.[3] In Rautenstrauch's programme, authorised for the Monarchy as a whole, scholastic theology was down-graded in favour of moral and pastoral studies, a traditional Protestant emphasis. The relative importance of religious dogmas could only be judged, wrote the pastoral theologian Giftschütz in 1787, in terms of their effect on Christian action and on man's improvement and happiness.[4] The alliance between Enlightenment and Catholic Reform could hardly be more clearly stated.

Not all the clergy, of course, embraced these ideas. Archbishop Migazzi of Vienna had ended his flirtation with reform trends when he rejected Febronius's critique of the Papal power in 1763. Embroiled by the 1780s in disputes with radical priests in his diocese, he argued that calls for a purported renewal of the Church did not strengthen its appeal but emboldened its enemies. Here Joseph's relaxation of censorship in 1781 was of crucial importance. It abolished provincial censorship organs and allowed free circulation of any material which did not systematically attack the Catholic faith. The result was a huge pamphlet literature in Vienna in which an unsophisticated public indulged a new-found taste for satire and irreverance at the expense of obvious authority symbols like the Church. While Joseph drew the line at a German-language edition of the anticlerical Voltaire, the new guidelines passed material like Ignaz Born's classification of religious orders in terms of insects and Eybel's hostile *What is the Pope?* There is evidence that in the increasingly turbulent atmosphere of Josephinian Austria Jansenist and Reform Catholic ideas were indeed yielding to anti-clericalism and scepticism among certain radical artisans in the larger towns. Genuine anxieties about the fate of the Church as well as a struggle over power fuelled the conflict of Pope and Emperor in the 1780s, the most dramatic aspect of which was Pius VI's visit to Vienna to remonstrate with Joseph in 1782.

Joseph wrote sarcastically to Catherine of Russia about this ostensibly fruitless visit, on the long daily conversations he and the Pope had had, 'talking nonsense about theology ... in words which neither of us understood'.[5] In fact, the forces of state reform and Church tradition were more evenly matched than Joseph implied. Both sides had powerful weapons. Vienna could threaten Rome with the withholding of bishops' temporal possessions, even, *in extremis*, with the summons of a council of Austrian bishops independent of Rome along Febronian lines. Rome could hint that Joseph was following Luther's road. Twice a point of confrontation came. When the Pope compared Joseph to Martin Luther the Emperor haughtily returned the letter to Rome, only to follow it himself in a visit of conciliation (1783). Again, when Pius demanded that the Josephinist Bishop of Ljubljana should recant his praise of the – thus implicitly heretical – Toleration Edict, a direct clash was averted by the bishop's timely death (1787). Ultimately, Joseph realised that as a Catholic sovereign he could not push matters to an open split.

No such restraint guided his policy towards his domestic opponents. 'As the provinces of the monarchy constitute a single whole,' he wrote in 1783, 'all the rivalries and prejudices which have been the cause of so many quarrels between province and province, nation and nation must cease. One thought should fill the mind.'[6] But for some years Joseph refrained from major initiatives outside his Austro-Bohemian lands. Then, in spring 1784, he launched several lines of policy more or less together. The crown of St Stephen, symbol of Hungarian sovereignty – though Joseph had declined to be crowned, to avoid the constitutional oath – was brought from Pressburg castle to Vienna, reportedly to the sound of thunderclaps in the offended heavens. A Hungarian census was ordered as groundwork for the introduction of the Austrian system of military conscription, but since censuses were conventionally concerned with the assessment of taxable resources the unprecedented inclusion of hitherto untaxed nobles in the count made it still more ominous. In addition, German replaced Latin as Hungary's administrative language, all officials being given three years to learn it. Resistance to these innovations was immediate and deep, and included the Hungarian Chancellor himself, to whom Joseph scathingly replied that he would not be put off by side noises. He showed the same intransigence to the Tyrol where the military conscription system was also being introduced for the first time.

Initially, the hard line appeared to work. The disorder predicted by Joseph's advisers did not occur or rather, it came from a different quarter, from Transylvanian Romanian peasants under Horea, a peasant himself who had met Joseph and claimed to be acting in his name against the unjust lords. Their rising, easily crushed, led Joseph to extend his abolition of personal serfdom to Hungary (1785). Flushed with success he now turned against the Hungarian counties, forbidding their assemblies to meet without his permission and making their deputy sheriffs government nominees, subordinate to a new network of ten Royal Commissioners. The year 1784–85 is the turning-point in Joseph's reign, when initiatives piled on each other in domestic and foreign affairs. Judging by letters to his brother Leopold Joseph interpreted this period very much along the lines of the pro-Enlightenment *Journal Général de l'Europe* in 1785:

> It is not surprising that the reforms are undergoing contradictions and giving rise to murmurings. But an enlightened and firm government sets itself above such murmurings and continues to attend to the people's weal despite themselves.[7]

Later events were to show such nonchalance was premature.

The Crisis of Enlightened Absolutism – to 1795

In the middle years of Joseph's reign, while domestic opposition fumed inwardly, the foreign pot began to bubble. That Joseph's reforms were intended primarily to strengthen the state as the instrument of his own martial glory has been a commonplace first voiced by contemporaries. Was this not Frederick the Great's notorious rival, who said on his final leave-taking with his troops that his first desire had always been to be a soldier?

Yet as so often with this complex man everything is not quite as it might seem. Joseph's letters from the campaign trail of the War of Bavarian Succession (1778–79) breathe a spirit of repugnance for war, 'a horrible thing ... much worse than I had visualised ... the ruin of so many innocent people'.[8] Foreign diplomats in the 1780s believed that his martial appetite was in decline. It is likely, as with his favourite general Lacy, that Joseph was always more military administrator than pugnacious warlord, a man whose travels had told him that Hungarian linen socks issued to Austro-German troops gave them blisters and much more of the same. He had, it seems, no master plan in foreign affairs but sought opportunistically to profit from events to consolidate his territories. Here a key theme of Austrian policy applied, the need voiced by the great Habsburg general Prince Eugen of Savoy (1663–1736) to round off the scattered imperial lands. Thus the Austrian Netherlands and even Galicia were seen as potentially dispensable, while gains in Bavaria remained the most attractive goal, as the war of 1778–79 had indicated.

The diplomatic setting for these rather indefinite purposes left something to be desired. Prussia under Frederick II appeared an irreconcilable foe. France, which had replaced Britain as Austria's ally after the Diplomatic Revolution of 1756, remained a fickle friend. Russia under Catherine II, the other potential ally, was disconcertingly expansionist towards enfeebled Poland and Turkey. In these circumstances the defensive agreement concluded with Russia in May 1781 came to dominate the reign. It seemed to offer Austria protection against Prussia and the chance either to contain or profit from Catherine's designs. In fact, the limits on Austria's freedom of action imposed by her anti-Prussian fixation made her the weaker partner in the alliance and besides, eighteenth-century enlightened statecraft put little value on the depopulated, impoverished Balkan lands Austria would have gained from a partition of Turkey. Whether acquiring, say, Serbia and Bosnia at that time would have made the

Monarchy's later 'South Slav problem' more tractable, or speeded its emergence, is a matter of speculation.

Joseph's own ambitions lay initially elsewhere. He hoped to make the Austrian Netherlands more competitive with their Dutch neighbours, even front-runners for the new American market, an ambition which required revision of the treaties of 1648 and 1713 closing the Scheldt to international commerce. Yet despite Russian diplomatic support – French support was not forthcoming – Joseph was unable to bully the Dutch into yielding their rights. In 1785 he accepted a compromise, partly because he was already thinking of an exchange of his Belgian territories for Bavaria. The calculation was rational enough, but its clumsy execution left the heir to the Bavarian throne, whom Joseph had initially squared, scurrying to Frederick's side, enabling Prussia to assemble a League of German Princes against Austria's pretensions (1786). This abortive deal over his Belgian subjects' heads was an inauspicious backdrop to what followed. On 1 January 1787 Joseph imposed on the Austrian Netherlands the kind of administrative streamlining he had pushed through in Hungary two years and Lombardy one year previously. The Estates of Brabant took the lead in opposing this flouting of their traditional constitution. Backed by popular demonstrations, they pressed the viceregal pair in Brussels, Joseph's sister Marie Christine and her husband, to suspend the reforms. Joseph could see in his Belgian opponents only men manipulated by 'designing lawyers, bigoted priests and a few men of higher birth, who are new-fangled dabblers in what they call patriotism'.[9] The viceregal pair were rebuked for weakness and the implementation of a hard line was entrusted to successive military commanders. Joseph had proceeded much more abruptly than in the Hereditary Lands.

It was two years before the Belgian discontent burst out into open revolt, bringing the succession of major domestic initiatives finally to a halt. The middle third of the reign saw much legislation in economic and judicial matters. In the former Joseph was as eclectic as his predecessors. While the tariff of 1784 set import duties at 60% and forbade the import of certain products altogether, quite in the spirit of Austrian mercantilism, in the domestic economy state controls and direct sponsorship of industry were reduced. The restlessly enquiring Emperor had already learnt from his early travels in the Banat, then directly administered from Vienna, that a state-run economy did not work. The relaxation of guild regulations, already apparent in the toleration of rural artisans in the 1730s and the looser controls allowed

for 'commercial' guilds in 1754 (as opposed to 'police' guilds producing for daily consumption) was continued in edicts of 1784–86. On
another front Joseph's policies showed the possible influence of physiocrats, whom he had met in Paris in 1778, and whose advocacy of
free trade in grain Kaunitz had experimented with in the Duchy of
Milan in the 1770s. Whatever the inspiration, the new cadastral
(land) survey ordered in 1785 led Joseph on to plan a simplified tax
system centred around a single tax on land, reflecting the physiocrats'
core belief that the source of wealth lay in the land, not trade, as the
mercantilists believed. When told it would take the 200 trained land
surveyors available 44 years to carry out the work, he enlisted peasants, equipped with basic instructions and kit, and had three-quarters of Austria's communes covered by the end of 1786.

Meanwhile, the first part of the new Civil Code appeared in
November 1786 and the Criminal Code in 1787. Many emphases of
an older world still present in the Codex Theresianus of 1766 now disappeared. Capital punishment and the crimes of sorcery and usury
lost their place, while adultery, blasphemy and sodomy were no
longer serious crimes and the disabilities attaching to illegitimacy
were greatly reduced. More attention was to be paid to the motives
of offenders and penalties were to be the same for all, regardless of
social status. The abandonment of the sovereign's traditional *Machtspruch* or right to intervene in the legal process disguised a certain tendency for the power of the state to rise while that of the old social
order declined. All crimes were declared crimes against the state
and Joseph reserved to himself, not the judges, the right to interpret
the law in case of doubt. One reminder of the climate in which he was
acting may be useful: the authorities hesitated to enforce court judg-
ment against as lordly a person as the choleric Transylvanian Count
Wesselényi, who had sent 600 men against a disliked neighbour's
mansion, before knowing Joseph's mind.[10]

Few images of Joseph's reign have been as evocative as those of
noble offenders cleaning the streets like common malefactors. From
now on elite resentment, foreign complications and popular disillusion were to complement each other as the Monarchy allowed itself
to be embroiled in a costly and unsuccessful Russo-Turkish war. The
background was Joseph's visit to Catherine in the Ukraine in 1787.
In fact, the tightening of the links with Russia this visit implied was
more Kaunitz's preference than his own, for contrary to Joseph's
image it was the Chancellor who was the more averse to a reconciliation with Prussia after Frederick's death the previous year. But when

the Turks were provoked into declaring war on Russia Joseph came to his ally Catherine's aid, even setting himself at the head of the opening campaign. It was a disaster. Reluctant to engage the enemy for 'a few unimportant conquests' at the cost of his subjects' lives and the 'true capital' of the state,[11] Joseph appeared indecisive, while disease devastated his troops in the swampy terrain on the Hungarian–Turkish border and its location gave Hungarian mal-contents leverage to press for restoration of their constitution. As treasonable links between Hungarian opposition leaders and Prussia developed, the Prussian envoy in Vienna argued that the Porte should be won for the cause of Hungarian secession.

The Hungarian crisis was particularly ironic in view of the good-will which Joseph had once enjoyed in certain Hungarian quarters. His centralising approach had sometimes worked to Hungary's advantage, as in the reintegration of Transylvania under the Hun-garian Chancellery, while his support of religious toleration was calculated to win the backing of Magyar Protestants. Examples were the Calvinists Ferenc Kazinczy, destined to be the foremost reviver of the Magyar language but an official in Joseph's Germa-nising school system, and Count Sámuel Teleki, one of the ten new Royal Commmissioners. But Catholic aristocrats of Freemason sympathies like Counts Károly Zichy, Transylvanian Chancellor till 1782, and Károly Pálffy, combined Hungarian–Transylvanian Chancellor, 1783–87) were initially equally loyal; in 1780 Hungary had some 900 Freemasons, in thirty lodges. As time passed, how-ever, many were either alienated by Joseph's failure to recognise, as the Lutheran Berzeviczy put it, that Hungary was a free country, or were swamped by the tidal wave of opposition. Their position was further compromised by Joseph's refusal to abolish existing dis-crimination in favour of Austrian economic interests or to endorse the Hungarian Chancellery's pleas for more investment and a credit bank. The initiative passed to those who would accept reform only on the basis of noble constitutionalism and to the majority of nobles who really did not want reform at all, though they might clothe their opposition in libertarian language from Montesquieu, whose specific references to Hungary had first taught them to see their traditional rights as making up a 'constitu-tion'. From autumn 1788 county assemblies met, in defiance of gov-ernment orders, to debate the withholding of supplies for the Turkish war. Shortly, they were to have a new grievance, the tax law of February 1789.

The tax law resulted from the Josephine cadastral survey, which had been intended originally to serve as a base to rectify the unequal taxation of peasant and noble land in the reform of 1748. Yet in its final form it went much further, for it replaced all obligations to state and lord of rustical peasants paying at least 2 florins a year in tax by a single tax amounting to 30% of the gross value of peasant produce, of which 17.8% was to go to the lord and 12.2% to the state. It amounted to a universalisation of the Raab system and a completion of the abolition of serfdom. Joseph had forced through this extension of the Tax Commission's original brief against the advice of his Chancellor Count Chotek, who resigned, and of the head of the Tax Commission, the reform-minded Count Karl Zinzendorf, who called it a violation of the rights of property; disagreeing with the bourgeois councillor Eger, Zinzendorf feared an undermining of the landlord–peasant nexus on which, he claimed, society depended.[12]

This remarkable measure lies at the heart of judgements of Joseph's rule. The common charge that the land survey on which it was based was over-hasty and slipshod may be unfair. A Polish reassessment in 1930 found it largely reliable in Galicia. However, in most cases it offered nobles far less than they had previously received in peasant services; and they feared the reform's extension to their dominical peasants. Galician nobles would have lost perhaps 60% of their income, while Austro-German landlords' share of peasant income had averaged from 25% to 42% instead of the 18% now permitted. Lacking resources to cultivate their demesnes, most nobles would have to turn them over to their peasants, completing the reshaping of the *Gutsherrschaft* system which had been advocated by reformers since the middle of the century. That does not make the legislation of 1789 anything less of a leap into the dark. If the switch to peasant-based agriculture had appeared profitable on the early Raab estates and those of a few great nobles in Austria and Poland, some modern historians believe, on the basis of the very limited capital resources available to the great bulk of landlords and the experience of the next half-century, that it would not have been so on a wider scale. Nor was Chotek's concern that impoverished nobles could no longer perform the administrative duties still expected of them mere special pleading. Noble alarms were understandable, particularly in Hungary where many nobles forced off the land could not have sought refuge in government service (as they were to do in the next century) because of Joseph's introduction of German as the

official language. By the autumn of 1789 a wave of Hungarian protest, strongest where nobles and Protestants were most numerous, in
the north-east and east, was calling for the first meeting of the Diet
since 1767. Meanwhile, Brussels fell to Belgian insurrectionaries
in December.

By this time Joseph was a dying man. The once vigorous monarch,
now sleepless, emaciated and plagued by suppurating abcesses, was
suffering from fluid on the lungs, alternating fevers and chills, a failing stomach, liver and kidneys and eventually dropsy to boot.
In January 1790, the Belgians declared their independence; the Tyr-
oleans were in uproar against conscription and religious innovation;
inflation was rising and regular income had fallen to 35% of state
expenditure. New exactions to finance the war, restrictions on Free-
masonry (1785) and on the press, and Count Pergen's police harrass-
ment as Lower Austrian Governor, then in 1789 'police minister'
(a new post) had strained links with reform-minded elements. Only
the capture of Belgrade by Field Marshal Laudon in October 1789
temporarily halted the ribald mockery on the streets of Vienna for
the dying Emperor. Seeing the end approach and learning of the
Prussian–Turkish offensive alliance of January 1790 Joseph revoked
all his Hungarian reforms except for toleration, abolition of personal
serfdom and the new parishes; seemingly oblivious of his brother
Leopold's secret hatred he begged him in the name of friendship to
speed from Tuscany to his side. This Leopold carefully forbore to do,
arriving in Vienna on 12 March, three weeks after Joseph's stoically
borne final illness had drawn to its close.

But enlightened monarchy did not end with Joseph's death.
As Grand Duke of Tuscany since 1765 Leopold had arguably been
truer to the famous picture of 1769 showing the two brothers seated
at a table bearing a copy of Montesquieu's *Spirit of the Laws*. It was
precisely Joseph's high-handedness which Leopold most disliked.
His papers show that in addition to the judicial, religious and social
reforms common to enlightened despots he envisaged setting up a
consultative Tuscan assembly along representative lines. A somewhat secretive, fastidious man who combined high purpose with a
certain deviousness, he worked resourcefully to defuse the multifar-
ious crises his impetuous brother had conjured forth. While summoning the provincial Diets and trying to appease their grievances, he
negotiated with the Turks and Prussians in order to deprive domestic opposition of potential external support. By authorising Serbs to
hold a National Church Congress at Timişoara and recreating an

'Illyrian' Court Chancellery where Croats and Serbs were represented he played the card of 'divide and rule' against the Magyars.
Meanwhile, he retained his own hidden agenda, in which as much
of Joseph's social reforms as possible were to be salvaged.

The Convention of Reichenbach restoring relations with Prussia in
July 1790 was followed by the recovery of Belgium and peace with
Turkey on the basis, effectively, of the *status quo ante* at Sistovo in
August 1791. Leopold could now pick and choose how to respond to
the Diets' predictable demands for restoration of old powers, a
tougher line to peasants, easier noble credit and, less predictable perhaps, from the Bohemian Diet, a bigger role for Czech in education.
Basically, the suspension of the 1789 tax edict did the trick in keeping
noble indignation in check in the Austro-Slav lands. The fact that
only Tyrol and Galicia complained about the role of the *Kreis* administration under Joseph showed how far this aspect of state bureaucracy had won acceptance. Hungary, of course, was another matter.
There some 500 pamphlets testified to a bewildering variety of opinions – progressive and reactionary, Magyar and non-Magyar,
noble and bourgeois. The loss of Prussian support through the Reichenbach Convention, however, shattered the confidence of the one
group with the cohesion and status to impose its programme on the
Diet: the middle nobility. The result was a compromise. Hungary
was recognised as an independent state with the right to be governed
by its own laws, to hold triennial Diets and to demand the King's
oath to the constitution. But only small gestures were made to newer
accents in the opposition movement, like the desire for more use of
Magyar in education and officialdom, and none at all to the call for
an elected senate to replace the Lieutenancy Council as focal point of
the administration. Noble immunity from taxation was reaffirmed;
even the nobility's enlightened wing never got beyond a mild paternalism on social questions. 'The French example shows how little
the dim eyes of a people long held in a dark dungeon can endure the
sudden light of truth', as one Calvinist *bien pensant* remarked.[13]

There is intriguing evidence that Leopold's own attitude to social
change was more robust. He lent secret support to an anonymous
press campaign of German-speaking Hungarian burghers against
the nobility. Having suspended the tax edict, he maintained pressure
on the Diets of the Austro-Bohemian lands to come up with their own
proposals for the abolition of *robota*. Leopold's support for stronger
bourgeois representation in the Diets and dispensing with Pergen's
ministry and detention without judicial warrant point in the same

reformist direction. What kind of Monarchy Leopold ultimately envisaged remains, however, unclear because he suddenly sickened and died, on 1 March 1792. He was the last Habsburg sovereign more interested in change than conservation.

Under Leopold's son Francis II enlightened absolutism finally gave up the ghost. A stolid if honest young man, Francis spent the first half of his long reign fighting against the French Revolution. With Pergen and his methods restored to favour, a conspiracy theory became received wisdom in which foreigners, Freemasons and similar sect members were all objects of suspicion and supervision. This paranoia was not wholly baseless. Jacobin France was as disturbing to contemporaries as Bolshevik Russia was to be. The combined result of the Austrian Enlightenment, Joseph's reforms and the revolution in France had been to diffuse a certain restlessness in quite wide ranges of the population, though coherent intellectual radicalism was a matter only of small groups in the larger towns. Bohemian peasants were reported to be avid for news of France in 1789 and full of hate for their lords in 1793. Research has revealed individuals in almost all provinces of the Monarchy and all branches of the professions, including clerics, civil servants and army officers, who sympathised with what they thought the French Revolution was trying to do and deplored the unbending negativism of the authorities. A poignant illustration is the case of army officer and engineering professor Andreas Riedel. An acquaintance of Leopold and former tutor of Francis, he was made a baron by the latter just as he was turning from pro-reform memoranda to the authorities to conspiratorial mobilisation of support for his views.

In Hungary disillusion with the tepid outcome of the 1790–91 Diet provided a somewhat wider basis for reform-minded members of the Magyar-speaking intelligentsia to split off from the movement of the middle nobility. 'Intelligentsia' is perhaps an anachronistic label to apply to a merely nascent category in late feudal Hungary, combining government and estate officials, well-educated professionals and teachers, a part of the clergy and noble and bourgeois elements, perhaps 15,000 in all. Of these two to three hundred may have been mobilised through social networks and reading clubs into the secret Society of Reformers organised by the ex-Franciscan friar Ignác Martinovics in 1793–94. Its programme, written by Martinovics, was national independence under enlightened noble aegis. But Martinovics also wrote a passionate hymn to peasant emancipation from feudalism for a second body (the 'Society of Liberty and Equality'), unknown to the first and seen by some historians as a vehicle of Hungarian bourgeois revolution. Too much should probably not be made of what would have been a minority of an already tiny minority of Hungarian 'Jacobins'. Martinovics confessed at his trial that he had only 'quite general conceptions' of how he would govern when the radical insurrection came.[14] The matter became academic when he was arrested in summer 1794, with some 50 others as well as 26 Austrians, after a spy's setting up of the drunken lieutenant Hebenstreit, author of a revolutionary effusion in Latin hexameters; how guilty of concrete treason the Austrians were is not clear. Martinovics was hanged and Riedel incarcerated in the Spielberg prison in Brno, to die a respected citizen in Paris in 1837.

Joseph II and the Historians

Helpful as it is to take the story of enlightened absolutism's rise and fall on to 1795, it is Joseph's personality and achievement which remain the focal point of enquiry. Historical debate on this score has been as revealing of the historians' own times as of Joseph's. Seen alternately as forerunner of liberalism and wilful free-thinker in the nineteenth century, then National Socialist *avant la lettre* by the Nazis, Joseph could appear in the affluent, utopian 1960s as a man behind the times who turned against the new thinking he himself had prompted. In conservative critiques, which have been the most consistent, he has always been the exemplar of a shallow rationalism that mistook vindictiveness to nobles for egalitarian principle, educational philistinism for enlightening the masses and an arid state-shackled religion for the subtler needs of the human soul. Above all in this view, by imposing a rationalistic Natural Law and a schematised administration in place of traditional institutions, he detached law from the actualities of life and eased its subordination to an abstract concept of sovereignty identical with the monarch's despotic will. Thus conservatives can criticise Joseph as both libertarian and despot, since for them professions of enlightenment merely cloak the power urge of individuals or interest groups looking to profit from social destabilisation. Hence their stress of *popular* alienation at the assault on custom and tradition, particularly in the religious sphere.

The argument *ad hominem* is not illegitimate. Joseph's meddling waspishness, cheese-paringness and philistinism are a matter of

record. Was there not, though, in the very cynicism which led him
to believe people would soon forget their childish whims if government stood firm, as much bumptious naïvety as nastiness? Joseph's
complex personality has largely escaped the attention of the psycho-
historians. Only François Fejtö has emphasised the peculiar mix of
passion and reticence underlying Joseph's ill-starred emotional life
leading to an only half-convincing sardonic sang froid and resignation to widowerhood and state service, though Derek Beales has
shown the scars of his close but difficult relation to his mother. But
that 'something so good-natured and frank in his appearance and
behaviour' noted by Keith, the British ambassador, and others,
should not be lost sight of. We are not dealing with the cold, abstract
benevolence of a Robespierre or Saint Juste.

Personal solicitude often broke through in the Josephinian
reforms, even where state interests were directly concerned: in the
novel permission to soldiers to marry and raise a family, in the special
regulations for the humane treatment of young prisoners, in the fact
that the denunciation of crime expected as a civil duty was specifically not to apply between parents and children. Nor was Joseph
always the exacting task-master, expecting more work for no extra
reward, or the gung-ho dogmatist commonly depicted. He raised
judges' salaries from 800 to 3000 florins a year and modified several
of his early measures on ministerial advice, like the philistine decision
to downgrade Freiburg University to a *Gymnasium*; 'I am human and
can err', as he said perhaps too grandly to the head of the Court Education Commission Gottfried van Swieten in effectively apologising
for his 'bad moods' on another occasion.[15] The aggressive foreign
policy in the Balkans was as much Kaunitz's as his own. In domestic
matters Emperor and advisers seem much of the time to have worked
together in devising thoughtful solutions to problems previously sta-
lemated by prescription or taboo. Thus in the discussions on the place
of illegitimacy in the Civil Code Joseph and Kaunitz's tolerance and
awareness of economic factors in extra-marital affairs read impress-
ively. Josephinism was more than a one-man band. It was the culmi-
nation of a generation of thought in Austrian governing circles about
the improvement of society and the strengthening of the state, which
presupposed that gains in knowledge and techniques enabled a different approach to the management of the Monarchy from that followed in the age of Baroque.

But how different was that approach to be? On this question the
judgements of the non-conservative camp have been much less

consistent than those made of Joseph by the Right. The nineteenth-century view of a liberal Emperor fighting for civil freedoms could not survive the Russian Mitrofanov's magisterial source-based biography of 1910 which set Joseph firmly in the tradition of enlightened despotism. Austrian liberalism itself decomposed into separate liberal, nationalist and socialist movements. The emphasis was still on change, however, whether in Viktor Bibl's portrait of an authoritarian reformer under the Third Reich (1943) or in two other well-known works of the 1940s, A.J.P. Taylor's *The Habsburg Monarchy* and François Fejtö's *Joseph II*, which, while cleaving closer to the nineteenth-century tradition, saw Joseph as radical rather than liberal: the 'royal revolutionary' for Fejtö, 'the Convention in a single man' for Taylor. In the light of modern research the French revolutionary analogy is misleading. Josephinism had nothing to do with creating a new social order along the lines of 1789–94; nobility was not to be abolished, nor the Catholic Church to be displaced by worship of a Supreme Being. True, Joseph went out of his way to encourage middle-class entrepreneurs, but particularly by ennobling them more readily – 18% of his ennoblements were of this type, compared to only 7% of his mother's. A decree of 1782 explicitly reminded the peasants that the Emperor's reforms did not mean they should cease obeying their masters. True happiness lay within, urged the new school textbooks. Joseph increased the number of parish priests, so that no-one should have to walk more than an hour to church. His scorn for the bourgeois rebels of Brabant shows he had no concept of the middle class as an independent source of social power. Most of his leading advisers remained aristocrats and he once expressed a preference for noble administrators, as less subject to material pressures. The social vision was Sonnenfels's, not Rousseau's.

Historians' increased awareness of the context of an ongoing Austrian enlightenment has led since the 1960s to an intriguing change of front. No longer the revolutionary, Joseph has been seen by some historians as turning on the burgeoning Viennese free press he had initially liberated to help him against his clerical enemies. Writers came to feel that they had been used. 'It is unlikely that genuine Enlightenment will be achieved in a country where the ordinary reader can only get books which insult church dignitaries ... and in every third line praise the gracious sovereign', wrote Joseph Grossing in 1785 in connection with Joseph's despotic methods in Hungary.[16] Ernst Wangermann sees evidence of radical intellectual influence even in artisanal ranks. In the face of such tendencies the regime responded with measures against the Freemasons (1785), orders for the strict teaching of Catholic dogma (1786), the creation of Pergen's police ministry (1789) and the censorship regulations of January 1790. The tragedy of Joseph's reign, argues Wangermann, is that his reforms had helped create a critical public opinion prepared to turn its scrutiny on the government; but when this point came Joseph repudiated his noblest handiwork. Paul Bernard has shown his continued interference in the judicial process, despite the abolition of the sovereign's right of *Machtspruch*, including some half-dozen cases of arbitrary imprisonment for political reasons.

Fascinating as these perspectives are, we should see Joseph's break with the progressive publicists towards the end of his reign as a repudiation of a particular wing of Enlightenment rather than of Enlightenment in general. The fact is that the fracturing of the reform movement was already taking place as a result of its own divisions and not because of the withdrawal of Joseph's support. Crucial to its earlier growth had been the Reform Catholic/Jansenist strain in eighteenth-century Austria which had proved so effective in dissolving the ideological base of the old alliance of throne, altar and aristocracy. Reshaped in terms of a utilitarian government, flanked by a service nobility and clergy, the Habsburg elite under Maria Theresa and her son had acquired in it a credo which could appeal to the rising middle class and even some better-off peasants. The crisis of Reform Catholicism, as the intellectual avant-garde turned to Deism and free thinking, reflected the splintering of the reform consensus as a whole.

In this context, Joseph's repudiation of the more radical bourgeois and plebeian currents of the latter 1780s was arguably realistic. Viennese literary production should not be romanticised. Often it followed earlier western stereotypes of unworthy priests, wicked, lascivious nobles and fabled Moroccan or Hottentot observers of Viennese society; some of it fell into the 'Grub Street' genre of salacious journalism by frustrated egos identified in pre-revolutionary France. Calls for involvement in public affairs of 'men of insight' and 'patriots' glossed over the inadequate information of even the best-educated non-official literati about a multi-national realm which made concepts of patriotism highly problematic. The mystical appeals to a new realm of light and truth which were common in Freemasons' discourse (Mozart's *Magic Flute* was written in 1791) offered no basis for real social action. The subsequent fate of the enlightened publicists of the 1780s suggests their lack of cohesion.

Alongside men like Riedel who became more radical, some others like Haschka or Richter gravitated to more conservative positions. Set against the record of human cruelty and folly, Joseph's repressions, of which the most discussed is the harassment of a publisher of anti-government tracts named Wucherer, appear less heinous. Pergen's police ministry had few resources and no executive power over provincial governors.

The most that was attainable by way of reform in late eighteenth-century Austria was an alliance of enlightened nobles and bureaucrats, with elements of the nascent bourgeoisie in subaltern role. The Monarchy's ethnic structure made even this more problematic than in nearby Poland, where arguably it was briefly achieved in the ill-fated constitution of 1791. Seen in this light, Joseph's alienation of noble reformers like Zinzendorf and the Hungarian Berzeviczy, both economic modernisers, was more fateful than his break with the littérateurs of Vienna. Why did Joseph forfeit their support? Was it mainly a matter of his personal defects, his impatience, arrogance and authoritarianism? Or was he attempting the impossible in going beyond the dubious Enlightenment of his fellow monarchs, Frederick and Catherine, who never challenged the interests of the mainstream nobility? Was there a possible middle way?

For Mitrofanov in 1910 the answer seemed plain. Joseph represented the cul-de-sac of absolute despotism which had taken reform as far as was possible without cutting the ground from under its feet. His radicalism and his authoritarianism were inseparable. The way ahead to liberalism was barred. Modern research has somewhat softened this antithesis both by revealing the general pressures for reform existing independently of the dynasty and by focusing on the enigmatic figure of Leopold. Could Joseph's brother, had he lived, have reconstructed an alliance of reforming elites, stabilising a period of forward-looking transition and setting a precedent for benign evolution? The speed with which Leopold was able to defuse the numerous imbroglios of his opening months demonstrated the underlying strength of the government's position. Yet other aspects of the reign suggest scepticism. Leopold made little progress in getting the Austrian estates to accept the principle of *robota* abolition or broader bourgeois representation, and in Hungary his secret dealings with the anti-nobiliar opposition were fraught with risk. The tactic of *reculer pour mieux sauter* which he was plainly following could well, at a later stage, have led to a renewal of confrontation which might have forced him to adopt his brother's stubborness or retreat to the more traditional line of his mother. The social base of reform monarchy did not extend widely enough into the middling elite strata, particularly in Hungary, for a corresponding middle course to seem in hindsight a good bet. Berzeviczy once remarked that English society had taken centuries to evolve its liberal traditions. At least Leopold, unlike his brother, showed an awareness that reform required a social base and not just moral invocation.

This does not necessarily make Leopold a more significant figure. Posterity, an often sentimental judge, prizes glorious failure more than judicious success. It was Joseph's most provocative moral stances, whether as scourge of noble ill-doers or of bureaucrats who did not give their all, which fixed his legend in the minds of later generations. Joseph's problems were two-fold. Though probably a good, if exasperating man, he was not a great one, in the conventional sense of one sure of himself and his destiny. At crucial moments, as in his dealings with the Belgians, he could be hesitant. Second, unlike his brother, he failed to see that the dynasty was ultimately one institution among others and had to respect others' traditions in the cause of reform. Thus his legacy to his successors could not be a working whole, a 'going concern', but only parts of a system in uneasy juxtaposition: traditions of social reform, religious tolerance, bureaucratic state service and German-orientated centralism. The parts had a strength which made them basic ingredients of the Habsburg polity for generations to come. But how to reconcile them with the Monarchy's irreducible pluralism of tradition, or adapt them to new circumstances, became the chief task of Habsburg statecraft. In this way Joseph's reign set the agenda for the future.

The Josephinist Legacy

Incomplete though it was, Joseph's achievement itemised at the end of the previous section far transcended his pitiful death. Bearing a relation to his purposes, if linked to other factors, was the quickening of economic and national life towards the end of the century. Estimates give 237,000 textile workers in Bohemia and 529,000 in 1798, while they nearly doubled in Lower Austria in the 1780s. These were, of course, largely female domestic workers since female employment provided extra means of subsistence for rapidly growing populations, helping them, Komlos speculates, to escape the Malthusian trap. But concentrations of factory workers were also growing, like the 500 carpet workers of Reichenberg in Bohemia in 1775 who became 2500 by 1794. The protectionist tariffs of 1775 and 1784 helped spur this activity, such that in the Monarchy as a whole by the 1780s finished goods made up 65% of exports and only one-sixth of imports. The French wars later had a similar effect. The Josephinist state helped industry also through granting peasants freedom of movement, which eased labour problems, letting confiscated monastic premises and liberalising the guilds. Meanwhile, the removal of the state from direct sponsorship of enterprises may have been responsible for the perceptible growth in industrial professionalism, suggested by a higher proportion of bourgeois entrepreneurs and capital, more attention to managerial skills and more stable work-forces.

Agriculture also registered gains. From about 1780 grain yields in Hungary began to rise for the first time since the Middle Ages, from three or four to some five times the seed sown. Advanced techniques were taught in the Lutheran pastor Sámuel Tessedik's college in Szarvas (1780–1796) and in colleges founded by the enlightened counts Széchényi and Festetics. In the Austrian lands the spread of all-year-round stalling of cattle, first practised in England and Holland, led to substantial expansion and rebuilding of farmsteads. In Lower Austria alone, 22,000 new buildings went up between 1800 and 1810, and by 1815 60% of the province's houses were made of stone. The rise of late eighteenth-century agricultural prices and the importance given to peasants in physiocratic doctrine was reflected in an upgrading of their lifestyle, at least for the *Bauern*. Anecdotal evidence that even day labourers were demanding white bread as a condition of employment in 1797 should be set against the finding that the average height of Austrian army recruits decreased from the 1760s. Diet regulations of state institutions no longer measured the amount of bread inmates could eat, as they had earlier. Coffee had become a regular breakfast drink of rich Austrian peasants and the fork had joined the spoon as a regular item in the peasant household. Further afield, in Hungary, peasants in the west of the country were beginning to use native builders rather than build their own homes, to discard their linen outer garments for lighter materials and to own brightly painted domestic furniture. Here the Danube was the dividing line between old and new. In much of the Monarchy the traditional 'folk costumes' subsequently so much admired date from this time.

The picture is somewhat different in the towns. Meat consumption declined in the later eighteenth century, along with real wages, though statistics for the latter must be tentative. Workers held that 9 florins a month was adequate to maintain a family, but a Schwechat factory worker, near Vienna, might earn only 50–60 florins a year and a coachman 20 florins with food. Nonetheless, the taste for novelty, like coffee for Viennese day labourers – if probably a cheap substitute – is recorded in the towns, too. By 1802 Karl Zinzendorf no longer considered sugar a luxury, as he had in 1772. Sandgruber's explanation of changes in consumption despite stagnant real wages, in terms of harder work, is fuller for the countryside, where anyway many incomes rose. Rising taxes which forced peasants to produce more for the market might lead them to stop spending time making their own linen clothes but to buy cotton ones instead – a complete reallocation of time, replete with implications for market demand, which in fact rose.

Where peasants belonged to non-dominant nationalities improved peasant education and status had ethnic consequences, enhanced by the stimulus the intellectually omnivorous Enlightenment gave to the study of non-dominant history and culture. Though at the higher levels of schooling Enlightenment acted as a Germanising force, at the rural level the better provision of elementary schools, operating effectively in the mother tongue, undoubtedly strength- ened ethnic awareness. In the towns, where the 'main schools' were overwhelmingly German, the impact was more mixed. Bohemia, where school attendance rose from two-fifths to two-thirds in Jose- ph's reign, is an instructive case. Though the municipal reform of 1784 made German the administrative language of Prague, separate university chairs were established for pastoral theology in Czech and German (1778) and for Czech language and literature (1791), while there was an unprecedented boom in Czech-language textbooks. Enlightened administrators gave the Czech peasants a role-model in the village judge Jan Vavák, among other things author of one of sev- eral poems commemorating Joseph's turn behind the plough at the Moravian village of Slavíkovice in 1769 – a much depicted anticipa- tion of the art of the photo-opportunity.

In Prague, both an intellectual and a popular Czech cultural revi- val emerged, if on different lines. For men like the Reform Catholic priest Dobrovský, protégé of Bohemian aristocrats, the task was to explore the roots of Slav philology and literature and to rehabilitate Czech history, including the role of the martyred heretic Jan Hus. For men like the editor and publisher Kramerius the task was to minister to the needs of Czech artisans through the rising media of journalism and theatre. From 1784 Czech plays were being regularly performed in Prague. Kramerius's prolific publishing activity concentrated on the translation of Josephinist texts, including Joseph's purported death-bed remarks. That one of these promised 'the people' that God would protect them from oppressive bailiffs best conveys the nature of Kramerius's work and audience.

Unsophisticated as this sort of thing was, Kramerius's writings were beginning to shape a modern Czech consciousness, its radical undertow overlaid by tactical caution. While he equated the previously often derogatory term *lid* (people) with the more august *národ* (nation), and identified the common folk, not the nobles, with the latter, he also supported the regionalist demands of the feudal Diet in 1790 and he denounced the course of the French Revolution he had initially praised. This resembles the deference of contemporary Irish Catholic leaders to the Protestant Grattan Parliament, and had a similar cause: the native population's lack of social and psychological resources for self-assertion. To complete the picture, there developed among the peasantry a cult of the good Joseph II. In the most popular novel of the Czech national revival, Božena Němcová's *Granny* (1855), the grandmother of the title recounts how as a peasant child she had met the simply dressed, kindly Emperor Joseph who had given help against an arrogant official and only at the end revealed his identity with a silver coin as souvenir.[17]

The very different Hungarian response to Josephinism had its own ambivalences. Important literary works lambasted Joseph's reforms in the spirit of old noble values. In one the uncrowned Joseph was the 'hatted king'; in another a country gentleman in Buda confronted dandified noble youths decked out in foreign fashions and disdaining their mother tongue. Yet the very quality of these works testified to a literary awakening bearing in part at least an enlightened stamp. Two-thirds of the books published in Hungary in the century appeared after 1765, while the number of printing presses in roughly the same period trebled to 51. Pest, with its eight bookshops and 'commission for urban embellishment' was undergoing by the 1790s the process of cultural efflorescence that Vienna had experienced a generation earlier. Whether in the first dispassionate enquiries into Hungarian linguistic origins, the pioneer works in Hungarian on topics like physics (1777), natural science (1783) and physiology (1791) or the beginnings of Magyar journalism and theatre the characteristic didactic tones of Enlightenment may be heard. 'Let us therefore broaden our minds, Gentlemen, so that growing in wisdom from a study of . . . the entire globe, we may see as in a mirror the strengths and weaknesses of our own country': thus the poet Bessenyei, a member of Maria Theresa's Hungarian Bodyguard, in his 1778 pamphlet *Magyardom*.[18] After the foundation of the first Hungarian language newsapaper, the *Magyar Hírmondó*, in Vienna (1780) groups of like-minded enthusiasts appeared in Bratislava, Pest, north Hungarian Košice (Kassa) and the Transylvanian capital Cluj inspired by Bessenyei's dream of establishing a nation-wide society dedicated to the systematic development of the Hungarian language. By 1792 half of Hungary's 18 newspapers were in Magyar, the largest with a circulation of 1300.

Despite their predominantly enlightened allegiance, these journals could also turn against the government at the time of the Austro-Turkish war. Many of them sided with the Diet in 1790. This alienation, though, was not irreversible. In retrospect Berzeviczy called Joseph 'of glorious memory', and the nineteenth-century reformer Wesselényi, whose father had been imprisoned by Joseph, was to record that as a man he blessed Joseph's name, while wishing as a patriot that he had acted through the law. Men like Kazinczy believed Joseph's reforms would ultimately benefit backward Hungary by the stimulation they afforded. The young Joseph Kármán's vivid account of how ardent young intellects, returning from abroad, could be sucked back into a world of hunting and greyhound racing from whose torpor only wild revels could rouse them shows the horror some had of stultifying tradition.

There is, then, a tragic note in the collapse of the Hungarian reform movement after 1792 not found elsewhere in the Monarchy. The split between monarchical, noble and bourgeois versions of Enlightenment doomed all to frustration. The voluminous reform materials prepared by commissions of the 1790–91 Diet remained unused because Francis declined to call the 1793 Diet which was to have discussed them. Some reformers were executed; others, like Kármán and the brilliant poet Csokonai, died young. Aristocratic patrons of change drew in their horns. Sámuel Tessedik was forced to close his pioneering agricultural college. As in contemporary England the French revolutionary wars snuffed out the flickers of reform.

The most unreserved Josephinists came from the smaller peoples of the Monarchy. Even in Croatia, whose Magyar-patterned noble Diet in 1792 submitted itself to the authority of the Hungarian Lieutenancy, the Bishop of Zagreb Vrhovac was a convinced Josephinist, like the Ljubljana *lycée* professor Anton Linhart and his Freemason patron Baron Zois, forerunners of the Slovene awakening. Slovene and Ruthenian were taught in the general seminaries of Ljubljana and Lvov respectively; the stipends of Uniate clergy, previously poor relations to their Catholic counterparts, were raised. Increased confidence encouraged the projection of theories of a proud Roman ancestry for Romanian 'Wallachs' (whose *Libellum Valachorum* of 1791 asserted, albeit unavailingly, the claim to equality in Transylvania) and of a 'Great Moravian Empire' of the ninth-century ancestors of the Slovaks. Rajić's influential history of the Slavs appeared in 1794–95. The Monarchy's Orthodox inhabitants had most to gain from the new concern for the periphery. Their schools in the Banat, Serbian and Romanian, increased from 205 to 452 within five years of the Hungarian school law of 1777, under the dynamic educational reformer Emanuel Janković. The Karlowitz church province acquired a Catholic-style consistory (1782) and a seminary, while permission was granted for the first Serb newspaper to appear, in Vienna. All this, of course, was not without an *arrière-pensée*. The Serbs were to be westernised no less than the Jews. Riots in Novi Sad when traditional burials with open coffins were forbidden on health grounds showed some of the strains attached. But just before his death in 1811, the leading Serb intellectual pioneer of the day, the ex-monk Dositej Obradović, declared he owed his achievements to the unique spirit of Joseph of blessed memory.

This moral conquest of the periphery has been insufficiently emphasised by historians. The Bohemian Diet in 1790 might bluster that there was no such thing as the Austrian Monarchy. But this was an escape from a reality increasingly expounded by the new school of statisticians and ethnographers who discussed its features with a thoroughness not unmixed with pride. Riegger, Demian, Lichtenstern, de Luca, Schwartner and Rohrer are the key names here. This almost proprietory attitude to the Habsburg lands as a whole came more naturally to German speakers than any other group. There *was* some heightening of cultural consciousness, as among other nationalities. Martini used the expression 'national spirit' approvingly. But there was as yet no full appreciation of the problematic nature of such a concept in multi-national Austria. While some Austrian Jacobins recognised that ethnic diversity ruled out a 'rapid, powerful and general revolution along French lines', Riedel could write to Leopold II of a 'National Assembly' for the whole Monarchy representing 'the supreme majesty of the nation' though consisting of representatives of 'various nations'.[19] Besides, it was not national cultural questions which preoccupied German speakers after 1792 but the struggle against reaction.

In this their fortunes were mixed. Pergen was able to restore a ministry of police and a re-censorship commission from 1803 banned 2500 works published in 1780–92. Robota remained. But in the early years of Francis's reign reformers like Martini, Zinzendorf and Sonnenfels retained office and influence. It was Martini who saw to it that the Austrian Jacobins were tried by due process of law and Zinzendorf who protested against limiting Hungarian professors' right to raise awkward questions in their teaching. Above all the process of legislative codification which conservatives had almost stopped in its tracks at the end of Maria Theresa's reign went on to its stately conclusion in the General Civil Code of 1811. If it omitted to define the responsibilities of the sovereign, much discussed in freer times, the Code still declared all individuals, as possessors of innate rights illuminated by reason, to be citizens, hence not subject to slavery or serfdom. With recourse to the moral philosophy of the north German Protestant Kant (otherwise virtually banned from Austrian places of learning until the 1860s), the codifiers distinguished sharply between public and private law. In the latter the citizen was to be free to do whatever he chose with his own, provided the interests of others were not affected. Here was a major endorsement of notions of civil liberty within the framework of the bureaucratic–absolutist state.

This is important. It is perhaps too easy to ascribe the authoritarian elements in the Josephine Enlightenment to Joseph's own domineering personality, or see them, with Mitrofanov, as the Achilles' heel of enlightened despotism. An authoritarian streak ran right through the Enlightenment as a whole, and not just in its governmental or central European manifestations. The zest for social and moral discipline can be seen also in the Rousseau who advocated a civic religion whose violators would be punished by death. This regimentation is certainly alien to the liberal understanding of the late twentieth century, but it was not so far from the liberal practice of the nineteenth. In the Enlightenment, which began the process towards liberalism, a dialectic was at work. As the moorings to one society, the *ancien régime*, were slackened, so the outline of another, with its own disciplines and structures, was foreshadowed. The condition of the transition, in the Austrian context, was the replacement of the feudal and Tridentine props of a 'court-orientated society' by a framework placing more weight on civic equality and citizenship. Civism was the key to a new kind of state power, which made genuine concessions to its people in such things as individual religious conscience and economic freedom.

Of course, Joseph's work remained a torso. The boast of civic equality was dubious once the coping stone of his reforms, the abolition of feudal labour service, had been removed under Emperor Francis. He never envisaged a public opinion truly independent of the purposes of government, nor saw the problem of where civic loyalty should be directed in a multi-ethnic society. But we should note the interconnections thoughtful contemporaries perceived in their daily life. Far from the burgeoning intelligentsias of Vienna, Prague and Buda-Pest, young Joseph Kármán commented on the role of new fashions and new aspirations to 'refinement' in multiplying needs and undermining traditional mores among the nobles of rural Hungary.[20] The pace of change varied in different parts of the Monarchy but its psychology was similar. The cake of custom was broken. That so many at the centre of the state were in favour of the dual goal of 'happy citizens' meant a conjunction of political and social trends deeper than the shipwreck of Joseph's last years would suggest. This, of course, could support the critique that he betrayed those trends; in a hindsight closer to the realities than modern historians can be, near contemporaries were kinder. The spirit of conscientious public service that was the Austrian Enlightenment's main legacy came to be dubbed, fittingly, 'Josephinian'.

3   Metternich's Austria: Pyrrhic Victory Abroad, Social Question at Home

The period from the 1790s to 1848 is the least discussed in modern Austrian history. This is a pity because if ever irreversible patterns were set in the Monarchy's long slide to dissolution it was most probably in these paradoxical years, when an ossifying elite repudiated Joseph's radicalism while steady progress was made towards many of his goals. In much of the empire (Francis called himself Emperor of Austria from 1804) the lineaments of a centralised bureaucratic state using a German lingua franca became clearer. The Josephinist state church and the commitment to primary education were consolidated, while a limited economic modernisation got under way. Yet in the absence of the nexus between centralism and social reform which had characterised the Josephinist experiment, the Monarchy's lumbering advance gave it no real place in its polyglot subjects' hearts. The sense of a lack of inner vitality, of deviation from the European norm, which was to haunt the Monarchy's last decades, was already the subject of recrimination well before 1848.

The Anti-revolutionary wars

The protracted wars with revolutionary and Napoleonic France brought out both the strengths and weaknesses of Austrian Europeanism. On the one hand she alone of continental powers joined Britain in all five anti-French coalitions between 1792 and 1815, during which her peoples united behind the dynasty despite French revolutionary blandishments. Yet the impact of the reformer Johann Philipp Stadion (1806–09) cannot be compared with that of his Prussian contemporaries, Stein and Hardenberg, under whom serfdom was abolished and real administrative reform achieved. The patriotic movement of the doomed campaign of 1809 had less lasting effect than stirrings in other German lands. Austria's crab-like progress from enforced pro-French neutrality after this to Prussia and Russia's side at the battle of Leipzig (1813), for all Metternich's diplomatic skill, bespoke the caution of a wounded and still vulnerable protagonist in these great events.

These wounds had grown more grievous as the conflict lasted. Leopold, who had initially greeted the French Revolution, felt obliged for the sake of his sister Marie Antoinette to adopt a threatening posture; an Austro-Prussian alliance in February 1792 encouraged French revolutionaries to declare war on encircling 'reaction' in April. French belligerence, the conservatism of Leopold's son and successor Francis (1792–1835) and numerous points of contact of Habsburg and Imperial lands with an expansionist France in Belgium, Italy and Alsace made co-existence impossible. To the dogged Thugut, Austrian foreign minister from 1793 to 1801, fell the difficult task of relating the balance of power politics of the eighteenth century to a new, revolutionary challenge, for the second and third partitions of Poland were taking place (1793, 1795) at the same time as France advanced in the Austrian Netherlands and old ideas of a Belgium/Bavaria swap revived. Austria participated only in the Third Partition whereby Poland disappeared from the map. But Napoleon's advance through north Italy to the Austrian Alps (1796–97), then his victories at Marengo in north Italy and Hohenlinden in southern Germany (1800), ended Austrian participation in the first and second anti-French coalitions respectively, through the treaties of Campo Formio (1797) and Lunéville (1801). How, lamented Thugut after the former treaty, could one challenge the energies of a Bonaparte with the typical Viennese, who cared nothing for 'the honour of the Monarchy' or its longer-term future, provided he could stroll the old city bastions (now a recreational area) and eat his fried chicken in peace.[1] Actually, the treaties retained some traditional balancing features. Austria lost Belgium and Lombardy but was compensated by the acquisition of Venice and its provinces in Istria and Dalmatia, four million subjects gone for one and a half million gained, as Thugut sourly calculated.

However, the Third Coalition, formed with Britain and Russia in 1803 and ending for Austria at the field of Austerlitz (December 1805), was a different story. By the Treaty of Pressburg Austria was obliged to cede Dalmatia to France, the Tyrol to Bavaria and lost the remaining *Vorlande*, gaining only Salzburg in paltry exchange. This time Vienna itself was occupied by the French. Though the equable Viennese do not seem to have resented their uninvited guests, the upper reaches of Austrian society were goaded into a self-assertion not unlike the Prussian response to defeat at Jena (1807). Austria's most successful general, Francis's brother the Archduke Karl, already minister of war, was empowered, as Generalissimo, to carry out military reform. Count Johann Philipp Stadion, an anti-French Rhinelander from a family with a tradition of service to the Holy Roman Empire, became foreign minister, ironically in the year when Francis, under French pressure, declared this Empire at an end (1806); this act and his prior assumption of the title of Emperor of Austria were, however, also designed to deprive Napoleon of a possible weapon for his German ambitions and to safeguard Vienna's position. A censorship relaxed at Stadion's request brought out a stream of publications appealing to the 'public spirit' which had made revolutionary France so formidable and which Stein was seeking to mobilise in Prussia. Joseph Hormayr's *Patriotic Journal for the Austrian Empire*, founded in 1808, and Sartori's *Literary Annals of the Austrian Empire* (1806–10) gave intellectual underpinning to the new patriotism. The government itself commissioned a volume of patriotic poems in honour of the *Landwehr*, the militia called into being for the Hereditary Lands by the Archduke Karl's reforms. Meanwhile, German-speaking intellectuals flocked to the Austrian capital. The Catholic converts Friedrich and Dorothea Schlegel headed the religious and Adam and Johannes Müller (unrelated) the political champions of a revalued medievalism, affirming the virtues of an organic society based on hierarchy and faith. The Prussian Friedrich Gentz, a one-man conservative think-tank and advocate of the need to remove the French threat to the European balance of power, wrote the official proclamation of war on France of April 1809, calling on Austrians to fight for 'all those sweet, holy and eternal things bound up with the concept of a particular fatherland'.[2] Crowds fought for copies of the order of military command with which Austria began the war.

For once, enthusiasm appeared little different in the Monarchy's non-German lands. French emissaries had differed as to whether Hungarian noble dissatisfaction with Vienna could be turned to French advantage, one of them claiming that the generals, ministers and orators of revolutionary France were household names to the Hungarian gentry, reactionary though they were! In the event, Napoleon's appeal to the Hungarians to rise, issued in French, Latin and Hungarian, fell on deaf ears. The Hungarian noble radical Batsányi, resident in Paris, who appears to have corrected its Hungarian style, proved isolated among his peers. The Hungarian Diet, which had protested in 1807 against the Crown's refusal to heed its grievances, in 1808 had empowered the king in advance to summon the feudal levy if needs be, and the call-up was duly successful the next year. Bohemia was also quiet. The ever loyal peasant Vavák, whose earlier attempt at a *Landwehr* song – 'we still have our Czech blood ... we have our crown and our King sits on the throne' – was thought by his betters to be too warlike for the Czech 'national character', promptly obliged with a second version: 'How could we have things better? Among us is no want, no misery, no constitution, only peace. There is also plenty to drink ... Our masters treat us in a regular manner ... Brothers, no moaning! Let us say joyfully: Up with Bohemia's monarch, long live all social orders!'[3]

All this was to no avail. Austria went to war in April 1809 before the Archduke Karl's preparations were complete and he became, even after his success at Aspern, the protagonist of peace. The issue was decided by Napoleon's occupation of Vienna and victory at Wagram and lack of effective support from coalition partners Britain and Prussia. In the subsequent peace of Schönbrunn Austria lost much of her Slovene and Croatian territory to new, French-ruled, 'Illyrian Provinces', forfeited Salzburg and the Innviertel to Bavaria and yielded her gains from the third partition of Poland to the equally new 'Duchy of Warsaw'. Into the bargain, Francis's own daughter, Marie Louise, was to marry the Corsican upstart, a humiliation as embarrassing as his abandonment to execution of Andreas Hofer, loyalist leader of the 1809 Tyrolean revolt against the new Bavarian masters. The patriotic propaganda was banned and Hormayr imprisoned in 1813 on suspicion of plotting a new Tyrolean rising. Indeed, the whole attempt to create a spirit of pan-monarchical patriotic defiance of France had an air of insubstantiality, since it was *German* national feeling to which the great majority of those concerned appealed. Had not the Archduke Johann, active in the Tyrol, exclaimed that he was German in heart and soul? Emperor Francis was sufficiently uncertain of the Czechs to order the closure of secret societies set up by Bohemian military and political leaders as a means of injecting patriotic values into the population. The ultimate effect of the long wars against revolutionary France was to fix definitively the conservative character of the Austrian state.

Metternich, Francis and Conservative Absolutism

Externally, too, concern to combat resistance to established authority came to overshadow older traditions of policy, like the anti-Prussian line of Kaunitz or Thugut and the support of Balkan Christians against Ottoman rule. Following Thugut's fall in 1801 the influence of the balance of power theorist Gentz and the young diplomat Metternich came to the fore. Austria did not support the Serb rising against the Turks in 1804, destined to be the first stage in the recreation of an independent Serbia. Where the *status quo ante* was irrecoverable, as in Germany, Vienna's policy was directed at maintaining as much of her traditional preeminence as possible. This meant thwarting both new aspirations for a more 'national' organisation of Germany and traditional Russo-Prussian or Russo-French power deals liable to entrench the influence of flanking states in the German centre of the continent. But this runs ahead: in the first instance Napoleon's humiliating hegemony had to be challenged and overthrown. The prospects for this in the first post-1809 years seemed slim. As France's ally, Austria had to participate militarily in Napoleon's grandiose anti-Russian expedition of 1812. Meanwhile the German national movement, against which Austria (much less so Prussia) now shut her face, was growing apace among patriotic notables and the student *Burschenschaften*. Yet in these years Metternich, who had moved from the Paris embassy to take over foreign affairs in the Vienna Chancellery in 1809, made the reputation he never subsequently allowed Europe to forget. Skilfully taking advantage of Napoleon's Russian failure he positioned Austria first as intermediary between the French and the other powers, then as a neutral mediator and finally as an armed one, till aligning her openly with the fifth anti-French coalition of 1813–15, all the while without provoking Napoleon into a preemptive strike. Under Field Marshal Karl Schwarzenberg Austrian troops joined Russia and Prussia to inflict Napoleon's first major defeat at the battle of Leipzig in October 1813; eventually three hundred thousand were under arms. The other two powers' alliance at Kalisch in February that year risked enabling the Russian presence in central Europe which Metternich feared, but he was confident enough to go along with it so as to draw the Russians west against the French, while expecting to frustrate their ambitions in Poland later. The claim to have tipped the scales against Napoleon gave Austria, however, high prestige in the coalition and laid the basis for Metternich's conservative influence in the post-war era. Indeed, historians have often called it after him.

This exaggerated the underlying strength of Austria's position in 1815. The empire that had seemed on the verge of extinction in the mid-eighteenth century took too complacent a view of its European role into the nineteenth; its victory proved a Pyrrhic one. Its best military leader, the Archduke Karl, a man with a more pressing sense of the Monarchy's underlying weaknesses and more nuanced attitude to the French Revolution than Metternich's, had been definitively side-lined by Austria's escape. His pessimism about opposing the spirit of the age had no doubt influenced his preference for avoiding war with France, but his offensive military strategy and his reforms as war minister were innovatory: the development of military medicine and archives, the reduction of life-long military service to 14 years, the abolition of the harshest punishments in new regulations of 1807. The common soldier came under consideration for the first time. But flogging was retained and Karl's endeavours to abolish sale of commissions failed, while inflation-hit pay remained at Maria Theresan levels. The army that emerged from the Napoleonic wars was hardly equipped to underwrite an Austrian paramountcy in Europe. Besides, the issue in 1811 of a new paper currency at a nominal value one-fifth that of the paper money withdrawn – effectively a forced devaluation by 80% – showed that the Monarchy had not overcome her endemic financial problems. War-induced inflation had swelled the volume of paper notes in circulation from 35 million florins in 1795 to 337 million in 1802 and 1060 million by 1811.

The peace terms of the Congress of Vienna (1814–15) reflected, anyway, only a qualified victory for Metternich. They endorsed his support of dynastic legitimacy in France and Italy, and put in place of the defunct Holy Roman Empire a toothless enough body, a 'German Confederation' (the *Bund*) of 39 states with a Diet at Frankfurt, under Austrian presidency. But he was unable to prevent the advance of Russia into central Europe through the creation of the Congress Kingdom of Poland under the Tsar, or the compensation of Prussia for this by the acquisition of half of Saxony. The definitive exchange of Austrian possessions in the Netherlands and south-west Germany for the northern Italian provinces of Lombardy–Venetia created a territorially united monarchy for the first time. But it was also a less German one just at the point when Prussia was strengthening her German credentials by taking over the Rhineland.

Prince Clemens von Metternich (1773–1859) was, next to Emperor Francis, the most important political figure in the Empire from the settlement of 1815 to the revolution of 1848. Arguments that as Chancellor (from 1824 State Chancellor) his influence was largely confined to foreign policy overlook the interlinkage of domestic and foreign policy in a polity several of whose constituent peoples straddled its borders. Metternich's Chancellery had a section on domestic matters with direct access to the Ministry of Police, and he himself took on the task of monitoring intellectual trends and managing the Monarchy's ideological stance (including, in modern parlance, its 'image') at home and abroad. He approached this work with the mental equipment of an eighteenth-century rationalist *grand seigneur* untouched by either the liberal democracy or romantic reaction of the French revolutionary period, concerned to preserve the balance of the body politic against the gusts of enthusiasm from whatever quarter. In international politics this led him to advocate the so-called Congress system of periodic meetings of the Powers (1815–22) to coordinate the fight against revolutionary tendencies. In central Europe he secured the confederal Diet's acceptance of the Karlsbad decrees (1819), which limited free speech and the autonomy of universities, where liberal and German nationalist ideas were strongest. In the Monarchy itself balance for Metternich meant ending the disproportion between its Austrian and Hungarian parts by lessening centralism in the former lands and reining in Magyar separatist tendencies in Hungary. To this end he advocated building up north Italian, 'Illyrian' and Galician entities (based on regional not national loyalties, however) which could then, by the most ambitious of his several reform drafts of this period (1817), become sub-units of a new Ministry of the Interior, with the hint of Hungary and Transylvania's potential reduction to similar status.

Metternich was thus aware of the problems which had long plagued Habsburg administration: its lack of coordination and the confusion between policy-making and its implementation. By proposing a system of ministries he was repudiating the time-consuming tradition of collegiate bodies through which the Monarchy had hitherto been governed. Ministries could efficiently discharge the day-to-day running of government business, while a small elite body advised the monarch on general policy for the state as a whole. The second goal had been the principle behind Kaunitz's *Staatsrat* of 1761 but in the interval this highest organ had continually allowed itself to be drawn into the detailed application of government policy. Francis's habit of settling matters directly with individual departments and his concern with minutiae had prevented the development of any kind of governmental *esprit de corps*. By the year 1802, 2000 files are said to have piled up for the Emperor's attention. Metternich's proposals for administrative reorganisation were thus not new. The Staats- und Konferenzministerium (1801) and revamped Staatsrat (1808, 1814) were all failed attempts to embody the idea of a central consultative forum unburdened by the trivia of the daily round.

Exalted notions of Metternich's statesmanship have been almost as common in some twentieth-century quarters as was his denigration as the evil genius of reaction in the nineteenth. The man who told the Duke of Wellington in 1824 that he felt all Europe to be his fatherland has been portrayed by his chief biographer Heinrich von Srbik as the guardian of Austria's European role in a system which recognised state and national individualities but subordinated their separate egoisms to the wider good. This fairly reflects Metternich's self-image but is somewhat uncritical. The Chancellor's generalised nostrums bespoke static assumptions. Human nature did not change, he opined; the mass of the people were always conservative and the oscillation of the forces of change and stability permitted only a cyclical view of history; hence, revolutionary utopias were a dangerous folly attractive only to naïve idealists (professors, religious radicals – Metternich played a role in the Papal condemnation of Lamennais in 1834) or self-interested egoists 'who enter the house they have set on fire not to save the valuables but to make off with them'.[4] Equality was a chimera, for what equality could there be between a wise man and a foolish one? Monarchy and sound religion cemented the bonds of loyalty necessary in a hierarchical society; democracy dissolved them. Metternich's *aperçus* were not without sociological force. He recognised the aristocratic base to the unique constitutionalism of pre-1832 England. He had, too, some awareness of the limits of the possible; when Adam Müller blamed all Europe's discontents on the Reformation, he remarked that he was not going to take on Martin Luther. Conscious of the need to rely on more than censorship in the battle for ideas, he overrode the police chief Sedlnitzky and allowed the leading German newspaper of the day, the mildly liberal *Augsburger Allgemeine Zeitung*, into Austria in the 1820s, getting its cautious editor Collin to accept Austrian government material for fear of losing his concession. But does this justify the claims of a higher political wisdom?

Clever as he was, Metternich's imagination was limited by a marked complacency, both intellectual and social. 'Such is *my character*', he wrote to one of several mistresses in 1813, assuring her of the magnitude of his passion; 'if it is unlike others', so much the worse for them ... time will prove to you ... what I am and what I can be for the friend of my heart'.[5] The conviction of his superior rationality, which made him reluctant to abandon doctrines

gradually outstripped by events, was already an irritant to his colleagues. Count Franz Anton Kolowrat complained of him as a pompous
pedant who was constantly telling everyone that two and two made
four, not five, and that all actions had consequences. The claim on his
behalf that his criticisms of Josephinian centralism in Austria put him
on the same wave-length as the early ethnic nationalists[6] seems to
misunderstand both Metternich's quite impractical bid to substitute
regional for national loyalties (as in Galicia) and the necessarily cautious tactics of the nationalists concerned.

Metternich falls short of greatness in another sense. He was a
weaker man than he imagined, who allowed Emperor Francis, one
of the most influential mediocrities of modern times, to frustrate
even his modest reform proposals. Francis, the prosaic son of an
enlightened father, humanised by a somewhat sardonic humour and
the old tradition he clung to of receiving petitioning subjects personally in Viennese dialect, was unswayed by the exasperation his pedantic administrative methods aroused in his abler brothers, the
Archdukes Karl and Johann. The problem was that the Emperor
could get his way. He had something of the suspiciousness and *amour
propre* of the mediocre, which made him prefer disjointed government
to a coherent system under a leading minister less easy to control.
Hence the Archduke Charles was driven into political retirement
after 1809; Metternich's reform plan of 1817 was put away in a
drawer; a Kingdom of Illyria was set up briefly (1816–23) but had
a shadow existence before abolition; Galicia gained a Diet (1817)
and a Ministry of the Interior lasted for some years, but only for the
non-Hungarian lands. The failure to use the favourable outcome of
the war to shape strategic decisions for an empire which was still pliable and loyal must be accounted a major factor in its ultimate fall.

An unreformed Austria failed to fund the army needed to lend
weight to Metternich's diplomatic goals. Whereas military expenditure took half the state's income in 1817, this had fallen to 23% by
1830 and 20% by 1848. Between the last two dates the troops in the
important Italian sector fell by half, to less than 50,000 men. Indeed,
army strength was always well below its nominal complement of
400,000, and it was regular practice to furlough soldiers at harvest
time. Metternich had only his own persuasiveness to rely on in foreign affairs. Increasingly, it was not enough.

The Eastern crisis of 1821–29 provided the first major evidence of
this. The Greek revolt against their Turkish overlords put the principle of Great Power hostility to rebels under strain for the Tsar, who

could not take kindly to the Turkish response of hanging the titular leader of Orthodox Christians, the Ecumenical Patriarch, on his cathedral door in full regalia on Easter Sunday. When Castlereagh was succeeded by the more liberal Canning as British foreign secretary the next year (1822), Metternich lost a possibly sympathetic ally. Alexander's successor, Tsar Nicholas I, distrusted him. Russia began to look to Britain as a partner in imposing a settlement on the Turks. Together with Britain and France she destroyed the Turkish fleet at Navarino in autumn 1827 before launching a ground war on Turkey the next year. Austria played no part in the Treaty of Adrianople (1829), which paved the way for the creation of an independent Greek kingdom three years later.

The 1830 July revolution in France, putting the 'bourgeois monarch' Louis Philippe on the throne, produced wide-ranging echoes, from revolts in Belgium, Russian Poland and the Papal States to pressures for further constitutionalism in the German *Bund*. Keeping the lid on liberal and nationalist tendencies in Germany and Italy remained Metternich's special concern. In the former country his line was that this goal could only be achieved by Austria not appearing to push her special interests while at the same time frustrating any combinations by others. Though most German rulers shared his anti-revolutionary fears, so negative an approach cut against the grain of a society experiencing economic growing pains and slow rise of a public opinion. Besides, Austria's defensive posture appeared to many, particularly south Germans, to risk drawing Germany into war in defence of over-exposed positions, notably an Austro-French war over Italy – a scenario that came about in 1859. New ideas were budding, like the Prussian hegemonist ambitions of the first architect of German customs union, Prussian finance minister Motz, or the 'Tria' schemes of middle-ranking south German states like Bavaria and Württemberg for an independent role alongside Austria and Prussia. Hindsight suggests Austria might have sided with the south German over the Prussian scheme. In fact, Metternich dismissed both, preferring an Austro-Prussian dualism but under Austrian lead. There are parallels with British illusions towards Europe after another Pyrrhic victory, in the Second World War. Following the famous Hartburg festival of German liberal-cum-national sentiment in 1832, the Austrian Chancellor was able to get six Articles through the Frankfurt Diet, further establishing the monarchical (i.e. anti-constitutional) principle in German government and, in 1834, a court of arbitration to which rulers could appeal against importunate assemblies. Yet with Bavaria insisting that arbitration was not binding on a diet against its will, little was achieved. The fact was that the *Bund* constitution of 1815 permitted, indeed encouraged, member states to grant constitutions, with their attendant assemblies, as many middle-sized ones had done. German public response to the temporary threat of war with France in 1840, which produced the famous patriotic song 'The Watch on the Rhine', showed the nationalist bogey was untamed.

The war scare with France arose over a new twist in the Eastern question, which, like the German question in one form or another, became a fixture of the international scene. In 1834 the British Whig foreign secretary Palmerston orchestrated a liberal Quadruple Alliance of Britain, France, Spain and Portugal as a counter-blast to the conservative Austro-Russian agreement of Münchengrätz the previous year. Münchengrätz, soon endorsed by Prussia, pledged support for the status quo in Poland and Turkey. Yet in 1839–40 when the Sultan was threatened by his nominal Egyptian vassal, Mehemet Ali, it was to Palmerston and a conference in London that Tsar Nicholas turned to sort out the matter, not to Vienna. Metternich, now 67, was prostrated by chagrin and took five weeks to recuperate. This last great episode of his diplomatic career showed his declining influence.

By this time Emperor Francis was dead. Domestically, the chief feature of his reign was drift. Metternich was joined in an ageing troika by the minister of police Count Josef Sedlnitzky (from 1817 to 1848) and by Kolowrat, the Staatsrat member with responsibility for internal affairs (1826–48), who called his sovereign the personification of suspicion. A pervasive censorship, which divided all books into four categories, only one of them fully tolerated, helped to foster a climate in which things were assumed to be forbidden unless expressly permitted. Francis sought to buy up the copyright of a play by Austria's most famous dramatist, Franz Grillparzer, after seeing it several times; the play celebrated a loyal servant of a medieval Hungarian king, but presumably Francis felt it could also be seen as showing up a monarch unworthy of such loyalty. Only exceptionally were foreign newspapers allowed into Austria, while the leading Austrian paper, Metternich's creation, the *Oesterreichische Beobachter*, simply did not report the military successes of the revolutionaries in Congress Poland in the spring of 1831.

Yet such censorship was as much paternalist as repressive in intent. Francis and Metternich shared a view of a contented, docile citizenry who should be protected from the machinations of foreign radicals. Theirs became the Austria of *Biedermeier*, originally a style in furniture which came to be associated with a whole epoch of cosy bourgeois domesticity, good music and a theatre of local colour, comedy of manners and the escapist 'magical' genre which took the audience to other worlds only to reveal that there was no place like home. Beethoven, Schubert, the classical tragedian Grillparzer, the satirical *farceurs* Raimund and Nestroy represent the Vienna of this time, and hardly a journalist or social thinker of note. Part of the price for the authorities' apolitical idyll was respect for a certain sense of civic dignity in broad strata of the urban population, in other words, maintenance of the enlightened idea of citizenship, as enshrined in the 1811 Civil Code. The Josephinian church settlement also survived, for it made the Church for the most part a tame organ of the state. The logic of conservatism inclined Francis to an accommodation with the Vatican after his visit to Rome in 1819 but its practical implementation moved at a snail's pace, despite Metternich's efforts. Two textbooks on church law and history put on the Papal Index in 1820 were not finally withdrawn from Austrian universities and seminaries until 1833 and then the state authorities could not decide how openly they should acknowledge the change of course. Two different proposals over this, left hanging in the air in 1837, were put on the desk of Austria's first minister of education on 1 May 1848!

Education was another field where the heritage of the reform movement was far from lost. Voices questioning the utility of schooling for peasant children were not heard, partly because peasant sons were more than ever needed for the priesthood at a time of falling vocations, partly because the argument that the uneducated became disproportionately social pests and mendicants won the day. Indeed, the second *Ratio educationis* for Hungary in 1806 extended the principle of compulsory free education to girls as well. In Bohemia 93% of children of school age were being educated by 1834. The parallel expansion of secondary education swelled the ranks of non-noble notables (officials, professionals and experts of various kinds) till the category acquired its own name – the *Honoratioren*. Thus this term, previously applied, in the Hungarian case, to all who lived from intellectual work, by the 1830s was confined to non-nobles who did so, though their lifestyle took on noble aspects. To speak of the emergence of a homogenous bourgeoisie thereby, still less of a fusion of elites through common education, would misrepresent the relationship of estate managers, large-scale merchants, small-town burghers and professionals at this time, but historians now ascribe a bigger role to pre-1848 elements in the shaping of the later bourgeoisie than they once did. The number of state officials and professionals (excluding clergy and elementary teachers) is estimated to have risen in the Austro-Slav lands from some 17,300 to 36,775 between 1790 and 1846 and from 5,000 to 24,000 in Hungary over a similar period.

One result was to create the trained bureaucracy for which the Enlightenment had striven. From 1774 educational qualifications for various government grades were successively established but only after 1800 did they reflect practice rather than aspiration. New service regulations emphasised (as Joseph's exhortations had not) unquestioning obedience to superiors, while constantly revised academic programmes increasingly side-lined politically suspect theoretical and historical disciplines. Uniforms were made universal, even for the members of provincial diets. Conservative as it might be, however, the imperial bureaucracy retained the 1787 principle of advancement by seniority of service, not social rank. Between 1840 and 1870 only 10% of departmental secretaryships were to be held by members of old established noble families. Hence, perhaps, in part, the bureaucracy's preponderant commitment to economic liberalism against traditional guild privileges and Francis's own preferences. Early nineteenth-century Austrian government was both continuator of the Josephinian project and its subverter.

How far Emperor Francis was aware of these contradictions is unclear. He appears to have been sustained by a belief in the special character of the Viennese, exempting them from the ills of the times. Yet in the midst of these seeming certainties he could retain an invincible paranoia. On Christmas Eve 1830 he ordered troops to ring St Stephen's cathedral in the capital, on reports that conspirators had timed an uprising for the midnight mass. For his part Metternich believed that hundreds of thousands of Italians belonged to secret societies. This lurching in leading figures from complacency to paranoia exposed the inner uncertainties of a regime which claimed to be at the heart of Europe while sedulously keeping out European influences. For all that, Francis's Austria was not the Russia of Tsar Nicholas I. It is the very sense of its potential normality, in European terms, which makes the caution and unimaginativeness of the Franciscan era seem a chance missed.

Industrialism Takes Root

This impression is increased when the economic fortunes of the Monarchy in the early nineteenth century are considered. Metternich's
cyclical view of history overlooked the beginnings of irreversible economic change. The Austrian case lends support to Sidney Pollard's
suggestion that European industrialisation should be seen as a single
process, in which bursts of economic activity moved, not from one
state to another, but from region to region across boundaries, as
favourably endowed areas were drawn into a network of reciprocal
relationships, at first dependent on forerunners' expertise but later
able to open up fresh outlets of their own. The marked regionalism
of Austrian industrialisation, the heavy reliance on English techniques and entrepreneurs, the role of proto-industrialisation in the
growth of textile manufacture, the development of the iron industry:
all this can be related to a wider pattern, particularly now that the
Rostowian model of dramatic take-off to industrialisation is no
longer seen as the standard path to this goal.

Growing interest in the Habsburg economy of the first half of the
century reflects confidence that its scale in that period can now be at
least approximately quantified. Whether it is Rudolph's estimate of
3.3% annual industrial growth between 1830 and 1845, based on
quinquennial production figures, Komlos's annual index of 2.5%
growth over the same period, Gross's deductions from accelerating
coal consumption from the 1820s or Good's conclusion that industry
advanced at 2.3% a year between the 1820s and the 1850s, a general
pattern seems to emerge. It is one of a widely diffused and subsequently sustained upturn from post-war depression in the late 1820s.
Forty per cent of industrial production was in textiles, with the
mechanisation of cotton spinning gathering pace in the 1820s and
that of wool in the 1830s. While the eighteenth-century staples,
wool and linen, made limited progress, cotton production grew at
7% a year. Austria had 157 cotton mills in 1847 and more cotton
spindles than the German *Zollverein*. She also by then made more
pig-iron per head than Germany, Bohemia having doubled
its output of iron and quadrupled that of coal since the 1820s.
Of two thousand industrial enterprises in 1841, those with modern
equipment were already producing three times as much as those
without and craftshops combined. Though her tally of steam engines
lagged far behind the French (550 to 4114 in the mid-1840s) her
industrial output per capita was on a par and her percentage of

people in industrial or commercial employment, at 17%, compared with Germany's. Here Hungary is not included. Of course, the scale was still very small relative to what was to come – a million tons of coal produced in 1850, for example, compared to 43 million in 1913.

How had this come about? The Monarchy had several of the traditional prerequisites for industrialisation. Its population increased by 40% from the late eighteenth century to 1848, to some 33.7 million. More to the point was the particularly rapid growth in German Bohemia, whose strong traditions of domestic textile industry made it easier to support larger families than on the land, thereby creating a reservoir of labour. The presence of coal and iron in largely German parts of Bohemia and Moravia, as in Styria and Upper Austria, enhanced the highly regional bias in Austrian development, for cultural dominance, proto-industrial traditions and natural resources went together.

Communications also improved greatly in these years. Some two thousand miles of main roads were built and the network of side roads grew two and a half-fold. Large areas of the Hungarian plain between the Danube and the river Tisza were opened to trade, while a canal linked the Danube (now regulated) with the Moldau and thence the Elbe, Bohemia's outlet to the North Sea. Regular steamships began to ply the Adriatic in 1818 and the Danube in 1831. Government was relatively quick to see the importance of railways. Not long after Salomon Rothschild's *Nordbahn* from Vienna to Olmütz (Olomouc) in Moravia had been begun in 1836 official plans provided for an additional three main routes south, south-west and west, to be built by the state if necessary. Austria's engineering tradition, expanded in the Enlightenment, had continued to develop, with the foundation of polytechnics in Prague (1807), Vienna (1815) and Graz (1844). Their teaching staff were not just pedagogues. The Prague mathematician Gerstner planned the first, albeit horse-drawn, railway in Austria, from Linz to Budweis (České Budějovice) on the Moldau, later built by his son (1832), while the Viennese polytechnic professor Riepl brought back experts from a study tour of England to introduce the iron-puddling process to Austria.

This example suggests the crucial role of foreign and particularly English techniques in early industrial development in the Habsburg lands. Count Karl Zinzendorf had praised Manchester as early as 1769. The Lombard Count Confalonieri, returning from England in 1819, ordered from there an engine for a steam-boat on the Po, gas-making apparatus and information on the Lancasterian schools system. He became involved in the Carbonari movement, was imprisoned in the notorious Spielberg prison in Brno and received a visit from Metternich, intrigued to plumb the workings of the revolutionary mind. Early borrowings often had to be surreptitious: a Brno company in 1805 claimed to have spent 70,000 florins on purloining the secrets of wool-spinning machines from England. As time passed English skills could be transmitted more openly and in person, though they were also often mediated through German agents, particularly Rhinelanders. Between them the British engineers Edward and John Thomas, Thomas Bracegirdle and David Evans, and Joseph Lee helped set up what became the three leading firms in the Bohemian machine-building industry. Englishmen were involved in the pioneering Moravian iron works of Vítkovice, the start of the Danube and the Adriatic steamship companies, the construction of the first bridge over the Danube at Budapest and the supply of gaslighting to Vienna. It was a time when British prestige was at its height and the Hungarian aristocratic reformer István Széchenyi could write to a native audience, 'Bless a thousand times the ashes of [Adam] Smith and [Arthur] Young and their immortal works which will certainly be known to the reader'.[7]

Economic liberalism pervaded the upper reaches of the administration itself. 'All kinds of compulsion and restriction are the mortal enemies of industry', opined the Hofkammer; 'only where a liberal administration leaves free play for the spirit of enterprise will it raise its mighty head and take bold wing'.[8] Frequently central government overrode local authorities when these withheld the issuing of factory licences. A perceptible embourgeoisement of industrial enterprise followed, though great nobles could still be preponderant in certain fields like the iron industry and the new, agrarian-orientated sugar beet manufacture. Three-quarters of the sugar beet factories founded in Hungary before 1848 were on noble properties and estates often maintained their own machine workshops and made their own paper.

It was in the textile industry that middle-class entrepreneurs came most clearly to the fore. A trading background was more common than one in banking or handicraft. Thus Moravian carpet factories, when not foreign-owned, were founded by Jewish wool merchants; early Slovene industry was pioneered by Ljubljana wholesalers; Jews again built on their traditional mercantile roles in Hungary, which varied from local hawker and regional factor to the long-distance merchant supplying – alongside Balkan Christians – Hungarian agricultural produce to central European cities. In Croatia the pillar of the first attempts to modernise a sluggish economy, Ambroz Vraniczany, was likewise from a merchant family dealing in transporting grain from the inner plains to the Adriatic ports. On a humbler note, Č. Daněk, one of the first Czech-speaking entrepreneurs, learnt his trade as a simple employee in Evan and Lee's textile factory workshop.

Industrialisation remained too weak to produce uniform patterns. The craft workshop and domestic industry were still numerically dominant over factory enterprise but the guilds were under increasing pressure. Even before the legislation of 1809–11, which continued the undermining of their legal prerogatives begun in the eighteenth century, official policy aimed to blur the distinction between factory owners and master craftsmen by easing the grant of citizenship (*Bürgerrecht*) which the former required to be legally able to operate town-based plants. Guilds remained; in remoter parts of Hungary they were even being set up for the first time. The more 1848 approached, however, the less they functioned on wholly traditional lines. Hungarian research, confirmed by Austrian, has shown the tendency for newly formed guilds to be mixed by trade, for guild members to work only part of the year at their craft and for masters to employ their apprentices contrary to regulations, when they had them at all – and there were only 0.67 apprentices per master in Hungary in 1846 and 1.3 in Austria in 1837. Competition was increasing between guilds and inside them. Masters were being supplied with their materials by merchants or found themselves being employed by others on a piece-work basis – 30 or 40 at a time in the textile trade in Vienna. This was the beginnings of proletarianisation.

A feature of the decline of the guild system was the movement of craft activity from the chartered 'royal' towns, where it was originally confined, to the less regulated countryside, a process following a little later in Hungary than in Austria. But the distinction between guild production and 'peasant industry' is not always easy to draw. A guild organisation could encompass part-time peasant workers who wove the cotton yarn spun by their wives, or made boots and shoes from their own leather. Other activities might supplement guild crafts, like the many varieties of mason who worked in brick or wood as opposed to the stone of the guild member, or the market women who sold the food most day-labourers actually bought, rather than the dearer beef or bread of the guildsman. Swelling populations pursued their humble livelihoods with a moving pertinacity and resource. About the south Hungarian town of Szeged in 1848 were employed 800 peasant masons of various kinds, 800 boatmen, 200 carters, 200 navvies, 120 millers, 100 tile-brick burners, 80 preparers of paprikas and 50 each of women fish cutters and loaf bakers for wayside sale.[9] Some of these trades had taken on corporative forms, with fishermen binding together to buy river leases, and amalgamations of boat owners which might leave individuals employing 100 to 150 men. The most potentially dynamic branch of Hungarian peasant industry – textiles – was, however, largely snuffed out by competition from the Austro-Bohemian lands.

In these lands the already mature domestic textile industry provided a base for the transition to manufacture and the industrial system. The process moved at different rates as the cotton, then woollen and finally linen branches were mechanised. Though there were 350,000 linen domestic workers in Bohemia in the mid-1830s, seven times more than there were factory workers, the former figure already represented a decline. The turning-point in the iron industry came with the use of coke-fired hot ovens in the Vítkovice works in 1836; for some time, however, Bohemian production remained behind that in the technically more conservative Alpine lands, with their ample reserves of charcoal. Other industries to be mechanised included paper making and sugar refining from the late 1820s and brewing and steam-milling from the end of the period. But growth also occurred in industries organised on more traditional lines and centred in the capitals Vienna and Prague: leather, glove-making and silk among them.

From this outline the wide regional variations in type and distribution of industry will already be apparent. One of the most developed regions was actually Lombardy-Venetia, soon to be detached from the Monarchy. In the German–Slav lands the key role of Bohemia was coming to the fore. By 1848 it had nearly half their cotton mills and mined 50% of their coal. While its domestic textile industry achieved the transition to factory status, that of the Alpine lands gradually declined. Meanwhile, the Hungarian lands produced about an eighth of the Monarchy's industrial wealth in 1841: inner Hungary then had just eleven steam engines. However, in the quickening 1840s iron replaced food processing as the most developing sector and the fact that by that time Hungary imported as much from Austria as it exported suggests its rural self-sufficiency was ending. Pest, its largest town, actually grew faster than Prague in this period. In Croatia, on the other hand, where even the lime kilns and sugar refineries beginning to dot the great estates of Hungary were still rare, trade in agricultural products remained as for centuries the chief source of non-landed wealth.

Even in the most advanced parts of the Monarchy would-be entrepreneurs could feel isolation and frustration. Count Buquoy, a reforming Bohemian aristocrat, complained in 1814 of the 'huge obstacles' and 'sad experiences' of those who in 'public spirit' advocated useful innovations.[10] Lack of credit was a universal problem. The Austrian National Bank, set up in 1816 to finance the withdrawal of the already devalued currency of 1811, lent largely to the state; successive proposals for provincial Estate banks were rejected as a threat to government credit, except in Galicia's case, a possible sop to the Poles. While there was no lack of private banks of mercantile origin these, like the National Bank, tended to confine their loans to the state and the wealthiest families, to the tune of an estimated 50 million florins between 1825 and 1846. The Rothschild brothers, ennobled by Francis in 1817, played a key role here. It did not help matters that Hungarian aristocrats, unless they waived an archaic legal right, could send their creditors packing by having their bailiffs shake a stick at them. Minor Hungarian landlords often resorted to pawning, as mortgage finance was hampered by the traditional system of 'aviticity', which made inherited land inalienable. It seems that in the Monarchy as a whole entrepreneurs responded to credit difficulties by self-finance, reinvesting even in times of recession, for want of alternative outlets. The earliest savings bank in Lower Austria dated from 1819, followed by Bohemia in 1825 and Hungary in 1836. Their resources, however, were not large. In 1848 the capital of Hungary's 35 savings banks amounted to 49,469 florins. Dissatisfaction with the financial situation was one of the leading complaints of would-be reformers on the eve of revolution.

More immediately explosive was the discontent felt at the social consequences of economic change. The resilience of the guild system had been sapped, and government work-houses, with a tradition dating back to 1671, had always wavered ineffectually between punishment and training for the outcast poor. Of 30,000 artisans in Vienna in 1845 a half had valuables auctioned off for non-payment of taxes. Journeymen, unable to become masters, became increasingly mutinous; in the larger Hungarian towns they were the tinder which sparked off social affray. Domestic workers suffered likewise from factory competition. The wages of embroiderers had declined to a quarter or a fifth of their 1800 levels by 1835. Entire communities of glass-workers in the Bohemian Erzgebirge uplands were brought to the brink of famine in the winter of 1843. Factory workers, not surprisingly, came off better. Zenker in the late nineteenth century estimated an average weekly wage of 5 florins for Viennese male workers in the 1840s on which, according to the English traveller Turnbull, it was possible to eat, drink and smoke to one's heart's content. Turnbull, however, was writing of the countryside. Bearing in mind the high rents in the towns, a contemporary calculation showed that a family with three to five children living on that wage would spend more than half its surplus cash on the mid-day meal alone. The real problem of factory workers was that because of Austria's weak competitive position they had little more security of employment than home-based craftsmen.

Economic uncertainty interacted with social hardship. Urban provision was quite inadequate for the inflow of people from the countryside. The failure of Vienna's housing stock to match the influx of population led contemporaries to compare it to a rabbit warren above ground. Horrors were enacted in the industrial suburbs beyond the old city in Vienna, claimed the radical Violand, about which young Viennese women wept sentimentally in reading the Parisian novels of Eugène Sue, unaware how close they were to home. His passionate account of conditions before the revolution of 1848 speaks of Viennese families living in the sewers and coming out at night to steal, also of the under-class forcing itself on public attention in the depression years 1845–46 by its flagrant prostitution, with the girls accompanied by their partners carrying benches and pillows for the performance of their 'horizontal side-line';[11] three hundred of the latter were eventually arrested and drafted into the army.

To what extent were workers' problems already threatening the social order before 1848? Crime increased in the Hungarian *Alföld* with the influx of day-labourers working on river regulation and drainage schemes. Miners as always were rumbustious, though they tended to be concentrated in remote places. Salt miners in Transylvania struck in 1804, 1807 and 1810, iron workers in 1837; the 7–8000 miners and 3000 auxiliary workers of the huge precious minerals complex in Transylvanian Zalatna were continually bubbling. There was a demonstration against unemployment in Vienna in 1816 and a government enquiry into unemployment following disturbances in Brno in 1831, little enough to be sure. Otherwise it was not in the capital but Bohemia that discontent swelled into organised protest in the 1840s, first in machine-breaking and attacks on part-time rural labour brought in to undercut wages, then in the Prague cotton printers' action of 1844, which grew into a controlled demonstration by a thousand workers from several cotton-printing works in front of the Viceroy's palace. Prague emissaries with an organisation apparently based on workers' benevolent funds played a role in sympathy movements among the textile workers of north Bohemia. Meanwhile part-time railway construction workers near Prague entered the city and destroyed Jewish merchants' shops. The episode excited Marx and Engels and belied official assertions that the labour question was a foreign affair. It gave an ageing government another problem to deal with, to add to those it faced where the great majority of Habsburg subjects still lived, in the countryside.

Reforming Landlords and Resentful Peasants

The population living from the land fell relatively in this period – from about 75% to approximately 71% of the total – but in absolute terms it grew considerably, while land under plough in Alpine Austria increased 30% between 1789 and 1830. Estimates of annual agricultural growth rate for the Monarchy as a whole vary between 0.5% and at least 1% a year. Whatever the precise figure, the pressures exerted by population growth for improved performance imposed strains on the social order on the land which helped burst it apart in 1848.

Agrarian growth did not come primarily, as the Enlightenment had envisaged, from a new class of peasant proprietors. The maintenance of the seigneurial relationship in the countryside, underlined by the prohibition of commutation for *robota* on Crown estates in 1821, put paid to that. In the absence of decent credit facilities peasants could, anyway, only redeem their services by selling much of their land, which was sufficient discouragement, while the same factor doomed the peasant plots created on the Raab model to disappointingly slow growth. Agrarian improvement was thus mainly a noble affair.

Most significant was the advance in communications. The Danube Steamship Company played a key role in the doubling of value of Hungary's agricultural exports to Austria between 1831 and 1845. Along the Danube, 147 depots sprang up, even more densely at Győr than at Pest, which itself had a thousand steamship sailings up-river a year and over a thousand merchants to Győr's 272 (1846). Just over half the latter dealt in both grain and livestock, a sign of Hungary's lack of specialisation compared to more advanced countries. Indeed, many small Hungarian merchants might band together to export a single cargo up the Danube, when profits could be of the order of 40%. Railways made an equally rapid impact. The *Nordbahn* was carrying about 211,000 tons of freight by 1846, nearly 30% of it agrarian produce. Much that the eighteenth century had conceived in terms of drainage and canals was now accomplished, often by magnate initiative, like Count Ferenc Zichy's regaining of hundreds of square miles of marshland around Lake Balaton. Most spectacular, albeit a state-aided project, was Count István Széchenyi's regulation of the river Tisza begun in the 1840's which aimed to save 5000 square miles of regularly flooded land for arable use.

Meanwhile, the professionalisation of estate management proceeded apace. The Georgikon on the Festetics estate in west Hungary, with 1414 pupils between 1797 and 1848, and the Schwarzenberg school at Krumlov in south Bohemia were perhaps the most famous of estate training schools. By the 1840s estate managers like František Horský and Antonín Komers, the overall directors of the Schwarzenberg and Thun estates respectively, were important figures in their own right. The tiny provincial agrarian societies set up under government sponsorship in the 1760s were succeeded from the 1800s by voluntary provincial bodies, often with branches and containing hundreds (in the Alpine provinces, thousands) of members. Those of Styria (1819), Tyrol and Vorarlberg (1838) and Upper Austria (1845) were a particular cause of the Archduke Johann, living with his ex-post-mistress bride in the semi-retirement the nineteenth century reserved for all Habsburgs with a touch of imagination.

Nineteenth-century Habsburg farm management added to the nostrums of the Enlightenment the cause of convertible husbandry, practised by the 1840s by some 170 Bohemian estates covering 7% of the arable land. Even on the most advanced estates, though, it was combined with the three-field system improved by the use of root crops on the fallow. Other new crops were tobacco and sugar beet, while potatoes made great gains. Nobles' industrial speciality came to be agricultural processing. Twenty-five per cent of Bohemian potatoes and 60% of Galician went on distilling alcohol, and breweries and saw-mills were also popular. Probably the biggest activity of early nineteenth-century landlords, however, was the keeping of merino sheep for their fine wool. Prince Esterházy had

150,000 sheep in 1819. By various means the senior Schwarzenberg line increased the rental income on its 32 estates from 30–40% of total income to 70% between the 1820s and 1840s, or from about half a million to a million florins.

Change for the peasantry was altogether more modest, particularly for those involved in the seigneurial relationship. The Hungarian peasants who participated most in the market were those who combined proximity to good transport routes with some prior special status, whether as members of old free communities or of 'village towns' which had redeemed their servile obligations. While two-thirds of Hungarian peasants practised a three-field system in 1828 (as against just over a quarter in 1720) they had a quite rational resistance to innovation in many spheres. They tended to shun the merino or, in their parlance, 'noble' sheep because they still needed a multi-purpose animal which would be as good for meat as for wool. Even serfs, however, were affected by their masters' drive for greater productivity because it called in question the efficiency of traditional *robota*. The great Hungarian reformer István (Stephen) Széchenyi's estimate that unfree labour (including journey time to work) was only a third as productive as paid labour was widely accepted, and sometimes used by progressive nobles in laying down what peasants should pay to commute their services. Even the keenest reformers, however, did not commute all the *robota* they were due. Permission was necesssary from the conservative state; peasants might be reluctant to commute something they thought might soon be abolished; and landlords could not wholly dispense with forced labour themselves, particularly for routine tasks like carting or road-mending. Growing employment opportunities on public works or building meant landowners often complained of labour shortages, particularly near Vienna. In Hungary, because of poor regional integration, labour scarcity could subsist with unemployment. Thus unpaid labour, though widely criticised, remained a substantial element in the farming even of the largest landowners. On progressively farmed Hungarian estates, which have been likened to islands in a sea of backwardness, it commonly provided about 45% to 50% of labour requirements. A corollary of the labour shortage problem was that wages for agricultural labour tended to rise in the final Pre-March decades, so-called from the March revolution of 1848.

If agrarian reformers wanted less *robota*, many middling landowners wanted more. Lacking the credit resources of the larger estates, they could only exploit greater market opportunities by increasing unpaid labour and if possible the size of their demesne. This was particularly true of Hungary and Galicia. At the least such landowners asserted their claims over uncultivated land and sought to restrict peasants' rights of pasture and step up pressure for dues. Additionally, they might try to appropriate peasant land. It has been estimated that in Galicia nobles usurped 6% of peasant land between 1781 and 1848 and increased peasants' obligations by 40%. In Hungary the major issue was control of land cleared by peasants and 'remainder' land cultivated by them but not deemed 'urbarial' by the legislation of 1767. Urbarial or registered peasant land was only 28% of the total in 1828 as against 65% in noble hands. At a time of mounting population such figures spelt a message of diminishing plots and expansion of the cottar class. By 1828 cottars were twice as numerous as urbarial peasants, whereas in 1777 the numbers had been approximately equal. By the 1840s only 3.5% of Moravian and 7.5% of Styrian peasants held a full plot and 64% and 61% respectively held less than a quarter.

But nobles did not have it all their own way. Behind the frequently inadequate statistics – which make it difficult to estimate the proportion of those altogether landless – a tussle can be made out between two dissatisfied social groups still unevenly matched, to be sure, but less so than before. Hungarian peasants actually controlled considerably more land than was ascribed to them in the urbarial registers and their share, on the whole, was growing. Partly it was a matter of the large areas of cleared and 'remainder' land not officially registered. Partly it was that landlords were transferring noble land to peasant use in order to claim *robota* with which to cultivate the rest of their demesne. These operations greatly increased the scope for conflict over *robota* services. Moreover, this legally murky terrain was being opened up at a time of increased peasant literacy and readiness to resort to lawyers, petitions and deputations. Between 1826 and 1848 a third of the communities of Somogy county in west Hungary were engaged in litigation about linking up the separate strips of their plots (commassation), in the great majority of cases peasant-initiated. Well might members of the Galician Diet in 1840 oppose the expansion of village schools which, they ironised, would only help their peasants bring more complaints against them. The traditional noble–peasant relationship in the Habsburg Monarchy before 1848 was being undermined both economically – through the increasingly disputed role of *robota* – and culturally – in the peasants' escape from a letterless world.

A government which retained the corpus of eighteenth-century pro-peasant legislation but administered it in a conservative spirit risked alienating both noble and peasant. The tragi-comic saga of the Upper Austrian 'peasant tribune' Michael Huemer alias Kalchgruber shows a cumbersome regime caught between the residual liberalism of some officials, the inquisitorial spirit of the police and the eccentric paternalism of Emperor Francis. Kalchgruber was the most remarkable of several Alpine village headmen who, falling foul of the authorities for questioning their high-handed approach, claimed that they had the Emperor's personal commission to keep him informed. Instead of serving out a two-month detention in 1821 he disappeared and was not caught till his death 28 years later, despite a large price on his head and ordinary peasants' ready ability to contact him to write down their complaints. Characteristic of Emperor Francis was that while expressing his exasperation at this state of affairs, he still had the complaints investigated. One of the last of Kalchgruber's near hundred petitions to Francis and his successor claimed Francis had told him he would never deviate a tittle from Joseph II's 'imperial plan'.[12] As another composer of petitions to on high assured Francis in 1828, his subjects were not donkeys but kept a good eye on their sovereign's acts and omissions, which was why they were compelled to take defence of their possessions in accordance with article 344 (of the Civil Code)![13] Both this writer and Kalchgruber had been prosperous farmers. Heavy state taxes, high prices, chicanery in the matter of estate services, occasionally harsh communal poverty all contributed to Alpine peasants' discontent; but the foremost sentiment would seem to have been resentment at their experiences at the hands of often corrupt estate managers and arrogant government officials. At stake was the dawning aspiration of a social group to be treated with dignity and, as it saw it, fairness.

Peasants at the other end of the Monarchy, in Galicia, were also at opposite poles to their Austro-German counterparts in terms of development. Contemporary officials and radicals alike depicted them as little different from the beasts they tended. Yet there were similarities, too: in the stubbornness with which Haynko Liush endured thirteen spells in prison in the 1830s and 1840s for protesting at illegal *robota* demands and being made to work on Ruthenian holy days; in peasants' visits to Vienna; in the solidarity with which 'the loudest and most arrogant shouters' in a manorial rent strike of 1847 bore the beatings inflicted on them by the District Commissioner.[14] Galicia produced the most dramatic anti-landlord protest in the

Pre-March era, when in 1846 Ruthenian and Polish-speaking peasants turned on Polish noble rebels against Austrian authority and
hundreds of landlords were massacred.

In between Austro-Germans and Galicians both geographically
and in terms of development, the Czech peasantry remained something of an enigma in this period. There is pathos in the lives of the
Veverka cousins, inventors of the swing-plough (1827) which a
German estate manager tried to pass off as his own discovery. Both
of them were forced by economic difficulties to sell their farms
before dying relatively young in poverty, symbols of a talented
people whose time had not yet come. A bleak picture of peasant life
emerges in the account of the Czech lawyer and patriot Brauner,
published in 1847: family feuds due to economic pressures were the
norm rather than the exception; doomed marriages were rashly
entered into by the unemployed and unskilled; foster mothers were
envied when a ward died in infancy because they would get more
funding to replace it; peasants deprived themselves to educate one of
their sons out of their class, to the neglect of the agricultural skills
Brauner believed the schools should teach. A few localised labour
strikes were the Czech peasant community's only overt protests in
these years.

As so often, Hungary played a distinctive role. Whether in the two
hundred or so peasant disturbances in multi-national Transylvania;
in the Serb revolts of 1807 in Srem and the Banat – where teachers
and priests stirred by their co-nationals' rising against the Turks
had a broader agenda than their peasant followers; or above all in
the mainly Slav peasant movement in north Hungary of 1831, the
combination of social grievance and ethnic difference lent a special
vigour to protest in Hungary. Slovaks and Ruthenians believed the
Tsarist forces moving against rebels in Congress Poland in 1831
would intervene on their behalf. Forty-five thousand participated in
the disturbances, sparked off by rumours that nobles were spreading
the current cholera epidemic by poisoning the wells. A hundred and
nineteen had been summarily hanged by the county authorities
before the central government could call a halt. The prominence of
cottars and their wives in the violence and the role of petty nobles,
who wrote the Hungarian-language appeals for support to the surrounding towns – where workers responded – show how what were
essentially *Bauer* grievances could become the focus for a broader
movement. The lack of sophistication of the great majority was paralleled in Serb peasants' enthusiastic response to the displaying of

Rajić's *History* (see p. 65) in anti-*robota* protests in 1814 and Magyar peasants' denial that the limited peasant reforms of 1836 really were what King Ferdinand had ordered.

The 1836 reforms abolished the carting duty of the 'long haul' and granted Hungarian peasants the security of tenure and inheritance rights that Joseph II's legislation had given their Austrian counter-parts. They represented the noble Diet's more considered response to the 1831 revolt, and increasing recognition of the untenability of the old order. For many this was making a virtue of necessity, for they wished to win compensation for waiving their privileges before they were swept away for nothing. The Lower Austrian Diet's 1845 peti-tion for the abolition of *robota* thus began with sharp criticism of the erosion of noble rights. The Galician Diet had set up a commission of enquiry before the 1846 *jacquerie*. Yet the principled case for change had also been put with unalloyed vigour by Count István Széchenyi. In his *On Credit* (1830) and other works he had exposed the incompat-ibility of feudal privilege and *robota* with successful economic systems based on free association and rational use of labour, concluding that present conveniences must be abandoned for the sake of longer-term rewards. Increasingly from 1830 absolutism faced a dual challenge. Discontented peasants looked back to Joseph II. Educated reformers looked forward to a society run, effectively, on western bourgeois lines. Even the very circumscribed economic 'modernisation' of the Monarchy which was taking place posed questions which a creaking administration was unable to answer.

Government at an Impasse

This administration's nadir followed Emperor Francis's death in 1835. His eldest son and successor Ferdinand was a good-natured but retarded epileptic, during whose reign real power was exercised by a *de facto* regency of the Archduke Ludwig, who presided, and the bitter rivals Metternich and Kolowrat, with general responsibilities for external and domestic matters respectively.

Part of the reason for this stagnation was that Metternich was a better intriguer than butcher. Faced with the Chancellor's insuffer-able air of superiority, Kolowrat withdrew with a diplomatic illness to his Bohemian estates, but was allowed to return to ensconce him-self in the rejigged *Staats- und Konferenzrat* which was to have been Metternich's instrument of power (December 1836). Each affected a role. Metternich convinced himself that Kolowrat was selling out to liberals, Kolowrat that he was a reformer saving Austria from last-ditch Armageddon. While Kolowrat fumed at Metternich's patronage of the reestablished Jesuits, Metternich railed at the underfunding of the army which damaged his diplomatic clout. Both men schemed to get their supporters into other positions, particularly the Hofkammer, though its head from 1840, Baron Karl Kübeck, deplored their rivalry. Not surprisingly, the decision-making process lost out.

It is not that the Pre-March government was wholly inactive. Kübeck was a man of parts, a tirelessly industrious civil servant who had risen from humble origins and was well acquainted with the principles of Adam Smith and Ricardo. His plans for the economic modernisation of the Monarchy had the firm support of Metternich, himself a progressive manager of his estates. They advocated that the entire Monarchy should join the German customs union or *Zollverein* which had been developing under Prussian aegis since 1818, and later they called for the abolition of the tariff barriers between Austria and Hungary. They sponsored, too, a state railway-building programme and the buying out of private lines, which became a major cause of the dangerous budget deficit of 1847. All these were projects calculated to unite the different parts of the Monarchy, while increasing the weight of its economically dominant German speakers. The concept was Josephinian. In the event they were sabotaged by the very diversity they sought to overcome. Bohemian industrialists opposed joining the *Zollverein* because they feared competition; Hungarian nationalists opposed a customs union with Austria. Neither took place. A conservative government which had abandoned Josephinism's dynamic social policy had no powerful vision with which to override the objections of interest groups, whether economic or national.

This social conservatism was authority's Achilles' heel at a time when growing social malaise required it to change gear. Instead, the emerging working class was either disregarded or treated as a political rather than a social problem. Factory workers were deemed subject to the Servants Ordinance of 1810. The Hofkammer's attitude to early police views (1803) on the difficulties of supervising a large body of people 'with principles peculiar to themselves' was that since workers were kept busy by their employers, their 'repellent demeanour' boded no ill.[15] The only attempt above provincial level to regulate labour, in 1842, remained a dead-letter because it did not provide for inspectors. Government claims of paternalism were undermined by fiscal and tariff policies which kept up prices and the increased taxes on articles of mass consumption imposed in 1829. While the share of the land tax in overall revenue continued to decline, the income tax paid by a few was replaced in 1840 by a stamp duty affecting all. The communal system of poor relief which Joseph II had substituted for religious charities suffered because the communes lacked resources and fiscal autonomy. The chance to overhaul it after the Viennese unemployment demonstrations of 1816 was passed up in favour of authorisation of private charities, of which there were some thirty in Vienna by 1848, mostly small-scale. But a proposal to entrust the provincial diets with charity work in 1845 was turned down as politically dangerous. Factory workers organised their own benefit funds, but only the printers received official approval for a general support fund, in 1843.

Older solidarities were therefore weakened while new ones were undeveloped and subject to some official distrust. This, and often lackadaisical government, exacerbated the social crisis of the 1840s, brought on by European-wide depression. Thus the soup kitchens organised privately in urban centres in 1846–47 were eventually discontinued on government orders.

The chief social issue facing the Monarchy remained, of course, the reform of the semi-feudal situation on the land. Something had to be done about *robota*. Indeed, Kolowrat had raised the question of its abolition in 1832, though under Francis discussion was still-born. Kübeck was another closet land reformer. But despite Francis's removal from the scene and the Galician rising of 1846 the Patent passed after it did no more than remind provincial authorities that peasants could commute their dues and services to their lord, if he agreed.

Why this dampest of damp squibs? Macartney has written that the solution to the peasant problem before 1848 'required nothing more than an adjustment of class relations which need not have entailed any modification of the structure of the Monarchy (a question to which no peasant devoted a thought)'.[16] This correctly pin-points the immobilism of the regime but is perhaps a little too dismissive of the problems involved. These were of three kinds. Most obvious were the technical. How much compensation were nobles to receive for loss of services and in what form? Would patrimonial jurisdiction also be abolished? Would peasants be emancipated without ownership of the land they had cultivated, as had happenened in the Baltic provinces of Russia in 1816, or with ownership of only part of it, as in Prussia in 1807? Could compensation take the form of the cession of part of former rustical land to the lord, as the Patent of 1846 allowed? In this case what became of the Josephinist principle of maintaining the peasant farm?

But a deeper problem, second, was that the peasant question did involve the structure of imperial government, as contemporary radicals pointed out when they argued (personalising as usual) that Metternich could not offend the aristocrats who bolstered his power. To be sure, this critique overlooked the fact that Pre-March Austria was a *bureaucratic* absolutism, which distanced itself politically from the landed class almost as much as from any other and was correspondingly disliked by it. Metternich was to deny in 1849 that there could be an Austrian eqivalent of the British House of Lords. Yet precisely because of this political estrangement from the nobility the government could hardly afford to alienate it on another front as well. The radical critique was oversimplified rather than false. Besides, those nobles who *were* friendly to reform often envisaged it on lines unacceptable to government. The Bohemian Count Leo Thun, for instance, desired changes on the land in the direction of peasant proprietorship, but with the maintenance of noble patrimonial powers for the sake of moral and social cohesion. The Josephinist policy of *Bauernschutz* (peasant protection) should thus be given a Christian conservative twist necessary in the face of bureaucratic economic liberalism *à la* Kübeck. Thun, with his interest in the Czech language and his bitter private criticisms of the dead hand of centralism, was the forerunner of the Bohemian school of conservative federalists of the second half of the century. This kind of criticism could hardly enthuse Vienna.

Thus, while peasants may not have been interested in structural issues, in Macartney's terms, others were. The problem of 'serfdom' for these people became bound up with the reorganisation of the Monarchy. The third and biggest problem for Vienna was that by the 1840s the abolition of serfdom had become the chief plank in the programme of Hungarian gentry nationalism. Many Hungarian patriots had come to believe that 'feudalism' was their country's curse, responsible for its economic backwardness and political weakness. Only the sweeping away of distinctions of birth and embrace of a common patrimony could mobilise Hungarians to reclaim control of their own destiny. The peasant question was no longer just one of class but implied a national position which challenged the central position of bureaucratic absolutism – the authority of Vienna.

Thus by 1848 the disjuncture between the conservative and radical wings of Josephinism had led to an impasse. The conservative commitment to a centralised, bureaucratic, part-industrial state had yielded fruit. The dropping of the radical goal of peasant proprietorship, however, had allowed the cause of social reform to be taken up by Hungarian gentry or, in the western lands, provincial aristocrats, not to speak of emerging petit bourgeois and professional elements in the non-dominant peoples. In their hands it nearly always bore a national or federalist character incompatible with Josephinian centralism. That Metternich probably understood the seriousness of this national issue more than his colleagues reflects the relatively broader perspective he brought to bear, which led contemporaries to identify him as the *éminence grise* of the Austrian *ancien régime*. Kübek, by contrast, remained a rigid German centralist, seeing the Bohemian aristocracy as the chief cause of the Monarchy's problems and even believing that Emperor Francis was too liberal in his dealings with Hungary. Count Kolowrat, the would-be conciliator, was little more imaginative as far as Magyar nationalism was concerned. But it was Metternich, by his dogmatic social conservatism, who had done most to create the conditions in which nationalism could flourish. The interlinking of social and ethnic questions, and hence of liberalism and nationalism, became the burning question of the last years of the Pre-March regime. How this was so will be explored below.

4 *Liberalism and Nationalism*

The intellectual life of the Habsburg Monarchy in the first half of the nineteenth century reflected its social development. Increasingly, old and new were admixed in ways more easily understood in hindsight than by contemporaries. New literary languages were being born and others revived at a time of unprecedented inter-communication through onmarching German. An often feudalistic liberalism and a generally antiquarian nationalism emerged in a spirit of opposition to the regime but with mostly unclear goals. Slowly, however, a new dispensation was evolving, as a spiritless centre forfeited the power to shape the aspirations and allegiances of its subjects.

The fortunes of German are a pointer to the age. Its progress cannot be put down just to state fiat, though its imposition as the official language of Galicia did help integrate the Polish elite into the Habsburg framework. Its role as the predominant language of the non-rural economy in Hungary, Croatia and Bohemia came to it naturally through German-speaking entrepreneurs and skilled labour, incoming or local; Pest was still at least half-German in speech in 1848. The popularity of German travelling theatre companies and of German novels and literary reviews, as well as the educational system, help explain why Radičević and Preradović, considered the leading mid-century lyric poets in Serbo-Croat, began their adolescent verse in German. Patriots' harping on feminine patronage of alien literature receives unexpected support from modern social linguists' claim that young women are more susceptible to linguistic fashion than young men. It was in these circumstances that Goethe could see Czech literature, much as Matthew Arnold did Celtic, as a fertilising tributary of his own culture. Yet in this he was mistaken. The failure of Joseph Hormayr's pan-Austrian periodical, which could draw on contributions in German from almost any Slav or Hungarian writer it chose, showed that German had become the instrument of an expanding commercial framework rather than of a common Austrian culture.

A conservative administration sought to fill the moral vacuum that threatened the state by the traditional means – religion. Regular church attendance and periodic communion were compulsory for

all secondary school pupils. The works of the great Protestant philosopher Immanuel Kant were not taught in Austria because they were
held to make the existence of God, the moral law and immortality
dependent on mere human reason. Not its Czech nationalism, but
its sympathy with the heretic Hus was what initially troubled the
censors in František Palacký's *History of Bohemia,* appearing from
1836. But a Josephinian Erastian church had lost the capacity to
offer its flock a vigorous independent spirituality. Reduced to a
department of state, defending its institutional interests but unable
to identify these with the hopes and fears of society at large, it had
little more concrete to propose on the problems of industrialisation
than that Protestant migrant workers should be kept at bay, while
its leading battle in the Pre-March period was to impose Catholic
rules on confessional inter-marriage. This proved particularly divisive in religiously mixed Hungary.

Two exceptions to this pattern should be noted, though their influence was limited. One was the circle associated with the Redemptor-
ist monk Klemenz Maria Hofbauer (1751–1820) who after settling in
Vienna in 1809 worked to free religious life from the straitjacket of
what the Vienna nuncio Severoli once called Joseph II's infernal legislation. The other was the brilliant priest-mathematician and
Prague university professor Bernard Bolzano, whose homilies to
packed student audiences demonstrated the continuing appeal of
freshly presented religious ideas. Bolzano believed in an objective
moral reality, and derived from it man's duty of service to the community in the interests of a better world for which he should be prepared to die. A German speaker himself, he stressed the need to
promote a common identity of all Bohemians and as a corollary
to raise the social and cultural level of the neglected Slav majority.
His expulsion from his chair in 1821 was thus a blow to constructive
thinking about problems facing the Monarchy on more than one
level. Through the residual neo-liberalism that survived the Franciscan blight he was spared severer punishment, it seems, by the tacit
protection of the Archbishop of Prague.

The snuffing out of challenging religious thought spelt nemesis for
the intellectual influence of the dominant church. It was replaced by
anti-clericalism, which began to acquire a mass base in Czech Bohemia in this period, by vague sympathy for Protestantism as the religion of liberty, or by personal faith clearly distinguished in the
holder's mind from the official church. Members of the actual Protestant minority became disproportionately active in reformist circles;

Palacký was from a Moravian village that had preserved its dissident beliefs through the period of proscription; the founders of cultural Panslavism Jan Kollár and Pavol Šafárik and of the Slovak literary language L'udovít Štúr, were all Slovak Lutherans. Rationalist Enlightenment influences could be strong among educated Protestants. The unpublished writings on Biblical history of the youthful Lajos Kossuth, later Hungary's national leader and a Lutheran, included scientific rebuttals of the Flood and the claim that the Creation story must be mythical since no man was present to record it at the time![1] It is significant that priests did not play a large leadership role in the national movements of the Catholic peoples, except perhaps the weakest, the Slovenes, though in a more passive sense, as subscribers to early patriotic periodicals, as in the Czech lands, their part was certainly important. The two Czech publicists who entered seminaries, Karel Havlíček and František Kampelík, both later withdrew. Among the Orthodox peoples of the Monarchy clerical leadership continued to be the norm, under men like Metropolitans Stratimirović and Rajačić for the Serbs and Bishop Şaguna for the Transylvanian Romanians. But in the wealthier Serb community it was no longer absolute.

On the whole, moral authority was wielded by the very ideas and images the establishment sought to ban. This ban was nowhere near as complete as contemporary references to a 'Chinese wall' around Austria suggested. Indeed, government propaganda in the 1840s presupposed a knowledge of forbidden material in its readers and censorship was flexible enough to allow individual scholars works they needed. Travellers reported all the latest French and English books to be available in Vienna. But to young people growing up in the provinces the restrictions on their mental horizons were real enough, as the later historian Anton Springer recorded of his experience as a *Gymnasium* student in Prague, where he learnt nothing of Goethe and Schiller because they were Protestant writers. The shock of discovery of his loss began the course which led him to die a Lutheran subject of the Second Reich. This was the danger of a censorship which was more vexatious than absolute. If there was hyperbole in Baron Andrian-Werburg's claim in 1842 that every word spoken in Germany echoed in Austria a thousand-fold, the outside world continued to intervene in ways mundane and dramatic, from Lancasterian pupil-teaching methods and Rumbold soup-kitchens to the risings of 1830 in France and Poland, with their inevitable excitement for youth. John Paget, travelling in western Hungary in the

1830s, found a country inn hung with portraits of English parliamentary reformers. An account of the fledgeling American democracy was a best-seller in Hungary at this time (though a translation of de Tocqueville's famous book on the subject was banned). The Czech journalist Havlíček, forbidden to discuss internal politics, discussed the Irish home rule movement instead.

Stirrings of a new political consciousness began to take on organised form only towards the end of the Pre-March era. Bodies like the Juridical–Political Reading Union (*Leseverein*), with 467 associates in mid-1845, Concordia and the Lower Austrian Commercial Association, all formed between 1839 and 1841, were the first in Austria to discuss general public issues, linking the western half of the Monarchy to the more vigorous tradition of public debate in semi-parliamentary Hungary, where Széchenyi's Casino, operating like a London 'club', went back to 1827. Smaller nationalities began to acquire platforms through the first successful vernacular newspapers, appearing among Croats and Transylvanian Romanians in the 1830s and Slovenes in the 1840s. In secondary schools and seminaries societies proliferated. Abroad disaffected *émigrés* assaulted the regime in anonymous tracts and in the Leipzig *Grenzboten,* edited by the Bohemian German Kuranda.

Collectively, these developments made a powerful impression. They seemed to confirm views of the 'restless striving' and 'irresistible' force of the age which were, after all, shared by many in government as well as its critics. Did not Kübeck record on a conversation with minister Pillersdorf in 1832 that the political revolutions with which they were confronted were but 'symptoms of a greater, deeper revolution in society itself'?[2] Regime fatalism grew with a reform consensus emerging in educated circles in much of the Monarchy by the 1840s. There was a sense of present malaise, but of living on the threshold of a new age, of being about to follow more dynamic lands into a world already partly known vicariously from their experience. In this new and juster world, to which education held the key, greater attention should be paid to peasants and workers, censorship should go, religious liberty should be extended and government more open. These convictions seemed powerful and coherent before the revolutions of 1848, which they helped to foster. Only with hindsight did their vagueness and the limited support behind them become apparent.

Who, after all, read the new newspapers? The most influential of all opposition papers in the Monarchy, the *Pesti Hírlap*, had under

Lajos Kossuth's editorship some 5000 subscribers and may have been read by a quarter of the estimated 50,000 Hungarian newspaper readers of the time. While the first great Czech journalist, Karel Havlíček, raised the circulation of the *Pražské Noviny* from 150 to 1600, other famous editors like the Croat Gaj and the Romanian Barițiu had to be content with 350 to 800 at most. These paltry figures bespoke a wider interest in public affairs, to be sure, than when these were the preserve of nobles attending the provincial diet, but one only enlarged to include a narrow film of secondary school graduates and wealthy merchants. How, too, could a society starved of free debate turn often borrowed and ill-digested ideas to constructive use?

Indeed, Austrian circumstances made it difficult to transcend the Josephinist agenda, and what has been dubbed 'liberalism' was often no more than this, with the addition of details plucked from contemporary western programmes, like the call for a National Guard and trial by jury. Yet backward societies *can* sometimes adopt a new philosophy almost as a didactic exercise, or blue-print for a desired new order. Such was the case with Count István Széchenyi (1791–1860). Man always strove to improve his destiny, wrote Széchenyi, but his striving was no longer for heroic success in war, love or faith but for machines, trade and associations; the passion to calculate was the idea of the century. The underlying principle behind all British horse-racing, he assured his readers in his first book *On Horses* (a theme aimed at their bucolic tastes), was the search for profit![3] In later books entitled *Credit*, *Light* and *Stage* Széchenyi argued for the abolition of *robota* to assure a supply of free labour, the restriction of entails to ensure mortgage credit and the principle of association to pool resources for the infrastructural investment Hungary required. The grand seigneur Széchenyi was more venturesome economically than politically, notably in his Danube chain bridge to link Buda and Pest and his river regulation and drainage schemes. But political conclusions were drawn by the high-principled lawyer Ferenc Deák, the kind of flinty moderate any constitutional liberal movement needs. It was Deák's achievement to argue the case for converting a medieval, noble constitution to a modern one, by extending the right to landed property, parliamentary representation and public office to all classes, limiting royal intervention in the legislative process, ending the cumbersome mandating of MPs by county assemblies and asserting the accountability of government. Deák was a liberal of the purest water. In his first major speech, on the death penalty in 1829, he defended the leader of a robber band on the grounds that in tender, character-forming years the orphan boy had had the misfortune to fall among desperate men and that as society should never use punishment merely for revenge he should be spared to devote his energies to the fatherland.[4] Why were principled liberal ideas so eloquently expounded in Hungary in the so-called Reform Era (1825–48)? Hungary had both the incentive to reform a lagging feudal order and the means to do so, in its constitutional institutions and self-confident noble class. And though the revolt of 1831 leant weight to liberals' occasional invocations of Spartacus to frighten their conservative fellow nobles into reform there was in fact little danger of the nightmare of all moderates – a successful revolution from below.

Széchenyi's closest counterpart in the Habsburg lands, if ultimately more radical, was the Lombard Carlo Cattaneo who like him invested the pursuit of capitalist agriculture and joint-stock enterprise with a moral aura, for what was credit but trust and association but brotherhood? Lombard liberalism was propagated by a growing press and burgeoning associational life; over a third of Italy's periodicals of 'useful knowledge' were being published in the Monarchy in 1833. As an awe-struck observer of a steam-powered Venetian factory commented: 'Our age lacks neither poetry nor monuments. What can better signify that God has placed man first and most beloved among his creatures.'[5] Elsewhere it is harder to speak of a classical liberalism. Austro-Germans were both economically stronger and politically weaker than Hungarian nobles, which gave a narrower focus and greater petulance to their criticisms of the regime, fixated as they were on the dead-hand of bureaucracy and censorship and the 'soul-destroying' educational system which bred them. The most famous of opposition essays, Baron Andrian-Werburg's *Austria and its Future*, published anonymously in Hamburg in 1843, disregarded the *robota* system and called effectively for a wrongly maligned aristocracy to be given the political clout it had in 'Germanic' England. This meant upgrading the power of the provincial diets while admitting the bourgeoisie and peasantry to them on equal terms, as in the Tyrol. The reconstituted diets were to supervise autonomous communes below and depute members to sit in an Imperial Estates body with undefined powers. This was at least politically comprehensive, if in the somewhat elitist spirit of trying to save the ship of state from the 'light-minded folly' of its crew,[6] as a like-minded aristocratic reformist, Count Anton Auersperg, put it tartly in 1847; under a pseudonym he was also the poet of protest

Anastasius Grün. Baron Anton Doblhoff, leader of nascent opposition in the Lower Austrian Diet, was another Whiggish figure, whose salon provided a forum for political discussion.

Middle-class dissent was quite distinct. It could spring from exasperation at regime mishandling of the social crisis of the 1840s (the Viennese lawyer Alexander Bach), the Josephinist traditions of middle-rank civil servants, or from the bourgeoisie's conviction that it now represented all that was best in the German nation, as with the German Bohemians Schuselka and Kuranda, editor of the Leipzig *Grenzboten*, favourite organ of the many Austrian literary exiles. But Schuselka's work already betrayed the awkward mix of bourgeois triumphalism and deference which was to dog nineteenth-century German liberalism. Nobles had had their day, he wrote, but the special 'nimbus' attaching to their name might yet make them the 'spiritual leaders' of the nation, as once with the sword.[7] The tension between radicalism and gradualism was not resolved, as also that between Schuselka's advocacy of an Austrian central representative parliament and his German nationalism. His economic writings condemned Metternich's courting of Russia for obstructing German control of the Danube artery, the key to German hegemony in what came later to be known as *Mitteleuropa*. This hegemony presupposed industrial protection, another breach of classical liberal theory. The complicated position of Germans in general and Austro-Germans in particular, perched between the advanced west and backward east, prevented them from simply endorsing the liberal programme from a position of strength, as did the English and French, or from one of weakness, like the Hungarians.

The smaller nations of the Monarchy lacked the professional and business men or reformist nobles for a liberal political culture. Significantly, the first Transylvanian Romanian newspaper was set up with the aid of the one substantial Romanian merchant community, in Braşov, while the middle nobility became the backbone of the Illyrian movement in Pre-March Croatia. The very fact that publications of the minor peoples existed at all did help encourage a slightly wider sense in these communities that a new dawn was breaking – 'I give thanks to God that I have lived to see literary gazettes and newspapers in our national language', one Romanian priest wrote to Bariţiu.[8] But the upbeat mood of progress hardly went beyond the ideas of Josephinism, at least among the Orthodox peoples. For the Czechs a skilful editor like Havlíček expressed the pragmatic radicalism of an underdog plebeian nationality when he commented

in February 1848 that any form of government would do which
recognised that power derived from the people. Revealingly, Havlíček supported the Irish leader O'Connell against the English,
whereas the Magyar liberal noble Eötvös criticised both sides.
Where a small nation enjoyed privileges its reformism was correspondingly qualified – the Illyrian National Party expressed no
view on *robota* in its 1847 programme except that compensation
should be paid. A general predisposition of educated opinion for
change on the eve of 1848 could thus disguise a wide range of policy
stances, not least incoherence.

But a heightened national feeling was common to all reformist tendencies. For contemporaries the links were manifold. Did not civil
equality logically presuppose national equality? Was not the nation
the highest form of free association? The other side of the coin was
that nations could only be truly free when all their inhabitants
enjoyed full civil rights. That Hungarian freedom *vis-à-vis* Vienna
could not co-exist with serfdom in Hungary was the insistent theme
of the Hungarian liberal noble reform movement. Finally, the call of
critics of the regime for a reinvigorating spirit to sweep away the cob-
webs of bureaucratic absolutism was, Andrian-Werburg freely
acknowledged, the call for a *national* spirit. This it was that would
breed the manly self-reliance and independent temper which reformers associated with free institutions. The work of Schuselka
abounded in calls for Germans to be vital, noble, strong, bold and
lovers of the mountain woods rather than soft, cowardly, unnatural,
tame, servile, base, corrupt infatuates of the city and the fashions
of foreigners.

The intellectual climate of the last years of absolutism is therefore
not easily summarised. Contempt for the regime was general but
divisions between aristocratic and bourgeois or conservative and
radical reformers are not so straightforward. While there were intriguing continuities with the late eighteenth-century reform, the difference between the two periods was the far greater articulation
which the national theme had meanwhile acquired and which calls
for separate inquiry.

The Rise of Nationalist Ideology

The most consistent theme in the scholarly literature on nationalism
emphasises its modernity. 'Nationalism is a doctrine invented at the

beginning of the nineteenth century', began Elie Kedourie's famous critique in 1960. Subsequent work by social scientists regularised the distinction between traditional and modern society, the latter requiring that individuals should *achieve* their social role instead of having it *ascribed* to them by immemorial custom. Standardised rules and procedures, including standardised languages, must take the place of traditional local norms in providing the social framework. It is the competition over which of the old folk cultures are to become the bearers of such modern 'high cultures' that gives birth to nationalism.[9] Nationalist claims of continuity with a known past are thus given short shrift in modern scholarship. Understandably, too, in view of its uglier excesses, nationalism's modernity is often seen less in its links with the rationalist Enlightenment than its role in easing the stresses of transition, through irrational appeals to past golden ages and present cultural exclusivism.

There can be some foreshortening in such approaches. The liberal associations of early nationalism have already been mentioned. It is no accident that men of the Enlightenment like Sonnenfels and Gottfried van Swieten hailed patriotism as the supreme virtue for officials or that the Freemason Ignaz Born called his Vienna Grand Lodge a patriotic work. The redirection of loyalties from faith to fatherland was not checked by the Franciscan reaction. In the secondary schools, colleges and universities increasingly attended even by the magnate class as noble academies declined, a kind of *esprit de corps* developed, subtly integrating noble and non-noble elements into a new kind of elite which, Moritz Csáky has argued for Hungary, saw its claim to national leadership in terms of 'patriotic' commitment as much as ancient blood. If among young Magyars the social mix rarely went below the middle class, a fifth of Czech national activists born in the 1820s were already of peasant stock, and a third of Vienna university students in 1848 were officially recorded as coming from poor homes. The nascent movements of the Monarchy's non-dominant nationalities were led preponderantly by educated sons from the upper levels of the common people, whose fathers were teachers, Orthodox or Lutheran parish priests, estate officials, millers, occasionally merchants. The intellectual energy and cultural breadth of the ablest products of the educational system could be remarkable. Lajos Kossuth's future right-hand man Ferenc Pulszky was familiar at fourteen with A.W. Schlegel, Tasso, Calderon, Sir Walter Scott, d'Holbach, Voltaire, Rousseau and Klopstock and all of Kotzebue and Lessing. L'udovít Štúr, founder of literary Slovak, knew nine languages. A liberal nationalism, centred around the notion of patriotism as the opposite of servility, in which all could share regardless of class or creed, became part of the ambience in which educated young people grew up.

Paradoxical as it might sound, nationalism was thus an international movement whose ideas originated from Germany and were recycled in the Monarchy's polyglot institutions by Slavs and Magyars. Slovak nationalism was born in the Lutheran *lycées* of Bratislava and Budapest, attended also Magyars, Serbs and the 'father of the Czech nation', František Palacký. The Slovak writer–linguist Šafárik taught in the Serb *Gymnasium* of Novi Sad, while the founder of Yugoslavism Josip Juraj Strossmayer was trained in Pest and Vienna, where the greatest of Slovene poets, France Prešeren, learnt his patriotism. Few creative writers worked in a monocultural framework. Vuk Karadžić, founder of modern literary Serbian, spent most of his life in Vienna; the leading Serbian novelist Jakov Ignjatović grew up in central Hungary; the best German Bohemian writers of this time stressed motifs from Czech history and the Austro-German poet Anastasius Grün translated Slovene folk-songs. How could nationalism in such circumstances be other than the call to emulation? As interpreted by the young it challenged all national groups to implant the principles of freedom and progress in their own land, in order to prove their fitness for membership of the European community of nations. It was fraternal, rational and universalist.

That youthful nationalists would share liberal hopes for change stemmed also from their social situation. They were, or hoped to be, upwardly mobile, with everything to gain from the ending of serfdom in broadening the basis of their nationhood. All, or almost all, supported fuller religious equality. All, in principle, approved of civil rights for Jews, although attempts to forge a Czech–Jewish alignment in the 1840s foundered on Czech scepticism at the concept of a Czech Jew and Magyar patriots tended to link emancipation with Jewish cultural assimilation. Never before or since was it so easy for Zagreb intellectuals of Orthodox background to function as Croatian patriots.

Yet ultimately nationalism was more than the application of liberal principles in an ethnic setting. What, after all, was one's fatherland? Was it a territorial–political unit, like the kingdom of Hungary, the province of Bohemia or indeed the Monarchy as a whole? Or was it the domain of one's mother tongue, essentially a cultural concept? Liberal nationalism, with its stress on patriotism as civics, implied the former. In practice, nationalism in the nineteenth-century Habsburg Monarchy moved increasingly towards the latter. Confusion between the two remained, however, to inflict mischief in the political sphere.

In the emergence of language as the key criterion of nationhood, the major role was played by the *romantic* concept of the nation as a cultural group with its own distinctive contribution to make to the development of mankind. Here the nation was envisaged as the framework through which values were transmitted from generation to generation. Maturity was a matter of acquiring these values, of becoming rooted in a particular tradition. Since traditions were handed down through language it was language which defined the truly important groups into which mankind was divided, not the usurpations of princes. Most important, the songs of a humble peasant could penetrate just as profoundly into the human condition as the writings of enlightened sophisticates. J.G. Herder (1744–1803), the German Lutheran pastor whose work sowed the seeds of what historians term romantic nationalism, was first inspired by Latvian folksongs when ministering in Riga. He went on to plead the cause of the Red Indians and to call on the 'Slavs, now sunk so low', to rise from their 'enervating slumber' and renew their peaceful, industrious ways on their ancestral lands.[10]

It is romantic nationalism's appeal to the past which has drawn forth historians' charge of anachronism. But this charge itself is somewhat undiscriminating. Patriots of the early nineteenth century were not operating in a framework of 'modern' urban industrialism but in small Baroque towns dominated by Counter-Reformation churches, noble diets and the palaces of magnates, Bans and Palatines. The Illyrian movement of Pre-March Croatia was hatched in the homes of old Zagreb, now a picturesque backwater. The Czech pioneer Dobrovský spent much time on the estate of his magnate patron, Count Nostitz; his successor Palacký began his career working for another magnate and was long the Official Historiographer for the feudally structured Pre-March Bohemian Diet. Views of national continuity in these venerable circumstances lacked proof and plausibility when they ascribed current resentments of German hegemony to the dark ages – but much less so where the early modern period was concerned. When Ljudevit Gaj founded the Illyrian movement in Croatia in 1835 he stood closer to Ritter-Vitezović's patriotic *Croatia rediviva* (1700) than to our own day. The subordination of an administrative unit called Croatia, regret at its failure to include all

Croats and awareness of a broader south Slav dimension were common to both situations. Nor is it clear, in psychological terms, why the very similar expressions of bitterness by seventeenth- and early nineteenth-century Czech writers at German superciliousness towards their language should not point to a common structure of resentment, at least for those writers. The current orthodoxy, which discounts elements of continuity between nineteenth-century and early modern nationhood in Europe, is rather too sweeping.

What was wholly novel was the proto-liberal climate of the first half of the nineteenth century. In this ambience 'patriots' were able to make their concerns a vital public issue which henceforth never left the region's agenda. But it is still worth saying that tradition was not wholly 'invented'. Where there was no precedent for nineteenth-century concepts like Czechoslovak or Illyrian nationhood these projects failed. Nationalism took hold insofar as it built on existing realities, historical, linguistic or social. It reshaped them qualitatively to form new, more powerful identities but the process should not be absolutised. It was possible for national consciousness to exist below the ranks of the privileged before the nineteenth century, as witness the avidity with which the Czech peasant Vavák read patriotic chronicles in his youth. May not the pathos of Gaj's famous song 'Still Croatia has not fallen' (1833) be seen as a plausible comment on Croatian history from the standpoint of an educated young man of the time? For nations which had once possessed their own states and social elites nationalist claims of *re*birth and *re*vival were not empty of content.

To be sure, there were peoples in the Monarchy – the Slovenes, the Slovaks, the Ruthenians, the Transylvanian Romanians – who had no traditions of political nationhood or centuries of a native elite to look back on. These were the classic 'nations without history' in Friedrich Engels' influential phrase. But these groups comprised under a quarter of the Monarchy's total population and it would be wrong to see even them as mere ethnic raw material, lacking any experience of forms of 'high culture'. The Bible had appeared in Slovene in 1584 during the later suppressed Slovene Reformation and Slovak Protestants continued to use the Czech Kralice Bible of 1579–94. Nor did it strictly matter, from the standpoint of romantic nationalism, that such people lacked a state past. Its basic rationale lay in the dignity it accorded the common people, their memories and folk ways. There was a democratic germ in this revaluation of the culture of the previously humble and despised. The romantic theme, quite correctly, was that tradition was not only a matter of the privileged orders; at the level of human psychology and empirical fact all communities have a history. Besides Palacký's roots in a region where Czech Protestantism and traditions of the Slav apostles remained alive, Šafárik inherited his migrant Czech Protestant forbears' recollections of Hus and Comenius; Kollár came from the High Tatra mountain region where Slovak was reputed to be purer than elsewhere. Such stray strands of sentiment and the sense of worth and meaning normal, healthy individuals feel in their lives could, for an educated minority exposed to Herderian ideology, become a real factor in psychological emancipation from the thrall of a dominant culture. They were elements out of which people who might once have considered themselves Hungarians of Slav stock, for example, could 'construct' themselves a new 'Slovak' identity.

Of course, the emerging intelligentsias of the 'nations without history' did not confine themselves to arguing their democratic right to exist. Transylvanian Romanians enthused over their distant Roman ancestry, Slovak and Slovene patriots over the shadowy realms of the ninth-century Svatopluk or sixth-century Samo respectively. Such windy bragging was arguably forced on them by the rules of the ethnic game set by the more powerful players, who played on their alleged lack of 'state-forming capacity'. In Herderian theory, or the Italian revolutionary Guiseppe Mazzini's vision of fraternal nations fighting for freedom, nations contributed jointly to a common Humanity. In practice, as national ideologies crystallised there were clashes in interpretations of past history and present interests. The on the whole generously emulative spirit of multi-national colleges bore much the same relation to attitudes in the wider world as does student idealism to the politics of our own day.

Modern historians' stress of the extent of myth in nationalist ideology was foreshadowed at the time. For dominant Germans who for two centuries had seen most Czechs as lower-order *Stockböhmen* the emphasis on the glories of the pre-1526 Czech state was antiquarian nonsense. One need not be a Burkean conservative, however, to feel that the present is not the only guide to the future but that what men have done in the past fits in somewhere too. There could in all honesty be two ways of making sense of the early nineteenth-century world. In one, the trends of the present pointed unequivocally to an ever-increasing role of German language and culture as the vehicle of economic progress and scientific knowledge. Here the non-German world represented a receding past and the perspective for a questing spirit was assimilation to Germandom. In the other prospect the time-span was broader and the social purview wider, so that the as yet unassimilated non-German masses loomed more centrally as an equally undeniable reality and one, moreover, which linked the non-German intellectual satisfyingly with an immemorial past. Was it perverse to hope that, 'awoken' to the spirit of the age, these masses might convert their numerical superiority into a more active role in the state, righting the wrongs of history and ushering in an age of equality and fulfilment? This was the nationalist perspective. Neither standpoint had yet won out. The choice between ethnic assimilation to a dominant culture still confronted almost all educated members of smaller nationalities personally.

Individual examples best illustrate the process. The autobiography of the Prague-born German art historian Anton Springer shows how assimilation operated: 'a Slavic dialect was my mother tongue', he wrote 'but I became a German as by natural power ... we [children] never even dreamt of the possibility of Bohemian schooling'.[11] Urged by his brother, who had become a Czech patriot, to read the fledgeling Czech literature around 1840, Springer was repelled by what he felt trivial and mediocre and confirmed in his German orientation. In a similar case the important natural scientist, Jan Evangelista Purkyně, became a Czech national revivalist and his brother a German. On the other hand, German was Ljudevit Gaj's mother tongue, while the composer of the first Croatian opera, Vatroslav Lisinski, had translated his name from its baptismal German, Ignjat Fuchs. Further east, Şaguna, the great patriot bishop of the Romanian Orthodox population of Transylvania, lived his adolescent years as a Hungarian-speaking Roman Catholic. His change of identity was a personal response to his family's origins from the Balkan Vlach community, whose speech resembled Romanian.

Choices can be burdensome. Often much self-justification is entailed. The situation remained fluid and the future obscure. The thought of 'national death' in an indifferent, even hostile world preyed on the minds of patriots. In these circumstances the work of cultural uplift which romantic nationalism inspired did not go forward in a spirit of mutual benevolence but of considerable psychological tension, bitterness and frustration. Patriots of different nationality, though still linked by the web of German culture, began to grow apart. To the extent that the authorities followed tendencies veiled partly by little-known languages and the patriots' caution, they were not unduly concerned, and could even support one language movement against another to exacerbate divisions in the potentially oppositionist educated classes. This was short-sighted. The switch in emotional allegiance to the mother tongue distracted from notions of imperial loyalty that the Enlightenment had fostered and in the longer term offered an alternative organising principle hostile to the interests of a multi-national state. However, the 'national idea' for non-dominant peoples at this time remained in stage B of its development in Miroslav Hroch's helpful typology, between stage A of mere antiquarianism and stage C of the mass movement: of interest only to a backbone of clergy, small numbers of intellectual workers, professionals and students, some urban commercial elements (increasingly) and fewer prosperous peasants. Thus it is that the apparently featureless landscape of much of the Pre-March Monarchy acquires its abiding interest – in the slow-motion grapplings of a sclerotic establishment with its still puny rivals for public esteem.

Developments in the Non-Hungarian Lands

The deceptive quality of these years – the fissile material bubbling away under a calm exterior – was most marked where Hungarian liberties did not obtain, particularly in Bohemia. The two areas which gave the authorities their most ostensible cause for concern were those which had been most recently incorporated, Lombardy-Venetia and Galicia.

Policies in these provinces reveal the limitations of Metternich's decentralising goals. Francis may have obstructed them but it was Metternich who remarked that Italians needed titles, ribbons and silent senators. The 'kingdoms' of Galicia-Lodomeria and Lombardy-Venetia were empty shells run from Vienna, the former regaining a diet on the lines of the Hereditary Lands (1817), the latter two central and a number of provincial 'Congregations' whose members were chosen by the Emperor from the wealthiest inhabitants. True, the Italian provinces were not administered through German, as was Galicia and its new university at the capital Lvov (Lemberg, L'viv). But most higher officials were non-Italians and the Austrian censorship humiliated a culturally advanced people: in 1847 Dante, Boccacio, Alfieri, Goethe and Victor Hugo were all variously forbidden fruit for university students.

Economically, both Italians and Poles believed, probably rightly, that they were being exploited, though figures for local revenue and expenditure are difficult to calculate and certain items, like central expenditure for the public debt, were omitted from nationalist reckonings. However, with less than a fifth of the population, the Italian provinces provided between a quarter and a third of Habsburg revenue, the stamp and poll taxes and the salt and tobacco monopolies being particularly unpopular. Revenue per head was less than a third the Habsburg average in backward Galicia but this still meant a sharp rise compared to the demands of the old Polish state. In return Galicians received a more efficient administrative and educational service, but not much else as early attempts at economic development came to be dropped. Lombardy-Venetia was far more advanced, serving as a source of raw materials and a receiver of Bohemian and Moravian textiles. But its flourishing silk production, exported crude or spun, was subject to an unpopular mulberry tax, and Venice's stagnation was only partly alleviated by free port status (1830) and the railway bridge from the mainland (1846). Venetians remained resentful of favoured Trieste and Lombards of being cut off from other markets by imperial protection.

Patterns of protest reflected the different traditions of Galician nobles and the more bourgeois society of north Italy. An early crackdown on the secret Carbonari society in Venetia in 1820–21 was followed by fretful calm. By contrast, the 1830 insurrection in Russian Poland lent wings to a pan-Polish revolutionary movement organised from exile and drawing inspiration from romantic patriotism. The radicalism of the pro-peasant Polish Democratic Society (founded in Paris in 1832) appealed to poorer nobles and student youth, grouped in the underground Assembly of the Polish People in the homeland. But the arrest of most of its Galician activists in the late 1830s led to the Assembly's suspension by more cautious members closer to the line of the *émigré* aristocrat Adam Czartoryski, who hoped to use international diplomacy to advance the Polish cause. Government concessions in the 1840s to the economic programme of the Galician Diet leader, Prince Leon Sapieha, a moderate reformer in the Széchenyi mould, suggest that Vienna may have been trying to outflank the revolutionary opposition. Any such strategy was, however, thrown off course by the Galician rising of 1846, set in train by the Polish left. The connivance of certain local officials in the bloody peasant *jacquerie* against nationalist nobles discredited pretensions to official paternalism, particularly since contemporary

European opinion wrongly believed the central government to be implicated.

This embarrassment may be part explanation for the government's reluctance to crack down on the burgeoning opposition movement in Italy which followed. Liberal national enthusiasm mobilised by the election of a popular Pope in 1846 and by mounting economic ambitions clashed with Austria's opposition to railway links with the rest of Italy, and the mishandling of the economic crisis of 1846–47 enhanced the sense that her rule damaged Italian national interests. At the annual congress of Italian scientists, held at Venice in September 1847, well-received comments on the disastrous quality of the potato crop played on potato's other meaning in Italian – as a dismissive term for German.

At the other end of the ethnic scale the Ruthenian and Slovene peasant peoples still gave the authorities little cause for concern. There were some stirrings. Grammarians, ethnologists and folklorists wrote on Ruthenian themes in Polish, German or Latin in the 1820s and in the next decade a patriotic literary circle in the Uniate seminary in Lvov published an almanac, the *Nymph of the Dniestr* (1836), which marked the beginnings of Ruthenian vernacular literature. The Lvov police chief's comments bely Polish charges that Austria sought to play Ruthenians off against them. 'We already have enough trouble with one nationality (the Poles) and these madmen will resurrect the dead and buried Ruthenian nationality.'[12] Not by chance the first Slovene weekly paper, edited by Janez Bleiweis, was for farmers (1843). Yet the literary language now being arduously hammered out between different provincial traditions could already produce the masterpiece of the unhappy school-master Prešeren's 'Sonnet Wreath', where the last lines of fourteen sonnets made the first lines of the next, all together composing the fifteenth – in which the object of Prešeren's unrequited love was immortalised in the mother tongue she despised.

The Czechs were a different matter. Bohemia exemplified regional alienation from the centre – the mixing of *sotto voce* distaste for authoritarian rule with implicit appeals to alternative values which gives the period its distinctive character. While the withdrawal of great magnates from Vienna after 1809 affected other provinces too (doubtless most famously in Archduke Johann's commitment to Styrian agricultural improvement) language and history gave the tendency a special edge in Bohemia. The Czech Museum, a learned society which was a crucial vehicle of the early Czech revival, was founded by Count Kaspar Sternberg in 1818, under whose patronage Palacký first made his name. Count Leo Thun could strive to become bilingual in the 1830s, though his estates lay in German-speaking Bohemia. The patriotic role of sections of the Irish Protestant Ascendancy class and of the Swedish-speaking elite of nineteenth-century Finland offer some parallels to the Bohemian loyalties of such lofty figures.

The alliance of provincial-minded aristocrats and Czech plebeian patriots that was foreshadowed in Kramerius's conservative turn in the 1790s thus took firmer shape in this period. By the 1840s three generations of Czech patriots had appeared, growing in confidence. That of Dobrovský (1753–1829) matured in an atmosphere of Enlightenment rather than romanticism and wrote about Czech more than in it; Dobrovský to the end had bouts of pessimism about the future of his native tongue. The turning-point came with the second generation, associated with Josef Jungmann (1773–1847), translator of *Paradise Lost* (1811) and author of a five-volume Czech–German dictionary (1835–39) which gave Czech the range required for a modern literary language. Jungmann's middle years, from about 1800 to 1830, saw the tension between continuing assimilation and mounting assertion press hardest on thoughtful Czechs, when despite growing Herderian influence Czechs still wrote their mother tongue more, as Count Thun put it, 'from an obscure feeling of national honour' than with any firm hope or concerted plan.[13] The pressures are often felt in Jungmann's correspondence: 'the sad thoughts which oppress you oppress me also', as he once wrote.[14] The constant refrain of German malevolence, an unsympathetic government, the need for divine guidance for a desperate people with few friends: all this suggests an embattled spirit for whom the struggle to save a fragile nationality outweighted other, non-Slavic solidarities. Under Jungmann's influence the concept of Czechdom became definitely wedded to the Czech language, bringing a narrowing of focus *vis-à-vis* the Bohemian German Bolzano's hopes for a bilingual Bohemian nation – though Jungmann sought to blur this fact by heady appeals to Panslavic ideas of the brotherhood of the Slavs. Thus distant Russians became in Jungmann's emotional world closer than German Bohemians. Parting company with Dobrovský and the great Slovene linguist Kopitar, he denounced as national treason all scepticism about the Dvůr Králové manuscript made public in 1817, ostensibly a collection of medieval poems revealing a higher level of Czech culture than had previously been suspected – and also a glowing anti-German patriotism. They and subsequent finds had actually been forged by their discoverer, Hánka. The forgeries and the intellectual cover-up, not abandoned till the end of the century, can be related to the Polish historian Chlebowczyk's claim that non-dominant groups' unequal struggle against assimilation initially required a phase of romantic myth-making to succeed.[15] If in retrospect contemporaries' fears for their mother tongue seem exaggerated, it should be remembered that in 1817 there were nearly as many native speakers of Irish as Czech. It boded ill that the numbers of those choosing to study Czech in Bohemian secondary schools when this option was conceded in 1816 soon fell after the initial novelty.

By 1837, however, the leading figure of the third generation of revival, the historian František Palacký (1798–1876), felt able to say that the national language's survival was assured and the controversies on its grammar and vocabularly resolved. Czechs, he argued, along classic liberal nationalist lines, should now turn outwards and identify their cause with that of wider human progress. Indeed, Czech literature was now popular enough for Czech plays to be performed in some 140 centres and mature enough to produce a Karel Mácha, whose highly personalised poetry, notably his *May* (1836), showed no trace of the stock patriotic didacticism of his contemporaries; the Pre-March radical editor Karel Havlíček could turn away from pan-Slav pieties and assert Czech democracy over Russian tsarism. Palacký himself was a genuine liberal, if at the conservative end of the spectrum like his French historian-politician counterpart Guizot, whose minority Protestantism and patrician temperament he shared. But Palacký's life and work show how hard he found it to escape the querulous round of nationalist apologetics. The more one reads him repeat that Czech history consists in a constant struggle of peaceful Slavs and marauding Germans, that Germans brought Bohemia certain good things, to be sure, but also feudal bondage, that Czechs did not merit before they were corrupted the charge of being of a cruel, deceitful and thieving nature, that taunts of early barbarism are eloquently disproved by the manly nobility and elevated patriotism of the Dvůr Králové manuscript (which Palacký never disavowed), the more one wonders if this tedious battle had to be fought. The answer is probably yes. Nationalism has played its great role in modern life because it touches so closely on primal forces of human nature – feelings of identity, inadequacy, hurt and self-esteem. Overarching theories of nationalism are useful insofar as they help us to situate and grapple with these issues of human feeling, not if in lofty abstraction they allow us to evade them. The result in Palacký's case was, however, predictable. Germans found his manner insufferable.

Even the small circles committed to a common Bohemianism on Bolzano's lines were fraught with mutual suspicions. No 'genuine Czech' , Alfred Meissner wrote to his fellow Jewish member of the bi-national *Rother Turm* group, the 'Bohemian' novelist Moritz Hartmann, would forgive Hartmann's poem *Bohemian Elegies* calling on Czechs to weep on Germany's shoulder and forget their old resentments. For his part, Hartmann declared that the anti-Semitism of Czech workers in the 1844 riots was enough to make him a loyal servant of the regime. German irritation did not at first find systematic intellectual expression. But a certain amount of grumbling in high places after the first volume of Palacký's *History of Bohemia* (1836) – ironically in German – led to the Czech Museum being grilled by the provincial authorities on its alleged neglect of German speakers. Palacký's chief accuser, Professor Exner of Prague university, engaged in private sarcasm against the ivory tower patriotism, as he saw it, of some of his Czech colleagues:

> True, more than a quarter of the population [of Bohemia] is German; but they are intruders; ... true, Czech monarchs summoned them, only to the disadvantage of the Czechs; ... true, [the Czechs] cannot attain their goal as long as a powerful Austrian Monarchy survives, so long as they cannot attach themselves to the great Slav Mother, but ...[16]

In the 1840s, however, the social base of Czech patriotism began to broaden, in the influx of Czechs into the previously aristocratic Union of Bohemian Industry and the setting up of a Czech-dominated technical section of the Union and of a prestigious Czech social club in Prague (1846). Enterprising young men arriving in the city and marrying into families on the verge of losing their Czech began to reverse its long process of Germanisation. Czech-speaking professionals like Brauner, the theorist of the Bohemian Diet's legal continuity, Strobach, and the Czech leader in the Industrial Union, Trojan, were all millers' sons. The ostensible Czech underdogs had a closer relationship with the Bohemian nobility than their German-speaking bourgeois rivals. Ensconced as Count Sternberg's protégé and editor of the Czech Museum's Czech and

German journals, Palacký was well placed to popularise the first as a patriotic monthly while the other dwindled into an academic quarterly. German-speaking nobles welcomed a patriotic 'Bohemian' history in their struggle from 1838 to restore the alleged past partnership of King and Diet. 'The good of the country is the goal, a strong monarchical government is the means and a constitution of estates is the condition', exclaimed the Diet's champion Wurmbrand in 1844.[17] Called to address Diet members, Palacký mixed forthrightness and flattery with a sure hand. Feudalism like absolutism had had its day but aristocracy as a fact of nature could rejuvenate itself by allying with the new force of public opinion, in its national guise. It was as close as Palacký could come to politicising the Czech cause in the circumstances.

The revived activity of decrepit organs like the Bohemian and Lower Austrian Diets in the 1840s showed the vacuum at the heart of government. The regime's rejection of a Lower Austrian Diet petition against censorship in 1845 signalled its fear of opening the floodgates. Beyond a dispirited Church and a nascent and still partly foreign industrial sector it no longer had the support of any social group. The dramatist Bauernfeld's play *Of Age*, staged in Vienna in 1847, transparently portrayed Metternich as an aged guardian vainly denouncing the new ideas his ward has acquired, which another character affirms are simply 'in the air'. It escaped censorship because Kolowrat wanted to spite his rival. In the same year a letter from Joseph Hormayr to Palacký ironised on the gratitude which Czechs and Magyars were supposed to show for their association with Austria and a thousand years' attempted Germanisation of the Slavs. Coming from the man who jouralistically had tried hardest of all to create a common Austrian patriotism Hormayr's private disillusionment is as telling as Bauernfeld's public mockery. The Austrian *Vormärz* (Pre-March period) is a time when too much water was allowed to run under the bridge.

Pre-March Hungary

At the start of the century even Hungary's distinctive traditions did not seem immune to the processes of cultural symbiosis affecting the western lands of the Monarchy. German booksellers like the Landerer business in Pest and Bratislava and the Heckenast firm in Košice led the way in the book trade; Hungary's leading historians of the period, Engel and Fessler, wrote in their native German; even writers of Magyar mother tongue (Gaál, Toldy, Mailáth) made German their literary medium. Magyar culture lacked clear hegemony in its own land. Between 1777 and 1848 the Pest university press published 1349 works in Hungarian to 1323 in Latin, 924 in German and 624 in Serbian. The Magyar cultural revival, like the Czech one a little later, proceeded from bilingual circles.

It was certainly vigorous. Controversy over Kazinczy's modernisation of the literary language had died down by 1819, permitting a plethora of specialist lexicographic activities which fed into a comprehensive dictionary in 1839 that helped to diminish 'cultural cringe'. In a few decades some of the finest works of Hungarian literature appeared: József Katona's historical tragedy *Bánk Bán* and Mihály Vörösmarty's verse epic of Hungary's origins, *Zoltán's Flight*, preceded the lyricism of the acknowledged national poet Sándor Petőfi (1823–49), while the realist novel began in the 1840s with József Eötvös. Cultural life became institutionalised through bodies like the Academy of Sciences (1825), the Pest Theatre, later the National Theatre (1837) and the First Hungarian Academy of Fine Arts (1846). A key development was the emergence of a national urban centre in Buda-Pest, where five-sixths of all journals sent through the Hungarian post in 1842 originated. In this city of a hundred thousand inhabitants noble reformers' vision of a Hungarian civil society transcending feudal bonds appeared to grow before their eyes.

The gradual strengthening of national consciousness undermined Emperor Francis's attempt after 1811 to revert to eighteenth-century practice and dispense with the Diet. After years of county protests – met with the imposition of royal administrators and, where necessary, enforced conscription and tax collection – Metternich advised the summoning of the Diet in 1825. Yet not for the first time his apparent flexibility proved purely tactical. It rested on the mistaken assumption that Hungarian parliamentarism could be kept in its traditional noble libertarian bounds, absorbed in wrangles with the executive about the priority to be given to royal business or its own grievances. After the European upheavals of 1830, however, and the appearance of Széchenyi's economic critiques, the county preparations for the 1832 Diet saw the outlines of a liberal opposition which was prepared to put the peasant question at the top of its agenda. True, majority desire to retain aviticity (p. 86) showed noble reservations about real change, which government further manipulated through the votes of the impoverished 'sandal nobility' (enfranchised as a pliable element in 1819) to get reformists' mandates revoked. The gains of the 1832–36 Diet were thus ultimately modest: a right in principle for peasants to redeem their *robota* services permanently and to own their land, and a symbolic breach of noble tax exemption – all were to be liable for the toll on the new Danube chain-bridge linking Buda and Pest.

The Diet was nonetheless a turning-point. The arbitrary jailing of leading reformers Wesselényi and Kossuth won breathing-space but no more. The authorities shrank from blocking the attendance at the Diet of up to 1500 young assistants of the delegates, for the most part exuberantly reformist, as their presence was sanctioned by custom. Hungarian society was in flux and the executive's attempt to treat the Diet like a medieval assembly, weighting votes according to their casters' importance and amending bills at the very point it approved them, did not correspond to the evolving reality. It was the liberals who offered a coherent way out of the contradictions: generalisation of property rights and accountability of government to a parliament representing all classes. Ferenc Deák's pious fiction that these principles derived from the core of the traditional constitution itself assisted their gradual progress. With government chastened by the exposure of its weakness in the Near Eastern crisis of 1839–40, the Diet of those years was able to pass most of its predecessor's vetoed peasant legislation and also laws on credit, commerce and factory enterprise which extended the range of capitalist norms.

The creation of a broader 'public opinion' around this programme, encompassing non-noble professionals and even previously pro-Vienna lesser nobles, was the work of the 1840s, chiefly of the landless noble and *Pesti Hírlap* editor, Lajos Kossuth (1802–94). Kossuth's editorials emphasised socio-economic renewal. The Defence Association he founded to agitate for protection of Hungary's infant industries in 1845 was Hungary's first experience of popular mobilisation of opinion. Implicitly, though, the programme and the nature of its support required the restructuring of the state as well as of the economy. Only in a Hungarian national state prised from the hands of the Austrophile and largely magnate administration could bourgeois professionals and impecunious nobles like Kossuth himself come into their own. Hence the laws passed by successive diets to replace official Latin by Magyar, culminating in that of 1844 making it compulsory in administrative, judicial and educational spheres. The removal of discrimination against Protestants in public office and mixed marriages was another step towards uniting educated Magyars into a potential national ruling class.

In these attacks on the old hierarchical system of government, the liberal nationalist opposition went well beyond the modernisation programme that 'young conservatives' were increasingly willing to endorse. The strategy of the latter, backed by Chancellor Apponyi from 1846, included support for Hungary's capitalist development, *voluntary* redemption of labour service by serfs and taxation of nobles, together with selected items of the liberal programme like trial by jury and abolition of capital punishment. But though the 'young conservatives' also supported Metternich's wish to abolish the customs barrier between Austria and Hungary, Metternich opposed the state aid Hungary needed for development. He was dismissive, too, of Széchenyi's attempts to draw closer to the government, after the once idolised 'father of the nation' had failed to convince Deák and other moderate nationalists of the dangers lurking in Kossuthite radicalism.

Széchenyi's central warning was against Magyar hubris and for the need for careful handling of Hungarians of non-Magyar mother tongue. The language movement had undermined the old notion of a common identity of all Hungary's inhabitants. 'We Hungarians are not a nation', the German-speaking and loyal Hungarian Berzeviczy had written combatively to the linguistic nationalist Kazinczy in 1809, forseeing the threat to older loyalties.[18] Not all non-Magyar speakers were equally concerned. For many German speakers the 'national question' remained secondary because of their sense of cultural strength, for nearly all Hungarian Ruthenians because of their cultural weakness. Other non-Magyar movements drew largely on the same contemporary themes as their Magyar counterpart, whether the Hegelianism of the Slovak patriot Štúr or the classical liberalism of the Romanian editor Bariţiu, who visited western Europe in 1845. Did not Hungarians deny such people the liberal national rights they claimed for themselves? Magyar reformers judged matters differently. From the standpoint of scale to which Eric Hobsbawm has drawn attention, surely the 'national idea' only applied to nations of a certain size, effectively those with 'historic' traditions like their own. Hence it was not hypocrisy in Magyar eyes for Baron Zay, head of Hungary's Lutherans, two-thirds of whom were Slovak, to emphasise the religious identity of his Slav co-religionists at the expense of their language while his Magyar compatriots were stressing their language rather than their religion.

Slovaks were simply not a 'nation' for them, at best a 'nationality'. Magyar polemicists did not fear that the non-Magyar movements could replicate their own liberal nationalism, rather that they might attach themselves to illiberal forces – clerical or Panslav – more powerful than they were themselves. This was the theme of Zaj's pamphlet attacking 'Slavism' of 1841.

Ironically, though Panslavism (the doctrine of the unity of the Slavs) had a predictable appeal to the weak and isolated Slovak intelligentsia, it was in these years that Slovaks under Štúr's lead finally established a separate literary language, decisively repudiating a common national identity with their closest Slav cousins, the Czechs. Czech reluctance to modify their own literary language contributed to this, and also a feeling that a home-grown speech would more effectively ward off Magyarisation, particularly among those lesser gentry who still spoke Slovak at home. Štúr belonged to the Slovak Protestant minority but in the spirit of the times this did not militate against his central Slovak dialect winning acceptance against the older Catholic Slovak standard devised by the priest Bernolák in the 1780s. But internal *rapprochement* was only the beginning of the Slovak struggle. 'Just as Hungary constitutes one country, so its inhabitants form one nation', wrote the director of the Košice school district in opposing permission for the Slovak cultural society 'Tatra' in 1847.[19]

Romanian nationality in Hungary also showed some decoupling of ethnic and religious loyalties. Romanians emancipated themselves from Serb hegemony in the bi-national church province of Karlowitz; the first Romanian bishop of Arad was nominated in 1828. But there was something in the Romanian experience which cannot be so easily fitted into liberal categories as they were understood in the mid-nineteenth century. This was the personality of Bishop Şaguna, who became administrator of the Romanian Orthodox diocese of Transylvania in 1846, with the aim of bringing his flock of 700,000 Karlowitz's standards of clerical training and sobriety. Şaguna combined powerful forces: the element of romantic commitment to the nationhood he had reclaimed, together with a deep dedication to the regeneration of his ancient Orthodox faith. His life is a case-study in the use of rational organisational techniques thought 'modern' in order to invigorate cherished values from the past, a process social scientists have dubbed the 'modernisation of tradition'. Previously Habsburg Romanian patriots had been very largely Uniates, with whose cultural mission Şaguna now aligned his church.

The south Slavs posed Magyar nationalists a more immediate threat. Even these nationalists accepted that Croats were not a mere 'nationality' but had historic rights of their own. However, they admitted these rights only for the three counties of Croatia proper, not the three Slavonian counties. Besides, half the flock of the Karlowitz Serb Orthodox province lived in Croatia-Slavonia. The Croat position seemed weak, which helps account for the 1844 Hungarian Diet's decision to include Slavonia in its official language law, albeit with a period of grace for Magyar to be learnt. Much milder linguistic pressure in the 1820s had helped spark off the Croat movement, together with patriots' awareness of their country's economic weakness and its elite's susceptibility to German culture. Count Drašković's *Dissertation* (1832) was the first political pamphlet to be written in Croatian and likewise the first major call to national self-assertion. The subsequent course of the Croat movement followed a line not available to the racially isolated Magyars. This was the 'Illyrian' programme for linguistic unification with other south Slavs with which the editor Gaj sought to rally his fragmented fellow-countrymen; the historical name chosen was hoped, in the modern jargon, to be safely inclusive. The weekly paper he founded in 1835 adopted a new spelling (based on Czech diacritic marks) and soon abandoned the *kajkavski* speech of Zagreb itself for the *štokavski* dialect which all Serbs and two-thirds of Croats spoke. Though the movement was ostensibly for south Slav cultural *rapprochement*, Gaj himself was a restlessly political animal, as his secret anti-Austrian memorandum to the Tsar (1838), his contacts with Serbia and his eventual work as an Austrian agent show. He was of bourgeois stock, like most of the early 'Illyrians'. Quite quickly the movement's centre of gravity shifted towards the Croatian middle nobility under whom what had always been its main impulse became more evident – the use of modern linguistic motifs to invigorate an essentially Croatian struggle for autonomy, based on Croatia's 'municipal rights', the equivalent of Hungarian county autonomy. This tendency interacted with the rejection of the Illyrians' wider south Slav concerns by nearly all Serbs and most Slovenes.

Thus Magyar nationalism faced in Croatia a mirror image of itself. The patriotic movement institutionalised itself culturally in the *Matica Ilirska*, economically in the Economic Society and socially in reading rooms in the main towns. Theatre, art, music, even opera were cultivated. At the political level battle ensued for control of the county assemblies and the Croatian Diet against 'Magyarone' adherents of *kajkavski* and the traditional order, often with their roots among the petty gentry. In a topsy-turvy relationship the arch-conservative Magyarones supported the radical Kossuthites in Hungary and the more liberal Illyrians supported the Hungarian conservatives. To be sure, in undeveloped Croatia the Illyrians remained unforthcoming on the peasant question. Forbidden by government to use the name 'Illyrian' in 1843 they became four years later the National Party. By 1848 they controlled the Diet.

Vienna's mild slap on the wrist for the Illyrian movement — for it was no more than this — showed the government's dilemma as far as nationalism was concerned. It had permitted Illyrianism in the first place as an exercise in 'divide and rule' against the Hungarians but then worried that it might get out of hand. Meanwhile, the Hungarian liberals achieved their greatest successes hitherto in the Diet of 1843–44, with laws on official Magyar, on full equality for Protestants and on the right of all to own noble land and hold public office. Yet most of their proposals, like those for municipal and penal reform and a state credit bank, were frustrated by the central government and the upper chamber. Moreover, they had not spelt out how redemption for the labour services they wished to abolish should be organised and paid for, and they remained divided between supporters of county self-government as a national tradition, like Kossuth, and the 'centralist' school of Eötvös which believed this institution smacked too much of the feudal past. Hence government felt emboldened to simply override reform opinion and install commissioners to manage many of the opposition counties. Even when Deák smoothed a compromise enabling a united opposition party programme to be drafted in 1847 the liberals still won only an uncertain lower chamber majority in the Diet elections of the autumn of that year. After a generation of endeavour the fate of the Hungarian reform movement still appeared to be in the balance.

Does this tentativeness about reform in a country of deeply conservative social traditions help justify the government's foot-dragging? Or does it suggest that it could have been bolder without opening the flood-gates? To be fair, contemporaries were up against problems unprecedented in scale and scope. The linguistic movements challenged former concepts of Hungary as a multi-cultural state; politically, a systemic change was proposed from an order of feudal origin to liberal parliamentarism; economically, the issue was not only the fate of a rural regime based on forced labour but also building a modern communications and commercial network, which unpacked

Hungary's relations to Austria and a wider world. It would be wrong to see government as wholly passive in response. Metternich in particular was quite fertile in expedients in the 1840s on the Hungarian front. Is there a case to revise the conventionally negative verdict passed on him and the Pre-March regime?

Not really. The defenders of Metternich have been as guilty of myth as his accusers. His tactical dexterity has been too readily taken for strategic insight, his comments on the nationality problem for more than the attitudinising and wishful thinking they chiefly were. In the earlier part of his career Metternich did have a strategic conception; it was to balance the Monarchy's nationalities in a mildly decentralist framework, in which German culture would provide a sheet anchor more acceptable than Josephinist fiat. There was something of the eighteenth century in this concept of the state as a mechanism in equilibrium; and insofar as it involved eroding the special constitutional position of Hungary it was as remote from historical reality as Joseph himself. Later, Metternich recognised the need for a distinctive Hungarian policy. But it is precisely in these Pre-March years that a dubiously principled conservative tradition was founded, whose authoritarian bias lasted longest in Dualist Hungary and occupied Bosnia. It operated by attempts to break up opposition by secret funding of press organs, cultivation of cliques of notables, isolation of alleged extremists or radicals and a rhetoric of civil rights and respect for nationality which disguised strictly hierarchical assumptions: all in the interests of building conservative groupings whose policies had little chance of alleviating social discontent. Particularly damaging to claims for Metternich's high statesmanship is the failure to give the Hungarian 'young conservatives' full backing on economic issues. As often later the regime presented itself as the patron of rational economic development against nationalist illusion without being prepared to back its claims in practice. Privately Metternich considered Hungary an economic swamp. His distrust of the basically loyal *grand seigneur* Széchenyi and playing off of Kossuth against him in the early 1840s was also short-sighted.

Of course, a different governmental course would not necessarily have brought long-term success. Though nearly all the Monarchy's burgeoning patriotisms were sincere in protesting their loyalty to it, this loyalty presupposed that Vienna would back their partisan goals, which were often in conflict. This was particularly true of Czech Austro-Slavism *vis-à-vis* the Germans. In the case of the Magyar liberals, a definite wish to weaken Hungary's ties with the rest of the Monarchy can be seen. Liberals, for example, prioritised a rail-way link from Buda-Pest to the Adriatic before one to Vienna because they wanted to build up Hungary's foreign trade rather than an internal Habsburg market. Among southern Slavs Gaj flirted with treason, while many Habsburg Serbs – and the Dalma-tian Catholic Matija Ban – devoted their lives to the fledgeling Serbian state.

The view mooted later in the century of a falling away from Austrian to narrower nationalist loyalties may thus take a prior Aus-trianism somewhat for granted. Told that someone was a patriot, Emperor Francis once notoriously replied, 'Is he a patriot for me?' The goal of Austrian Enlightened despotism had been to extend such essentially dynastic loyalty to the concept of a Habsburg state. But stripped of their reformist dimension after Joseph II's death, ideas of a wider Austrianism lacked the energising power to override the traditions of centuries. When proto-liberal sentiment, suffused with patriotism, began to seep into the empire, it was on these latter identities that it worked. The immobility of government in the Met-ternichian era in difficult circumstances can be understood. What-ever policy had been followed, social mobilisation would no doubt eventually have shaped national–cultural identities threatening to the cohesion of the Monarchy. Yet there was complacency and lack of imagination. Liberal state traditions can work to counteract ethnic diversity, as was shown by nineteenth-century Britain, France and Canada, if in less taxing circumstances and with the Irish exception. Pre-March government's aversion to new European impulses was a strategic mistake. The pattern of the 1848 revolutions showed how far the rot had spread, and their defeat soon proved a Pyrrhic victory.

5   1848–49

Few events appear to hindsight as well signalled as the European revolutions of 1848. In the Monarchy, following on the Galician tumults of 1846 and the altercations in Hungary came febrile disturbances over the tobacco tax in Lombardy-Venetia from December 1847. Further afield, opposition to the July Monarchy in France, the home rule movement in Ireland and liberal nationalist fervour among educated Germans and Italians all seemed to be reaching a climax. The continent's political life was beginning to beat to a common pulse, just as the economic woes of 1845–47, brought on by the failure of the potato crop, were the first instance of European-wide depression. For all the disturbances in Italy, which had led to a revolution in Naples and the granting of a constitution in Piedmont-Sardinia, it was logical that it should be the February revolution against Louis Philippe in France, home of European revolution since 1789, which sparked off the wider conflagration.

The First Phase

Significantly, the first response in Vienna to the climate of uncertainty following Louis Philippe's fall was a run on savings banks. A secretive regime which had devalued savings in 1811 and 1816 was suspected by the middle classes of being nearer bankruptcy than it actually was. Petitions for change, of mounting insistency, came from the Commercial Association, the Reading Union and the university students, but encountered a government which thought concession would be a sign of weakness under pressure. Liberal elements in the Lower Austrian Estates decided to use a Diet meeting scheduled for 13 March to press for the educated reform consensus: a free press, a citizens' militia or National Guard to calm restless spirits and some kind of united imperial Diet to approve the budget and monitor legislation. On that day a crowd of thousands, initially largely middle-class but radicalised by angry students and an injudicious salvo which left several dead, intimidated Metternich into resignation and his colleagues into granting a free press and the arming of the students – the so-called Academic Legion. By this time, late evening, the crowd had been transformed by workers flowing in hour by hour from the suburbs to the inner city. Within two days of further popular pressure a National Guard had also been formed and a constitution promised. Eventually the National Guard numbered upwards of 40,000 and the Academic Legion some 6000, not all of them bona fide students.

These events were linked in an intricate chain reaction with those in other centres in the Monarchy. Kossuth's declaration of 3 March in the Pressburg Diet that only constitutionalism in Austria could guarantee a constitutional Hungary helped spur the Viennese revolution; the events in Vienna in turn encouraged 20,000 demonstrators in Buda-Pest on 15 March to march on the royal castle and win an end to censorship and – shades of the storming of the Bastille – the release of the castle's single prisoner, the peasant tribune Mihály Táncsics. The Hungarian Upper House no longer dared resist Kossuth's programme for a Hungarian government responsible to the Diet and the gamut of liberal reforms, including the abolition of serfdom. A delegation set out by Danube steamer from Pressburg which secured the Emperor's consent to a separate government on 17 March. On the same day, an expanded town council meeting in Zagreb commissioned a delegation to the Emperor whose address called for the convocation of a Diet for a reintegrated Croatia, including Dalmatia and the Military Frontier. Privately Ljudevit Gaj had already set out for Vienna on the evening of the 16th to urge the appointment of a Military Frontier officer, Josip Jelačić, as Croatian Ban. As Vienna was already thinking along the same lines, this was approved on the 23rd.

Elsewhere the Vienna events had the same radicalising effect. In Prague a petition issuing from a bilingual meeting of 11 March organised by the clandestine Repeal club was being conservatively redrafted – alleviation of the peasants' lot rather than *robota* abolition, a toning down of the demand for political union of the Czech lands – before the news from Vienna prompted reinstatement of the more radical wording. When this petition received an evasive answer a second trumped it by demanding a separate ministry for the Czech lands along Hungarian lines, and this time gained a positive response from a punch-drunk central government, though only for Bohemia (8 April). Equality of the Czech and German languages was a staple of all these demands. In north Italy the news from Vienna provoked a drive for outright secession. Venice was evacuated by Austrian troops without a struggle on 22 March, Milan after five days of street fighting the next day. The Venetians promptly declared a republic under Daniele Manin. The Milanese sought union with Piedmont-Sardinia. Only in Galicia, where the dominant Poles were unsure of their own peasants and the exiled national movement's attention was initially fixed on Prussian Poland, were the pressures no more than might have been expected (autonomy petition, 18 March; National Council in Lvov, 14 April); but the highly strung Governor, Franz Stadion, bombarded Vienna with reports of impending doom.

A key to the quick initial success of the European revolutions of 1848 lies in the cumbersome policing mechanisms of the *ancien régimes*. In the face of large, agitated crowds the authorities had to yield unless they were willing to resort to the bloody instrument of troops, which they no longer had the self-confidence to do – except for Field Marshal Radetzky, a formidable 81-year-old, in Milan. In Vienna with some 1100 military police guards, there was a Civic Guard, numbering 14,000 prosperous bourgeois, but only a third were armed and they took the demonstrators' side on 13 March. There were doubts, too, about the loyalty of the mainly Italian garrison in Buda. The speed with which petitioners formulated their goals showed the pervasive influence of the liberal alternative to the *ancien régime*. Their programme had three facets. Socially, it called for the freedoms of speech, the press, association and assembly, the abolition of serfdom, and public justice by oral procedure and jury trial. Institutionally, it demanded representative assemblies, parliamentary budgets and National Guards, with ministries responsible to the assemblies. At the level of nationality it located freedom in the transfer of sovereignty from monarch to people, a term implicitly or explicitly linked to the language group.

Of course, not all these elements were present in each declaration or petition. Smaller nationalities were slower to mobilise and called only for a regional autonomy, while being more radical than their larger neighbours in their social demands. Thus Slovak leaders called for a Slovak territory in northern Hungary on 10–11 May, Serbs for a Serbian Vojvodina or Duchy on 13 May, Romanians for a share in an autonomous Transylvania two days later. These were great popular meetings, 30,000 peasants being present at the last-named according to some reports, and the religious associations of the venues (Karlowitz for the Serbs where Metropolitan Rajačić presided, the Uniate centre Blaj for the Romanians) lent them a traditional air suspect to German and Magyar liberals. In fact, insofar as autonomy calls cloaked further aspirations ('Dacian' unity with

Wallachia-Moldavia or the closer union of south Slavs in general) this was a matter of younger, more secular-minded elements; only in the Yugoslav case were such thoughts a real factor. The Supreme Ruthenian Council, set up in Lvov on 2 May and dominated by Uniate clergymen, was too aware of the novelty of its cause even to glance in the direction of its Ukrainian kinsmen in the Tsarist empire. It held out for language equality and a division of Galicia which would leave its people in a majority in the eastern half. Weakest of all the 'non-historic' peoples were the Slovenes, a number of whose call for a united Slovenia carved out of four existing provinces never became a serious bone of contention in 1848.

By the time these minor programmes were being formulated, developments in the larger nations had already moved into a second phase, compressing into weeks a radicalisation of the crisis that in the great French revolution had taken years to unfold. On 23 March King Carlo Alberto of Piedmont-Sardinia invaded Lombardy, turning the struggle in north Italy into an Italian national cause. German patriots meeting in Frankfurt called for elections to a German national assembly to prepare a German constitution in place of the Confederation of 1815. The Frankfurt Assembly duly met on 18 May, posing obvious problems for the relationship of Austria to the prospective German state. Meanwhile in Vienna the relative conservatism of the press law of 1 April (which prescribed large deposits for editors) and the draft constitution of 25 April, with its upper chamber subject to executive influence, increased distrust between government and the young radicals of the Academic Legion. Conservatives' attempt to disband the central committee of the National Guard brought about a mass demonstration and the flight of the Emperor to Innsbruck (15–17 May); then their closure of the university to undermine the Academic Legion led to the Legion's members clashing with army troops, who backed down (26 May). The result of these episodes was the promise of a wide parliamentary franchise with no second chamber and the setting up of a Security Committee with representatives of the National Guard, the Academic Legion and the city council. For three months it was to exercise almost a dual-power role alongside a wary government.

In Bohemia a related situation developed, with a national twist. The merger of a Governor-sponsored commission, where Czechs were a small minority, with the largely Czech Wenceslas committee inherited from the March petitions created the influential National Committee, whose German-speaking members had all left it by

May. The Czechicisation of what had originally been a bilingual movement for liberal reform reflected the growing weight of the lower middle class and the 3500-strong student body, both largely Czech in composition. By June the Czech trend had developed along two quite different lines: one in the Prague Panslav Congress uniting some 385 participants, two-thirds of them Czechs or Slovaks, to consider the place of the Slavs in a changing Europe; the other the 'Whitsun Uprising' of 12–17 June in which the military commander in Prague, Prince Alfred Windisch-Graetz, clashed with members of the Czech student society *Svornost*, whose militancy had been heightened by the May events in Vienna. The students, assisted by young workers and artisans, threw up barricades and a week's desultory sparring claimed some 43 lives.

In hindsight Windisch-Graetz's June bombardment of Prague was the opening round of counter-revolution. At the time, though, its conservative implications largely eluded the Viennese because it was directed at upstart Czechs. Hungary was still further distanced from the Whitsun events, engrossed in implementing the Diet's 'April laws' which had codified its revolution: an autonomous government responsible to a Hungarian parliament, abolition of serfdom and patrimonial jurisdiction, reintegration of Transylvania, modernisation of credit, municipal and press conditions and much more. Hungary's own radicals, grouped in the Democratic Club, were the guiding spirits in large demonstrations in early April and again in May against the central Vienna government and the Habsburg military. But they were also preoccupied with defending Hungarian liberties, as they saw it, from Slovak bands in the north and, even more so, mutinous south Slavs steeled in the traditions of the Military Frontier. Besides, attention in Vienna and Buda-Pest was directed towards the Austrian and Hungarian parliaments, due to open on 22 July and 5 July respectively, as the most spectacular symbols of revolutionary success. By early summer 1848 the various groups who were to play out the revolutionary drama to the end had all made their first moves, but the overall shape of events and their likely course was still beyond the ken of almost all participants.

Conservatives, Liberals, Radicals

Contemporaries' confusion was not surprising. Social and national conundrums overlapped. Of these the former were the better understood and, probably, taken by themselves, the easier to handle. At its simplest, the reconstitution of the social order that the revolution seemed to demand involved three groups, the conservatives of the *ancien régime* whose best times were long past, the masses whose time had not yet come and the assorted ranks in between whose (roughly) liberal ideology appeared to be the spirit of the age. The failure of the last-named to seize their opportunity is the core problem for analysis of 1848.

In understanding the initial timorousness of conservative forces in 1848, it is hard to exaggerate the corrosive effects of bureaucratic absolutism on two of the chief props of traditional conservative rule – aristocracy and church. A key result of Josephinism had been to break the link between nobility and political power, at least in Austria. Austrian nobles neither held the reins of local government, like their English counterparts, nor dominated the state administration, like their fellows in Prussia and Russia. The fissure between nobles identified with state service on the one hand or supporting provincial traditions on the other (which took its special form in Hungary in the tension between Habsburgophile magnates and nationalist gentry) crippled the landed interest as a solid base for conservative ideas and contributed to apathy towards public affairs. At the height of the radical regime in Vienna in the summer of 1848 a conservative diarist noted that as always at this time of year the aristocrats were living in their castles in the country. All but a handful of Hungarian conservatives abandoned active politics in March 1848.

As to the Church, the cooptation of leading figures like Archbishop Milde of Vienna (1832–53) into a Josephinist framework had produced a loyal instrument of state policy, but one with little independent spiritual authority. The consequences in 1848 were three-fold: first, the anti-clericalism which led Milde to quit Vienna after a bout of mock serenading in April; second, an anti-Josephinist trend among some ordinary clergy canalised by Sebastian Brunner's combative *Wiener Kirchenzeitung*; and third, a minor strand of radical Christianity illustrated by the university theologian Anton Füster and his identification with the revolution. Of these, the brightest future beckoned the second tendency, but not just yet. Nor could Catholicism offer authority stronger support elsewhere in the Monarchy. Ljudevit Gaj taunted Haulik, bishop of Zagreb, with his lack of influence, and an end to clerical celibacy was one of the Croatian 'National Demands' of 25 March. Educated opinion in 1848 Hungary was preponderantly agnostic and the fact that everywhere church spokesmen were among the most reluctant to give up their privileges, notably the church tithe, did not enhance the Church's prestige. The schismatic German Catholic movement proved a nine days' wonder in the Monarchy. Where Catholic fervour was evoked, in north Italy, it was for the national cause.

The authority of the *ancien régime* therefore rested essentially on the state bureaucracy alone. Yet this body's Josephinist heritage made it a less than certain support of conservative principles. The year 1848 revealed many of its members to be, if not exactly closet liberals, then willing to man the new ministries which replaced the old conciliar organs during March and April. While Metternich took flight to England and men like the Hofkammer director Kübeck retreated to private estates, Count Ficquelmont and Barons Pillersdorf and Krauss became respectively foreign, interior and finance minister in the new regime. Nor were the imperial family and the court united, for all the talk of a reactionary 'camarilla' around Emperor Ferdinand; the Archdukes Franz Karl and Johann argued for Metternich's resignation on 13 March, the Archdukes Albrecht and Maximilian against.

There were outposts of conservative sentiment in the diplomatic corps and to a lesser extent the army. For Prince Felix Schwarzenberg, in March the Austrian minister in Naples, the system of election to the Reichstag had excluded almost all prominent persons of property, intelligence or political experience. Though army generals had little cause to love a regime which had relatively neglected military spending, they accepted the Reichstag as a new imperial institution rather than from constitutional sympathies. Their basic conservatism leaps out from Radetzky's proclamation to his troops after the murder of the Austrian minister of war by a Viennese mob in early October:

> Soldiers! Open your eyes to the abyss that yawns at your feet; everything is in flux ... property, morality, religion are threatened ... Everything that is holy and dear to man, everything that the state is based on and which it upholds, people are determined to destroy.[1]

But for six months after March such sentiments were stilled and the liberals had time to do their thing.

Who were the Habsburg liberals? By and large they were what the German-speaking world termed *Honoratioren* or local notables – officials, landowners, doctors, lawyers, apothecaries, writers, editors, university lecturers, grammar school teachers and the like who had acquired elements of a common culture through the expanded educational and bureaucratic systems already described. Financiers and industrialists, a class still too recent or foreign to chance its arm, were virtually absent in their ranks, though not so liberal nobles. For the further east liberalism penetrated the continent, the more it reflected the aspiration *towards* a bourgeois society rather than its achievement. Liberalism was as much the product of the diffusion of ideas as of new social classes. It was its success in furthering these ideas, through a self-consciously 'progressive' European public opinion, which enabled it to transmit concepts – attenuated, to be sure – across ethnic or social barriers.

But styles of liberalism differed not just between west and central Europe but in the Monarchy itself. Habsburg liberals of 1848 came, roughly, from three different milieux. In Vienna and the Austro-German lands, for all the role of individuals like the Pre-March Diet opposition leader Baron Doblhoff, minister of the interior from July to October 1848, the middle-class orientation already dominated, in the sense of ennobled bureaucrats and professional people, sometimes of minor noble stock. Such were the lawyers Alexander Bach and the Frankfurt deputy Karl von Mühlfeld, doctors Ludwig von Löhner and Adolf Fischhof, writers or editors Franz Schuselka, Ignaz Kuranda and Ernst Schwarzer. Lombardy-Venetia was not dissimilar. In Hungary, on the other hand, the liberal drive was led by traditional nobles, though many of these, being landless or almost so, functioned as civil servants or members of the free professions – a kind of substitute middle class where the actual townspeople still often spoke German. Whereas 60% of members of the Vienna parliament were bourgeois, 74% of the Buda-Pest parliament were noble. Polish liberals in Galicia had a similar backgroud to Hungarian, Croatian liberals somewhat less so, for Gaj came from bourgeois stock and the influential Vraniczany was a rare case of the liberal entrepreneur.

The third pattern was that of Czech Bohemia, followed in this respect by the Slovenes and Transylvanian Romanians. Here a professional middle class was preponderant as in Vienna – but its leaders, Palacký, Rieger, Brauner and Trojan, had rural rather than urban origins. A married clergy permitted a variation: Bariţiu, Bărnuţiu and Cipariu were all sons or grandsons of Romanian Uniate parish priests. Serb liberals, by contrast, had deeper roots in a Balkan Orthodox mercantile tradition extending to the Serb colony in Pest itself. Svetozar Miletić, live-wire of the younger generation of

1848 activists and the son of a boot-maker and grandson and great-grandson of merchants, illustrates the genre.

Despite these social variations liberal programmes showed a strong family likeness. For one thing, once the old order had fallen, the model of bourgeois civil society was the only alternative available. Moreover, leaders' desire for a peaceful transition through rational deliberation put a premium on the common values of the educated minority, regardless of whether liberal dogma, elite self-interest, or non-dominant groups' sense of vulnerability were in play. Thus it was Brauner who expunged the socially radical demands from the first draft of the Prague petition of 11 March. Liberals' tendency to define their programme by reaction to others applied not only in relation to the conservatives on their right, but to radical democrats on their left. The division between liberals and democrats opened up by the turbulent Viennese *journées* of 15 and 26 May and reflected to an extent in other major Habsburg cities, proved to be an important inner fissure of the revolution.

Democrat was no more precise a term than liberal. Democrats, however, generally accused liberals of seeking to curtail, even abort the revolution before its term. They wanted a clear assertion of the sovereignty of the people (which usually made them strong nationalists), a single chamber elected by universal male suffrage and vigilance against 'reaction' in the name of an uncompromising 'justice'. In Lombardy-Venetia they were strongly republican. Predictably, they were strongest in large centres where more complex social structures belied a simple distinction between notables and masses. Not all critics of the liberals became fully fledged democrats. Often those known as 'the Left' in the parliaments of Vienna and Buda-Pest might be better seen as advanced liberals, men who sympathised with some or more of the radical ideas in circulation, or were simply more nationalistic; the Left in the Zagreb Diet were probably just liberals, none of whom unequivocally opposed compensating landlords for *robota*.

Democrats sometimes, and parliamentary leftists more often, might have the same social background as the liberal notables, differing from them only in temperament or life experience – a Baron Andreas Stifft in Vienna, the 30–40 gentry radicals in the Hungarian parliament, the eight Polish nobles who voted against compensation for *robota* in September 1848. But they were also, particularly the more radical, recruited from the young – the Academic Legion was a bulwark of Vienna radicalism (many students being of humble origin), from more marginal educated groups (junior doctors, language or music teachers, non-established writers, actors) or from the traditionally underprivileged Jews. The variety of background and terminology (left, democrat, republican etc.) indicates that we are dealing with a diverse phenomenon, with its own internal stresses. A republican lawyer like the Venetian Manin was much warier of unleashing the lower-middle-class resentments of urban radicalism than an agitator like the Viennese Democratic Association leader Tausenau. On the Monarchy's periphery, if radicalism can be said to exist – and there were individual Serbs with knowledge of France and an emotional commitment to European revolution – it took a purely national form – uniting the nation meant being one with the people. At bottom, though, radicals shared a certain reserve about the masses. 'The will of the people often yields to prejudices', wrote the Czech radical Sabina.[2] One of these which radicals did not yet sanction was the popular anti-Semitism which boiled over in Vienna, Prague and Buda-Pest in the revolutionary year.

Isolated Austria's unfamiliarity with the liberal/democrat divide of west European politics since c. 1830 helps explain her liberals' consternation at the radicalisation of events after March. The explosion of uncensored journalism – 172 new newspapers appeared in Vienna from March to December 1848 – the mock serenading which disposed of foreign minister Ficquelmont as well as Archbishop Milde, and the prominent role of students and workers seemed just as anarchic to upper-middle-class liberals as to conservatives. Anastasius Grün, who refused to address student revolutionaries at the start of the revolution, and the dramatist Grillparzer who left Vienna in June having published an unpopular poem in praise of Field Marshal Radetzky, were only two scions of Pre-March liberalism swiftly disillusioned. All the Czech national leaders denounced the Whitsun rising in Prague; indeed, Palacký and the journalist Havlíček were too cautious even to go to the petition meeting of 11 March. For Széchenyi, in April minister of public works in the new Hungarian government, the Hungarian radicals were the 'ultra-barricade', 'steam guillotine' party.[3]

It is tempting to place this recoil of the notables from popular politics in the broader context of a somewhat bookish German political culture, combining the traditions of enlightened despotism and Germany's celebrated universities. Assuming their role was to teach the people how to adjust to the new stage in a Hegelian evolutionary process, men like the north German playwright Hebbel, resident in

Vienna since 1846, were alienated by the events of May, with their apparent challenge to the state, 'the precondition for all human thought'.[4] The mordant mockery in Anton Springer's famous history of 1848, for example, of the Reichstag's wranglings as to whether to 'request' or 'demand' Emperor Ferdinand's return from Innsbruck, has made it a classic text of the political immaturity thesis. For the Germanophile Springer, however, the barbs had specifically Austrian targets and it is hard to deny that there was an extra dimension to Austrian political gaucherie. How could the revolutionaries of March have left the cabinet government created by their pressure in the hands of old regime bureaucrats with an average age of 67, not to speak of Count Hoyos (69) as commander of the National Guard or Count Colloredo-Mansfeld (71) as head of the Academic Legion? Not till July did a Pre-March bourgeois dissident, Alexander Bach, enter the government, revamped under Baron Anton Doblhoff, the standard-bearer of noble Whiggery. Deference to the half-witted Emperor embraced almost the whole population; his portrait was borne by one of the leading barricades of 26 May, dubbed without irony 'the imperial–royal barricade' in a popular lithograph. No Viennese radical dared to stray outside the formula of 'constitutional monarchy' and probably few wanted to, though perhaps the most radical figure in Vienna, Hermann Jellinek, spoke of it, in his ideal, as having republican institutions. Tradition died hard.

Moderate liberals were particularly amazed at the self-activation of the urban workers. In March and April movements for the reduction of working hours and/or the raising of wages, sometimes accompanied by strikes, broke out among artisans in Vienna, Prague and Buda-Pest, as well as Vienna railway machine workers, north Hungarian miners and Buda-Pest shipworkers. They deployed pathos rather than menace. 'We are not rebels', read the 'Ardent Entreaty to the Burghers of Prague from the (Cotton) Printers' in May. 'Everyone has the right to joy, freedom and education', appealed the Viennese book-binder journeyman Friedrich Sander earlier in the same month.[5] Many artisanal claims were, in fact, met. The Hungarian government brokered a settlement of journeymen's grievances, feeling as it did little sympathy with the largely German guild masters of Buda-Pest. But the growing problems of unemployment as business fell off met at best a traditionally paternalistic response; one May proposal in Vienna was for the prosperous to pay a kreuzer a day for the relief of the poor.

More positive was the attitude of the Vienna radical left to the workers, whose plight was one of the issues of justice democrats felt should be addressed. Louis Blanc and the utopian socialists were known, mainly through the account of the conservative sociologist Lorenz Stein. The Security Committee proclaimed the right to work and organised public building projects in the capital which employed 20,000, often incomers from outside, by mid-June. Democrats also successfully campaigned for the revision of government franchise proposals to include all but servants and those on public relief. In the longer term mainstream left thinkers envisaged alleviations in terms of hours and wages and more trade schools, with workers' respect for the right of property as the *quid pro quo*. Most condemned the Paris workers' rising in June, as all did the communist idea, if some approved a vaguely conceived 'socialism'. When Karl Marx came to Vienna in early September 1848 the radical publicist Julius Fröbel argued against him that the time was not yet ripe for Austrian workers to break ranks with the radical bourgeoisie, as western workers had done. Hermann Jellinek, a young Moravian Jewish intellectual with theories of 'organised society' or 'social democracy', and Friedrich Sander, with his notion of socialism as a science, came closest to later socialist positions. The provisions of the Workers' Association which Sander set up in June for informative lectures and entertainment, including songs and 'declamations', were some way from the *Communist Manifesto*. The suspicions between this fledgeling movement and even radical bourgeois appeared in disputes with the Security Committee over wages for public work, resulting in clashes with the National Guard. No consensus existed over the new-fangled 'social question' in 1848.

The peasant question was different. Centuries of elite apprehension lay behind the swift preventive action of conservatives and liberals at the outset of the revolution. Within days of the Vienna revolution Kossuth pushed much more generous terms through the Hungarian Diet than he had proposed as recently as 6 March: abolition of all dues and services of feudal origin, compensation being coyly left to 'the honour of the nation', implicitly, the public purse. On 20 March Bohemian nobles petitioned for the abolition of *robota*, which was announced on 31 March, with effect from 31 March 1849; similar measures followed for the Austro-German provinces. On 22 April the Galician Governor Franz Stadion went one better and announced abolition inside a month. An entire social institution was being unceremoniously buried. With it went patrimonial jurisdiction.

The possessing classes feared social upheaval. The 15,000 peasants assembling on the outskirts of Pest, actually for a fair, scared the Diet in Pressburg. But prudent though the authorities' concerns were, as striking as the very extensive refusals of *robota*, reclaimings of disputed woodland and the like – vastly outnumbering cases of physical violence or calls for division of noble land – were the 580 peasant petitions of Bohemia, the 306 of Moravia, 112 of Croatia, 50 of Carniola and so on which flowed in to the authorities. Appeals for public order in the vast, mainly peasant gatherings of the minor peoples were heeded; Hungarian peasant disturbances slackened off as the convocation of the Hungarian parliament drew near. Generations of official *Bauernschutz* (peasant protection) and spreading literacy had left their mark.

Yet the partial inuring of peasants to ordered procedures was far from making them liberals, as the parliamentary elections showed. Finding the gentry electors awaiting them at the polling place (the elections were indirect and this was the second of the two stages), the peasant electors of one Galician constituency declined to join a poll with people of other ranks, declaring an election to be unnecessary, as the Emperor was their good lord. But should His Majesty really desire general elections he should deign to order them for each social group separately.[6] Galician peasants abstained from voting in 21 constituencies. Such attitudes help explain why the Polish noble minority was able to win more seats to the Vienna parliament than peasants did (50 to 35). In the Alpine and Czech lands class divisions were less acute and literacy and internal differentiation among the peasants greater. Peasants followed advice to vote for educated professionals to represent them in the Reichstag, while voting for their own kind – but always rich peasants – in the Diet elections. Altogether, roughly a quarter of the 383 members of the Vienna parliament were peasants, a proportion never again equalled in the Monarchy. The Hungarian parliament had but two peasant representatives, one of them the fiery radical Táncsics. About one in three Hungarian adult males, or 10% of the total population, met the franchise requirements (which included six years' schooling); but a third of these did not register and half of the remainder did not vote. There was, after all, only one polling station per constituency and in 60% of seats, after withdrawals, only one candidate was left.[7]

Yet peasants still looked to parliament to clarify the hasty anti-serfdom moves of March and April. They benefited most specifically

Bauern on rustical land (p. 00) rather than cottars or manorial peasants, but even here there were problems of definition. Vinyards were deemed dominical though their peasant cultivators considered them theirs, as they did land they had cleared and, in Hungary, the 'remainder lands', in peasant hands but not registered as such in the 1767 Urbarium. The fate of common woodland and pasture, largely dominical, was especially important, because of the 'servitudes' entitling peasants to cut wood and pasture livestock on it. Above all, how was the issue of compensation, which peasants opposed on principle, to be settled?

Such questions were immediately put before the new parliaments by Táncsics in Buda-Pest, and in Vienna through a deceptively simple motion for the abolition of serfdom from an educated Silesian peasant, Hans Kudlich. Nobles had their answers. Servitudes, for example, should be abolished along with *robota*; both were part of the feudal past. How, anyway, as a Polish noble asked, could the so desirable mutual interdependence of the social classes be maintained if peasants were totally self-sufficient in wood and pasture and had no need to turn to their former lords? This argument, significantly from a democrat who voted against compensation for landlords, exposes the social reality in the more backward parts of the empire. Under-capitalised nobles could not pay for market rates for the labour they needed now that *robota* had been abolished, nor could they substantially increase the amount they leased out since the demand from tenant farmers was limited. According to contemporary calculations Hungarian landlords had only a quarter of the draught animals and implements necessary to farm their land – previously these had been provided by the serfs. Investments of 180 million florins (on top of their existing debts of 200–300 million) would be needed to make up the deficiency.[8] In these circumstances landlords clung desperately to compensation and any other device which would give them access to a supply of cheap labour from dependent peasants. The emancipation measure of the Vienna parliament of 7 September therefore favoured landlords on most disputed issues, including compensation, the decisive vote passing by 174 against 144 votes of peasants and their tactical allies on the left. By contrast, peasants' servitudes were abolished without compensation. Of the indemnity calculated, a third was to be met by peasants, a third paid by the state (actually the crownlands) and the final third remitted to cover the lords' now lapsed patrimonial expenses. The terms were higher for dominical peasants who wished to redeem their land. In Hungary the state was to meet the full cost, but the question of dominical peasants – increasingly mutinous – remained in the air.

The emancipation settlements were considerably more generous to peasants than those of Prussia in 1807–11 or Russia in 1861. Largely respected by the counter-revolutionary regime that followed, they showed the ability of the liberal revolutionaries to impose a new order on the land based on property, not privilege. By contrast, the liberals usually felt able to side-line the more narrowly based social movement in the towns and absorb its radical sympathisers on a pan-nationalistic ticket, as with the poet Petőfi and the Democratic Society in Hungary and urban radicals in Cracow, Lvov and Milan. (The exception was Venice, where the radical republican Manin remained in control.) In Vienna in August 1848 even the radicals of the Academic Legion were passive when the bourgeois National Guard turned on workers resisting wage cuts on the public works projects in Vienna. Lower-middle-class artisans demonstrating for cheap credit also got short shrift early in September. However, pressures from below were important in pushing the city into a fateful confrontation with a government whose hard line towards the new Hungarian government made it suspect to the Viennese. Early in October Vienna rose again in revolt. The Reichstag's moderate majority decamped to the small Moravian town of Kremsier and the court to Olmütz, while Windisch-Graetz took the capital by storm at the end of the month.

Brief as this October radical episode was, it played a crucial part in aiding the revolution's slide into reverse. Even without the nationalist complications, it seems that the social forces behind the Austrian revolution of 1848 were insufficiently coherent to succeed. However, the point is academic because nationalism was an integral part of the revolutionary year, and the confrontation in Vienna in autumn 1848 owed much, as has been said, to the Hungarian question. The nexus in revolutionaries' minds between freedom and nationhood necessarily made new national as well as new social structures central to the new dispensation.

Germans, Magyars and Slavs

In the French Revolution, still the paradigm for political sophisticates in 1848, it was the patriotic fervour of the *levée en masse* which sustained a movement threatened by social divisions and foreign attack. Should the revolutionaries of central Europe therefore seek to unite their people in the comradeship of war against 'reaction'? All national leaders believed events gave them both the opportunity and the duty to strengthen national unity, many Poles and some Germans through an expected clash with Tsarist Russia, many Serbs through a trial of strength in the Balkans. The consequence of such beliefs for revolutionary cohesion in the multi-national Habsburg polity was quite different from what it had been in France. How could central European political structures be reshaped without shattering the euphoric brotherhood of the 'Springtime of the Peoples'?

The course of the German national movement in 1848 illustrates the problems. In Vienna the identification of sovereign people and nation, attraction of ideas of national citizenship for non-elite groups and stimulus of events elsewhere in the German-speaking world all stimulated a popular celebration of Germandom, German colours, German flags, German cockades. ('National' dress had a symbolic role for all peoples in 1848.) Yet there was a deep conflict of interests. The more integrated Germany which the Frankfurt assembly was to bring about, and which presumably only Austria's German provinces would join, threatened to divide the Monarchy in two, provoking the government to declare its commitment to imperial unity. In the event the elections to Frankfurt which the government had not dared obstruct saw only a minority of the more radically German nationalist Viennese candidates returned. Moderate Austro-Germans shrank from weakening a Monarchy in which they played a leading role, while denying that this meant a lack of German feeling. Was not a strong Austria a vital German interest, as an instrument for the transmission of German culture to the Slav and Balkan worlds which might otherwise fall under Russian or even Hungarian hegemony? This was a continuation of the *Mitteleuropa* argument first developed from the economic standpoint by Friedrich List in the early 1840s, with his notion of the Danube as a German sea. It did not lack, either, for radical adherents, glimpsing a Greater Germany under Austrian aegis, as in Julius Fröbel's September pamphlet *Vienna, Germany and Europe*.

The problem was that this Austro-German self-image cut little ice with other Germans. True, homage was paid to Austria's historic role through the appointment of the Archduke Johann as imperial regent at Frankfurt, where the head of the putative new central government was also an Austrian, Anton von Schmerling. But the isolationist

Metternich years had side-lined Austro-Germans during the German *Vormärz* and this could not be quickly undone. There was only one Austrian representative in the German Pre-Parliament (which preceded the Frankfurt assembly) and two in the June congress of German democrats. Hence the disregard for specifically Austrian interests shown in the main motion on the issue debated at Frankfurt, in October. It proposed that Austrian provinces joining the new German state could be linked to other Habsburg lands only by 'personal union', or a shared sovereign, and was passed decisively, though more Austrian deputies voted against than for. Amendments and counter-motions designed to shape an outcome less destructive of Austrian unity – the most interesting proposed German and Austrian states bound in close treaty alliance – were heavily defeated. Non-Austrian Germans either did not care about Austria's alleged mission on their behalf or believed she was about to break up. Outsiders saw the dilemma insiders refused to admit – the sheer implausibility of eight million Austro-Germans dominating a multinational empire of over thirty millions while allying it on their own terms to a German state equally large.

How, though, was post-revolutionary central Europe to be organised? Habsburg Slavs and Magyars had their own visions, ultimately just as utopian. Slavs dreamt of a federalised Austria, giving pride of place to its Slav majority and preserving the European balance of power against German or Russian hegemony. Kossuthite Magyars believed an alliance of the region's 'historic' peoples was the only safeguard of the revolution, linking a united Germany with a liberal Hungary.

The Slav programme, which has been dubbed Austro-Slavism, was a largely Czech-led affair. The more radical agenda of Polish exiles, which shrewdly enough saw Russia as the mainstay of European reaction, was quickly stalled by the reluctance of new liberal regimes in Prussia and France to take on the Tsar. The gist of Austro-Slavism was for a federation of equal Habsburg peoples, as a barrier to both German and Russian hegemony. Expressed in Addresses to Europe and Emperor Ferdinand drafted by the Prague Panslav Congress, its most famous formulation came in a letter of Palacký of 11 April declining, 'as a Bohemian of Slav race', to participate in the planning process for the Frankfurt assembly. Palacký's letter threw down the gauntlet for a century of Czech–German struggle, for it apprised a largely unsuspecting German world that Czechs did not see themselves as a regional appendage to it, but sought a destiny of their own opposed to a German *Mitteleuropa* or German dominance in Austria.[9] This shock, together with the Panslav Congress, the Whitsun uprising and the offer to Palacký to become Austrian minister of education (though he refused), raised Austro-German opinion to a pitch of indignation. 'The Czechs have thrown off the mask, showing us the grimacing face of their national hate', wrote the Vienna *Constitution* in early May.[10] The national 'coming out' of neighbours they had thought of as compatriots seemed to Prague Germans at first masquerade, then bad dream come true. Friedrich Engels's articles of 1851-2 present a bleakly considered example of German scorn. 'Dying Tschechian nationality ... made in 1848 a last effort to regain its former vitality' through a Panslav movement which, wrote Engels, 'intended nothing less than to subjugate the civilised west under the barbarian east, the town under the country, trade, manufactures, intelligence, under the primitive agriculture of Slavonian serfs.'[11]

The majority German response to the Czech movement in 1848 under-estimated a people who were no longer the rustic *Stockböhmen* of two generations before. The cautious, pro-Habsburg stance of Czech leaders in 1848, which infuriated German radicals, reflected the disciplined pragmatism of a movement with its feet on the ground which knew its limitations. It could not afford to be compromised by outbursts like the Whitsun rising, hoped to play on the Slavophile sympathies of Count Leo Thun, the new Bohemian Governor, and in the bourgeois spirit of the age wanted to build a nation on property and education, not slogans. It was easier to incite the masses than to educate them, Havlíček urged. Hence Czech politicians' support for compensation of landlords in 1848. Yet four-fifths of the 580 Bohemian peasant petitions were in Czech and the boycott of the Frankfurt elections preached by Czech leaders was completely successful in Czech areas. Here was a sense of purpose.

On the other hand, the vision underlying this pawky prudence far outran it. As Springer observed, the Slav programme of 1848 was really the most revolutionary of all, for its concept of national fraternity through ethnic federalism presupposed the greatest change in the status quo. But the Czechs could not persuade even their Bohemian German neighbours to this perspective, as the foundation of a back-lash League of Germans of Bohemia, Moravia and Silesia in April showed. The simplest call for national and language equality involved a can of worms. If it meant officials should speak both languages, then the bilingual Czech intelligentsia would get all the jobs, because Germans thought learning a minor language like Czech a waste of time. And did national equality imply a 50 : 50 relationship or, as Havlíček once posited, one reflecting the Czechs' 60 : 40 majority? Outside Bohemia, complications multiplied. Moravian Czech speakers still considered themselves closer to Moravian Germans than to Bohemian Czechs, at least for administrative purposes. Other Slavs were at a lower cultural level than Czechs and often bitterly divided – Poles versus Ruthenians, Russians versus Poles – though a compromise was patched up between the first two groups at the Panslav Congress by which Ruthenians postponed their demands to split Galicia in return for promises of equal treatment. Serbs and Croats, too, though at a high point in their chequered relationship, skated over rival claims to eastern Slavonia. At bottom, the Austro-Slav programme for a federal, constitutional Monarchy represented a forlorn Czech hope, repeated in 1918 and 1945, that the rest of central and eastern Europe would follow their own decent priorities. In particular, it misjudged Habsburg dynastic circles, too readily crediting their professions of loyalty to the principles of constitutionalism and national equality they had conceded early in the revolution.

What of the Hungarians? Priding themselves on political skills gained through their constitutional heritage they dismissed both the illusions of Austro-German hegemonism and the Slavs' trust in the dynasty. The Kossuthite mainstream in Hungarian politics after March doubted the dynasty's loyalty to the April laws. If the revolution survived, Austria's Polish, Italian and German provinces would gravitate elsewhere, leaving Hungary to enter into an alliance with the new Germany (such as the Frankfurt parliament offered Hungary on 3 August). But Kossuth knew the Viennese government would contest developments like these. His policies in the spring and summer of 1848 can be seen as a bid to build a polity strong enough to resist eventual attempts by 'reaction' to destroy it.

Perhaps this is to impose too much clarity on a fluid situation, in which many Hungarian politicians, including the prime minister Count Batthyány, hoped against hope that a clash with the dynasty could be avoided. Special Hungarian illusions surfaced: might Ferdinand exchange his exile from ungrateful Viennese in Innsbruck for residence in Buda castle, shifting the Monarchy's centre of gravity to Hungary? But the driving force came from Kossuth as minister of finance, skilfully maintaining his position between Batthyány and the radicals of the Society for Equality. By floating a loan to raise troops (the *honvéd*) ambiguously related to the imperial army and laying conditions for deployment of Hungarian soldiers in the Italian war, he pushed Hungary's rights under the April laws up to and perhaps beyond their uncertain limits. Ostensibly, the *honvéd* was needed to defend Hungarian integrity against Slovak guerilla bands and separatist threats from Croats and Serbs. But Hungarian suspicions that dynastic circles were in collusion with their south Slav opponents suggest that their determination to arm was directed also against Vienna.

Hungarian–south Slav relations in 1848 are the most tangled skein in the revolutionary labyrinth. Modern Hungarian historians who criticise the Batthyány government's high-handedness towards Slovaks and Romanians (whose protests over the union of Transylvania with Hungary in May were ignored) still blame Ban Jelačić for the breakdown of the relations with Croatia. It is not clear they are wholly right. The fact that Kossuth promised the Croats respect for their historic rights (28 March) loses weight since the nature of those rights was disputed, as over Slavonia. True, the Croats had not waited for signs of Hungarian good or ill will, like other non-Magyars, but had immediately sought their own kind of constitutional relationship to Vienna, while formally reaffirming loyalty to the Hungarian crown. Yet Jelačić was not quite the dyed-in-the-wool Habsburg loyalist and reactionary Hungarians have painted him. He was an Illyrian patriot of sorts, who had the Serb Orthodox Patriarch Rajačić install him as Ban and momentarily turned to Belgrade for a loan when the Habsburg court seemed deaf to his pleas for protection against Magyar pressure. Ill-defined plans for some kind of union between Croatia and the autonomous province demanded by the Hungarian Serbs were part of the south Slav agenda. But his patriotism and dynasticism were tightly linked and he made himself available to be used by Vienna against the Hungarians when it should wish. This imperial circles long hesitated to do. But neither did the court clearly come out on the side of the Hungarian government in its conflict with the Hungarian Serbs, so that imperial troop commanders asked which they should support – the government in Buda-Pest or its Serb opponents.

It is fairly clear that dynastic circles indeed had no intention of putting up with the April laws, especially as interpreted by Kossuth. The royal Palatine, Archduke Stephan, privately said as much in urging their acceptance in the first place: the point was to avert revolution – and times could change. In late July the conservative cause was enormously boosted by Radetzky's defeat of the Piedmontese at Custozza; Johann Strauss's *Radetzky March* had its première on 15 August. Manin's Venetian republic now paid the price in isolation for its excessive reliance on the Piedmontese dynasty. However, it was not only the court that was anti-Hungarian. The same Austro-German opinion that opposed the merger of Austria's identity in Germany refused to accept an empire linked only by personal union with Hungary. While Jelačić was promised reinstatement as Ban and urged by the war minister Latour to go on the offensive against the Hungarians, the Emperor reinforced his rejection of Kossuth's bills with an Austrian government memorandum accusing Hungary of breaking the Pragmatic Sanction. Unable any longer to balance loyalty to nation and throne, Batthyány resigned on 11 September. Now, in the fundamental act of defiance, Kossuth led parliament in enacting the financial and military measures to which Ferdinand had refused assent. As a royal commissioner sent to Buda-Pest was murdered by a mob (28 September), a National Defence Committee dominated by Kossuth prepared to meet 50,000 invading Croat troops under Jelačić's command.

In this late summer countdown to war the interrelatedness of the Monarchy's problems was displayed more starkly. Hungarian representatives sought a reception by the Vienna parliament in the hope of exploiting German radicals' sympathy for the common cause of freedom. They were refused admission through the efforts of Czech MPs denouncing Hungary's policies to non-Magyars. But the mood of the Vienna streets, wound up by economic hardship and the agitation of the democratic clubs, identified with the Hungarians, against whom an imperial manifesto of 3 October declared war. A mob's brutal murder of war minister Latour on the 6th provoked the Emperor's second flight. Radicals held sway in Vienna and, in control of the National Guard and a new, largely working-class Mobile Guard under the Polish revolutionary József Bem, they awaited the assault they knew must soon come.

The Conservative Dénouement

Though now in their most radical phase, the Vienna revolutionaries were less favourably placed than the Jacobins of 1793–94. The clubs of revolutionary Paris had been widely duplicated in provincial centres, and by abolishing compensation for seigneurial dues the

Jacobins were also able to influence the countryside. By contrast, Austrian provincial politics in 1848 was confined to adjusting the balance between nobles, bourgeois and peasants in the diets; Brno alone of provincial cities concerned itself for the fate of Vienna in October, while the issue of compensation had been already settled against the peasants. Only the Viennese equivalents of the *sans-culottes* rallied to a lonely cause, at the very time that debates in Frankfurt were revealing the widening rifts in the German national camp. Frankfurt, however, sent a number of fraternal delegates to the beleaguered city. The workers in the Mobile Guard showed more enthusiasm than the bourgeois in the National Guard, which had already lost many of its members. Observers commented on the good order which prevailed.

If there was anywhere where dynamic leadership might fuse social and national themes to sustain a revolution it was Hungary. The Hungarian parliament showed some awareness of the linkage when on 15 September it abolished the tithe on vineyards, but it postponed concessions to manorial peasants on the grounds of national emergency, a line of reasoning quite different from the Jacobins'. Many Hungarians recognised another linkage, solidarity between their cause and that of the German left, but would this lead them to bring succour to the Viennese democrats? Three times Hungarian troops crossed the border with Austria, only twenty miles from Vienna, the last time engaging in unsuccessful combat on the site of Vienna's Schwechat airport. However, the Hungarians could not quite bring themselves to all-out commitment on this score. Partly the reason was lack of resources; partly it was because they still claimed loyalty to Ferdinand. For that matter the Viennese revolutionaries, claiming the same loyalty, never officially requested their aid. This reluctance of revolutionaries to break the umbilical cord to the dynasty is a constant refrain of 1848, in which traditional deference and pragmatic motives no doubt both played a part. They certainly each contributed to Széchenyi's despairing mental breakdown in September, for he had always believed the Magyar cause would be lost unless it had the dynasty on its side against the Slavs.

The failure of Viennese–Hungarian cooperation, however, could leave only one outcome open. On 31 October Windisch-Graetz took Vienna, where perhaps two thousand had fallen. The Frankfurt radical delegate Robert Blum and National Guard commander Wenzel Messenhauser were among those executed. On 6 December all democratic associations were forbidden. But the chief consequence of these events was the appointment of the tough-minded Prince Felix Schwarzenberg as Austrian prime minister (24 November) and Emperor Ferdinand's abdication in favour of his 18-year-old nephew Franz Joseph (2 December). To prosecute the war with Hungary under a new ruler not bound by Ferdinand's promises made obvious sense.

The Hungarians proved formidable opponents. Kossuth's organising skills were largely responsible for building the 50,000 troops opting for Hungary at the start of the conflict into an army of 170,000 by June 1849, with 508 field guns and an output of 500 muskets a day. Jelačić and his successor Windisch-Graetz proved ineffectual commanders, to the extent that the Hungarians could retake Pest in April, while József Bem, now in Hungarian employ, reconquered most of Transylvania, where Romanians fought on the Habsburg side. Politically, however, the story was less uplifting. Senior politicians like Batthyány, Deák and Eötvös withdrew from active politics once the conflict with Austria began and the unease felt by many Hungarian politicians at the breach found echoes in a peace party in parliament, even among the 300 more committed MPs who followed its withdrawal eastwards to Debrecen. Kossuth was at odds with his best general Arthur Görgey, who inclined to the peace camp. In the Austrian-occupied areas Hungarian county administrations (essentially unreformed in 1848–49) generally collaborated unquestioningly, and successive attempts at a *levée en masse* ran up against much peasant indifference; the distinguished twentieth-century writer Gyula Illyés has wittily described how his humble grandfather was alternately hero and traitor as he hid from Habsburg and Hungarian recruiting officers.[12] One further concession to the peasants, Kossuth's decree of April 1849, putting the onus on landowners to prove their land's manorial status, was side-tracked by local officials; proposals of June to abolish all remaining feudal services remained on paper.

Could Hungary's struggles against reaction attract international attention? Sympathy, perhaps, in Britain and France but no help. The British Foreign Secretary Palmerston supported Austrian integrity in the interests of European equilibrium. Louis Napoleon's election as President in France ended Venice's hopes of a French expedition. Recognition from the distant United States arrived too late. The central European climate, too, was growing colder. In November 1848 the King of Prussia dismissed his liberal cabinet. The following April he rejected the *kleindeutsch* (little German) solution of a German imperial crown excluding Austria offered him by the Frankfurt parliament which, losing its *raison d'être*, melted away. The Frankfurt offer to the Prussian king had been prompted by Felix Schwarzenberg's assault on the revolution's liberal–national principles. His dissolution of the Kremsier parliament by imperial decree (4 March) and declaration that the whole Austrian Monarchy should enter the new Germany (9 March) also precipitated the final break with Hungary, since the imposed constitution which was to replace the Kremsier constitutional draft covered the whole Monarchy, Hungary included. On 14 April the dethronement of the Habsburgs was proclaimed in the Calvinist high church in Debrecen, with Kossuth assuming the rank of Governor of an independent Hungary. The young Emperor Franz Joseph responded with a public appeal for Russian aid and on 17 June General Paskievich entered Hungary at the head of 200,000 Tsarist troops. This was the dénouement which Széchenyi had feared.

Against it, the activities of a talented set of Hungarian agents abroad availed little. In May Teleki, Pulszky and the doyen of Polish exiles Adam Czartoryski met in Paris, joined now by the disillusioned Czech leader Rieger, to plan concerted resistance to Habsburg reaction. But their agreement, which smacked somewhat of Slav-style federalism and would have included autonomy for Hungarian Serbs and Romanians, was firmly repudiated by Kossuth. Not till late July did the Hungarian revolutionary government bring itself to approve a nationality law granting language rights to its non-Magyar subjects. Shortly after, on 13 August, Görgey surrendered to the Russians at Világos, while Kossuth sought refuge across the Danube in Turkey. Venice laid down its arms on the 24th. The conservative restoration was for the time being complete.

1848–49 in Perspective

A sense of anti-climax still pervades perceptions of the 1848 revolutions in central Europe. Greeted at the outset as the means by which the region's peoples would narrow the gulf separating them from their more advanced neighbours, they came to be seen as confirmation of immaturity and ineptitude. They were the turning-point that failed to turn.

There is much for this view. The fusion of national and social radicalism to sustain revolutionary momentum rarely occurred in the

Monarchy, because of diverse national aims and conservative social structures. Where the aspiration to bourgeois transformation existed, as to a degree among educated Magyars, it was weakened by the tension between the need for popular mobilisation and their largely noble mores. Where social and national goals coincided more fully, as in the non-dominant communities, these were usually too backward for bourgeois aspirations to exist in force. Hence the fitful splutterings of revolution in the region, where even radical movements sometimes appeared to have half an eye cocked to the imperial institution and, apart from Kossuth and perhaps the Venetian leader Manin and in a military sense József Bem, leadership lacked charisma. In Hungary many liberals watched unfolding events with a sense of foreboding and in Austria with mounting distaste. Nestroy satirised the new order in his play *Freedom in Krähwinkel*; he had always said Progress talked big. 'God knows how this will end, for who could have thought that Austria would be so bold in rising to seek a constitution, but this is a time when hours bring about what years could not':[13] these words of a Serb notable from the Slavonian county town of Požega in mid-March 1848 illustrate the bemusement many must have felt when the currents of European history swept over the 'Chinese walls' into their sluggish backwater. Liberalism in the Monarchy in 1848 was often a reactive creed, a grasping for new guide-lines by leaders of societies where the positive pulse of a new bourgeois order beat feebly.

Yet failure, no less than success, usually needs qualifying. Fifty-five years were to pass before France again had a constitution as democratic as that of 1793; in the Habsburg Monarchy much of what the revolutionaries sought was reinstated in less than twenty. There was no peasant Vendée (*pace* German–Hungarian views of the Slavs) and no counter-revolutionary tradition lived on; after all, the Hungarian revolutionary government executed 122 opponents all told and Robespierre's Terror 17,000 in Paris alone, though Hungary dethroned its king in a third of the time. Major achievements which survived the following reaction included an abolition of serfdom more radical except any but the Jacobins', and in Austria at least a sharp reduction in local landlord influence, an overhaul of the educational system, a leap forward in teaching through the mother tongue, and formalisation, challenged only for a few years, of notions of national and language equality – for the clauses of the Kremsier constitution to this effect were taken over by the constitution which replaced it.

Above all, the experiences of 1848–49, catalysed by an expanding press, encouraged wider politicisation, social initiatives and new reading habits which could later be suppressed but not forgotten. At least a hundred thousand copies were sold of L.A. Frankl's poem 'The University', written in March 1848. Besides the mass participation of students and youth, the first women's political association was founded in Vienna and the first women's meeting and deputation organised in Prague. Most significant, perhaps, in the longer term, was the stirring of non-dominant groups; upwards of 200,000 signed the Ruthenian petition for the partition of Galicia; Czech-language periodicals quadrupled from 13 to 52. 'Newspapers are the mirror of the national present and future', enthused the editor of *Napre-dak* ('Progress'), the new voice of younger Serbs; 'from them we see most quickly, easily and best what must be safeguarded, what aimed for and altogether what must done to attain spiritual and material happiness'.[14]

This earnest patriotism reminds us that it is after all the record of nationalism rather than liberalism which has cast its shadow over the memory of 1848. This was the year which gave the lie to images of a world of nations living in fraternity. Why was this so? Spokesmen of the non-dominant peoples denied the charge that through narrow nationalism they had sold out liberal solidarity to the Habsburgs. Political freedom without recognition of nationality meant nothing, claimed Havlíček; where a foreign tongue dominated there could be no liberty, only an aristocracy of language. The smaller nations were only asking for what the larger ones claimed and invoking the liberal principle of equality, wrote Palacký to Frankfurt: 'the rights of nations are the rights of nature'. Besides, the dominant nations' reliance on historic rights was illiberal. 'You say you want democracy, and at the same time you want the thousand year old Hungarian state; but the two are incompatible', protested a Romanian to the Hungarians.[15] Thus non-dominant polemicists tended to argue from first principles, deploying the very liberal, rational theses they were accused of betraying, in an attempt to counter the reactionary image Germans presented of them to the western world. *Napredak*'s young collaborators, conceding that they could not achieve this goal by sticking to their mother tongue, sought entrée in the Paris periodical *La Pologne* of the East Europeanist Cyprian Robert. The aim was to demonstrate that their nationalist aspirations could be set in a liberal framework. Indeed, historians' conventional counterposing of liberalism and nationalism in 1848 is an unhelpful cliché, since both principles were intertwined for all revolutionary participants, often with an unabashed assurance which raises modern eyebrows. As the first article of the constitution of the League of Germans of Bohemia, Moravia and Silesia stated, 'We believe in the holy spirit of Humanity . . . We believe that this spirit has become incarnate in the German people'.[16] To separate off the 'nationalist' from the 'liberal' elements in this bizarre claim is to miss the point. It is better seen as an instance of that deep-seated human self-righteousness which knows no ideological boundaries.

German and Magyar perspectives on the revolutionary débâcle were more sociologically orientated than those of their opponents. Linking the Slavs' pro-dynastic role in 1848 to their allegedly priest-ridden peasant societies, they saw liberalism as the creed of a more developed social order, not just as a set of abstract principles. Slavs could not attain such development unaided but only by aligning themselves with their more dynamic neighbours. Their interest lay in recognising this fact and abstaining from demands which would conflict with German-led civilisational advances from which all would benefit. This approach required the non-dominant peoples to defer their national claims to a future time, meanwhile putting their trust in the goodwill of their more developed mentors. Given traditions of ethnic arrogance on the one side and resentment on the other this was hardly likely to happen. Indeed, German radicals like Engels appeared to deny the Slavs any future at all. Dominant groups' acquiescence in formulas proclaiming national and language equality must be taken with a pinch of salt. The German-dominated Styrian Diet made such a declaration but promptly opposed the Slovene minority's request to address it in Slovene as their language was purportedly inadequate to the occasion.

Yet it may be unwise to base a conclusion on national relations in 1848 only on contemporary polemics. In practice things could be different. While Magyars and non-Magyars in Hungary were poles apart, Germans and Slavs reached a form of compromise in the Kremsier constitutional discussions of early 1849. Czech MPs did not insist, for example, on the promise of their own government in Prague made on 8 April the previous year or on any of several proposals made to federalise the Monarchy, whether on the lines of the historic crownlands or, less favourable to Czech historic claims to all Bohemia, of ethno-linguistic units – Palacký himself had submitted schemes of both kinds. On the other hand the draft eventually followed, by the Moravian German Mayer, conceded the crownlands and the provincial governors substantial powers, while creating ethnic *Kreise* of some half-million inhabitants apiece within the larger crownlands. This allowed a measure of autonomy to Bohemian Germans – but also to Slovenes and Italians in German majority provinces. Mayer's work has been called an exercise in federative centralisation.[17] Essentially, the Kremsier settlement showed give and take on both sides, with the rather greater concessions of the Slavs suggesting that they were still willing, as the less developed party, to defer in practice to a German lead tactfully given. Particularly interesting in this respect is their acceptance throughout 1848 of an electoral franchise weighted towards the towns, seats of enterprise and literacy – but also of German preponderance.

As the most wide-ranging agreement reached between Germans and Slavs in the Habsburg Monarchy the Kremsier constitution has aroused much interest. In time the traditional underdogs could have been expected to press against its Germanocentric limits; yet power adjustments are easier within an established framework of cooperation, as Quebecois–Anglophone relations in Canada since 1867 so far demonstrate. In the Habsburg case, however, there were factors – beyond sheer complexity – which must temper appraisal of the Kremsier accord. The radical German nationalist Left remained in Vienna in October 1848 and did not attend the rump Kremsier parliament, whose brief, too, excluded the Hungarian half of the Monarchy. Moreover, there is ample evidence from 1848 for the chief hazard threatening multi-ethnic polities when long-entrenched patterns of ethnic hierarchy begin to shift: a backlash from the historically privileged group in which the perceived challengers are both luridly diabolised and contemptuously dismissed. German anti-Slavism oscillated in this fashion in 1848. Almost hysterical German overreaction to the Slav movement was mixed with disparagement and an eventual sigh of relief as old certainties resumed their hold. The later relaxation was as ill-founded as the earlier alarmism.

It is the injection of the poison of national hatred into all camps which was the most damaging legacy of 1848, rather than any blows it dealt to overarching ideas of Austrian patriotism, whose prior weakness it merely exposed. Thereafter pragmatic national leaders might still see the Monarchy as the framework for their aspirations, but in a psychological atmosphere which militated against genuine cooperation. In this way the role of 1848 was to bring to a head in the most confrontational way possible tendencies which had been growing in the Pre-March era. The real missed opportunity, if any, probably came in the long decades of ostrich-like government inactivity after 1815, when national movements developed in an atmosphere conducive to mutual ignorance and distrust. That said, the folly of the state coup against Kremsier and its constitutional settlement can hardly be overstated. Austrian conservatism revealed its immaturity no less than Austrian liberalism.

6   Eventful Transition, 1849–67

In 1850 Metternich told his fellow conservative Count Hartig that sixty years after the French Revolution a new order had still not arisen in Europe.[1] No-one could have made this claim by 1870. The map of Europe worked out at the Congress of Vienna had been redrawn and in the new Germany and Italy, the new Austria and Hungary, parliamentarism ostensibly held sway. Not surprisingly, the international and constitutional struggles of the 1860s long claimed the lion's share of Austrian historians' attention. Our own age, more sceptical of Whiggish theories of progress and preoccupied by issues of economic growth, has introduced new perspectives, in which the neo-absolutist 1850s loom larger than before. Were these years an instance of the 'modernising autocracy' which has so interested social scientists? How far did they sow the seeds of later change? The balance between liberal and conservative motifs is a leading theme of the essentially transitional period covered in this chapter, echoing at a distance the ambiguities of Louis Napoleon in France and Bismarck in Prussia.

But the division into liberals and conservatives hardly does justice to the array of bureaucratic centralists, Catholic clericals, aristocratic federalists and small-nation nationalists who jostled on the Habsburg stage. The fact that by 1867 the German-speaking bourgeoisie had emerged apparently triumphant from among so many competitors merely increased its providential sense of superiority *vis-à-vis* these rivals: only its economic and cultural strength could modernise a Monarchy full of 'reactionary' Slav peasants. Aspects of this way of thinking were not confined to liberals. Part of the neo-absolutist programme of the 1850s was to relegitimise notions of imperial unity through stress of the state's developmental role, with heightened emphasis on German language and culture as means to this end. A barely conscious shift of focus was under way, whereby the German-speaking elite and its allies were accorded almost a parallel role to the Emperor as upholders of the state. It was a shift which, by updating Josephinian notions of the empire as a progressive force, was to help extend its lease of life into the 'Dualist' epoch for a time, following the collapse of the old unitary Austria in 1866–67.

For the internal transition to Austro-Hungarian constitutionalism in 1867 was mediated by external defeat. International politics was the handmaiden of the new central European order, as Austria's defeats by France in 1859 and Prussia in 1866 set in train Italian and German unification and the retreat from absolutism at home. This need not mean that diplomacy and war should dominate accounts of these years. The greatness of Austria's nemesis, Otto von Bismarck, was to seize the opportunities offered him by changing times to resolve the deadlocks of 1848. The economic rise of the region's German-speaking bourgeoisie strengthened moderate liberalism against both artisanal radicalism and traditional elites, while Prussia's leadership in the *Zollverein* helped make her and not Austria the chief focus of German middle-class patriotism. The contours of a possible compromise between government and the better-off ranks of the bourgeoisie sharpened as the international radicalism bequeathed by 1848 *à la* Mazzini or Kossuth lost appeal. In the Monarchy this became a compromise between Franz Joseph, the Magyar gentry and the Austro-German liberals at the expense of the Slavs, producing many losers and some Pyrrhic victors. The Monarchy's reincarnation in 1867 as constitutional 'Austria-Hungary' was a substantial achievement, which enabled it to present itself as a 'modern' European state in a way Tsarist Russia never achieved. But the modernity was partial and the birth pangs of the new order traumatic and fateful.

The Rise of Neo-absolutism

Modernisation of any kind may seem an inappropriate theme in approaching the court and government of Franz Joseph's early reign. Many of their leading characters would not have been out of place centuries before: the interfering royal mother, the Empress Sophie; the ecclesiastical confidant, Archbishop Rauscher; the seemingly indispensable military man of perhaps more style than substance, Count Grünne; the plebeian minister risen by talent, Baron Kübeck. Franz Joseph himself had little modern about him. A conscientious, somewhat unimaginative young man, who identified state, dynasty and self, he was only briefly distracted from the chores of absolutism by his marriage to the sixteen-year-old Elizabeth, a princess of fairy-tale beauty, in 1854. Yet alongside these timeless figures there were men in the young Emperor's first government who were more identifiably of their age, like the ministers of trade, finance and public works, Karl Bruck, Philipp Krauss and Andreas Baumgartner respectively, even the minister of the interior Alexander Bach, who was to cleave ever closer to the old elite. The justice minister Anton von Schmerling had been a member of the Frankfurt Assembly. The very existence of a ministerial cabinet with a prime minister, Prince Felix Schwarzenberg (1800–52), in place of the advisory 'conferences' of Pre-March, showed the compromises tradition had had to make with the revolution.

Yet Schwarzenberg was no liberal. His formative influence over the young monarch stemmed precisely from his mentoring role as conservative strong man. For Schwarzenberg, too, was in his way a type. A great aristocrat and bachelor roué who had turned his energies and talents to affairs of state, he treated the constitutional principles he had mouthed on entering office in November 1848 with the cold realism of the man of power, though he was not personally in favour of a full return to Pre-March absolutism. He was also foreign minister, whose title of 'minister of the imperial house and foreign affairs' aptly expressed the Emperor's view of the intimate link between foreign policy and the throne.

Unchallenged at home, the Emperor and his chief minister faced in Germany the liberal–conservative tension mentioned above. So seductive was the liberal 'spirit of the age' that the very Prussian government which had sent the Frankfurt parliament packing adopted, in its programme for a German Union of May 1849, many of Frankfurt's *kleindeutsch* principles: German parliamentary institutions, the Prussian sovereign as chief executive and a confederal tie with Austria. Failing to win acceptance for his own looser tripartite proposals (for Prussian, south German and Austrian spheres), Schwarzenberg threw down the gauntlet. Prussia must give up the Union scheme, accept the reconstitution of the old confederal Diet and admit to it the whole of the Habsburg lands under conditions of customs union. Her acquiescence at a meeting of late November 1850 became the 'humiliation of Olmütz' in Prussian liberal mythology. Yet when the Confederation was indeed restored under Austrian presidency at the Dresden conference of March 1851, Schwarzenberg abandoned his wider scheme to include in it all the Habsburg lands and plans for a customs union also went no further.

Why did Schwarzenberg not press home his advantage? For earlier Austrian historians like Srbik who saw him as the champion of a dynamic vision of *Mitteleuropa*, the 'empire of seventy million' under

Austrian primacy, the aftermath of the Olmütz victory was a puzzling anti-climax. The hostility of Russia and France to an Austrian hegemony is part explanation. But some more recent historians have questioned how far Schwarzenberg really was committed to the *Mitteleuropa* idea, a scenario more properly traceable to his trade minister Bruck's enthusiasm for central European customs union. Though Schwarzenberg's style differed, his policy like Metternich's may ultimately have been to work with Prussia in Germany rather than demote her. In this view the demands for the incorporation of the entire Monarchy in a reconstituted Germany were largely spoiling moves against Frankfurt's and then Prussia's initiatives.[2] Insofar as Schwarzenberg was in earnest about his declared central European aims, moreover, he may have been constrained from pressing them more firmly by the enhanced role of public opinion after 1848. It became harder to conduct external policy in isolation from domestic and Austria's absolutist trend was hardly compatible with a stronger role for her in Germany. The obverse of this was Schwarzenberg's reluctance to break wholly with all the constitutional structures inherited from 1848–49. His sovereign, who quite lacked insight into the domestic–external equation, thus did more than set the internal clock back when he sided with Kübeck against Schwarzenberg in the muffled debate of 1851–52 on snuffing out the constitutional legacy. He also helped scupper the Austrian position in Germany.

Until 1851 the imposed constitution of March 1849, named after the then interior minister Stadion, remained nominally in force. Indeed, its moderate liberalism was amplified by further reforms in this period: introduction of oral, public legal procedure and jury trial; improved rights of association and assembly; the important 1849 provisions for communal self-government; and implementation wherever practicable of mother-tongue education, including at the secondary stage. For conservatives the entire liberal preoccupation with rights marked a philosophical aberration as distasteful as revolutionary excess. Archbishop Rauscher argued that prior to rights were duties, to which a people could be awakened only by the Christian faith and the prospect of eternity.[3] A common view saw liberalism not as a rational creed corrresponding to a new and practicable social order but as a principle of dissolution tending inevitably to the final shipwreck of socialism, that 'criminal code ironically translated into a doctrine of virtue', as Kübeck called it.[4] But neither Windisch-Graetz, who lacked real achievement to his name, nor Metternich, back in Vienna from 1851 but too old and vain, could provide leadership for conservative sentiment. Kübeck, however, was at the heart of government and had the young Emperor's ear. He succeeded first in having the Reichsrat referred to in the Stadion constitution set up and then in turning it under his chairmanship into a rival organ to the council of ministers. His memoranda formed the basis of decrees of August 1851 declaring the ministers responsible to the Emperor alone (rather than the parliament held in prospect by Stadion) and finally of the formal abolition of the Stadion constitution by the 'Sylvester Patent' of the last day of the year.

The Sylvester Patent set out the structures of a centralised, absolute Monarchy. Only at commune level would an elective element remain, though even here the old feudal estates could remove themselves from communal jurisdiction. Judicial and administrative powers at district level were recombined and the jury system soon abolished. Schwarzenberg's premature death in April 1852 ended the ministerial system, already weakened by the protest resignations of Schmerling and Krauss in the previous year. He was to have no successor as prime minister, for the former ambassador in London, Count Buol, replaced him as foreign minister only. Ministers were not to take collective decisions, but became mere instruments of the imperial will, meeting together under Franz Joseph's chairmanship or that of his nominated deputy, the Archduke Rainer. The ministry of war disappeared altogether, transformed into an administrative department of the High Command. The press law of 1852, which imposed very heavy deposits for journalistic ventures; the reintroduction of secret, written judicial process through the revised criminal procedure regulations of 1853; the shift of powers from the district to the provincial authorities in 1854; above all the omnipresent role of the newly created gendarmerie under Baron Kempen were further steps in the assertion of government authority across the board.

Open absolutism only deepened the centralist trend already apparent in the provinces. Hungary, its rights deemed forfeit by rebellion, had become just one crownland among many, divided into five districts which remained under military rule until September 1850. Hungarian counties were assimilated to the pattern of the Austrian *Kreise*, all but minor officials being appointed from Vienna. With the introduction of Austrian financial and judicial structures came the Austrian Civil Code of 1811. Administered apart from Hungary as separate crownlands were Croatia-Slavonia, the Military Frontier, Transylvania and a Serbian entity, Vojvodina, with the Banat in southern Hungary which had been set up in 1849 in illusory fulfilment of promises of Serb autonomy during the struggle against Magyar rebels. Actually, Serbs were barely a quarter of the population in 'their' territory. These arrangements applied almost equally in Croatia, whose people's loyalty in 1848 earned merely symbolic rights – to call the reorganised Zagreb court by its ancient name, to call an almost powerless Jelačić Ban. In the words of a Hungarian noble, the Croats received as reward what the Hungarians had as punishment, though the Croatian language, hard-pressed as it was, was not like Magyar wholly replaced by German in administrative practice.

The treatment of nationality became one of the sorest points of neo-absolutism. The Sylvester Patent omitted reference to the guarantees of national and language equality which had figured in the Kremsier and Stadion constitutions. Early attempts to advance the cause of non-German languages in the schools were steadily reversed. By the late 1850s the official goal of secondary schools was clearly to prepare their pupils to receive a wholly German-language education by the upper forms, with non-German languages used in lower forms only when needed to smooth the path. So-called nationality secondary schools were gradually to be eliminated. Even at primary level, German was increasingly emphasised as a tool for transition further up the educational ladder in town schools, in 'main schools' and in mixed areas. Of course, not all of this was resented; the Pre-March situation was not totally reinstated and many parents undoubtedly wanted to ensure that their children learnt German well. However, centralism meant the suppression of non-German voices even when they were expressed in German – of the pro-Czech paper *Union* and the Croat *Südslawische Zeitung* as well as of *Národní noviny* and *Slavenski jug*. By 1855 there were 78 'political' periodicals left in the whole Monarchy, far less than in Vienna alone in 1848. The story of Karel Havlíček's last stand editing a regional newspaper after the closing down of the Prague liberal press, of his Tyrolean imprisonment, broken health and death in 1856 shortly after his release – he was 32 – was to become one of the classic themes of Czech national martyrology. Support even for cultural patriotism was closely watched by the authorities; collections for the Czech national theatre project launched in 1845 stagnated in the neo-absolutist years.

The neo-absolutist period has always been associated with the interior minister Alexander Bach (1806–93). He was the architect of its streamlined administrative structures and uniform chain of command; the eclipse through bureaucrats of the semi-autonomous role of communes and quasi-national *Kreise* envisaged by Stadion; the control of public opinion through censorship; and the police and informer networks. It seems likely that Bach was one of those bourgeois liberals disillusioned by the indiscipline and chaos, as they saw it, of the popular movement of 1848. Whatever his sincerity in maintaining, during a long and embittered retirement, that he personally envisaged the restoration of some kind of central representative body once his work of consolidation was done, the fact is that as a man of action and ambition he chafed for the opportunity to make his mark irrespective of political creeds. If neo-absolutism came to be linked to his name (the 'Bach system') this was a tribute to his energy and prominence but also reflected the fact that he made a convenient fall-guy for a regime of which he was only part. Thus the alien Austrian officials of the 1850s in Hungary were 'Bach's hussars' in the scornful Magyar jibe not just because of his role in appointing them but because of the irony of this Viennese bourgeois dressing up the mainly humbly born Czech and Slovene 'Germanisers' in a fanciful version of Hungarian noble costume, complete with sword and spurs. Tsar Nicholas I too snubbed him at Olmütz. Bach's political potential remained circumscribed by his radical past.

Bach shielded himself from noble disdain in part through increasing piety. After Schwarzenberg's death it is Archbishop Rauscher who has been seen by many as Franz Joseph's leading confidant. Distrustful of the press, the modern opinion former, the regime turned to its forerunner, the Church. In 1850 Franz Joseph cast away Josephinist controls on Austrian clerics' contacts with the Vatican and the publication of Papal Bulls, and opened negotiations with Rome on the neuralgic question of Austrian marriage law. The resulting Concordat of 1855 accepted Catholic canon law over civil law in marriage questions, including mixed marriages, prohibited the teaching of Catholic children by non-Catholics and entrusted school inspection to the clergy; it also lifted state controls of the training of priests. The Church continued to be unhappy about the equality granted to non-Catholics in 1848, one of the very few civil rights reaffirmed by the Sylvester Patent. The Papal Nuncio's calling of an assembly of bishops on his own initiative (1856) also annoyed the absolute state. The renegotiation of the union of throne and altar was therefore not without strain, but Rauscher's belief in this 'union of forces' made sense to a regime which instinctively sought security in old verities as well as Bach's new broom. The year 1848 had done what 1789 had not and finally opened men's minds to the evils of godlessness, Rauscher wrote to Metternich. This was wishful thinking. The revival of religion among intellectuals *à la* Chateaubriand or Schlegel in the wake of the French Revolution was not repeated after 1848. For many of the German-speaking bourgeois needed to operate Bach's new centralising bureaucracy, the Catholic hegemony restored by the Concordat was inwardly distasteful.

There were other tensions in neo-absolutism. Despite the strong Catholic convictions of the minister of education and religion, Count Leo Thun, several of his reforms had more of a liberal character. Thus *Gymnasien* were upgraded by becoming eight- instead of six-year institutions, with a final state examination (the *Matura*) for university entrance. Universities themselves were largely entrusted to the autonomous direction of the teaching professors and granted the *Lehr- und Lernfreiheit* of liberal slogans, that is, tutors could lecture on and students attend whatever they chose. Behind both reforms was the 'neo-humanist' inspiration of the founder of the University of Berlin, Wilhelm von Humboldt – that young minds should be formed by free engagement with the noblest products of classical antiquity – as mediated through the drafts of the liberal Prague professor Exner, prepared before Thun assumed office in July 1849. Thun made these his own because he shared the dreams of his largely German advisers (often converts from Protestantism) that a revivified Austria might become the leader of the 'Catholic movement' in Germany, a Germany in which the Humboldtian reforms had been generally acepted across the confessional divide. The Catholic cause was to be served not by the lifeless regimentation of the *Vormärz* but by the intellectual power of its exponents, winning out over the religious apathy and crypto-liberalism of the Josephinist academic establishment. Indeed, freedom of student choice had to be modified to ensure a law degree syllabus (law was the entrée into Austrian state service) grounded in positive history instead of the natural law philosophy which had led the way to revolution. Thun's university reform and its reception shows the complexity of influences on Habsburg government in the 1850s. His German orientation made sense at a time when Austria still claimed leadership in Germany, but it was resented by Austrian Catholics and Josephinists alike, who united in defence of the Pre-March university system. Divisions in the leadership led to press polemics, in which even crypto-liberal views could gain a hearing; Professor Hye, associated with 1848 and forced out of his chair, wrote scathingly that the social contract theories so incriminated by the critics of natural law in fact had their origins in the classical and Germanic law they trumpeted, indeed, in the Bible itself.[5] On the other side, Thun was forced to make many exemptions for Catholic monks from the new state examinations meant to upgrade the quality of secondary school teachers.

A second tension was between the university reform's German orientation and the Monarchy's non-Germans. The Bohemian Thun's attempt to enlist Czech support for his conservative programme involved appointing the nationally conscious Czech J.J. Tomek to the chair of history at the University of Prague. But conservative and Austrophile as he proved, Tomek was also deeply suspicious of the emphasis on the legal history of the German Reich which was part of the new official ideology. Thun's pursuit of a German and a Slav strategy at the same time betrayed a mistaken assumption that a people like the Czechs could still be slotted into a pan-German framework, given some recognition of their cultural identity. After 1848 this was not so. The fate of the Austrian History Research Institute, founded in 1855 following J.A. Helfert's appeal for a 'history of the Austrian state and people as a whole', showed that hopes for a common Austrian national feeling were unrealistic. In practice the Institute never attempted such an ambitious task but became a specialist centre where young scholars acquired technical skills they then deployed to bolster the historical profile of their own nationality.

Like most authoritarian regimes, therefore, the Austria of the 1850s was not as monolithic as it seemed. Ultimately, only the will of the Emperor united possessions too diverse to give rise to a shared philosophy of government. The young monarch saw his determining role as natural and inalienable by family tradition. Yet the neo-absolutism of the 1850s was not traditional. Almost everything about Austria's position, domestic and international, was shaped by what had happened in 1848–49. Some issues were old ones in new guise, but there were others which had little or no precedent. Once part of a common European pattern, Austrian absolutism was now reciprocated among major European states only by Russia and France, the latter ruled by a parvenu adventurer. It operated, moreover, in a world of railways, steamships and joint stock banks, from which the age-old relations between lord and serf had been expunged. These, rather than the rooting out of conspirators and constitutionalism, were the kind of factors which would shape Franz Joseph's reign.

A Case for Economic Modernisation?

It is here that nineteenth-century perceptions of a 'Bach system' find their place. They pinpointed what was new about neo-absolutism – the enhanced role and confidence of the Austro-German bourgeoisie from which Bach sprang. Obstacles to an economic forward strategy favoured in the Pre-March period by Metternich and Kübeck, like serfdom and the special status of Hungary, had been removed by the events of 1848–49. The rational systematising spirit inherent in the Enlightenment now had its head. Bach's activities read like a Josephinist fantasy come to life. Whether in the grandly conceived state geological and meteorological institutes, the reorganising of state medical services, the new veterinary tax, the first regulations against cruelty to animals, the classifying of roads, the embanking of the Austrian Danube, the regulation of the Hungarian Danube and the Tisza, the new forest law or in a host of other fields the neo-absolutist state inaugurated, upgraded or brought to fruition projects redolent of enlightened absolutism.

Yet its ability to do so related to something new, the quickening impulse of European capitalism by mid-century being transmitted from the west to the centre of the continent. The latter benefited from the receipt of cheap, high-technology products from the former, while acting as industrial suppliers to more backward neighbours on their east, where their lower wage costs and proximity to the markets enabled them to hold British competition at bay. The pace of transmission of new technology constantly rose. Where it had taken nearly forty years for the first Austrian steam engine to follow Watt's invention, the Bessemer process for steel, first successfully implemented in Britain in 1856–60, was introduced to the Vítkovice iron-works in Bohemia in 1863. This had much to do with the development of communications; many historians have seen the railway, and the iron industry it promoted, as the trigger of central European industrialisation. Yet railway expansion was bound up with the more flexible banking system emerging in the 1850s to provide the unprecedented investment sums involved. This in turn was linked with the new means of facilitating commercial and financial contacts: the electric telegraph, the modern postal systems spurred by Rowland Hill's penny stamp (the Austro-German postal union was founded in 1850), the Austro-German currency union of 1857 and the standardisation of Austro-German commercial law in 1862. The Austrian ethnographer Czoernig in his book *Austria's Transformation* (1858) marvelled that Russian acceptance of his country's Crimean peace proposals had been learned in Vienna virtually at the same time as it had been communicated in St Petersburg.[6] More sympathetic to the official line than modern historians, he saw the Austria of 1847 as closer to 1758 than to the present.

The beginning of any reform from above had to be acceptance of the abolition of serfdom. The final settlement (1849 in Austria, 1853 in Hungary) required landowners to be compensated, but under terms far less onerous to the peasants than in the Russian emancipation of 1861. Obligations of pure feudal origin were not compensated at all; the remainder, according as they were held to derive partly or wholly from landlords' rights of property, were subject to 'modest compensation' or redemption at full market value. Thus the 'modest compensation' for *robota* was fixed at only a third of the value of a day's free labour. In Austria the resultant sum was to be divided three ways, following the principle of the 1840 legislation. In Hungary and Galicia the state met the whole cost of the compensation. Altogether between 37 and 41% of Hungary's taxable land passed into ownership of some three million peasants, including their families.

How important was peasant emancipation as a turning-point in the Monarchy's agricultural development? Komlos has calculated that *Vormärz* agricultural growth has been underestimated and that the replacement of *robota* by more productive free labour increased agricultural output in Austria only by 2.4% and in Hungary by 1.2%.[7] Though the case appears to put too much faith in uncertain statistics, the assumption that forced labour was already being supplanted by wage labour under the *ancien régime* is correct. Social analysis also undermines the idea of a sudden growth spurt. The great bulk of newly enfranchised peasants were not in a position to make swift changes in their methods of cultivation. Direct taxation, swollen by local and other surcharges, amounted to about 40% of their income as estimated by cadastral values, admittedly somewhat out of date. A division of common pasture, meadow and forest lands weighted against them, particularly in Galicia and Hungary; the limitation of full emancipation to rustical or urbarial peasants; difficulties in proving the status of peasant land when, for example, Hungarian vineyards and 'remainder' lands were not registered as urbarial in the 1767 yardstick survey, though they had had urbarial obligations: all this meant that only a minority of the rural population had a chance of prosperous peasant proprietor status.

Hungary's case is particularly instructive. Tentative comparisons suggest that the 1853 Patent deprived peasants of some 3-4% of the land they would have won under the revolutionary legislation of 1848 and made them pay compensation for about 20% more of the land they did obtain.[8] All told, up to three-quarters of Hungary's peasant families were either cottars, who received their small plots on less favourable terms, or manorial peasants whose position remained unchanged unless they could demonstrate they had a contractual status. This rural majority had little future except as a class of farm-servants or labourers. Signs of peasant mutiny appeared in Hungary in the second half of the 1850s, as the negative features of the settlement became apparent, and again in the early and mid-1860s; more and more court cases were contested in its long-drawn-out implementation. Military intervention was enforced against the wine peasants of the Croatian county of Zagreb in 1862. About a third of the settlements reached by 1864 required judicial process because local agreement proved impossible.[9] The changes in peasant agriculture in Hungary remained confined to the generalisation of the use of iron ploughs in western Hungary and a transition from the sickle to the scythe for the cutting of hay which, by increasing the hay harvest, enabled cattle to be stabled also in summer. But a shift from the three-field system to partible agriculture did not yet occur, since peasants lacked confidence to move out of the village community with its rigid cropping patterns; consequently, the percentage of fallow land remained high.

In Bohemia the pace of change was quicker. The first agricultural schools for peasants as opposed to farm managers were set up in 1850, with parallels in other Austrian provinces. Between 1848 and 1868 the proportion of fallow in Bohemia fell from 21.6% to 6.2%. But the emergence of a class of prosperous peasants came only in the second half of this period and the growing use of farm machinery after 1860 was almost exclusively a matter of larger landowners. It is this category which is usually credited with agricultural expansion, on the strength of the investment capital flowing into its hands via the compensation procedure. The sums were certainly large. Of the 290 million florins paid to landowners in the western half of the Monarchy the various branches of the Schwarzenbergs received 1,870,000 and of the Liechtensteins 1,100,000. No doubt the initial development of the Bohemian sugar beet industry owed something to this financial injection. In 1858 three-quarters of sugar beet works in Bohemia were noble-owned and production had increased nearly six-fold over the decade, though the cutting edge was provided by factories of the bourgeois Skene and Schoeller. Increased grain production in Hungary, however, was due rather to the sharp rise in grain prices from the late 1840s, for the bonds through which compensation payments were transmitted were issued with a delay in Hungary and their stock exchange value soon declined. Far from encouraging landowning credit the regime transferred peasant payments arriving early from the regional compensation funds to the central treasury, and opposed calls, particularly from Bohemia, for a noble mortgage bank. What agrarian uplift occurred is thus best seen as part of the broader pattern of economic change in central Europe as a whole.

The most striking feature of neo-absolutist economic policy was the effort put into railway construction, first under direct state auspices, then from 1854 through generous state cash guarantees to private companies. On the eve of revolution Vienna was only connected to Prague. Budapest was reached in 1852, Ljubljana and Trieste after the completion of the world's first mountain railway over the Semmering pass in 1854, Passau on the Bavarian border in 1861. Hungary, previously neglected, opened up rapidly, with an arc of major towns from the south to the north-east joining the European rail network in the 1850s: Miskolc, Oradea Mare (Nagyvárad), Debrecen, Timişoara, Arad and Szeged. By the early 1860s Budapest had been connected with Zagreb and Prague with the Bohemian industrial centres of Reichenberg, Pilsen and Kladno. Altogether the Monarchy's railway network, excluding Lombardy-Venetia, grew under neo-absolutism from about 1500 to 4700 kilometres at a cost to the state (by the end of 1856) of some 291 million florins, or 20% of total state expenditure. Such sums had no precedent outside the military sphere.

Indeed, the effort overtaxed state financial resources, leading to an 1854 Patent arranging for future lines to be built by private capital with a 5% state interest guarantee. Within four years the state's ownership of total mileage fell from 70% to insignificant proportions. Much private railway capital came from abroad. The government actively encouraged the foundation of the first great Austrian financial institution, the Oesterreichische Creditanstalt, modelled along the lines of the Parisian Crédit Mobilier, with interests in long-term industrial loans as well as short-term deposits. Anselm Rothschild was a big contributor to its 100 million florins capital, alongside illustrious aristocrats. Neo-absolutism's complaisance to business interests was shown too in the state-sponsored chambers of commerce set up in leading towns in 1850, in the favourable terms businessmen obtained in the selling off of state property and in the effective abolition of the guilds as a barrier to free trade in 1859 – initially delayed by traditionalist elements. In general the economic role of the state was plainly coming into line with *laissez-faire* precepts, limiting itself to infrastructural measures and international commercial agreements. The most important of these were the abolition of the internal Austro-Hungarian customs barrier from 1850 and the reduction of Austria's external tariff in two general tariff revisions and a trade treaty with the *Zollverein* (1852–54). What were the results?

Until the European recession of 1857, the first unconnected with harvest failure, progress was undoubtedly good. Iron production rose by 7% a year in the Monarchy in the 1850s and coal consumption by 10% a year from 1851 to the slump of 1873. The mechanisation of cotton weaving finally got under way at this time and by the end of the fifties had also penetrated the Brno woollen cloth industry. Even where further advances in mechanisation were to await the 1860s, as in brewing, paper making and flour milling, growth was still aided by concentration of production in larger units. Overall, there were 630 steam engines in the Monarchy in 1852 and 2841 in 1863. The rise was proportionately greater in Hungary which was experiencing an inflow of Austrian and foreign capital, leading to rapid growth of the iron industry and the expansion of what was to become the great Hungarian milling industry – Buda-Pest already had 14 flour mills in 1860. In the first eight years after the revolution the capital of the Danube Steamship Company increased nearly fourfold, so that by 1856 it transported 1.3 million passengers.

Were, then, the much maligned fifties a turning-point in the history of the Monarchy? While the decade was not as black as nineteenth-century liberals and nationalists painted it, most recent research warns against overzealous rehabilitation. Three lines of argument deserve notice.

One, stemming from the emerging consensus about the gradualist nature of the Monarchy's nineteenth-century economic growth, would deny any particular energising role to the post-1848 years. It can also carry a sub-text refuting Marxist-derived views that only the sweeping away of 'feudal' checks on the bourgeois mode of production could set rapid progress under way. Thus Komlos plays down the effect of the 1850 customs union similar to those cited above minimising the impact of peasant emancipation. The gain to Hungary from the union he calculates at only 1.5% of her GNP and for Austria at a mere 0.8%. Huerta extends the argument to the Monarchy's tariff reductions and *Zollverein* treaty of 1852–54, whose significance has been exaggerated, he suggests, because many duties were comparatively unaffected and the *Zollverein's* trade with Austria was relatively low.[10] It is argued that, if anything, Germany's economic lead over Austria accelerated from this time, for example, in cotton spinning. Sandgruber has asserted that given the favourable European conjuncture the historian's problem is to explain why there was not a neo-absolutist boom rather than why there was.[11] Official statistics may mislead. But the very uncertainty of statistics makes the non-specialist uneasy over Komlos's precise calculation that *robota* accounted for only 4.4% of Hungarian field labour before 1848,[12] the figure on which he bases his low estimate of the impact of emancipation on Hungarian agriculture. It sits oddly with what we know of the backwardness of much middle-gentry agriculture in pre-1848 Hungary and its subsequent failure to meet the challenge of capitalist farming. More generally, it may be that the impact of infrastructural change, such as the 1850s attempted, is not easily measured quantitatively.

In a second set of arguments, the claims to efficiency of an innovative bureaucracy look less solid under the microscope of regional studies like those of Mirjana Gross for Croatia and Christoph Stölzl for Bohemia, or Harm-Hinrich Brandt's magisterial survey of the neo-absolutist regime. Croatians appealed in vain for a branch of the National Bank, a commercial bank or mortgage facilities; the merchant-orientated chambers of commerce were unpopular with the vastly more numerous Croatian artisanry, few of whom bothered to vote in council elections. While Zagreb stayed railwayless, the forests under-exploited and the Sava unregulated, peasants, as throughout Hungary, still had to perform the old unpaid *corvée* on roads, saw livestock numbers decline and resented the alcohol tax which burdened one of the few chances they saw of earning cash to pay their increased taxes. The demands of the central administration for paperwork were certainly novel but also often impracticable. The sense that more backward lands were as heavily taxed as richer ones, as appeared the case with per capita direct taxation in poor Hungary and relatively prosperous Bohemia by 1864, acted corrosively. By 1859 only 13% of Hungarian direct taxes were being collected without force or threat of force. It seems – a not unfamiliar tune – that authoritarian modernisation savoured more of bluff and bluster the further away one moved from the centre of the action.

The beleaguered bureaucracy which risked being overwhelmed by these problems was far from the formidable force of the history books. Criticised for its numbers and expense, it was in fact a rather small and stingily paid body, apparently swollen only because the state had taken over duties formerly provided by patrimonial jurisdiction. The real expense of the domestic administration was the gendarmerie, not to speak of the army, whose access to costly new equipment was protected by the Emperor. Above the hapless ranks of office clerks and clerical assistants, with their annual pittances of 300 and 216 florins (£30 and £21.60 respectively), even the academically qualified personnel were in large majority set in the lower ranks of the administrative hierarchy. The disjuncture between their salaries and the rising incomes of free professionals and tradesmen at a time of inflation, as also between the role-model demands made of them and their growing demoralisation, were often pointed out to Bach. A spirit of reform on the cheap, however, pervaded the would-be model administration.

Alongside these critiques a third accuses the 1850s regime of failing at the most sensitive point for all governments but particularly Austrian ones – finance. The famous tax-yield hike from 150 million to 280 million florins by 1858 was no solution set against military expenditure at 257 millions in 1855, a fiscal system unwilling and technically largely unable to tax capitalist income and a peasantry probably taxed to the limit. The most palpable signs of financial weakness were the discount on Austrian paper currency abroad, the so-called silver *agio*, and the periodic need in times of crisis to enforce the acceptance of this currency at nominal value. Fiscal policy thus amounted to a series of expedients to avoid bankruptcy and reduce the debt and the *agio*. Deflation, loans (most notoriously the 1854 forced loan of 508 million florins) and finally the selling off of state land and railways were successively sabotaged by the expenses of Crimean War mobilisation (1853–56) and war in Italy (1859). In 1858 40% of regular state income was going to pay off the state debt.

The root cause of these embarrassments – inability to control military spending – reveals the tension at the heart of neo-absolutism: between traditional and 'modernising' authoritarianism, bourgeois and aristocratic values. Franz Joseph's willingness to let Bach and Bruck do their thing was conditional on their streamlined state appearing to strengthen his own authority. The reservations of the high aristocracy against a fully fledged bourgeois programme come out vividly in the comments of the chairman of the ministerial conference, Archduke Rainer, on Bruck's proposal of 1857 for an Institute to finance the renting out of noble estates. It would, he wrote to a sympathetic Emperor, endanger the security of large estates, weaken the position of peasants whose well-being was vital for the army and in all likelihood provide a means for Jews to evade the prohibition on Jewish landed property which the regime – to the Rothschilds' fury – had enacted in 1853. Brandt has argued persuasively that the two elements in the ruling circles thus frustrated each other's developmental strategies, Bruck by rejecting the aristocrats' pleas for provincial mortgage credit banks, the conservatives by blocking plans such as that just outlined.[13] The key limitation on the ambitions of bourgeois 'modernisers', of course, was their exclusion from the spheres which Franz Joseph considered the most important in the state, the army and foreign policy.

An Empire Overstretched

To be sure, there was a powerful case to be made for the 'primacy of foreign policy' in a state like the Habsburg empire. Lacking internal solidity and exposed in the heart of the continent, Austria had survived historically through successful alliances within the European state system, most notably with Britain. Despite the latter's withdrawal from Metternich's would-be European Concert after 1821 the pattern of international politics remained on the whole favourable in the Pre-March years. The conservative alliance of the eastern powers, whereby Tsarist autocracy and Prussian deference kept each in basic sympathy with the Metternichean status quo, was not challenged by a sustained Franco-British entente. Thus despite Austria's growing domestic weakness her position in Germany and Italy could survive until and indeed beyond the 1848 revolutions.

In the 1850s all this began to change. Napoleon III, determined to upturn the 1815 settlement, was prepared to play the Italian nationalist card against its chief architect, Austria. Prussian subservience to Habsburg primacy in Germany could no longer be relied upon. Worse still, a new front now opened up in the Balkans as Nicholas I, taking for granted the acquiescence of the young ruler he had succoured in 1849, threatened to turn Russia's claim to protection of Ottoman Orthodox Christians into a scheme for the partition of European Turkey. War between Russia and Turkey (October 1853) and the Anglo-French decision to come to Turkey's aid (March–April 1854) faced Austria with an embarrassing choice. Russian occupation of the Danubian Principalities and appeal to Slav nationalism seemed to threaten her vital interests, and led her first to put pressure for Russia to withdraw from the Principalities, then to occupy them herself (August 1854). But having incurred Nicholas's bitter enmity thereby, should she go on to enter the war against him? Buol, the Austrian foreign minister, concluded a treaty with the British and French in December 1854, only to alienate them in turn by avoiding military action. In the Paris peace conference which concluded the Crimean war in 1856 Austria reaped the disfavour of both sides.

In retrospect, it seems that she was in a no-win situation. Mere neutrality appeared an inglorious option for a great power, and Buol feared that whoever won would take advantage of Austria's passivity to impose their own solution on areas of importance to her. But which way to jump? The pro-Russian alignment favoured by the military party was difficult to achieve honourably, given tensions over the Balkans: Austria's maturing interest in Bosnia as a strategic adjunct to Dalmatia and her fostering of Balkan Catholic Slavs and Albanians date from this time. Yet the full-fledged alliance with France urged by Austria's ambassador in Paris ran counter to Napoleon's ingrained radical streak, his patronage of Italian nationalism and his preference for an alliance with England. The logic holding Austria back from ultimate commitment is thus clear enough and was mirrored in the mutually cancelling emphases of Buol and Franz Joseph, for and against a pro-French alignment.

Perhaps Austria's chief mistake was her failure to carry Prussia along with her. The historian Srbik argued retrospectively for a policy of 'strict neutrality', galvanising German support to defend the interests of a Germanic *Mitteleuropa* and building on the Austro-Prussian treaty of April 1854.[14] Indeed, it is true that the conservative Frederick William IV of Prussia judged Austria's western alliance of December 1854, after Buol had promised him he would not turn his back on Russia, to be a breach of faith. A.J.P. Taylor has said that the real stake in the Crimean war was not Turkey, but central Europe.[15] The episode showed that the confederal Diet restored by Austria in Frankfurt was an impotent shell and that Austria had no policy for Germany except to expect the other German states, including Prussia, to follow her lead. This encouraged sharp observers like Bismarck in their willingness to envisage new structures for central Europe.

The balance of the war was thus strongly negative for Austria, both diplomatically and in costs of mobilisation. Russia turned to genuinely neutral Prussia and even to France. Napoleon III's influence swelled, enabling him to dally with nationalist movements ever more boldly, presiding over the autonomy of the Danubian Principalities (1859) and concluding a secret anti-Austrian pact with Cavour, the prime minister of Piedmont-Sardinia, in 1858. Faced with French diplomatic pinpricks Austria allowed herself to be provoked into declaring war in April 1859, partly because financial weakness suggested a quick knock-out blow against Piedmont before the French arrived. Unfortunately, the command of the Austrian troops was entrusted to an elderly and unwilling retired general, Count Gyulai. After the indecisive battle of Magenta, the Emperor assumed the command personally, only to be decisively defeated at Solferino in June, in a battle so bloody that it spurred the creation of the Red Cross.

The broader diplomatic background told the same tale of miscalculation. It was assumed that Prussia would have to take the field once Austro-German blood had been shed, but Prussia was offered only a share in the command on the Rhine front. She abstained. Kossuth's exiled emissaries, having found no entrée for their energies in the Crimean war, seized the new opportunity. While Klapka dangled before princes Cuza of Wallacho-Moldavia and Michael of Serbia a plan for Danubian confederation against Vienna, Kossuth himself secured French commitment to a free Hungary and a Hungarian Legion on condition of English neutrality, which, helped by the return of a Liberal government in London, he remarkably achieved. Garibaldi was to lead an incursion on the Dalmatian coast and strike inland to meet up with the insurgent Magyars of the Danube plains. But these combinations came to naught when Napoleon and Franz Joseph, each apprehensive of untoward complications, suddenly concluded the truce of Villafranca only three weeks after Solferino. In the final treaty of Zurich in the autumn Austria retained Venetia, but ceded Lombardy to Piedmont.

Military defeat and financial extremity – the convertibility of the Austrian currency only just achieved had to be abandoned – exposed the shifting balance of forces in the Monarchy. Depression from 1857 had seen a downturn in iron and textile production, adding the resentments of the new industrialists to those of artisans and aristocrats, and the sullen response of Franz Joseph's Slav subjects on his 1858 visit to Prague. These factors lay behind the

Emperor's manifesto of July 15, three days after Villafranca, with its reference to advancing domestic prosperity by the 'appropriate development of spiritual and moral resources' and to 'reasonable adjustments in legislation and administration'. It was to be the beginning of a tortuous path to constitutionalism.

Franz Joseph intended to yield as little as he could. The first changes were only in personnel, with the replacement of Bach and Kempen by conservative aristocrats; Count Agenor Gołuchowski, a Pole, became minister of the interior. Yet the underlying financial problem led Franz Joseph on 11 November 1859 to write to Bruck promising a committee to examine the state debt and a strengthened Reichsrat. After restrictions on Jewish acquisition of landed property were withdrawn, Protestant sensitivities courted and all crafts thrown open to free competition by the *Gewerbeordnung* of December 1859, the assembling of the 'extended Reichsrat' in May 1860 signalled, officially, the 'final act in the reform process'. Though it was hardly a representative forum, for its 38 extra members (including 10 non-nobles) had been nominated by the Crown, the invitation to non-bureaucrats to discuss public affairs amounted to a repudiation of the neo-absolutist course. Brandt has argued that for men like Bach neo-absolutism constituted an attempt to create the infrastructure of a bourgeois order in advance, for the time being, of bourgeois political norms;[16] this is reminiscent of Lenin's hope to build socialism in a still backward society. Events had shown that the Monarchy lacked the financial muscle to do this while maintaining its overextended positions in Germany, Italy and the Balkans. Defeat on an Italian battlefield was a harshly appropriate way of exposing this truth.

Constitutionalism at an Impasse: The Beginnings of Habsburg Pluralism

Each imperial concession was accompanied by the warning that it was the last. This was mainly illusion. Once the neo-absolutist chain was slackened there was no chance of preventing the contestants of 1848 from returning to the public stage, albeit in somewhat changed roles. The demands of the Germans and Magyars were no longer so radical and the Slavs, who had helped rescue the dynasty from them in 1848, were no longer its allies. The germs of a different solution to constitutional deadlock were thus present, in which Franz Joseph might do a deal with the dominant peoples at the Slavs' and Romanians' expense. By 1867 this had come to pass. However, the grudging spirit in which constitutionalism had been conceded left its mark on the outcome.

At first the pendulum swung to and fro as the Emperor measured advice from different quarters against the response of public opinion. Determined to preserve ultimate power, he had nonetheless deduced from earlier failure the need to compromise with the most powerful currents of his realm. These in 1860 appeared to be the neo-liberal tendency represented by the Austro-German bourgeoisie and the 'old conservative' wing of the Hungarian, Bohemian and Polish aristocracy.

Hungary's importance was self-evident. It had suffered the most sweeping changes under neo-absolutism and seen the strongest resistance to it. But collaboration had not been absent there. Aurél Kecskeméthy, Bach's confidant and government press official, recorded his joy on his appointment in 1854 at entering 'the great body which in fact rules over this vast empire', adding later, 'there is no Hungarian politics ... only an Austrian politics is possible'.[17] For most Magyar officials who served under Bach – still a majority in the two most Magyar of inner Hungary's five departments – the mood was doubtless more akin to the tight-lipped realism of Baron Zsigmond Kemény, that an Austro-Hungarian equilibrium was the best that could be hoped for, given that the Kossuthite independence course had proved an illusion. For the great bulk of Magyars, however, even this grudging acceptance of national setback was too difficult. The opposition was split three ways. Kossuth's emigration band succeeded in maintaining a high profile owing to its leader's charisma, but the very empathy with which Kossuth responded to the sociopolitical issues of the more advanced world around him distanced him from the Hungarian gentry from whom he sprang. In emigration he became a democrat, believing liberal goals only attainable with the support of the 'people' as a whole. The fruits of advancing industry offered hope of overcoming Malthusian pessimism, though their unequal distribution was the 'great social problem' of the age.[18] Along with the Polish Left in exile, Kossuth is the prototype of the twentieth-century refugee leader whose agenda straddled two worlds, one relating to western radicalism, the other to a far away homeland. His Hungarian programme of 1851 with its call for universal suffrage and Danubian federation retained the support of disadvantaged peasants and small gentry but aroused unease in the ranks of the *bene possessionati.*

Whatever their doubts about Kossuth's radicalism, the anti-Austrian resentments of the last-named had been exacerbated by their difficulties in making the transition to capitalist farming. Hence frustration and weakness held the middle gentry to the path of political abstention maintained by Ferenc Deák, in retreat on his Zala estate. Deák declined to follow Kossuth's progression from east European liberalism to democracy, like the other figurehead of moderate opposition, József Eötvös, whose *The Influence of the Leading Ideas of the Nineteenth Century on the State* (1851–54) identified the incompatibility of notions of equality or general will with true liberty as the fatal flaw in the French revolutionary legacy. No less a realist than Kemény, Deák saw the unlikelihood of returning the Austro-Hungarian relationship to the merely 'personal union' implied by the April laws of 1848. But until the Hungarians could negotiate on more equal terms he took his stand on the continuing validity of these laws and was thus condemned to passivity. Meanwhile, the potential strength of the moderate opposition lay in a national cultural identity that had emerged strengthened by misfortune. Curiosity about the national past launched the documentary series of the *Monumenta Hungariae Historica,* while the romantic historical novels of Mór Jókai (1825–1904) soothed the wounded national psyche. The consolidation of a self-standing culture through Magyar is no doubt part-explanation for the national tongue's growing attraction for young German speakers in Hungarian towns, reported to Kossuth at this time, and for the increasing identification of conservative magnates with the national cause.

It was this conservative group who in 1859–60 negotiated the restoration of Hungarian autonomous institutions and steered the extended Reichsrat's aristocratic majority towards a federalist resolution: the basis of the Diploma abruptly issued by Franz Joseph in October 1860. With the 'October Diploma' the constitutional era in the Habsburg Monarchy may be said to have begun. A pan-imperial Reichsrat of a hundred members with the right to consent to taxation and a brief on customs, trade, currency and communications; the grant of all competences not specifically assigned it to the Diets, which delegated its members; recognition of Hungary's special status by provision for non-Hungarian Reichsrat delegates to meet separately to discuss non-Hungarian matters: these were its principal features. Though this federal programme fell far short of

Deák's demand for the restoration of the April laws, he initially with-held a total condemnation. The decisive challenge to the October Diploma came from a different quarter, the Austro-German liberal bourgeoisie.

Why was this group able to exert such influence so soon after a decade of restrictive absolutism? Many 1848 liberals had continued to work quietly in the Bach administration, and men like the finance official Ignaz von Plener or the Prague law professor Leopold von Hasner responded to appeals to enter the political arena in 1860 out of a Josephinist sense of public service. But wider factors were at work. Better communications were fusing the local urban elites of the *Vormärz* into a common bourgeoisie, in which commercial and industrial elements now played a greater public role. There were 34 factory owners in the urban and rural curias of the 1861 Bohemian Diet. The taking down of the Viennese city walls in the late 1850s, and plans for an elegant inner ring road (the Ringstrasse) where they and army parade grounds had been, all suggested a certain updating in the balance of social power and values. Austro-German liberals shared too a confidence as members (as they saw it) of the senior branch of the great German nation, whose modern bourgeois civilisation they deemed the sole guarantor of progress for Slav peoples constitutionally incapable of achieving it themselves. The federalising October Diploma was thus particularly provoca-tive to Austro-German susceptibilities. Gołuchowski's replacement in December 1860 by the Diploma's leading opponent, Anton von Schmerling, with his predecessor's recently bestowed title of state minister, was a sign that Franz Joseph was becoming aware of the importance of not alienating German opinion. His rethink resulted in the 'February Patent' of the following year, which osten-sibly fleshed out the October Diploma but in fact turned it on its head. Where the Diploma had left the provincial diets all powers not specifically allotted to the Reichsrat, the Patent did the reverse, and with 343 members the Reichsrat became closer to a con-ventional parliament.

Suspicious of the federalist Diploma, Hungarian opinion was out-raged by the more centralist Patent. To be sure, Deák succeeded in getting a narrow majority of the resummoned Hungarian Diet to present its view in the form of a petition to the throne rather than a stark resolution, but the view itself was uncompromising: Hungary stood by the April laws. Since the royal riposte exasperated the Deákist 'petitioners' as much it did the 'resolutionists', the Diet was prorogued in August 1861. Hungarians boycotted the Reichsrat and bureaucratic absolutism was effectively reimposed upon them.

Unlike in 1848 this time the Slavs and Romanians followed the Magyars' anti-Vienna lead. The 1850s had brought small-nation patriots bitter experiences. Seeing for the Czechs only a choice between denationalising German liberalism or the Slavic Tsarist knout and putting his liberalism before his nationalism the disillusioned Czech activist Pinkas told his son not to bother about his father's cause.[19] In a world where power seemed to rule over ideals the Czech radical Sabina turned informer, the Croat reformer Tkalac looked to Bach. Czechs avoided Germanised *Gymnasien* and moved increasingly into the business field and private law, just as the concentration of Transylvanian Romanian patriots on legal studies was aimed at building an intelligentsia to face the new challenges. In the sterner climate Jakub Malý, member of a Czech conservative circle which included besides Professor Tomek several survivors from an earlier generation of 'national revival' like Kollár, Šafárik and Čelakovský, argued that nations could no longer claim rights simply for existing; they had to justify themselves by showing they had something to contribute to the current, changing world.[20]

In a way, this was quite a positive injunction. It showed that even pro-regime Czechs like Malý now viewed things from a Czech perspective rather than that of the official Austrian patriotism. Malý was right to say that the Czech nation had grown up and that its nationhood was no longer just the cause of a clique of enthusiasts. Ludwig Przibram's recollections of the Old Gymnasium in Prague in the 1850s show how the positive support which Czech had enjoyed in education before the return to absolutism had an impact surviving subsequent re-Germanisation. The Croat writer Šenoa's short story about a young Slovene devotee of German literature won by a pretty peasant girl to appreciation of 'our Prešeren', though propaganda, no doubt reflects how the achievements of the national movements up to and including 1848 could jolt complacent absorption into a German world.

In fact, at the grass-roots level national awareness had continued to grow after 1848. The Czechs again are the classic example. With the ending of patrimonial authority local power passed to peasant-dominated communal councils from the Germanised aristocracy, whose participation in public life often declined. Analogously, the withdrawal of aristocratic German speakers from the Union for

Bohemian Industry, though meant as disapproval of Czech national-ism, left the Union far more Czech than it had been before. The movement for agricultural improvement had a markedly Czech character, aided by a Czech medium agricultural school for peasants (1850) and the patriotic charge which devolved on the specialist press after the proscription of Czech political newspapers. Thus *Hos-podarské noviny* ('Economic News') and František Šimáček's *Posel z Prahy* ('Messenger from Prague'), both enhanced by the editors' reli-ance on scores of local correspondents, often teachers, urged peasants not to think a knowledge of German the only road to success. The Czech national implications of Šimáček's advocacy of democratisa-tion of local agricultural societies appear from the organised entry of seventy peasants into the Mladá Boleslav branch of the Patriotic Economic Society in 1857, forcing it to operate thereafter in Czech. In a period of apparent German ascendancy many profes-sional Czechs chose to return to a half-forgotten mother tongue, like the composer Smetana, while first-language German speakers opted for a Czech national orientation, including the founder in 1862 of the patriotic Czech gymnastic society or *Sokol*, Friedrich (Jindřich) Fügner. Such seemingly quixotic conversions testify to the importance of *local* majorities over wider trends in shaping indivi-dual identity.

In these ways the ground was prepared for the breakthrough of Slav movements with the onset of constitutionalism. The federalist stances affirmed in the resolutions of the Czech, Croat and Galician Diets of 1861 reflected the national–cultural reality which had actu-ally strengthened in the years of ostensible Germanisation. The Cze-chicisation of Prague as if overnight, with a nationalist town council (1860) and switch of guild bodies to functioning in Czech only, should be understood in the context of a bilingual city whose Czech majority was no longer prepared to accept the dominance of German in public life. Czech associations pullulated; in the Prague suburb of Smíchov twelve such bodies had emerged by 1869 which with the three German had a combined membership little short of half the male population of 7600. In Zagreb the demonstrative turning of the permanent theatre from German to Croat and the Diet's vote for a south Slav academy and university (1860–1); among Slovenes the dozen reading rooms by 1864 and advance from just three nationally conscious Reichsrat MPs in 1861 to a majority in the Carniolan Diet in 1867 showed other Slav peoples following parallel tracks. Only the primacy of local majorities can explain such rapid mobilisation.

After all, what idea could be simpler for Slav communities to grasp than the claim for language equality and local autonomy in a federal Monarchy? In the stronger Slav nations, among Czechs, Croats and Poles, the appeal to federalism was naturally reinforced by references to historic constitutional rights.

Thus at the dawn of the constitutional era three blocks confronted each other: Austro-German centralists, Slav federalists, and Magyars standing under the April laws. Many Slavs, disillusioned with Vienna, were now prepared to trust Magyar liberals' disavowal of their 1848 chauvinism. Though there were still Austrophile wings in the Croatian Diet and the Vojvodina Serb assembly that met in 1861 the leading politicians in each case – Bishop Strossmayer and the Novi Sad lawyer Svetozar Miletić – stood for conditional reincorporation in Hungary and Serb–Croat cooperation. The price was to be Croatian autonomy, and for the Hungarian Serbs counties redrawn to give Serb majorities, with Serbian as their official language. Slovaks demanded the same in their own assembly of the same year. Only the Transylvanian Romanians were unwilling to approve the reintegration of their province in Hungary, for they heard no encouraging noises from Magyar liberals: religious leaders looked to Vienna to support them in the Transylvanian Diet; 1848 liberals envisaged the province's repartition on national lines; while some radicals even hoped for a duchy of their own, uniting all Romanians in the Monarchy. This last involved abandoning the concept of Transylvania altogether, a bold step when all peoples if they possibly could tried to evoke some historic claim rather than rely only on a 'natural right' to self-government. Even the Slovenes, a non-historic people *par excellence*, toyed with the idea of dropping vain calls for 'united Slovenia' in favour of a historic 'inner Austrian' unit in the Alpine lands where at least they would form a substantial proportion (43%) of the population.[21] With Slavs' adoption of pro-Magyar positions came adoption of Magyar tactics. The Czechs too withdrew from the Reichsrat on the grounds that no parliament in Vienna had the right to legislate for the lands of the Bohemian crown, joining forces thereby with anti-centralist 'feudal conservative' aristocrats in strange alliance.

The efflorescence of manifestos from Slav nationalists failed to move the Austro-German centralists. State minister Schmerling's sang-froid over Magyar non-cooperation – 'we can wait' (September 1862) – applied still more to the non-dominant groups. In this opening phase of would-be constitutional life a gulf of contempt cut

Germans off from Slavs no less than in 1848. The memoirs of Ernst
Plener, son of Schmerling's liberal finance minister Ignaz and later
German liberal leader, record at length his efforts to educate himself
on the social question at this time, but of any attempt to understand
what lay behind Slav nationalism there is not a word. Partly it was a
matter of the dogmatic identification of civilisation with German culture, famously attacked by the Czech leader Rieger in the 1861
Reichsrat, but doubtless reinforced by sights such as Przibram
reported of bored Ruthenian MPs in sheep-skin national dress earning extra cash by railway portering and voting with their Uniate
archbishop who alone knew German. Partly, Germans might have
have weightier grounds for scepticism about non-dominant appeals
to the rights of the age. After all, Czech and Croat claims to accept a
central government but not a central parliament would make it in
practice very difficult to reform bureaucratic neo-absolutism; Romanian leaders opposed elections to the Transylvanian Diet in 1863
because they wanted the court to nominate the members and assure
them a majority. But the stereotype of reactionary Slavs mouthing
liberal slogans they did not understand was overdrawn. There *were*
true liberals in the non-dominant ranks: Miletić, for example, who
fought to transfer power in the Hungarian Serb community from
the Orthodox hierarchy to the educated bourgeoisie and urged that
non-Serbs must have the vote in the proposed Serbian autonomous
zone; or Canon Franjo Rački, the brains of the Croatian National
Party and formulator of the 'Yugoslav' idea of Serbo-Croat *rapprochement* – more so perhaps than his famous patron Bishop Strossmayer
whose offer to help fund a south Slav university and academy in
Zagreb electrified educated Croats. Above all, František Palacký,
despite his tactical alliance with the Bohemian aristocrats, could present his small-nation nationalism in a liberal perspective with a
sophisticated understanding of the dialectic between centralism and
decentralisation in the modern world:

> Railways and telegraph, almost miraculously overcoming natural
> physical barriers, draw all nations, all governments and all out-
> standing talents of the entire civilised world closer together ...
> But ... the more that which is related attracts the more that
> which is alien repels; the greater the nations' contacts the more
> they see, feel and become aware of their natural differences ...
> Hence the principle of nationality too has its eternal task in the
> economy of the world.[22]

Such was German complacency, however, that the eventual abstention of all other nationalities from the Reichsrat – except for the Transylvanian Romanians – did not invalidate it in their eyes. For the rump that remained there were enough problems for liberal consciences under Schmerling's regime, which lasted till 1865: the absence of ministerial responsibility, the disregard of the Reichsrat's right to approve the state budget, the growing financial crisis under Ignaz Plener's deflationary course, the proclamation of martial law in Galicia following the Polish uprising in Russian Poland of 1863. But the Emperor was more open to the wider realities, particularly the unsustainability of the impasse with the Magyars. Secret negotiations led to an article by Deák in the 1865 Easter number of *Pesti Napló* setting out his terms: a self-governing Hungary ready to accept more common affairs with a constitutional Austria than were allowed for in the April laws. While Franz Joseph hoped to bring the Hungarians into the ring on more restrictive terms than this, with a powerful role for the Hungarian Old Conservatives, Deák sought to retain the initiative by finessing between the conservatives and the 'resolutionists' to his left and bolstering liberalism in Austria as a safeguard for Hungary's freedoms. Schmerling's system had no place in either scenario. He was dropped for a federalist-tinged Bohemian aristocrat Richard Belcredi, who declared the operation of the February Patent suspended. What would replace it was to be considered by newly elected diets whose composition reflected the government's turning away from the German liberals.

When the Hungarian Diet met in December 1865 Franz Joseph's speech from the throne showed him to be still far from conceding the Deákists' case, though they had won 180 seats to the Old Conservatives' 21 and the resolutionists' 94: common affairs should be dealt with in a common parliament additional to the Austrian and Hungarian parliaments instead of in joint delegations of the latter, as Deák had proposed. In the trial of strength between monarchical and Hungarian claims head counts would not sway the balance, any more than in Prussia where Bismarck had just uttered his derisive *mot* on the decisive role of iron and blood *vis-à-vis* parliamentary majorities. Accordingly, all sides realised that the resolution of the Monarchy's constitutional disputes awaited the outcome of a bigger national problem than that of Slavs or Hungarians, in which Bismarck had a pivotal role. The key to central Europe's future still depended, as in 1848, on the course of the German question. It was about to be answered.

Towards Sadowa and the Compromise

In the traditional Prussian *kleindeutsch* view, the unification of Germany mimics the conventions of drama. On the one side is the young challenger Prussia, emboldened by economic leadership through the *Zollverein*, the rallying of the German liberal middle classes and Bismarck's fixity of anti-Austrian purpose to take up the national cause; on the other the ageing Austrian champion, isolated, wavering between different counsels and ill at ease with the new nationalist spirit, yet unable out of dynastic pride to acknowledge her loss of German primacy except on the battlefield. There was a 'struggle for mastery in Germany' and the right side won. Revisionist historiography disputes this. The pro-Austrian *grossdeutsch* cause, envisaging a central Europe organised on more federative, universalist principles than the Prussian-dominated nation-state of 1914 and 1939, would have been better for Europe and also for Germany, it claims. But pro-federalist interpreters are more prepared to rehabilitate Austria's potential cause than her actual policies. If the Austrian historian Helmut Rumpler denies these policies represented the malign will to anti-national power of the *kleindeutsch* view, it is because he stresses more their inconsequentiality. They were a prestige-driven attempt to keep Austria's end up in Germany rather than anything more purposeful.[23]

But maybe Austrian ineffectuality suggests difficulties in the *grossdeutsch* cause. Many revisionist views have a modern sub-text (interest in *Mitteleuropa* and European federalist visions in the wake of Soviet decline) and raise two problems when applied to the past. One is practical. Was the ancient German federal tradition embodied in the 1815 *Bund* reformable, so as to produce a polity agreed on Germany's defence forces in an unpredictable world, meeting burgeoning expectations for some kind of elected representative body, and reconciling the interests of Austria, Prussia and the middle-sized German states, the last of which (on whose mediating role much revisionist work is based) had their own diverging interests? Austria's main contribution to the plethora of plans on this score, the grandiose scheme for a congress of German princes to debate closer confederal union at Frankfurt in 1863, had been initially opposed by Rechberg, foreign minister from 1859 to 1864. As a proponent of the Metternichean tradition of partnership with Prussia, he realised Prussia would resent it as a bid to assert Austrian primacy on the German question. Franz Joseph and state minister Schmerling by contrast were initially enthusiastic; in the event King William of Prussia's refusal to appear negated the congress. Austria's proposals for a weak, indirectly elected assembly, chamber of princes and executive Directory of five (countering Bismarck's wish for Prussian parity in a dual Austro-Prussian hegemony) are open to the charge of 'organised impotence'.[24] Her attempt to join the *Zollverein* on its renewal in 1865 was frustrated by Bismarck's opposition.

The second problem of *grossdeutsch* revisionism is conceptual. What kind of system would a federal *Mitteleuropa* under Austrian aegis have been? For contemporary Austrophiles like Constantin Frantz, as retrospectively for inter-war historians like Srbik, the project meant in practice German dominance over all other peoples of east-central Europe and the Balkans. The tragedy of Austria's exclusion from Bismarck's Reich was thus to undermine German hegemony in the Monarchy and in the region as a whole. Yet the domestic difficulties Schmerling's German-tinged centralism was encountering showed how problematic such a (by no means benign) project already was before 1866; it was Austria's internal weakness which sabotaged her policies on the German stage. A desire to keep her hand in with German patriotic opinion led her, after the failure of the Congress of Princes, into a joint Austro-Prussian war against Denmark (1864) to prevent the integration of the majority German duchies of Schleswig-Holstein into the Danish state. Acquiring distant Holstein at the convention of Gastein in 1865 she failed to exchange it for a deal nearer to hand, largely because of the anti-Prussianism of foreign ministry official Biegeleben, the real conductor of Austria's German policy under Rechberg's weak successor. This gave ample openings for a man of Bismarck's skill to pick a quarrel with Austria over Holstein, go to war on the issue and drive her from a reshaped Germany. That Bismarck resorted to war after the Frankfurt Diet had, unsurprisingly, voted down his confederal proposals seems less important than that he had well prepared the diplomatic ground for the military outcome he had long envisaged.

For Austria faced the looming contest alone. Her international diplomacy had been lamed by Franz Joseph's hostility to the new Italian state, which his potential ally Napoleon III regarded as his protégé. Having rejected French advice to sell Venetia to the Italians and thereby remove the danger of a two-front war, against Prussia and the Italians, Austria ended up by offering to hand over Venetia anyway, but to France and for nothing. This was the key provision of the Austro-French treaty of 12 June 1866, by which France promised neutrality; the indirect transfer of Venetia to Italy, via France, was meant to preserve Austrian dignity. But Italy was already on Prussia's side, though in the war that followed she lost quickly on land and sea. The decisive encounter was on the Prussian front near the Bohemian village of Sadowa (Sadová), where von Moltke's troops with their breech-loading rifles pushed the Austrians into disorganised retreat with the loss of 43,000 men killed and wounded (3 July 1866). Napoleon III's decision not to intervene in a contest which had confounded his expectations screwed up the pressure on Austria to cut her losses. The Peace of Prague spared her territorial demands, which might alienate France, but excluded her from a reorganised Germany under Prussian leadership. Venetia, however, was lost. The Austrian northern commander Benedek was sworn to silence, then made the public scapegoat for the defeat, which ended his country's attempt to figure simultaneously as an Italian, a German and a Balkan power.

External defeat made it harder for Franz Joseph to resist internal reform, all the more so if, as suggested by the appointment of an anti-Prussian Saxon, Friedrich von Beust, as foreign minister in September, he wished to challenge the verdict of Sadowa. But at least Franz Joseph could choose between the conflicting programmes pressed upon him. Deák's proposals for a 'dualist' arrangement between Austrian and Hungarian constitutional states had the advantage of simplicity and, after Sadowa, moderation. By contrast, the Czech federalists' call for the division of the Monarchy into five units (two in the Alpine lands, Bohemia-Moravia-Silesia, Galicia and Hungary-Croatia) must have seemed neither simple nor moderate. Moreover, it was opposed by Poles and Croats, who thought they could do a separate deal with Vienna, and by many Slovenes. Austro-Germans were mainly centralist in sympathy but among them 'autonomists' under the Styrian leader Kaiserfeld were willing to accept the Magyars' dualist programme. Everything pointed to the latter course. In February 1867 Beust replaced Belcredi as state minister and Count Gyula Andrássy was commissioned to form a Hungarian government responsible to the Hungarian Diet. Following the Diet's implementation of Deák's programme, more or less, in Law XII, Franz Joseph was crowned King of Hungary on 8 June. The process was eased by the continuing haemorrhage of support among Kossuth's exiled ranks; Andrássy himself, condemned to death in 1849, had returned with a pardon only some years before.

The Compromise, as it came to be known, provided for three common ministries to deal with foreign policy, defence and the financing of the common government. In addition various economic issues, including the inherited state debt, tariffs, currency and certain indirect taxes, were declared to be 'matters of common interest' and made subject to negotiation with a view to common regulation every ten years, along with the 'quota' fixing each state's share of common expenses. As in Deák's programme, control over the common ministries was not to be exercised by any common forum but by 'Delegations' of the Austrian and Hungarian parliaments, meeting alternately in Vienna and Budapest and deliberating separately. Thus the Compromise presupposed a parliamentary regime in Austria but was itself concluded between the Hungarians and the monarch, building a certain assymetry into the Austro-Hungarian relationship from the start. This appeared in the less than rigorous procedure for its approval in Austria. Belcredi's promise that the deal with Hungary would be submitted for discussion to the Austrian provincial diets was effectively evaded; to smooth acquiescence, government pressure secured German majorities in place of the pro-federalist Czech majorities elected to the Bohemian and Moravian Diets after Schmerling's fall. Moreover, the Reichsrat's 'assent' to the Compromise was sought only after Franz Joseph had already ratified Law XII of the Hungarian parliament.

The Slavs in particular resented the bitter pill which condemned them to play second fiddle to the Magyars in Hungary and the German speakers in Austria. In late May 1867 Palacký and his son-in-law Rieger made a Slav pilgrimage to Moscow, symbolic of their fury rather than a commitment to Panslavism. In 1869 Rieger handed Napoleon III a memorandum urging French support for the Czech cause, without whose satisfaction Czech support against German expansion (threatening France as well as the Slavs) could not be expected. But the Czechs as yet had scant international purchase. The French ambassador to Vienna dismissed their claims of persecution as the greatest lie of the age and pronounced federalism the death-knell of Austria. Prague was under a state of siege throughout the late 1860s.

The pill was barely sweetened for Croats by the Emperor's requirement that the Hungarian government should negotiate separately with them over a kind of sub-dualist autonomy inside Hungary. The Hungarians held all the cards, particularly when they weaned away Serbian support for the Yugoslav alternative Strossmayer had secretly been negotiating with Prince Michael of Serbia – already before the latter's assassination in June 1868. (Serb–Croat relations in the 1860s showed all the wary ambiguities of 'Yugoslav' brotherhood, as shown by the Zagreb Diet's ingenious 1867 resolution that the Serb nation in Croatia was 'identical' and 'equal' with the Croat). Later packed with a Unionist (pro-Hungarian) majority over Strossmayer's National Party, the Diet duly passed the *Nagodba,* as the Hungaro-Croat compromise of 1868 was called, guaranteeing Croatian as the official language in Croatia and permitting a modest autonomy in non-economic affairs. The significance of this was undermined, however, by making the Croatian *Ban* the appointee of the Hungarian government. Hungary, too, by a subterfuge deemed illegal by all Croats, reserved the port of Fiume (Rijeka) to itself, as its outlet to the sea. Hungary's other non-Magyars, lacking recognised historical claims, received no institutional recognition whatever. Franz Joseph's request that Transylvania's reincorporation into Hungary should be carried out in a way satisfactory to all its nationalities remained no more than a pious hope. Solemn Czech and Polish declarations in their respective diets in 1868 and a small-scale Croat insurrection of 1871 in the Military Frontier (shortly to be abolished) were exercises in impotence. After a generation of constitutional and national upheaval Austro-German and Magyar liberals had been unequivocally rewarded and the others sent away empty-handed.

There was a certain logic in this. Franz Joseph had been on a learning curve since 1859, though, still unwilling to abandon the traditional pretensions of his House, he bore the major responsibility for the humiliation of Sadowa – 'even I could have done as well as that' was the comment of ex-Emperor Ferdinand in his Prague retirement.[25] Lacking the creative ability to shape events, he showed some shrewdness in adapting to them and settled after many zig-zags for the more plausible liberal rather than 'old conservative' course. Could aristocratic anti-absolutism work in Austria when something very similar had failed to keep abreast of events in pre-revolutionary France eighty years before? True, the conservatives found allies against centralism in the nascent nationalisms of non-dominant groups, but the alliance was hardly a natural one and Czechs and Poles, Croats and Serbs were often divided over the permutations of their rather vague federal creed. Czech state right was a historical theory; Hungarian state right was a political reality embodied in the institutions of a self-conscious nobility. Franz Joseph's choice in 1867 made sense at the time.

But to say this is to recognise that the Habsburg dynasty had compromised its hegemonic power and made an deal with the strongest of its subjects. This was the decisive turning-point in the modern history of the empire, which now became the Dual Monarchy, Austria–Hungary. The transition was not without promise. The aura of absolutism surrounding the dynasty had made constructive criticism of its policies difficult, particularly in foreign affairs. Moreover, the Austrian state continued to appear to most other Europeans something of a land apart, like autocratic Russia. Shorn of the incubus of irresponsible absolutism, Austria–Hungary might hope to develop on lines reflecting her civilisational superiority to Russia and underlining her relative Europeanism and normality.

There was another side to the coin. The realism of the Compromise was to reflect the balance of forces of the time. This balance could change. Whether the 1867 constitutional settlement would become a straitjacket or a framework for flexible adaptation was to be a key question for the future Dual Monarchy. Josef Redlich famously noted the fusion of bureaucratic absolutism and liberalism at the birth of the Austrian constitutional era, embodied in the ambiguous figure of Schmerling, a civil servant who said he would rather have been an army officer.[26] Could further compromises gradually infuse more democratic elements into the new system? This raised the issue of the hierarchical relationship between dominant and non-dominant peoples that the settlement entailed. How was the multi-national community to be maintained? If by the cohesion of a dominant culture, which the English liberal historian Lord Acton in 1862 saw in Austria's Germans, would such cohesion be weakened by the paradox of 1866–67 – that this group gained hegemony at home just when it was excluded from the heartland of German power? And if it was, would the fragility of Austro-German dominance spread ethnic resentment wider or spur efforts towards a more challenging alternative – a democratic association of equally entitled nations? In 1867 such questions still lay beyond the horizon.

Part II
Constitutional Monarchy, 1867–1918

7 Liberalism

The Dual Monarchy shuffled into life under a cloud of defeat, its starting point almost as elusive as that of the Austrian Empire it replaced. Practically speaking, it might be said to have begun with Andrássy's appointment as prime minister of a Hungarian responsible government on 20 February 1867; symbolically, with Franz Joseph's coronation in Budapest in June; formally, with his approval of the Hungarian Law XII/1867 in July or even with the Viennese Reichsrat's passage of the Compromise legislation in December. The first Austrian constitutional prime minister, Prince Karl (also Carlos) Auersperg, so disliked the new birth that he balked at its christening and the name Austro-Hungarian Monarchy (or Empire) was not agreed until after he had resigned. Eventually, Austria-Hungary emerged as the standard form. Common institutions like the army were dubbed first Imperial–Royal (or k.k. after the German words *kaiserlich–königlich*), and later Imperial and Royal (k. und k.) as Hungarians strove successfully for grammatical equality. Not till 1911 was the Imperial War Ministry to change its uncompromising title. While Hungary remained Hungary throughout, the rest of the Monarchy was recognised as 'Austria' only in 1917, remaining till then officially merely 'the Kingdoms and Provinces represented in the Reichsrat', sometimes, in a pompous unofficial neologism, Cisleithania or the lands on *this* side of the river Leitha separating the two countries. Nomenclature reflected the turning of the tables on the old centralised empire.

Yet the five decades of the Dual Monarchy which followed are perhaps the best remembered in the whole history of Austria and its neighbouring peoples. Vienna had known artistic fame before. Now, in addition to classic operetta, Mahler and Schoenberg, the architecture of the Ringstrasse, and the artistic outpouring of the *Sezession* and Viennese modernism came powerful intellectual currents. Dualist Vienna was home to the founder of modern psychiatry, Sigmund Freud, of linguistic philosophy, Ludwig Wittgenstein, of marginal economics, Karl Menger, of political Zionism, Theodor Herzl – as also to the young Hitler. For Hungary, too, these were the years of development of the Budapest metropolis, when regular translation made Hungarian authors like Jókai and Molnár part of the cultural patrimony of an international public. In the Czech lands the music of Smetana and Dvořák gave the Czech name a platform after two and a half centuries; in the south Slav world the graceful lower town of Zagreb arose and Ivan Meštrović's monumental sculpture lent an unwonted glamour on a world stage to the south Slav identity whose aspirations were becoming increasingly familiar through diplomatic imbroglios. The Dual Monarchy saw a time of unprecedented economic expansion and cultural advance. Its problems sprang from growth, not the stagnation of most empires of the past.

The constitutional arrangements by which the reconstructed Monarchy functioned imposed on the Emperor–King a dual persona vastly more complex and important than the dual religious allegiance of British monarchs or modern Belgian sovereigns' joint Fleming–Walloon identity. Franz Joseph often presided over the common ministerial councils which offered the only forum in which Austrian and Hungarian politicians debated together. On important issues he might also chair Austrian or Hungarian cabinet meetings, the latter in Hungarian – rare breaches of this language etiquette conveyed his deep displeasure. But crucial as the personal role of the monarch was, the Dualist system could not have survived half a century of accelerating change without some form of ideological prop going beyond dynastic tradition and deference. The rationale on which it was founded combined dynastic loyalty with the principle of German liberal hegemony in Austria and Magyar liberal hegemony in Hungary. Liberalism was made easier for Franz Joseph to swallow because, for all the excesses of the 1850s, the dynastic tradition was essentially Josephinist. Josephinist doctrines of legal equality, impartial administration and restraint on special interests of creed or class could be given a liberal twist if reinterpreted from the standpoint of the subject rather than the state. The converse was also true. Liberalism gained acceptability because it incorporated so much of the baggage of the central European bureaucratic state.

There were asymmetries in the underlying rationale of Dualism, however. While Magyars were to be dominant in their own state, it was supposed that they would ultimately defer to the German culture which dominated central Europe as a whole, not in the sense of full assimilation but through accepting the guiding role of German industry, German science and German letters in wider regional development. Had they not forgone their dream of a totally independent state? In this sense the ideological underpinning of the 1867 settlement had a German flavour. Austro-German liberalism latched on to Josephinist traditions but gave them the support of an entire civilisation. Behind the elegant massivity of expanding Habsburg cities, the railway network that fanned out to enclose the far-flung empire in its web of pastel-coloured stations, the richly moulded opera houses that sprang up in its provincial and would-be national centres, was the driving impetus of German bourgeois culture. In the early Dualist years this dominant role of Germandom was felt so strongly by some that Dualism was not inwardly accepted at all. Many Austro-German liberals remained unitarists at heart, while in military circles there was still a yearning for Austria to reverse her defeat in 1866 as leader of the German cause.

Though German cultural hegemony under Dualism ultimately had relevance for autonomous Hungary too, it impinged directly on the non-Germans of Austria. The early architects of Cisleithania intended the new polity to be as far as possible a projection of triumphant German *Bildung* and *Besitz*, the values of 'culture' and 'property' stemming from the German Enlightenment. So powerful was the impact of developments in an increasingly dynamic German world that Habsburg Germans found it almost impossible to distinguish between liberalism and German liberalism. Nor was this as immediately damaging to the role of liberalism as an integrative force as might be thought. German economic and cultural power was a fact, against which the habitual railings of non-German nationalists should not always be taken at face value, any more than twentieth-century denunciations of American imperialism. But in the middle and longer term Austro-German liberalism's inability to fashion itself a supra-national identity proved its Achilles' heel. Integration failed. The history of Dualist Austria thus becomes a study in the erosion of German liberal hegemony and the emancipation from it of the non-German nationalities, in a process in which political, social and cultural motifs intertwined. The result was the development of fully structured and culturally cohesive Slav communities increasingly resentful of their subaltern role.

The decline of German hegemony in Austria had important repercussions in Hungary because it upset the premise on which the Dualist settlement had been based: the cooperation of two dominant nations. Hungarian self-confidence and relative influence grew as a result, to the extent that some commentators have seen Hungary as eventually the dominant partner within the Monarchy. Insofar as this was so, however, and the point can be exaggerated, it reflected events in Cisleithania as much as in Hungary itself. This chapter and to an extent the second half of this book will be weighted to Austrian events not just because Austria was the more populous half of the Monarchy but because, if the above premises are correct, it was the fate of (Austro)German liberal hegemonic pretensions which provided the motor-force of events in the area as a whole. The starting point for discussion must therefore be an exploration of these pretensions, their doctrines, values and social base.

But before this is undertaken a very important background theme must be broached. The emphasis of the following pages will be on the Monarchy's domestic circumstances, partly because these aspects of its life have been less thoroughly treated in English-language surveys. However, Austria-Hungary's destiny continued to be interdependent with that of other European countries, and the historian cannot overlook this fact simply because the vast majority of Habsburg subjects did so. True, the crises which had threatened the state's very existence in mid-century had seemingly been resolved by the events of 1859–61, 1866–70 and 1870–71, and a Balkan settlement was to follow at the Congress of Berlin in 1878. The vital role of the Habsburg empire in terms of the European balance of power, which had underlain Anglo-French support for its integrity in its darkest hour in 1848–49, continued to be widely acknowledged in calmer times. As the Italian publicist Luigi Palma put it in 1883:

> The Austrian state is a geographical and historical unity of such a kind and is so placed between the Russian colossus and the might of Germany that with regard to general security its existence and bounds are of great interest not only to its own peoples but also to the other European states.[1]

Nonetheless, the case for Austria as a European necessity lost something of its force after the unification of Germany. It was no longer a question of Austria filling a central European vacuum into which otherwise either France or Russia might slip to achieve the continental hegemony. After 1870 the balance of power theme became narrower in focus: Austria-Hungary might be viewed by France as a counterweight to Prussia/Germany in central Europe or by Italy as a guarantee against anarchy in the Balkans. As part of an informal 'Crimean coalition' surviving the Crimean war she also offered the other interested parties, Britain and France, a barrier to Russian ambitions in the Balkans and at the Turkish Straits. Finally, for the

Three Emperors' League of the 1870s she played her part in affirming the League's conservative principles, particularly in its joint commitment against Polish nationalism. Thus the general strategic importance of the Monarchy in the nineteenth-century European state system can after 1866–70 be broken down into concrete roles in particular sectors. This way of looking at it leaves open the possibility that the Monarchy's real significance might come to lie not so much in the general over-arching indispensability still often asserted as in discrete sectoral functions that could more easily be eroded or displaced. Put bluntly, the failure of her mid-century German policy did tend to weaken her Europe-wide importance and give her more of a regional, especially a Balkan role.

These subtle and in the longer term disadvantageous shifts in the Monarchy's international position are, however, largely the fruits of hindsight. For most contemporaries foreign political issues held little interest. The reasons for this apathy towards foreign affairs were various. The former spokesmen for international radical links, scattered over Europe by the earlier explosions, either returned with the collapse of their causes, like a Magyar Klapka, a Czech Frič, or died in exile, like the Croat Tkalac. Meanwhile, the 1867 Compromise left the Emperor–King effective control of foreign affairs, so that the foreign political process, as conducted by him and his advisers, with occasional confidential discussions in the Common Ministerial Council and less frequent reports to the Delegations, remained veiled from public view. Conventional diplomacy was an arcane business, the last domain of the old aristocracy. Public indifference to it was reflected in other European countries.

Besides, Austria-Hungary was a huge realm which for its subjects offered almost a world in itself, like the Soviet Union before 1989. Civil service or academic or military careers could be pursued in successive different ethnic milieux without leaving the state. Despite the development of railways and steamships, foreign travel was still a rarity right up to 1914. Even the few thousand of the international elite in each of the Great Powers rarely left the beaten track of the Bohemian and south German spas, Switzerland and the Riviera. Franz Joseph never visited Britain. The mass economic migration that eventually set in mainly concerned the lower classes and took most of them to a New World long detached from the politics of Europe. Above all, the 1867 settlement had bequeathed the educated elites of Austria-Hungary a task which sufficiently absorbed their energies, namely to take over from the imperial bureaucracy the leading role in the building of bourgeois society. This was the liberal challenge.

The 1867 Settlement in Austria

The catastrophes of the twentieth century still cast their shadow over talk of German liberalism. Indeed, its Austro-German form may appear compromised from the start by the circumstances in which it gained what power it did, as a side product of a compromise between Franz Joseph and the Magyars. After Sadowa German speakers remained unhappy onlookers at the dismantling of the unitary 'Austria' where they had held pride of place. The young Ernst Plener chided his father for acquiescing in the new order: to imagine one could combine continuing imperial unity with two responsible governments was to hope to square the circle.[2] In the absence of the Czech abstentionists, who were even more strongly opposed to the Compromise, and with the Poles ranged on the government side to secure regional concessions, German liberals in the Reichsrat yielded unwillingly to a *fait accompli* which Magyars presented as simply a deal between themselves and their king.

Yet Austro-German liberals were not entirely passive in 1867. They took their opportunity to link the Reichsrat's ratification of the Compromise in December with a move for more far-reaching constitutional revision than Franz Joseph or his advisers had expected. A framework was created in many ways more liberal than in Imperial Germany which permitted a rapid development of a pluralistic society.

Thus the Reichsrat's 'Basic Law' of 21 December 1867 approving the Compromise was accompanied by four others that aimed to turn the largely consultative structures of 1860-67 into a fully fledged constitutional monarchy. In keeping with the doctrine of ministerial responsibility all royal acts were to require a ministerial countersignature. Though still indirectly elected by the provincial diets, the Reichsrat now gained the power to initiate legislation. It was flanked by an upper chamber, the Herrenhaus, which contained life peers nominated by the Emperor alongside hereditary elements. Civil rights, ignored in the October Diploma and February Patent, were elaborately listed and a special court (the Reichsgericht) was set up to superintend their observance, to be joined in 1876 by an Administrative Court (Verwaltungsgerichtshof) with power of redress against maladministration. Separate laws detailing rights of association and assembly complemented the press and communal laws of 1862 in fostering freer social development. With the reinforcement of the 'twin-track' principle in local government, elected communal and municipal (sometimes also, as in Bohemia, district) councils took control of a wide range of matters like education, health, welfare, transport, industrial policy and public amenities, alongside appointed government officials whose chief function remained control of the police. Legal issues, too, figured prominently in the settlement. Judges were made irremovable; administration and judiciary were finally separated at all levels, and the introduction of trial by jury in political press cases (1869) presaged its wider restoration in the 1873 code, which generalised oral, public procedure, separation of judge and prosecutor and other safeguards. The liberal state was to be the *Rechtsstaat*, the state based on law.

For all liberals the affirmation of the legal state required the removal of the special privileges secured to the Catholic Church by the 1855 Concordat, a veritable Canossa in their eyes. This was achieved by the three 'confessional laws' of May 1868 which ended Catholic tutelage of education, gave religious bodies (including Judaism) equal status, and restored civil marriage, thereby easing Catholic pressures on non-Catholics in mixed unions. Vienna was festively illuminated when the legislation finally passed. In 1870 the formal repudiation of the Concordat by the Austrian government followed the declaration of Papal infallibility at the Vatican Council, which most Austrian bishops had initially opposed. Indeed, the Austrian Catholic Church retained Josephinist instincts, so that liberal–clerical polemics lacked the intemperance of the later Prussian *Kulturkampf*. The fortnight's gaol sentence imposed on Bishop Rudigier of Linz for calling for resistance to the confessional laws (he was pardoned by the Emperor) remained an isolated case; the habits of a state church still held.

The recurrent liberal image of clerical darkness versus contemporary light encouraged the new regime to ambitious plans for education. The May 1868 school law made eight years of primary education compulsory. Regulations of 1872 approved the old 1848 demand for academic freedom in the universities. New universities were founded in Zagreb in 1874 and Czernowitz, capital of the Bukovina, in 1875. It was in its provision for education and civil rights that Austrian liberalism came closest to its self-image as a universal ideology of human freedom. Far more of the provisions of 1848 found embodiment in the Austrian settlement of 1867 than in the constitution of the German Reich; indeed, the Basic Law on human rights was often a verbatim repeat of the Kremsier draft, including the Kremsier declarations concerning equal rights to language use in school, administration and public life, which became its famous article 19. In the hands of liberal-minded figures like the old-1848er Anton Hye in the Reichsgericht, article 19 served as a basis for precedent-creating judgments broadening individual freedom, as Hye saw it, but in fact advancing the legal position of non-dominant groups.

That liberals were serious about systemic reform can be seen from their attempts to bring even so traditional a body as the army into their purview. The liberal war minister, Major-General Baron Kuhn (1868–74), strove to assert his, hence parliament's, authority over all other military authorities. The head of the army high command, Archduke Albrecht, became a mere Inspector-General, the General Staff was opened to all officers, losing its allegedly elitist function, the Emperor's military chancellery was denied direct contact with army organs. Military schools were to provide a more humanistic education to officers now charged (1873) to get to know their men and forward their personal development, while measures were taken to encourage more reserve officers (generally bourgeois professionals) to make the army their career. Regular barracks and mobile kitchens for manoeuvres made life more bearable for the troops. Much of this did not work. Kuhn was partly discredited by the poor mobilisation during the Franco-Prussian war and the failure to introduce more efficient breech-loading rifles quickly enough. Archduke Albrecht – whom Kuhn in his diary accused of 'Spanish absolutism, bigotry, ultramontanism, falseness and Jesuitness'[3] – together with the military chancellery head, Friedrich Beck, engineered Kuhn's fall. Beck, presiding over a restored General Staff from 1881 to 1906, became the formative influence on the Dualist army. His chief reform, the move to its territorial organisation (1882), showed, however, that times had changed. The old practice of moving troops about, as far as possible outside their home area, was based on ruling-class suspicions outdated in a more citzenship-orientated climate, where many conscripts' experience of army life was becoming more positive.

In other ways, too, the Austrian settlement of the post-Compromise years remained a liberal torso. Unlike the constitutions of France and Belgium following the 1830 revolutions, the 1867 'Basic

Laws' – the word 'constitution' was avoided for Franz Joseph's sake – formally exalted not the sovereignty of the people but the sacredness and inviolability of the monarch. The Reichsrat's right to impeach ministers was never concretised through a law on ministerial responsiblity and in practice they were responsible to the emperor who appointed them. Franz Joseph retained full control of foreign affairs and the army, subject to parliament's rights – not negligible but untested – to approve the number of conscripts, the military budget and treaties entailing public expense. Even on the religious front, a liberal preoccupation, a government memorandum of 1874 stated bluntly that the Catholic Church could never be, as liberal theory purported, a mere voluntary association like others; it would continue to have a special role in official eyes, reflected in the use of state power where appropriate to enforce church wishes – if only because such a relationship allowed the state a greater control over it than liberal associational rights implied. The qualification was significant. The state in constitutional Austria continued to enjoy an exalted authority out of line with western perceptions of liberalism. The ultimate state *Aufsichtsrecht* or right of supervision over all voluntary activity within its bounds was questioned by none. Through the traditional practice of the government informer or *Vertrauensmann* the authorities kept tabs on the social pulse and felt free to intervene against particular associations or organisations as they saw fit. Press freedom, likewise, was guaranteed by the 1867 settlement only 'within the law' and deposits could be forfeited for pieces held to counter the interests of the state; when the rebellious Crown Prince Rudolf contributed secret articles for a left liberal daily in the 1880s, the Jewish editor Szeps had to rewrite them because such criticisms would never have got past the censors. Ministerial decree (*Verordnung*) remained more pervasive than parliamentary law.

No doubt Josephinist tradition helped reconcile Austrian liberals to such practices. But so did the fact that they were exercised very largely against their own opponents, both national and social. In an eighteen-month period in 1868–69 Czech nationalist editors were sentenced to a total of 73 months in prison. Likewise, the Association Law of 1867 did not allow unions for purposes of wage-bargaining. Liberals preferred the model of the Workers' Educational Societies founded widely in the late 1860s under the influence of the community credit and self-help ideas of Schulze-Delitzsch. When several of these bodies in larger towns, however, began to move in a socialist (Lassallean) direction they too attracted the distrust of the authorities. Thus the Vienna Workers' Educational Society set up in 1868 called for universal suffrage, state aid to cooperatives and a militia in place of a standing army, a programme denounced by interior minister Giskra as utopian fantasy after 20,000 workers demonstrated in its favour in 1869. The eventual liberal response showed evidence of double-think. The 1867 Association Law was amended so as to permit wage-bargaining, which effectively legalised trade unions, but the Vienna Workers' Educational Society was dissolved on another pretext, as a 'political society'. Not only the working class but the greater part of the lower middle class was excluded from the conventional political process by the narrow electoral franchise, limited to payers of 10 florins in direct taxes. Even those who had the vote found their influence circumscribed by the weighted representation of the curias. Thus the seventy members of the landowners' curia to the Bohemian Diet in 1872 were elected by just 445 landowners; votes of urban voters in the third curia counted four times heavier than those of rural electors in the fourth. This was the liberalism of a propertied elite.

It is not surprising that native authors as much as outsiders have often contrasted the liberalism of the regime established in Cisleithania in 1867 unfavourably with its more robust west European models. But perhaps caution is necessary. Bourgeois parliamentarism was not really so strong in Louis Philippe's France or the aristocratic England Cobden and Bright failed ultimately to subvert; nor was nineteenth-century German-speaking liberals' preoccupation with establishing a *Rechtsstaat* (rather than seizing power) so much of a timid legalism as has often been implied: recent historiography has noted the successes of the *Rechtsstaat* framework in promoting a more modern and pluralistic society. Undoubtedly Austrian circumstances gave Austrian liberals' respect for state and imperial authority a special dimension: how easily, for example, the popular Viennese ebullience which greeted the passing of the 1868 confessional laws could change to a chastened, almost hang-dog mood when Franz Joseph appeared to show his displeasure. But what was the yardstick for judgement of an authentic liberalism? Austrian liberals themselves noted with some puzzlement that British practice was less sure a guide than they had imagined: ministerial responsibility for one was not really secured by the musty notion of impeachment borrowed from English history. Their conclusion, sensibly enough, tended to be that the English secret lay in English social development rather than exact constitutional prescription.

Indeed, nineteenth-century European liberalism as a coherent body of doctrine becomes more elusive the more it is examined. Easier to pinpoint are those people who thought of themselves as in some way part of the liberal current of history, and the social and historical context they occupied in various European countries. In this sense the best way to understand Austrian liberalism is to ask: who were the Austrian liberals?

Austro-German Liberals and Their Beliefs

Until recently discussion of Austro-German liberals remained limited both in bulk and perspective. Older works like those of Franz and Eder present a narrowly based bourgeois elite of academics, professionals and commercial elements, respectively dogmatic or unscrupulous, but sharing alike an interest in trumpeting nostrums drawn from other societies, particularly England, which were ill-adapted to Austrian circumstances. The critique contains truth but is somewhat overdrawn. The make-up of Austrian liberalism was not so different from that of the movements it sought to emulate; like them, if more briefly, it was for a time a hegemonic force whose influence went beyond the bounds of its bourgeois core. Indeed, in its 'golden age' from 1860 to 1880 it showed clearly the three-fold division visible in all major European liberalisms but most emphatically in the English exemplar: between aristocratic 'Whigs', mainstream bourgeois liberals and assorted radicals.

The English Whigs, essentially an upper-class grouping of conservative-liberal landowners, had clear Austrian counterparts. The brothers Prince Karl Auersperg, prime minister in 1868–69, and Prince Adolf Auersperg, prime minister from 1871 to 1879, certainly had the authentic *grand seigneur* quality of the English Whig elite. Friedrich Beust for one doubted the ideological convictions of Prince Karl Auersperg, with his monocle and stiff nasal speaking style, his private stall at the Noble Theatre in Prague, his sense of family honour – he was responsible for the death of a favourite nephew by pushing him into a fatal duel. Yet there were two things only of which Karl Auersperg declared he was proud shortly before his death: the 'enlightened' tradition of his family and his role in passing the confessional laws of 1868. From a distant relative, Count Anton von Auersperg (the poet Anastasius Grün), came the most famous definition of liberalism in this period, significantly vague and attenuated as it was:

the man of liberal temperament was the man who honoured what was right even if he found it where he did not expect to find it; for freedom was inseparably bound up with the sense of the rightful, permitting 'the peaceful development of reform' which would avert the 'revolutionary upheavals' of the previous century.[4] If a tempered rationalism was one half of Austrian Whiggery, the other was allegiance to Austria itself and the imperial idea, given a certain constitutional twist. The Emperor, having granted constitutional liberties and standing above the parties, now willed parliament to exercise them by voting according to its own conscience. Thus understood, imperial authority became a symbol of the Austrian identity which remained the constitutional aristocracy's strongest emotional commitment. As Karl Auersperg floridly put it in 1862:

> Pledged unshakably to the endeavour to nurture and increase the strength and influence of the imperial state, the Herrenhaus will uphold before all the power of its Supreme Lord, because its members are ineluctably convinced that the monarch's power is the mighty lever for the advancement of the interests of the peoples entrusted to him by the grace of God and for the achievement of political concord and political equilibrium among all ethnic groups of the far-flung empire.[5]

Favoured by the curial system, landowners of similar centralist, German sympathies were organised in the Reichsrat and the provincial diets as the club of the Constitutional Large Landowners, one of the constituent groups of the ruling liberals.

The core of the liberal party, however, was middle-class. The *Bürgerministerium* (bourgeois ministry) of 1868 was so named because that is how contemporaries saw its essential focus of gravity, though three of its nine members were aristocrats. Franz Joseph's amusement as finance minister Brestel dropped his dagger between his legs during the cabinet's ceremonial presentation to him is a piquant detail of the social symbolism of transition. The bourgeoisie that the new ministry represented was broader than had previously played a role in Austrian politics. The industrial and commercial classes now appeared in some force, just as with their luxurious apartments along the emerging Ringstrasse they were muscling in, as it were, on the old privileged orders' terrain of social display. In the Schwarzenbergplatz palace of the former locksmith Franz Wertheim, designed by the architect of the *Votivkirche*, the production of Wertheim's

twenty-thousandth safe in 1869 was celebrated with a specially commissioned polka score from Johann Strauss the Younger. Wertheim
was a Vienna councillor and Lower Austrian Diet member before
becoming an imperial councillor in 1871 and holder of the Iron
Crown, V Class. Other industrialists who underwent ennoblement
and ended up in the upper chamber included the steel works owner
Franz Mayr and the Protestant sugar beet manufacturer Alexander
Schoeller. That said, businessmen did not aim for the heights of the
political world. Though at 17% they formed by far the largest single
group of readers of the leading liberal daily, the *Neue Freie Presse*, in
the mid-1870s, they provided only one figure among liberal parlia-
mentarian chiefs, the Moravian sugar beet manufacturer Alfred
Skene, of Scottish descent.

The great bulk of these liberal leaders came from educated professionals. The role of Josephinist officials like Ignaz von Plener declined
relatively, while that of private lawyers, academics, doctors, journalists and other writers and publicists increased; Eduard Herbst, generally acknowledged as the leading figure in the liberal
parliamentary party in the 1870s, was a lawyer. Free professionals
were to account for two-thirds of the higher taxpayers of Graz by
the end of the century. Education was the common denominator.
At a time when Beust was planning the creation of new peers to
ensure the passage of the Compromise legislation through the Herrenhaus in 1867, the *Neue Freie Presse* called for political recognition
of these strata by opening the upper chamber 'to the nobility of the
intellectual bourgeoisie, the nobility of bourgeois labour, the nobility
of science and art'.[6] To a considerable extent this was done. Six professors of Vienna University alone were called to the Upper House
between 1867 and 1869 (one was a rogue conservative); six also sat
in the Reichsrat in the parliament of 1867–73. The strong representation of historians among them (Adolf Beer, Alfred Arneth, Franz
Krones) matched the trend elsewhere for the political salience of historians in liberal movements, a Dahlmann and Gervinus in Frankfurt in 1848, a Macaulay in England, a Guizot in France, not to
mention the Slavs Palacký and Rački in the Monarchy itself. But liberalism's rationalist base had an appeal to scientifically trained intellectuals, too. Rokitansky, first elected Rector of Vienna University
(1852), President of the Academy of Sciences (1869–78) and head of
the Vienna Medical Faculty as student numbers rose from 590
in 1859 to 2248 in 1885, was perhaps the most forceful exponent
of liberal principles in the Upper House. Eduard Suess, professor of

geology at Vienna from 1867, was another whose enthusiasm for scientific method – and shock at popular contempt for it – helped propel him into public life, as member successively of Vienna city council, the Lower Austrian Diet and the Reichsrat.

Perhaps the most characteristic feature of early Dualist liberalism was the heightened role of the press. The mushrooming new organs were, as elsewhere in Europe at this time, very largely liberal, if in the specifically Austro-German way which has been described. 'Austria as a great power, Austria as a pillar of defence for Germany, Austria as a constitutional state, Austria great, German and free – this is the basic political concept which enthuses us and will guide us in all things', as the opening number of the *Neue Freie Presse* intoned in 1864.[7] By 1874, the circulation of the *NFP*, at 35,000, had been overtaken by another liberal paper, but it remained the most influential, with some 500–600 employees, 200 of them domestic and foreign correspondents, and strong links with literary and academic circles. Liberal editors hobnobbed with liberal politicians in Vienna's Café Daum. In this way the liberal press provided a network which drew together the different strands of the expanding liberal world, creating and subserving the public opinion which liberal theory put at the heart of its social vision. Though from 1869 Catholic press associations were formed in several of the leading towns of the Monarchy their papers only had a fraction of the circulation of their liberal rivals.

What were the ideas propagated by the expanding liberal media? Liberals believed that they were living in a new epoch freed from the shackles of age-old ignorance and bigotry. Politically, the rejection of past prescription meant that the new, unitary constitution could not be impugned by federalist arguments based on historic provincial rights. Economically, it meant *laissez-faire* and self-help. 'The state has fulfilled its task', claimed the Lower Austrian Chamber of Commerce in 1867,

> if it removes all obstacles to the free, orderly activity of its citizens. Everything else is achieved by the considerateness and benevolence of the factory owners and above all by the personal efforts and thriftiness of the workers.[8]

Culturally, it meant an often blunt challenge to the intellectual claims of religion and its public role. 'Knowledge and faith are two entirely different things', argued Rokitansky; 'knowledge is grounded in fact, faith on authority. Knowledge rules progress; faith may make claims only in the internal domain'.[9] Professor Beer, himself of Jewish origin, could call the 1870 proclamation of Papal infallibility a declaration of war on the civilised world.

There was a certain air of generality about these notions. Outside business circles liberals' knowledge of the economic principles they invoked tended to be shallow and formulaic, conditioned by a sense that these principles – like opposition to protection – applied in their full force only in 'advanced' industrial states to the west. The felt disjuncture between Austria and 'modernity' helps explain why conservative liberals like Giskra made bold to deny that there was a western-style 'social problem' in Austria at all. More positively, *laissez-faire* never meant an unwillingness for infrastructural improvements at public expense; here liberalism stood for the cult of modernity and science-based utility but also, it should not be forgotten, for the conviction that new knowledge could and should be used for human betterment. The liberal scientist Eduard Suess, whose campaign for a better Vienna water supply sprang from a personal sense of responsibility for the prevention of typhoid, records in his memoirs how a book-seller colleague on the Vienna city council wept after the final vote approving the project was taken, saying 'Now I can die happy, for I have contributed to a good cause'.[10]

As befitted a largely bookish community, bourgeois liberals put great weight on self-development through *Bildung*. Education (only a tame equivalent of the German word) was to be the solvent of the tensions in liberal philosophy, enabling transition to the future utopia from the patent inequalities of the present. To be sure, the conception was hierarchical. Improved primary schools would prepare the masses for humble roles as agriculturalists, artisans or workers, with trade schools and *Bürgerschulen* training a somewhat higher level of commercial or clerical skill. The higher education sector, fed from the classical *Gymnasien* and to a lesser extent the *Realschulen* (which also taught Latin but more science and no Greek), remained the domain of an upper middle class which now saw itself as an aristocracy of the spirit. In an 1885 memorandum ridiculing the Austrian practice by which mere Extraordinary Professors could sit and vote in professorial conclaves the famous Vienna classicist Theodor Gomperz condemned a false democracy which permitted those who had not reached the top of the greasy pole to opine on the affairs of their betters and cast votes which could not be objective but only the expression of the group interest of their kind. It was the radical liberal

John Stuart Mill's error, said Gomperz, to pay too much attention to the struggle of interests, as opposed to the ethical cultivation of the individual on which true social reform depended.[11] The liberals of Gomperz's *Bildungsbürgertum* were indeed often formidably talented. Cajetan Felder, mayor of Vienna, was variously a lawyer, university teacher and interpreter (he spoke thirteen languages), a world traveller, author of a standard work on butterflies, collector of fifty thousand portraits and at the end of his days a member of the Austrian Academy of Sciences. Moreover, Felder had scaled Etna in his youth, Ernst Plener Mont Blanc; Gomperz was proud to have been among the first up the Grossglockner. His comparison of the 'sublimity' of the glacier world to the pleasure of great art shows how liberals found substitutes for the emotive power of the traditional religion they had usually rejected.

The elitism of bourgeois liberals was increased by their close sense of association with a German-dominated empire. The state belonged to them in a way it could not to a Czech or a Pole. 'The Germans in Austria', exclaimed Professor Beer in the Reichsrat in 1884, 'start from the conviction that the state comes first and then the liberty of the individual'; they were 'sustained by a single thought, by the Austrian state idea'.[12] Whether Slav peasant peoples were inherently incapable of developing along modern bourgeois lines was a moot point in German periodicals. Education minister Stremayr's parliamentary remarks of 1876, in allowing the possibility that Slavs could better themselves through German, were therefore as conciliatory in German eyes as they were unacceptable to Slav nationalists:

> They [the non-Germans] can preserve their nationality, can cultivate their language ... but they must nonetheless acknowledge, gentlemen, that it would be truly an enemy of their own nationality who would deprive the Czech, be it the lowliest in the land, of the possibility of rising to a position where he could, through use of the German language, participate in the great affairs of the empire.[13]

The elitist sense of belonging to the vanguard of culture was probably the trait which most united the Austro-German bourgeoisie, for their essentially attitudinal 'liberalism' involved little uniformity on other core values. Quite rare was the sceptical view of government authority common in west European liberals. That it was to be found in Eduard Herbst helps explain why many of his contemporaries condemned him as doctrinaire. A few, like Adolf Fischhof, author of an 1878 work on federalism, or Moritz von Kaiserfeld, leader of the Styrian 'Autonomists', diverged from conventional centralism. Degrees of anti-clericalism varied from forthright support for a 'free church in a free state' to the more traditional Josephinism of an Ernst Plener and the caution of an Arneth, who held shrewdly that the clergy should not be too deeply antagonised because the end of feudal authority had increased their local influence. Gomperz's individualism may be contrasted with Plener and Beer's explicit criticism of this term, and liberal 'triumphalism' with the influence on many liberals of Schopenhauer's pessimistic doctrine of individual will – as an affirmation of suffering man's existential quest. The self-conscious high-mindedness of many, too, was belied by others' greed and corruption, exemplified in minister Giskra's comment on the 100,000 florin bribe he took in the Lvov–Czernowitz railway affair – that it was only the bourgeois version of aristocratic tipping!

However, in the hour of its bloom, liberalism was not just an elite affair. It had wide influence in the lower middle classes, and even on the peasantry in some regions. Particularly in the larger towns, the mood of these artisans, inn-keepers, petty officials and merchants, journalists and the like was sharper than among more prosperous bourgeois, their endorsement of 1848 was less qualified and their satisfaction with the 1867 settlement correspondingly reduced. There is a case for arguing that these groups indeed were no longer liberals but 'radicals' or 'democrats', the latter term given clear currency in the many Democratic Clubs established in 1867 in Vienna. It seems, however, truer to contemporary perceptions to see them as branches of a still common movement, like the radicals in the British liberal movement or a Gambetta in France. It was in the name of 'the liberal party' that the *Neues Wiener Tagblatt*, favoured paper of the Vienna lower middle classes, accepted the 1867 constitution, with the intention of improving it so as to make it representative of 'the people' rather than 'property' alone. Calls for a broadening of the franchise, more checks on church power, stronger safeguards for the freedom of press, assembly and association, even a just solution to the 'social question' were not essentially different from a consequential liberalism. In 1867 ideas of solidarity within all sections of the middle class and beyond still held sway.

The fate of these solidarist ideas is crucial to an understanding of Austrian liberalism's subsequent fortunes. The Dualist era began with a dramatic explosion of working-class organisation, with work-ers' educational societies in 22 towns by 1869 and Democratic clubs and Viennese workers cooperating vigorously in mass meetings urging radical liberal issues; the great demonstration of December 1869 was initially proposed by the leader of the Vienna democrats. The upper middle classes, too, sought to influence workers' attitudes, through bodies like the Union for Economic Freedom (1867) which suggest their initial belief that they spoke for general interests and that only ignorance of economic laws accounted for socialism. How-ever, as it became apparent that the workers' organisations were fall-ing into the hands of Lassallean socialists they were increasingly harassed, culminating in the trial for treason of the Vienna Educa-tional Society's leaders in 1870 and the dissolution of the society, whose branches had 35,000 members. The Paris Commune of 1871 only swelled liberals' anti-socialist paranoia – though institutional repression was led by the non-liberal interior minister Count Taaffe and was mainly opposed by the liberal press: bourgeois juries fre-quently acquitted socialist editors. Meanwhile disengagement of democratic and petit bourgeois elements from the workers' cause fol-lowed gradually, fuelled by mounting suspicion on both sides. It was more or less complete by 1873.

In differential reactions to the emergence of a working class in these years can be seen the germs of the break-up of ideas of a united middle class serving the interests of the whole society and the move towards quite separate upper-middle-, lower-middle- and working-class politics by the 1890s. Another incipient line of fissure was the national question. 'Democrats' and other radicals felt that on this as other issues men of goodwill should strive for reconciliation, but their support of the interests of the 'people' over those of the elites made them naturally partial to the appeal of national over more traditional loyalties. In the liberal camp as a whole a tendency emerged, the *Jungen*, which identified its 'youthful', progressive energies with a heightened stress on Germandom and came increasingly to dominate the annual liberal party conventions. In 1873 supporters formed a separate 'Progressive' club in the Reichsrat.

Liberalism was therefore institutionally splintered. There was no organisation based on formal membership and local branches in the modern sense, coordination being limited to electoral committees of liberal notables operative at election times and then at most at a pro-vincial rather than all-Austrian level. Once elected, members of par-liament joined parliamentary fractions or 'Clubs' expressing their

particular shade of opinion. Thus in 1873, the first parliament to be
directly elected, the liberal or Constitutional Party, as it named itself
officially, had three main clubs, those of the Whiggish large landowners, the centrist Left and the Progressives, in addition to five
Democrats. The Vienna town council was still more diverse. In one
sense, this liberal fragmentation reflected a measure of strength.
Throughout Europe at this time liberals were slow to organise as a
single party because they felt themselves to be the expression of an
age, speaking for all. Yet in Austria the sheer number of fronts on
which liberals felt called to fight, against upper class 'reaction',
priestly 'ultramontanism', 'phraseological' republicans, 'street
demagogic' workers – in the *Neue Freie Presse*'s polemical language – reflected the region's belated development *vis-à-vis* western
Europe. Traditional social forces remained stronger, while a new
socialist foe, conjured up in part by German intellectuals' observa-
tions of western bourgeois society, had had time to mature and
could not so easily be assimilated into an itself infant liberal political
culture. British liberalism developed over decades before it faced a
fundamentally hostile socialist critique. Austrian liberals faced a
treble whammy from left, right and, beyond, the 'Cloud-cuckoo-
land' of Slav nationalism.

It is hard not to see in the hectoring scorn of the *Neue Freie Presse*
a certain iron in the soul of Austrian liberalism almost from the
moment of its birth, beset as it saw itself by so many interrelated
threats. For ultimately liberals believed the hydra had a single
brain. 'Reaction' through demagogic and federalist slogans could
turn workers and Slavs into grist for its absolutist mill. Such paranoia was not dispelled by the clerical *Vaterland*'s cry in 1868: 'For
the present ruling class we want humiliation, comprehensive
humiliation.'[14] The fraught atmosphere in which liberals achieved
hegemony made it very hard for them to see that hegemony as an
instrument by which, as in liberal theory, middle-class wealth,
education and power would eventually spread down to the population at large. Liberal values came to be a talisman to be jealously protected rather than a trust to be shared. Hegemony
made liberals, at least of the *Neue Freie Presse* stamp, alternately
arrogant because it was theirs, and aggressively fearful because it
was challenged. This was ironic because the hegemony of liberal
values was for a time real, even in the despised non-German
lands, and differently regarded might possibly have provided a
basis for better things.

Liberalism in Non-German Lands in the 1860s and 1870s

Reaction had a natural home in the Monarchy's Slavic provinces, in the German liberal view. In fact, there too for the most part a free press, free association and better education were the slogans of burgeoning lay intelligentsias, mimicking with varying degrees of intensity trends in the metropolitan core. Only in Hungary did a markedly distinctive version of liberalism emerge, and one whose existence was recognised by Austro-Germans. Indeed, it aroused in them mingled feelings of admiration, envy and censoriousnes. Noble-led Hungarian liberalism inherited from the centuries-old struggle against Habsburg absolutism, now crowned with apparent success, both a robust confidence and a cavalier forthrightness in pursuit of the rights of the Magyar state *vis-à-vis* non-Magyars. Austrian liberals smarting at the loss of hegemony in the monarchy as a whole found salt rubbed in the wound as Hungarians lectured them for failing to curb pan-Slav fantasies in their half of the empire as they had been suppressed in Hungary. From the perspective of Vienna Hungarian liberalism seemed both fraudulent and effective, a double irritant indeed.

It was the role of the 'gentry' in this liberalism which was its most characteristic feature. The gentry were the old middle nobility, hailed by Kossuth as the heart of the nation. Adversely affected by the post-1848 land reforms, which had forced great numbers of them to sell up estates they could no longer afford to run, they found outlets in the administrative apparatus of the new autonomous state, which doubled in size by 1875. About half of central government civil servants at the grade of secretary and above in 1867 were nobles, only 10% of whom were landed. Wealth and education were still too narrowly distributed to provide for a broad-based bourgeoisie. About 200,000 people in all paid taxes derived from land, industry and artisanal work in 1868, while of the 128,000 educated enough to be considered members of an 'intelligentsia' in 1884 only 25–30% were calculated to be book-readers. As one-tenth of these actually wrote books themselves the picture emerges of a very small segment of the population mutually sustaining a cultural life detached from the preoccupations of the great bulk of the population. In his memoirs the Orientalist and traveller, Ármin Vámbéry, painted a vivid picture of cultural lethargy and parochialism even at the level of the Hungarian Academy of Sciences in the 1860s. Such characteristic institutions of *haut bourgeois* enlightenment as the Academy thus still reflected the aspiration to cultural modernity rather than its reality.

To an outsider like the journalist Ludwig Przibram at Franz Joseph's Hungarian coronation, the nobles decked out in bearskins or carrying animal heads who rode by in procession reflected their country's medieval values; he saw no bourgeois elements in the ceremonial.[15]

Yet the successful and patriotic career of Vámbéry, the son of a rabbi, showed the attractions Hungarian liberal nationalism could have for ardent young men of urban German and Jewish background – German speakers had long had a Hungarian political identity and Jews found noble liberalism a more congenial creed than the anti-Semitism of traditional urban burgher elites. In the assimilation to Magyardom of these groups lay one line of potential recruitment for a new Hungarian middle class though one, as Vámbéry's memoirs show, which would retain a strong sense of being outsiders.

Dualist Hungary had to accept common institutions with Austria more developed than in the 1848 April laws on which Deák had originally stood. But the Budapest government retained control of the voting, recruitment and provisioning of the Hungarian soldiers of the common army; and it gained the right to set up a separate Hungarian force, the *Honvéd*. Prime Minister Andrássy, once hanged in effigy for his rebellious role in 1848–49, made himself the channel through which the common ministers corresponded with Hungarian ministers, who unlike their often bureaucrat Austrian counterparts, followed the English practice of always sitting in parliament. Libertarian traditions asserted themselves, too, in a relatively greater liberty of the press and judiciary, which did not always accept government fiat, and the common habit, as in eighteenth-century England, for leading politicians to seek to prove their popularity by winning their seats in 'open' constituencies rather than the Hungarian equivalent of 'rotten boroughs'.

Yet where they deemed it necessary Hungarian politicians enforced their wishes with an unsqueamish ruthlessness. They bullied the Croats, suppressed movements of peasants who thought the new era opened up a new social dispensation as in 1848 and prosecuted local government organs which publicised Kossuth's opposition to the Compromise. As in eighteenth-century England – again – the impossibility of allowing an opposition victory, whether of Jacobite Tories or Kossuthite nationalists, meant a parliamentary system based on permanent one-party rule, sustained through partially managed elections. Alongside the two hundred or so open constituencies where voters were too numerous to be effectively controlled, there were enough in the government's pocket to ensure the pro-Dualist Deákist Party a substantial majority, often in non-Magyar parts of the country, to counteract the popularity of the opposition in the open constituencies of the Magyar central plain. When the opposition nonetheless made a gain of some forty seats in the 1869 elections the government's response was a law of 1874 slightly tightening the franchise, which at roughly one in four adult males remained static till the First World War.

It was characteristic of this society that the main advocates of a fuller liberalism, Ferenc Deák and the minister of education and religion József Eötvös, should also have been nobles. For supercilious Austrians were wrong to think there was no liberalism in Hungary worthy of the name. The vision of a better society, in which the motherland would claim the heritage of the most advanced societies of the day, has haunted 'modernisers' throughout the recent history of eastern Europe, and the 'reform period' of 1825–48 still cast an afterglow on the early years of Dualist Hungary. Deák himself preferred the role of elder statesman to that of minister, throwing his prestige in the scales when he thought the liberal conscience of the majority party he had created was in danger, not always successfully. Thus while he advocated the idea of the 'unitary Hungarian political nation' against non-Magyar federalism, he believed that the state should not fund a Magyar language 'national theatre' while refusing support to a Serbian one in Novi Sad. He failed to convince his colleagues.

Eötvös, as a minister and president of the Academy of Sciences, had more direct opportunity to shape the new polity. 'The nation must take its part in the great struggle whose aim is the establishment of civil freedom and western civilisation in this part of Europe', he lectured the Academy.[16] He shared the positivist creed of the day that laws of society awaited discovery which would be no less beneficial to mankind than the laws of science had proved. Citizens should be equipped to play their part in the new society by an expanded educational system, in which state schools would be founded to supplement existing provision (largely church-based) where needed; an approach quite similar to that of Forster's Education Act of 1870 in England and Wales. The churches should be democratised, with lay majorities in church assemblies responsible for the administration of church schools and property, and episcopal control of Synods charged with specifically doctrinal issues. Justice would be done to Hungary's ethnic mix by a nationality law granting local authorities the right to ordain their own language of business, with safeguards for minorities, while making Magyar the language of the central organs. The concept of the liberal national state, conceding substantial autonomies to its subjects in school, church and nationality, but retaining the right of supervision in the interests of the whole, was central to Eötvös's vision of a modern society.

A creditable amount of this was achieved before Eötvös's death in 1871 in the School Law, the Serb and Romanian Church Statutes and the Nationality Law, all of 1868. Some aspects proved impracticable. Leaving the financing of the new state schools to the 'honour' of the local communes ran up against their poverty and lack of public spirit. The Nationality Law did not satisfy non-Magyars, who had demanded a form of territorial autonomy based on the redrawing of county boundaries along ethnic lines; yet it went too far for many Magyars. Eötvös was aware of the limited resources of expertise and goodwill at his disposal, at one point beseeching his son on his studies in Germany to put him in touch with any able young Hungarian he might meet there. Indeed, his opposition to federalism in multi-ethnic Hungary, which he recognised to be the truly liberal solution, was based on the fear that the Magyar minority was as yet too weak to control a decentralised Hungary. Even Eötvös's liberalism had its limits.

Eötvös died in 1871, Deák in 1876. Their principled liberalism found no major torch-bearer. By contrast, an adulterated version of the creed was shaping itself to suit Hungarian elite interests, whose two main characteristics were already discernible by the mid-1870s. On the one hand a centralising national state continually expanded its sphere of influence. On the other, a Hungarian bourgeoisie was encouraged to develop through policies of economic liberalism and far-reaching toleration of Jews, conditional on Jewish readiness to assimilate to the Magyar-language community (still barely 45% of the whole), while drawing on the prior need to heal the Catholic–Protestant split among ancestral Magyars. These themes went back to the modernising aspirations of the Pre-March reform movement and could thus satisfyingly be presented as a fulfilment of its goals. But success as so often brought complacency. Liberalism passed from being indispensable catalyst of a liberal–national synthesis to become a pragmatic policy tool. As prime minister Tisza told his Debrecen electors in 1878:

> By liberalism I have never understood ... that without regard to other matters ... we should abruptly and at any price choose to

implement the most liberal course, whether or not it corresponds to our circumstances.[17]

Hungarian circumstances in practice were understood to require the strengthening of the Magyar character of the state and protection of the position of the Magyar-speaking 'historic' classes. Peasant hopes that the autonomous government would undo the pro-noble bias in the neo-absolutist land reform were dashed. Indeed, the permission given agricultural labourers to strike over wages in 1871 was withdrawn in the 1876 Penal Code and the Agricultural Servants' Law (1876) allowed masters to administer corporal punishment. Successive local government measures increased the powers of the centrally appointed county high sheriffs, made local decisions subject to governmental review and instituted county administrative committees effectively to run the counties in place of the unwieldy county assemblies and their traditionally elected officials. One of Tisza's first acts as prime minister was to close the Slovaks' three secondary schools and their cultural organisation *Matica slovenská*. The provision for use of non-Magyar languages in local government contained in the 1868 Nationality Law remained in practice a dead letter.

This was the hard-nosed face of Hungarian 'liberalism' which Austrians alternately envied and deplored. Yet in an important regard they overestimated its instinct for power. A remarkable memorandum of 1867 gave Franz Joseph the right to the so-called *Vorsanktion* (he had to approve all Hungarian legislation before its presentation to parliament), allowed him a similar control over all civil service and church appointments beyond a certain grade, and specified further fields like policy towards the Orthodox communities and the former economic *regalia* where his consent was required. It serves as a reminder of the complex situation in which Magyar liberalism found itself, facing as it did potential enemies in the Austro-Germans, the King–Emperor, the non-Magyars and the Magyar lower classes. There had to be an element of illusion in its apparent triumph.

If Austro-Germans overestimated Hungarian liberals they underestimated Slavic ones, except in the case of the Poles, where liberals were indeed weak. Galicia showed analogies to Hungary in the presence of a powerful native nobility, but its patriotism was still more conservatively weighted than in Hungary's case. Galicia's economy was more backward than Hungary's, very large landowners – the so-called Podolians in the largely Ruthenian east – played a comparatively bigger role and landless nobles a lesser one, and there was little equivalent of mass Magyarisation of German and Jewish bourgeois, though some Jews did Polonise. Even in the small middle class the association of progressive politics with nationalism left less space for a bourgeois politics of civic improvement. Thus a democrat or left liberal strand in Galician politics existed more as a pressure group than as a political force, acquiring its organ in Tadeusz Romanowicz's journal *New Reform* from 1882. Political power remained with the noble party dubbed *Stanczyk*-ites, who gained legitimacy through extracting concessions like the replacement of German by Polish in the administration and in the universities of Cracow and Lvov (1868–70). Effectively the Polish elite won a kind of sub-dualism denied the Czechs, which fell short of the autonomy demanded by the Galician Diet's Resolution of 1868 but crucially ensured its loyalty almost till the end of the Monarchy. Administrative Polonisation helped it to keep control of a Ruthenian minority somewhat over 40%.

German underestimation of Slav liberals elsewhere is not particularly surprising, given continued Slav weakness in the towns which were liberalism's natural domain. Though Czechs had begun to gain majorities on municipal councils in inner Bohemia in the 1860s, this development did not mean Czech control of the economic sphere so closely connected with liberal ideology; besides, Moravian towns were still politically German and long remained so. Outside Bohemia-Moravia the chief towns of the Slavic provinces were very small from a Viennese perspective. Ljubljana had 22,000 inhabitants in 1869, Zagreb about 20,000, the Hungarian Serb centre, Novi Sad, only 12,000. Even in populous Prague the petit bourgeois Czech society depicted in Jan Neruda's touching *Tales from the Little Quarter* (1867) is overwhelmingly one of underdogs, for all the salons of Palacký, Rieger and Brauner. Deference showed in the refusal of the radical editor Julius Grégr's own father, a successful estate official used to official German, to write reports in Czech. The homely nature of this society is well conveyed in the career of Vojta Náprstek, advocate of industrial schooling and women's rights and a bibliophile whose book collection, opened to the public, became the nucleus of the Czech national ethnographic museum. But this was no conventional Maecenas but a returned American emigrant whose industrial school was largely financed by the three houses bequeathed him by his innkeeper mother.

Yet at a level largely beyond German bourgeois ken the non-dominant Slav societies were shaping their own version of liberal civilisation. From the 1860s their associational life and journalism blossomed apace, with keynote papers founded in this period often surviving until Nazism brought the bourgeois age to a close: Grégr's *Národní Listy* in Prague, *Pozor* (later *Obzor*) in Zagreb, *Slovenski Narod* among the Slovenes. If these peoples still lacked a strong capitalist bourgeoisie they were developing professional sectors of doctors, lawyers and secondary school teachers with the faith in education and progress and opposition to authoritarianism and clericalism characteristic of their kind. Already in the 1861 Bohemian Diet there were 20 Czech lawyers to 25 German and 8 of the 21 founding members of the Young Czech Party in 1874 were lawyers. All six main speakers at the monster Slovene anti-Dualist demonstration of 1869 had doctorates. The local government system introduced in Austria in the 1860s gave further scope for training in an orderly political process and was particularly important in the case of Bohemian Czechs. Czech businessmen tended to operate at this local level, but so did rich peasants who had benefited from the accelerated development of the sugar beet industry from the 1850s.

Nowhere were the liberal proclivities of these people clearer than in their attitude to the churches. Anti-clericalism among Czechs could build on the Hussite and anti-Jesuit heritage which reached particular heights in 1866–67, even if it was in part a case of the 'invention of tradition'. Svetozar Miletić incurred the wrath of the Serb Patriarch Maširević over his bid to turn the institutions of Serb Orthodox church autonomy into instruments of modern nationalism. Though Metropolitan Şaguna remained the most central figure in his community there are some signs of lay efforts to marginalise him too, for example in the cultural organisation *Astra* founded in 1861, a typical product of the liberal nationalist age.

As among German speakers the degree of anti-clericalism was a touchstone of an emerging moderate/radical division among non-dominant liberals. What became known as the 'Old Czech' leadership of Palacký and Rieger had forged a kind of alliance with the federally minded Bohemian nobility, in large part because of Palacký's unease at the social weakness of the Czech middle class. This brought on their heads the taunts of 'Young Czechs' hostile to the degree of complaisance towards the Catholic Church that this entailed, though Young Czechs also favoured universal suffrage and a constitutional approach more orientated to 'natural' rather than 'historic' rights. The tendency had first appeared in 1863 when the future Young Czechs supported the Polish insurrection against

Tsarist rule. It should be noted, though, that Old Czechs saw their emollience towards the Church as purely tactical. Palacký and Rieger were classical right-wing liberals, favouring constitutional process, free trade and the right of their nation to equal participation in the 'progress' of the age. Rieger had drafted the Kremsier constitution's articles on civil rights: his famous speech on the sovereignty of the people saw the 'will of free nations' as expressing itself in the choice or tacit recognition of the wise and valiant leader – hardly democracy![18] Czech politicians admired gradualist England and were uneasy about authoritarian Louis Napoleon even when they sought his aid for their cause. Prijatelj has argued similarly that the leader of the corresponding 'Old Slovene' faction, Janez Bleiweis, never changed the free-thinking opinions of his younger days, though he refrained from any public criticism of the Church. The Young Slovenes who emerged from 1868 shared their Czech counterparts' condemnation of what they saw as opportunism and advocated principled reliance on the 'national idea' and Slavic solidarity. Such stances did not differ from the nationalism of German liberalism's radical wing.

Of course, what non-dominant activists *thought* was not necessarily yet of immediate political relevance. The actions of so small a group as the Slovenes were decided by their circumstances; 'beggars can't be choosers' might be the motto of small-nation opportunism. Whereas the Old Czechs felt strong enough for principled abstention from the Dualist system which violated 'Czech state right' (they maintained their boycott of the Reichsrat and the Bohemian Diet till 1879), most Slovene MPs signed up for Dualism in return for a local railway and funds for a dictionary. The decision of his colleagues to oppose the German liberals' confessional legislation on tactical grounds so disgusted one Slovene MP that he contemplated defecting to the German camp, as had the scholarly Dežman in 1861, appalled at what he saw as the intellectual narrowness of the national movement. Indeed, Slovene liberals, an urban minority in a pious countryside, were to cooperate with Ljubljana's Germans to keep Slovene clericals from municipal power till 1908.

Yet where they saw a chance, Slav liberals could be active in the most unpromising terrain, like 1870s Croatia, 85% peasant and 80% illiterate. The slight revision of the 1868 Hungaro-Croat compromise with which a long constitutional wrangle between the two countries came to an end in 1873 seemed to some educated Croats to offer a window of opportunity under a new native Ban, the poet–bureaucrat Mažuranić, himself more Josephinist than liberal. Their programme included: responsibility of the autonomous Croat government to the Sabor, a university in Zagreb (opened in 1874) and a school law (1874) which wrested control of primary education from the clergy and was influenced by the People's School movement led by a secular-minded visionary heavily indebted to progressive German pedagogy. Hungarian obstruction and inherent difficulties of an undeveloped society soon soured the mood.

As significant were the signs that Czech and Slovene radical liberals were not isolated from their people. The *Tábor* assembly movement of 1868–70, gathering altogether over a million people in the Czech lands and up to 25–30,000 in the largest Slovene meeting in protest at Dualism, showed that Slav activists could stir their masses if not yet the authorities. It was an important pointer. There were non-dominant regions, among Ruthenians and Slovaks for example, where nothing of the sort was on the cards. Slovakia at this time offered the case of a community under such heavy elite pressure that many of its tiny nationally conscious intelligentsia (two to three hundred in one estimate) despaired of making it competitive along modern lines; the father of Slovak nationalism L'udovít Štúr had himself fallen back on Panslavism and impotent maledictions before his death in 1856. But the Czech, and to a lesser extent the Slovene, example was beginning to show that in an easier environment it was possible to create a simulacrum of a modern society, with its network of associations, journals and schools. To the extent that the Austro-German liberals pooh-poohed this they miscalculated.

Cisleithanian Politics, 1867–79

Of course, the arrogance of the dominant German liberal culture was in part a response to its difficult position. Its proponents were a minority perched between Magyars and Slavs on the one hand and the Emperor on the other, who had no intention of sacrificing his prerogative to people he knew to be unrepresentative. The chequered political course of the so-called liberal era up to 1879 accurately reflected this balance of forces.

Basically, the Emperor was prepared to tolerate the main thrust of liberal legislation on church and school matters and civil liberties, but had no intention of allowing any encroachment on his control of the army and foreign policy. He was unhappy about a doctrinaire

German centralism which drove Slavs into destabilising opposition or which might upset the dualist relationship with Hungary. Here the issues of Czech 'historic rights' and the decennial economic compromise with Hungary were uppermost. Domestic and foreign political issues clearly interacted. At the international level the Bismarckian settlement did not bed down immediately any more than did constitutionalism inside the Monarchy. The relation of the Powers to the rise of Prussia/Germany and the unresolved Eastern question proved the pivotal issues. Finally, the economic crash of 1873 was bound to influence the fortunes of a liberal movement closely connected with the onmarch of modern capitalism.

The triangular relationship between German liberalism, Slav nationalism and the Emperor showed itself early, when the first Austrian constitutional prime minister, Prince Karl Auersperg, resigned in autumn 1868 still in a huff over Chancellor Beust's negotiations with Czech leaders behind his back some months before. Whether Beust acted on his own initiative or not he was in tune with Franz Joseph's wish for a Czech reconciliation and his free-wheeling role vis-à-vis the prime minister was not yet compatible with the norms of constitutional government. Auersperg was succeeded by Count Eduard Taaffe, whose ministry came to deadlock on essentially the same issue fifteen months later. Five bourgeois ministers pressed the case for direct elections to the Reichsrat and three (including Taaffe and another noble) opposed. A directly elected Reichsrat instead of one deputed by the Diets would, the cabinet majority believed, remove a vestige of federalism and put the coping stone on the Dualist system. It seems the Emperor wanted to keep the disagreement under wraps and perhaps lean on his centralist ministers, but Taaffe eventually had to resign – a Pyrrhic victory for the left in the event, for the attempt of Taaffe's short-lived successor, the former education minister Hasner, to enforce the centralist line led to Poles, most Slovenes, clericals and others joining the Czechs in abstention. The Emperor thereupon more or less instructed Hasner to resign, to be followed in April 1870 by a Polish count of more federalist stamp, Alfred Potocki.

Potocki's domestic agenda was soon overtaken, however, by pressing foreign political concerns. In reality, these had never gone away. If historians no longer believe that Beust's aim was to prepare for a war of revenge with Prussia, he and Franz Joseph did wish to rebuild Austria-Hungary's Great Power status and await events. This meant fishing for the support of southern German states and for a French alliance, and also, on the Emperor's part, the ambition to compensate for his previous losses by Balkan gains, preferably in Bosnia. The two issues, the German and the Eastern, were linked in that Bismarck could not buy off Austria's hostility, as he would have wished, because he was unwilling to support her against Russia in the Balkans. Austro-Russian rivalry in the region reached a new peak during the Consul-Generalship of the ambitious and somewhat unscrupulous young Hungarian Béni Kállay in Belgrade (1868–74) who schemed with Hungarian premier Andrássy to separate Serbia from Russia (and also from the Croats) by, among other things, the bait of support for a Serbian occupation of Bosnia. The Bosnian gambit seems to have been largely a Hungarian one and in its ingenuity and dubious sincerity interesting for the vigour with which the fledgeling Hungarian state defended itself from a sea of perceived enemies.

Andrássy was to play a powerful role, too, in the Crown Council of 18 July 1870 which debated Austria-Hungary's stance in the event of the looming Franco-Prussian war. While the Archduke Albrecht, present as Chief of Staff, wanted war with Prussia and Beust wanted mobilisation (to enable Austrian intervention in the event of a stalemate), Andrássy insisted on complete neutrality and had his way, helped by reports of military unpreparedness. The complementarity of Hungarian and Prussian interests went back at least to 1790. Bismarck had warned the Hungarians that their new status was in danger from Austrian resurgence.

Prussia's victory over France, the adhesion of the southern states to a united Germany and the enthusiasm with which these events were greeted by German Austrians made for a dramatic change in Austrian domestic politics. Fearing Prussian designs on his own dubiously loyal Germans, Franz Joseph abandoned accommodation with the liberals and turned to the Slavs. Potocki was dropped as unsuited to the purpose and in February 1871 the famous Hohenwart–Schäffle government took office. Its driving force was the minister of commerce, Albert Schäffle, a Württemberg Protestant with social reform interests who shared with prime minister Count Karl Hohenwart (later leader of the Reichsrat's conservative clericals) only a dissociation from Austro-German liberal traditions. The new administration's overriding task was to reach an accommodation with the Czechs, though it also established the precedent of a cabinet minister with a brief for Galicia, one of the final steps by which Poles were reconciled to the Dualist system. Negotiations with the Czechs yielded a draft law on nationality relations in Bohemia and an agreement on Bohemia's constitutional position in the Monarchy. The former proposed an administration which would operate bilingually at the provincial level and monolingually locally – with safeguards for local minorities. The latter reinstated the autonomous Bohemian Chancellery abolished in 1749, but allowed for Bohemian participation in a central Reichsrat legislating for 'common' matters like commerce, finance and citizenship. These 'Fundamental Articles' would have put Bohemia somewhere between the 'sub-dualist' position Croatia enjoyed in Hungary and full equality with the Magyars in a 'trialist' Monarchy.

However, the deal fell through. Formally, the necessary majorities in the Diets and the Reichsrat existed; it is a reflection on the superficiality of Austrian constitutionalism that each basic change of course (towards federalism in 1865, centralism in 1867 and federalism again in 1871) was initiated from above and subsequently endorsed through managed elections. But the announcement of the Fundamental Articles on 6 October 1871 unleashed a storm of Austro-German fury. Bismarck himself made known his displeasure at the alleged weakening of German interests. More telling still was Andrássy's charge that the concessions to the Czechs undermined the Dualist system and the position of Hungary. The Emperor abandoned the initiative and the Hohenwart–Schäffle ministry resigned. With it ended the most ambitious attempt between 1867 and 1918 to respond to the non-dominant peoples' dissatisfaction with the Dualist system. The Czechs resumed their political abstention.

Franz Joseph had no alternative but to return to the liberals. The head of the new government was Prince Adolf Auersperg, whose brother had held the post in 1867–68. Two years later the Emperor yielded, too, on the liberal wish for direct elections to the Reichsrat. During the 1870s German liberals used their Diet majorities in Bohemia and Moravia to maintain as far as they could German medium secondary schools in the market towns of Czech-speaking areas. Yet all this was again a Pyrrhic victory. Auersperg's was not really a parliamentary government but depended more on the Emperor's goodwill than on that of the liberal party, sections of which, as in the British Labour governments of the 1970s, became increasingly frustrated by the inability to agree on or impose their doctrinal nostrums. While the leader of the largest liberal grouping, the Club of the Left, Eduard Herbst, adopted a quasi-oppositional role as the keeper of the liberal conscience, his 'old liberals' came more and more under attack from the *Jungen* who in the spirit of the times called for a 'sharper tone': a specifically German national orientation of the liberal state, with a broader franchise and a social aspect. Herbst condemned what he saw as the nationalist heresy, the more easily because he unconsciously assumed German hegemony was natural and needed no prop. But the stock market crash of 1873 weakened liberalism's prestige in non-bourgeois sections of the population and influenced the foundation of a 'Progressive' Club by restive liberals in rivalry to the Club of the Left.

In these growingly murky waters Herbst's mainstream liberals crossed the Emperor on two policies close to his heart. One was the decennial economic compromise with Hungary, renewed in 1877 to a chorus of public bickering which riled Franz Joseph – the stock market crash had made much Austrian business suspicious of free trade and the free trade interests of Hungarian landowners. But the Emperor's decisive break with the liberals came over foreign policy, where Beust had been succeeded as the Monarchy's foreign minister by Gyula Andrássy in 1871. Andrássy's policy oscillated between a Magyar patriot's natural suspicion of Russia and cooperation with her in the conservative Three Emperors' League, concluded between Austria-Hungary, Russia and Germany in 1873. The potential rivals pledged to consult on points of friction, the most obvious of these being the Balkans. Serb Orthodox peasants' revolt against Turkish rule in Bosnia-Herzegovina in 1875, by pressurising first Serbia and Montenegro and then Slav Orthodox Russia to intervene militarily on their behalf, greatly strained this relationship. In the treaty of San Stefano of March 1878 the victorious Russians decimated the European Turkey which Andrássy had wished to preserve and set up the large south Slav state he opposed, albeit a big Bulgaria rather than the larger Serbia which Vienna especially feared. Moreover, San Stefano violated the understanding Andrássy thought he had reached with his Russian couterpart at Budapest early in 1877 before Russia went to war. In the event, with British support and Bismarck's mediation Andrássy was able to get Russia to retreat from San Stefano and accept at the Congress of Berlin in July 1878 a smaller Bulgaria and an Austro-Hungarian occupation of Bosnia-Herzegovina. This *de facto* annexation (for Turkish suzerainty became an empty form) removed Bosnia from Serbia's grasp, gave Dalmatia a strategic bulwark and pleased an Emperor smarting at previous territorial losses.

It is the domestic headaches the occupation brought which are the chief concern here. Hungarian and Austro-German liberals objected to the acquisition of Slav lands both on national and financial grounds. Herbst's stress of parliament's constitutional right to approve a treaty entailing public expense made a mockery of Franz Joseph's prized prerogative in foreign affairs and forced Auersperg to tender his resignation: he could not guarantee parliamentary support for the government's Bosnian policy, which armed Bosnian Muslim resistance (August–September 1878) made still more expensive. In the end enough liberals were won over to pass the army credits and the treaty, but Herbst led a defiant minority to the last. A stop-gap ministry succeeded Auersperg while a non-liberal, Count Taaffe, negotiated with the Czechs for the ending of their abstention. The Bosnian crisis therefore fed into a realignment of Austrian politics at the same time as Bismarck was orchestrating the downfall of the liberals in nearby Germany. The specifically Austrian twist was the dissatisfaction of the Czechs with the results of abstention, a policy already abandoned by the Young Czech minority (a separate party from 1874) and now given up by the Old Czechs in return for promises far short of their 'historic rights': essentially language concessions, a Czech university, and a lowering of the franchise. In the elections which followed the Czech–Taaffe deal the liberals lost nearly fifty seats and Taaffe took office backed by a Czech–Polish–clerical block of 179 to the liberals' 174 (September 1879). It was the end of the German liberal hegemony in Austria.

Some of the criticisms to which Austro-German liberals have been subjected are contradictory. They have alternately been rebuked for a pawky timidity and accused, with Herbst, of dogmatic intransigence. Older criticism often reflected a conservative and Catholic distaste for liberalism itself, as the arid individualistic creed of an urban minority remote from popular concerns. Many Austrian liberals themselves have joined the chorus of disapproval, lamenting like Baron Chlumecky immediately after 1879 their immature inflexibility or like Ernst Plener in his memoirs their inability to resemble the homogenous political class of an idealised British parliament. Maybe too often liberals are criticised for being liberals, for wanting a say, in other words, in high policy like the Bosnian issue. But this defence does not void the argument that a German liberal parliamentarism was simply impracticable in such a culturally and economically heterogenous state, where only the dynasty enjoyed general acceptance. From this viewpoint the liberals' chief inflexibility was towards the non-Germans, which gave Franz Joseph legitimate cause to withhold his full confidence. But even their Germanism was perhaps not as purblind as hindsight has made it seem. Though today's western nations are a small minority in the contemporary world their economic and cultural hegemony is such that few can imagine its fundamental reversal. The main theme of this chapter has been that a similar mindset was shared by nineteenth-century Austrian liberals. And not only them. Bismarck, one of Herbst's most scathing critics, himself believed the Austro-German hegemony could be maintained.

Indeed, though he consistently declined to intervene in Austrian domestic politics, Bismarck's decision to opt for a German–Austrian alliance in 1879 was undoubtedly intended, among other things, to bolster the Monarchy's German character. This alliance, concluded in October and presented to the German emperor as a defence against a Russia still smarting from the Congress of Berlin, was more probably aimed to detach Vienna from a possible western orientation (the so-called Crimean coalition) and prepare her for a revived league of the three conservative eastern powers which Bismarck sought. It was a defensive alliance offering mutual support against Russian attack and benevolent neutrality in the event of attack by any other power. Andrássy endorsed it gladly, then retired, weary of parliamentary assaults on his Bosnian policy. This treaty of the 'central powers' inaugurated the era of alliance-building which ended in the slide to war of 1914. Ambiguous from the start towards Russia (Austria-Hungary wanted German support against her in the Balkans, Bismarck wanted to avoid this by reconciling the two rivals), the 1879 treaty was clear at another level. Barring minor frictions, it tied the Monarchy definitively to the German Reich, as a junior partner of the 'central powers'. The year 1879 therefore inserted a potentially fateful fissure into the Austrian polity, between a domestic orientation working against traditional German hegemony and an international stance tending to reinforce it. Over time, this helped strengthen both German and non-German alienation from the state.

For Austro-German liberals the 1879 alliance only sustained their feeling that their fall from power (though paralleled in Bismarck's Reich) was a violation of the natural order, an artificial result of political manipulation. Many who subsequently moved far from liberalism took with them from this event a poisonous sense of treachery and conspiracy. Meanwhile German cultural and economic power long remained, in fact till 1918. But it had never been as hegemonic as German speakers liked to assume. That 1879 was never reversed politically reflected the fact that at the grass roots German centralism did not have the economic, social or cultural underpinning that such a project required. This the following chapters will show.

8   Economics, 1867–1914

Between the censuses of 1869 and 1910 the population of Vienna rose from 600,000 to two million and that of Budapest from 270,000 to 913,000. Meanwhile, the Monarchy's railway network expanded seven-fold to 42,000 kilometres and its coal production five-fold to 55 million tons. Four million people left the empire, of whom about a third returned. Just in the second half of the period, 1890–1913, capital in financial institutions increased from 8.8 to over 38.5 billion crowns (the Krone, introduced in 1892, was half a florin). The eradication of epidemic disease, rise of great business conglomerates, organisation of mass interest groups of all kinds and emergence of still recognisably 'modern' patterns in communications, sport and entertainment contributed to a scale of change unmatched before or since, even in the inflated indices of communism.

These advances were not uniform. One overview influenced by theories of long-term economic fluctuations has seen sharp growth till the stock market crash of 1873, followed by the 'Great Depression' till 1896 and an upswing to the First World War. The two years named do mark a down-turn and up-turn in price levels in the Monarchy as in most of Europe, but in many other respects the notion of depression throughout the intervening period is misleading. A more differentiated picture for the Monarchy would see depression ending in 1879 and would pick out perhaps four cycles thereafter, with periods of expansion in the early 1880s, early to mid-1890s, then in 1904–07 and 1909–13. That this periodisation, though derived from Austrian experience, suits Hungary too shows the high degree of integration between both parts of the Monarchy. Interdependent economic development was one of the shades of the unitary Monarchy which continued to haunt the age of Dualism, benignly or malignly according to political taste. Hence a discussion of Dualist economic development must take its political implications into account, separating out what happened in the empire's main regions before considering the benefit or otherwise of the common economic ties.

Industrialisation in the Dual Monarchy: Cisleithania

Nothing so inflated the confidence of Austrian liberalism in the immediate post-Compromise years as their industrial boom, and nothing so weakened it as the crash of 1873. The *Gründerzeit*, as they became known (literally: founding time), resulted from a combination of favourable factors: a mushrooming financial sector willing to invest in the economy, an expanding rail network making demands on the iron industry and technical innovation in a swathe of coal-consuming industries, the whole interacting to produce a leap forward led by heavy industry with the railways at its core. In these years Austrian lines grew by 150%: long arms radiated out from Vienna to reach Innsbruck, Pilsen and (by a direct route) Prague for the first time; provincial capitals in the Alpine lands were linked up; there was a criss-crossing of Bohemia and particularly the Sudetenland; Graz was attached to the west Hungarian network and the Eastern line pushed on from Lvov towards the Russian frontier.

As in the 1850s railway expansion spurred financial innovation: the efflorescence of banking institutions was the mark of the *Gründerzeit*. With the eclipse of most private bankers after the financial crisis of 1857–58, finance grew from 1867 through the multiplication of joint stock banks, though the established Creditanstalt, associated with Anselm Rothschild (1803–74), and the Niederösterreichische Escomptegesellschaft maintained leading roles. Utilising high profits, the banks helped sponsor the growth of joint stock companies, 1005 of which received charters in the years 1867–73. Vítkovice, controlled by Rothschild, led the way in the adoption of the Bessemer process by the Monarchy's other major iron works by 1870, along with puddling, the rolling mill and increasingly the use of coke in preference for charcoal. Chief among these other works was the Bohemian Iron Company centred at the coal-mining town of Kladno near Prague, which had emerged from amalgamation of three predecessors in 1857.

The growing fusion of coal and iron industries was a natural tendency. Vítkovice was close to Austria's chief anthracite area around the city of Ostrava on the Moravian–Silesian border. Kladno, by contrast, was a lignite or soft coal area like the larger Teplice–Most–Duchcov field in northern Bohemia, which had important exports to nearby Germany. Coal production received powerful impetus from technical modernisation in a series of industries in the 1860s, like flour milling, sugar refining and paper making, all of which increased demand for it. Sugar beet deserves special mention as a rapidly advancing, largely export industry with a twelve and a half-fold increase in acreage planted between 1857–58 and 1872–73. In the textile industry, too, mechanisation made strides, becoming predominant in the cotton-weaving centre of Reichenberg in north Bohemia by the end of the decade and entering the linen industry in the 1870s.

The speculative side to this impressive progress – only two-thirds of the 1005 charters mentioned above led to actual foundations – was revenged in classic form in the crash of May 1873, with plunging share prices, panicky crowds mobbing the banks, fraud exposures and 152 suicides registered in the immediate aftermath. In the next six years of severe depression it was the boom sectors of finance and heavy industry and the related building trade which were worst hit. The most lasting legacy of the crash was the distrust of *laissez-faire* liberalism it bequeathed and the caution it instilled into the banks over too active and direct a role in promotion of industry. It did not help that depression coincided with the trial of directors of the Eastern railway in Galicia, where labyrinthine patterns of sub-contracting and shoddy construction exposed the dangers of the system of state interest guarantees for private capital. The economic historian Adolf Beer showed why doctrinaire liberalism lost ground when he opposed anti-corruption legislation: no law could protect fools; people should use the same common sense in buying shares as in buying food.[1]

From 1880 the Austrian economy began to recover more strongly. Again railway expansion led the way, this time under state control and with extensive renationalisation of private lines. Between 1873 and the turn of the century, 13,637 kilometres of track were added. Bank capital also rose, in larger but still far fewer joint stock banks compared to the *Gründerzeit*. The nine Viennese 'big banks' held somewhat under half all bank share capital in 1900 and two-thirds in 1913. It was a pattern of concentration which pointed to the restructuring Austrian industry as a whole had undergone from the 1880s, as a long-term response to the depression and also to the growing tendencies towards protection and concentration elsewhere in Europe, above all Germany. Austria-Hungary adopted a more protectionist tariff in 1882. The iron industry was the most striking example of concentration; by 1911 just three firms produced 92% of Austria's pig iron. The number of Austrian coal mining firms fell by 58% in the four decades to 1913, by which time eight of the 186 sugar firms accounted for 35% of production. According to the industrial census of 1902 three-quarters of workers in machine plants in the Czech lands were employed in enterprises of more than a hundred employees. Concentration was far from universal, however. Many industries retained small or medium-sized units of production, like clothing, leather and wood products, or chemicals, glass and construction respectively; others, above all textiles, were polarised between large enterprises and a host of handicraft concerns. In the 1902 census more than half of the Czech lands' cotton weavers and a fifth of its cotton spinners were revealed to be domestic workers. Yet overall Austrian concentration was surprisingly advanced, bearing in mind the more backward provinces of Galicia, Bukovina and Dalmatia. Indeed, the 1902 census showed that the proportion of workers employed in enterprises with over a thousand employees was already higher than in the comparable German census of 1895.

In this concentration of industry the leading Austrian banks played a not insignificant part. Alexander Gerschenkron has linked banks' role in central European development with the need of later industrialising countries for larger investment in order to fund more advanced technologies. Hence the commonness of the 'universal bank' in Germany and Austria, in the sense of a bank prepared for an industrial as well as commercial role, financing enterprise as well as discounting bills and receiving deposits. Rudolph has entered the qualification that Austrian banks remained leary of an entrepreneurial role after 1873 and contented themselves with cultivating relationships with already successful firms, to whom ostensibly short-term credit, through repeated renewal, could become long-term in all but name; in such relationships banks might contract to sell a client's produce on commission and receive a seat on the board. This in itself, however, went beyond British banking practice. Moreover, from about 1890 the links of finance and industry began to become tighter, with banks increasingly willing to sponsor the conversion of private firms to joint stock companies and their merger into more powerful concerns. Joint stock companies doubled to 780 by 1912, holding, in Rudolph's view, as much as half of all Austria's industrial capital. In other estimates the nine Viennese big banks held more than half of joint stock capital in 1914 and banks participated in 146 new joint stock foundations in the preceding seven years.

A further aspect of industry's ties with finance was bank sponsorship of cartels, whereby firms in particular branches came together to regulate prices and/or output or market share. Starting with one for iron rails in 1878 there were some two hundred cartels in Austria by 1912, with a supervisory Kontrollbank set up by the big banks in 1914 to be the coping stone of the process. But the tendency to cartelisation applied to the banks themselves, for a major bank like the Creditverein would have a number of smaller, provincial banks in tow and in turn enjoy links with outside capital. This was in addition to the extension of their own branch network by which from the turn of the century the joint stock banks succeeded in advancing their share of savings at the expense of the savings banks and credit associations.

Alongside the tendencies to concentration, bank involvement and cartelisation which marked Austrian industry before 1914 an equally important feature was the shift of power from the Alpine to the Czech lands, and particularly Bohemia. Many factors contributed to this: the switch from charcoal to coke in the iron industry which helped the Czech lands with their better coal reserves, closeness to German markets and through the Elbe–Hamburg route to the wider world, the success of the sugar industry which became more exclusively Czech-based with time, and the emergence of Prague as a financial, food-processing and metallurgical centre. Meanwhile, the Moravian capital Brno yielded primacy to Bohemian Reichenberg in textiles. By the twentieth century 56% of Austrian industrial workers were in the Czech lands and more than 75% of output came from there in chemicals, mining, textiles, sugar and glass. Bohemia had become (after Lower Austria, which included Vienna) emphatically the wealthiest Cisleithanian province in per capita income terms, at an estimated 761 crowns in 1911–13, ahead of the next top placed Austro-German land (Salzburg) at 641. Yet interestingly this did not initially involve any displacement of Austro-German economic dominance in the Czech lands. Of probably the two most dynamic figures in Bohemian–Moravian industry, the Czech-born Emil Škoda, who opened his armaments factory in Pilsen (Plžen) in 1900, counted socially as a German just as much as the manager of the Prague Iron Company, Karl Wittgenstein, father of the philosopher – eloquent testimony to the perception of Germans as managers and Czechs as workers. Even in the sugar industry, closest to the Czech-speaking population, the refining sector was largely in German hands and received more support from government and the Viennese banks. Only in the twentieth century did this situation begin to change significantly.

Indeed, the new century saw much development. Austria's financial assets more than doubled, investment may well have been 13% of

GNP and per capita national income rose annually at an estimated 5.4%. During the 1904–07 upswing employment went up by a third in iron and steel and 23% in cotton. New industries like electro-technology made their mark, industry became electrified, and Porsche began producing his cars. Whatever else their problems, the last years of Habsburg Austria were not a time of economic sclerosis.

Industrialisation in the Dual Monarchy: Magyars and Slavs

Hungarian economic development under Dualism bears many family likenesses to Austria's, but as of a younger son constantly reaching the point where his elder brother has been some years before. With qualifications, one may speak of Austria's relationship to Germany in similar terms and posit tentatively a central European economy sharing certain structural traits. Close bank ties with industry, an overall complementarity of financial flows and markets, despite mutual rivalries, and other resemblances rooted in elite acquaintance with German culture and educational norms: all this shaped a more intimate regional nexus than central Europe has known since 1918. It is a context which has subtly influenced historical perceptions. The deficiencies of Hungary's industrialisation compared to her neighbours have been more emphasised than very real contemporary fears that she might not industrialise at all. For though immediately after 1867 patriotic rhetoric stressed liberalism's catching up goal in the struggle for life, it was mixed with a real apprehension based on Hungary's age-old status as an agrarian land, with the consequent 'centuries of omissions', the capital shortage, poor communications and ignorant work-force, not to speak of the relative shortage and remoteness of minerals, located mainly in Hungary's mountain rim, in Slovakia and Transylvania. Indeed, Hungary's textile industry, a mainstay of industrialisation elsewhere, had already been decimated by Austrian competition – by 1900 it was to supply only 14% of the country's domestic needs.

The first spur to real growth was provided by corn exports stimulated by the 'miracle harvests' of 1867–68 and by the rapid rise of Budapest's flour milling industry. A third of Hungary's joint stock foundations in the *Gründerzeit* were in flour milling and Budapest production rose eight-fold by 1879. Half Germany's flour imports were coming from the Monarchy by the middle of the decade, mainly from Hungary. When Germany introduced protection in 1879 exports were sustained by the Austrian market, which rose 10% a year till 1896. The west Hungarian town of Győr, which had been the traditional seat of the corn export market, was replaced in this role by the capital, whose rapid growth was stimulated by government policy to make it the focus of a veritable spider's web of radiating railways. Hungary's railway effort fell little short of Austria's, with nearly six thousand kilometres built in the *Gründerzeit*, and another thirteen and a half thousand by the end of the century. Significantly, the Hungarian government pursued railway (re)nationalisation earlier and more vigorously than the Austrian and by 1891 84% of the chief lines were under state control, a percentage not quite reached by Austria in 1913. The resulting progress in economic integration was indicated by the fall in regional wheat price differences. Reaching 120% in the first half of the century, they stood at a maximum of 40% (in 43 markets) in 1875 and 24% by 1891-92.

Railway (and bridge) building naturally acted as a stimulant to the iron industry which grew at 4.5% per annum to overtake flour milling in terms of value added before 1914. Thus the problems caused to Hungary's first leading sector of corn and flour by German protection and American competition did not stall the economy, which from the late 1880s began a decade of rapid growth. Most historians date Hungary's industrial breakthrough to this time. Investments and credit institutions trebled in these years, iron ore, coal and crude iron output doubled and Budapest joint stock companies increased four-fold. It is not possible to explain this advance without stress of the Austrian link and particularly Austrian capital exports to the eastern half of the Monarchy. After the brittle boom of 1867-73, when 60% of Hungary's industrial capital was of foreign, mostly Austrian origin, recovery came from 1880 with further injections of Austrian capital, amounting to half of all Hungarian share capital in the 1880s and 2.7 billion crowns by 1893. The transfer of Zsigmond Kornfeld from the management of the Creditanstalt's Prague branch to head the Hungarian General Credit Bank in the Rothschild interest in 1878 encapsulates the close links in the empire's financial system. Like Vienna, Budapest in the 1880s developed its league of recognised 'big banks', eventually five in number, which held 58% of bank capital on the eve of 1914. Bank profits in the 1880s exceeded 10% a year.

The period of rapid growth mentioned above brought the Hungarian economy into something of a paradoxical position. Two industries – flour milling and mining/metallurgy – were technologically at a European level, with 80% of metallurgical output coming from three giant plants (including the state railway iron works inherited from neo-absolutism and employing 13–15,000 workers in the 1880s). But after them there was little; textiles and sugar trailed far behind their Austrian counterparts and only one-fifth of modern leather production was in native hands. Budapest likewise had its modern financial sector, its impressive boulevards, bridges and railway stations, its 'Underground', the first in continental Europe (1896), but it was ten times larger than any other Hungarian town. This lop-sided progress provoked a question. Was the time ripe for Hungary to break free from the division of labour stemming from the Austro-Hungarian customs union (roughly, Austrian textiles for Hungarian corn and flour), break the pattern of uneven development and aim to be a fully fledged industrial nation? Or could it be argued that the customs union was at least partly responsible for the progress Hungary had made and that fuller economic maturity would be more safely pursued in its framework, adapted where necessary? The second position was that of the Liberal Party establishment and it was the one which prevailed, even after the Liberals' fall in 1905, until 1914.

Broadly speaking, Liberal governments combined a *laissez-faire* approach to business interests with the view, in the words of Prime Minister Lónyay in 1873, that 'the state is obliged to perform that which exceeds the powers of private enterprise, but not to do everything for everyone'.[2] In practice, this reserved the state an important role in infrastructural development. The post-Compromise government retained control of the state enterprises it inherited, and was energetic in nationalising the railways when interest guarantee payments to private companies began to burden the budget. Substantial sums also went on the regulation of the Tisza and Danube rivers, which saved 3.6 million hectares (nine million acres) or nearly 13% of Hungary from the threat of flooding. No fewer than eight iron bridges were built over the Tisza in the 1880s. Government also sought to tackle the problem of an unskilled work-force through a network of commercial and industrial schools, while facing the problem that aspiring youth was more attracted to traditional humanistic education with its allure of prestige and safe clerical employ. A highly skilled master craftsman had less status in Hungary, the education minister Trefort lamented in 1882, than an unemployed and impecunious lawyer.[3] All told, Hungarian governments in the latter half of Dualism (1890–1914) employed around 12% of the industrial work-force and were responsible for 20% of all invest-ments. This was doubtless economically more important than the 76 million crowns (2% of total industrial investment) calculated to have gone to industry through the subsidies, tax exemptions or preferen-tial rail rates promoted by pro-industry laws like those of 1881 and 1907; or the ten-yearly renegotiations of the economic compromise with Austria, for all their patriotic charge. There the main problems concerned the common bank of money issue, the Austrian National Bank (renamed the Austro-Hungarian Bank in 1877 and put on a basis of full parity in 1898), and Hungary's quota to the cost of common imperial affairs. Successive increases of the original 30% figure testified to Hungary's relative economic advance.

As Hungary entered the new century it seemed a good case could be made for the Liberal policy of working for economic emancipation from within the customs union. Already by the 1880s the percentage of raw agricultural goods in Hungarian exports to Austria had fallen to 63% as opposed to 90% in the 1840s. Hungary now produced all her own rails and most of her locomotives and railway coaches and was no longer overwhelmingly dependent on Austria for investment. While the volume of Hungarian shares held in Austria hardly grew between 1892 and 1912, those held in other countries quadrupled to reach 3.8 billion crowns, half of them in Germany. Finally, impor-tant as it was to have ready access to foreign funds, 75% of Hungar-ian industrial capital by 1914 came from domestic sources. Yet the narrowness of the industrial base in a vast rural hinterland continued as before. The intention of some of the emphases above has not been to leave a rosy picture of Hungarian economic development, but rather to highlight the potential for political dissension that lay behind it. The relative successes and continuing shortcomings alike fuelled the appetite of Magyar nationalists, making Hungary an object of resentment and/or desire for emulation in the other half of the Monarchy. The negotiations over the customs union became fraught with a tension which spread over into Austrian internal poli-tics. Hence the focus must switch to the way in which Czech eco-nomic development, too, prepared the ground for national strife.

The economic development of the Czech lands for long only seemed to confirm Czechs in their position of social underdogs. That does not mean nothing significant was happening. The fierce resentment of non-dominant peoples against their former masters is one of the most pervasive features of the modern world. Czech activists were aware of the importance of economic power in the ethnic struggle; one talks of economics but thinks of nationality, the *Národní Listy* commented in 1878. The way forward for the Czechs, logically enough, lay through agrarian modernisation and the development of agrarian-related industry. Still two-thirds noble-controlled in 1858, sugar beet production (if not refining) became a preserve of the peasantry of north and north-east Bohemia and adjacent Moravia in the 1860s. The first explicitly Czech joint stock sugar company was founded in Hradec Králové in 1863. Since sugar production at this time was 60–80% more lucrative than corn growing the attraction for farmers is obvious, but that they were able so quickly to build an industry as a base for a rich and politically active Czech peasant stratum requires further explanation. The Czech countryside already had a decades-old tradition of literacy; by the end of the century Czechs were the most literate nation in the Monarchy. They were thus in a position to benefit from the messages of patriotic agronomes like the former Schwarzenberg estate manager František Horský, when in the constitutional era these began in pamphlet and lecture to adapt the lessons of generations of scientific estate management to peasant benefit. The existence from 1862 of district self-government gave rich peasants an organisational–political base. Finally, the foundation of the Živnostenská banka – Živnobanka for short – in Prague in 1868 provided them with a financial mainstay.

The Živnobanka remained the most important single fact in Czech economic life until the Second World War. It was particularly successful at absorbing the savings of Czech small investors directly or as prop to the proliferating local savings banks and credit societies, and directing them to Czech business needs. As early as 1870, for example, it took responsibility for the tax payments of 18 sugar mills. The first real attempt at Czech economic self-assertion came in 1887 when the Prague chamber of commerce, having only recently acquired a Czech majority, called for an end to the neglect of Czech interests by the Austro-Hungarian Bank. The conventional view of such charges of neglect is that the bank's acts complained of (it was usually a matter of refusal to discount bills of Czech organisations) had social rather than ethnic motives, because the bank was unaccustomed to dealings at the humble level of most Czech associations. Needless to say, contemporary Czechs would not have found this distinction very convincing; when Czechs won a majority in the Bohemian Diet in 1883 the proportion of peasant savings bank bills discounted by the provincial branches of the Austro-Hungarian Bank rose sharply.[4] The linkage of socio-economic and ethnic issues was to be further complicated by the migration of up to half a million Czech work-seekers to German Bohemia and Vienna in the last two decades of the century which over time turned once near homogeneous districts into zones of ethnic tension.

However, it was only from about 1890 and particularly the turn of the century that potential began to be converted into actual Czech economic power. A factor here was the consolidation of a Czech bourgeois grip on Prague, where important light and engineering industries were developing. In 1890 Czech commercial banks held less than 2% of the capital in the Czech lands to the Sudeten German banks' 8%, with Viennese banks holding the remainder; by 1913 the Sudeten German share was unchanged but the Czechs' was now over 20%. From another angle, the Živnobanka's net profits in the Czech lands, from being less than a third those of the Creditanstalt's Prague branch now exceeded them nearly five-fold.[5] Raising its equity five times from 1905 to 1911 (to 80 million crowns) it held 35% of Czech capital in 1913. But other important Czech banks had appeared on the scene, like the Czech Industrial Bank (1898), the Prague Credit Bank (1899) and the savings-bank-orientated *Sporobanka* (1903). These four banks, and particularly the Živnobanka (which developed interests in other Slav lands), were now seen in Viennese circles as a factor to reckon with, and in the jockeying for position which characterised European banking relations in the pre-war years, in which national and international motifs intertwined, the Živnobanka both wrestled with the Creditanstalt to prevent Viennese cartel control over sections of Bohemian industry (for example, in metallurgy) and cooperated with the Viennese banks on other issues.

The Czech case, economically as in so much else, is an object lesson for the mobilisation of a non-dominant community. No other non-German people in Austria can really be discussed in the context of industrialisation at this time, except perhaps the Slovenes. Straddling German speaking central Europe's outlet to the Adriatic at Trieste, in a traditional iron mining region, the Slovene people, heavily agricultural though it remained in occupational structure, had living standards closer to those of its Austro-German Alpine neighbours than to those of Galicians or Dalmatians. Ljubljana with suburbs grew from around 30,000 to 65,000 under Dualism but local capital, initially German in character, predictably lost out in this period to the financial centres of the Monarchy. Toussaint Hočevar has argued interestingly that this was not the end of the story. In ways which have Czech analogies, he suggests that, alongside big capital from outside, a network of local savings and agrarian societies could develop which was uniquely able to tap into practical need and ethnic sentiment at the grass roots. Eventually, under the aegis of the Slovene national–liberal mayor of Ljubljana, Ivan Hribar, and with the organisational help and 48% stake of the Vienna branch of the Živnobanka, local interests were able to found the Ljubljana Credit Bank in 1900, as the city's first independent commercial bank, and that in Slovene hands.

The capital of the Ljubljana Credit Bank was diminutive in relative terms (500,000 crowns), but Hočevar's thesis of an economic twin-track of big and local capital retains its interest. Austro-German economic strength was not able to dominate the far-flung Dual Monarchy just of itself, any more than German language and culture had been able to do in the old unitary state. An element of dialogue was necessary. Moreover, this dialogue had to bridge not only ethnic fissures, but also the gap between urban and traditional sectors in a still largely rural Monarchy.

Dualist Agriculture

In 1910 26% of Austria's and 18% of Hungary's working population were employed in mining and industry, as against 53% and 60% in agriculture. The latter percentages had fallen over the previous twenty years (from 62% and 67% respectively) but the Monarchy as a whole was still an *Agrarland* in the expressive German phrase. After all, scythes and sickles were a key part of Austrian iron production. For some provinces this was overwhelmingly so; the 1910 figure for agricultural employment in Croatia was 82%. What industry the outlying provinces had was largely agrarian-related, the chief exception being the oil industry of Galicia which had begun to develop strongly around the eastern towns of Drohobycz and Borysław after the railway arrived in 1883. Production spurted briefly in the early twentieth century to 5% of world output. Symptoms of regional backwardness were that the Galician oil industry was largely financed from Vienna and that a refining as opposed to an extractive sector remained in its infancy. 'Our youth has acquired a mania for bureaucratic careers', exclaimed the advocate of Galician industrialisation S. Szczepanowski in 1888, rueing the neglect of economics for politics.[6]

Traditionally, Galicia had had a flourishing textile centre in the majority Jewish town of Brody, also in the east of the province. But Brody fared ill against Austro-Czech competition in the free trade era. With more than a quarter of Cisleithania's population Galicia had only 6% of its industrial output. As late as 1912, less than one in five of its 320,000 'workers' worked in modern industrial enterprises. The coal mines around Cracow and Chrzanów had not yet prompted a significant iron industry. Much capitalist production actually took place on noble estates, as in Croatia, where in 1890 40% of all industrial workers (defined as working in businesses of more than twenty employees) were in forest enterprise, mainly on the great estates of eastern Slavonia, to which the 15% working in saw-mills might be added. The overall figure was less than ten thousand!

There were people in both provinces who put the case for industrial development, Ziblikiewicz and Szczepanowski in Galicia in the 1880s, for example, or the Zagreb chamber of commerce in Croatia. But force of circumstances was against them. The Polish large landowners who dominated the Galician Diet after 1870 were suspicious of economic changes which might loosen their grip. At odds with the peasants over the grossly unequal share of the pre-1848 forest and common land they had received from the neo-absolutist regime, they long felt little incentive to tackle peasant illiteracy with the energy of Hungary's long-standing minister of education Ágoston Trefort (1872-88). In 1890 the province's illiteracy still stood at 67%. In Croatia the limited autonomy secured Croatia by the 1868 *Nagodba* left all major economic powers with Hungary, which blocked proposals to create a separate economic department in the Zagreb mini-government. Khuen-Héderváry, Ban from 1883 to 1903, even got the Hungarian trade minister to condemn the Zagreb chamber of commerce for exceeding its competence in publishing a statistical survey of Croatia-Slavonia as a whole. By feeling a Magyar but also a Slavonian landowner, he favoured the economic interests of this conservative and in large part German- or Magyar-identifying class against those of the fledgeling Croatian bourgeoisie. That said, given the Monarchy's common market, wood was possibly the only competitive product Croatia had; a number of concessions granted for Croatian economic projects in the 1860s were not acted upon because native capital was just too weak.

In areas where social–political tensions were less inhibiting a better balance could be struck that enabled a division of labour between town and country and between different interest groups in the countryside. In the Alpine lands and the more prosperous parts of Hungary west of the Danube it meant large landowners concentrating on timber and grain, and peasants on stock-rearing, viniculture and market gardening. The logic of this was that noble land had always contained a disproportionately large share of forest, while peasants could provide the intensive labour which stock-rearing required. Woods covered 35% of Austria, 28% of Hungary proper and 36% of Croatia. This division of labour reflected the continued economic importance of large estates throughout the Monarchy. The Schwarzenberg family, for example, still held 117,000 hectares after the peasant emancipation. Altogether 0.1% of Bohemian landlords owned 36% of the land and 0.16% of Hungarian some 32% (1895). Hit by the fall in market value of compensation bonds, however, many nobles had to sell up in full or in part. The middle gentry in Hungary, owning between 200 and 1000 holds (a hold equalled 1.43 acres), shrank to 7000 families by 1900, losing land to peasants but particularly to the large estates of over a thousand holds, whose share of the land more than doubled to 19.4% by the end of the period. Galician large landlords gradually sold off land to peasants, so that their share fell from 43% of arable and 90% of woods and pastures before 1866 to 41% of all land by 1889, and they disposed of another 122,000 hectares by 1902. The idea of a polarised development, with the great estates and an emerging prosperous layer of the peasantry gaining at the expense of middle landowners and smallholders is attractive in these circumstances, but the empirical evidence is thin, at least as far as the peasantry is concerned. Different estimates for Hungary see the peasant share of the land either slightly falling, or rising by 300,000 hectares. In Galicia it is possible that the process among the peasantry was more one of homogenisation than polarisation, as population pressure generalised a tendency towards smaller plots. An important factor here was that, unlike in earlier times, there was litle possibility of adding to the cultivated area. Indeed, after 1860, this area in Bohemia began to contract. The exception was Hungary, where the land added by the great river regulation projects of the neo-absolutist and early Dualist periods were hailed by contemporaries as a second 'occupation of the fatherland'.

The provinces with the smallest proportion of estate land were those of Alpine Austria. Yet it was these who showed the way in capitalist development, through the systematic commercial exploitation of the forests which were their main resource. The forest statute of 1855 smoothed the way. By 1899 wood had become the largest item

in Austrian exports. On the Hungarian and Galician plains, however, the chief tendency was the growth in cereal production, particularly of wheat, profiting from the greater ease of transport which
rail afforded this bulky commodity. There was a large increase in
the area under crops aided by the river regulation schemes in Hungary and by the general decline in fallow, down from 21.6% to 1% in
Bohemia (1848–1908) and from 22% to 9% in Hungary (1870–
1914). Sixty-two per cent of the *Alföld* went under plough, as compared to just 5% in 1720. The three-field system, general in the
1850s in the west of the Monarchy in its improved form (i.e. with
root crops, and clover in the fallow) yielded more and more to convertible agriculture, certainly on large estates. By the twentieth century clover covered 8–12% of the cultivated area and the land
devoted to root crops had nearly doubled. Agricultural machines,
which for so long had been an aristocratic rarity, finally achieved
something of a wider breakthrough in the last third of the century,
particularly in threshing, with 290,000 or 9% of farm units reporting
their use in 1902 – mainly animal powered. Probably optimistically,
the Hungarian agricultural census of 1895 no longer even had a category for wooden ploughs. Thus it was not just crop production which
grew – by some 65% between 1868–75 and 1904–13 – but agricultural productivity, traditionally little better than stagnant. American competition dented but did not reverse this ascent, and when
world wheat prices began to rise again from the end of the century
the expansion of wheat lands resumed.

Peasants shared with large estates in cereal production, but in
stock-rearing they were largely on their own. Sheep and wool, seen
before 1848 as a noble concern, declined in importance, particularly
after Australia began to make its impact. By contrast, cattle and pigs
became more profitable. Hence the Monarchy produced 286,000 tons
of beef in 1850 and 675,000 tons in 1910. Dairy cattle also had a bigger
role. After all, each Viennese drank nearly a pint of milk a day in 1913,
four times more than eighty years previously. Another preserve of
peasant production was wine, but the phylloxera disease that affected
crops from the late 1870s dealt the industry a blow that forced many
viniculturalists into other fields, particularly market gardening.
Peasants could be resourceful in developing new lines. Poultry, for
example, came to be nearly as valuable in Hungarian exports as
grain. Interestingly, in the case of Hungary at least, it was not the
rich peasants who proved the most entrepreneurial. These tended
to use their wealth in traditional ways, to buy land and maintain a

lifestyle they felt appropriate to their local status. It was the owners of 30–50 holds of land, enough for a cushion against the daily grind or the threat of a ruinous harvest, who aspired most creatively to better things. Such people were perhaps the chief beneficiaries from the marked expansion of peasant credit facilities in the second half of the Dualist period. Notoriously, rural credit had been a noble affair, so that even institutions intended for a broader stratum like the Galician Peasant Credit Association (1863) or the Small-Farmer Land Credit Institute in Hungary (1879) did not in fact serve their needs. It was the local credit societies, often organised on Schulze–Delitzsch or Raiffeisen principles and multiplying from the 1880s, which got to grips with the problem of cheap credit in small sums. On the eve of the First World War there were no fewer than 8356 of these in Austria and over 3000 in Hungary, most of them attached to a central organisation. By this time specialist agricultural education had also made strides, particularly in Austria, where student numbers in the 192 middle and lower agricultural schools in 1907, at 7518, stood nearly three times higher than twenty years before.

Plainly, the Monarchy's agrarian performance was not negligible. Sandgruber estimates a doubling in the value of output between 1850 and the pre-war decade, while estimates of a rise in Hungarian agricultural production vary between 1.8% and 2.2% a year for the Dualist period.[7] Yet though Bairoch's well-known agricultural figures for eleven countries show the Monarchy advancing relatively faster from its 1840 base than all but Germany, Switzerland and Sweden, it still finished ahead only of Italy, Russia and Spain.[8] Uncertain as such international comparisons must be, this mixed result draws attention to weaknesses in the Habsburg rural economy which also deserve attention.

What pulled the Monarchy down was the nosedive of all regional indices as it stretched away to the south and east, towards Russia and the Balkans. Thus fallow land was twice the Hungarian average in Transylvania, credit societies there were four times smaller in resources and a two- or three-field system was five times more prevalent than west of the Danube. Wooden ploughs, illiteracy and usury held their redoubts in such regions. The fierce denizens of the arid mountains bordering Montenegro in southern Dalmatia revolted in 1869 against a military service none had till then dared impose on them, as likewise Herzegovinian Serbs in 1882.

Many of these disparities were, of course, historically rooted. Here the economic implications of liberalism may be noted, which could operate in the more advanced parts of the Monarchy too. Land as a means of production was not indefinitely extendable like capital. Opening it fully to the market meant a likely transfer of small, unviable plots to larger hands. The loss of peasant servitudes, removal of prohibitions on usury and dividing up the core peasant homestead, and legal bias against collective property rights (as in the *zadruga*) combined with a continuing increase of population under Dualism to swell rural proletarianisation. Industrialisation reduced some of the traditional earning options of the rural poor, like domestic industry or the carting of goods. The lifestyle of small upland peasants in the Austrian Alps became unsustainable, as the rural population fell not just relatively but absolutely and family farms dealt with labourers' 'flight from the land' by relying on their own members, breeding a lasting anti-liberal animus. In Hungary, expanded commercial wheat-growing, facilitated by the railways, meant a harder life for peasants than the more laid-back pastoralism, made still harder as American competition grew. Dalmatia's ship-building industry was eclipsed by the turn to steam and her other mainstay, wine, smitten by phylloxera. If industrialisation did offer alternative employment, in the purely agrarian provinces emigration was often the only safety-valve, estimated at 720,000 between 1896 and 1910 for Galicia alone.

Peasants' preparedness to uproot themselves and migrate to the unknown – though networks soon sprang up to guide their way – belies views of them as resistant to economic change. This is not necessarily contradicted by their often tepid response to reform initiatives which came from outside, like the Austrian laws of 1868–69 setting aside funds for drainage, or the commassation law of 1883 (to amalgamate the different strips of land into which peasant plots were usually divided), even the 1873 law on rural association, which later blossomed. Heavy peasant indebtedness, too, could result from the aspiration for improvement rather than mismanagement, it has been argued for the Alpine lands, while the poverty of the Galician peasantry or the struggling farmers of south Bohemia (sometimes dubbed Bohemia's East Elbia) came from circumstances, not apathy; south Bohemian potatoes were simply not as profitable as other Czech regions' sugar. Regional lags in development could produce processes curiously out of phase with each other. While the Budapest market was increasingly deserted by big businessmen as old-fashioned, the number of markets in rural centres continued to grow; and in rural Croatia the movement of artisans from the towns into the countryside, which further west had been a feature of proto-industrialisation much earlier, now proceeded apace, and was linked with the doubling of shops in Croatian villages. This was, in context, modernisation, but that protean concept put on particularly diverse forms in the polyglot Habsburg realm.

A Case for the Austro-Hungarian Economy?

Is an overall balance possible? David Good, in his innovative *The Economic Rise of the Habsburg Empire* (1984), has commented on the negative tone of much discussion of economic development in the Habsburg lands. The history of the later Monarchy is implicitly constructed around a theme of failure, and a variant of this motif has been present also in the account given above, with its emphasis on the inability of Austro-German liberal capitalists to establish an economic hegemony as leaders of Austro-Hungarian industrialisation.

Accounts highlighting the Monarchy's relatively sluggish economic progress commonly point to both objective and subjective factors. Austria-Hungary was rather poorly endowed in mineral resources for its size. It was an all but landlocked realm, from which it was easier to reach the main sea-routes down the Elbe to Hamburg than via its own chief port of Trieste. Though the Danube gave it a certain geographic unity this was not complete, for Galicia-Bukovina and Dalmatia lay beyond the mountain ranges which girt the river basin and the Danube flowed into the Black Sea, a commercial backwater. Besides, nationality squabbles reduced the possible economic benefits of 'Danubian' unity, for Hungary notoriously pursued its own railway and freight tariff policies; while even that unity, as Oscar Jászi famously argued,[9] could lock different parts of the Monarchy into complementary arrangements which kept the agrarian east undeveloped, thus diminishing market demand for the dual state as a whole. The negative influence of the Monarchy's conservative social elites and hide-bound social structures has often been adduced, and used as part explanation of a lack of dynamism on the part of its business leaders. While there has been general recognition of the great regional diversity in the empire and the tendency of overall figures to mask higher performance in certain parts of it, these very facts have been turned against the Monarchy's leaders, in that they failed to overcome the economic disparities.

These arguments are plausible and mainly true. The difficulty is to know the yardstick by which success or failure is to be judged. Economic history is particularly awkward territory in this regard, since its quantitative aspect invites comparisons which are less regularly ventured in political or cultural fields. But even statistical comparison is swayed by frameworks of assumption which can lead, for example, to studies of the French nineteenth-century economy in the 1950s from the standpoint of economic failure and in the 1980s from a standpoint of relative success. In the case of judgements of Habsburg economic performance two yardsticks appear to have been influential. One is the practical example of Germany; the other is the theoretical model of a successful capitalist economy.

The German comparison, common to contemporaries and historians, reflects what has been said about Austro-Germans' role in the Monarchy and their self-image as bearers of German civilisation in east-central Europe. The sense of relative economic backwardness paralleled the Monarchy's weakening as a German power, but is given objective force by modern estimates that Austria grew at least a percentage point faster than the *Zollverein* in the Pre-March years, even if figures suggesting her national income exceeded Germany's in 1800 seem over-speculative.[10] Against this background Imperial Germany's later spurt ahead came to be viewed in Austria in a climate of self-disillusion. (Hungarian economic history, it should be said, has its own special brand of masochism, in which most pages bear tables showing Hungary at the bottom for the particular item in question.) May one not, however, invert the terms of the problem? More surprising than the Austrian fall-back behind Germany by 1900 was surely the weak German position a century before, considering her natural resources, unequalled university system and more favoured location. Indeed, German frustration at her lag behind her neighbours at that time proved to be the most powerful force in nineteenth-century Europe.

The comparison of the Habsburg Monarchy with Germany is not only inevitable, but has the benefit of pointing to an important debate on how industrial society expands. In one set of views, industrialisation processes fan out from the original industrialiser: the emphasis may be, as in Pollard, on international trade – the exchange of finished goods for raw materials – through which societies originally peripheral to the industrial core acquire the means to industrialise themselves and enter into similar relationships with their periphery; or it may be, as with Gerschenkron, on the transmission of technology, whereby late industrialisers can use the advantages of the newest techniques to catch up with the core. In each case, late industrialisation succeeds. In the so-called underdevelopment view, on the other hand, which has roots in Marxism, the spread of modern industrial society is seen as inhibited by unequal relationships between core and periphery, perpetuating the latter's status as supplier of raw materials to the former. Examples of both kinds of development are not hard to find. While Germany and other now developed European countries were once peripheries to the first industrial societies in north-west Europe, in the Third World there are many societies which seem to have little hope of escaping from their current economic marginality. Is there indeed a line to be drawn beyond which the distance of one society from another, economic/cultural/political, will tend to make any relationship between them exploitative rather than, as in Pollard's model, collaborative? Was the Habsburg Monarchy a case in point, with the difference in performance from its west to its east not so much a matter of time lag, eventually remediable, as of developmental divide likely to grow further with time? If so, the comparison with Germany is indeed one between German success and Habsburg failure.

Many Hungarian nationalists at the time and since argued for the notion of an underdeveloped Hungary kept in a semi-colonial position by the customs union with Austria. The picture presented above of the Hungarian economy in the Dualist period gives little support for this view. The framework provided by the customs union for the inflow of Austrian capital and a secure market for Hungarian exports did not prevent a gradual loosening of Hungary's economic dependency on Cisleithania. Hungarian GNP grew an estimated six-fold in the years 1850–1913, as against five-fold for Austria. Her strengthened relative position led to successive increases in the Hungarian contribution to common expenses from the original ratio of 70 : 30 to 63.6 : 36.4 by 1907. Nor was this progress confined to western Hungary and Budapest. Once Transylvania acquired a fuller rail network by the 1890s (twice as dense as neighbouring Romania's) it too began to advance. It could of course be argued that Hungary's progress under the Compromise was due less to the continued economic ties with Austria than the self-government she had won, which the multinational Monarchy denied to its other peoples. But the majority of Hungary's political leaders resisted nationalist pressures for the abandonment of the customs union, and Czech capital was able to make great strides without political autonomy.

Habsburg multi-nationalism does not therefore seem to have doomed her non-German peoples to the permanent dependence of underdevelopment theory. Within the customs union national movements could act as a useful spur to social mobilisation, particularly in the stimulus they gave to the development of associations and rural banks. David Good has argued interestingly that regional differentials in savings bank deposits and income per capita were narrowing in the Monarchy in the later Dualist period and may be taken as proxies for a similar process in living standards as a whole. He suggests a possible exception was eastern Galicia. Yet even here Galician backwardness was not the result of a classic draining of the periphery's resources by the metropole. The province contributed 10% of state revenues but received 16% of state expenditures, benefiting from the remarkable rise under Dualism of the proportion of the Austrian budget devoted to infrastructure – from 12% to 42%, by far the largest item being railways. Besides, if east Galicia, along with Dalmatia, was the most backward part of the Monarchy it saw a substantial mobilisation of the traditionally subordinate Ruthenian peasantry; east Galicia became (and was to remain) the leading sector of the wider Ukrainian cultural and nationalist movement of the twentieth century. It was from this area, too, that hundreds of thousands of Jews moved westwards to Budapest and Vienna, or sometimes to Vienna via Budapest. En route the Monarchy provided a framework in which significant numbers of a ghettoised, traditionalist, Yiddish-speaking community were transformed into a dynamic component of Magyar and Austro-German business and culture – one of the most dramatic metamorphoses of modern times. Though the bulk of the Monarchy's citizens continued to live in straitened circumstances in this period, it did provide them with more *elements* of contact with west European norms than most of them were to experience after its collapse.

That the Monarchy was better than what came after is of course a negative defence. Some of the criticism of its performance has been motivated by the view that it could have done much better, if entrepreneurial capitalism had been more genuinely embraced. In its stronger form this view sees the tendency towards cartelisation and protection, or attempts at government aid to industry, as distortions of the free market principle, threatening to lead to misallocation of resources. In a weaker form the emphasis is on the anti-capitalist ethos of leading social strata. Neither position is wholly convincing. Rudolph argues that Austro-German and Czech banks pursued a cautious policy towards direct involvement in industrial promotion after the crash of 1873, particularly in the next 15 years.[11] This is unsurprising, and the implied comparison with German dynamism only works if it is assumed that most modern businessmen like taking risks. While the image of the charismatic entrepreneur may be helpful in promoting the cause of managerial salaries, the German sociologist Weber at roughly this time was outlining his famous thesis that modern society was not based on charisma but on bureaucratic rationalism. Finance appears to be a success story of the Dualist epoch, both in the state and private sectors. The pre-1867 turbulence of state finances came to an end, capped by Austria's successful adherence to the gold standard in 1892, while equally against precedent is the lack of signs of a general credit shortage in the Monarchy's last decades. Cartelisation provided a control over a necessary process of rationalisation; it was, besides, like many other aspects of Habsburg business organisation, an import from the highly successful German economy.

As to the conservative ethos of Austrian society, this was very true of the aristocracy and court, as elsewhere in pre-1914 Europe. But not for nothing did Viennese parlance refer to the 'first society' of the aristocracy and the 'second society' of non-titled wealth: Austrian society's many fissures limited the social influence of an aristocracy which was as removed from political power as any in Europe. The economic position of the great estates had not been broken, but it did not appear to impede the economic progress of Bohemia, any more than did the gross maldistribution of land in Britain.

One very important exception must be made to the above argument. In Hungary power and influence undoubtedly lay with a coalition of gentry and aristocrats whose preferred framework of rule limited economic options. The industry which developed under their aegis had an agrarian flavour, and after the elite became converts to protection their policies meant high food prices for the poor, subsidising of the well-off and no hope of a breakthrough to a modern industrial democracy. In 1914 Hungary was still like Britain under the Corn Laws. Budapest, after Minneapolis the greatest corn-milling centre in the world, was an impressive central European city with financial and cultural institutions to match, but all this rested on a shaky base. Far more than in Bohemia the unequal land system in the countryside that was the quid pro quo of noble–bourgeois cooperation had destabilising implications. Hence most modern Hungarian historians, while accepting that Hungary did indeed develop within the Dual Monarchy, lament the lop-sided nature of that development.

To accept this perspective is to agree that structural limitations, even deformations, were built into the Monarchy's economic modernisation. Much criticism can be turned away, but not all. Hungarian industrialisation inevitably bore the stamp of the age-old agrarian society regarded apprehensively by Hungarian themselves at the outset of the constitutional era, just as Austro-German industrialisation combined the legacy of old superiority complex towards the Slavs with a later inferiority complex towards the Reich Germans. Czechs and some other Slavs organised economically on the basis of the national consciousness that had begun to bud in the romantic age. Economic development cannot be separated from the social and ethnic matrix in which it occurred. It is these social and ethnic themes which must next be explored.

9 Society and Social Movements

Liberalism and industrialism remained half-cock ventures in the Dual Monarchy. But they were still the most sustained influences chipping away at the structures of a highly traditional society. The result was the curious hybrid wittily observed in Robert Musil's famous novel *The Man without Qualities*: 'By its constitution it was liberal, but its system of government was clerical. The system of government was clerical, but the general attitude to life was liberal.'[1] Musil was right. Austria was indeed a society where the liberal values of the 1867 settlement were prevented from achieving hegemony by the peasant, petit bourgeois and worker majority, but where the post-liberal regimes shrank from repudiating the liberal baggage entirely. In Hungary the pattern was somewhat different and will be discussed later. This chapter's concern is with the evolution of Cisleithanian society, its mix of conservative and liberal motifs and the political system which came to take the place of German liberal rule.

The Traditional Elites

At the pinnacle of Austrian society the life of the Emperor himself epitomised the ambiguous impact of liberal forces on a conservative core. Certainly, Franz Joseph was a conservative by background and temperament. The etiquette at his court was severe: the weekly family dinners for those of the three score or so Habsburg Archdukes present in Vienna could see some leaving unfed, as it was the convention for each dish to be removed as soon as the Emperor had sampled it — and he ate quickly. Except under the *Bürgerministerium* and when hunting (his only real pastime) Franz Joseph always wore military uniform. Though pious, he was enough of a Gallican traditionalist to shrug off over-zealous Papal pressure, dismissing a threat of spiritual sanctions over the liberal church laws of 1874 with the simple reply that his conscience was clear. While his view of 'my peoples' was purely dynastic, he matched it with an unbending sense of duty, rising from a simple iron bed to start working through state papers by 5 a.m., including the usually lengthy memoranda addressed him by his ministers under the title 'All Highest Submission' at the rate of some 4000 a year; his lifestyle retained bedroom chamber-pots but abjured the telephone.

Yet for all his traditionalism Franz Joseph for most of his reign was formally a constitutional monarch, if the constitutional spirit hardly breathed from the charge he gave his new prime minister Prince Adolf Auersperg in 1871:

> Concealment of nothing from me, no innovations, unity, strict adherence to the programme laid down which will receive my support. I will tolerate no departure from it.[2]

Nonetheless, Franz Joseph developed constitutional habits to the extent of consulting on particular issues only the ministers responsible for them – though this also involved a non-recognition of collective ministerial responsibility. He stomached some policies he did not much care for, like the liberals' anti-clerical legislation of 1867–74. He even, at the age of 77, was prepared to create new peers if necessary to steer a universal suffrage bill through the Austrian upper chamber. If he never appears to have contemplated the *coup d'état* that Bismarck by the 1880s was saying was the only answer to Austria's problems, this no doubt reflected part constitutional propriety, part the real power an ethnically divided parliament in fact left him, part limited imagination. He was intelligent enough, though, to realise his limitations; he lacked, he had said after Sadowa, a 'happy touch'.[3] For the rest, his relations with his ministers retained a cold-blooded streak. Notoriously, the talented commerce minister Bruck had cut his throat on finding a curt dismissal notice on his desk in 1860. Ministers for Franz Joseph were still ultimately instruments of his rather than any popular will.

The Emperor's aloofness no doubt owed something to his own bleak experiences in the pursuit of duty. His brother, the Archduke Maximilian, who had accepted the Mexican throne against Franz Joseph's advice, was shot by Mexican rebels in 1867. His child wife and first cousin, Elizabeth of Bavaria, grew up into a beautiful woman he adored but she developed a neurotic restlessness and compulsion to travel which kept them increasingly apart. His very intelligent and highly strung son and heir, Rudolf, committed suicide with a 17-year-old girl in turmoil at his father's conservatism and his likely gonorrhoea in 1889. When Empress Elizabeth was stabbed to death by an Italian anarchist nine years later, the anguished Emperor exclaimed: 'Is nothing spared me on this earth?' For such a man the routine of daily devotion to duty offered as much solace, perhaps, as the more human yet decorous friendship with the actress Katharina Schratt, introduced to him by the Empress, to whom he wrote engagingly self-deprecating letters: 'note the picture of the great statesman pondering at his desk', as he enclosed the latest official photos.[4]

The education of Rudolf offers the most interesting example of liberal influences on his father. It was to be entrusted to believers, not free-thinkers, but was to give Rudolf a familiarity with the spirit of the age, which happened to be the climacteric of nineteenth-century European liberalism. The result was a young prince whose notebooks and essays were a compendium of progressive conventionalities. Yet while never abandoning these views the adult Rudolf could organise the horse-whipping of a German radical nationalist who had attacked aristocratic horse-play. He was caught in a bind not confined to the nineteenth century whereby would-be royal reformers find themselves trapped between the desire to draw closer to the people and an inability to renounce the ways of their exalted station. One Habsburg, Johann Salvator, most talented of the Archdukes but blocked in his attempts to modernise the army, did indeed renounce his title, and as Johann Orth qualified for a career as a merchant seaman. On his first voyage as captain, accompanied by his long standing ex-ballet dancer lover, he disappeared off Cape Horn in a midwinter hurricane in 1890.

Such tensions were less marked in the aristocracy, partly because of its lack of initiative, lambasted by Rudolf in an anonymous pamphlet in 1878. Though Austria had one of the highest rates of ennoblement in Europe – with 5761 cases between 1849 and 1914 – it was the very largely self-contained 300–400 families of the older aristocracy with entrée at court which constituted what contemporaries called the 'First Society'. Composed of 'genial, friendly, hospitable incompetents', in a common view,[5] they were helped by their redemption payments to retain the bulk of Austria's large estates, particularly in the provinces where serfdom had been most pronounced. One hundred and sixty families with the title of count or above held 22.5% of Bohemia, over half of it owned by just fourteen of them; the same groups held only 9.6% of Lower Austria. The leading Austrian aristocrats, it has been suggested, were alone in Europe in matching the wealth of their British counterparts, yet the fullest figures are available for the senior branch of the Windisch-Graetzes, whose estate of 30,000 hectares (72% forest) was less than a third those of the Schwarzenbergs and Lobkowitzes.

It showed an income averaging 316,000 florins in 1862–68 rising to 1,525,000 crowns in 1900–03, with estate personnel increasing from 134 to 224 over roughly this period. The estate does not appear to have been particularly well managed; loan repayments took over 60% of income over long periods. But rising prices around the turn of the century, particularly of cattle, mostly made up for any short-comings. Even the debts of over two million crowns run up by an heir were more of an embarrassment than a disaster, and he was packed off to Brazil. It seems the great estates, which were, of course, nearly always entailed (though not in the Windisch-Graetzes' case), had too much going for them to be at much risk from the business cycles that regularly knocked out industrial and commercial enterprises.

Thus the high nobility retained a sound enough economic base to nourish their sense of social superiority. Unlike most of their German counterparts, they continued till the end of the nineteenth century to be educated largely by private tutors, appearing in secondary school only to take the final *Matura* examination; when they began to send their children to school (the Schwarzenbergs never did) it was to the prestigious *Schottengymnasium* in Vienna or to board in private Catholic foundations, often strict and spartan, but fostering the strong identification with Catholicism which became in the liberal age part of aristocratic self-identification in a way it had not been before. The sense of being a caste apart comes out best in a Hungarian example: a seven-year-old Esterházy asked his governess at a retainer's funeral, 'Do gentlefolk die too?'[6]

How far did aristocratic sense of superiority reflect a real leadership role? In economic terms aristocrats were no longer at the cutting edge of innovation. Earlier, the first Bessemer engine in Austria had been introduced on a Schwarzenberg estate in 1863, and the Archduke Friedrich owned 12% of Silesia and Austria's fourth largest iron works in 1880. But after a quarrel with Rothschild in the early 1860s the great magnates who had done so much to finance the Creditanstalt tended to withdraw from an active role. In the upper ranks of the army, too, they shrank from 56% to 14% between 1848 and 1914, though much less so in the diplomatic service, or more representational positions, as in their near monopoly of provincial governorships. Even the premiership was effectively reserved to them till the late 1890s, with a man like Prince Adolf III Windisch-Graetz (PM 1893–95) notoriously playing the figurehead; family tradition has him answering all the Emperor's questions with 'as your Majesty commands'.[7]

The aristocracy were assured a genuine political influence, however, by the curial system and the partially hereditary nature of the Austrian upper chamber, alongside life peers. The Large Landowners' Curia, elected by a few thousand proprietors paying over 250 florins in direct taxes, played an important parliamentary role, as did its equivalents at diet level. It was shifts in allegiance here which determined whether the key province of Bohemia had a Czech or German majority and which helped end the dominance of the German liberals in the Reichsrat in 1879. But this very role betrays the landed curias' openness to regime manipulation, exploiting the aristocracy's traditional loyalty to the throne – a loyalty overriding its internal division between the so-called feudal conservatives, who were federally inclined, and the 'Constitutional Large Landowners', who aligned themselves with the Austro-German liberals. The division was particularly acute in Bohemia, where the 'feudal' magnates, though speaking German for preference, supported the cause of Czech state right. In fact, the Bohemian feudal conservatives' loyalties exposed them potentially to a double dependency, on the Emperor above and the Czech peasantry below, who largely controlled local government after the 1862 communal reform. Hence the unmistakable note of gratification with which Count Heinrich Clam-Martinic, a federalist leader, informed Prince Georg Lobkowitz in 1867 that a peasant of his estate had greeted him in Czech and they had conversed together in the count's first-class train carriage, the lower-class carriages being all occupied.[8] Such complaisance would have been much less likely in Galicia, where the Polish aristocracy had an almost total grip on power at local, diet and university level. Noble estates in Galicia were not subject to communal jurisdiction; the middle class was weak and the magnates could present themselves as pillars of native culture with far greater confidence than their Germanised Bohemian peers, while reducing Ruthenian Diet representation to a minimum. Nor did Polish nobles' regional hegemony debar them from a wider Austrian role. They provided Austria with two prime ministers, the influential finance minister Dunajewski (1880–91), common ministers of foreign affairs and finance and many other leading figures.

Traditionally, dynasty and aristocracy had been flanked by army and Church. The military ethos of honour, loyalty and hierarchy paralleled that of nobility, and gained all army officers the right to direct access to the Emperor and his court. Their elaborate duelling code, set out in numerous works on etiquette, continued to bolster their mystique despite the criminalisation of duels in Austrian penal law, not least because it enjoyed Franz Joseph's tacit approval. Parliamentary control over the armed forces, except financial, remained a chimera. Nonetheless, the nexus of army and nobility, which had seen 60% of noble second sons enter it in the second half of the eighteenth century, gradually weakened. Factors were, if not the requirement of secondary school graduation for officer candidates from 1868, then the generally hard circumstances and poor pay of army life, only limited favouritism for aristocrats and military under-funding by finance-conscious parliaments. In 1914 20% of reserve officers were actually Jews. As in other European armed forces the artillery and the navy were particularly notable for a bourgeois ethos. Overall, the army with its elaborate organisation of its multi-national intake, whose hair was to be cut back 6.5 cm in front and 2.5 cm at the back, who were to have 4.5 square metres of barrack space and 22.4 kilos of straw in their pallets, was closer to the bureaucratic than the aristocratic spirit; and won the plaudits of the future socialist president Karl Renner for its relative democracy.

Despite its gospel of humility and the origins of its clergy – between 1815 and 1870, 47% of graduates of the Viennese archdiocesan seminary were sons of landed peasants or artisans, with only one high noble and day-labourer apiece – the Church's links with elite society were also traditionally strong. Twenty-four bishops and archbishops presided at Crown Prince Rudolf's wedding. Its bishops, twelve of whom held the title 'Prince-Bishop', often enjoyed the incomes and the lifestyles of aristocrats, like the Croatian bishop of Djakovo, Josip Juraj Strossmayer, whose art collection became the nucleus of the Croatian National Gallery and whose bequests set the Yugoslav Academy on its feet. Many of them by tradition *were* aristocrats; Schwarzenberg, Cardinal Archbishop of Prague, was always known as 'the Prince' to his staff. Moreover, the Church like dynasty and high aristocracy claimed to stand above nationality. Its sees cut across ethnic and even state lines (witness the Archdiocese of Breslau) with the sang-froid of African colonial empires. For all this, the Church had also suffered as a pillar of elite power. It had been badly mauled by its liberal foes through the loss of the Concordat and curtailing of its educational role, and a low point in vocations in the mid-1870s in Vienna and Prague dioceses, particularly from the sons of teachers, testified to a certain crisis of confidence. Besides, it was increasingly divided on national issues. Strossmayer himself headed the Croatian national movement in the 1860s and was suspected of Panslavism by the Emperor. In a celebrated incident in 1888 Franz Joseph publicly rebuked him for sending greetings to the anniversary celebrations of the Russian Orthodox Church at a time of Austro-Russian tension, only to be startled when Strossmayer repeatedly answered back: 'No, I really think you must have been mad . . . I repeat, your Majesty, my conscience is clear.'[9]

Yet the weakness of the Church and its elite links was more apparent than real. Neither Strossmayer, known as a liberal Catholic, nor even the radical union of Czech parish priests formed in 1902, doubted the principle of the alliance of Church and state. Feudal conservatives did not take their support of Czech federalism to the point of sharing Czech Hussite nostalgia: Cardinal Schwarzenberg prided himself that he had stopped the 'heretic' Hus from being commemorated in the Czech National Theatre rebuilt in 1882.[10] At the grass roots among peasants and artisans the Church was strong, and a hundred Catholic associations were founded in Vienna in the 1870s. Drawing on the romantic restorative motifs of the Catholic revival of the early nineteenth century, Catholic thinkers led by the ex-Lutheran convert Vogelsang (1818–90) were elaborating the idea of an organic, corporative society in which the different natural groups (*Stände*) of peasants, craftsmen and merchants could overcome the atomisation of liberal society. Aristocrats like Alois and Alfred Lichtenstein played a role in developing these ideas which were to feed into the Christian Social movement, while aristocrats were naturally dominant in the feudal conservative strand of Catholic thought represented by *Das Vaterland*. What was distinctive about the late nineteenth-century period was that these forms of anti-liberal mobilisation, particularly the Christian Social tendency, increasingly sought an adjunct in popular opinion, not just the dynasty. This entailed the use of the liberal techniques of association, assembly and the press; the first Austrian *Katholikentag* met in 1877. As Count Waldersdorff laid down in 1869, conservatives should use the constitution to remedy the misfortunes it had brought.[11] One of Austrian bourgeois liberalism's main contributions was to sponsor the means by which other social forces could fight against it.

Peasants, Petits Bourgeois and Workers

At a less august level the population at large had made the transition towards modern demographic norms from the 1870s, with a fall first in the death rate, then the birth rate yielding a figure of 28 million by 1910. Tuberculosis took over from epidemic diseases like cholera and smallpox as the major scourge. The high age of marriage in the Alpine lands reflected the distinctive pattern of Austrian development, more orientated to small-scale production, where at its peak around 1850 marriage had come five to seven years later than in factory Britain. One consequence was the high illegitimacy rate (reaching two-thirds of all births in Graz), a significant contributory factor to the bleakness of many lives.

Peasants remained the largest social group. The impact of economic liberalism on them had been a powerful one. Cumulatively, the burden of compensation payments, the loss of peasant servitudes and from 1868 the liberals' ending of restrictions on interest rates and on the breaking up of the household plot had widened the gap between solid peasant proprietors and the less successful majority, a tendency reinforced by the steady rise of population and taxes. In the first half of the Dualist period 81,000 peasant farms went to compulsory auction in the four largest Alpine provinces and nearly 50,000 in Galicia. Meanwhile, the number of peasant holdings rose by 20% in the Czech lands and by 30% in the Alpine lands, suggesting an increase in dwarf holdings as farms were sub-divided. Most striking in this regard was Galicia, where four-fifths of peasant holdings were less than five hectares (12.5 acres) by 1902. By this time 19% of Galicia's rurally employed – and 36% of Bohemia's – were landless.

A three-fold differentiation between prosperous peasants, smallholders and landless can thus be made. But it fails to do full justice to the situation in the post-emancipation decades, especially in the small-holder category. For many people in this swelling group were drawn into dependent relationships with cash-strapped landlords desperate for cheap workhands. Small-holders offered them a reserve army of labour that only needed to be called on at certain times, like harvest time, and might then be paid by a share of the crop harvested rather than in cash. Better-off peasants might provide landlords both labour and payment in return for a lease of extra land. In such ways a variegated transitional system could be created, more advantageous to employers than a fully capitalist one based on permanent agricultural labourers. One neo-feudal feature was the extension of old farm-servant roles, which under serfdom had been essentially youthful and temporary, either through life-long bachelordom, as often in the Alpine regions, or the Bohemian *Deputatisten* who now remained in dependent employ after marriage, working as a family group.

Increasingly, as urbanisation and emigration sucked up the local labour supply, travelling seasonal labour was used, exploiting particularly the hordes of Galicians who tramped from domestic poverty to neighbouring Bohemia and elsewhere.

Galicia displayed the plight of the landless and dwarf peasants at its worst. About half the rural population relied wholly or in part on working for others, whereby employers had the legal right to inflict corporal punishment. Agricultural labourers got on average 50 kreuzer (2p) a day in winter which could buy four pounds each of rye flour and potatoes. Summer work was paid with a share of the harvest, most often every twelfth sheaf, much lower than in neighbouring Russia. 'Why should one wonder that our people are often skinny and weak, slow to work, happy to lie behind the oven, greedy for liquor?', wrote a Ruthenian village mayor in 1885, lamenting the loss of servitudes which allowed for a richer diet.[12] In Bohemia and the Alpine provinces corporal punishment was less applied but rural wages were not much higher, except in Lower Austria, and they fell in real terms from about 1880. The memoirs of the future socialist leader Renner, eighteenth child in a German Moravian rural family, show how social differentiation in free market conditions eroded village solidarity and scattered his own siblings to bleak apprenticeships, failed small businesses and makeshift marriages in the towns. Perhaps the most drastic effect of the penetration of the liberal economy into a once virtually subsistence sphere was the crisis of the *zadruga* in the Monarchy's south Slav lands. Croatian legislation gave individual members, and creditors, of these joint households the right to dispose of their posited share in them; thereby it legitimised and accelerated an existing tendency to secret division, spurred by increased indebtedness and mobility playing in turn upon the internal feuds which anthropologists suspect had been common even in the patriarchal past. 'Come now brother,' as one irate *zadruga* member recalled writing from America to his brother in Germany, in a deposition to the authorities of 1891, 'help me pay that off if you want a share of the house and the plot to that he told me I and the Croatian Land can go to hell he won't give me anything towards it.'[13] In the 1880s the Croatian agricultural population grew by 12% but active male *zadruga* members fell by 11%, though remaining numerous in remoter areas like the largely Serbian Krajina of recent notoriety.

Poorer peasants could try to solve their difficulties by migration to the towns or further afield, for example to seasonal work in Germany, or increasingly to north America. But there were also more direct outlets, like the Croatian disturbances of 1883 and the east Galician farm labourers' strikes of 1902–03 and 1906, which succeeded in winning an increase of the labourers' harvest share. By 1900 even in Galicia two-thirds of children of school age were attending school. The days when peasants would buy only salt and liquor had gone, and village stores, themselves previously rare, sold articles of clothing, rice, white flour, paraffin, oranges and other things previously unknown or made at home. Associational life had arrived, through the reading clubs common to all parts of Austria, and often linked with them the burgeoning singing societies, agrarian circles and peasant credit societies. Nostalgia or satire provides an index of social shift, whether it be Galician ridicule of the umbrella-wielding or newspaper-reading peasant or a Slovene author's distate for the 'tasteless neo-Frankian' dress and 'not always in character' modern songs which were displacing his people's folk ways.[14]

Initially change came to the peasant world from outside, from progressive intellectuals, priests, teachers and rural artisans, whose ideas were taken up most enthusiastically by the upper reaches of the peasantry and the young. This marked the beginning of the end of the aristocratic role as sponsors of innovation in the countryside which had been exercised through the provincial agricultural societies from Enlightenment and *Vormärz* times. These bodies had been overtaken by the variously named peasant 'Kasinos' or circles multiplying in the Alpine provinces and Czech lands in the 1870s, and Galicia and the south Slav lands a decade or two later. There were, for example, 898 of these with 41,000 members in Galicia in 1901 and double that number twelve years later. The chief impulse in Galicia had come from a radical intellectual, Bolesław Wysłouch, an independent-minded priest, Stojałowski, and the Ukrainian peasant journal *Batkivshchyna* (1879), edited by the son of a primary schoolteacher. In Croatia the peasant movement was launched by two university graduates, the brothers Ante and Stjepan Radić. Not surprisingly, the first provincial groupings of these peasant organisations came in the more advanced lands to the west, in Moravia and Bohemia and several Alpine provinces in the 1880s. But the formation of peasant parties occurred within a more limited period, with the Galician PSL (Polish People's Party, 1893) in the lead, followed by the German and Czech Agrarians (1899). That Galicia should organise earlier says something about the role of intellectuals and ideas in backward areas: new ideas under modern circumstances can take root far faster than new social structures, and regions made conscious how far they lag behind will always feel the attraction of overhaul through 'enlightenment' and remoulding of consciousness. Hence the importance of journalism to the peasant or 'populist' movement in Austria, as to other movements of the previously non-dominant at this time; the heart of a movement was usually its central organ and its leaders the editorial board. Hence, too, the didactic idealism which makes movements like those of the late-nineteenth-century Habsburg peasantry strangely moving to a later age.

Despite the culture clash implied by the very words 'urbanity' and 'civilisation' and the anti-liberal demands of peasant programmes (agricultural protection, restrictions on land subdivision and interest rates, more religious influence in the schools), peasant populism ironically also brought peasant values closer to those of liberalism: in the enthusiasm for education, thrift and temperance; in the development of bureaucratic organisation in the cooperative movement; and finally, in that movement's need to adopt capitalist techniques to compete in the market-place. Ernst Bruckmüller has noted, however, that as peasant movements gradually outgrew sponsorship by others, so liberal motifs of independence and individuality tended to decline in favour of the leadership of charismatic personalities. The curious tension between liberal and non-liberal elements here apparent took, with hindsight, its darkest form in the fillip given by peasant movements to anti-Semitism. It was in many ways the resentment of peasant reformers of the Jewish middleman role as lessees of noble estates in Galicia and of most of the province's 17,000 taverns which exacerbated traditional prejudice, as also the rivalry which developed when the cooperative movement sought to displace Jewish shopkeepers with its own village retail outlets, often with intimidation. Rural anti-semitism in Hungary had similar roots.

Unlike peasants, the artisans and shopkeepers of the petite bourgeoisie had on the whole been liberals' unruly allies in 1848 and again in the 1860s. But in a common historiographical view the last decades of the nineteenth century were to see them begin a reactionary Odyssey away from the modern world towards a mix of anti-capitalist nostalgia, cultural philistinism and racial prejudice – leading eventually to Fascism. No doubt this précis of conventional views is overdrawn, but it has a prima facie plausibility in central Europe and may serve as a backdrop to more nuanced discussion.

Economically, the threat to Austrian artisans from large-scale capitalism should not be exaggerated. Often this produced new products which did not compete with theirs, they could themselves exploit new technologies (for example, the sewing machine), or they could find a niche sub-contracting work from large-scale industry. Austria had few large cities and to the end of the century in most small towns old burgher values remained dominant. In some areas modern industry hardly existed. In 1895, 4784 craftsmen and 'industrialists' under the Split chamber of commerce in Dalmatia employed between them 5691 workers![15] But significant pressures from factory industry did exist. Textile handworkers decreased rapidly in Dualist Vienna and in the clothing and shoemaking trades master craftsmen were often reduced to the status of dependants working on commission for large producers under the so-called *Konfektion* system; many artisans turned to shopkeeping, and though Paris-style department stores did not yet challenge them in this role, a tendency for large producers to market their own products did. Insecurity was at a height in the Depression years of the late 1870s and 1880s, when the self-help solutions in terms of better education and credit recommended by liberals were less attractive than the call for the repeal of liberal anti-guild legislation. But many artisans remained prosperous, and the average Viennese artisan in 1898 was 2.2 times more likely to be a taxpayer than a skilled or semi-skilled worker.

What of the idea of a shift to the right of petit bourgeois *political* values at this time? Crossick and Haupt's argument that this depended on the particular environment has resonance for Austria, where the evolution of the Slav- and German-speaking petite bourgeoisie ultimately diverged. In the Czech lands this section of the population gravitated towards the Young Czechs in the 1880s and later the Czech National Socialist Party, whose initial anti-Semitism lost ground over time: Czech National Socialism remained a force of the left centre with a triple commitment to nationalism, social reformism and democracy and a lower-middle-class base, expanding to include patriotic civil servants and schoolteachers. In Vienna, by contrast, the anti-Semitic focus remained central and eventually sowed fascist seeds. Artisanal protests mounted at the end of the 1870s against the peddling of new factory products, usually by immigrant Jews. In 1885 the anti-Semite machinist Joseph Schneider took over the presidency of the toothless craft associations which had replaced the guilds abolished in 1859. Eighteen anti-Semites were elected to the Viennese city council in 1886. In Schneider's programme of 1890, approved by 4000 artisan delegates, *Konfektion* (allegedly mainly Jewish) and the retailing of any handwork product by other than artisans would have been forbidden and the definition of handwork widely extended. By this time the artisan cause had become intertwined both with the Christian Social movement, represented by the Society for Social Reform (1887), and the German nationalist movement of the anti-Semite Georg Schönerer, cooperating under the general term of 'United Christians'. The social world beneath the liberal upper bourgeoisie of the capital was a confusing flux of local allegiances, expressed through the pullulating network of district clubs, artisanal, Catholic, nationalist and anti-Semitic, most of which an able opportunist, the ex-liberal Karl Lueger, eventually succeeded in mobilising under the banner of the Christian Social Party.

Though Lueger's demagogic skills were admired by Hitler, John Boyer denies that his artisanal supporters had already made the transition to a comprehensive anti-modernist reaction. Politically, Viennese artisans felt betrayed by the bourgeois liberal establishment, which had undermined the ideology of a united *Bürgertum* by high voting qualifications and indifference to their economic difficulties. But they did not at once jettison the beliefs that had once bound them to the liberals – in particular their suspicions of clericalism. On the cultural front, too, Josef Ehmer has ingeniously argued that the growing artisanal stress on family values at this time was not a reversion to guild traditionalism, as might be supposed. Guild tradition had been focused on the guild and not the family, and sons had rarely been apprenticed to their fathers. The growing trend to father–son inheritance in certain guilds in the late nineteenth century was actually an approach by better-off artisans to the strongly familial lifestyle of the contemporary bourgeoisie. It reflected a distancing from traditional relationships between masters and journeymen; only 9% of craft workers lived with their masters in early twentieth-century Vienna. Master craftsmen were increasingly educating their sons in higher commercial and technical colleges, and if these then returned to the family business they often referred to themselves as their fathers' business managers or associates, terms unknown to guild tradition. Alternately, they might pass laterally into the expanding clerical petite bourgeoisie, which was easier than the rather slight chance of ascent to the bourgeois ranks above. In a world which had created many modern pressures without yet creating modern affluence, it was easier still to fall into the proletariat. This explains the anti-socialist animus Lueger injected into his mobilisation of the Viennese and then the Austro-German lower middle class.

The world of the early socialist movement in the 1860s was barely distinguishable from that of the embattled journeyman. His prospects had become too uncertain with the emasculation of the guilds in 1859 and employers' flouting of traditional qualifications. Prospects of guild restorationism lacked the attractions of the burgeoning workers' educational associations, increasingly influenced by Lassallean or Marxist thought, to a still largely artisanal work-force facing problems of insecure employment, wage pressure, harsh working conditions and bad housing, nourishment and health. Worst, in comparative terms, appears to have been housing. Rents in Vienna rose three and a half times faster than consumer prices in the nineteenth century, swallowing from a quarter to a third of workers' income there (and in Cracow and Graz), as opposed to an eighth to a tenth in London. Four-fifths of Graz small housing still had no running water in 1900. The sole employment protection in force at the outset of the Dualist era prevented children under ten from working. Hours in Galician textile factories were then up to 17 hours in summer and 14-15 hours in winter. The expectation of life in Cracow for 1859-68 was estimated at 26 years; infant mortality in German north Bohemia in the 1880s exceeded 30% and over a third of all Viennese deaths over the age of 15 at this time were from tuberculosis. Not surprisingly, the 'social question' was endlessly debated from the 1860s, with answers ranging from the shiftlessness of workers to Marxist schema of universal history. Since by the early 1870s relations had already broken down between the nascent workers' movement and its brief allies on the democratic liberal left the former was exposed to the full force of a hostile consensus. Meanwhile, it suffered from the fact that most of the workers themselves, downtrodden and uneducated, still took their harsh lot as the way of the world or divine dispensation.

How then did the socialist movement take shape? In the German- and Czech-speaking areas its early members were overwhelmingly artisans, with a small number of educated professionals from artisanal roots, several of them, like Oberwinder, Scheu and Most, from Germany. Motivation might vary: the pioneer woman activist Adelheid Popp (1859-1939) had been set to clothing work from ten years old, with terrible spells in hospital and a workhouse. The Prague-born Karl Kautsky's on the whole petit bourgeois family tree included spirited people like his grandfather who gave up tutoring the nobility for the poorer but freer life of a theatrical scene painter and requested a copy of Darwin before he died. Further afield, in Galicia, Poland's insurrectionary traditions enabled student youth to take up socialism as early as the 1870s when an undeveloped economy ruled out much more than a guild-conscious movement among workers, except in Lvov; one defendant in a Polish trial could say that unlike in the West the first socialists in Poland came from the best families who, brought up as Polish patriots, embraced socialism as the highest form of science.[16] Only in the following decade did such sentiments begin to turn men like Pernerstorfer and Viktor Adler in the Austro-German intelligentsia in the same direction, to become bourgeois leaders in the second generation of Austrian socialism, which they saw as the moral and intellectual spirit of the age. Yet the moral dimension had been present from the start for the early worker socialists, whose careers show moving parallels in the arduous struggles against educational disability and eventual rise to positions as trade union or party organisers:

> The enemy we hate most deeply ...
> It is the ignorance of the masses,
> Cleft only by the spirit's sword.[17]

The emphasis on self-discipline and diligence, the anti-alcoholism and the high-minded semi-religious language of much early socialism distinguish it from the radicalism of the late twentieth century, which has sometimes criticised it in consequence for conniving at the myth of the undeserving poor. The criticism goes to the heart of socialism's uneasy balance between its two poles, as moral vision and materialist critique.

Not surprisingly, the unsympathetic state chose to emphasise socialism as cold-blooded nihilism. Implicitly, it denied the relevance of civil rights to those who sought to overthrow existing society; explicitly it exploited the illiberal provisions of the neo-absolutist Penal Code of 1852, which criminalised anything which could be construed as exposing the ruler, the form of government and the administration to contempt or ridicule, or rousing hostility against other nationalities, religions or classes. This produced the absurdity of the state prosecutors of an anti-clerical regime accusing socialist agitators of denying the immortality of the soul (the *Tauschinsky* case in Graz in 1874) or the constant prosecutions of Viktor Adler in the 1890s for bringing the authorities into disrepute by teasing state commissioners who were heavy-handedly intervening in socialist meetings: 'Learn something, before you come here to supervise our gatherings!'[18] Plainly the bottom line for the authorities, as the Galician governor Count Potocki rebuked the Polish socialist Limanowski, was the passage from being a 'theoretical socialist' (which an Austrian prosecutor once said might make for a good discussion) to actually meeting other socialists for 'militant' socialist purposes. Here it was fear of the infection of the 'uneducated masses' that was at stake, what a Graz judge in 1884 called 'the struggle between the state idea and the unbridled mob'.[19] Running through official attitudes of the constitutional state to socialism is a clear sense that the lower orders were still considered beyond the pale of civil (bürgerlich) society. They bespoke a dual theme in Austrian history: the sense of social backwardness vis-á-vis the West and the corresponding exaltation of the state as the bedrock of social progress. On the other hand, the socialists on trial were vigorously defended by their lawyers (usually but not always left liberals) and were quite often acquitted by juries, to the extent that the state as far as it could bypassed jury trials in prosecuting them. And of course, the prosecution charge that the transformation of private into communal property would not take place as harmlessly as socialists depicted was not as silly as some of the other objections to socialism. The problem for any new political movement is that its tenets are examined for their logical rather than their emotional content, which tends to happen less later as they become part of the landscape.

The waves of persecution which followed the workers' educational societies' movement of the late 1860s and the Neudörfl socialist congress of 1874 made such domestication of socialist organisation very difficult, and encouraged internal feuding and a shift towards anarchism. Terrorist actions in 1883–84 produced anti-anarchist legislation which in practice was directed at socialists also. The patient work of Adler in reconciling supporters and opponents of constitutional means led eventually to the launch of a united Austrian Social Democratic Party on Marxist lines in the Hainfeld congress of 1889. Austrian socialists now committed themselves to work within the law without disguising that their goal remained the overthrow of the existing order. For fear of the Austrian law forbidding political associations to have branches, the organisation of the new party developed only gradually, with provision for a party executive coming in 1892 and individual party membership through party branches only in 1909. Meanwhile leadership was provided by the

Arbeiterzeitung's editorial board and organisational back-up by the workers' educational associations and trade unions. The unions thus became the backbone of the workers' movement. Founded in 1893, the Austrian Trade Union Commission had established itself with 135,000 members by 1902. This was still only a very small proportion of the work-force, however; trade union influence could only be partial. Exploitation in small industry continued, and the legal factory norm of eleven hours exclusive of breaks was no great gain. But the Sunday rest day was recognised in 1895, as also the right to May Day celebrations, which had caused a huge sensation in 1890 when 200,000 workers marched peacefully through Vienna for the first time. The trade union movement urged such self-discipline also on the issue of strikes, which it advocated only when strictly necessary and well prepared. As a result they increasingly ended in compromise.

The establishment of the socialist movement was assisted by the adoption of the bourgeois associational principle on a hitherto unpractised scale. The movement spawned organisations to cover every aspect of life: for abstinence, sport, students, young workers, women, Alpinism, stenography, education, libraries and much more. It had its own emphases: football and cycling rather than fencing and gymnastics, though the latter had its place. Many of these activities, too, were conducted in several languages, because socialism was an international movement and its most remarkable achievement, in the Austrian context, was to organise itself on a federal basis, in 1896, with a German party corresponding to the Czechoslav, Yugoslav and Polish socialist parties which had emerged under its aegis. By far the largest of these Slav parties was the Czech which had organisational roots going back beyond Hainfeld. To a period which Hans Mommsen has dubbed 'naive cosmopolitanism', when Czech working-class leaders were more prepared to acquiesce in German leadership, had succeeded a greater self-assertion of Czech consciousness based on the increase in Czech skilled workers and the general rise of the Czech movement, particularly in Prague. In Galicia the national question had always been on the agenda, so that the Polish Socialist Party of 1893 was both a socialist and a nationalist party. The Yugoslav Social Democratic Party (1896) was largely Slovene – there were 76,000 Slovene workers in 1900 – but its name signalled a broader ethnic consciousness, stimulated in large part by the Slovene presence in dynamic Trieste, the third city of Austria, and their conflict there with the Italian majority. All these complexities Adler had deliberately skated round at Hainfeld, which wrapped them up in a single bland sentence:

> The Social Democratic Workers' Party in Austria is an international party; it condemns the privileges of nations as it does those of birth, possession and origin and declares that the struggle against exploitation must be international as is exploitation itself.[20]

In consenting to Slav pressure for the formal federalisation of the common Austrian party in 1896, the German leadership was acknowledging that words were not enough if they were to avoid the fate of the trade union movement, whose leader Anton Hueber had provoked a Czech secession by his intransigent centralism the previous year.

The creation of a multi-national party was the most dramatic evidence of Austrian socialists' desire to create a new kind of society, distinct from the liberal capitalist world it condemned. But as with the other anti-liberal movements discussed above, their enterprise owed more to their ideological foes than they seem to have realised. It is ironic that in scornfully dismissing 'the adulterous farces and the unworthy flaccidities of the operetta' as culturally appropriate for 'the moneybags of the present time' the socialist journalist and Workers' Symphony Concert member Gustav Seekow should implicitly be invoking a high culture that was also, after all, bourgeois.[21]

Anti-liberal Politics, 1879–93

The sheer variety of the anti-liberal movements just described help undermine the German liberals' charge that their ejection from power in 1879 was an unnatural manipulation. But their bewilderment was not altogether myopic. The mobilisation of peasants, petits bourgeois and workers, as of the non-dominant nations to be described below, was only in its early stages in 1879. The unrepresentative nature of the liberal regime prepared the ground for its fall, but the timing was such that the immediate recipients could only be the traditional forces embodied in the person of the new prime minister Count Eduard Taaffe, a childhood friend of the Emperor, who remained in office for the next fourteen years.

It is ironic that an increasingly articulate age should have been presided over by a man who held no particular views himself except loyalty to his monarch and the desire to keep the imperial show on the road. This was dubbed 'muddling through', by maintaining the contending interests in the state in what Taaffe called 'well-modulated dissatisfaction'. Under his 'Iron Ring', or governing coalition of Poles, Czechs and Hohenwart's largely German clericals, a moderately Slavophile domestic course was balanced by suspicions of Russia and the eclipse of the Three Emperors' League in foreign policy. Slavs, particularly Czechs, received some linguistic concessions; Catholic conservatives achieved modification of the 1868 liberal school law; the guild system was partially reinstated and the free disposal of peasant plots restricted; hours of labour were regulated and health and accident insurance introduced. In hindsight most historians have given the benefit of the doubt to the mildly cynical *grand seigneur* whose tactical ingenuity (the Empress once called Taaffe an acrobat who was using her husband as a balancing pole)[22] enabled these mainly sensible reforms. By contrast, contemporary Austro-German liberals, none more so than Crown Prince Rudolf, were vituperative towards a man they felt by pandering to Slav nationalism had opened the way to 'reaction'. The clash with Rudolf's earlier apparent sympathy for Czech aspirations is to be explained through his typically liberal assumption of a German civilising role in Slav emancipation; concessions to Czechs which aroused German resentment, divided the two peoples and drove Austro-Germans to look towards the German Reich were not what he had had in mind at all. The central charge of Taaffe's critics was that he undermined the alleged German state-building element for party advantage in what one contemporary called his 'blind hatred' of liberalism.[23]

This critique begs the question as to whether the aspirations of non-dominant groups can ever be satisfied without a backlash from the former masters. Taaffe does not in fact seem to have thought of excluding the German liberals from power in 1879, while there were also moderate liberals who thought the Left should cooperate with him to avoid a purely right-wing government. Attacks on them as traitors by more radical figures, however, convinced them that they could not claim a party mandate to enter a Taaffe-led coalition government, and even those liberals who were initially in the new ministry as individuals soon felt they should resign. Liberal intransigence spread beyond the radicals in the Progressive club; leading right-wing liberals like Ernst Plener believed dogmatically in the identity of the liberal party, German culture and the constitutional state, hence that the present situation was unnatural and the Right's narrow lead could be undermined by uncompromising opposition. Liberal division enabled Taaffe to push through a decennial parliamentary settlement for the army (December 1879) even though this required a two-thirds' majority, and thereafter he appears to have overridden the Left with a degree of ruthlessness.

In addition to concessions to the Czechs – the Stremayr ordinances (1880) allowing use of Czech with the authorities throughout Bohemia; a Czech university (1882); control of the Bohemian Diet (1883), and a broader 5 florin tax franchise – the government now made legislative concessions to the Catholic Right. Anti-usury laws were reintroduced (1881), the liberal school law was amended to permit only six instead of eight years' compulsory schooling in rural communities and to ensure Catholic teachers in Catholic areas (1883) and in the same year entry to certain crafts again required formal qualifications. Reflecting the new vision of Catholic social reform, factory inspectors were introduced (1883) and working conditions regulated (1885), forbidding wage labour below the age of twelve and in factories before fourteen, partially prohibiting night labour for women and children and limiting adult male hours to eleven a day, not including breaks, with Sunday rest. The adult male hours showed the rather modest nature of the final provisions after fears of competition had whittled them down. Meanwhile civil rights were suspended for socialist agitation in Vienna and a couple of other industrial centres from 1884–85, while an Act generalised the suspension of jury trials for 'anarchists' (widely interpreted) in 1886. Finally, the Austrian Right sponsored insurance schemes similar to those of Bismarck for accident and sickness (1887–88). Workers were to contribute 10% and two-thirds to the two schemes respectively and the funds were to be administered on a territorial basis rather than the 'brotherhoods' of craft guild tradition which Catholic social reformers had advocated.

The territorial solution adopted was attractive to federalists, both conservative and Slav, indicating the differences of emphasis which existed in the right-wing majority. Taaffe for one was opposed to too strong a shift to the right, and in foreign political terms the Monarchy in no way acted as a Slav power, continuing to cleave to the German alliance. Taaffe's preference was probably to detach the 'constitutional large landowners' from the camp of the Left into a 'centre party'; this was after all the decade in which most English upperclass Whigs split away from Gladstone's Liberal party. Since, too, Czech MPs had an uneasy relationship with their aristocratic allies and only reluctantly went along with the attack on the 1868 school law, the ultimate right-wing goal of reintroducing church-controlled education was unattainable. It was probably the 'feudal conservatives' who came off best of all groups in the 1880s, for to liberal cries of hypocrisy they secured the exemption of their farm and forestry workers from the laws providing for insurance and regulation of working hours. East Galician Polish landowners were the most insistent here.

The damage inflicted on the German Left by the Taaffe regime was thus more psychological than material. Despite right-wing attacks on ruthless 'Manchesterism', most liberals had never been out-and-out *laissez-faire*ists. Indeed, Plener's memoirs make plain how the petit bourgeois element of their electoral support made several liberal leaders go easy on the finer points of liberal principle. What hurt the Left was that Taaffe had shown Austria could be ruled without the self-appointed 'party of state'. Hence their response initially took a symbolic form, in the demand that German – in practice accepted by Slavs as the lingua franca – should be officially recognised as the 'language of state', rejected after acrimonious parliamentary debate in 1884. But the Czech majority in the Bohemian Diet from 1883 was more than symbolic, and when the Diet rejected German Bohemians' call for the province's partition on ethnic lines, Plener led his supporters out of it in 1886.

These traumatic times for German liberals were reflected in their constantly changing political structures, facilitated by the loose nature of party political organisation in the Monarchy. The legal prohibition of party branches, provincial differences, the curial system and preference for alternative networks of local 'notables' played their part here. For the most part the 'clubs' into which candidates divided when elected were organised only at the parliamentary level, and the politically minded minority learned of their views through sympathetic newspapers. Meanwhile, the cooperation of parliamentary clubs under a 'party' label was regulated through varying provisions for joint executives and intraparty discipline.

Under the shock of the Stremayr decrees, which obliged German Bohemian towns, in principle, to operate bilingually, the Progressives merged their identity with other liberals in 1881, as the United Left. In fact, the name was a misnomer. The humiliation of exclusion from Germany in 1866, followed by the loss of hegemony in Austria, had left a bruised and divided community in which many yearned for a 'sharper tone' than liberalism's seemingly ineffectual appeal to German superiority. National and social radicalism went together in this mood, with sympathy for universal suffrage, a sense of the neglect of the *Volk*, and an admiration for dynamic Wagnerian Germany over stuffy Austria. The 'Linz programme' of 1882, which called for universal suffrage (but requested hiving off an autonomous Galicia and Dalmatia to assure a German majority) was an expression of this approach. The fact that its leading signatories included the future progenitor of Austrian fascism, Georg von Schönerer, and two Jews, the future Social Democratic leader, Viktor Adler, and the famous historian, Heinrich Friedjung, shows the appeal but also the contradictions of attempts to deepen the national content of Austrian liberalism. For the problem of the 'sharper tone' was that it was just that, a heightened emphasis of existing liberal themes, and its spokesmen could make real headway only by acquiring distinct ideological baggage of their own. This became apparent after the 'Iron Ring' increased its majority in the parliamentary elections of 1885, and the United Left broke up into the 'German–Austrian Club' and the more nationalist 'German Club'. Within two years the German Club had itself split, with an emerging wing under Steinwender turning the idea of the *Volk* in a petit bourgeois, anti-Semitic direction. Schönerer meanwhile took anti-Semitism much further, making it the basis of his increasingly strident pro-Hohenzollern Pan-German League. Those who stuck to the old liberal line regrouped in 1888 as the United German Left under Plener's leadership.

While the Austro-Germans went through these unavailing permutations, their arch enemies, the Czechs, were also unhappy. The Old Czech leader Rieger spoke of their gains as crumbs picked from the table and, indeed, the Bohemian Diet had little real power. 'Parisians celebrated the New Year with 1129 cases of drunkenness and 234 acts of hooliganism of various kinds; in Prague there were three drunks and one hooligan. And we want to be a nation!', the leading Czech daily commented ironically on Czech passivity in January 1885.[24] Moreover, the Old Czechs found themselves in hock to their aristocratic partners, the Bohemian 'feudal conservatives', whose economic interests ran counter to those of the Czech-speaking peasantry, threatened by competition from Hungarian grain and a world sugar crisis. Thus economic and national themes interlocked. By 1887 Rieger was pouring out his heart to the Czech representative in Taaffe's government:

And we can't fob off the people with empty promises for ever!...
The weakness and impotence of our M.P.s exasperates them; they
keep pointing to the importance of the Bohemian Crown... – and
its painful dependence nonetheless... And always it is the Czech
[parliamentary] Club which is the whipping horse, from which
miracles are demanded![25]

In 1888 Rieger, fearful of Young Czech and Pan-German radicalism,
begged an interview with Franz Joseph, who told him that it was up
to him to deal with the Young Czech threat. But the Old Czechs, a
party of notables almost as much as Plener's liberals (Rieger, by
training a lawyer, recorded himself as landowner in the census)
were vulnerable to the Young Czechs' ability to appeal to professionals, the petite bourgeoisie and above all discontented peasants.
In the Bohemian Diet elections of 1889 the Young Czechs made a
dramatic advance in the rural curia, defeating the Old Czechs there
by 30 seats to 19.

Thus it was that at the end of the decade Rieger and Plener began
to negotiate more seriously over a Czech–German reconciliation.
Rieger wished to reassert his authority as Czech leader and take
some heat out of the situation, Plener to gain the decentralisation for
Bohemian Germans which had eluded frontal assault. The compromise of 1890 gave Bohemian Germans the principle of provincial
institutions divided and administrative and judicial boundaries
redrawn on ethnic lines, a veto in the Diet on their vital interests,
and a Bohemian Judicature with 15 unilingual judges – obviously
Germans – alongside 26 bilingual ones. Stremayr's bilingual bogey
was partly repelled. However, the Young Czechs had not been consulted. They orchestrated a storm of protest which helped them to a
sweeping victory in the parliamentary elections of 1891; Rieger's
party won only two seats. The compromise became effectively a
dead letter.

The eclipse of the Old Czechs imperilled Taaffe's majority and led
him to a disingenuous dalliance with Plener over terms on which
German liberals might return to government. Plener hoped to separate Taaffe not only from the Czechs but also the clericals, so as to
restore something like the 1870s alliance of German liberals and
Poles; Taaffe hoped to detach the most conservative wing of the liberal camp. Ultimately he could not bring himself to any substantial
deal with Plener but instead, in 1893, produced a most unexpected
rabbit out of the hat – a proposal close to universal suffrage. True,

the curias of the large landowners and the chambers of commerce would remain, but 247 of the 353 members of parliament were to be chosen by all literate male taxpayers over 24 in a combined urban and rural curia, with an overall electorate up from 1,770,000 to four million. The rationale of the bill's inspirer, the able bureaucrat turned finance minister Emil Steinbach, was that a wider electorate would be more interested in socio-economic than in nationalist issues. But the secretively prepared plan backfired because it was instantly repudiated by all parties but the Young Czechs. In November 1893 Franz Joseph dismissed his long-serving prime minister.

In 1895 the liberals lost their majority in the Viennese city council to the Christian Social Party. In the 1897 Reichsrat elections Plener's group, most direct descendants of mainstream German liberalism, won barely twenty seats. Christian Social success in Vienna was brilliantly orchestrated by a former left liberal, Karl Lueger (1844–1910), who knew best how to replace increasingly questioned liberal principle by the politics of interest, utilising the new associational networks to mobilise a mass movement of the *Mittelstand* against the liberal bourgeois notables. The *Mittelstand* were those who claimed bourgeois status but felt excluded from or neglected by the liberals: not only anti-Semitic artisans, but teachers, the lower ranks of municipal and state civil servants and last, the growing cohorts of commercial employees with some secondary education, who aspired to work their way up the firm but in a harshly competitive climate feared remaining little higher than their non-bourgeois janitors; since Taaffe's time conservative social policy had sought to shore up their position. Lueger's success was not only achieved against the liberals. Clerical conservatives appealed against the Christian Socials to the Vatican, and Franz Joseph vetoed his election as mayor of Vienna for two years before yielding in 1897.

It is significant that the only concrete intersection of domestic and external factors in this period involved the Vatican on an ultimately minor issue. The liberals' attempt to intervene in high politics over the Bosnian occupation (1878) was not repeated. Their partly Slav successors left the alliance with Germany untouched as the cornerstone of the Monarchy's foreign policy, and the main event in this field was a sustained clash with Russia over a Balkan issue. Of course, Catholic Poles had no reason to be Russophile but this was also the time when their Croat co-religionaries saw their influence in occupied Bosnia finally squeezed out under two Magyar joint finance ministers entrusted with its administration, József Szlávy (1880–82) and Béni Kállay (1882–1903).

The period began, however, with a revival of the Three Emperors' League orchestrated by Bismarck (1881). Despite his failure to win Russian approval for the Monarchy's right to annex Bosnia (in return for Austrian recognition of Russian interests at the Straits), foreign minister Haymerle felt constrained to sign, partly because Gladstone's new Liberal government (1880) was a less secure partner than Disraeli's Conservatives had been, partly because the Austro-German treaty of 1879 was formally upheld. In the event Austria-Hungary was able to establish her Balkan interests through secret treaties with the rulers of Serbia (1881) and Romania (1883), Serbia, for example, pledging to respect the status quo in Bosnia and consult Vienna on diplomatic initiatives. This was elite power politics; King Carol of Romania was a Hohenzollern, King Milan Obrenović of Serbia wanted Austrian support against his turbulent subjects. The entente with Russia was, however, shattered by the Bulgarian crisis of 1885–88, as the tussle for influence over this state twice brought the two states close to war, once when Russia despatched a general to Sofia in quasi-viceregal role (1886) and again after a German Roman Catholic, and officer in the Austro-Hungarian army to boot, Ferdinand of Saxe-Coburg-Gotha, was elected Bulgarian prince (late 1887). In the middle of this imbroglio the Three Emperors' League was not renewed. Security against Russia was sought in two 'Mediterranean agreements' of 1887 between Austria, Britain and Italy and in extension of the terms of the Triple Alliance by which Italy had joined the two central powers in 1882, of which more below (see p. 370–1).

Little of all this preoccupied party politicians or parliamentary debate. In the Hungarian House of Lords Andrássy urged more bellicosity on Count Gustav Kálnoky, Haymerle's successor as foreign minister. He had no counterpart in Austria. There Taaffe achieved his goal of moving Austria away from the German liberalism most of her citizens disliked without questioning the German alliance or committing her either to federalism, anti-capitalism or clericalism. Doubts about his stewardship spring mainly from the fact that the discontent his policies provoked was by no means 'well modulated'. What is striking is the intensity of disenchantment in a time which in hindsight seems relatively stable: the Cassandra cries of the Crown Prince ('our sad time, when reactionary tendencies hostile to culture arise in every land'),[26] Plener's gloomy hubris, and Rieger's anguished frustration, which was paralleled in the contemporary correspondence of the Croat leaders Strossmayer and Rački.

Of course, much of the 1880s saw economic depression and none knew the Bulgarian events would be the dog which did not bark in the night. Foreign minister Kálnoky shared unease at the Monarchy's state, at the absence of strong leadership and the 'deep sickness'[27] of German Bohemian estrangement, threatening the empire's cohesion. These agitated tones were linked to awareness of a quickly changing world, throwing up multiple social and national questions. A harsh assessment of the Taaffe era might be that its comparative stability was due more to a temporary balance between shifting forces, German hegemony and Slav revival or capitalism and anti-capitalism, than it was to particular foresight on his part. The absence of a Slav challenge to the Austro-German alliance as the cornerstone of the Monarchy's international stance, such as the Young Czech leader Karel Kramář was to launch a decade later (also in French and English journals), implies anti-centralist forces were not yet ready for a comprehensive critique of the way the empire was run. For all Taaffe's tactical skill he remained too out of sympathy with the social and ethnic currents he dealt with to impinge upon them or check the gradual festering of their mutual relations. In this sense, his incumbency was a time of drift.

Liberal Survival

That liberalism's influence did not vanish with its political defeats in 1879 and 1895 has long been a commonplace. Awareness of the continuing hold of liberal values through press, education and law has been complemented more recently by research into the cultural and intellectual achievement of the Viennese *fin de siècle*, and into elements of continuity between liberal and post-liberal political structures.

Thus John Boyer has shown the many points of contact between the Christian Social Party and the liberal regime it displaced, setting in context Karl Lueger's relative moderation as mayor of Vienna from 1897 till his death in 1910, including his racial pragmatism: 'I decide who is a Jew', as this anti-Semitic leader once notoriously remarked. Lueger's effective aim, according to Boyer, was to restore the notion of a united Viennese *Bürgertum* which had carried the liberals to power in the 1860s but had faltered through their elitism. Artisans, teachers and lower civil servants they had alienated were reintegrated by judicious attention to their prejudices and pockets (anti-Semitism for the artisans, higher salaries for officials). The massive public works programme begun under the liberals (Danube regulation, water supply) was continued in the municipal gas works of 1898, the tramway system from 1902 and the electricity plants of 1908. Meanwhile, a good working relationship established with the inherited core of liberal city officials and with the central government enabled lower-middle-class Christian Social activists to outgrow their social resentments and play the notable on public occasions. Lueger did squeeze Jews out of the city administration by denying them promotion, but his assurances that he meant no other threat to their civil rights were widely believed by sidelined Christian Social true believers and by Jews.

Pieter Judson and Lothar Höbelt have extended continuity arguments to the provincial towns, though here the continuity was between liberalism and German nationalism. A small town club might change its name from Friends of the Constitution to German National Association, an Alpine provincial capital might have a liberal council in the early 1890s and incline to Steinwender's nationalist *Volkspartei* a decade later, but the personnel might not have changed much, allowing for individual opportunism, transitional coalitions, 'middle parties' and the like. Facilitating realignment was that the liberals had always had a strongly German character and had, Judson argues, sought to shore up their position after 1879 by leading the fight to defend allegedly imperilled German interests (the most important national defence body, the German School Association (1880), remained under their control), while on the other hand the nationalist concept of national *Besitzstand* (assets) had a liberal core. It represented material interests which had been built up by the liberal bourgeoisie – their stake in trade, industry, the educational system and so forth. Höbelt, too, stresses that neither in their pre-modern methods of party organisation nor their ideas did liberals and nationalists differ markedly, except on one issue. Liberals rejected the anti-Semitism which had been central to Schönerer's movement from the 1880s and which figured prominently in the *Volkspartei*, first as an optional, then (from 1896) compulsory article of party dogma.

These were survivals of liberal practice. More emotive for contemporaries was a sense of the survival of liberal principle, of a *Rechtsstaat*, constitutionality and civil rights, with their intimately bourgeois liberal associations – the German word *bürgerlich* means both civil and bourgeois. The law continued to enjoy immense prestige. Around half of Austria's university students studied it, for it was the basic degree for a career in public life; the succession of able, legally trained bureaucrats of at least mildly liberal views and reformist plans who figured in public life – a Steinbach, Baernreither, Koerber, Redlich or Sieghart – was one of the most consistent features of Dualism. The Basic Laws of 1867, which included a declaration of national and linguistic equality, gave the interpretation of legal texts an important place in political life; indeed, it may be said that the attempt to devise legal answers to political problems was a characteristic feature of Austrian political life. It helped that the historical school of law, with its notions of a law rooted in the *Volk* rather than rationalism, had less currency in Austria than in Germany and that Franz Joseph adhered conscientiously to the letter of the law as a constitutional monarch. If he was no liberal, the scrupulous, not to say pedantic bureaucracy he exemplified was an aid to constitutional habits of mind. Divided as of 1873 into ranks I to XI, this body consisted for the most part of poorly paid clerks who would never climb higher than grade X but who were expected to view their work as a 'profession', from a moral rather than economic point of view. Besides, hours were short, six a day except for financial officials who worked an hour or two longer. Wage rises came in 1855, the 1860s, 1873 and 1896, yet even after the last rise those in the bottom category could only reach 1000 crowns a year (about £50). Even more static were pensions, with the first major modifications of Joseph II's regulation coming in 1866 and 1896. On the whole, the pawky tight-fistedness of the authorities was relaxed slightly in the Dualist period, with extension of pension rights to lower categories, less mean terms for widows and inclusion of allowances in the pensionable salary.

A more enthusiastically liberal element was the press. Boasting a combined circulation of some 120,000 around 1900 the two leading liberal dailies, the *Neue Freie Presse* and the *Neues Wiener Tagblatt,* far exceeded the 6000 each of their Catholic counterparts, the conservative *Vaterland* and Christian Social *Reichspost,* and the 24,000 of the socialist *Arbeiterzeitung.* Both superior journalistic skills and the articulation of some underlying sentiment must explain these figures, which reached well beyond a large Jewish readership, naturally attracted to the liberal universalist values of writers often Jewish themselves. Certainly, the liberal press was an immensely impressive affair in terms of sheer bulk and breadth of coverage. The *Neue Freie Presse* serialised original novels by leading writers. One worker, struck with a copy of the left liberal *Die Zeit*, riposted with the 216-page Easter number of *Neues Wiener Tagblatt* and got six months' jail for breaking his interlocutor's shoulder blade.[28] When in 1895 Bismarck in retirement chose Moritz Benedikt to spill the beans on his successors, the celebrated *Neue Freie Presse* editor duly reported a three-hour conversation conducted without notes more or less word for word.

The liberal complexion of the press may have owed something to the persistent humanistic bent of Austrian secondary education, particularly in the prestigious *Gymnasien*, with their emphasis on the Greek and Latin classics. Certainly, post-primary education shared points of contact with liberal values, notably the earnestness – Austrian secondary curricula were notoriously overcrowded, with up to thirty hours a week of scheduled lessons – but also the claim to high-minded liberality: secondary school and university authorities often responded huffily to government enquiries about alleged political activities of their students. Thus while liberalism declined as a political force, a growing proportion of the ablest youth received an introduction to its values: the number of university students increased over twice as fast as the population as a whole between 1851 and 1909, from 5646 to 25,941, with the share of nobles falling to 4%.

With these surviving supports in administration, press and college, not to speak of an expanding economic base, the German-speaking liberal bourgeoisie expressed itself in a remarkable cultural efflorescence associated with its one major urban centre, Vienna. In keeping with Austria's pragmatic intellectual tradition, literature played a relatively minor role in this cultural flowering, though a figure like Arthur Schnitzler in internationally famous stories evoked the stifling pressures of bourgeois morality and also older codes like the cult of duelling honour. The physicists Ernst Mach and Ludwig Boltzmann, the former the pioneer of jet propulsion and of the mechanics of hearing, showed the creative strength of Austrian natural science but also of its wider intellectual culture, for both speculated on the relation between scientific knowledge and 'reality'. Mach's thesis that this knowledge was also a form of sensation, hence that an objective reality was ungraspable and the 'I' undiscoverable, has been seen as an aspect of intellectuals' search for meaning in a diffuse, multi-lingual society ruled by a remote and unaccountable bureaucracy. Other aspects of the Austrian experience in this view were Schoenberg's search for a language of music in his twelve-tone scale, and the investigation into the meaning of language by the future founder of logical positivism, Ludwig Wittgenstein. The fundamental insights of the economists Carl Menger and Friedrich von Wieser into 'marginal utility theory' have also been given an Austrian social context, whether in the bent for calculation of a commercial bourgeoisie or of a rationalist bureaucracy.

Of course, the idea of a specific social base for Austrian creativity is still plausible hypothesis rather than established truth. The discovery of genetics by Gregor Mendel in his Moravian monastery garden shows that intellectual originality can have purely individual roots. But clearly there were energies in Austrian cultural life that belied the image of a royal palace which still shunned electric light. In art and architecture Vienna was in the avant-garde with people like Otto Wagner (1841–1918), a pioneer of urban planning and the spare, functionalist building style, and his disciple Adolf Loos; the founder of the Vienna *Sezession* school of art nouveau, Gustav Klimt (1862–1918); and the expressionist painters of gaunt erotica, Egon Schiele (1890–1918), and Oskar Kokoschka (1886–1980). The best-known of Vienna's innovators claimed to have invented not just a new style but a new science. This was the father of psychiatry, Sigmund Freud (1856–1939), whose cultural breadth, studies of female sexual neurosis, and fondness for classical tags and analogies (*ids* and super-egos, the Oedipus complex) indeed reflected the social and intellectual climate of his surroundings.

Explanations of this cultural vitality usually do locate it in the socio-political ambience of the German-speaking bourgeoisie. The major ones all stress various aspects of the creative use of disadvantage. For Janik and Toulmin disadvantage lay in the problems of a multi-cultural society and unaccountable polity, impelling interest in themes of communication, language and meaning; for Schorske and the Hungarian scholar Hanák it lay in the fall of the liberals from political power, leading to a turning in of younger generations of the middle class to the subjective world of art and theory; for Beller the issue is preponderance in the liberal bourgeoisie of Jews, driven to advance the cause of a higher culture which would give them a home after centuries of persecution. All these approaches are suggestive but they may imply a more pervasive alienation on the part of the bourgeoisie as a whole than was in fact the case in late Dualist Austria. This society was not as 'autocratic' as Toulmin and Janik presuppose even if parliamentarism functioned inadequately. There was a vigorous free press and a predictable administration, while awe before the Emperor did not stop Friedjung writing a famous book on the

Austro-Prussian conflict which laid the blame for Austria's defeat fairly plainly on Franz Joseph's shoulders. Besides, though the public was not privy to the private thoughts of its sovereign, he was hardly a man of mystery; what you saw was very much what you got. Kafka's nightmarish bureaucratic world owed more to his personal circumstances than the Austrian reality.

Schorske's linkage of bourgeois cultural creativity with political withdrawal and impotence also perhaps underplays the extent to which generational shifts of interests in entrepreneurial families were a European, not a specifically Austrian tendency. The fact, too, that the novel Schorske takes as emblematic of liberal retreat to an inner cultural world, Adalbert Stifter's *Nachsommer* (1857), was published before Austrian liberals ever came to power, suggests that the argument is intuitive rather than empirical, attractive though it remains for a society more interested in Mahler's stormy career as Director of the Vienna Court Opera than in political events. Beller's thesis, by contrast, is based on a numerical analysis of candidates matriculating from Vienna's *Gymnasien* in the Dualist period. Arguing that Jews comprised 64% of Viennese students of liberal bourgeois background, he concludes that the Viennese cultural movement was essentially a Jewish phenomenon, driven by a traditional Jewish respect for learning, strong desire to prove themselves in the face of prejudice and unconditional support for liberalism, because only a liberal society was worth assimilating to. The fact that about half Vienna's doctors, lawyers and journalists (the 'free professions') were Jews in 1900 though Jews were only some 10% of the population overall lends weight to this argument. But Beller does stack the cards in his favour by excluding all (largely non-Jewish) public employees and teachers from his definition of 'liberal bourgeoisie' on the grounds that Lueger received much support from this sector, as Boyer has shown. Boyer, however, himself turns the argument the other way, suggesting that the relation between Lueger and public servants shows a continuity between liberal and Christian Social Vienna – a more plausible interpretation in view of the long Josephinist–liberal tradition of Austrian public service. To identify liberal survival in Austria with Jewish commitment to universalist values seems to narrow it unduly.

Yet the Jewish question was indeed a touchstone of the growing conflict of values. The tensions between the universalist vision of civil society, which gave freedom to organise to all potential groups, and the particularist concerns of historic social groups, uneasy at change, often came to a head in the attitude taken to the Jews, a people marginalised and despised in the traditional context but seemingly central in the new. Much anti-Semitism was an index of underdevelopment and insecurity in a society in flux which was exposed to all but environmentalism of the ideologies extant today, yet was vastly less equipped to cope with them. A better point of comparison than modern Europe might be the contemporary Middle East, where the devout artisans of the Teheran bazaars in 1979 faced a choice between the ayatollah, the Marxist *mujaheddin* and the Shah. Such a comparison suggests that Austrian anti-Semitism was an aspect of a general disjuncture between old values and new, in which religion assumed an important symbolic role. A curious example of this disjuncture was the diametrically opposed treatment of Darwinism in textbooks for science and religious instruction.

Thus turn-of-the-century Austrian citizens received sharply opposed ideological messages. Local solidarities were no doubt often still strong enough for one or other of these to block out the others, usually to liberalism's disadvantage. Making liberalism's fate even more problematic was that would-be progressives increasingly felt they could have the advantages of a non-conservative world-view without sacrificing a sense of rooted particularism. The ideology which offered them this was nationalism. This was, of course, an aspect of the continuity between liberal and nationalist movements which historians like Judson and Höbelt have been examining. It requires a fuller study of the nationalist agenda.

10   Nationalism

In commemoration of Franz Joseph's Golden Jubilee in 1898 the Czech Academy produced a bulky volume outlining 'The Intellectual and Artistic Development of the Czech Nation' over the period. Introducing it with reference to the 'forces stirring society', the 'irresistible advance of population' and the 'general enhancement of social circumstances', the Secretary of the Academy promised readers a detailed portrayal of

> the complex and minutely organised deployment of materials denoted by the familiar phrase 'industry and commerce', the accelerated increase of means of transport and communication, the advancing significance of financial institutions, the multiplication of associations of all kinds . . . [1]

It is appropriate to remember the wider social context here floridly appraised when considering the remarkable 'rebirths' of non-dominant peoples in the nineteenth-century Habsburg Monarchy, of which the Czechs were without doubt the paradigm case. The Monarchy's notorious national problems have often seemed exotic and bizarre to west European commentators. In fact, they were a natural consequence in a multi-national state of the developmental processes common, in varying degrees, to Europe as a whole. National 'mobilisation' of previously subordinate peoples paralleled the mobilisation of peasants, workers and artisans in 'modernising' societies.

Thus nationalism was the ethnic side of the coin in a two-fold process undermining Austro-German liberal hegemony. As in the self-assertion of non-bourgeois social groups, so also the non-dominant nations used techniques of organisation and association pioneered in the German camp. Yet in the case of nationalism the dialectical linkage was even closer; non-German nationalists shared with German liberals not just techniques but ideology, for they too derived their faith in national development from the concept of progress. It was this conjunction of elements – the liberal pride in being on the right side of progress together with the emotive sense of historic roots and values – which gave nationalism its power, as a kind of secular religion. The prominent Austrian writer Hermann Bahr, expelled from Vienna University for a fiery Pan-German speech in a Wagner commemoration in 1883, recorded in his memoirs his father's bafflement that a proponent of progress could be anything but a liberal. But the younger generation was identifying progress increasingly with the aspiration for a dynamic nationhood rather than a more abstract concept of advancing humanity.

As so often developments among the non-dominant nations are best seen in a context set by the German-speaking minority. It is on the non-dominant groups, however, that the emphasis here rests, mainly on those of the Austrian half of the Monarchy, as these came to pose a greater threat to the would-be hegemonies than did the non-Magyars in Dualist Hungary. A fuller treatment of Hungary awaits the next chapter.

National Mobilisation: Towards 'Internal Sovereignty'

Central as socio-economic development was to national mobilisation in the Habsburg Monarchy, the relationship can be oversimplified. Some of the pitfalls of an over-glib distinction between 'traditional' and 'modern' society are present in the well-known 'functionalist' thesis of Ernest Gellner. Gellner sees the national ideologies of non-dominant peoples like the Habsburg Slavs as arising in response to a modernising situation, which brought them into the industrial towns on terms of inferiority to the Germans, obliging them therefore to turn their folk culture into a 'high culture', with claim of equal rights, if they were to avoid permanent helotisation. Helpful as the concept of a 'high culture' is, this perspective overlooks the fact that Slav linguistic ideologies were formulated in the romantic period before significant industrialisation had taken place. Indeed, different aspects of 'modernity', like bureaucratisation, urbanisation and industrialisation, are conflated in Gellner's theory, producing an over-deterministic view of the relationship of ideas to social processes. It cannot explain, therefore, why the contact of dominant and non-dominant cultures in an industrialising situation produced linguistic assimilation in South Wales and Spanish Biscay, while 'high cultures' emerged in groups like the Habsburg Ukrainians or Romanians without substantial economic change.

Thus it is best to see Habsburg nationalisms as a compound product, successively assimilating new elements as 'modernity' itself evolved. At an early stage, an ideological core was formed around the Herderian concept of language as the spirit of a unique people, itself fusing Enlightenment and romantic motifs. Then, the sociological process of mobilisation of ethnic groups opened wider strata up to such ideas through expanding education, media, associational life and social change. Finally, in the political sphere, liberal constitutionalism formally validated principles of national and language equality.

Of course, the Habsburg national movements, even those of the non-dominant groups, differed greatly according to the size, history and development of the peoples concerned. And if Habsburg nationalisms nearly all claimed liberal roots, they reflected at second hand the ambiguities and shortcomings of liberalism itself in still largely illiberal societies. Most significant was the divide between Austria, where the German hegemony was effectively breached, and Hungary, where the Magyars were able to evade even formal commitment to language equality and up to a point restrict the ethnic mobilisation of non-Magyars. Nonetheless, even in Hungary the erosion of liberal principles did not go far enough to arrest that mobilisation effectively (except possibly in the case of the Slovaks) or to eject the issue of national equality from political life. To a greater or lesser extent the intellectual, social and political issues outlined above were a real factor in the development of all the Monarchy's peoples.

The central point of patriotic endeavours remained language. Our modern age does not share the nineteenth century's love affair with philology, but there is a romance in the linguistic transformation of peasant geese into salon swans. The issue was the elevation of languages previously used 'to speak of simple household matters, such as old women talk about', as a Transylvanian Romanian had put it in 1813,[2] into all-purpose vehicles of modern culture. Should the required standard grammar be based primarily on an existing prestigious dialect, as had happened with Tuscan in Italy, or should it attempt the broadest possible compromise between different dialects, achieving accessibility at the cost of naturalness? Should the spelling system reflect its current pronunciation or its history? Should the new terminology required be drawn from native roots and related languages or from classical or prestigious modern tongues? These were all complex problems and their successful resolution in the second half of the century was a considerable collective achievement.

In some cases, of course, language modernisation had been achieved before 1850 (Germans, Poles and Magyars) or substantially so. The Czechs finally dropped the Gothic script and the German 'w' for 'v' in the late 1840s. Jungmann's great dictionary had created a modern vocabulary; the contribution of the following decades was to put it to use, sifting out unviable neologisms, gaining confidence to drop excesses of anti-German purism and in the process creating a sophisticated conversational Czech which educated people actually came to speak. Others had more work to do. Scripts and orthography proved relatively easiest to solve, with Croats and Slovenes adopting the Czech system of diacritical marks (č, š, ž) in 1836 and 1839, and Romanians and Serbs finally deciding to drop the Cyrillic alphabet or to accept a modified form of it respectively in the 1860s. Dialects were trickier. Czechs continued to claim Slovak as a form of Czech, and till the 1880s some Croats held out hopes that the Slovenes would come round to a related view. Slovak and Slovene consolidated their separate status in somewhat different ways, with the Slovaks making their central dialect the literary norm and the Slovenes gradually expanding the dialect base of theirs into a consciously contrived standard no-one actually spoke. The problems of Croatian were particularly acute because regional language differences masked important rivalries between Croats and Serbs and between Croats themselves – there were for some time separate linguistic schools in Dalmatia and Rijeka critical of Gaj's reform. The whittling away of the concessions originally made by Gaj to the dialect speech of Zagreb itself, leading to an ever purer form of *štokavski* (the dialect of most Croats but all Serbs), led to accusations that Croat identity was being betrayed in a spirit of starry-eyed Serbophilia. This is still a live issue. Most bizarre was the difficulty Ruthenians had in deciding between a form of Russian (prestigious but alien) or of Ukrainian (the reverse) as their literary tongue, a battle which moved in Ukrainian's favour from the 1890s. While this dispute remained unresolved in 1914, by that time elsewhere only a handful of communities geographically isolated from their compatriots (like Burgenland Croats of western Hungary) persisted in using non-standard dialects for writing purposes.

Some of the most impressive work in the language movement was done by lexicographers. Where an army has worked on the *Oxford English Dictionary* for most of this century, Bogoslav Šulek, admittedly in wide consultation, laid down in his German–Croatian dictionary (1860) equivalents for nearly all the terms in the famous German dictionary of Heinsius and went on to develop the Croatian vocabulary for botany (1866), military matters (1870–75) and chemistry. The numerically small Slovene people turned to their Slav brothers to build up their alternative to German cultural domination. One-third of all the words in the modern Slovene dictionary of 1962 are derived from other Slav languages. But these exercises were only a means to an end. They had no point in the minds of patriots unless the languages taking shape became the real instrument of mental culture of the peasant masses currently suffering a double exclusion, through speech and class, from 'the march of progress going on over their heads'. Consequently, the history of non-dominant nationalist movements must trace their attempt to expand their influence from an original pocket of intellectuals in a provincial capital till it prevailed throughout the area where the rustic mother tongue was spoken. Here the romantic concept of the nation as a community of culture expressing its 'soul' through language merged with the liberal principles of enlightenment and association: an expanding network of schools, press and associations became the basis for ever wider radiation of the 'national idea'. Modern historians have called the process 'national integration'.

Bohemian Czechs, for example, more or less caught up with Germans in terms of denseness of a secondary school network by the 1890s, but Moravian Czechs not till the eve of war. As Moravia was gradually won for the fold Czech patriots raised anxious eyes at the lagging third province. The appearance of a volume entitled *Silesian Songs* in 1903, appearing to reveal the unquenchable hatred of horny-handed Silesian Czech miners for their German masters, thus aroused a storm of enthusiasm, not wholly quenched by the revelation that the anonymous author – Petr Bezruč, itself a pseudonym – was a long-standing postal official in the Moravian capital Brno who had once spent two years in the same employ in Silesia.

As self-conscious Czechdom sought to widen out its bounds, so Slovenes aped them at a lower level. Secure in their Carniolan base where they had won control of the Ljubljana town council and the provincial assembly in the early 1880s, they changed the balance of primary schools in Slovene-speaking south Styria by 1914 and won division of the state *Gymnasium* in Gorica; Ljubljana had the only wholly Slovene eight-year *Gymnasium* (1905) though it was private. But in Carinthia and Trieste even Slovene primary schools proved out of reach in the face of hostile German and Italian majorities respectively. What could not be achieved officially could be partly made up for by voluntary organisation, spearheaded, for Trieste Slovenes, by a daily newspaper. In Hungary voluntary association was the only way forward for non-Magyars whose school systems shrank under state pressure. The growth of local savings banks, cooperative societies and cultural bodies helped keep a skeleton structure of non-Magyar consciousness in place. In the process Romanians in Transylvania and in Hungary proper merged political parties and strategies which till the 1880s had been separate, a good example of integration. Thus Hungary and the Czech lands represented opposite poles of ascendancy pressure. Galicia stood mid-way between the two. There Ukrainians were able to develop a primary school system in proportion to their numbers, but the Polish-dominated Diet (and their own backwardness) meant there were only eight Ukrainian *Gymnasien* in the province in 1911-12 and 70 Polish ones.

The broadening of the base of the national movements was social as well as territorial. Initially, industrial migrants from the countryside could be absorbed into their new ethno-linguistic milieux and open to the argument (as in Bohemia in the 1870s) that capitalists should not be allowed to divide them by exploiting national differences. Socialism came more naturally to them than nationalism, leading some nationalists like the Old Czech leader Rieger to oppose universal suffrage on the grounds that it would give the vote to workers and socialists, 'elements which are concerned only with filling their stomachs'.[3] But as between 1880 and 1900 some half a million Czechs moved to German-speaking areas for work, the majority to German Bohemia, the tendency for them to assimilate to Germandom declined over time. Partly it was obstructed by German employers' preference for segregating a supposedly more malleable Czech work-force. Partly Czech workers grew less willing to trade off denationalisation for work as they acquired more skills, raising the contentious issue of Czech 'minority schools' in German areas. The transition of Czech national leadership from the Old to the Young Czechs and the rise of the 'Progressive' movement of innovative intellectuals and student youth in the 1890s enhanced the attraction of nationalism for Czech workers. Successive pressures led to the federalisation of the new Austrian Social Democratic Party in 1896 which has already been described.

Socialist policy on the national question stressed the need for propaganda in the mother tongue. Nearly a quarter of the some 130 Slovene periodicals published between 1906 and 1912 catered for worker or artisan interests.[4] Socialists made a sharp distinction between medium and content, but in the Habsburg context such journals fed into and strengthened the pattern of ethnically organised social life. They help explain why from the end of the nineteenth century the earlier tendency to Italianisation of Slovene workers in Trieste declined. The life's work of the writer Ivan Cankar (1876–1918) catches the flavour of the time. Himself of working-class background, a socialist but also a Slovene and Yugoslav patriot, he was inspired by residence in Trieste to sense and then proclaim the indomitable vitality of the common Slovene people in an intensely felt synthesis of their double exploitation, social and national. Similarly in Budapest the Slovak and Romanian wings of the Hungarian Social Democratic Party had a press and an intellectual support which gave them a large role in the life of these minority nations, though less success in stemming assimilation.

Rivalry between socialists and nationalists for workers' support helped maintain ethno-linguistic loyalties among them. Self-conscious nationalism was important here because socialist concessions to ethnic identity were in part aimed to counter it. By contrast Welsh workers developed a substantial labour-orientated press in Welsh in the nineteenth century, but without a language movement this press gradually declined as knowledge of English grew. National language consciousness was not the functional product of a Gellnerite situation. The widening of national movements' social range thus depended on their simultaneous *deepening*, in the sense of the existence of a body of activists working for the goal of the modern nation (as they saw it) using its own language in all walks of life. The drive to what the Polish historian Chlebowczyk vividly calls 'internal sovereignty ... the right to live and work creatively in one's own national community'[5] was the ultimate motor of east-central European nationalist movements in the nineteenth century, sustaining them before the idea of 'external sovereignty' or independence appeared remotely possible. There had to be people committed to the belief that their traditional ethnic group could mediate modern civilisation to its people without the systematic interposition of another culture or language. Individual bilingualism was acceptable. National bilingualism was rejected as a stepping-stage to absorption. The issue was in good measure psychological. The tiny educated elites of non-dominant peoples at the outset of the national revivals had been brought up on dominant assumptions, usually internalised in their own communities, of their cultures' inadequacy as instruments of a full modern life. Hence the overriding obsession to demonstrate the reverse.

What at first seemed an idle dream to many national revivalists or an idle threat to their opponents proved easier of accomplishment than either side had thought. Alongside social factors came two psychological ones. One was the importance of *local* majorities. The power of the German economy and the German *Weltsprache* remained remote abstractions unless they were translated into dominance of the village school or small town theatre, which increasingly ceased to be the case. The second was that the non-dominant cultures did not have to match the actual range of the dominant ones; they needed only the potential to do so in a particular case. Put crudely, the fact that the revival had made it possible for any play by Shakespeare to be satisfactorily translated into Slovene was more significant for Slovene self-confidence than that not all of them had been. After all, the intellectual appetite even of most educated people is soon sated, and for the average Slav 'cultural worker', in the telling contemporary phrase, it sufficed that there should be expressionist poets in one's language without having to read them oneself, let alone that there should be as many as in French or German. Literary histories reflect this human trait to see likeness even where the scale of things is quite different. Such works proceed from romantic to realist to naturalist to modernist/ expressionist schools, with some four or five authors usually singled out for detailed treatment in each category, regardless of whether the literature concerned is that of seventy million Germans, eight million Czechs, three million Croats or one and a quarter million Slovenes. This mind-set made it easier for small-nation intellectuals to think they had 'arrived' and were now indeed *Kulturvölker*, with all the energising impetus that gave.

The above remarks are not intended to diminish the real achievements of the non-dominant revivals. As early as the 1850s fifteen plays of Shakespeare had been performed in Czech. Organisations sprang up for Czech-speaking lawyers (1864), philologists (1868), doctors and natural scientists (1869) and chemists (1872), while bilingual societies founded for architects and engineers and for mathematics and science lecturers in the same years quickly became purely Czech. In 1868 the Czechs opened their National Theatre with a Smetana opera: they had over 800 amateur dramatic societies by the 1880s. Even nationalists failed to grasp the implication of events, as when Rieger aroused Young Czech derision in 1883 for saying an educated Czech needed a perfect command of German. Cultural 'internal sovereignty' arrived sooner than expected. Other non-dominant movements' achievements were patchier than the Czechs' but hardly less heroic. August Šenoa (1838–81) edited the first high quality Croatian literary monthly, *Vienac,* on all-European rather than just German models, pioneered the Croatian historical novel and became, through his voluminous short stories and novels of contemporary life, the 'father of Croatian realism'. But he also, for a time, was responsible for the repertoire of the Croatian National Theatre, formed in 1861, which meant knowing the entire European repertoire and reading some sixty new scripts a year, from which together he had to provide about forty-five annual productions. The reception of the Modern movement in Zagreb from 1895, in full sympathy with international trends, shows, however, that his life's work in the interests of a modern Croatian literature had not been in vain, though for most of it probably 80% of Croats were illiterate.

Such glaring unevennesses run through the history of non-dominant communities in east-central Europe in the last century, and indeed later. There were remote or backward areas where social mobilisation had barely started, like the Bukovina, where a mainly Ruthenian or Romanian population continued to accept the dominance of official German as in a throw-back to absolutist times; or occupied Bosnia where perhaps two thousand in a population a thousand times larger had completed secondary school by 1914. Even in a more developed zone like Slovenia a leading historian can cast doubt on the long-term success of revival, giving a bleak picture of an economically struggling ethnicity of low-status peasants and workers, its surplus population regularly creamed off by emigration, its industrial capital nine-tenths owned from outside, and its share of the population on its language territory in decline – from 89% in 1846 to 77% in 1910.[6] This view contrasts somewhat with that presented earlier in this book and is perhaps over-pessimistic. By what process could the core Slovene lands of Carniola, and adjoining territories where local government and basic education had likewise come into Slovene hands, now be denationalised? Nazi brutality in the Second World War suggests that the Slovenes had indeed changed the terms of the situation, such that their enemies felt only the repudiation of all modern norms could reverse it. The Nazis thus acted out the warning Palacký had given in 1865 that to suppress a nation conscious of itself was akin to murder.[7] They showed that Palacký's words were not empty rhetoric, but pinpointed a real achievement of nineteenth-century non-dominant nationalism. The groups concerned had acquired a new kind of consciousness which was encoded in the process of social development, and could only be finally destroyed by challenging that process itself.

The Psychology of National Conflict

Nationalism looked at from the inside, as activists saw it, was a constructive, cherishing project. This was the aspect the doyen of modern nationalism studies, Hans Kohn, had in mind when he wrote 'the age of nationalism brought to private and public life a new morality and dignity'.[8] But the shadow side Kohn went on to note is also implicit in the defensive assumption behind the cherishing. Against whom were patriots protecting ther own? A fruitful line of modern research into matters of ethnic identity is the concept of boundaries, self-definition by exclusion of others: 'us' and 'them'. The age of nationalism was also an age when ethnic stereotypes held sway, alternately vainglorious and demeaning.

Engels's characterisation of Slavic backwardness in 1848 helped to set the terms of the German stereotype. The liberal *Westermann's illustrierte deutsche Monatshefte* in 1875 still ascribed Slav–German tensions to the lack of a Slav bourgeoisie, from which it followed, since the journal identified modern civilisation with bourgeois culture, that German intercourse with Slavs could only concern material processes and not 'sensibility in the broadest sense'.[9] The partial exception often made for the Czechs, who were felt, like an attentive child, to have absorbed certain Germanic qualities of hard work and thrift, was hardly flattering. Such mind-sets were reflected in the fact that the first professor of Slav philology at Berlin from 1874, the Croat Vatroslav Jagić, had no students for several years, while the taste for a remote and exotic Slavdom (Dalmatian 'Morlaks', Bosnian Muslims, Montenegrins) was fed by a minor German travel literature. Meanwhile, as in other imperialist scenarios of the period, individual Germans (or Hungarians and bicultural Croats) did pioneer work in exploring the traditions of the peoples they hoped to draw within their sphere of influence: men like Carl Patsch, founder of the Institute for Balkanology in Sarajevo, and the Magyar medieval Balkan historian and Bosnian administrator, Lajos Thallóczy.

German scorn was matched by deep-rooted Slav resentment. 'A German will as soon do a good turn to a Slav as a snake will warm itself upon ice' was cited by Anton Springer as a traditional Czech saying in 1865.[10] Palacký's view of Czech history as the interaction of a peaceful peasant society and aggressive German militarism – which allowed for moments of attraction as well as repulsion – was simplified in conventional formulations to the claim that Czech history in essence was nothing other than a thousand-year struggle against Germanisation. This fact, as the well-known realist writer Jakub Arbes began a pamphlet in 1895, did not need exposition.[11] Two years later the leading poet Antonín Sova thus addressed the German historian Theodor Mommsen, who had said apropos of the Badeni affair (pp. 306–7) that the thick skulls of the Czechs understood only blows:

> Arrogant spokesman of slavery.
> Do you behold naught else but the blossoming
>   peaks of your country,
> And all beyond would you leeringly crunch
> Beneath war-chariots of the conquerors . . . ?
> Since you have forgotten to proclaim unison
>   and humaneness . . .
> In an age when a myriad slaves hunger with an
> all-human suffering . . .
>   . . . our grandsons shall forget not . . .
> And will lay bare your words, where is sealed
>   the downfall of your race . . .[12]

Spokesmen of other Slav nations felt a like frustration. The ruling Germans and Magyars wanted to helotise the Slavs, complained Strossmayer to his friend Rački in 1867. Magyars, a nation of Calvinists, Jews and Freemasons, saw Croatia's yoke as their freedom.[13] The leading Dalmatian Croat paper greeted Easter 1889 with the words

> Croatian nation, old in suffering and torment, have cheer in Easter, do not give up the ghost, hope for better days! Already you have trod your heavy way of the cross, already you have drained your bitter cup: your enemies thrust you into the grave . . .[14]

These sentiments came from a quarter considered to be one of most *kaisertreu* in the Monarchy! Non-dominant frustration and resentment found frequent outlet in satire at overbearing Germans' expense. The theme of German pedantry and arrogance was the same in all Slav nations' gibes, but the humour varied according to the traditions of the people concerned: mordantly savage, as in the skits of the Bosnian Serb Kočić (1877–1914) on the occupation's *kulturtregeri* ('culture bearers': an ironic play on Austria's self-claimed 'cultural mission'); or slyly subversive, as in Jaroslav Hašek's famous character Švejk – a Czech army private whose apparent dumb subservience disguised an ingenious ability to send up his German and Hungarian superiors. Mockery is the best weapon of the weak.

The drip-drip of ethnic disparagement went together with perhaps the most significant feature of the mental climate of the nationalist age, the ineradicable conviction in all groups of others' relentless hostility. It was no wonder 'the German' harped on about Croats as lazy simpletons, commented a Croatian reformer in 1869 – after all, this was the enemy who had been swallowing Croats for centuries; the trouble was when Croats believed it.[15] 'The Ruthenian people is in extreme indigency...our enemies...fleece us of everything we have, of our entire patrimony', claimed the opening editorial of the Ruthenian journal *Batkishchyna* in 1877.[16] Such emphases had roots in the very doctrine of the national soul. If nations were the concrete expression of humanity and progress and if their nationality resided in their soul, which in turn inhered in their language and culture, then it followed that non-native speakers were aliens who could only obstruct the people's progress. It was on these lines that the idealistic progressive and Yugoslav-minded Croat educationalist Ivan Filipović blamed 'foreigners' for Croatia's economic weakness. Here is the emotional origin of anti-imperialist nationalism in disadvantaged societies in the twentieth century. National aversions dragged in those who wished to stand above them; as the journal of Polish democrats wrote of sharpening Ruthenian self-assertion in 1891: 'recognition of these [Ruthenian] rights need not...go so far as to yield to candidates who display hatred to the Polish nation'.[17]

Casual assumption was reinforced by the conscious polemic of press and pamphlet. All groups had neuralgic points, whether the Slavic nature of Carniola for Slovenes, which Germans denied, the nationality of Polish-speaking Uniates or Ukrainian-speaking Catholics for Ruthenes, the prior claim to settlement in Transylvania for Romanians and so on. But two ongoing rivalries stand out. The Serb–Croat conflict showed the difficulties a language-based view of nationality could produce. For both these south Slav peoples the Herderian orthodoxy by which they were really one 'Illyrian' or 'Yugoslav' nation clashed with popular sentiment and sociological reality, leading to arguments on both sides that the true identity was Serb or Croat, the others being merely Catholic Serbs or Orthodox Croats respectively. The latter position was held only by one wing of the Croats, the so-called Party of (historic) Right founded by Ante Starčević (1823–95) in opposition to Strossmayer's Yugoslavism; it attacked Austrians, Hungarians and Serbs with the petulance of weakness. Serb hegemonist assumptions were more widespread, but Croatian charges then and now that they were malevolent in nature are not wholly fair. When Vuk Karadžić argued in 1849 that Croats were truly only the speakers of the *čakavski* dialect spoken in Adriatic pockets, he was genuinely trying, on the Herderian assumption of the linguistic base of nationhood, to locate two strands in Serbo-Croat which might have given rise to the two nations. If Croats did not accept his intellectual case, obviously flawed now and provocative then, Karadžić was willing simply to divide the two peoples by religion. But this solution left out the Bosnian Muslims and seemed unscientific and demeaning in the nineteenth century, to both sides. Serb–Croat competition over the Muslims after they came under Austrian rule in 1878 finally put the lid on Strossmayer's Yugoslavism and made the Party of Right the popular force in Croatia for a generation. In turn, a 1902 article by a Bosnian Serb stated that Croats, having stolen the Serbian language and retaining no identity apart from their non-Slav religion, could only throw their hand in with pan-Serbianism.[18] It led to anti-Serb riots in Zagreb.

A still more fateful rivalry was that between the Czechs and Germans. Sneering at the Slavic Congress held in Prague in 1868 the *Neue Freie Presse* apprised Czechs that they did not delude themselves about the coming struggle between Czechs and Germans. Bohemia was the classic centre for the contest for national *Besitzstand* carried out by bodies like the *Deutscher Schulverein* (German School Association, 1880) and its Czech equivalents along the language borders and in mixed areas. The *Schulverein* reached a peak of 107,000 members within a few years of its foundation. Unlike bodies like the Slovene Society of Saint Mohorije, numbering 85,000 members in 1910, the various school protection associations explicitly organised their large memberships for purposes of national contestation. But could the promotion of national cultures ultimately be separated from national confrontation? And what place was left for Austrian-identifying individuals who straddled nationalities, or for Jews who did not fit the prevailing linguistic definitions of nationhood, the Yiddish mother tongue of most Galician Jews not being officially recognised? In the face of Gentile nationalism Jews could move three ways, to the supra-national Austrian patriotism of the Galician-born Viennese rabbi Joseph Bloch, assimilation to the nationalism of the milieu, most marked in Hungary, or Jewish nationalism, which challenged Polonophile Jews in Galicia (with three MPs in 1907) or provided a Zionist dimension in the Bar Kochba movement of Jewish students in Prague (1899). The Zionist pioneer, Theodor Herzl (1860–1904), himself showed the role of inter-group reactions in nationalism, when anti-Semitism drove this assimilee of German liberal culture (who called his barmitzvah a confirmation) to champion a people of whose own culture he knew little.

Of course our view of nationalism in the Habsburg Monarchy might be overshadowed by hindsight. Could one argue that for the bulk of ordinary people in their daily lives the polemics and interactions referred to above would have seemed remote, and that opinion polls would have shown them to have had social issues at the top of their agenda, as in Scotland today? Our society tends to assume that people's common sense counteracts the massive volume of media-generated images of violence. If this is true, would not the same basic decency have informed most personal inter-ethnic dealings in the society under study here?

There is empirical evidence for such surmises. Radical nationalism à la Schönerer never came near winning majority support. The level of ethnic violence in the Habsburg Monarchy was low compared to modern or nineteenth-century Belfast, let alone the thousands of fatalities in the social movements of Tsarist Russia. Moderation and a sense of the possible characterised the mainstream in both Czech and Polish academic historiography, under Goll and Pekař, and the Cracow Historical School respectively. Pekař accused Masaryk of romanticising Czech history in 1912. Alongside the powerful working-class movement, the Church was an even more influential force for national forbearance, whose diocesan boundaries ignored linguistic lines. Its official view saw the nation, as an extended family, as a legitimate object of love but condemned over-emphasis on it as un-Christian.

These glosses do not carry full conviction. It is unwise to oppose social and national concerns of the ordinary electorate in the late Habsburg period too strongly. Thus Czech peasants in the 1880s became dissatisfied with the Old Czechs' neglect of their social concerns, and contemplated common action with German peasants. Yet at the same time they blamed the Old Czechs for failing to deliver on the Czech lands and their state right. When an Agrarian Party finally came into being in 1899 it was just as nationalist on constitutional issues as the bourgeois nationalists had been. The processes described in the previous section had created a framework whereby all demands tended to be voiced through a national prism. It was not necessarily a question of intellectual conversion of the masses to nationalism in the sense activists gave it. Rather, as Owen Chadwick has argued for religious secularisation in the nineteenth century, changes in social and political structures eroded the context in which pre-nationalist loyalties had operated and gave a new weight to ways of looking which were not in themselves all that new.

The Church provides a good example of this process at work. As Czech–German tensions heightened, the line it had always drawn between legitimate patriotism and its excess proved too abstract to stop priests from effectively endorsing their own camp's views. Bishop Brynnych of Königgrätz (Hradec Králové) could write to Franz Joseph on the withdrawal of language concessions to the Czechs in 1899 that he was born in a Bohemian village and Bohemian was his mother tongue. These words were intellectually empty but emotionally and politically supercharged. The first number of the journal of the Czech priests' organisation founded in 1902 left a wide enough door open for nationalism in all conscience: 'The priest serves God, to be sure, but he also serves the people and so must take both interests into account.'[19]

How is late Habsburg nationalism to be summarised? On such a vast topic perhaps only negative generalisations should be attempted. In most people's lives it no doubt played second fiddle to other concerns nearly all the time. That is not to say that its influence was not ineluctably in the ascendant. The reason for that lay in its role in the process of development. The greater the pace of change, the more salient it became. Hence its relative weakness among Hungary's marginalised minorities. But here an interesting exception proves the rule. In her fine study of Transylvanian villagers the anthropologist Katherine Verdery cites the case of the self-made Romanian entrepreneur Ioan Mihu. When a fellow Romanian to whom Mihu had sold a once-Magyar home made to sell it back to another Magyar, Mihu is said to have expostulated: 'I snatched this property from the jaws of the wolf and you propose to hand it back again.'[20] Mihu's national consciousness had grown with his success. Verdery also notes that for Romanian peasants after 1918 poverty under Romanian landowners was seen as a God-sent misfortune;

it was no longer so resented as it had been under Magyar masters. A tentative conclusion on this theme might be that one should modify the common view that the social and national concerns of the masses are either opposed, with the latter a false consciousness, or simply overlap, with one the reflex of the other. National identity for the majority was real and social processes were making it more relevant.

Nationalism in Contemporary Perspective

Whatever our modern perspective, the question remains of how nationalism was understood by educated contemporaries, including those less caught up in it themselves. It is important to remember that nationalism had still not acquired all the fateful overtones it has for a modern audience, nor were some of the intellectual disciplines now brought to bear on it fully developed. Even after the events of 1848–49 Palacký could speculate as to whether national conflicts might yet become as divisive as religion had been two centuries before. How was the 'age of nationalism' interpreted by those who lived through it?

In any age most people continue with routine and can seem quite passive towards the ingrained ideas which underlie their daily lives, regardless of practical difficulties. This human trait helps explain why in the Habsburg monarchy an unreflective endorsement of the 'national idea' could obtain even in unpromising circumstances. In June 1914, with several acts of student terrorism already recorded in the Monarchy's south Slav provinces, the government chief inspector in Bosnia could begin a report on nationalist disturbances in Mostar *Gymnasium*: 'Every friend of healthy national development rejoices when youth is nationally minded, when it has ideals and dreams for these are the most beautiful prerogatives of youth.'[21] Though the Habsburg Monarchy ultimately provided a number of the most famous discussions of the nationalist phenomenon, there was also much triteness. One of the difficulties politicians encountered in dealing with it was that old ideologies like religion and philosophy had little to offer, contemporary disciplines like philology and history promised more than they could deliver, while the social sciences were still in their infancy.

The churches' failure to find an original angle on nationalism is particularly noteworthy, since their social role remained important. Throughout the period no advance was made on either of the two traditional positions. One was that held by the government and the bulk of the higher clergy. It emphasised the union of throne and altar, the role of church hierarchies in ensuring their flocks' political loyalty and the religious aspect of ethnic identity – as against the more secular model of linguistic nationalism. In this perspective, for example, the autonomy granted the Serbs in southern Hungary from 1690 had a religious character and was not violated by the growing centralisation imposed on Serbs after 1867 in the name of modern state norms. Moreover, a wedge could be driven between Serbs and Croats in the nascent Yugoslav movement by recalling their religious differences. But in the event, this approach proved double-edged. Too tight a control over the Karlowitz Serb Patriarchate – as in the appointment of unpopular patriarchs – tended to discredit the hierarchy in the laity's eyes, encouraging the rise of the anti-clerical Radical Party among Hungarian Serbs. A similar tell-tale development was the protracted boycott of church functions by Bosnian Serb activists from 1897 in protest against the Orthodox hierarchy's pro-government politics. The union of throne and altar against nationalism was becoming anachronistic and harming the Church more than the nationalists.

The alternative tradition, of the Church as the upholder of its people, easily took on nationalist overtones in this period. It was not just a matter of ethnic churches, like those of the Orthodox Serbs and Romanians, or the Ruthenian Uniates, in whose development Metropolitan Sheptickyj played an important role. Catholic churchmen, as seen above in Bohemia, could also come to understand themselves as ethnic spokesmen, if few matched the Biblical eloquence of the Croat Bishop Dobrila in Italianised Istria, who preferred, he said, to graze his flock with Moses on stony Sinai than to swim in comfort at Pharaoh's court, leaving his people to thorns and oppression.[22] Strossmayer's advocacy of Serb–Croat brotherhood rested on the simplest of Biblical postulates: unity in love. On withdrawal from active Croatian politics in the 1870s Strossmayer from 1881 began campaigning for the use of the Slavonic liturgy in the Catholic Church, with a view to reunion of the Roman and Eastern Churches but also of the religiously divided Slavs. The campaign eventually won over almost the entire Croatian and Slovene episcopate, showing how seamlessly Catholicism could be enlisted in what became effectively a nationalist cause, asserting the Croatian language over Italian in the Monarchy's coastal provinces. A Catholic theology rising above platitudes and balancing the claims of nationalism and internationalism in a serious manner was not attempted until Ignaz Seipel's *Nation and State* in 1916, which, like the Austro-Marxists, advocated recognising national rights on a personal rather than a territorial basis.

Philosophers were no readier to engage with nationalism at an analytical level. Before the Czech movement had got under way the famous Bernard Bolzano, professor in Prague in the *Vormärz*, had advocated a single Bohemian nation of Czechs and Germans but on the somewhat patronising premise of Bohemian German tolerance for their backward Slav brethren. Viennese thinkers of the later nineteenth century were uninterested in ethnic themes and tended to the dismissive attitudes to non-dominant nationalism common among established cultures. Dismissal could take different forms. It could be scathing, as in the dramatist Grillparzer's epigram on mankind's progression from humanity through nationality to bestiality; bluffly naïve, as in Hermann Bahr's pronouncement that left together in a room without the bureaucrats any half-dozen Germans and Czechs would quickly reach agreement; or shrewdly – but still too glibly – witty, as in his fellow novelist Robert Musil's later claim that the nationalist turmoil which disrupted Austrian constitutionalism should not be taken too tragically:

> But between whiles... everyone got on excellently with everyone else and behaved as though nothing had ever been the matter. Nor had anything real ever been the matter. It was nothing more than the fact that every human being's dislike of every other being's attempts to get on – a dislike in which today [1930] we are all agreed – in that country crystallised earlier, assuming the form of a sublimated ceremonial that might have become of great importance if its evolution had not been prematurely cut short by a catastrophe.[23]

Certain Austro-German politicians made contributions to the study of nationalism but hardly any professional thinkers.

If any intellectual discipline epitomised the national aspirations of the nineteenth century, it was history. Palacký, Strossmayer's right-hand man Canon Rački and Hrushevsky, the first professor of Ukrainian history at Lvov, all became leading nationalist politicians. History provided the raw material for the historical dramas, novels, paintings and sculptures which remained the staples of popular taste in their respective spheres till the end of the Monarchy.

It followed that history, like its kindred science philology, was too closely involved in the nationalist age to offer an objective comment on it. On the contrary, it provided continual grounds for nationalist polemic, particularly on issues of 'state right' debated between Czechs and Germans, Austrians and Hungarians, and Croats and all comers. Nineteenth-century history-writing was weighted to issues of ethnic emergence and development in the dark age, medieval and early modern periods; Palacký's famous *History of the Czech Nation* stopped in 1526. With the fading of romanticism and liberalism as intellectual driving forces in the last third of the century the emerging academic history of the universities and learned bodies took on a more positivist, critical form, certainly among the larger nations. However, its preference for the scholarly article rather than the broad synthesis made it incapable of reversing popular historical conceptions derived from the romantic period. Masaryk could say to public acclaim in 1918 that Tábor (the centre of radical Hussitism and symbol in his view of the continuity of Czech history and mission) would be the programme of the new Czechoslovak Republic.

The social sciences, prominent now in the investigation of ethnic issues, had barely emerged as independent disciplines in the Habsburg period. Moreover, of the social theories that did circulate the most influential – variations on social Darwinism – will seem to modern observers crude, if not pernicious. The *Struggle of the Races: A Sociological Enquiry* (1883) of the Galician Jew Theodor Gumplowicz was probably the study most noted by contemporaries. Observing in human history the same 'definite, unalterable laws' and 'iron necessity' as in all other natural processes, Gumplowicz argued that all ethnic groups, whose mutual hatred he stressed, sought to overpower those weaker than themselves, whether by destruction or assimilation. Though this in theory implied an eventual world civilisation, such a consummation was so far off that one could affirm 'an eternal racial struggle', in which centuries of bloody racial wars lay ahead before even a 'European race' would emerge from the Germanic, Romance and Slavic contenders.[24] Significantly, Gumplowicz was cited in the article which sparked off the Serb–Croat riots in Zagreb in 1902. The maudlin self-pity of much non-dominant journalism was partly fed by the prospect of being among the weaker peoples doomed to extinction, though escape routes naturally had to be offered, whether through the achievement of 'state right' or reinterpretations of the stereotypes foisted upon one. Thus the inaugural address of the Rector of Zagreb University, Natko Nodilo, in 1890 conceded Bismarck's claim that Slavs were feminine people but urged his audience to take pride in this feminine sensibility, unlike cold German reason, and not to fear the fate world history had meted out to Egyptians, Arabs and now Turks.[25]

Influences from European colonialism meanwhile reinforced the vogue for ethnic and civilisational generalisation with disparaging force. Béni Kállay's 1883 address to the Hungarian Academy of Sciences on Hungary's place between East and West distinguished between the Orient of anarchic individualism and despotism and the Occident of ordered civil society. In his administration of Bosnia as joint finance minister from 1882 to 1903 he deemed the Serbs in particular to pose an oriental threat to his pro-consular style of rule. His fellow Magyar Khuen-Héderváry, Croatian Ban in the same period (1883–1903), once dubbed Croats as well Orientals. As professionalisation drew historical study into a cautious positivist shell, the vogue for sweeping speculation passed to the nascent social sciences. Overall, intellectual contributions to the problem of nationalism were probably no more helpful than hospital treatment is supposed to have been before the later nineteenth century.

Here the figure of Tomáš Masaryk deserves attention, as the most impressive personality among non-dominant groups in the age of nationalism. His ideas too were of their age. Believing that the decline of influence of the Catholic Church made the union of throne and altar (which he condemned as 'theocracy') untenable as a way of governing the empire, he sought in typically nineteenth-century manner to replace his lost Catholic village faith with another over-arching moral vision. This he found in the aspiration towards 'democracy', which was the goal towards which world history was moving since the national revivals, the eighteenth-century Enlightenment and ultimately the Czech Hussite Reformation and its legacy of 'humanism'. Masaryk combined nationalism with internationalism, and a romantic Herderian belief in national missions with the positivist spirit of the later nineteenth century, reflected in his curiously pawky, didactic style. His democracy echoed John Stuart Mill's in that it presumed the people, liberated from Habsburg 'theocracy', would choose high-minded experts like himself to preside over them. Masaryk's eclecticism and subjective view of Czech history have opened his intellectual reputation to criticism, both before 1914 and again, with the additional charge of Platonic elitism, more recently. It is true that his view of democracy was based on a nineteenth-century act of faith, like Gumplowicz's belief that no 'truth', such as he had to tell, could harm mankind. If he escaped the trap of social Darwinist 'scientism' it was because of his old-fashioned Herderian view of nations as moral entities. This moralism required Czechs to justify their national claims and led Masaryk to a sense of the need for fair treatment of the German 'other'; but he accepted nationalist categories, to the extent of denying that Jews could be Czechs. In the Monarchy as it was, however, Masaryk offered a humane counter both to state right approaches to the national question and the fatalistic assertion of the law of the strong.

If there was one section of the educated elite which made a genuine contribution to the national problem it was lawyers. This was not so surprising. The fact that the faculty of law was by far the biggest in all Austrian universities reflected the historical importance of law and notions of civil equality in political development since the Josephinian Enlightenment. Article 19 of the Basic Law of 1867 explicitly recognised the equality of all nationalities and languages in Cisleithania, while promising citizens the right to use the local language in dealings with the authorities and at school. These provisions, to be sure, left much unclear. Were they merely a declaration of principle requiring further legislative provision to take effect, or were they already enforceable? Were the two different terms used (local language and provincial language) intended to be different or synonyms? Did the rights spoken of apply only to individuals or could cultural associations and such like also be 'juridical persons' entitled to request language rights? In all these cases the German position, which wished to restrict the implications of article 19, was for the first of these alternatives.

In the event, the judgments of the Reichsgericht and the Verwaltungsgerichtshof (Administrative Court) tended to favour a broader explication of the Basic Law. Thus three Czech-speaking communes in the otherwise German province of Lower Austria were recognised as juridical persons in 1877, with the right to petition for their own Czech schools. Communes' right to receive correspondence in their own language from a hostile provincial authority was deduced from article 19 without the passage of enacting legislation. Indeed, case law built up in the mid-1880s effectively supplied a charter of provisions for the founding of Czech minority schools in Bohemian German areas, interpreting the law in ways certainly not anticipated by its drafters. The courts accepted Czech as a local language entitled to rights with as low as 0.4% of local speakers in the town of Cheb (Eger). All this was recognition of the reality of rising Czech and other non-dominant aspirations. It broke with the German liberal position that nationality and language were purely personal matters and offered effective support to smaller nations' attempts to organise to claim their rights. How far these rights were actually won continued to depend on each group's political strength in the local situation, however. Slovene language rights varied greatly in the different provinces in which they lived; thus the Carinthian authorities in particular succeeded in blocking Slovene rights to their own schools or the use of Slovene in courts or in the provincial diet. The continued importance of the Austrian provinces even under Dualist 'centralism' should always be borne in mind.

The tendency was to chip away at German hegemony. An interesting decision was the rejection of a German speaking Reichsgericht judge's argument in 1884 that even if a Czech doctor was not officially employed by a Bohemian German town council, he must fill in medical forms for the council in German, because as a professional person he had a duty to know German to perform his duties competently. This old assumption that German was indispensable to professional life was increasingly losing ground, leading to complaints by a number of government ministers in this period who believed the functioning of the empire depended on a common language of the educated classes. But German speakers did not lose out every time. They were allowed to deny any language rights for the hundred thousand or more Czech migrants to Vienna, where Czech was not deemed to have acquired 'local' roots, and they themselves were the recipients of minority rights in other areas, like Italian-speaking Tyrol. On the whole, the decisions of the higher courts seem to have combined broad-mindedness, practicality and a sense of the times, though inevitably not to universal satisfaction, as witness the controversial contrast in the treatment of Czech speakers in Cheb and Vienna. The recording of language in Austrian censuses from 1869 also showed thoughtfulness. There was a deliberate attempt to prevent the politicisation of the census by avoiding a rubric on nationality and relating the language rubric to 'language commonly used' rather than mother tongue; this of course was open to the charge that it favoured larger nations who dominated the work-place, and in practice the language given came to be accepted as evidence of national affiliation. But formally the principle was maintained.

Ultimately, the mounting aspirations of non-dominant peoples could not be satisfied by piecemeal extension of article 19, in the paternalist spirit of an old 1848 liberal like the long-standing

Reichsgericht judge Anton Hye. But could the flexibility of the Austrian legal system shown in case-by-case scenarios inspire a more comprehensive approach to ethnic problems? Growing recognition of national organisations as legal persons did indeed point a way forward, for a system of guarantees of rival nationality rights within an agreed framework. The Czech–German compromise in Bohemia in 1890 had built on this principle to provide for separate educational councils for the two nations, national curias with veto powers in the Diet, division of the Supreme Court in Prague into bilingual and monoglot German members and so forth. It had been repudiated. But as the politics of the post-Taaffe era became increasingly mired in the nationality swamp it is not surprising that a fresh attempt was made, the biggest initiative in internal Austrian politics since the Hohenwart–Schäffle government of 1870–71. The result was the Badeni crisis of 1897.

The Politics of Nationalism: To the Badeni Crisis

The back-drop to Austrian politics in the 1890s was the need to compensate for the loss of the Czech component in Taaffe's previous 'Iron Ring' majority of Poles, Old Czechs and German conservative clericals. No more than in contemporary Germany did the sovereign intend to yield his prerogatives to a parliamentary majority but there was a clear convenience in having one, though social mobilisation made it harder to obtain by weakening the parties of 'notables'. Thus the Old Czechs could not simply be replaced by their victorious Young Czech rivals, who were like a red rag to a bull for the Emperor – 'a lot of strange customers have come to the surface and we must take energetic measures against them', was his comment.[26] This casts light on the petty persecutions which followed, culminating in the imposition of a state of siege in Prague in 1893–95, a mass trial of radical youths and attempts to smear the Young Czechs by association with murderers of a police informer.

In default of Czechs, moderate German liberals returned to government after Taaffe's fall (autumn 1893) for the first time since 1879, in coalition with Poles and German clericals. The government's driving force was not the prime minister, Prince Alfred Windisch-Graetz, but the finance minister Ernst Plener, leader of the United German Left. But Plener had never had a happy touch with non-dominant nations and his hopes of ministerial achievement were soon dashed by a bizarre ethnic clash. The new government inherited a commitment to set up parallel classes in Slovene in the German *Gymnasium* in Celje (German: Cilli), a small, mainly German town in Slovene-speaking countryside in south Styria. Though the budgetary expenditure involved was a mere 1500 crowns (approximately £75), on the issue of principle Plener's party withdrew its support from the coalition rather than accept this Slavic advance, and the government duly fell after only eighteen months. After an interval the Polish Count Kasimir Badeni assumed the premiership.

With the failure of Windisch-Graetz's government – which in Austrian terms has been seen as a parliamentary one, in that several of its ministers had a parliamentary party rather than civil service base – the problem of a parliamentary majority returned. Shrewdly, Badeni saw that the Young Czechs might now be won, for their radicalism was losing its edge with success; having already had their support for his creation of a Fifth Curia of 72 members based on universal suffrage in 1896, he next envisaged cementing this by granting Czech a role in the so-called 'inner service' of the administration: communications to officials from Czech-speaking citizens should not only be answered in Czech (this right was guaranteed by the Stremayr ordinances of 1880) but handled internally in it. The famous Badeni decrees of April 1897 effectively offered the Czechs linguistic equality with the Germans in Bohemia.

Yet Badeni's initiative showed many of the weaknesses of the Austrian system. First, like the regime bureaucrat he was, he proposed it to help with an immediate problem rather than as part of an overall solution to the Czech–German problem. Badeni needed a parliamentary majority to strengthen his hand in negotiating the decennial economic compromise with Hungary, due that year. Besides, a full Czech–German reconciliation which opened the way to genuine parliamentarism would have tied premier and emperor more firmly to the majority will; Badeni's aim was to stand above parties like Taaffe but with a securer base, incorporating both German liberal and Czech support. Second, his typically Austrian method of negotiation with the parties, through confidential intermediaries, was liable to come unstuck when exposed to public scrutiny. Criticisms that Badeni finessed clumsily in this regard, failing to square the Germans about his intentions, are perhaps not quite fair since leading Germans were aware of what was going on and would have refused direct contacts anyway. In fact, a bigger mistake was probably an anonymous interview he gave in which reassurances to the Germans provoked the Young Czechs to rush out a contentious list of 35 demands. Worse still was the failure to anticipate the impact of the parliamentary elections of March 1897, when the mainly Slavic Right, with Young Czech support, won an outright majority and pressed for a parliamentary government of the Right, increasing the German sense of embattlement. Germans began parliamentary obstruction; Badeni closed the parliamentary session, but used the summer not for a cooling-off period, but for the state authorities to harass the German protests against the decrees.

The result was a huge wave of German indignation, fed also from the Reich – 860 professors of Reich German universities decried the victory of Czech barbarism over German *Kultur*. There were genuine grounds for German alarm, because the decrees called for all officials in Bohemia to be bilingual within four years – Czech officials were of course bilingual already – and offered no incentives to achieve this feat. But the most remarkable aspect of the protest was its strength outside Bohemia in the Alpine German lands and particularly Graz, where the Slovene Celje affair still rankled. The role of students and radical journalists in whipping up feeling was marked. By the time parliament reassembled in the autumn German obstruction was so vehement that the government took the hazardous step of illegally changing the standing orders so as to suppress it, including the use of police. Social Democrat MPs now led the way in storming the speaker's rostrum, which had been barricaded off, crying that the revolution was being tamed. While Czechs called on the Emperor to carry out a constitutional *coup d'état* to force through national equality, the German clericals withdrew their support from Badeni. On 28 November Franz Joseph accepted his resignation. Not for the first time he abandoned a government whose bold policies encountered resistance, an act he quickly regretted.

In formal terms, the issue of language use in Bohemia dragged on for a considerable time. Badeni's successor, Baron Karl Gautsch, a long-standing education minister, issued 'provisional decrees' in February 1898 which went some way to meeting German objections by dropping the principle of official bilingualism throughout the province. But psychologically the damage had been done. Gautsch soon made way for a Bohemian aristocrat of German orientation, Count F.A. Thun, who revoked both Gautsch's and Badeni's decrees altogether in 1899. In theory the Czechs were back to square one; in reality, the use of Czech in internal administration grew but they were already embittered.

Thus the episode is important as much for its psychological impact as the reality. The astonishing scenes in the Austrian Reichsrat lived on in the memory to tarnish the cause of parliamentarism, whereby one might note that the Pan-German member of parliament Karl Hermann Wolf fought three duels during the Badeni affair, including one with the prime minister himself. Obstruction continued as a standard tactic deployed by all groups against unwelcome measures, so that the Reichsrat came to function through the operation of article 14 of the 1867 Basic Law, originally intended to allow for legislation by decree in time of emergency. Used thirty times in all before 1897, this provision was invoked 75 times in the next seven years, and for five of the seven annual budgets. Not for nothing did Prince Karl Schwarzenberg write to the future foreign minister Baron Aehrenthal in February 1898, 'the growing recognition that the parliamentary form of government has had its day can only help us genuine conservatives'.[27]

The Badeni crisis discredited not only Austrian parliamentarism but what was left of political multi-nationalism. It completed the split between south Slav and German clericals begun by the Celje affair and aligned the German clericals by autumn 1897 with the German nationalist camp. Lueger's new Christian Social Party sided with the German nationalist protest against Badeni from the start. With the aid of the Fifth Curia it had sprung from 10 to 28 seats in the March elections almost to equal the conservative clericals. Only the Social Democrats were left to sustain an ostensibly supra-national position. The refusal of the five Czech Social Democrats elected in 1897 to sign a state right declaration by their fellow Czech MPs was the clearest signal of this.

Yet the Badeni crisis finally spurred Viktor Adler, the Austrian Social Democratic leader, to confront the national question he had previously evaded. He now feared nationalism's power to infect his own ranks. The Brno (Brünn) party conference of the Socialists in 1899 advocated the reorganisation of the Monarchy as 'a federal state of nationalities', the units being ethnic rather than the historic crownlands. Essentially, it was to be a cultural federalism, for political and economic matters would fall to the central organs of the state. The centre, too, was to arbitrate on the vexed question of minorities. These provisions hardly provided an operational blueprint. In effect the Brno programme was a tactic designed to hive off a divisive issue in the hope that party members' minds could then be redirected to the key concerns of socialists. But more thorough treatments of the national question were to follow from individual socialists, in the works of Karl Renner (1902 and 1906) and Otto Bauer (1907). Both these writers argued for what became known as the personality as opposed to the territorial principle in federalism: the national entities would group adherents of like mother tongue wherever they happened to live, as is the case with membership of modern churches. Bauer in particular gave his work an intellectual depth, in which a full rather than merely tactical integration of national and socialist aspirations was attempted. Only socialism, by freeing the forces of production from their capitalist shackles, could create the plenty whereby a nation's culture became the patrimony of all rather than a class. But this very plenty would make the autarchic barriers of statehood unnecessary, enabling nationhood to flourish in an international commonwealth. Bauer's eloquence tended to disguise a crucial flaw in theories of personal autonomy. If each ethnic group was responsible for its own cultural development would not the economically more advanced gain over the poorer? Indeed, Bauer's own book proposed that Germans might migrate to zones like the Ukraine, which would benefit from their civilisational skills, an eerie socialist version of *Lebensraum*.[28] Socialist ideas of personal autonomy and legal schemes for the allocation of national rights both treated nationality as a matter of cultural identity separable from economic issues. When the Czech liberal Albín Bráf argued in the 1890s that the Czech movement should move from equality of rights to economic equality or equality of power, he was showing how the national question could burst these conceptual bonds.

A last comment on the Badeni crisis takes us to an aspect of the many-sided nationality problem which finally presses its claims. The Badeni decrees were spurred originally by the wish to strengthen Cisleithania's hand in economic negotiations with Hungary. For Hungarian nationalism was patently the strongest and most successful version of the genre, whose impact on internal affairs in Austria (where Hungary resisted any moves to federalism), on the foreign political position of the Monarchy, as well as on the internal development of Hungary itself was almost universally considered the single most important issue facing the Monarchy. To this we must now turn.

11 Hungary

In 1815 Metternich had pronounced dismissively that Asia began east of Vienna. Such a jibe was harder to sustain of late nineteenth-century Hungary. It appeared a land opening rapidly to the norms of modern bourgeois society. Four hours forty minutes by train brought visitors from the Austrian to the Hungarian capital, while the train journey from Budapest to Venice in 1888 was actually an hour shorter than a century later. From Budapest at least twelve major lines radiated out to different corners of the kingdom, enabling centralised bureaucracy to side-line the ancient system of county autonomy. Intensified state health provision had played a part in the down-turn in the death rate in the 1880s, so that while six years in the quarter-century up to the cholera epidemic of 1873–74 had shown an excess of deaths over births no such case recurred thereafter. By 1913, cholera and smallpox had been removed from the official list of fatal illnesses. A law of 1876 regulated doctor supply and the number of hospitals increased nearly ten-fold (44 to 427) over the period. Overall, Hungary's population grew from 13.6 to 18.3 million between the 1869 and 1910 censuses.[1] For all this the advance was strictly relative; 45% of children still died before the age of five in 1910 and the increase in life expectancy from thirty to forty still left Hungary behind any society known today.

This youthful population – its average age was only 27 in 1910 – was also much better educated. Less than a fifth of children by then failed to complete at least four years' schooling so that illiteracy had halved from 1867, to 33%. It was already under 10% in Budapest by 1900. The capital, by this time the sixth largest city in Europe, showed its modernity in many respects. Nearly all its houses were of stone or brick, against 21% in the country as a whole in 1910. The first electric street-lighting had been installed in 1873, the first telephone in 1881, the first electric tram in 1887. The beautiful new city was visited by six million people for the Millenary celebrations of the arrival of the Hungarians in the Danube basin (1896), far exceeding the still respectable figures for foreign tourists in Hungary, which rose from 130,000 in the mid-1890s to a quarter of a million before the war. With its 600 central-European-style cafés, its theatres, opera

house, twenty-four daily papers (1900), eight thousand printers and
vibrant Jewish community in close touch with co-religionists in
Vienna and Berlin,the capital reflected ostensibly the aspirations of
a resurgent European nation. If regions like Transylvania to the
east and Croatia to the south lagged far behind Budapest, this situation had parallels enough in the Austrian half of the Monarchy. Was
not Dalmatian per capita income in the early twentieth century
barely 40% that of Lower Austria?

Thus by 1900 the chief causes of Austro-Hungarian estrangement
had to be cultural and political rather than social. A major factor was
almost complete Austrian ignorance of the daunting Magyar language, related only to Finnic among European tongues. By contrast,
virtually all well-educated Magyars had a command of German, but
they associated their debt to German culture with the German world
at large rather than the Austro-Germans, whom they tended to
despise for failing to keep control of Cisleithania's Slavs. Here lay a
neuralgic point in the Austro-Hungarian relationship: after 1867
many politically conscious Austro-Germans hoped initially for the
resurrection of the unitary empire over the corpse of the Dualist
experiment. Their resentment was deepened when the problems of
Dualism revealed themselves first in Austria's nationality wrangles,
not in Hungary as they had expected. Hungarians crowed over their
discomfiture instead of showing the understanding Austro-Germans
thought was due, in the interests of a common anti-Slav policy. The
Croatian crisis of 1883, sparked off by Zagreb demonstrations
against new bilingual (Magyar–Croat) public insignia, marked a
turning-point. Though Austro-German hopes that a chastened
Budapest might become more cooperative were not directly realised,
the crushing of Croatian protest seemed to be a final consolidation of
Dualism, a system the Austro-German upper bourgeoisie was now
reconciled to as a bulwark against Slav federal claims.

But if Dualism became more acceptable to the likes of the *Neue Freie
Presse* it became less so to the mass of ordinary Austrians. Hungarian
agricultural interests pressed for higher protection of grain, which
would enable them to dominate the Habsburg market at the expense
of Austrian producers and consumers alike. Greater Magyar confidence led to more pressure for political concessions, while ethno-
political division in Austria induced a humiliating sense of weakness.
Austro-German opinion became fixated with an apparently triumphant Magyar ruling class, which combined the old state rights
intransigence of the Magyar nobility with a novel economic weight.

For the gathering Austrian anti-Semitic movement the role of Magyarised Jews in the new Hungary only further enflamed anti-Magyar sentiment. Prejudiced sterotyping did pick on one feature of Magyar ruling-class politics which really existed, namely its powerful national drive, strengthened by the ability of traditional social leaders to infuse their values into broad sections of the developing middle class. If in some respects Dualist Hungary was becoming less different from the rest of the Monarchy than before, its dominant mentality was as distinctive as ever – and all the more resented.

Magyar Hegemony – a Unique Socio-ethnic Structure

The key to Hungarian distinctiveness in the Dual Monarchy was the stronger position of the Magyars as a dominant group, compared to the Austro-Germans. Here history and geography interacted. The thousand-year-old Hungarian state was a geographical unit, consisting of the Danube basin and its mountain rim, with semi-autonomous Croatia, a later addition, stretching between the rivers Drava and Sava towards the Adriatic in the south-west. Ensconced in the central plain, the Magyars had been able to maintain their historic hegemony over the non-Magyar periphery despite their reduction to a minority of the total population under Turkish rule.

In the Dualist period substantial assimilation to Magyardom took place through urbanisation, as towns more strongly bore the impress of a Magyar-orientated state. Their population grew from two and a half to three times faster than the countryside's, so that by 1910 just over a third of Hungarians lived in settlements of more than five thousand. Budapest was a particular magnet for the whole country. The great bulk of its growth between 1850 and 1910 (from 206,000 to 1,109,000 in its modern boundaries) came from in-migration. Yet despite the very varied origin of incomers, over the whole period the proportion of Magyar mother-tongue speakers in the capital rose from a third to 80%. The hundreds of thousands of Magyar identifiers who returned themselves in censuses as bilingual in Magyar and some other tongue give a clue to what was happening; very many of these people were former non-Magyars, or their children, who on moving to a town had opted for a Magyar identity. Besides urban assimilation, other processes worked to swell the Magyar proportion of the population, whether by absorption of scattered non-Magyar settlements in the central plain (Petőfi, born Petrovics, had sprung from one of these) or the comparatively high Magyar birth rate and lower rate of emigration than non-Magyars. The result was that an overall Magyar minority of 46.6% in 1880 had become a majority of 54.5% by the census of 1910.

The great bulk of this Magyar population was congregated in two blocks, the major one being the core area in the Danube basin, the minor one the Szekler-inhabited language island in eastern Transylvania. There, in 1890, Magyars constituted 7.4 million out of 8.4 million inhabitants. Another 900,000 Magyars lived outside these areas among 7.7 million non-Magyars, making up barely 3% of the six most strongly Slovak counties of the north-west. Yet even there Magyarisation made strides. In 1880 Slovaks had been the absolute majority in nine of the fourteen leading towns of what is now Slovakia, and the highest Hungarian percentage had not exceeded 28%. Thirty years later, there were five Magyar and only four Slovak majorities.[2] The Romanian case further illustrates the importance of towns to Magyar dominance. The nearly three million Romanians (1910) were the largest of the non-Magyar nationalities and formed an absolute majority in Transylvania, but their highest proportion in a town of any size was only 29% in Braşov, where 12,000 Romanians lived.

Altogether probably over a million people were assimilated to Magyardom after 1880. The matter has not ceased to be controversial, with Hungarian historians defending a distinction between voluntary and forced Magyarisation (*magyarosodás/magyarosítás*) which is quite correct in general terms. Undoubtedly, most assimilation occurred as a result of people's adaptation to a social milieu rather than political fiat, and for Jews and German speakers, who made up the bulk of the assimilees, it was generally seen positively, as an aspect of modernisation and/or Hungarian patriotism. Yet it is equally true that the social milieu was shaped in part by a specific dominant culture, whose attractiveness state power saw it as its duty to foster. This is why assimilation cannot be separated from the ideological intentions of the Dualist ruling class. Magyarisation was both its goal and, to the extent that it occurred, its legitimation. Whereas the Austro-German Dualist elite justified its role in terms of a vague and somewhat arrogant claim to *Kultur*, its Hungarian counterpart had a clearer and in its way less elitist goal: to make Hungary fully what it already was in the Hungarian language, Magyarland (*Magyarország*). Quite what role this left for the non-Magyar 'nationalities' (the term by which they came to be known) was a matter on which opinions could differ; it might be a matter of their leaders' acceptance of Magyar hegemony; or of the Magyarisation through education of their potential leaders; or ultimately of mass absorption into Magyardom. But no Magyar denied either that the nationalities were a present reality or that Hungary should be a national state, not an ethnic federation. Within these parameters all could enthuse for the ideal of building the national state. Hence the buoyancy of Magyar public opinion which arguably made Budapest intellectual currents more *engagé* than Viennese.

That this public opinion should be strongly influenced by noble traditions was natural in view of Hungarian history and the noble leadership of the 'first reform movement' of 1825–48. Now that Hungary had achieved a fair measure of autonomy in the bourgeois era they were prominent in the work of implementing the reform synthesis of liberalism, nationalism and capitalism. In a nationalist climate in which all peoples sought inspiration in history it was predictable that Hungarian publicists should exalt the national role of noble leaders, more particularly, in view of the titled aristocracy's pro-Habsburg allegiances, of the middle nobility or gentry, 'in which the patriotic and progressive spirit is incarnated' and who provided the 'democratic element in the past', in early twentieth-century presentations for the English-speaking public.[3] These phrases are symptomatic also of a tendency to equate English and Hungarian history as the pursuit of liberty, and make the Hungarian gentry stand service for the missing middle class in that regard. So strong were the English associations that the English word was adopted into Hungarian as *dzsentri* in the 1880s, displacing earlier expressions for the middle nobility as this social group adapted to the new bourgeois order. By the 1890s the emergence of another expression, *úri középosztály*, literally 'gentlemanly middle-class', showed how closely the development of a bourgeoisie in Dualist Hungary was bound up with the fortunes of the old gentry, *úr* being the inherited feudal term for someone in authority, equivalent to German *Herr*.

What underlay these remouldings of terminology was the economic crisis of the former middle nobility (p. 241). However, the expansion of a Hungarian state bureaucracy enabled many scions of bankrupt landlords to find clerical refuge in the modern world, where their gentry values would have made commerce unacceptable. It was to fit both the surviving middle landed class and these bureaucratised nobles that the term *dzsentri* came to be invented. *Dzsentri* lifestyle, incorporating the old noble code with its emphasis on honour, exercised a strong attraction for recruits to a bourgeoning middle class of non-noble origin, including free professionals, intellectuals, state and private employees and businessmen. Its embrace by those Jewish- or German-born held out the hope of greater acceptance in the wider society and appeared a logical concomitant of Magyarisation in a context where no Magyar bourgeois tradition existed for them to join. It was this heterogenous product of Hungarian economic expansion in the late nineteenth century, united only in deference to gentry values, that became known as the Hungarian 'middle class', or 'gentlemanly middle class'. Symptomatic of the influence of gentry mentalities is that even in a romantic hymn to scientific capitalism, the *Black Diamonds* (1872) of Mór Jókai, Hungary's most popular novelist, the coal-mine-owning engineer hero must also show his superiority over his noble detractor in a duel – which despite never having wielded a sword in his life he carries off with aplomb!

The *dzsentri*, and particularly its landed wing, remained the core component of this unusual middle class. Landed nobles provided half Dualist Hungary's government ministers and made up 64% of MPs in 1861 and 41% in 1914. Moreover, for the influence of traditional values on those who remained ostensibly bourgeois one need look no further than the only non-noble prime minister under Dualism, Sándor Wekerle (1848–1921), descended from a line of feudal estate managers of German origin and married into the nobility, whose lifestyle he followed; though known as Dualist Hungary's most skilful finance minister, he invested his wealth in a large estate, holding no stockmarket shares. He was active in the foundation of the *Országos Kaszinó,* founded in 1883 specifically to provide a forum where prominent nobles and bourgeois could meet.

The middle class as defined above was a small section of society. At its most numerous, in Budapest, it made up perhaps 12% of the population by the twentieth century, but countrywide, officials and intelligentsia amounted to not quite 4%, to which a business component of some thousands of relatively prosperous and tens of thousands of smaller businessmen and their families may be added. The Budapest estimate is based on housing statistics, for contemporary opinion saw middle-class status as entailing homes of three to six rooms, allowing for one or more maids to live in, a possible governess and an office where required for the husband's professional work. Below this limit began the lower middle class of artisans, small shopkeepers and petty officials and tradesmen, numbering 13% of the population in 1910, and most conspicuously debarred from higher status by the frequent need to let out part of their small quarters; 61% of Hungarian artisans at this time worked alone. Above the limit was the upper bourgeoisie, which has been put at not more than a thousand families in all, most of them Budapest-based. Such figures indicate that the spread of education – a trebling of the educated intelligentsia over the Dualist period – had produced a large body of qualified people living in straitened circumstances. The problems of middle-class impoverishment which in a less optimistic ambience fed into inter-war Fascism were already there, as income inequality grew for the professional classes, and an elite prospered disproportionately. By 1910 industrialists and financiers headed the capital's taxpayer lists. Men like Leó Lánczy, head of the Hungarian Commercial Bank, whose executives held 150 directorships between them as they moved into the sponsoring of heavy industry, or the Jewish Zsigmond Kornfeld, General Credit Bank director, architect of four state debt conversions and developer of the port of Fiume, show the power the financial sector came to wield. Both ended up members of the Hungarian House of Lords.

Jews played a vital role in the formation of the Dualist middle class. Increasing through in-migration from 1.8% to 5% of the population between 1815 and 1910, by the latter date they provided 23% of Budapest residents, nearly half Hungary's journalists, lawyers and doctors, and 85% of finance executives. An estimated 346 Jewish families acquired Hungarian nobility in the old Monarchy, though the fact that only two of them were Orthodox Jews at the time demonstrates the adaptation to the dominant culture that Jews were expected to make. By 1910 78% returned their mother tongue as Magyar. This was the basis of ruling-class support for tolerance. But the Jewish contribution to Magyardom was not only numerical and economic. The efflorescence of a cosmopolitan *fin-de-siècle* Budapest also owed them much, that Budapest where two-thirds of all copies of its two dozen dailies were read (in 1896), the heart of a Magyar language culture responsible for three-quarters of Hungary's 2000 periodical publications by 1914, up ten-fold since Dualism began.

The apparently successful integration of Jewry was only one aspect of a national evolution in which patriotic Hungarians felt entitled to take pride. Count Albert Apponyi put it thus in 1908:

In creating Hungarian democracy without revolution ... the Hungarian nobility has rendered to this democracy an invaluable

service; it has introduced a spirit of tradition ... The new middle
class ... the captains of industry and commerce, the mass of the
intellectuals ... all mingle with the old element in the proportions
and to the degrees which permit the ancient spirit to permeate the
new alloy and to communicate to modern aspirations ... its traditional character.[4]

Apponyi's euphoric statement shows the largely delusive preoccupation with national continuity that shadowed Hungarian elite politics. For the transition from the 'noble nation' of feudal times to the
language-based nation of the nineteenth century *had* been a revolution in conceptual terms. It meant that around half the people of
Hungary – the non-Magyar speakers – were in principle alien to
the national idea, hence that political arrangements had to be
manipulated to ensure a Magyar hegemony. Meanwhile, the aspect
of genuine Hungarian tradition which patriots stressed, namely the
struggle against Vienna, was so firmly inculcated by their rhetoric
that the 'gentlemanly middle class' who were its heroes remained
mostly opposed to the 1867 Compromise, requiring more manipulation to keep their Kossuthite instincts in check. Hungary's economic
progress complicated this situation further. It heightened national
self-confidence, increasing discontent with the ties with Austria and
encouraging more aggressive repression of the nationalities. The climate by the turn of the century became conducive to ideas of
'Magyar imperialism', whereby Budapest replaced an effete Vienna
as the focal point of the Monarchy and proceeded to extend its hegemony over the small peoples of the Balkans. Gusztáv Beksics and Jenő
Rákosi, himself a Magyarised German, were the chief exponents of
these notions. They showed an overestimation of Magyar strength
which was the first shadow over Apponyi's comforting perspective.

The second shadow was the compromising of Apponyi's vaunted
libertarian heritage by the need to defend a system which did not
enjoy majority support. From the start of the Dualist era Hungarian
liberals had made plain that if it came to a clash between liberalism
and nationalism the lesser evil would be to choose nationalism.
'We are attentive to our national minorities but have obligations to
ourselves as well, and to ignore these would be a crime against our
national existence' was how Count Gyula Szapáry had put it as minister of the interior in 1874.[5] Since conservatism was associated with
Habsburg absolutism, there could be no strong Hungarian conservative party, only shades of liberal, which gave Hungarian liberalism

an amorphous quality and turned it into the ideological fig-leaf for a governing machine. By the 1890s the problem lay deeper. Liberalism was losing its appeal not just for reasons of expediency but as part of a European-wide questioning of its precepts, which had played its part in Austria, as we have seen. In Hungary, however, the crisis of liberalism took a form which reflected the gentry heritage and the nature of the Hungarian economy. The result was an upswell of what contemporaries called 'agrarian' protest against a liberal system now dubbed 'mercantilist', with currents of political Catholicism and anti-Semitism joining in the fray.

The roots of agrarianism lay in the economic plight of the landed gentry and more widely the Hungarian middle classes. In general, the competition of North American grain during the 'Great Depression', in particular the down-turn of the economy in the early 1890s, no doubt also the example of German agrarian organisation through the *Bund der Landwirte* (1893) underscored doubts about liberal *laissez-faire* principles. Very important, too, was the role of the landed aristocracy which, though overshadowed by the more militant gentry in national mythology, had greatly increased its share of the land, while retaining a steady 12–16% of seats in the Lower House and supplying the majority of Dualist prime ministers. In aristocratic ranks were those who most hankered after the conservative banner a landed elite normally waves; the ideologue of agrarianism, Count Sándor Károlyi, came from one of the country's richest families. His nephew Michael Károlyi has described the splendidly *grand seigneur* response of his cultivated uncle when he found Michael influenced by liberal economic doctrines: it was to give the boy Karl Marx. The gambit misfired and Michael Károlyi later in life became 'the Red Count' and a 'class traitor'.

The agrarians' chief concrete demand was for higher agricultural tariffs. But at a more emotive level they were able to exploit mounting middle-class resentment of Jewish prominence in public life. Charges that the culture of Budapest was not really Magyar linked gentry romanticism and anti-Semitism in ways which retain an echo today. Finally, Leo XIII's determination that the Catholic Church should not leave modern society to the liberals and Hungary's version of the *Kulturkampf* (see below) led to the emergence of political Catholicism through Count Zichy's People's Party in 1895, and by 1903 a Christian Socialist movement, albeit within the framework of Zichy's party. Powerful thinkers like Ottokár Prohászka (1858–1927) and Sándor Giesswein (1856–1923) challenged the liberal intellectual hegemony from neo-Thomist positions; that is, like St Thomas Aquinas they sought to show how Catholic doctrine could be rationally expounded without contradiction of the world in which they lived.

From this brief account the irony of Apponyi's view of Dualist Hungarian society for the modern historian should be apparent. Apponyi correctly identified the central role of a kind of social synthesis in the Magyar hegemonic elite, but he blandly overlooked both the problems this synthesis posed for the body politic and the tensions within the elite itself. In this he was not alone. Government in Dualist Hungary required not only tactical agility but the rarest of political skills, the ability to recognise national sacred cows, and the courage to tackle them. This challenge was only imperfectly met.

Elite Politics in Dualist Hungary 1875–1905

The Hungarian half of the Monarchy did not lack talented statesmen. Ferenc Deák and Kálmán Tisza have already been mentioned. Deák, however, went increasingly unheeded before his death in 1876, at a time when the Dualist regime was still far from consolidated. State income from 1868 to 1875 rose more slowly than expenditure (22% to 58%), government bonds issued to bridge the gap circulated at 55 to 75 in the European money markets and the national debt increased two and a half-fold. Meanwhile, party political alignments were in flux and the dissension-fraught governing Deák party came to the brink of collapse. Kálmán Tisza's achievement was to pull this situation round.

Tisza was a member of the predominantly Calvinist nobility of eastern Hungary. His merit as a practical politician was to recognise that Hungary lacked the strength either to reject the 1867 Compromise – the line of the Kossuthite 1848 Party – or to press Franz Joseph to accept his own Centre Left Party's version of it: the Bihár programme of 1868, which would have shorn it of its joint institutions like the common army, tariff and Delegations. The end of international instability after 1871, too, deprived Hungarian nationalists of a possible bargaining counter. Persuaded of this, Tisza waited for the right moment to engineer a fusion with the Deákists, emerging as leader of a new governing 'Liberal Party' in 1875, while those of his former centre Left associates who refused to follow him formed a second anti-Dualist grouping, the Independence Party. Even in

Liberal ranks, however, the hankering for further autonomy gains *vis-à-vis* Austria was not absent and led to periodic secessions of Liberal 'dissidents' into opposition.

The famous conservative historian Szekfű commented between the wars on the confusion of thought in Dualist Hungary over the 1867 Compromise. Ostensibly, Hungarian politics divided into those who supported this Compromise (the 1867ers) and those who opposed it (the 1848ers) – rather as modern Irish party politics have been dominated by attitudes to the Anglo-Irish treaty of 1922. But while elements among the 1867ers increasingly moved towards an 1848 stance, thinking sufficient Hungarian pressure could win a 'rounding out' of the autonomy offered by the Compromise, 1848ers who claimed to recognise only the 1848 laws as a valid basis for Hungary operated *de facto* within the 1867 framework, which their leaders eventually accepted *de jure* through oaths of office to the Crown. The exiled Kossuth further muddied the waters, Szekfű maintains, by deliberately blurring the distinction between 1848 and 1849 in his constant declarations and letters home, thus lending his supporters in Hungary the aura both of the April laws, concluded at a time of national consensus, and the 1849 Independence War, in which many dignitaries of Dualist Hungary had fought in idealistic youth.[6] The fact that 1867ers could be disguised 1848ers and vice versa contributed to an artificiality and fissiparousness in Hungarian politics, as parties constantly split and realigned over patriotic symbols rather than concrete issues. Thus a high point in the campaign to 'round out' the Compromise was the concession won in 1889 whereby common Austro-Hungarian institutions were to be entitled imperial *and* royal instead of imperial–royal. While the two anti-Dualist parties united as the faction-ridden '1848 and Independence Party' in 1884, to the right of the liberals a conservative grouping under aristocratic influence existed from 1875, periodically reinforced by dissident liberals to form loose coalitions under such names as the United Opposition (1878) or Moderate Opposition (1881).

It is thus possible to speak of a three-fold party structure in which the governing liberals were flanked by anti-Dualists and conservatives/dissidents. The last group, though ultimately ineffective because of its internal divisions (centralist/decentralist; clerical/liberal) had a role as a safety-valve for periodic disaffection in a system which really amounted to one-party rule, because an anti-Dualist majority was unacceptable to the powers that be. Since, however, anti-Dualists would have won truly free elections – a contemporary remarked that Kossuthite arguments sounded to ordinary Magyar voters like a popular song and Deákist ones like chamber music[7] – electoral manipulation, concerted between Tisza and his county high sheriffs, was central to the system. Nonetheless, over the whole Dualist period the opposition still won 60% of all Magyar constituencies contested.

Thus Hungarian constitutionalism was not just charade. Tisza faced successive crises in his early years, over the renegotiation of the economic compromise with Austria (1876–77), then the Eastern crisis and the Austro-Hungarian occupation of Bosnia-Herzegovina (1877–79), in which defections or abstentions sharply reduced an ostensibly large majority; the economic compromise, where he had failed to secure Hungary a separate state bank, was passed by nineteen votes. Tisza himself was defeated in the east Hungarian Calvinist city of Debrecen in the parliamentary elections of August 1878. On the other hand, the fact that he won this election with a majority of 77 at the height of the military occupation of Bosnia, which was expensive, bloody and added Slavs to the Monarchy, shows ultimate government control when it mattered. In the 1880s Tisza was able to perfect his system of close administrative control, winning majorities of 225, 242 and 261 in successive elections before making them five-yearly instead of three-yearly affairs. Further centralisation of local government in 1886 (county high sheriffs could veto any decision of autonomous bodies); reform of the Upper House (1885) which introduced appointed life peers; above all, assertion of government control over the nationalities, could all be presented as liberal, in favouring modern expertise over traditional sectors, and as national, in terms of strengthening the Hungarian state. In the 1880s, too, Sándor Wekerle, as minister for finance, established a pattern of balanced budgets, largely by transferring the tax burden from direct to indirect taxation and giving it a markedly regressive trajectory. But the very success in stabilising an initially shaky polity fed a destabilising nationalism. Massive demonstrations against perceived concessions to imperial centralism in Tisza's 1889 army bill (modestly raising the common army's annual recruiting quota to 103,000) presaged his fall on an issue of national sentiment the next year. Dualism was damaged. Count Albert Apponyi transformed the Moderate Opposition into the National Party, supplementing agrarian conservatism with a campaign for the 'fulfilment' of the Compromise by concessions from Vienna – the same illusory attempt to have one's Dualist cake and eat it that Tisza had abandoned in 1875.

Tisza's successors were soon embroiled on another issue of ruling-class fissure. A *Kulturkampf* broke out over Catholic priests' violation of an 1868 legal provision that children of mixed marriages should be baptised in the religion of the parent of their sex. Traditionally ascribed to a moribund liberalism's search for an issue on which to revive itself, this episode has been seen by the left-leaning Péter Hanák as the first shoots of a political Catholicism deliberately aiming to embarrass the government. The outcome was the pious monarch's reluctant sanction of bills transferring registration of births from Church to state, and introducing civil marriage. But noting Franz Joseph's distance from his government the Upper House voted them down in spring 1893. Wekerle, who had become prime minister the previous year, resigned only to return basking in liberal–national favour when Franz Joseph's preferred successor failed to form a government. The confessional laws went through. However, the whole crisis threw the political realities of Dualist Hungary into lurid relief. The king retreated from confrontation with a genuine majority opinion, but a prime minister who had crossed him could not survive either, and a delay in royal approval of the civil marriage law was the signal for Wekerle to go.

With his successor, the Transylvanian Calvinist, Count Dezső Bánffy, Hungarian liberalism finally ran out of steam. Bánffy applied his unsubtle techniques as high sheriff of a largely Romanian county to the wider stage, making an increasingly intolerant nationalism the regime's most distinctive feature. Too much fantasising about the *Rechtsstaat* (read: civil liberties) could be dangerous, he declared, and his subsequent political testament of 1903 blamed Hungarian politicians for wasting time over Vienna before they had sorted out the non-Magyars. Bánffy set up a special prime ministerial department to deal with social movements and the nationalities, and prohibited place-name designations not in Magyar throughout the country (1898). Yet his nemesis was to come over Vienna and reflect the mounting 'agrarian' backlash in the ruling elite against capitalist 'mercantilism'. The terms won in 1898 for the continuation of the economic compromise included some long-standing Hungarian demands, but also (at Franz Joseph's behest) the 'Ischl formula', by which if further negotiations on the common tariff did not succeed the existing tariff should simply be extended. The nationalist opposition held that this deprived Hungary of its right to paralyse common institutions by withholding assent. To mounting street fury and parliamentary obstruction, Bánffy's majority of over 160 from the brutal elections of 1896 suffered melt-down in a backbench revolt which swept him from power (February 1899). However, with his departure his former ministers dominated the new government which now had a majority of 227. All the brouhaha of a claustrophobic political system had brought forth a mouse.

The new prime minister Széll, a one-time finance minister become banker and committee member of the agrarian interest pressure group, the OMGE, was well placed to defuse mercantilist–agrarian tensions. His 'Széll formula', swiftly agreed with Austria, won nationalist consent to temporary prolongation of the economic compromise by ingeniously declaring that *legally speaking* an independent Hungarian tariff now existed, though it happened to be the same as Austria's. Though in the Monarchy's perfervid climate this clause incensed Austrian Hungarophobes, it was essentially tokenism and the existing common tariff arrangments were subsequently extended to 1907. Széll went on in longer-term negotiations with Austria to win the higher grain tariffs the agrarians wanted, in the so-called Sylvester night agreement of 31 December 1902, haggled up to the deadline in a way which will be familiar to students of modern European institutions. But deceiving himself that he could build on this success to get through a bill increasing the size of the common army, Széll united against him the 'gentlemanly middle class', resentful that only 5–6% of the army's top command were Magyars, and the broad masses, who could be roused on an anti-Austrian ticket. Obstruction brought about his fall, and an intransigent defence of the common army by Franz Joseph in his Chlopy manifesto of September 1903. The manifesto rejected proposals of military concessions to Hungary with a – for Hungarians – demeaning reference to 'that spirit of unity and concord which directs the special characteristics of every ethnic group towards the good of the whole'.[8] The result of the crisis was the summons to power of the last strong man of Dualist Hungary, Count István Tisza, Kálmán Tisza's son, in November 1903.

A convinced Calvinist of puritanical temperament and iron will, István Tisza is one of the personalities of early twentieth-century Europe. His credo was uncompromising: 'only such a nation deserves national life as, when attacked in its rights and freedoms, neither asks if it faces superior force nor weighs the prospects of the fight but unhesitatingly sheds its blood in the life and death struggle'.[9] Like his father deeply convinced of the necessity of the union with Austria for Hungarian interests, he dreaded a twist of international politics which might make Hungary another Poland – but find the Hungarian political class locked in battle over dead-end obstruction and unable to respond. Tisza was a Hungarian Guizot, whose ultra-conservative liberalism linked the democratisation of Hungary to an educational process which would at some future time overcome present social divisions. Meanwhile, he advocated industrialisation as a means of modernising Hungary and absorbing the non-Magyars. Now he saw his chance, having suppressed a major railway strike in 1904, to seize the opportunity to rid Hungary's constitutional life from the scourge of obstruction. The uproar he caused by forcing through parliamentary proposals to ban technical obstruction and introduce a guillotine left him no choice but to go to the polls in January 1905. It is evidence that Tisza's idiosyncratic 'liberalism' had an idealistic streak that he did not try to fix them. As a result, he lost. Though most voters (410,000 to 268,000) still supported pro-Dualist parties, the governing Liberals won only 159 seats, against the 166 seats of the Independence Party (now including Apponyi) and 254 of all opposition groupings. Incidentally, 108 seats were not contested. Having failed to reach agreement with a dissident Liberal, Andrássy junior, son of the foreign minister of the 1870s, Franz Joseph responded by appointing a general, Baron Géza Fejérváry, head of a temporary government which the parliamentary majority – and indeed Tisza – refused cooperation as unconstitutional. Thereupon, on 27 July 1905, Fejérváry's minister of the interior, the career bureaucrat József Kristóffy, told a socialist delegation of his intention to introduce a bill for universal suffrage. It seemed the dynasty was willing to play the populist card against the whole political caste of gentry Hungary.

The Kossuthite tendency grew from an 'extreme left' rump of some twenty seats in the late 1860s to the relative independentist majority of 1905 because of the 1867ers' cumulative failure to harness gentry libertarianism and burgeoning national confidence to their cause. But there were also shifts in the Kossuthite ranks, aptly symbolised in the humdrum personality of Kossuth's son Ferenc, who returned to Hungary after his father's death in 1894 to lead a movement safely ensconced in the politics of gesture. A Hungarian historian has recently written of the 'preposterousness' of Dualist politics because of the gap between liberal self-image and reality, which swelled political duels over honour as real principle declined.[10] The verdict is severe but not unjust. Those who have been noted here as superior politicians all perceived the need to compromise on the independentist position towards Austria. With the partial exception of Deák, however, they did not depart from long-standing gentry attitudes to non-Magyars and the lower classes. This left them open to the populist gambit in 1905, because these groups had most to gain from universal suffrage. But was the Hungarian political elite simply less imaginative than Franz Joseph and his advisers or did it have more to lose? How culpable was the failure to do more on the social and nationality questions?

The Nationality Problem

One of the most dubious achievements of the Hungarian Dualist elite was to push the question of the 'nationalities' almost out of view in conventional political discourse. This had been far from the case at the time of the Compromise, when in addition to Croats some 35 non-Magyar nationalist MPs (there were also about 25 non-Magyar members of the governing party) upheld an alternative vision of a pluralist Hungary, where each national unit had its own official language. But this seemed even to the most liberal Magyar tantamount to partition, and in view of contemporary evidence of non-Magyar high-handedness (chiefly on the part of the Serb-dominated town council in Novi Sad), which anticipated what would happen in territories ceded by Hungary after 1918, it is hard to deny Magyar fears that what was at stake was not the extent of language rights but a struggle for power, potentially recreating the anti-Hungarian scenario of 1848–49. Dualist Hungary came into being in an atmosphere of unrest, in which the Hungarian Serbs' leader Svetozar Miletić and the *Omladina* movement of the nascent Serbian intelligentsia seemed to be preparing for a Balkan crisis they could use to jockey Serbia and the whole south Slav world into a bid for unification. As with Afrikaners, what became Magyars' systematic repression of ethnic rivals stemmed from an initial fear of being swamped. The Hungarian interior minister's 1869 comment that a Serb–Romanian pre-electoral conference to reiterate their stance on the nationality question amounted to 'the spreading of ideas hostile to the existing laws and aiming at deliberate disturbance of domestic calm, whipping up men's minds, indeed, even formal revolt' shows Budapest's intolerance of opposition.[11] Mayor Miletić and the elected council had already been deposed in Novi Sad.

Central European liberalism allowed the state the right of 'supervision' over autonomous bodies. Kálmán Tisza developed it into a means of effective persecution of minorities. Constant enquiries into the working of their cultural associations could lead to a total ban, as of the premier Slovak organ, the *Matica* (1875) or the state's taking over of the largest fund of the Serbian *Matica*. The traditional local autonomy of Transylvanian Saxons went in 1876. Criticisms of government nationality policy in the minority press brought the risk of prosecution for spreading ethnic hatred or endangering the constitutional order. Nationality primary and then nursery schools were obliged to make the teaching of Magyar compulsory (1879/1891), while the state established new Magyar schools in non-Magyar districts or, since its resources were limited, sought to cajole existing nationality schools, run – like most in Hungary – by the churches, to go bilingual. This was much easier when the churches concerned had mainly Magyar hierarchies, as in the case of the mixed Catholic–Lutheran Slovaks. Thus in 15 counties with a sizeable Slovak population the ratio of Slovak or partly Slovak schools to Magyar schools changed from 2016 : 1036 in 1876 to 502 : 3478 by 1908. Where the church hierarchies were outside direct Magyar control, as for the Orthodox Serbs and Romanians and the Uniate Romanians and Ruthenians, minority schooling held up much better, and there were even a handful of Serb and Romanian secondary schools. Nonetheless, here too government exerted its pressure through religious leaders, exploiting their rivalry with the local secular intelligentsia. The substantial autonomy the liberal Eötvös had conceded the two Orthodox churches, with a built-in lay majority in their National Church Congresses, was an irritant but could be circumvented. From 1875 to 1908 the Hungarian government sanctioned only one measure of the Serbian Congress and in 1881 Franz Joseph appointed a conservative Patriarch who had been heavily defeated in the Electoral Congress, in successive ballots.

These tactics won a fair measure of success. The nationalities turned to a Czech-style policy of abstention from the Hungarian parliament which simply left them on the side-lines. In 1878 only six and in 1887 one minority nationalist was elected. An assimilationist could compare secondary schools to sausage machines which took in Slovak boys one end and produced Magyar patriots the other. By 1900 93% of local officials and 97% of judges gave their nationality as Magyar. The constant pressure encouraged fractures in struggling political movements. Miletić's Serb National Liberal Party split after 1884 into the Radical and Liberal parties and what Serbian historiography calls an 'opportunistic' wing. Slovak political nationalism was moribund. Romanian politics were livelier but were checked for a time by the harsh response to their 1893 protest Memorandum, which Franz Joseph simply refused to accept, leading to eventual imprisonment of the 'ringleaders' for exercising the right of petition. Minority leaders, recruited from the narrow circles of the non-Magyarised intelligentsia, lacked the means to mobilise their overwhelmingly peasant populations. As late as 1910, 86% of Romanians were employed in agriculture as against 55% of Magyars.

Yet victories won in the name of the 'Hungarian state idea' came at a cost. Where earlier in the Dualist era all minority national movements had had wings which hoped for an accommodation with Magyardom (Vincenţiu Babeş, Budapest university professor, among Romanians; the 'New School' among Slovaks; the Serb Liberal leader and long-serving MP, Polit-Desančić), by the new century sullen bitterness was general among the still politically active. Disillusionment was particularly strong with the Hungarian independentist tradition, which in the 1870s still claimed to champion minority rights along with universal suffrage. A radical Magyar daily's obituary to Svetozar Miletić in 1901 ranted:

> A traitor has died ... The venomous spider gave out his death gasp in his own web ... The pen in our hand shudders from contempt when we put on paper the name of Svetozar Miletić.[12]

The one-time leader of the Independence Party, Lajos Mocsáry, who remained loyal to the earlier ideals, became so isolated that he was driven out of it in 1887 and subsequently accepted election as MP for a Romanian constituency.

By this time the Magyar nationalist tide was also washing against the walls of Croatian autonomy. By the terms of the 1868 *Nagodba* this autonomy was anyway limited to cultural and administrative affairs, giving Croatia's slender professional elite no instruments with which to overcome the country's chronic economic weakness, admittedly not their priority. A neuralgic point came in Budapest's attempt in 1883 to introduce bilingual insignia on public buildings, thereby breaching the Croatian interpretation of the *Nagodba*. Protests of increasingly indebted peasants quickly fed on the initial nationalist spasms. The attempt made since 1873 to govern Croatia through moderate Croatian nationalists broke down, and Tisza imposed as

Ban a Slavonian landowner who knew Croatian but was otherwise barely more Croat in feeling than Conservative secretaries of state for Wales have been Welsh. Count Khuen-Hédervâry, however, weathered the storm which greeted him, including a physical assault in the Croatian Diet. Neutralising the Croatian Serb minority by minor cultural concessions and controlling the Croat electorate (2% of the population) through the half of it who were state officials, he was helped too by the hostilities between the Strossmayerite camp in the Independent National Party (the National Party were Khuen's satraps) and the crusty Starčević's anti-Serb Party of Right. But both the old matadors of Croatian politics were vacating centre stage to pragmatic politicians with sights set lower. A merger of the two opposition parties in 1895 led to a split-off of Party of Right hardliners but only slightly dented Khuen's Diet majority. The turning-point, as so often in Dualist politics, could not come through parliamentary means but was mediated through mass violence: Croatian peasant riots in 1903 sent Khuen back to Budapest to deploy his fix-it skills, briefly, as Hungarian prime minister. Subterraneously, a 'New Course' was being prepared which would bury the hatchet between most Croats and Serbs for a time, and underpin an intervention in Habsburg grand politics designed to get the south Slav world out of the rut into which Dualism had consigned it. This initiative was the Serbo-Croat coalition of autumn 1905 which burst upon the wider scene with its offer to aid the Hungarian Independence Coalition in its struggle against Vienna.

The Serbo-Croat coalition, based on party agreements in Austrian Dalmatia and Hungarian Croatia, serves to illustrate certain trends which were at work also among the nationalities of Hungary proper. These amounted to a realignment of small-nation strategies in the direction of 'realism' and some strengthening of their economic base. The number of all Croatian credit institutions nearly doubled between 1902 and 1907 and share capital increased by 60%. In 1905 the leading pro-nationalist bank was headed by a Serbo-Croat coalition MP, while the speaker of the Diet and president of the Serb Autonomous Party was the wealthiest of Croatian Serbs and closely affiliated to their strongest bank. Though one could hardly speak of industrialisation in a society with only 23,804 workers in firms of more than twenty employees in 1910 (up from just under ten thousand twenty years earlier), the falling percentage of Hungarian share capital and rising percentage of Serbo-Croat-speaking entrepreneurs pointed to a greater economic awareness in the political class. A belated embourgeoisement in Croatian attitudes might be seen in the democratically slanted social Darwinism of its chief advocate, the Rijeka-based journalist Frano Supilo (1870–1917). Supilo sought allies for Croatia among Serbs, the Italian Left and ultimately the Hungarian independence movement against the onmarch of Germandom to the Adriatic. The terms of the deal with Croatian Serbs was to be Serb support for Croatian 'state right' in return for recognition of the Serbs as an equally entitled branch of a common nation. The terms with the Hungarian independentists were Croatian support for Hungarian state right against Austria but a fuller Croatian autonomy inside this framework, including the incorporation of Dalmatia. When politicians from smaller peoples were mostly condemned to passivity or fruitless twists and turns in the attempt to escape the reality of impotence, the Serbo-Croat coalition programme was a remarkably bold stroke and an important contribution to the Habsburg crisis of 1905–06.

Non-Magyars in Hungary proper had fewer resources. But between 1890 and 1915 their financial institutions multiplied over seven-fold and their capital nearly twelve-fold. That altogether this amounted to only some 6% of the capital in the country counted for less with the alarmed authorities than that it should have happened at all. For in the context of still largely monoglot peasant populations – only 13% of Romanians could speak Magyar in 1910 – the growth of non-Magyar economic networks made their millions even less penetrable for the state idea. Yet liberal assumptions remained too strong to permit simple repression. As a Magyar journalist wrote in 1904, the nationalities were now fighting with modern weapons:

> Anti-national schools can be closed, dangerous associations can be dissolved, agitators can be jailed; but state citizens cannot be forbidden to form societies and financial institutions and offer their fellow citizens loans.[13]

Thus any government attempts to weaken the nationalities economically were more a matter of omission than commission. Non-Magyars emigrated disproportionately – two-thirds of the 1.4 million officially recorded emigrants from 1899 to the war – and a top-level decision was taken at the turn of the century not to try to counter the departure of poverty-stricken Ruthenians from the north-east, where the pattern of migration flows began. But once abroad non-Magyars often developed a stronger national awareness than before and the United States became a battleground where Budapest sought to neutralise their potential influence through subsidising, for example, Slovak newspapers and working through biddable priests. Meanwhile, despite non-Magyars' greater relative poverty, ironically the transfer of land at home was often in their favour. Nearly 5% of Magyar gentry or magnate land in Transylvania passed to Romanians or Saxons in the last pre-war decade.

This helps explain why, though the nationalities continued to decline on all the indices under control of the state, their political role revived in the twentieth century. More crucial here perhaps was the influence of the Romanian kingdom, of the Czechs (particularly Masaryk) and of Serbia and Croatia on their respective kinsmen. The periodical *Hlas* among Slovaks, the pressure in the Romanian National Party to prioritise universal suffrage over Transylvanian autonomy, the Radical victory in the Serb Church Congress elections of 1902 all bespoke the end of sterile passivity. The minorities participated in the 1905 Hungarian election, winning nine seats, and again in 1906, winning 25. But how many more seats would they win under universal suffrage? This sub-text of the drama Kristóffy's franchise proposals unleashed indicated how the nationality problem had, after all, not been solved.

The Social Problem and the Anti-Climax of April 1906

Whereas the nationality problem was an old issue which the less discerning thought belonged to the past, the social problem had for some time been touted as the issue of an uncertain future. The leading liberal daily, the *Budapesti napló*, editorialised on 31 December 1899 as follows:

> The nineteenth century brought the rule of democracy, the triumph of rights and affirmation of the individual ... [B]ut enquiring knowledge bold beyond limits is passing from this into a new period ... The social revolution is besieging democracy, and the concept of collectivism assaults the sanctity of individual right ...[14]

A sense of unease at the social condition runs through turn-of-the-century Hungarian writing, often linked to concern at rising emigration. (In fact, most emigrants overseas intended to return and recent research suggests that more than the official figure of 30% did so.) What is also noteworthy is that 'the social problem' in a still peasant-majority country was so often cast in the imagery of urban socialism.

There were at least two grounds for complacency as far as the rural masses were concerned. Any unity among peasants had gone with serfdom. Non-noble rural Hungary by 1900 was divided into three great blocks which lived quite separate lives: the landed peasantry, the landless labourers and the farm-servants. Second, the fear and deference inculcated into the lower orders over the centuries retained its hold. 'The sword does not cut off the head which is bowed', ran a Transylvanian Romanian saying, while Hungarian farm-servants used their employer's full title ('His Excellency the Count') even as they cursed him privately![15] Hence the phenomenon of Hungarian politicians like Wekerle and István Tisza, both landlords, who took urban social issues seriously, but considered the peasantry to be no cause for concern.

The landed peasants were generally descendants of the urbarial serfs of feudal times. Divisible into rich, middle, poor and dwarf categories in the rough ratio $1:4:10:9$ they showed in the upper two levels (above approximately 30 acres) limited signs of a *rapprochement* to both bourgeois and noble lifestyles which produced, however, a distinctively peasant culture. It was at its most self-conscious in the *Alföld* which retained the three-field system and where rich peasants invested in buying more land rather than intensive farming. Peasant dress took on simplified forms of pre-1848 noble costume, older dance and tune types yielded to what is now thought of as typically Hungarian (like the *csárdás*), better-off peasants acquired the means to make or purchase high quality folk crafts. West of the Danube more intensive and mixed farming patterns developed but the same willingness to adopt their own niche in a stratified society applied.

Landless peasants in 1910 numbered some 4,350,000, a quarter of the total population. Largely descended from the old servile cottar class, they and dwarf peasants often found themselves providing neo-feudal services to their old masters; a modern anthropologist discovered that the dues an old Transylvanian Romanian woman recalled the landlord receiving in her youth were the same as her ancestors were supplying in the 1820s.[16] Because of the prevalence of great estates in the Danube basin Magyar peasants were disproportionately landless, just under a third of them being farm-servants living largely in overcrowded wooden barracks near the big house.

Work-time was conventionally from half an hour before sunrise to half an hour after sunset, all day every day, with a free period on Sunday afternoons, inducing an animal-like torpor in men who had lived thus all their lives. Farm-servants' wretched conditions gained them at least more security than landless labourers, who were lucky if they could secure a contract, partly in kind, from, say, April to September (the *summa*) or a ploughman's contract of two or three months. Their willingness to accept such terms seems to have earned them at best patronising contempt: 'Their moral character is of course inferior, and they are very little to be relied upon', wrote a government publicist in 1909.[17]

It was the third category, the labourers, who were eventually mobilised in ploughing strikes of 1891–92, 1897 and 1905–06 in three different regions of Hungary. The 1897 movement, which involved some 15,000 ploughmen, led on to the foundation of the Independent Socialist Party by a dissident socialist and former farm labourer, István Várkonyi, whose programme of compulsory letting out of estate land in small leaseholds was interpreted by poor and landless peasants as a step to the division of the land. Prime Minister Bánffy replied by outlawing agricultural strikes, imprisoning Várkonyi and banning his paper. Later would-be peasant leaders, the journalist Vilmos Mezőfi and rich peasant András Áchim, who both founded their own parties (1900/1905), gave their movements a less idealistic direction, incorporating elements of Magyar nationalism in place of Várkonyi's stateless vision. Both won seats in the 1905 election, in which the official Social Democratic Party failed to break its duck, though it was the best organised movement in Hungary.

Hungarian Social Democracy's travails were perhaps the clearest reflection of Dualist Hungary's peculiarities, hoist between an advanced *Mitteleuropa* and the Balkans. There was ample basis for a socialist movement in the Budapest metropolis, the most crowded of European cities after St Petersburg, where the average working day at the start of the period was at least twelve hours and deaths exceeded births. But industrial legislation of 1872 and 1875, while abolishing guilds, also forbade the organising of strikes (though not strikes themselves) and limited craft unions to educational and relief functions. Moreover, the multi-national work-force was hard to organise; the workers' movement was originally as much German as Hungarian. This meant it went through very similar stages to its Austrian counterpart: the initial general organisation in the capital, with printer antecedents, in the form of the General Workers' Society

(1868); its early government suppression (1871); struggling attempts to establish a workers' party in the 1870s and 1880s, dogged by persecution and internal quarrels; eventually, a more solid organisation, the Hungarian Social Democratic Party (HSDP), set up in 1890 in response to the founding Congress of the Second International the previous year.

Trade unions, emerging from the craft stage in the 1890s, helped the new party overcome legal constraints on organising, but since strike activity was restricted the actual base of the socialist movement, even more than in Austria, lay in the 'free associations'. Existing ostensibly to support newspapers or various organisational functions, in fact they provided the link between the party leadership and the unions, and the brains of both. The real role of the free associations in the nascent socialist movement was no secret to the authorities, but they resisted calls to modernise trade union law because this would remove the pretext for government harassment whenever desired. By 1905 the Trade Union Council numbered 71,000 members and the chief party organ, *Népszava*, now a daily, had 25,000 subscribers. Ethnic subordination made non-Magyars open to messages of exploitation and the development of a socialist press in their languages was particularly promising. Though Christian socialism was also in the field and the striking railway workers of 1904 had links with the Independence movement, the greater weight of the Marxist HSDP was reflected in the interest taken in it by the radical fringe of the intelligentsia. The title this tendency selected for its flagship journal, *Twentieth Century* (1900), like that of the Social Science Society founded in 1901, was symptomatic of its turn from an outworn liberal–national romanticism towards positivism, influenced by Herbert Spencer's sociology. There was a touch of the histrionic, though, in the embrace of modernity and rejection of Hungary's 'Asiatic' conservatism by the brilliant young poet Endre Ady (1877–1918), whose response to Rodin's sculpture, *The Thinker* – 'Never has Plato's two-legged, featherless animal lived in a more complicated, more confusing and more demanding world' – encapsulated the restlessness of many young intellectuals in what they felt to be a stuffy and hypocritical backwater.[18] The strongest mind in the bourgeois radical tendency and editor of *Twentieth Century* was Oszkár Jászi, son of Jewish converts to Protestantism in Transylvania, who was willing to cooperate with the socialists. Jászi did not mind that his own reform programme (land reform, universal suffrage, concessions to the nationalities) would be seen by socialists as the minimum programme to their Marxist maximalism. At the same time, he still had contact with elite figures of more conservative stamp who also desired Hungary's modernisation, if not on those lines. István Tisza was a member of the Social Science Society. Gentry Hungary may not have been the liberal–conservative England of noble dreams, but neither was it Tsarist Russia. Polarisation was not total.

This was the complex situation into which József Kristóffy threw his universal suffrage bombshell, gaining the support of a hundred thousand socialist-organised demonstrators before the parliament building on 'Red Friday', 15 September 1905. Like Austrian socialists at this time the HSDP had from its 1903 congress made the democratisation of public life through universal suffrage the focal point of its strategy. But fraught with factionalism and dogmatism its vision was less clear on the issues a democratic Hungary would confront. Its failure to mobilise peasants, compared with dissident socialists like Várkonyi and Mezőfi, owed much to its rejection of peasant dreams of more land as petit bourgeois individualism. Its views on the national question did not advance essentially beyond the position of a Magyar participant in its 1905 Congress: 'We do not know a national question but only a question of exploiters and exploited.'[19] Hence it approved mother-tongue propaganda and even national organisations within the common party (approved in 1905), but rejected a Serb proposal that the autonomy promised in the party programme should also specify national–territorial autonomy. Basically, the HSDP falsely assumed that modernisation would mean the erosion of ethnic difference.

Ultimately, the Social Democrats were a stage army in the wings; only 2–3% of the population was industrially organised. The Fejérváry programme would go through only if the Emperor and his advisers stuck to it and were willing to fight a general election on a progressive platform against virtually the whole Hungarian establishment, and incidentally the Austrian prime minister Gautsch, who feared universal suffrage in Cisleithania. The alternatives were military action against the Hungarians, for which plans existed, or a deal with the Independence coalition. Not surprisingly, a Crown Council on 22 August 1905 decided for the last option. The fact of the matter was that an Independence coalition containing lifelong 1867ers like Apponyi and Andrássy did not have the stomach for a long fight on the lines of Deák's famous tax-withholding campaign of the 1860s, much as they invoked it. In February 1906 the

Hungarian parliament was dissolved to much reduced protest, and early in April Franz Joseph reached an agreement which brought the opposition to power but on the terms Andrássy had rejected a year before: the customs union and common army would remain substantially unchanged. The fact that the premier of the Independent coalition government was to be the wily Wekerle, an 1867 Liberal who had jumped ship, underlined how far the Hungarian nationalist camp had moved from 1848 positions.

The crisis of 1905–06 in Hungary highlights several bizarreries of the country's political system. The independentist opposition, which had called over a generation for the democratisation of Hungary, sabotaged the most far-reaching proposals ever put forward to that end and accepted office to implement policies they had vehemently obstructed at the cost of the parliamentary traditions they professed to love. Half the MPs of the Liberal Party, all-powerful for thirty years, had defected within months of losing the January 1905 election and the whole party simply dissolved itself days after the king's deal with Wekerle. The Fejérváry government for a time made its chief negotiating partner a party, the HSDP, which had never returned a single member of parliament, though it was undoubtedly the best organised in the country; and later abandoned its possibly beneficent proposals just as its opponents were on their knees. In all this commotion socialists and bourgeois intellectuals were able to have only a negative influence on the course of events, in that fear of popular radicalism getting out of hand no doubt facilitated the eventual deal among the elites.

Probably this summary is too harsh. It is the substantial progress made by Dualist Hungary in many spheres which causes its political defects to stand out the more. Political crisis was not the result of stagnation but of lop-sided development. In this, early-twentieth-century Hungary may stand for the Monarchy as a whole. But as an autonomous Hungary was the defining characteristic of Dualism, so that Hungary's plunge into crisis in 1905–06 is the most telling portent of the growing difficulties of the late Dualist system as a whole.

12   Austria-Hungary in the Early Twentieth Century

The constitutional crisis of 1905–06 in Hungary was a still greater blow to Austria-Hungary's international prestige than the parliamentary scandals under Badeni. Following from that earlier crisis, the failure to renew the decennial economic compromise with Hungary on a regular basis had given force to the humiliating label 'Monarchy on notice to quit' hung about its neck by sceptical observers. Eventually, the Sylvester night agreement of December 1902 had confirmed the common tariff at least until 1907, but Hungarian pressure meant this arrangement was now referred to as a 'treaty' between the two halves of the Monarchy, with the intended implication that commercial union rested on no more than the mutual reciprocity of sovereign states. Hungary separately signed the international sugar convention of 1902. The uncertainty in which the Independence coalition's 1905 electoral victory now plunged the entire future of the Monarchy is underscored by assurances the German government felt it necessary to give both Russia and the United States at the time that it had no territorial interests in the event of Austria-Hungary's collapse.

Éva Somogyi's commentary on the minutes of the common ministerial council she has edited for these years illustrates the ambiguity which surrounded the whole 'Dualist' project. Did the council amount to a common imperial government and the foreign minister who summoned it to an imperial minister? Hungarian state right principle ruled this out. The Austrian and Hungarian prime ministers regularly attended, alongside the common foreign, finance and war ministers, but were they formally members, and how was their 'collaboration' in foreign policy specified in the 1867 legislation to be achieved? In the absence of a common parliament, constitutional responsibility of the common ministers was nominally fulfilled through reports made to periodic meetings of the Austrian and Hungarian Delegations, though the means by which these could call them to account were never adequately worked out. There was, besides, a common military council which met quite frequently without any basis in the 1867 legislation, and there were ways of presenting the joint military budget to the Delegations which effectively veiled what was going on. Yet despite or rather because of these semi-absolutist aspects of common government, the whole issue was so sensitive that the raising of the annual quota of army recruits which experts felt necessary to maintain military credibility could not be put through till 1912, though first broached in 1892. Somogyi argues convincingly that Austria as much as Hungary often put its own interests in the way of common government, but shows that both negotiating partners, nonetheless, remained strongly supportive of continued collaboration. The problem by the twentieth century was more serious than either side's wish to sabotage Dualist institutions; it was those institutions' inherent fragility. However, the unending national–political problems which fed the stoical pessimism of imperial administrators was not matched by economic or cultural decay. The late Habsburg Monarchy differed in this respect from the contemporary 'sick man of the Bosphorus' or the declining Soviet empire. It is the interplay between political crisis and relative buoyancy in other spheres which gives its last years their intriguing poignancy.

Early Twentieth-century Habsburg Society

Initially at least, the international back-drop against which anxious statesmen pursued their discussions figured little in the minds of contemporary citizens. The 1897 Austro-Russian agreement to put the Balkan question 'on ice', confirmed by cooperation between the two powers over unrest in Turkish Macedonia in 1903, would have appeared reassuring to all but the paranoid; during this period Russia's attention was concentrated on the Far East and the deterioration of her relations with Austria-Hungary came only from 1908. The Austrian industrial boom years of 1904–07 and Hungarian growth, second fastest in the world between 1906 and 1912, began in what seemed a relatively stable wider climate. Unlike the case of the *Gründerzeit* (1867–73), progress this time did not leave the periphery behind. There were 30 Polish secondary schools in Galicia in 1900 and 104 in 1911–12; Croatia began to escape the economic stagnation of the Khuen era; the number of associations in Bosnia soared from 266 to 950 between 1905 and 1912. Urban social life became more 'modern' in tastes and techniques, for the first decade of the twentieth century saw the introduction or popularisation of many things which were to dominate the next ninety years. There were 25,000 telephones in Vienna in 1905 and 40,000 in 1909; the capital boasted 2161 automatic dispensers in the latter year and 62 cinemas. Its first department store opened in 1900. The *Neue Freie Presse* adopted regular rubrics for motor cars and aviation which reported Blériot's flying demonstration at Vienna in 1909, watched by 300,000 people. New leisure patterns developed besides film: cycling encouraged 'dress reform' for women; competitive sport, at first frowned on by patriots as divisive, caught on, with the Czech Football Federation founded in 1901 and the first Austro-Hungarian football match held in 1902. Sea-side resorts gained ground on traditional spas, but modestly by later standards; Istrian Opatija attracted around 35,000 tourists a year.

Cultural life also felt the whiff of modernity. The creativity of the Viennese avant-garde has already been referred to. There was a shift from earlier styles of realism in literature, fussy representationalism in painting or décor and historicism in architecture (the eclectic imitation of past models) towards greater subjectivity or simplicity: symbolism, impressionism and functionalism. Conventionality was challenged by new tonalities in music and by emphasis on sexual themes in painting or lyric poetry. Franz Ferdinand once said every bone of the painter Kokoschka should be broken. These tendencies were general. In Hungary as in Bohemia the major shifts in cultural tastes did not come with the passing of the Monarchy but in the preceding two decades. Ady expressed the zest and impatience of a new age in Hungary, where the very title of the Galileo Circle of radical Budapest students founded in 1908 bespoke iconoclastic tendencies. The artists' colony of Nagybánya in Transylvania (1896) introduced French-style *'pleine-airisme'* and moved on through neo-impressionism to full-scale modernism by 1907, while the self-styled 'Activists' of 1913–15 sought a radical political engagement which would help prepare the brilliant political poster style of the short-lived Hungarian Bolshevik republic of 1919. In Bohemia the Czech Modernist manifesto of 1896 called for individual creativity in all spheres, including the political, repudiating thereby the herd-like allegiance to nationalist clichés deemed outworn. Poets like the symbolist Otokar Březina and homosexual decadent Jiří Karásek, who affected an aristocratic title, were a world away from the up-beat patriotism or folksy realism of previous schools, as was the anarchist and later communist S.K. Neumann. All were born between 1868 and

1875. The leading Slovene modernist writer Cankar's *Erotika* was burnt by agents of the bishop of Ljubljana in 1899. In Croatia the voluminous literary critic and impressionist poet, A.G. Matoš (1873–1914), living – like Ady – a Bohemian lifestyle in Paris for several years, marked a similar transition. The attraction of Paris for this generation of non-German artists and writers is to be noted as an aspect of the decline of German cultural hegemony. Alternatively, the composers Bártok and Kodály sought inspiration from the folk-songs of the remoter Hungarian countryside, their first programmatic collection appearing in 1906.

At more commonplace levels change was most marked in the extension of the principle of association to include ever wider sections of the population. Here the state-wide *Dachorganisation* or 'roof organisation', over-arching existing local associations, played its part. Cisleithanian industry, first organised in the relatively loose Industrialists' Club of 1875, then the Central Association of Industry (CVI) and the somewhat less protectionist League of Industrialists in the 1890s, acquired a Permanent Committee of the three bodies in 1903. In Hungary industrial interests came together in GYOSZ (1902) and commercial in OMKE (1904). Hungarian landowners were already organised in the association OMGE from 1879 and the Hungarian Landlords' League of 1896. Austrian agrarians gained a *Zentralstelle* from 1898, its main brief being to lobby for agricultural protection. Teachers and civil servants were other significant pressure groups which increased their organisational muscle in these years, with the Imperial League of Secondary School Associations in 1905 and primary school teacher bodies of liberal and Catholic orientation. Women's groups acquired their League of Austrian Women's Associations in 1901. The organisation of interest groups reflected people's need to protect their interests in a society where few were affluent.

Their development beyond national lines seemed to contemporaries to offer some hope for escape from the cul-de-sac of ethnic recrimination. The secondary school teachers' league, for example, drew members from eight ethnic groups which were proportionately represented in its leadership. In 1897, the year of the Badeni clashes, sugar beet growers and refiners formed a cartel, though the former were largely Czech and the latter largely German. Within national groups, too, the new century saw bourgeois national parties like the Young Czechs increasingly challenged by new parties based on class or creed. T.G. Masaryk's famous advocacy of 'small deeds' in place of windy nationalist megalomania resonated with the many young Slav intellectuals he influenced in the Czech University of Prague in the pre-war decades, and his own sympathy for working-class aspirations, if not Marxism, mirrored a wider trend of opinion deemed 'progressive' in contemporary terms and not dissimilar to left liberal trends elsewhere in Europe. It went with openness on 'the woman question' and predisposition to educational reform.

Public opinion, whether interest-group-orientated or reformist, organised in order to influence the state machine. It was not utopian to hope to do so, particularly in Austria. State and society were not separated by the gulf of autocracy in Tsarist Russia or the endemic corruption of many superficially democratised twentieth-century societies. The ease with which able people could move between the academic and bureaucratic worlds brought talent into the system, while enough of the spirit of Josephinism remained to turn the wheels of state, often grindingly slowly but on the whole benevolently and competently. True, attempts to speed them up made little headway, despite a major inquest of 1911 which found that nearly a third of officials sampled processed one file a day or less. But major reforms put Austria on the gold standard, thereby consolidating the improvement in state finances (1892), updated civil law procedure and the tax system (1896–98), and had a comprehensive system of social insurance, including self-employed, rural workers and the old, ready for the statute-book when the war intervened. The administration was not a tool in the hands of the rich and powerful. Thus the 1898 civil service law continued a practice of increasing bottom pay scales proportionately more than top ones and the 1914 civil service regulations (*Dienstpragmatik*) finally tackled the problem of promotion for officials stuck in the lowest grades. Dissatisfaction with the emphasis on rote learning and the classical languages in the *Gymnasien*, previously the most prestigious of secondary schools, led to the creation of the category of *Realgymnasien* in 1908, with equal rank and access to university education; syllabuses were revised, the seven grades of mark awarded for performance reduced to four to lessen stress and those for diligence abolished altogether! It should not surprise, therefore, that the quite numerous associations pushing for social reform agendas in such matters as housing, worker protection or industrial mediation were well disposed to state-orientated solutions, as was the Social Liberal Party, essentially a Viennese body of progressive bourgeois, founded in 1896.

Hungary was a somewhat different case. To be sure, an agenda of social modernisation was prominent there too, in the concerns of the Social Science Society and the magazine *Twentieth Century*. In less radical form it was embraced also by establishment politicians like István Tisza and Wekerle: a pet project of Wekerle's was the Wekerle Settlement on the outskirts of Budapest, founded on the Garden Village principle and inhabited by 20,000 people by 1920. In gentry Hungary, however, such agendas were not so congruent with state traditions as in neo-Josephinist Austria. Attempts to reform the classical *Gymnasium*, for example, had less success in Hungary, where this institution was identified with the gentry's prestige and its access to the bureaucracy; there were five times as many pupils in Hungarian *Gymnasien* as in *Realschulen* in 1912–13. But where gentry interests were not felt to be at stake, Hungary was no backwater. Girls were allowed to study at university before they were in Austria and by 1910 326 were enrolled, some 2% of the whole.

The feminist movement, for all its frustrations, illustrates the nature of social change as contemporaries saw it: something to be welcomed or deplored according to taste, and in the latter case deflected and ringed round with impediments as much as possible, but ultimately, for thinking conservatives, hardly avoidable. The Monarchy's first women's organisations and post-primary schools for girls were set up in the 1860s, followed by a new wave of activity around 1890, which saw the first (Czech language) girls' *Gymnasium*, in Prague, and first political meeting, on women's suffrage, in Vienna. Thereafter, the burgeoning movement became concerned with access to university education and professional posts (initially, as secondary school teachers and doctors); regular conditions of employment in public service like post and telegraph, where they had been admitted on a casualised basis in the 1870s; equal civil and political rights; restrictions on prostitution and the like. On all these fronts except the franchise some ground had been won before 1914. That feminist leaders like Auguste Fickert were disappointed in their hope of achieving 'the moral reconstruction of the world'[1] (1898) seems no reason to decry what was gained. Actually, Fickert's hyperbolic goal implied acceptance of anti-feminists' central premise – that women had a distinctive role unrelated to cold male rationality – but this was not so damaging in context as it might seem to later eyes: this male way of deflecting feminists' drive for a public role only opened it up in another form – for women as mothers to the nation's youth. Nationalism provided an eagerly seized opportunity for women's energies; there were 10,000 women members of the *Deutscher Schulverein* in 1885. Patriotism was a key element in Czech feminism, making it possible for feminist leaders to cajole Czech political parties into backing a woman's election to the Bohemian Diet in 1912.

Far more dramatic was the accelerating advance of Social Democracy. The primary spur remained harsh living conditions, compounded of age-old patterns of inequality and the proletarianising effects of capitalism in town and country, though from the turn of the century rising real wages brought workers some belated share in widening horizons. Between 1903 and 1913 trade union members in Austria rose from 154,000 to 424,000, a level of mobilisation well short of that in Britain or Germany but comparing favourably with France. Predictably, printers were the most unionised with 94% organised in Bohemia in 1908. This increased muscle gained improvements in working conditions but far from spectacular ones. Employers were also increasingly organised, and in face of this the Austrian Central Trade Union Commission dissuaded from strikes unless strictly necessary and well prepared; the movement grew more prepared to accept technological change within the framework of collective agreements.

All this was part of a move to the normalisation of socialism's place in society, incomplete to be sure. Unlike in autocratic Russia, it did not become the spawning ground of a revolutionary intelligentsia. Indeed, leading intellectuals of the three chief Habsburg nations subjected Marxism to telling critiques from different perspectives: the Austro-German Böhm-Bawerk economically, Jászi sociologically and Masaryk morally. Rather, the socialist model for both halves of the Monarchy came from Germany, though the German SPD's proneness to factional in-fighting was reflected more in Hungarian socialism than Austrian. The pragmatic, flexible leadership of Viktor Adler played a role here. The 'Austro-Marxism' which was to highlight Austrian distinctiveness in inter-war socialism was as yet not so apparent, except in the creative approach of Renner and Bauer to the nationality question. Nonetheless, the personality of Renner in particular reflected an Austrian patriotism underlying at least the German-speaking wing of what its opponents took to be a subversive movement. Renner's original inspiration came from the cry of Marx's rival Lassalle that Europe could only be saved by the People and Knowledge. What he later derived from Marx appears to have been a pedantic materialism which caused him in his memoirs to note carefully that the beauty of nature is a marvel of geological rather than divine law; the emotional driving-force remained his image of 'modern heroism' – the humble day-labourer or baker's apprentice with the boldness to set and achieve, as his life's task, the acquisition of understanding.[2] No fiery anti-militarist, Renner observed that Habsburg military service was a step up in the life of the common man. At the end of his long life, when President of Austria for the second time, he is said to have commented of Franz Joseph: 'The old emperor stands above everything.'[3] Life stories like Renner's help explain the moral power of the socialist cause, and its success in a basically quite conservative society.

Christian Socialism, the other mass movement to flower in the pre-war years, was for Renner a step away from modernity to a narrow artisanal world. This was not quite fair. Lueger's mayoralty in Vienna from 1897 to 1910 undertook major municipal gas and electricity projects and electrified the tramways. The threads he drew together in a post he retained till his death were diverse and included besides threatened artisans the eminently modern lower middle class of clerical employees, public and private, and many teachers. Moreover, the party's artisanal links began to fray as Christian Social politicians, seeing the wider picture, started to woo big business and weary at their first supporters' every call for protection. The Christian Socials showed signs of developing into a mass modern party of the middle class, on an anti-socialist ticket. This consummation still lay ahead, however, because the divisions in the middle class were as yet far from resolved and besides, the Christian Socials were a mass party of German speakers only. The ideological cement that Catholicism would be able to provide by the inter-war years had not yet set, though the Catholic revival was well under way which would update the corporatist teachings of its forerunner, the ex-Lutheran convert Vogelsang (1818–90), with a more modern social programme, strengthening the Catholic presence among students and intellectuals. 'As our enemy changes, so must our weapons', wrote Schmitz, leader of the growingly influential People's League of the Catholics of Austria in 1914, 'What unites us with the past is the commonality of principles, of ideology, of goals.'[4] A speech by Lueger in 1907 urging Catholics to reconquer the universities pointed to a future in which political Catholicism would return to the intellectual and political mainstream in several European countries. Religion, however, for reasons which have been explained, could not span nationality in the Habsburg Monarchy and non-Germans had their own Christian Social movements which, with the exception of the Slovenes, failed to achieve Lueger's movement's clout in their ranks.

Thus Christian Socialism was not yet a mature middle-class mass party; its anti-Semitism told the same tale. Lueger himself wore his anti-Semitism (and even his Catholicism) as lightly as many Marxists their revolutionism, but John Boyer has warned against assuming that at the grass roots anti-Semitism had eased. It was too convenient a scapegoat for groups resentful of change, whether artisans under competitive pressure, Catholic priests alarmed at their own and their church's loss of status, declining gentry circles in Hungary or German-speaking intellectuals faced with challenges to ethnic hegemony. The anti-Semitic party which won 17 seats in the Hungarian elections of 1884, following the alleged ritual murder of a Christian girl by a Jew, received its greatest electoral support not in areas with most Jews but where Catholicism and Magyar gentry opposition to the Dualist regime were strongest. Another ritual murder allegation played a sensational role in Czech society in 1899, where petit bourgeois anti-Semitism was rife, as was the peasant version in Galicia, with its 830,000 Jews (1900). Anti-Semitism was part of Ottokár Prohászka's intellectual armoury in Hungary. The most striking feature of anti-Semitism, however, was its pervasiveness in the most advanced Habsburg national group, with which the Jews themselves had most closely identified, the German. In German ranks it became a prevailing ideology not just among Christian Social artisans but the successor parties of Austro-German middle-class liberalism. It mattered little if the Pan-Germans of the racial anti-Semite Schönerer fell back from their electoral high point of 21 seats in 1901, when the leading German bourgeois grouping, the *Volkspartei*, had made anti-Semitism part of its official programme four years earlier. By 1907, *Volkspartei* objections to the inclusion of Jewish MPs from Vienna could obstruct negotiations for a common front of German post-liberal parties.

How could this happen among Germans, when anti-Semitism never breached the tacit alliance between Jews and the Dualist Magyar elite, and Czech anti-Semitism did not prevent the rise of a Czech-identifying movement among Bohemian Jews? The answer involves the all-important relation of national to social themes in the Habsburg Monarchy. While bourgeois anti-Semitism owed something to the relatively modest scale of Austrian economic development – the *Volkspartei* drew much support from small businessmen – it sprang even more from the difficult national position of the Austro-Germans after 1867/1879. Having forfeited their traditional hegemony in the Habsburg Monarchy and lost their potential nation-state in Germany – by contrast, Hungarians had won a state and Czechs hoped to follow them – their sense of dissociation between nation and state led to increasing transfer of emotional allegiance to the former, yet with strong overtones of frustration and resentment. Contemporary neo-Herderian ideology saw the nation in cultural terms, encouraging doubts extant through the century as to whether Jews could be Germans in this sense. But in the fraught circumstances of Austro-German identity the insistence on an allegedly purified concept of nationhood made the rejection of 'alien' Jewish influence the very touchstone of nationalist commitment. It is not surprising that it had its strongest roots in the emotional world of student politics. Austro-German student fraternities had begun denying Jews membership in 1878. Organisations more involved in the real world, like the *Deutscher Schulverein*, could not afford to be so cavalier, since in many places where 'Germandom' was threatened, most notably Prague, Jews were a high proportion of German speakers. However, many pre-war Austro-German politicians had had their political initiation in the heady atmosphere of student days and/or the rising Schönerer movement of the 1880s. All this contributed to a climate so saturated with anti-Semitism that prominent Jewish intellectuals like the satirist Karl Kraus or the posthumously famous Otto Weininger could make Jewishness the symbol of cultural corruption and the Jew's struggle to overcome it in himself the highest expression of his humanity – 'through dissolution to redemption' was the solution Kraus offered the Jewish community for the problem of anti-Semitism;[5] Weininger put it into practice by committing suicide at the age of 23, shortly after publishing a bizarre pot-pourri of anti-Semitism and anti-feminism, *Sex and Character* (1903), made famous by his death.

Anti-Semitism in its various forms pointed up the shadow side of Austro-Hungarian society. It showed particularly strongly a general feature of the pre-1914 European world: weakness in handling the new kinds of ethnic relationships caused by the expansion of some European nations *vis-à-vis* others, European and extra-European, in the age of capitalism. Anti-Semitism fitted into the habit of crude ethno-cultural stereotyping (white/black, Teuton/Celt or Slav, Protestant Nordic/Catholic Latin and so on), as shorthand explanation of differential development which seems, in hindsight, the least impressive intellectual feature of the age. In its half-baked racial and Social Darwinist theories – often linked to misogyny – it showed most tellingly the difficulty any time of major change has in getting to grips with what is really happening, in this case, intensified socio-ethnic mobilisation. The peculiarly neuralgic problems of Austro-German and German–Jewish identity intensified this difficulty. Some of the cultural efflorescence of turn-of-the-century Vienna, which has been presented as brilliant critique of a fraught society's pathology, seems to this writer to be trapped in that pathology itself, like aspects of Karl Kraus's satire or the mixed-up Kurt Cobain figure of a Weininger.

A key facet of unease in the late Dualist period was the sense of backwardness *vis-à-vis* more dynamic lands. It was the source of Ady's rage against Hungary's Asiatic state, the Czech modernist movement's railing against the philistinism of the Czech little man, Cankar's satire at the expense of the hollow pretensions of the nascent Slovene bourgeoisie. For Austro-Germans the model was invariably Imperial Germany, whether it was debates on *Gymnasium* reform or social legislation, the continued prestige of Goethe and Schiller and of German publishing houses used even by self-consciously 'Austrian' writers like Hermann Bahr, or rueful references to the energising power of a common patriotism to overcome economic sluggishness. Habsburg subjects, though inhabitants of a large empire, had the mentality of poor relations in awe of rich and powerful cousins. Plainly, in such cases attitudes could be overdrawn, and risibly so. A correspondent of a leading feminist periodical could write of an editor who had abused women protesting against his misogyny that such men would have been beaten to death in less apathetic France or Italy, or tarred and feathered in England. 'But in Vienna?!'[6] The conviction that the grass is always greener elsewhere can become a habit with societies which feel they are under-achieving. Hence the substantial economic and cultural gains of late Habsburg Austria were discounted in a somewhat one-sided self-image of stuffy stagnation, while the hubristic dangers of the missing sense of national purpose Austrians so much admired in the Germans – or resented in the Hungarians – were quite overlooked. Of course, the primary cause of negative self-stereotyping was despair at the state's continuing political failure. But has political failure itself been somewhat oversimplified? The politics of the years between Badeni and 1914 deserve more attention than they commonly receive.

Cisleithanian Politics 1900–14

The common view of Austrian politics in the Monarchy's last years is bleak. After the Badeni crisis an unmanageable Reichsrat fell prey to obstruction, by which irresponsible party politicians sought to extort concessions for their own group or frustrate those for others. In the political vacuum thus created the Emperor and bureaucracy resumed what was effectively a neo-absolutist role. The one hope of the time, that the parliamentary ship could be refloated by diverting attention from nationalism to social development, was dashed by the failure of the universal suffrage reform of 1907 to bring about any improvement.

This picture is not so much false as incomplete. Set in a broader time-span, Austrian political experience in these years casts interesting light on the fortunes of the parliamentary idea in east-central Europe on the way to its inter-war débâcle, as well as on the mechanics of parliamentary management in a multi-national setting. First, the frequent disruption of Austrian parliamentarism did not discredit it quite as much at the time as might be supposed because Austrians were more inclined to blame their own failings rather than the parliamentary system itself. It was still seen as a definitive part of European progress and power, adopted even by patriarchal Montenegro in 1905. Second, bureaucrats as prime minister were less symbolic of parliamentary failure in a country with Austria's Josephinist traditions than they would have been in Britain or France. Austria's twentieth-century premiers, all civil servants, divided into those who were indeed indifferent to the ideal of representative democracy, confining themselves to keeping the show on the road, and those who invested both energy and ingenuity in the effort to modernise Austrian politics and reshape relations between government and electorate. It is certainly true that ambitious bureaucrats coveted ministerial posts, though their influence could be equally great behind the scenes: Joseph Baernreither and Rudolf Sieghart are respective examples.

Ernest von Koerber, who took over the premiership in January 1900 after the final withdrawal of the Bohemian language decrees, was in the reformist camp. No more than his predecessors did he aim to set up a 'parliamentary' government in the sense of one consisting mainly of party politicians, but he relaxed persecution of the Social Democrats, was open with the press and sought to capture the public's imagination through a billion-crown programme of infrastructural development. Bills of June 1901 pledging large sums towards a railway to Trieste tunnelling through the high Alps and for canals linking the Danube to the Elbe, Oder and Vistula passed through an enthusiastic Reichsrat. Riding high, Koerber was able to get the 1902 budget approved without recourse to emergency article 14, the first time this had happened since Badeni. The Sylvester night settlement of economic relations with the Hungarians and a law increasing military recruitment followed. Koerber's administration showed how a bureaucratic government had actually to be in closer touch with Reichsrat opinion than a party-based one, because while a party government could operate with only half the chamber's support Koerber needed nearer nine-tenths – procedural rules allowed any fifty MPs to bring real debate to a stop if they chose to obstruct.

Nonetheless, Young Czechs resumed consistent obstruction in late 1903 and by the end of the next year Koerber had fallen. Why had he failed? The economic historian Gerschenkron has made so much of the 1901 investment programme as an exercise in developmental economics that he is hard put to explain why it subsequently languished, only the Alpine railway route to Trieste being completed in full. It seems, over and above Koerber's alleged lack of steeliness or the covert opposition of the finance ministry, that the strategy of displacing national by economic priorities may have been given too much weight, by contemporaries and historians. Such attempts might bring temporary alleviation but in the long term could not substitute for a direct settlement of the neuralgic national issues. After all, part of the attraction of Koerber's investment strategy, as Lothar Höbelt has pointed out, was to keep different parties sweet in anticipation of a share of the spoils. Once the course of a canal or its priority of construction had been fixed this rationale lost much of its force. Koerber was under no illusion about the importance of national questions, since his ministry's first initiative was to call a Czech–German conference, whose breakdown led on to a bout of Czech obstruction in the summer of 1900. His papers contain the draft of a plan for a constitutional *coup d'état* at that time, involving the imposition by decree of universal suffrage for 60% of the Reichsrat's seats, together with a Czech-German language settlement. But as so often before 1914 the authoritarian bullet was not bitten; the Czechs grew tired of waiting for change and after more abortive negotiations in 1903 decided to seal Koerber's fate.

The brief tenure of Koerber's successor, Baron Karl Gautsch, a long-serving education minister, was rocked by the Hungarian crisis and the Russian Revolution of 1905. The conservative Gautsch opposed universal suffrage for Hungary, for fear of the knock-on effect this might have in Austria. However, the radicalisation of the Russian Revolution and a massive socialist franchise demonstration in Vienna led to an abrupt turn-about in November, ordered by Franz Joseph himself. What had motivated the Emperor and why was opposition muted when most of the traditional parties stood to lose by the reform? A couple of broken windows in the imperial palace could do more to change Franz Joseph's mind than any amount of theorising, commented the German ambassador cynically. But additionally, the age had become attuned to think, willynilly, in terms of change, and the possibility of reactionary change in a socially mobile age was still barely a gleam in a few individuals' eye. Thus, when existing institutions faltered one could only go forward and hope to mitigate the effects. This seems to have been the mood of Young Czech, Christian Social and German liberal leaders, all afraid of starting off on the wrong foot in the new democratic age by appearing to have opposed it. Even most of the large landowner MPs, whom the loss of their separate curia threatened with electoral wipeout, eventually came to heel, 'with a heavy and bleeding heart' in their leader's words.[7] 'Yes, they lose much', was the Emperor's typically laconic comment to expostulation on their behalf; 'Sire, they lose everything', was the reply.[8] For other groups the pill was sweetened in various ways: compulsory voting, where provinces wished, to help the Christian Socials offset better socialist organisation; a larger Reichsrat to facilitate share-outs of seats between individual nationalities at the regional level; a limitation on future creation of life peers to reconcile the Upper House. Plural voting, however, was rejected. By these means a new Reichsrat of 516 members was established on a basis of universal but not fully equal franchise, for tax contribution was taken into account. Thus the 241 posited German constituencies had an average population of 40,000, while the 108 Czech MPs each represented on average 55,000 and the 34 Ruthene MPs 102,000 people. But overall Germans were now in a minority for the first time. That this subtle mix of democracy and continued ethnic ranking was eventually achieved in 1907 was surely a notable achievement of Austrian statecraft, more specifically of Baron Max Vladimir Beck, who assumed the premiership the previous year.

Beck (1854–1943), another career civil servant, was perhaps the most interesting of Cisleithania's twentieth-century leaders. Describing himself as a conservative, and a long-standing adviser to the arch-conservative heir to the throne Franz Ferdinand, Beck sought nonetheless to go with the grain of the times rather than against it. Believing a society as complex as Austria's could not be dictated to, he concluded that strong government was to be achieved by bringing the people and their parties closer into a step-by-step process of development centred on the new parliament, obliging them thereby to greater self-discipline and responsibility. He also announced his wish to work through a parliamentary government formed from party politicians. With two Young Czechs, a German liberal, two Poles and later also two Christian Social ministers this was achieved, and the decennial commercial settlement with Hungary due in 1907 was successfully agreed. The fact that the Christian Socials voted for it and thereupon joined the government despite Lueger's previous demagogic attacks on deals with hated 'Judapest' (a play on *Jude*, German for Jew) shows that Habsburg politicians could act more responsibly than they orated. Their party with 97 seats and the Social Democrats with 87 (50 of them German) were the chief beneficiaries of the reform which, as intended, acted to encourage amalgamations in a highly fissiparous political system. The Christian Socials, previously concentrated on Vienna, now became a state-wide party through union with Catholic conservatives in the provinces. The successor parties to the old German liberals also felt the need to regroup to enhance a position weakened by mass party competition, which had halved their share of the chamber to just 79 seats; at first Progressive and *Volkspartei* MPs only, later also German Radicals and German Agrarians joined in the *Deutscher Nationalverband* (German National League). Schönerer's Pan-Germans collapsed from 21 seats in 1901 to three, most of his movement having split off as the more pragmatic Radicals, led by Karl Hermann Wolf. Yet alongside amalgamations universal suffrage also allowed a brood of newer parties to grow from under the wings of the formerly hegemonic Young Czechs and Polish conservatives: Young Czechs with 18 seats now came third among Czech parties, behind Agrarians and Social Democrats but still ahead of sizeable cohorts of Clericals and National Socialists. Polish National Democrats and (peasant) Populists won 42 of the 80 Polish seats. The success of Social Democrats shocked Franz Joseph. The intended transposition of politics from a national to a social domain was not meant to produce a balance between socialist Left and bourgeois Right but to aid the amalgamation of bourgeois forces against the socialist threat. The governing elite did not yet envisage democracy twentieth-century-style.

For all its promise the Beck experiment foundered after only two and a half years. One bugbear was Franz Ferdinand who, feeling betrayed by his former confidant over universal suffrage, which he opposed, was further alienated by constitutional concessions Beck made to Hungary to secure the 1907 economic compromise. Attitudes to Hungary offer an interesting touchstone of Austrian conservatism at this time. Moderates, as Beck had become, preferred military or political concessions, if needs be, for the sake of economic agreement; hard-line conservatives would rather have sacrificed economic agreement. Despite the fact that the concessions Beck made were symbolic or hypothetical (the customs union was again called a 'treaty' and limitations were set on the executive's power to muzzle Hungarian county autonomy as it had in the 1905–06 crisis) Franz Ferdinand made a secret deposition that on his accession to the throne he would not feel himself bound by the latter commitment. Nonetheless, the Archduke's decision to work on the party closest to him, the Christian Socials, to secure Beck's fall only assisted a process which was already pending with the collapse of government policy in Bohemia. The Czech–German problem retained its deadly potency.

Repeated unavailing attempts to resolve the Czech–German dispute were a fixture of the Monarchy's last years. From the time of Koerber they took a similar form. A settlement of the language question recognising Czech- and German-speaking zones in Bohemia and giving Czech full status as 'inner language' of administration in the former would, government hoped, be matched by redrawn administrative boundaries to satisfy German desires for their own territory semi-autonomous of Prague. Concessions to Czech wishes for more powers for the Bohemian Diet would be balanced by some kind of veto right to the German Diet minority on matters of vital interest. All this was a long way short of Czech state right but then the Young Czech leader Kramář in a programmatic book in 1906 had more or less renounced this dream, arguing that Czechs would come closest to it by greater participation in the Austrian state at the centre, which would give Germans themselves cause to call for devolution. This 'positivist' approach went back to Josef Kaizl, briefly Austrian finance minister in the 1890s. At different times virtually all aspects of a possible package – even the ultra-sensitive issue of minorities inside the other side's heartland, like the Prague Germans – were agreed. Indeed, in Bohemia's sister province of Moravia a deal was actually struck in 1905, if somewhat different on language because the two communities were more interspersed; it reflects Jiří Kořálka's interesting view that a dominant minority might compromise its hegemony, as the Moravian Germans gave up their majority in the Diet, in return for guarantees that worse would not befall them. But in Bohemia, where tensions had always been greatest, the problem, as with a Rubik cube, was to fit in all parts of the solution at the same time.

In 1908 the breakdown came on the language front. Certain courts in German Bohemia refused to accept documents in Czech, 81 Czech towns then said they would not accept German and by the time the Diet met in September to consider Beck's proposals ethnic relations were in a trough. The Czech majority nominated only Czech officers, German deputies withdrew in protest, singing the Pan-German song 'Watch on the Rhine', Beck failed to get the support of the large landowner contingent (no doubt because one of his proposals envisaged democratising the Diet franchise too) and with Germans and Slovenes clashing bloodily in Ljubljana Beck prorogued the Diet in despair, the Czech members of his government resigned, followed by the Christian Social ministers, and one of the most ambitious and resourceful of Austrian prime ministers was out of office, never to return.

With Beck's fall the guts were torn out of Austrian parliamentarism. His chief successors Bienerth (1908–11) and Stürgkh (1911–16) did not attempt to form parliamentary governments; Bienerth repeatedly prorogued the Reichsrat at the first signs of obstruction, relying on article 14; Stürgkh initially professed support for parliamentarism, adding, however, that it was not a goal in itself but should serve state and people – a qualification which disguised a good dose of scepticism. The last major attempt to tackle the Bohemian question came in 1910 but on false pretences. The pro-Czech and pro-German wings of the large landowners reached agreement among themselves, which it was hoped could be extended to other parties. However, the large landowners' interest was mainly confined to refloating the Bohemian Diet, which was their only public forum after the loss of their Reichsrat curia; they did not have their hearts in a full national settlement because this would deprive them of their mediatory role and complete the process of democratisation at their expense. There is evidence that this was also Franz Ferdinand's view behind the scenes. In fact, all parties to the dispute felt they had an interest in delaying a solution: Czechs because they were on the rise and imagined that in a little time Czech migration to German Bohemian industrial areas would undermine the German project of a clearly defined autonomous zone; Germans because delay would drive the Bohemian Diet yet further into debt, forcing the Czechs into concessions to meet its bills to teachers and others. But as in a game of multiple chess other dimensions were also relevant. Would the Czechs have made concessions in Bohemia for the sake of a better deal in the Monarchy as a whole? There were, for example, over a hundred thousand Czechs in Vienna who were denied publicly funded schools. How important was the consoling regional might of the Second Reich in feeding German Bohemian stubbornness? So impotent had public forums become that Stürgkh's suspension of the Bohemian constitution in 1913 aroused only muted protest; a state commission took over the administrative functions of the standing committee of the Diet.

The Reichsrat elections called by Bienerth in 1911 had meanwhile not yielded the result he wanted. The clericals, both Czech and Christian Social, had declined and the Social Democrats and Czech radical nationalist parties had advanced. The tendency to party con-solidation visible after 1907 went into reverse as rifts reopened between the urban and rural wings of Christian Socialism, the Alpine elements in the *Deutscher Nationalverband* resented the predo-minance of the Bohemian Germans and even among the Social Democrats ethnic harmony began to dissolve. For socialists could not be wholly immune to the rising tide of nationalism around them, which increasingly coloured the way internal disputes in the move-ment were viewed. Czechs, for example, were inclined to condemn the (mainly German) leadership's caution over a general strike for universal suffrage in 1905 from the standpoint of their radical self-image as the nation of the martyred Hus; Austro-Germans were afraid to allow a Czech socialist candidate in Vienna to represent the large numbers of Czech workers there because this would provoke a German nationalist backlash. In these circumstances alienated Czechs began to found rival branches in sector after sector of the trade union movement, making the central Czech TU Commisson they had been conceded in 1896 the motor of an effectively separate body. Condemnations of this 'separatism' by the international trade union movement and the Second International, some of whose mem-bers displayed ignorance of who Czechs were, proved if any-thing counter-productive. Eventually in 1911 a pro-Viennese faction broke away from the Czech wing of the federal party, accusing it of separatist tendencies and setting up a 'centralist' Czech socialist organisation, based in Brno in less nationalist Moravia. When the federal party recognised this new Czech movement, the main body of Czech socialists broke off collaboration with Vienna, effectively seceding. 'Centralist' and 'separatist' Czech socialists stood against each other in elections (the separatists winning easily), as did Czech- and German-speaking socialists in Vienna and Bohemia; at least most Czech socialists voted for German socialist candidates on a second ballot if their own man was already eliminated; very few German socialists responded in kind. Before the war Ruthenian and Trentino Italian socialists had also split on the national question and the departure of Poles and south Slavs in 1916 completed the demise of the federal party. In fact, no genuinely all-Austrian party congress was held after 1905.

The socialists stopped short of breaching one taboo, their renunciation of obstruction. No-one else did. When Stürgkh prorogued the Reichsrat in March 1914, not to meet for two and a half years, it was the humble Slovenes who were at it. Circling the titanic Czech–German battleground a constellation of lesser conflicts spluttered frequently into fiery life: Slovenes, Ruthenes and Italians demanded their own universities; a Ruthenian student shot dead the Polish governor of Galicia in 1908; secessionist propaganda waxed among Italians from the nearby kingdom and among Ruthenes from Russia, where it often came in the cloak of Orthodoxy; Italians and south Slavs squabbled over the use of Old Church Slavonic in Catholic services, an ancient privilege revived for nationalist ends. Hence, cumulatively, Franz Joseph's *cri de coeur* of early 1914 that it was finally time to sort things out since parliamentary government had proved impossible in Austria. From the other end of the spectrum socialists had also put doomed hope in universal suffrage which would, Renner and Bauer argued, allow the Austrian bourgeoisie to emerge from under the petticoats of the bureaucracy in a proper democracy where issues of class and freedom would replace the German–Slav miasma. The conclusion of most contemporaries and later historians has been that a stifling bureaucracy and irresponsible political culture, grubbing for petty ethnic favours, maintained their grip.

True though this mostly is, perhaps the tone can be too censorious. Lothar Höbelt, the historian of Austro-German liberal–nationalist politics, has pointed out that for party politicians denied an input into foreign policy and defence matters, fighting for one's national share of the cake was the most obvious remaining field of action.[9] A diffuse society necessarily produced a diffuse politics, illustrated by the constant permutations and realignments of regional political groupings as between Bohemia, Moravia, Vienna and the Alpine lands. Moreover, development and democratisation actually eroded the basis of a kind of ideological party politics on *Kulturkampf* lines which had been operative between 1867 and 1893, when German liberals claimed to stand for 'progress' on anti-clericalism and schooling and a mainly Slav Right opposed them. By the twentieth century the social question had come to the fore, raising important issues like worker insurance, labour conditions, trade unionism and feminism which did not divide the Reichsrat in clear-cut ways. Indeed, in many aspects they fell into the competence of the provinces or other self-governing bodies which vigorously assumed important responsibilities, like Lueger's Vienna – or the enterprising British municipalities of this time. Their treatment was quite up to international standards. Despite Austrian feminists' complaints at their backward society, for example, Austrian girls were allowed to take the secondary school-leaving *Matura* examination and to study at university before their counterparts in Prussia. Altogether, provincial budgets increased three times faster than central government ones from 1865 to 1905, a figure to be set against images of an Austria sclerosed by the dead hand of state bureaucracy.

The fairest verdict on the politics of late Dualist Austria is no doubt failure with extenuating circumstances. Not all calculations had misfired. It is noteworthy that the Young Czechs, the Christian Socials and the *Volkspartei* all basically supported the universal suffrage governments, lending some support to the view that a move to mass politics could temper previous irreconcilabilities. The Czech 'positivist' willingness to work the system reflected, Jan Křen believes, rising social forces' sense that an equal role in a democratised empire would offer them a wider field than the state right doctrines of older provincial elites; not supra-nationalism but the Monarchy as quasi-national state for all was the goal. However, Křen also notes that these expectations were not fulfilled. By 1908–14 continuing government by central bureacracy and a forward policy in the Balkans reliant on Reich German support kept disillusioned Slavs in their place, resulting in the inner decay of positivism and its exponents' readiness to shift to separatism during the First World War. Masaryk later wrote that he had given up on the Monarchy from 1907, hoping the democratising currents of the age might shape an alternative for his people. While it is true that for the vast majority the struggle of the Austrian nations was to control the state rather than leave it, the endemic competitiveness that this induced lowered willingness for compromise. Moreover, where national compromises did occur, as in Moravia and Bukovina, they required individuals to enlist in one or other national register, so highlighting difference rather than softening it, as Gerald Stourzh has pointed out.

Too much optimism for the longer term should not therefore be read into Austria's relative placidity in the pre-war years. Nonetheless, a combination of economic advance, competent administration and a system of political share-outs helped to keep all groups from the brink of despair. This is why the jolts which threw the system in crisis did not come from Cisleithania but from Hungary and the south Slav lands, where these factors were less in evidence, not to speak of the growingly menacing course of events in the external world.

Hungarian Politics

Austrian public opinion resented Hungarian politicians for their perceived strength in pushing Hungarian interests. Arguably the real danger they posed the Monarchy lay more in their weakness – their inability to sustain the elite's national vision simultaneously *vis-à-vis* Austria, the Magyar masses and the non-Magyars. The limitations of Magyar nationalism had been shown by the outcome of the crisis of 1905–06, when the Independence Party agreed to enter government on Dualist terms, postponing its calls for a separate Hungarian army and pledging to work for electoral reform and the renewal of the customs union with Austria. Yet this exposure of gentry nationalism did not lessen the Hungarian problem. A frustrated Independence coalition was all the more likely to pick away at the constitutional scab to redeem itself with its supporters, while provocatively throwing its weight about against non-Magyars. Dualism was not directly challenged but made that much harder to run.

The climb-down of the independentists was reflected in the composition of the new government, in which ministers of pro-Dualist background predominated over 1848ers. They included the prime minister and former Liberal premier Wekerle, a wily pragmatist whom Franz Joseph appointed *faute de mieux*. The different natures of the two men are nicely caught in an exchange between them on the question of a proposed church to be built for Franz Joseph's diamond jubilee over the grave of the ancient Hungarian leader Árpád: when the well-informed but literal-minded monarch pointed out that the whereabouts of Árpád's grave were unknown, Wekerle replied that Árpád could be buried where His Majesty pleased.[10] Apponyi, who had fused his party with the independentists, and Andrássy, whose ex-Liberal dissidents had become the Constitutional Party, became ministers of education and the interior respectively. Traditional 1848ers held only two posts, Ferenc Kossuth himself being minister of commerce.

The new government inherited a weight of expectation based on Kossuth's name. Its tendency was to support powerful agrarian and business interests (as in state aid for industry) while making placatory gestures in insurance and cheap housing to workers whose organisations were being harassed. But absence of the 'national gains' which the Coalition had proclaimed as its goal led to a leeching of support, and pressure in the negotiations on the economic compromise for military and constitutional compensations for a higher Hungarian contribution to the common quota. Franz Joseph, mindful of his nephew's vigorous opposition, made only minor concessions and expected a quid pro quo through disciplining of extreme nationalists, which the Coalition was too weak to deliver. But other than Magyar nationalists were disaffected: non-Magyars by Apponyi's education law of 1907, which tied state aid to their primary schools (necessary to meet the higher standards imposed) to more teaching in Magyar; the Serbo-Croat coalition by the requirement that all state railway employees in Hungary–Croatia should know Magyar; the Social Democrats by Andrássy's electoral proposals of 1908, which offered twelve illiterate, unpropertied men one vote between them, while literates were to have from one to three votes according to their education and wealth. The socialist campaign of protest culminated in a general strike and giant demonstration in Budapest on 6 October. The traditional hold of the Independence Party on Magyar peasants, too, yielded to emerging regional movements, all calling for parcelisation of great estates among peasant lease-holders, but standing either in the radical Várkonyi tradition, like Áchim's Democratic Peasants, or in the peasant proprietor mould of István Szabó's National Peasant Party.

Mainstream politics, however, continued to be dominated by the nationalist agenda, which with the economic compromise concluded turned its fire against the common Austro-Hungarian Bank. Leading the small man opposition to 'sell-out' policies, Gyula Justh – who was genuine about universal suffrage – emerged as the rival in the Independence Party to Ferenc Kossuth, who had privately told the bank's director he did not believe Hungary was ready for its own bank of issue. When the Wekerle government's proposed compromise of two banks in a cartel relationship was rejected by Franz Joseph, Wekerle offered its resignation in April 1909. This was declined but only so that the Emperor could prepare the ground for a homogenous 1867 government to succeed it. The formal split-ting of the Independence Party in November, in which Justh took the majority of the MPs, was the precipitant for the Coalition's col-lapse and the restoration of the pro-Dualist Liberals to power. But now they were grouped in the 'Party of Work' founded by the new prime minister Khuen-Héderváry in February 1910, in which most of Andrássy's disbanded Constitutional Party – though not Andrássy himself – found their place. The Party of Work, using a set of newly minted county high sheriffs, duly gained a large electoral majority in May, with 55 seats for Kossuth's and 41 for Justh's Inde-pendence factions. The failure of the Independence coalition was a telling commentary on a nationalist tradition that contained too many contradictions and hypocrisies.

More contradictions followed when Khuen's vast majority was quickly paralysed by Justhite obstruction of a bill to raise the quota of recruits to the common army. Generally recognised as an overdue response to mounting international tension, the bill nonetheless touched a sense of unease about the health of gentry libertarian tradi-tions and brought Khuen down. His real successor was not the new prime minister, the financially shady Lukács, but the Speaker, István Tisza, whose use of troops to overawe the parliament while he forced through the outlawing of technical obstruction (June 1912) was a turning-point in Dualist Hungary and anticipated the authoritarian treatment of parliamentary impasse that was to become standard between the wars. It followed the forceful response, with six dead, to a huge, but not repeated socialist demonstration. In 1913 Tisza assumed the premiership himself. He then set the scene for the grimly awaited confrontation with the enemies of Magyar-dom and the social order through a comprehensive assault on civil rights, including a law on exceptional governmental powers, tighten-ing of administrative control over the electoral process, press and assembly, shackling of juries and proposed revision – held up by the war – of Hungary's relatively liberal criminal code.

The fact that Tisza was a conceptual rather than merely authori-tarian politician, deeply convinced of the necessity of *Kulturkampf* against godless, anti-national materialism, shows the extent of the gulf which had opened up between Left and Right. In August 1906 a struggle for control of the Social Science Society led to the departure of 37 of its establishment wing of conservative liberals, headed by Andrássy. Under Oszkár Jászi's influence it could now become the forum for a consequential bourgeois radicalism prepared to cooperate with the Social Democrats on universal suffrage, while favouring parcelisation of great estates and an uncompromising secularism; its Free School for adult worker education (1906) paralleled the movement of the same name in Vienna, and Jászi tried to enlist Hungary's considerable Masonic tradition in the cause, even founding his own lodge. The basis of Jászi's critique, like that of Cobden and Bright's Anti-Corn Law League in Britain seventy years before, was that the country was held back by a selfish aristocracy whose power was sustained through agricultural protection. Hence he also cooperated with Justh's party on the questions of a separate Hungarian bank of issue and customs area, seeing them as means to industrialisation and embourgeoisement. In 1914 Jászi founded his own Radical Party which in Hungarian circles seemed no more likely to break into mainstream politics than had the Democrats of the middle-class politician and Budapest Jew, Vilmos Vázsonyi. The fact that a distinguished American–Hungarian historian in 1988 could see the 1906 gentry parliament as 'after all, a representative assembly of Hungary at large,' while the reformers represented only 'a certain portion of the intelligentsia of Budapest – mostly Jewish and increasingly radical',[11] casts light on the difficulties a bourgeois reform movement in Hungary faced two generations after their British counterparts had triumphed.

Tisza's Hungary on the eve of war was thus a polarised society in which he sought to mobilise the forces of order, spanning the old Catholic–Protestant divide. His interesting wish to include non-Magyar notables among these only showed, in the outcome, the width of the gulf which previous policies had opened. Most effort went to wooing the Transylvanian Romanians, approached via church hierarchs, in negotiations of 1910 and 1913–14. But Tisza's willingness for concessions on church and school matters was met by Romanian demands for vastly more civil servants and MPs, Romanian education up to university level and a minister in the government on Galician Polish lines. Knowing they had Franz Ferdinand's backing, they stepped up their terms. Since only five of 33 Romanian National Party candidates had succeeded in the 1910 elections against nine pro-government Romanians, the sudden power shift in Transylvania would indeed have been too much for Magyar stomachs, in Tisza's phrase, but it was Magyar vainglory which had

created an illusory starting-point in the first place. Few acknowledged the unwelcome truth noted privately by the ruminative
ex-joint finance minister Burián in December 1914, that minority
national consciousness was spurred both by economic deprivation
and economic success.

The South Slav Question

Hungarian policy on the Romanian minority question engaged Austrian and indeed Reich German attention because of its impact on
independent Romania's loyalty to its 1883 alliance with the Central
Powers. Hungary's policy to Croatia had a still wider potential for
mischief. Her centrality to the Habsburg empire's south Slav problem is often overlooked. The eight-century-old Hungaro-Croat
union at its core had already lost most of the cultural force which
had all but fused the two aristocracies and made the Croatian noble-
man Zrinski one of the greatest Hungarian-language poets of the
seventeenth century. None of the 44 signatories of the Croatian modernist manifesto of 1904 had studied in Hungary proper, while a
Hungarian specialist on Croatia could write in 1918 that Croat-
speaking Hungarians were as rare as white ravens.[12] General awareness of the south Slav provinces had dissipated during the long and
apparently successful stewardships of Khuen-Héderváry in Croatia
and Kállay in Bosnia. The rise of the Serbo-Croat coalition in Croatia showed the limitations of this perception, as did the movements of
Bosnian Serb and Muslim notables from the late 1890s for freedom
from state tutelage in religious and school matters, which Kállay
tried unavailingly to suppress with his unique blend of suavity
and cynicism – lofty generalisations about Orientals' difficulties in
modern society mixed with bribery, spies and bullying.

The victory of the 'New Course' of the Serbo-Croat coalition in the
Croatian Diet elections of May 1906 was a turning-point in the south
Slav question. It put 'Yugoslavism' back on the Balkan agenda,
impacting on Croatian, Bosnian and Serbian politics, as well as
'Great Austrian' circles around the Archduke Franz Ferdinand. But
this victory was more the result of miscalculation than design by the
Independence government in Hungary, all but whose left wing
quickly forgot its understanding with the Coalition of autumn 1905.
Prime minister Wekerle granted the Coalition's request for 'free'
elections, i.e. without administrative interference, on the assumption

that the establishment Croatian National Party would win anyway. Their failure to do so startled contemporaries as a rare breakthrough of the popular will in a south Slav politics of dependency. To high-minded outsiders like the Scot R.W. Seton Watson, the Serbo-Croat coalition appeared as that force for principled decency challenging the corrupt exercise of power which liberal-minded people continually seek in the trouble-spots of the world. In his book *The Southern Slav Question* (1911) it became the focus for hopes of a just solution of south Slav aspirations in a 'Trialist' unit in a revivified Habsburg Monarchy. The Coalition, however, reflected its society. This had matured sufficiently to permit a resourceful individual (Supilo) to conceive of a challenge to the dominant interests in the region but not to the point of being able to sustain it in face of inevitable counter-attacks.

Four main kinds of politician emerged in this Habsburg south Slav milieu. Neglected in Yugoslav historiography have been the collaborationists of Khuen's old National Party, from semi-Magyarised aristocratic lineages, business interests close to big capital, or professionals more interested in the exercise of power than its source, like Khuen's cultural chief of the 1890s, the dynamic opportunist Izidor Kršnjavi. Then came opposition notables who had identified their own interest with that of their wronged people, the backbone of the Coalition but not natural radicals: professionals and businessmen, the latters' politics often intertwined with their local commercial concerns, like the Mayor of Dubrovnik Petar Čingrija, mortgage banker, newspaper proprietor and shipping company owner, but overshadowed by the dominant Hungarian and Austrian shipping lines. Third were radicals, a handful of campaigning individuals (including up to a point the pragmatic Supilo himself) and the often Masaryk-influenced intelligentsia of the Progressive Party, a minor wing of the Croatian part of the Coalition. Regional, ethnic and ideological disparities all had to be juggled in a coalition which the Dalmatian progressive Smodlaka called 'a conglomerate of all possible tendencies, including the most risible'.[13] Outside it, fourth, were the claimants to the Starčević Great Croat tradition, a bombastic reaction to national weakness, subtly led by his successor Dr Josip Frank towards Vienna, which Starčević had abhorred. Peasant and socialist movements were still crippled by the tiny electorate.

Unable to insist on its goals of a Ban responsible to the Diet or reunification with Dalmatia, the Coalition nonetheless took charge of the administration in Zagreb, with little by way of striking

reform: Supilo opposed universal suffrage because in Croatian circumstances this would strengthen clericals and the peasant party,
both hostile to the Coalition. But his whole Budapest-orientated
strategy was stymied by the 1907 railway regulations referred to
above, introduced by his nominal ally, Ferenc Kossuth. The Croat
delegation began obstructing in the Hungarian parliament; an
authoritarian Ban, Baron Levin Rauch, was appointed (January
1908) who failed to win a single seat in fresh Diet elections but
began planning to indite Serb members of the Coalition for high treason, to an enthusiastic chorus from Josip Frank's anti-Serb Party of
Right. It was the end of the New Course.

Rauch's father had been the Ban under whom the Hungaro-Croat
Nagodba had been forced through a packed Magyarophile Diet in
1868. Hungarian policy in Croatia under Dualism alternated
between two main tactics: one directly overriding Croat nationalist
feeling, the other working to dilute and degut it, as Khuen had
achieved with the National Party after 1883. In Bosnia, governed as
a common imperial land by mainly Magyar joint finance ministers,
the change of government in 1903 involved a similar shift, from Kállay's hard line to Burián's preference for heading off nationalism by
flexibility. The Serbs and Muslims were granted cultural autonomy
in 1905 and 1909 respectively and remaining elements of Kállay's
one-time pursuit of a *Bosnian* identity liquidated. But the pace was
no longer being set by Magyars alone. The region's fate was increasingly the concern of all the Monarchy's power centres, including the
Emperor's impatient and ambitious heir, Franz Ferdinand.

This revival of long-quiescent Balkan concerns went back to the
year of changes, 1903. Besides the passing of Khuen and Kállay in
Croatia and Bosnia and the threat to Near Eastern stability from
the Macedonian revolt, the return of the Karadjordjević dynasty to
Belgrade after Alexander Obrenović's murder had voided the secret
Austro-Serbian treaty of 1881 by which the last two Obrenović rulers
acknowledged Austrian hegemony. Austrian assumptions were given
eloquent expression by foreign minister Gołuchowski in 1901:

> Politically in complete disorder, financially on the verge of bank-
> ruptcy, militarily quite insignificant and weak, this country lies so
> much within our power that it will always be dependent on us.[14]

These words explain but do not excuse Gołuchowski's clumsy
demands that Belgrade repudiate a Serbo-Bulgarian commercial

treaty of 1904 and agree to buy arms from Austria instead of France. The Monarchy's trade war with Serbia (1906–11), which ultimately enabled Serbia to lessen her commercial dependence on Austria-Hungary, only raised the temperature further. Meanwhile Bosnian Serbs, at 43% the largest, richest and most confident Bosnian community, were making the running in the politicisation of the small Austrian-educated intelligentsia, with the convenient tactical ploy of a Muslim–Serb call for autonomy under Turkish suzerainty, which acquired added weight with the Young Turk revolution in Istanbul of July 1908. But clarifying Bosnia's position meant rethinking the whole south Slav world, the structures of Dualism, even the Triple Alliance – because of Italy's claims as an Adriatic and Balkan power. The Italian threat was particularly important to Franz Ferdinand, the great proponent of Habsburg naval power. Hence his concern with the economic regeneration of Dalmatia, one of the planks of his south Slav programme from its broaching in the pages of the *Neue Freie Presse* in 1906.

Roughly, three scenarios seemed possible. The one the Monarchy's leaders feared was a Yugoslav movement based on Serb–Croat cooperation and leading by force of gravity to the unification of south Slavs outside the Monarchy, around the Serbian Piedmont. This was why Franz Joseph regarded the Serbo-Croat coalition as an inherently disloyal organisation, as he had once regarded the Young Czechs; its members' contacts with Belgrade were zealously watched. (Actually, Belgrade distrusted the Coalition, and Croat aims.) The other two combinations foresaw either a union of Bosnia with Croatia and Dalmatia (Croatian 'Trialism') or Bosnia's direct attachment to Hungary, based on Hungarian medieval claims. The air was thick with self-delusion and disingenuousness. Though Aehrenthal (Gołuchowski's successor from 1906) favoured the Bosnian–Croat alternative, he did not intend this as a prelude to the Trialist statehood enthusing the Archduke's Croatian allies in the Party of Right, nor indeed did the Archduke. Nor were Croatian Coalitionists so Serbophile as to drop their own claims for Bosnia, which was tacitly put on the back burner between them and their Serb colleagues. 'Great Austrians', Hungarians and Croats could thus agree on Bosnia's annexation, approved by the common ministerial council on 19 August 1908. But the implementation was bungled. Aehrenthal's meeting with the Russian foreign minister Izvolsky in the Moravian castle of Buchlau on 15 September was differently interpreted by the two sides: by Aehrenthal as agreeing mutual support for each other's claims in Bosnia, and for the opening of the Straits; by Izvolsky as involving a prior European conference. These misunderstandings emerged after the annexation was proclaimed on 5 October, before Izvolsky had been able to complete his diplomatic preparations over the Straits. The bitterness of the Russian and Serbian response made war seem a likelihood for several months.

Such was the background for the campaign to discredit the Serbo-Croat coalition which climaxed in 53 of its Serb members going on trial for high treason on 3 March 1909. The Zagreb trial of 1909 and its pendant, the trial of the historian Heinrich Friedjung for libelling the Coalition, made a key contribution to the reversal of traditional images which was to take place in a wider European consciousness by 1918. The Habsburg establishment appeared corrupt and incompetent as it indicted Coalition members on the basis of forged documents supplied by the Austro-Hungarian Legation in Belgrade. In place of obscure Slav subversives stepped a series of impressive and dignified witnesses, including a high Serbian state official and Tomáš Masaryk, who exposed the fact that Friedjung had used translations of the forgeries to attack the Zagreb accused without verifying the originals; Aehrenthal stood revealed as the man who had given him them. Following the trials Rauch was replaced as Ban by Khuen's old collaborator Tomašić, who returned to the tradition of trying to tie nationalists into the Dualist structure, working with the Coalition majority in the Diet while aiming to cajole its more conservative members into a new government party. After two elections failed to produce a pliable majority, he too departed and in the face of mass secondary school strikes constitutionality was suspended and his successor declared government commissioner in 1912.

These details, it is hoped, will help explain not only why the Monarchy's last great foreign political act, the annexation, ran into the sand as far as its domestic consequences were concerned, but also something more general about the tail-twisting frustration of late Habsburg politics both for ruling and non-dominant groups. The balance of forces between Zagreb and Budapest did not permit the Serbo-Croat coalition to translate its moral and electoral victories into significant reform – the rise in the Croatian electorate from 2% to some 6% was in line with the Hungarian elites' tokenism on this question. The fact that by 1914 the Coalition was back in 'power' in Zagreb after a return to constitutionality showed that it had finally been made into an acceptable partner in running the status quo. But this too was a Pyrrhic and on past form temporary victory of the powers that be in their unremitting struggle to fit square pegs into round holes in their complex realm. The ironist Musil might find Austrian politics an amusing charade. Less sophisticated souls reacted differently, like Hitler staring intently at Czech parliamentarians as they obstructed the Reichsrat in a language he did not understand or the 'Young Bosnia' conspirator Čabrinović speculating how he would like to throw a bomb from the gallery of the Bosnian Diet into the middle of the prating notables. Actually, as Habsburg politics went, the Bosnian Diet from its opening in 1910 was a success story, as Serbs, Muslims and Croats pirouetted in shifting coalitions and the administration kept the show on the road.

'Young Bosnia''s terrorism, and the wider radicalisation of student youth in the Habsburg south Slav lands from 1910, was one response to the limited perspectives of constitutional nationalism in peripheral, backward societies – the semi-servile position of peasant *kmets* in Ottoman Bosnia was never abolished by the Austrians. The story of Franz Ferdinand's assassin in 1914, Gavrilo Princip, son of a poor carter who, expelled from a Bosnian Austrian school, walked to Belgrade to pursue his education, speaks for so much in the story of twentieth-century student youth in the third world. It is all there already, from the eclectic mix of anarchist, socialist and nationalist doctrine to the soulfulness of the socially and nationally deprived caught between old and new values. 'My life also is full of bitterness and gall, my wreath has more thorns in it than others', Princip wrote to a friend, 'Do read, you must read; this is the best way to forget the tragic side of reality.' One bookseller alone in Sarajevo, a town with some 900 secondary school pupils, sold in a year a thousand copies of Schopenhauer on honour, 150 copies of his *Metaphysics of Sexual Love* and 150 copies of the leading Serbian literary critic's work on Serbo-Croat nationalism.[15] Whatever distinctions can be drawn between Yugoslav and narrower Serb, less often Croat orientations in the student movement (it also developed a Slovene Yugoslav wing) are best seen in the context of youthful *élan* and the heady atmosphere caused by Serbian victories in the Balkan wars of 1912–13. Unlike the period of Masaryk's influence, student politics went on largely independent of father figures, though Supilo, having become disillusioned with the Coalition, hoped for a time to mobilise youth support and the Young Bosnian assassins eventually turned to officers in the Serbian army for their guns.

The introduction of violence into the south Slav student movement, beginning in failed attempts on the lives of the Bosnian

Governor and the Croatian Royal Commissioner in 1910 and 1912, seems at first a discordant note in the fractious but not murderous tenor of Habsburg politics. However, ideas of the essential restraint of Habsburg political wrangling should perhaps be glossed. The thirteen Slovaks shot dead by gendarmes at Černova in 1907, the assassination of the Galician Governor and ethnic riot victims in Ljubljana in 1908, the six dead in the Budapest socialist demonstration of 1912 and the frequent ethnic brawling and states of siege in Prague need a note too. Without awareness of the bitterness and continuing sense of ethnic subordination and injustice which infected the Monarchy's political life, the slogan of it as 'the prison of the peoples' is hard to understand.

The stuff of bitterness was to be found also in dominant circles. Late Habsburg politicians' language abounded in invocations of resolute, persistent will in order to cleanse the sickly body politic: 'purposeful' (*zielbewusst* and its Hungarian calque *céltudatos*) was their favourite word. Yet they mainly drew back from the authoritarian methods which were to follow the war. This is what gives the Archduke Franz Ferdinand his interest, for the bitterness of this pious, conservative dynast extended even towards pro-Dualist Magyars like Tisza. 'The voice of the people is the voice of cattle', as he was reminded by one of his advisers, Count Ottokar Czernin.[16] Czernin's suggestions for the Archduke's reign, in plans variously drawn up between 1908 and 1912, included the immediate arrest of Czech nationalist leaders and successive dissolutions of the Hungarian parliament until it yielded a majority to break gentry power, ironically through universal suffrage. The Archduke was in touch with non-Magyar leaders like the Slovak Milan Hodža and the Romanians Vaida-Voevod and Aurel Popovici, author of a famous plan for a federal Monarchy, *The United States of Great Austria* (1907). Yet he himself was not a federalist but if anything (for he left no blue-print) favoured recentralisation. This applied also to his south Slav work, which showed prescience in foreseeing the internal and external importance of the area but tied him to the anti-Serb wing of Croat politics and Dr Josip Frank's minority party. The cooperation was far from ideal because the Frankists' goal was a Trialist Greater Croatia rather than Great Austria. It was partly a victory for the Archduke's tendency that by 1911 an organisation of all the Rightist parties of the Croat-inhabited provinces had been formed, with a stronger clerical imprint and Slovene links; but it remained resolutely Trialist. Illusions on both sides, linked chiefly by hatred of Serbs.

Whether Franz Ferdinand would actually have proved the ruthless strong man had he come to the throne is not clear. There is some evidence that he preferred bullying subordinates to arguing his case with real rivals; Czernin, for one, was more moderate as a foreign minister in the First World War than his bombast would have suggested. But the Archduke certainly embodied those tendencies in the Habsburg governing elite which craved action and an end to drift. It used to be naively argued that Gavrilo Princip had killed a kindred spirit and proponent of south Slav Trialism in Sarajevo on 28 June 1914. In fact, the confrontation of the Serb nationalist peasant youth and the haughty Catholic Archduke carries with it a telling symbolism, even if any picture of the Monarchy on the edge of war and dissolution should also include the figure of the venerable, pragmatic and universally respected old Emperor himself.

Franz Joseph remained the ultimate arbiter of all important decisions. The image of the upright old man more than anything preserves the former Monarchy its reputation for old world order and decency, stuffy as it might be. Does not the aura which held back the gun even of a Bosnian assassin (Bogdan Žerajić, unable to fire on the old Emperor on his first visit to Sarajevo in 1910) work against arguments just advanced of a darker turn to Habsburg politics in the era of mass nationalism? But the emperor who told Theodore Roosevelt in 1910 that he was a creature from a past age recognised the constraints on his power of initiative imposed by new realities. Twice, in 1870–71 and 1897, Franz Joseph sought to readjust the balance in his realm by accommodating Czech Slavs, in accordance with the dynasty's traditional self-image as a supra-national and even-handed force. Each time he was beaten back, with German dissent making itself felt on the streets during the Badeni affair. Nor did he feel able to challenge the rigidities of Dualism in the Hungarian sphere, as when he refused to receive Romanian petitioners in 1893 or Cisleithanian Croats protesting against the treatment of Hungarian Croats in 1903. These were significant episodes. They spoke to the narrowing options available to government at the very time that public opinion in all the Monarchy's nations was becoming more volatile and demanding.

No doubt Franz Joseph's acquiescence in the shortcomings of Dualism was eased by the lack of imagination with which he is often charged. But to suppose that the alternative lay in the sixteen quasi-states of Popovici's federal 'Great Austria', or similar schemes, was to suppress imagination the other way, as to what could go wrong.

Positive signs, like the Moravian and Bukovinian provincial compromises of 1905/1910 and the by no means definitive Polish–Ruthenian agreement in Galicia of 1914 (which brought Ruthenians more Diet seats but hardly equality), do not outweigh more negative ones in Bohemia, Hungary and the south Slav world on the eve of world war. On balance the democratisation fuelled by socio-economic advance fed into rival nationalisms and undermined non-dominant notables with whom elites sought to do deals. Conservatives as apart as Franz Ferdinand and István Tisza realised this was not a time to add the complications of war to those of peace. But the former's bloody removal from the scene in Sarajevo on 28 June 1914 came against an increasingly tense international situation, and the formerly pacific Emperor and foreign minister Berchtold yielded to views like those of Conrad von Hötzendorf, who as Chief of Staff – with one break – since 1907 had consistently argued for war against Italy, then Serbia. The Gordian knot would be cut.

13 To World War and Collapse

Count Klebelsberg, Hungarian minister of culture in the 1920s, once commented that his countrymen had conducted their pre-war politics as if Hungary were an island in the middle of the Pacific.[1] Magyars, of course, had no ethnic kin outside the old Monarchy. But Panslavism and Pan-Germanism too were more matters of sentiment than practical politics. Most Czechs who knew Russia or its culture, from Havlíček to Masaryk, were anti-Tsarist, the 'neo-Slav' Kramář, with his Russian wife, being the exception. The Croatian journalist Josip Horvat wrote later of Croats' almost total ignorance of the Serbia they joined with in 1918. Though Franz Joseph Land was so named by Count Wilczek's expedition of 1874, and the Middle Eastern career of the Czech monk and adventurer Alois Musil – a cousin of the novelist – was as exotic as any in the imperialist age, Austria-Hungary's multi-ethnic composition did not prevent its remarkable self-absorption.

How is the general apathy towards foreign affairs to be explained in a state which has been judged just 'a product of foreign policy requirements and sustained by them'?[2] First, the judgement, though not uncommon, perhaps underestimates the role of the dynasty, the impress of German culture and the acceptance of the state by the Habsburg peoples themselves; till late in the day their nationalisms were more concerned with competition within the empire than with secession from it. But more to the point are factors already alluded to in Chapter 7: the veiled nature of the foreign political process conducted by the Emperor and a narrow circle of largely noble diplomats, the still restricted patterns of foreign travel even of educated elites, the self-sufficiency of a vast multi-national realm whose subjects' focus was on communal, class and ethnic construction, survival and pride.

However, Austrian uninterest in the outside world was repaid in kind. Jean Bérenger has stressed the Monarchy's lack of centrality to French concerns for all but the years 1866–70 of the post-1848 period,[3] though some debate continued as to whether or not it offered a buffer to German ambitions. Rising Balkan elites eager for western culture and their scholarship holders tended to by-pass Austria-Hungary on their way to Switzerland, Germany and above all

France. The British Foreign Office records list two volumes of 'General Correspondence' from Vienna for 1911, the same number as from Abyssinia and the Netherlands, compared to nine from Germany and 22 from Persia. Vague generalisations of support for the Dual Monarchy as a force for European stability hid a good deal of indifference. The decline of her strategic centrality after the creation of Imperial Germany has already been noted.

But in the aftermath of the 1878 Berlin Congress, the Monarchy's last unqualified foreign political success, any forebodings would have seemed misplaced. The Habsburg empire was in demand. That success had been a striking achievement of the informal Crimean coalition of Austria, Britain and France to check Russian ambitions. Yet within three years Austria-Hungary was in a renewed conservative Three Emperors' League with Russia and Germany; within four the Dual Alliance of 1879 with Germany broadened into a Triple Alliance including the old enemy Italy. There were in addition the secret treaties with Serbia and Romania in 1881 and 1883 respectively which coordinated the policies of these small Balkan states with the Monarchy.

The story of Habsburg international relations from then on till 1914 is one of the narrowing of these options. Some had their limitations from the start. The treaty tie with Italy through the Triple Alliance of 1882 was designed mainly to stabilise the new kingdom against internal unrest and French overbearingness. It was always a matter of head not heart for the Italians as long as three-quarters of a million Italian speakers were 'unredeemed' Habsburg subjects in Austrian borderlands from Trentino to Dalmatia. More importantly, the 1879 Dual Alliance with Germany and the 1881 Three Emperors' League reflected Bismarck's schizophrenic attitude towards Russia: his wish for support against a possible Russian threat but also his hope for a wider conservative solidarity which would defuse Austro-Russian tensions through the League. Thus Bismarck strenuously denied that the Dual Alliance committed Germany to favour Austria over Russia in the Balkans and much of his diplomacy was designed to avoid having to choose between them. At the height of Austro-Russian tension over the Bulgarian crisis of 1885–88 he helped mediate the 1887 'Mediterranean Agreements' whereby Italy, Britain and Austria compacted to resist any Russian infraction of the Balkan status quo. This arrangement gave the Monarchy security but at no risk to the Second Reich. It went with an extension of the terms of the Triple Alliance which promised Italy compensation in the event of any changes in the Balkans. Ultimately this proved an unwelcome complication for Austria, but for a time the Agreements brought Anglo-Austrian cooperation to a high point between two traditionally friendly powers.

It was in relation to Britain and France that Austria-Hungary's options narrowed most in the years that followed. The decisive factor was France and Russia's move towards alliance, consolidated by 1894, mainly in response to the power of the new Germany but with far-reaching consequences for the Monarchy. For the risk of confrontation with both Russian and French fleets now made it harder for Britain to envisage action at the Straits as presupposed by the Mediterranean Agreements. Unable to get a German pledge to restrain the French, Salisbury ultimately refused to renew the Agreements in 1897. A century of Anglo-Austrian cooperation on the Eastern Question was at an end.

As a Britain alarmed at German *Weltpolitik* overcame its colonial quarrels with France and Russia in the ententes of 1904 and 1907, the Crimean coalition was turned on its head. The western powers did not immediately agree to support Russian Near Eastern ambitions they had traditionally opposed. France long resisted the extension of her anti-German treaty with Russia to the east European sphere. But the logic of alliances – the felt need for friends in face of a feared enemy – had the potential to erode such embargoes. By the twentieth century the Dual Monarchy faced its regional conflict of interest with Tsarist Russia without a real option to the west. Here Anglophile Italy's disenchantment with the Triple Alliance reflected unease at Anglo-German estrangement as well as anti-Austrian irredentism. Italy's agreements with France of 1900 and 1902 were clear signs that she had an alternative alignment to hand.

Alongside the Anglo-German rift, Austro-Russian rivalry in the Balkans was the most important of Great Power tensions in the early twentieth century. Yet what made it such a neuralgic point for the old Monarchy, when it had accommodated itself to the loss of its former dominant position in Germany and Italy? There, though, was the rub. For many of those in charge of Austrian foreign policy Great Power status meant empire and its prerogatives, and the only remaining sphere where they could exercise these after their central European discomfitures was in the Balkans. Little as Austria wished to trespass on the independence of the Balkan states, wrote foreign minister Kálnoky in a despatch of 1884, she would intervene 'energetically and ruthlessly' to suppress anarchic or hostile tendencies in an area so wholly within her power zone.[4] The idea that the Dual Monarchy had no contact with the imperial mood of late nineteenth-century Europe is not quite correct. Béni Kállay was nothing if not a proconsular administrator of Bosnia-Herzegovina from 1882 to 1903, who exchanged advice and compliments with British and French authorities in Algeria and Egypt.

In an intriguing way Habsburg Balkan policy mirrored certain tendencies in domestic politics. In each case conservative rulers in a century attuned to a discourse of progress faced the mobilisation of Slav forces; in each they made similar distinctions between legitimate aspirations to be patronised and illegitimate ones to be opposed. The possibility of choice therefore presented itself; at the crunch conservatism could either take a liberal or a reactionary turn – conciliation or aggression – as represented domestically by the split between Baron Beck and Franz Ferdinand in Austrian politics. The existence of liberal and conservative polarities in Habsburg foreign policy has been stressed by the Hungarian historian Diószegi, but not quite in the way just suggested. For him the liberal tendency was represented by foreign minister Andrássy's would-be anti-Russianism of the 1870s, inspired by Hungarian national awareness and prepared to establish working relationships with the Balkan peoples under Habsburg aegis. By contrast, conservative foreign ministers like Kálnoky (1881–95) and Aehrenthal (1906–12) were more drawn to the ideal of entente with Russia underlying the Holy Alliance and the Three Emperors' League. Diószegi's account of how all three of these foreign ministers came to operate policies opposed to their basic convictions, whether Russophile or Russophobe, helps to show up the frustrating constraints which characterised every aspect of Dualist politics. But on the substantive issue his notion of liberalism seems to share something of his nineteenth-century compatriots' blinkers, for Andrássy's (and his disciple Kállay's) concept of a subaltern role for the Balkan peoples was more cynical than realistic. At bottom, liberal for Diószegi appears to mean anti-Russian, perhaps not an unreasonable position for a Hungarian to hold in the twentieth century or the previous one.[5]

On the other hand, Habsburg conservatives were perhaps less sanguine about cooperation with Russia than Diószegi's categorisation requires. The basic problem was that the Balkans simply could not be divided into neat spheres of influence with Austria in the west and Russia in the east. Bismarck pressed this solution as a way of reconciling his two alliance partners but no Austrian foreign minister endorsed it. The Bulgarian crisis was precisely over Austria's unwillingness to allow Russia total control over this state, for fear, among other things, of repercussions for her position in Serbia. But ideological convictions were also in play. 'Panslavism is ... identical with Russianism', asserted the St Petersburg ambassador in 1883: 'To suppose of a Russian foreign minister that he should totally deny the Panslav idea as such is to demand the impossible of him.'[6] That the Russian foreign minister in question was Giers, presented by historians as the archetype of a conservative anti-nationalist, only shows the barriers in the way of lasting Austro-Russian understanding. Kálnoky, who had resisted renewed Hungarian pressure for war with Russia, still thought (in 1888) that it was inevitable in the long run.

This background must be borne in mind when considering the three decades of relatively stable Austro-Hungarian relations from 1878 to 1908 and in particular the formal entente from 1897. The agreement of 1897 came about under the foreign ministership of Count Agenor Gołuchowski, as a Pole not a natural Russophile. It bound both powers to preserve the status quo in the Balkans on a basis of non-intervention; should European Turkey prove unsustainable they would agree on its future reorganisation. The agreement rested in fair part on Russian preoccupation with the Far East and Austria's lack of alternatives after the breakdown of the Mediterranean Agreements. Pressures from other Austrian diplomats, notably the St Petersburg ambassador Aehrenthal, to build more positively on the entente towards a conservative partnership with Germany and Russia, were resisted by Gołuchowski. Indeed, his high-handed policy towards Serbia helped inflame the Russian press against him. The change of Serbian dynasty in 1903 was fateful for Austria because, like western powers in the Middle East half a century later, she had sought to prop up her influence in Serbia through unpopular monarchs against nationalist sentiment. A maturing Serbia won the resulting tariff war (1906–11), after Austria-Hungary banned her livestock exports, by exploiting refrigeration and alternative export routes. Conservative underestimation of nationalism had its come-uppance here.

After Aehrenthal replaced Gołuchowski in 1906 he relaxed the feud with Serbia, as part of his Russophile course. However, by this time Russia set greater store by her new friendship with Britain than with the Monarchy and showed no interest in a resurrected conservative league. Peeved, Aehrenthal negotiated a Turkish concession for a railway from the Bosnian border to Salonika, thereby shaking the Austro-Russian entente severely early in 1908. Russia had not been consulted and had cause to doubt that this was a purely economic matter; Balkan railway schemes never were. All amity was to vanish over the annexation of Bosnia-Herzegovina and the misunderstanding between Aehrenthal and his Russian counterpart Izvolsky in Buchlau later that year (p. 363). A straw in the wind was that Britain associated herself with Russia's outrage, charging Austria-Hungary with acting outside the concert of the powers envisaged by the Treaty of Berlin (1878). But since France still held back the Triple Entente was divided, while the Monarchy had Germany's backing. A German ultimatum to Russia to withdraw its support for Serbian belligerence brought the crisis to an end in Austria's favour in March 1909.

The Bosnian crisis of 1908–09 proved a Pyrrhic victory for the Monarchy. By the time of Aehrenthal's death from leukaemia in 1912 relations with Italy and even Russia had improved but Serbia remained impervious to economic blandishments. Alone, she could not endanger Austria-Hungary, yet the possibility of the tail wagging the dog could not be excluded, as Great Powers measured their prestige by their ability to keep small states in tow. The crisis had sharpened the polarisation between the alliance systems. But to see Aehrenthal's coup as a failed exercise in prestige politics would be too harsh. The annexation of Bosnia was a logical step, in view of Bosnian oppositionists' play with the province's uncertain status and the spectre of Bosnian representation in a Turkish parliament after the Young Turk revolution of July 1908. Nor was Aehrenthal's wish to reassert the Monarchy's international profile mere bombast when it was increasingly being treated as an adjunct to other polities and interests – particularly German.

Aehrenthal was one of the rare Habsburg statesmen who tried to relate the Monarchy's internal and external problems. A 1907 memorandum of his had envisaged annexation in the context of the cession of Dalmatia and Bosnia to Hungary, in return for which Aehrenthal hoped Hungary would cease to obstruct the economic compromise desired by Austria. In other words, he had a programme. It was, of course, a conservative programme with little to say to the minor Habsburg nations. The union of Bosnia, Croatia and Dalmatia under Hungary was not intended to be a prelude to the realisation of Croat Trialist dreams. Aehrenthal's correspondence with fellow

Bohemian aristocrats exposed his deep anti-Semitism and anti-constitutionalism; he excised from the Gotha almanac of nobility any hint of his own partly Jewish descent. His action in supplying unverified, forged documents to the historian Friedjung with which to discredit Serb members of the Serbo-Croat coalition reveals a casually bullying approach, unsuited for the Monarchy's nationality problems. Unsurprisingly, the constitutional arrangments set in train after Bosnia's annexation were less dramatic than his proposals for the reshaping of Dualism: Bosnia-Herzegovina was given special status outside the Dualist system, like the Alsace-Lorraine *Reichsland* in Imperial Germany but with its own Diet.

Aehrenthal's foreign policy similarly showed the limitations of Austrian conservatism. While the renunciation of war with Serbia in 1909 in favour of economic penetration was realistic, it clashed with the frequent emphasis in Austro-Hungarian conservative statecraft on the need for ruthless, decisive action. As we have seen, conservatives never screwed their courage to the sticking point in decades of such talk in domestic or foreign policy – until 1914. This undermined their morale without reconciling their opponents. In the event, the Monarchy lacked the capital reserves for an effective Balkan economic policy. In fact, it was in need of capital injections itself; the closure of the Paris money markets to a Hungarian state loan in the pre-war years was a disturbing sign of the hardening of the alliance system to the old empire's disadvantage.

Aehrenthal was succeeded, somewhat unwillingly, by Count Leopold Berchtold, a career diplomat who had already retired to his Moravian estates at the age of 49. Russian diplomacy was secretly putting together a Balkan alliance based on Serbia and Bulgaria. It was not intended by the Russians to act against Turkey, but small-nation nationalism could no longer be reliably controlled. Berchtold's failure to act against this alliance as its aggressive designs became apparent can probably be defended. Why incur the opprobrium of attacking Serbia when the outcome of a Turkish–Balkan clash was still unpredictable? After the allies overran European Turkey in autumn 1912 far faster than anyone had foreseen, Berchtold succeeded in maintaining his fall-back position, including Great Power approval at the London conference of ambassadors (December 1912–May 1913) for an Albanian state blocking Serbian access to the Adriatic. But the second Balkan War of early summer 1913, this time over division of the spoils, saw Serbia, Greece, Romania (and Turkey) triumphing over Bulgaria and the first-named emerging with the lion's share of Macedonia and doubling in size. Serbia's victories were greeted with great excitement by Habsburg south Slavs, including Slovenes and Croats. Montenegrin and then Serbian encroachments on Albania in March and October 1913 were faced down by Austrian ultimatums, whetting the taste for armed diplomacy in any crisis. Historians have noted the slip down the slope of confrontational prestige politics.

This is the background to July 1914. The road to world war was not direct. The rival alliance systems long refused to gel into monolithic units. France had not supported Russia in the Bosnian crisis; Germany's then commitment to Austria – an easy one since there was no chance of Russia fighting – was subsequently modified. Franz Ferdinand usually advocated peace, putting priority on domestic reconstruction, and Conrad, champion of preventive war against Italy and Serbia, was removed from his post for a year from autumn 1911. But by 1913 the fronts were hardening. In that year France first committed herself to supporting her Russian ally in the Balkans. William II grandiloquently acclaimed the Austrian *démarche* against Serbia in the autumn. Besides, Germany herself now had intertwined economic and strategic interests in the Balkans and Near East, as her courting of Turkey continued and the Berlin–Baghdad railway pushed forward.

The narrowing of Austro-Hungary's options in the last months of peace is shown by her almost obsessive preoccupation with restoring her position among the small Balkan states. The preferred option was to reclaim Romania for the central powers, but pending the outcome Bulgaria was to be kept sweet as an alternative. In retrospect this seems a little like rearranging the decks on the *Titanic*, and after the assassination at Sarajevo on 28 June 1914 the official mind-set appears to have been focused on the inevitability of war. The diary of Thallóczy, a Balkan expert at the Joint Finance Ministry, shows his conviction that deep down the Romanians 'hate us', just as Serb nationalism was bred in the soul of Serb priests, teachers and merchants. The 'psychological moment' was there, he wrote on 7 July, and his main concern throughout was that the Serbs should be given no chance to wriggle out of a decisive war.[7] This was the fear of Conrad, too, whose disastrous decision to send the Monarchy's reserve forces to the Serbian front in late July, thereby exposing the Galician front to Russian advance, was due in large part to a wish to force on the war he wanted with Serbia, leaving Germany – or fate – to deter an eventual Russian intervention.

There was indeed an element of fatalism in the final slide to war. Franz Joseph seems to have envisaged it with equanimity since 1913, presumably on the same grounds of honour which had made him a tacit protector of the duel. Yet such attitudes were still premised on the assumption of German support; it was to Berlin that Habsburg eyes turned after the assassination, and the German thumbs-up of 6 July that sent them along the militant path. Nonetheless, there was an indirect Austro-Hungarian input into the decision for war, for weighing with Germany was the felt need to give support to their one remaining ally in its desire for a reckoning with Serbia. Only Tisza of leading Habsburg statesmen stood aside from the consensus for a fortnight, until he was swayed by the stand of Franz Joseph, fear that German support might not be available later and the argument that action against Serbia would deter the Romanians. Further than Germany and at a pinch, Russia, Habsburg statesmen do not seem to have looked in the crucial weeks, though Kann gives evidence that the Emperor realised the likelihood of European war. But the main impression is of hedgehogs scurrying across a road with eyes averted from the cars that might squash them. Plainly, Habsburg leaders knowingly risked a war with Russia. Overall, however, one is struck by the shrinking and regionalisation of Austrian perspectives, in line with the trend in the Monarchy's international role over the preceding Dualist decades.

All the more intriguing therefore is Bertholdt Molden's account of Aehrenthal's foreign policy, published in 1917. Here distant Britain's relentless reshaping of alliance systems in defence of her imperial hegemony becomes the primary factor in precipitating world war, though she hardly appears in Vienna's calculations of July 1914. Molden provides a basis for an Austrian version of the war guilt debate best associated with the monumental German series *Die grosse Politik der europäischen Kabinette* (1922–26), which by shifting the focus from the immediate back-drop of war to the European state system over the previous forty years undermined notions of a uniquely German belligerence. Indeed, in the work of the American diplomatic historian Paul Schroeder the disruptive role of British international policy is taken back further still, certainly to the Crimean War. The British fixation with balance of power politics and the unpredictable value judgements insinuated into diplomacy by English parliamentary Whiggery contributed to the undermining, first of Metternich's, then of Bismarck's European Concert.

There is something to be said for the Molden–Schroeder perspective. Britain's switch from an Austrophile to a Russophile allegiance in the twentieth century seems impetuous and over-coloured by her fixation with a German threat to the balance. That Austria-Hungary was a German client quickly became a dogma for the Foreign Office. The mixture of liberal idealism and acute British imperial consciousness that made Europeans distrust 'perfidious Albion' can certainly be seen in *The Times*'s Vienna correspondent Wickham-Steed's pre-war fears of Vienna's German links and, if less overtly, in the Scottish publicist R.W. Seton-Watson's conversion to support of Hungary's repressed Slavs. But Alan Sked has criticised the wider Schroeder thesis, noting that Austria began the wars of 1859, 1866 and 1914 and would have done better to have worked harder for an accommodation with Russia in the Balkans. Moreover, Seton-Watson (and his French counterpart, the Czechophile Calvinist Ernest Denis) continued to support the Monarchy strongly until 1914, albeit they hoped for liberal nationality reforms. The idea of the Monarchy as international victim is ultimately untenable. Schroeder himself admits that the cost of sustaining its allegedly beneficial international role when it adopted neo-absolutism became too high.

This book has been premised on the primacy of domestic rather than foreign policy, though plainly they intertwined. The Habsburg empire resorted to war in 1859, 1866 and 1914 in a context of mobilising national aspirations. This mobilisation was not so dynamic that a Bismarck or a Louis Napoleon could not turn it to their own purposes, at least for a while, but the Monarchy's structures were too cumbersome and conservative to permit it to follow suit; the partial neutralising of the Hungarian threat through the Compromise of 1867 only exacerbated the other problems. As Bismarck had shrewdly observed, the real danger to the Monarchy did not come from Russian Panslavism but its own Slav peoples. No doubt the distinction is a little too glib, but the Habsburg elite's excessive fusing of the external and internal threat to the German–Magyar hegemony amounted to a projection of domestic embarrassments onto the international scene. The perception of Panslavism as a restlessly aggressive foe besieging a too passive Monarchy helped push the latter to war, despite the fact that it was Austria-Hungary which acquired the only Balkan provinces to fall to a Great European Power in the nineteenth century, Bosnia-Herzegovina; that it was she that challenged a Russian hegemony in Bulgaria in the 1880s similar to the one she herself exercised in Serbia; that it was she which ruled over many millions of non-dominant Slavs. Fritz Fischer's thesis of the domestic roots of German belligerency in 1914 is surely relevant to Austria-Hungary also.

Not Without Hope: 1914–16

The early stages of the war brought Austria-Hungary the same domestic truce as other combatant countries experienced initially. Austrian party politics was anyway restricted by the fact that the Reichsrat remained closed; indeed, it had been turned into a military hospital before a shot was fired. But Hungary's hardier parliamentarism, too, suspended hostilities. Social Democrats found it easier to retreat from their former anti-war stance because Tsarist Russia appeared as the principal foe. When one saw a dagger at one's throat, Viktor Adler commented, the first duty was to remove it; class struggle had ceased in Hungary, a leading Hungarian trade union journal wrote in October 1914.[8] While famous writers like Robert Musil, Rainer Maria Rilke and Ferenc Molnár all engaged in war journalism, aristocratic daughters became nurses and their mothers hospital visitors. 'Soldiers,' exclaimed the Archbishop of Zagreb, 'God is calling you into war, God, the eternal truth is calling you.'[9]

The first flush of enthusiasm was also present among the historically non-dominant, though not universally. Serbs were victimised as the villains of the piece, their businesses set upon by Croat and Muslim mobs in Sarajevo after the Archduke's assassination and their Orthodox schools and gymnastic societies in Bosnia closed indefinitely. Czechs too suffered. Czech troops were indicted among other things for singing sad songs instead of happy imperial ones, in short for a general disloyalty possibly overdrawn by their critics, but lent credence by the apparent desertion to the Russians of all but a handful of the 28th Prague infantry regiment in April 1915. Only Czech socialists and Catholics were positive about the Austrian connection; the Živnostenská banka privately advised its customers that the Austrian state war loans were a bad risk. But such tactics now carried a heavy price. The bank's directors were put on trial and dubious prosecutions from December 1915 to July 1916 ended in death sentences, later commuted, for the Young Czech leader Kramář and the editor of *Národní Listy* among others. It was paralleled by the Banjaluka trial of Serb activists in Bosnia. From early in the war the revoking of constitutional liberties (actually begun on 25 July), expansion of the use of German, textbook changes and censorship had weighed heavily on the Czechs. In areas under military administration, like Galicia, now with a non-Polish governor for the first time for half a century, official Germanism weighed heavier still.

The hard line may have reduced ostensible disloyalty, but it called in question the pragmatic roots of Czech and Polish willingness to work the Habsburg system. For though only a handful of Czech public figures followed Tomáš Masaryk into exile in November 1914 (rather more Yugoslav politicians, most notably Supilo and Trumbić, took this course), appearances were somewhat deceptive. Masaryk's political base in his own minority Realist Party was small, but the bigger parties' Austrophilism was tactical, based on the assumption that there was no alternative to the Monarchy, except a Pan-Germanism which would be worse.

Loyalty was soon strained by the horrific experiences of total war. Austro-Hungarian military planning reflected the contemporary assumption that modern wars were short, if sharp. Thus too many skilled men were enlisted at once, leading to manpower shortages and production bottlenecks. The disruption due to sudden militarisation of the economy further depressed output, bringing reserves of war clothing to the point of exhaustion by autumn 1914. Having got his war, Conrad von Hötzendorf, the offensive-fixated Chief of Staff, proved less successful in fighting it. Disabused of his early reliance on vague German promises and Russia's own cumbersome mobilisation to hold the Tsarist colossus at bay while he fought Serbia, he proceeded to throw unassisted Austrian armies into an offensive against Russian Poland in late August 1914, only to have to beat a retreat which left most of Galicia in Russian hands. Here 350,000 troops were lost and yet more in an obstinate winter campaign in the icy Carpathian passes for the relief of the Galician garrison of Przemyśl, which nonetheless fell in March 1915. Meanwhile, three Austro-Hungarian campaigns led by the lack-lustre Potiorek against little Serbia had been humiliatingly repulsed, and when a third front opened with Italy's entry into the war in April 1915 an overstretched Monarchy found itself reliant on German aid against Russia. A joint Austro-German campaign under German command was in fact brilliantly successful in clearing Tsarist troops out of Galicia in the summer of 1915 and German forces dominated in the conquest of Serbia later that year. But attempts at individual Austrian campaigns by Conrad against Russia in the autumn and Italy the following spring were no more successful than before, though the latter brought forward the Brusilov offensive, in June 1916, yielding Russia 350,000 prisoners. All told, Conrad estimated the Monarchy had lost 2,083,000 men killed or permanently disabled by the end of 1915.

Yet these calamities should not disguise the fact that, human error apart, the Habsburg *system* worked quite well in these opening war years. By the spring of 1915 manpower had been redeployed and an equilibrium restored to the economy, with huge military orders stimulating growth far beyond traditional military suppliers. By 1916 iron production exceeded its 1913 level and coal production and consumption were up on 1914, with coal districts serviced by almost the required number of wagons, as opposed to only 69% the previous year. The munitions situation was also satisfactory, with 95% of gunshot required available in June 1915. The apparent health of 1915–16 has been compared to the rosy cheeks of the fever patient, however, for its inflationary roots were initially overlooked, partly because of the soaking up of funds through war loans. Ultimately, it was the preference in both Austria and Hungary for loans over taxation as a means of financing the war which produced higher inflation rates than elsewhere.

It is not easy to weight the scales as between hyper-critical contemporaries and some more recent and more positive assessments of the wartime Monarchy's performance. Perhaps the key to judgement is to recall that it remained, as ever, awkwardly poised between west-central Europe and the east. All but demoralised by a sense of weakness *vis-à-vis* Germany, the Habsburg war machine functioned far better and longer than the Tsarist. Legislation from the time of the Balkan wars allowed for compulsory recruitment of industrial labour in a military emergency and anyone who left his job was liable for call-up. Though some military administrators at first paid workers only at army rates, overall the military impact was as much paternalistic as authoritarian. It was the War Ministry which pressed for the setting up of commissions for wages in 1916 and complaints in 1917, despite private employers' unease. It too paid the bulk of workers' sickness and unemployment benefit. Strikes in military industries fell from 204 in 1914 to 15 two years later. On the German pattern, war-related industries organised *Zentrale* with staff funded by private employers but subject to Trade and War Ministry vetoes, for tasks which varied from obtaining raw materials abroad to widespread domestic regulation. Austria had 91 such *Zentrale* by the end of the war. Food production and, later, iron and steel were taken under direct state control and the war ministry and, in Austria, the *Kriegsüberwachungsamt* (War Supervisory Office) had considerable administrative powers. Ration cards, initially introduced for bread, eventually covered a range of foods and other items like leather. Disputes between civil and military authorities or between Austria and Hungary seem to have been no more venomous than in other countries. The most notorious concerned the shortfall in grain supplies to Austria from agrarian Hungary, where until military requisitioning was introduced in 1918 the Hungarian authorities dragged their feet, unsurprisingly so, as their own reserves were low and they continued to operate a parliamentary regime wary of public opinion. Actually, the tone of disputes in the wartime Habsburg realm seems gentlemanly, considering the horrendous issues at stake. This is not necessarily a positive point. Only in a society habituated to rule from above by a narrow social elite is it easy to imagine a record of such consistent failure as Conrad's being tolerated for so long.

The chief consequence of its undistinguished military record was to force the Monarchy into increased dependence on a supercilious German ally, 'the hidden enemy' as Conrad dubbed her. In addition to aid through troops and subsidy, by 1916 Germany was providing Austria with effective hand grenades, gas masks, steel helmets and trench mortars, while the Monarchy had given up its proud blue uniforms for less ostentatious field grey cut from German cloth. The fate of satellite in a German-dominated central Europe beckoned and was thrust into the forefront of debate by Friedrich Naumann's book *Mitteleuropa,* published in autumn 1915. Naumann, a north German liberal, clothed his proposals for an economic and in part political union in emollient language, but it included references to the smaller nations' role as planets to the German sun; the association's headquarters were to be in Prague. The goal was to make central Europe the German base for the world power status Naumann assumed the British, Americans and Russians already had. Reactions showed the cross-currents in the central European world. Austro-Germans were enthused, though not industrialists fearful of competition or the official class with its Habsburg loyalties. Hungarians, except for some agrarians and long-standing 'Central Europeans' like Wekerle, were opposed. Most interesting was the degree of Reich German negativity, from anti-imperialist Left Social Democrats to Pan-Germans more interested in *Lebensraum* in the east than cajoling Czechs and decadent Habsburgs – 'you say softly and

fawningly what ought to be stated firmly, coldly and ruthlessly'.[10]
Such attitudes showed that most Reich German nationalists
regarded the Monarchy as an effete liability with which they would
treat only on their own masterful terms. The higher costs charged
Austria for German fuel, ruthless pursuit of German interests in occu-
pied enemy territories and enforced unification of Austrian and
German military commands in summer 1916 – naturally under
German control – were not encouraging.

The Habsburg–German relationship merely added another level
of complexity to those arising from Dualism. These had got in the
way of wartime strategy from the start, with the Hungarian prime
minister Tisza opposing territorial concessions to keep Italy out of
the war because he feared creating a precedent for similar Romanian
demands on Transylvania. In the event, the Monarchy could screw
itself up only to an offer of Italian-speaking Tyrol and that at the end
of the war, far less than Italy was promised by the Treaty of London
of April 1915 which brought her into the fray on the Entente's side.
Ironically, victory threatened to burst the Dualist straitjacket.
Tisza's wish to avoid swelling further the number of Slavs in the
empire led to agreement that conquered Serbia would not be
annexed, but subjected to border adjustments and Habsburg economic control. Yet he did request the incorporation of Dalmatia
and Bosnia into Hungary, as a balance to the likely growth of the
Austrian half if conquered Russian Poland were annexed to the Monarchy. But this latter, the so-called Austro-Polish solution of the
Polish question, raised the spectre of a Polish Trialist unit, which
Tisza vehemently opposed. In the event, dominant Imperial Germany had other ideas. A joint German–Austrian proclamation of
5 November 1916 declared occupied Russian Poland an 'independent' state in alliance with the central powers, but economically in
the German sphere. This put in some doubt the position of Galicia,
whose relationship to the new Polish entity – its frontiers were not
fixed – remained problematic. The Polish question highlighted the
contradictions of Dualism.

Galicia impinged on internal Habsburg wrangles in two other
ways. For one, Tisza denied that the reconstruction of this war-
devastated province was a common imperial expense, which would
have involved Hungarian contributions. More immediately important was the impact any Galician settlement would have on the per-
ennial Czech–German dispute, which festered on through 1915–16
in the form of Austro-German nationalists' attempts to impose their

preferred solution of the Bohemian problem. Such an *octroi*, in the contemporary term, would involve making German a state language, confining official Czech to Czech-speaking areas, negating the Czech Diet majority through strong local government *Kreise* and, as always since the Linz programme of 1882, cutting Galician representation in the Reichsrat so as to entrench a German majority. Bourgeois nationalists' demands took shape in the uncompromising public 'Easter Desiderata' of 1916 and, slightly diluted, in proposals to the Christian Socials for a common German-speaking platform. Even Social Democrats were consulted by the leader of the German *Nationalverband*. But there was some opposition in Christian Social ranks to an octroi from above which would necessarily require the postponement of parliament's recall. While prime minister Stürgkh opposed recall, foreign minister Burián demurred that parliamentary government was a duty to the people and a means of accountability. Others felt the democratic violation more strongly. On 21 October 1916 Friedrich Adler, son of the socialist leader, assassinated Stürgkh in a restaurant, crying 'Down with absolutism! We want peace.'

The assassination of Stürgkh and the Prussian-orientated proclamation on Poland were signs of the Monarchy's increasing frailty as the war moved into its third year. Nonetheless, the central powers occupied many times more of their enemies' land than vice versa and Franz Joseph's last weeks of life saw a victorious allied campaign unfold against Romania, which had incautiously declared war and invaded Transylvania in August 1916. The Emperor died on 21 November, in the sixty-eighth year of his reign. Katharina Schratt placed two white roses on his breast. He was not to see the swiftly following decline.

Darkening Clouds

The new sovereign, Charles, son of Franz Ferdinand's brother Otto (died 1906), struck several contemporaries as younger than his twenty-nine years. A pious Catholic of conciliatory nature, his good intentions were not reinforced by gifts beyond the ordinary. Influenced by Franz Ferdinand's circle and inheriting many of his assumptions rather than his temperament, he was to struggle throughout his brief reign with mounting internal and external crisis.

It was the domestic crisis which loomed larger at first. The simple question, as the German ambassador reported to Berlin, was how much longer the Monarchy could continue to wage the war. Charles's accession coincided roughly with the transition to the third of the four stages of Austria-Hungary's wartime experience: after initial shock and apparent recovery began the remorseless slide into general shortage and privation which in the last stage was to become system seizure in 1918. Of course, this process unfolded at somewhat different times and rates in different sectors. Shortage became acute as early as spring 1916 in cotton, wool, leather and iron, in coal in the winter of 1916–17, in other metals, horses and troop reserves the following spring. The rise in production of war materials ceased, except for munitions, if the fall was not yet precipitate. Coal supplies in 1917 were only 5% down on those for 1916 but hoarding contributed to a fall in iron production by nearer 20%. Transport was a major difficulty, as train rolling stock ceased to be adequately maintained.

The worst crisis opened up at the human level. The impact of Entente blockade on clothing production had been underestimated, but the food crisis was more puzzling as Hungary only consumed 65% of her corn before the war. Overall wheat and rye production fell from 90 million quintals in 1914 to 79, 63 and 62 million in following years, the fall being particularly great in Austria. Production of potatoes, too, was 42% the 1914 figure by 1917. Old Prague women crowded trains to travel 50–60 miles into the countryside to barter clothes and shoes for them.[11] The bread ration for front-line troops was cut only slightly to 470 grams in 1917 but for other troops and Austrian civilians it was a different story which saw them down to 240 grams (at the lowest point) and 165 grams respectively. The Hungarian civilian figure was 210 grams. The setting up of a Joint Food Committee under General Landwehr in February 1917 did little to alleviate the situation. Though the Emperor talked to him several times a week, Landwehr did not have executive powers, indeed, had to be dissuaded from resigning early in 1918. As damaging as low production was uneven distribution, for exemptees from the bread ration (corn producers and those who bought directly off them) were roughly half the rest in semi-industrialised Austria, double them in Hungary and four times more numerous in slackly regulated Croatia.

Naturally, mass acquiescence began to falter. Major strikes in Austria in May 1917 led to the first wage increases (as opposed to *ad hoc* allowances) of the war. As mainstream socialist leaders were increasingly coopted into the official war effort and government–trade union cooperation developed, socialist agitation spread among the population, which was not as paradoxical as at first it seems: both reformist and revolutionary aspects of the socialist project were taking on a new relevance and a skilfully tacticising trade union movement never forfeited all influence over radical elements. The participation of Austrian and Hungarian socialist spokesmen in international socialist peace conferences was actively fostered by the foreign ministry, to little effect since their western counterparts were debarred by their governments from participating. More significant was the revival of trade unionism. By June 1917 there were 215,000 Hungarian trade unionists, nearly four times as many as the previous autumn, but there was also a movement for 'Engineer Socialism' among technical experts not formally allowed trade union membership. The eloquent rage expressed by Friedrich Adler in his trial, speaking for up to six hours at a time, throws in relief the enigma of early twentieth-century political systems – which over years could inflict on their peoples grotesque casualty rates on the fronts and semi-starvation at home, yet allowed a public forum for their own indictment. The experience of less articulate folk than Adler may be gauged from the short stories of the young Croat Miroslav Krleža, *The Croatian God Mars (Hrvatski bog Mars)* (1922), which paint a lacerating picture of peasant youths uprooted from traditional environments, transported vast distances to remote fronts and there subjected to brutal sergeants, corrupt officials, disease, mutilation and death. The Russian revolutions of February, then October 1917 cast their shadow over the authorities.

It was fear of driving the people too far which most motivated the new Emperor. But the baggage he had inherited from his uncle, and his own limitations, restricted his options in both halves of the Monarchy. Charles shared Franz Ferdinand's distrust of the Hungarian elite, and István Tisza in particular, as barriers to regeneration. Nor had the masterful Calvinist premier's determination personally to crown Charles Hungarian king endeared him to the deeply Catholic monarch. However, the young king could not pluck up his courage to dismiss Tisza. Not all criticisms of Tisza were fair. He was probably the least chauvinist of major Hungarian parliamentarians in his relation to Austria. The economic compromise he concluded with Austrian trade minister Spitzmüller at the end of 1916 included the extended twenty-year term the Austrians desired but with a smaller reduction of the Hungarian quota than Hungarian public opinion would have demanded in return, which explains why its provisions (to be implemented after the war) were not made public. Convincing himself that the war had strengthened religious, conservative sentiment, Tisza effectively disregarded Charles's April 1917 request to take an initiative in favour of electoral reform. The king took the plunge and dismissed him on 22 May, an act almost as symbolic as the young William II's dismissal of Bismarck in 1890.

Charles was unable to build on his boldness, however. He passed over as Tisza's successor the experienced Andrássy and chose instead a politically colourless aristocrat, whose government drew its support roughly from the same quarters as the Independence coalition of 1906–09, but with stronger links to bourgeois democrats and the Social Democrats, with whom the new minister of justice Vázsonyi (himself a practising Jew) reached a franchise reform deal. What blighted this apparently hopeful scenario was that Tisza's Party of Work retained a majority in the as yet unreformed parliament, which could not be challenged unless government and ruler were prepared to risk a general election. Hence official Hungarian politics gradually moved back into a conservative groove as, soon under another Wekerle premiership, the Tisza-ites succeeded in whittling down the electoral reform package, while in the population at large frustration mounted.

In Austria the most capable public servants available to Charles were probably Koerber, Stürgkh's successor as prime minister, and Max Beck. Since both had been unpopular with Franz Ferdinand, however, he dismissed the first and declined to appoint the second. The premiership fell to a Bohemian aristocrat, Clam-Martinic, almost an embodiment of the bankruptcy of the Czechophile 'feudals' of this class. For the paternalistic Austrianism at its heart now had nothing concrete to say even to 'well-disposed' Czechs in Clam's telling phrase, and he operated within the centralist assumptions of a pro-German octroi, albeit groaning that he could not now end his days on his Czech-speaking estate. Charles sensibly disavowed an anti-Slav diktat whose fate by now was almost over-determined: by the democratising influence of the February revolution in Russia and recent peace overtures, by fears that Czechs might sabotage war production and by Charles's own mounting dislike of an overweening Germandom. The alternative was to recall the Reichsrat. It met in late spring 1917 to hear Clam offer emptily 'in place of the part the whole, in place of cloudy, hazy political configurations the happy, tried and powerful state ... The programme of the government is

Austria!'[12] But differences with the Poles over Galician autonomy lost Clam the cushion of a parliamentary majority and he resigned in June. His successor was a German civil servant from the ministry of agriculture, Ignaz Seidler. This was the politics of mediocrity.

The Austrian government was in a 'no win' situation. It had given up the hard line. As the Bohemian military governor argued in July, militarising factories was effective against individual subversives but not a modern trade union movement. But its return to constitutionality merely gave Czech and south Slav MPs the platform to make declarations calling for statehood, in which the reference to the Habsburg framework was patently conditional, or rather a means for remaining Austrophiles and radical nationalists to slide over their differences. The Czech declaration of May 1917 was the work of the Czech Union, founded the previous autumn. For the first time the claim was for a Czechoslovak, not just a Czech state, which mirrored a key feature of Masaryk's programme in exile. As summer became autumn the balance in the Czech Union shifted against 'activism', or the readiness to engage in Habsburg politics, if only as a talking shop. Above all, this was a shift in the two great class-based parties, the Czech socialists and agrarians, towards the earlier established anti-Habsburg stances of bourgeois nationalist groupings like Kramář's Young Czechs. The autumn resignation as socialist party president of Bohumil Šmeral, the proponent of a merely cultural autonomy (and Czech communist leader of the 1920s) is a case in point. A related tendency among the south Slavs at this time saw the Austrophile Slovene leader Šušteršič eclipsed by the more social- and Yugoslav-minded Krek and Korošec, both of whom were priests. Among Habsburg Romanians the debate was largely over in the political class, which figured prominently in the 80,000 Romanians who had left Hungary with the retreating Romanian army at the end of 1916. Austrophilia among Poles, sorely tried by the erosion of Galician autonomy during the war, was dealt a heavy blow by the central powers' treaty with Russia at Brest-Litovsk in February 1918, which allotted areas disputed between Poles and Ukrainians to a new Ukrainian state.

The signs of dissolution for the Habsburg empire were thus palpable by early 1918. A great strike wave in Vienna and Budapest in January, induced by ration cuts, had a more nationalist reflection in Prague. But to avoid the foreshortening of hindsight, it must be said that there were still counter-signs at that time. South Slavs in particular were far from united in their goals. The Serbo-Croat coalition, the largest grouping in the Zagreb Diet, did not associate itself with the Reichsrat declaration of Austrian south Slavs for Yugoslav union of May 1917. Its Serb component preferred to remain passive as long as the Yugoslav state at issue might be one under Vienna's rather than Belgrade's aegis, and unlike Croats did not want to see Slovenes included in it. Besides, Italy was still opposed to the whole idea of a strong south Slav state on the Adriatic.

Indeed, the major problem facing anti-Habsburg nationalists in the Monarchy by early 1918 was how far they really had external support. Trumbić and Supilo had founded a 'Yugoslav Committee', based in London in 1915. Czech exiles had set up a body in Paris, renamed the National Committee in 1916, with the 32-year-old Edvard Beneš as secretary. Contacts had been established in Allied countries which had enabled recognition of Czech military units (mainly formed from prisoners of war) in Allied armies and the inclusion of reference to liberation of 'Slavs and Czechoslovaks' in the Allied war aims transmitted to President Wilson in January 1917. But a year later the secret wing of the exile movement in Prague (the so-called Mafia) beseeched Beneš for news: in its absence Prague was desperate, trust suffered and nobody now believed, Beneš was told, that the Czechs had any connections with the Allies at all. The request followed on a Lloyd George speech of 6 January 1918 and Woodrow Wilson's Fourteen Points for peace, both envisaging the federalisation of the Monarchy rather than its dissolution. They seemed to confirm Slav nationalists' suspicions that the western Allies were only using them to put pressure on Austria-Hungary to break away from Germany in a separate peace.

There were grounds for this fear. Indeed, the Emperor Charles's diplomacy since his accession had been premised on the hope he could reach agreement with the West. In the most dramatic initiative of his reign he had despatched his brother-in-law, Prince Sixtus of Bourbon-Parma, to a secret meeting with the French President Poincaré in February 1917. This meeting led on to a letter from Charles intended for Poincaré which spoke of his wish to support France's 'just claims' over Alsace-Lorraine at a future peace conference. Later contacts numbered J.C. Smuts, a member of the British War Cabinet, and the pre-war Austrian ambassador to Britain. None made real progress, because for all his irritation at the Germans Charles saw his overtures as opening the way to a general peace, while the Allies were only interested in dividing him from Berlin.

Besides, Italy, brought into the secret by Lloyd George, renewed unacceptable territorial demands. The Sixtus episode was to boomerang on the Emperor in April 1918 when his foreign minister Czernin charged the French with secretly talking peace, only for premier Clemenceau to reveal Charles's own dealings. Embarrassment was compounded because Czernin, not knowing the Alsace-Lorraine letter was genuine, pressed his sovereign into a public denial of it as a forgery.

The immediate significance of this affair was to force the Monarchy to prove its loyalty to the Germans by deepening the alliance of the central powers (the Spa agreements of May 1918). Deprived of any prospect of a separate peace on the Monarchy's part, about which British diplomacy at least was already sceptical, the Allies became converted to the need to destroy it. The fact that Czernin should not have known the crucial details of his sovereign's Alsace-Lorraine letter (he knew of its existence) throws a glaring light on Austro-Hungarian circumstances and the potential they contained for irresponsible absolutism. It is true that Lloyd George kept the Sixtus affair to himself in Britain too but unlike the Emperor Charles he had got where he was through a political process requiring proof of skill and experience. There are rather rare times when the untidy multiplicity of historical experience seems to sort itself into a pattern; the normal cross-currents are resolved and history starts to flow unambiguously one way. That the well-meaning Charles should have been pushed into the part of mendacious autocrat illustrates the fate that was now upon the old Monarchy. As all indices increasingly pointed to its ruin the democratic rhetoric of the Czech national movement's reply to Czernin's 2 April charge of treason acquired a sheen of plausibility, going beyond the hot-house emotion of a Prague public meeting:

> The unending battle approaches its culmination . . . And with firm, unshakeable confidence in the ultimate triumph of our sacred rights, with confidence in the . . . triumph of right over force, of freedom over bondage, of democracy over privilege and of truth over lies in great historical events, we raise our hands and solemnly vow . . . We will endure until we hail the freedom of our people . . . free in their own homeland.[13]

It was true that the non-dominant groups were more clearly aligned with notions of 'democracy' and 'self-determination' than their opponents. This was the concomitant of patterns of social mobilisation over the previous century. For many sorely tried Austro-German and Magyar workers there could be of course an equivalent socialist teleology. The miseries overwhelming the old order increasingly legitimised these no doubt selective ways of interpreting the historical drama, as a clash between past authoritarianism and future democracy. Masaryk himself saw the struggle between the central and the western powers in these terms.

Collapse

Heading the indictment against the Monarchy was its failure to provide for its subjects. The wheat harvest inherited from 1917 had been little worse than that of 1916 but this time there was a collapse of barley yields too, German aid was much reduced, Bulgaria denied she could help and the million tons' supply of grain specified in the central powers' treaty with the Ukraine at Brest-Litovsk failed to materialise. Sensation was created when General Landwehr hijacked supplies from Romania intended for Germany (April 1918). The effect was short-lived. In June only 45% of the ration could be covered, so that in Vienna it was halved again, while Plzeň, seat of the Škoda armaments works, with no bread or flour available for five days saw riots in which five were shot dead. Only the summer harvest temporarily relieved pressure.

Even front-line troops, with often paper-soled shoes, could no longer be cushioned with strong rations, which were cut by more than a third in April. Their average weight on the Italian front was eight and a half stone. And there were fewer of them. Though the army nominally still had four million men on its rolls in October 1918, only half a million were at the front, mainly facing Italy. There Conrad's final disastrous offensive of June 1918 (the Battle of the Piave) lost 142,000 in nine days, reducing combatants to 147,000 men, according to one source. Many troops were engaged on the 'inner front' in 1918, requisitioning grain and pacifying disturbances, but mutinies and desertions led the military authorities finally to see the need to counter the ideological challenge to age-old dynastic loyalty. However, a very largely new officer corps – because the professionals had been killed off early – proved an unreliable instrument in the propaganda task. All told, the army called up more than 8 million men (and 100,000 women) in the war, of whom 1,016,000 died,

1,691,000 became incapacitated or missing and 478,000 succumbed in enemy captivity.[14]

As the system fell into malfunction, prime minister Seidler, who had begun office by dismissing the only Czech in his cabinet, now told the Reichsrat (July 1918) that he did not wish to deny Slav charges he was following a pro-German course: 'the German people are today the backbone of this polymorphic state, and they will always remain so'.[15] In practice this meant moving to create the nationally homogenous *Kreise* in Bohemia that the Germans had been demanding for thirty years. In Hungary Tisza's resistance to substantial franchise reform increasingly bore fruit. As late as September on a tour of the Monarchy's south Slav lands he banged the table to tell regional politicians they would never get Trialism.

All this was tailor-made to suit the propaganda of exiled Slavs and Romanians about the unreformability of the old empire. Though the western Allies came to support partition for their own reasons, reflecting the wish to weaken Germany through its Habsburg partner, the exiles had given their alternative self-determination approach so high a profile and developed arguments so congruent with western democratic values that the Great Powers had less compunction than might have been expected about the fateful change of regional strategy they made in the summer of 1918. They also set about propagating the new line with a remarkable vigour which owed something to the commitment of individuals like R.W. Seton-Watson and Ernest Denis to Masarykian ideals as well as to the more *realpolitik* calculations of a Northcliffe, head of Britain's propaganda ministry. Dismissal of the role of the exiles would be as wrong as the exaggerations of it in the Monarchy's 'Succession States' between the wars. British contacts with exiled politicians over the war years may have gradually drawn them, Calder argues, into a pattern of engagement in exile plans beyond their conscious intentions. Certainly – contrary to Vienna's assumptions – the Foreign Office seems throughout the war to have been little more committed to preserve the monarchy than to destroy it, so that it was accessible to exiled partition plans from the start. Even Woodrow Wilson, of whom this was not true, was influenced in his turn to self-determination by the military potential of the Czech Legion in Russia in summer 1918, as a lever against the Bolsheviks, who threatened his vision of a liberal democratic world order. Hence the recognition of the Czech National Council in Paris as 'basis' or 'trustee' of or '*de facto*' government of a Czechoslovak state by France, Britain and America (29 June,

9 August, 3 September). The recognition of the Yugoslav movement was somewhat vaguer. It took the form of approval of the resolutions of the Congress of Oppressed Peoples in Rome in April, calling for a Yugoslav state and appearing to reconcile Italian–Yugoslav differences – wrongly as it turned out.

A direct result of Allied endorsement of nationalist aspirations was to embolden their spokesmen in the Monarchy. Thus a late September statement of the Czech National Council, founded earlier in the war but revived in July, stated baldly that the only good thing which could now come from the war was an Allied victory; shortly afterwards, Czech MPs left the Reichsrat. The Serbo-Croat coalition and the spokesmen of the Yugoslav Reichsrat Declaration finally united in a National Council in Zagreb in early October. German-speaking socialists too at a conference of 8 October called for a National Council of German Austria. This was a victory of Otto Bauer's left tendency over the Habsburg patriotism of Karl Renner. A Marxist sensitive to historical shifts, Bauer had for some time believed the socialists' traditional approach to nationality questions must yield to full-blown acceptance of the inevitability of national self-determination. His approach had no counterpart among Hungarian-speaking socialists, however, who advocated limited cultural autonomies in a single Hungarian state.

In government circles gloom deepened. Something had to give. In the second half of September the Bulgarian front broke before an Allied offensive from Salonika, forcing Sofia out of the war. No transport was available to send Habsburg troops to plug the gap. The Common Ministerial Council of 27 September decided for peace at any price. Germany, having shot her last bolt with the offensives of spring and July, agreed to a parallel approach to Woodrow Wilson, requesting an armistice based on his Fourteen Points of 8 January 1918. The Fourteen Points, of which the tenth envisaged the Dual Monarchy's federalisation (shorn of her Italian and Polish lands) had of course been outstripped by later promises to the Czechoslovaks and Yugoslavs. An air of unreality surrounds Habsburg politics in this final stage. Burián, again foreign minister after the Czernin affair, seemed to suppose that the Polish independence called for in the Fourteen Points could be acquitted in the framework of the Polish puppet state which the Monarchy was still discussing with Germany. Indeed, agreement on an Austro-German customs agreement was finally reached on 11 October. These were the negotiations of ghosts.

The ghosts were still held in sufficient awe by their subjects for order to be preserved. Thus a general strike organised by Czech socialists for mid-October was nipped in the bud, and the socialists put in their place by the bourgeois-dominated National Council. But the authorities could no longer influence events in a positive sense. On 16 October Hussarek, Dualist Austria's last prime minister, presented a proposal for federalism. Despite the fact that it loyally excluded Hungary from its provisions, premier Wekerle took the opportunity to state that Hungary would no longer feel herself bound by the 1867 Compromise. There was no other response. The so-long-debated issue of a federal Austria was now *passé*. Unreality took on a new dimension when the Monarchy declared Wilson's answer to its note, which by reiterating American commitments to Czechoslovak and Yugoslav independence doomed it to extinction, to be an acceptable basis for negotiation. It was this Habsburg response, however, which precipitated the final showdown. Prague citizens, logically assuming that Vienna had now recognised their independence, took to the streets on 28 October. The National Council decided to preempt any disturbance, declared independence and brought out a musical band to distract the crowds. Later, having notified the appropriate fire and water services, Praguers proceeded to dismantle the statue of the Virgin Mary on the Old Town Square in Prague, leaving that of Jan Hus, erected opposite her in 1916, in sole possession of the field. The police and military authorities did not interfere.

Peaceful takeovers also occurred in Cracow between 28 and 31 October and Zagreb on the 29th, the first to a Polish state already proclaimed in Warsaw, the second to an entity which declared itself part of the 'national and sovereign state of Serbs, Croats and Slovenes'. Ljubljana and Sarajevo followed suit, the Yugoslav state finally coming into being in Belgrade on 1 December. On 31 October a coalition government assumed control in German Austria. Events were less peaceful in Budapest, where the quixotic Károlyi formed a National Council, combining his Independence Party, the Social Democrats and Jászi's Radicals, and was appointed prime minister by Charles on 31 October, the same day that Tisza was shot dead in his home by marauding soldiers. Hungarian Romanian and Slovak leaders had already declared their allegiance to Romania and Czechoslavakia respectively, though in these cases alternate periods of negotiation and force ensued before the new arrangements were consolidated. This was also true of east Galicia, where Ruthenes proclaimed independence on 1 November and were promptly attacked by Poles. Italy, having at last broken through the Austro-Hungarian front at Vittorio Veneto in the last days of the war, looked to secure the territories promised her in the Treaty of London, which included some 600,000 south Slavs in Gorizia, Istria and Dalmatia. In view of the centuries of conflict and complexity underlying the old empire, however, the immediate circumstances of its collapse must be declared remarkably free of bloodshed and violence.

So rapid was this collapse that by the time an armistice was arranged at Padua on 4 November only the army still acknowledged Charles's authority. But it was melting away or being rounded up by the Italians. Károlyi found separate terms imposed on him by the French commander of the Allied Balkan forces. The final humiliation for the Emperor was to accept the republicanism of the two core peoples of his former realm, the Austro-Germans and the Magyars. On 11 and 13 November respectively he 'renounced' his state duties, without making a formal renunciation of the throne. Indeed, when his wife was finally allowed to return on a visit to Austria in 1982, sixty years after his premature death in a damp, drafty Madeira mansion, she had still not renounced it either.

Assessment

Tolstoy's famous disquisition on history in *War and Peace* was spurred by his revulsion at what he took to be the historians' simplistic and morally offensive assumption: that a single individual like Napoleon (whom he despised) could have set in train the sufferings of millions in the Napoleonic Wars. Historians are now more sophisticated than Tolstoy assumed; the idea that great processes regularly operate beyond the will or actions of individuals has become a commonplace. It remains moot whether it is more consoling to see tragic events as functionally inevitable or as due to avoidable human error or malignity. But Tolstoy was right to rebuke historians for evading big questions on big events.

In the case of the Habsburg Monarchy and the First World War the big issues concern the outbreak and conduct of the war but above all the break-up of the old state at its end. What is the balance between individual and structural factors, and between shorter- and longer-term ones, in shaping what came about? The relative cohesion of the Monarchy's wartime administration has been contrasted above with the disastrous personal qualities of its Chief of Staff

Conrad von Hötzendorf. Franz Joseph's age, Tisza's stubbornness, the mediocrity of Berchtold, Stürgkh and Potiorek, the naivety and inexperience of Charles himself also need mentioning. On the other hand come weighty structural factors, if short-term at first view, including the numerical superiority of the enemy and the unfavourable strategic position of the central powers, which pinioned them between two and in Austria-Hungary's case three fronts and exposed them to effective blockade. This made an Entente victory the more likely in the longer term once the quick knock-out blow Germany had planned for failed in summer 1914; and military defeat in such a total war meant almost certain political collapse. Moreover, the qualities of Habsburg leaders cannot simply be separated from the system they rose in. Tisza's stubbornness was directly related to his view of what he was trying to defend. That most of the generals chosen by Franz Joseph soon failed the test of war reflected his preference for soldierly form over substance; his unease with his quite able war minister Auffenberg from 1911, for instance, owed something to the poor figure Auffenberg cut on parade. The importance of notions of aristocratic honour in leading the Monarchy into an ill-judged war, the continued social elitism in conducting it (to his embarrassment, Károlyi's squadron's departure to the front was delayed till his first child was born), the number of obscure aristocrats or run-of-the-mill civil servants who served as premiers at the time of supreme trial: all this suggests the longer-term structural weakness of a conservative state ship-wrecked on the reefs of a war of the nations. Contemporaries lamented their society's backwardness and historians from the region have often echoed them.

Powerful as it is, the theme of the Habsburg odd-ball out of step with twentieth-century Europe does not go quite to the heart of the matter. After all, out-of-touch generals, skewed relations between officers and men, emphasis on honour and the like were rife elsewhere in the Great War, including democratic Britain and France. Austria-Hungary's conservatism was indeed distinctive in the continued semi-absolutism of the monarch and his ministers in the conduct of foreign policy. A theme of this book has been, however, that in many aspects of development the Dual Monarchy was following related trajectories to other European states and, if anything, slightly narrowing the gap, while inside it Hungary was gaining on Austria, and the regions – marginally – on their metropoles. A modern study has even dubbed the performance of the Austrian wartime armaments industry 'extraordinary'.[16]

But there is a weakness in this line of argument, too, if pushed too far. It opens itself to the amusing satire of Robert Musil:

> There in ... that misunderstood state that has since vanished ... there was speed too, of course, but not too much speed ... The conquest of the air had begun there too, but not too intensively ... One went in for sport, but not in madly Anglo-Saxon fashion. One spent tremendous sums on the Army; but only just enough to assure one of remaining the second weakest among the great powers ... [17]

Austria-Hungary cannot ultimately be summed up as a middling central European society whose modernisation successes should receive more attention. The distinctiveness over which contemporaries agonised was a key structural feature. At its core, however, was not just socio-economic backwardness and the region's authoritarian legacy, but their interaction with the nationality problem which retained throughout its determining place in the old empire's evolution.

This, of course, is not a new perspective. But it was one not always fully understood, at the time or since. The persistence of widespread poverty through all the remarkable economic and educational advances of nineteenth-century Europe is indeed its most significant feature, and a key theme of this book. Stalin in his famous 1913 pamphlet on nationalism understandably dismissed the petty sqabbles over the language of railway signs in Bohemia. But to oppose what contemporaries often dubbed the 'stomach question' (*Magenfrage*) to nationalism as the real underlying issue of the time mistakes nationalism's deceptive nature. At the level of ideology, the interests of nationalist activists were often remote from popular concern. But in its concrete social impact nationalism operated more as an organisational than an ideological principle: should a society be organised through this cultural code (in Habsburg circumstances, language) or that one? As long as the bulk of Slavs were illiterate peasants social organisation beyond the village level could only be carried on through a traditionally dominant language. Social mobilisation made it possible for modernity to find expression in Czech or Slovene or Romanian. At the popular level nationalism was thus a matter of the means of expression rather than the content. It was quite possible for 'the masses' of contemporary parlance to prioritise social issues while wishing them to be settled in a national framework. Indeed, the more their ambitions grew, the more the felt need for this national dimension followed, as it became apparent that a ceiling on their language's use was a ceiling on their own mobility: also that the standard socialist solution of national 'cultural autonomy' still kept non-dominant languages under the hatches by reserving the higher economic and political spheres to the traditionally dominant speech. This is why by the latter stages of the war the bulk of Social Democrats had moved from cultural autonomy to self-determination without feeling any contradiction with their socialism. The social and national questions fused along the lines of the ancient split between dominant and non-dominant ethnic groups.

Of course, in real life there is give and take. Common sense suggests that Slovenes, say, will see the practical advantages of learning German, while German speakers will show tolerance of the actual mother tongue used in a Slovene area, in appropriate contexts. This was the perspective long accepted by speakers of non-dominant tongues and assumed for longer by the great majority of German speakers. However, experience shows that the intertwining of constantly recurring practical difficulties with the psychological heritage of previous inequality (resentment and backlash) makes the settlement of problems involved in such give and take far harder than common-sense scenarios suggest. This underlies the tension between Josef Redlich's statement in his famous work on the Habsburg state problem that an 'organic solution' could still have been found 'if seriously striven for, with the help of the one great creative idea of a federation of equally entitled peoples', and his acknowledgement that the dissolution he and like-minded people had hoped to avert was 'in all probability long unavoidable'.[18] The difficulties of multi-ethnicity even in what was traditionally thought the benign environment of British-style liberalism, in Quebec and in Britain itself, give an academic flavour to claims for the Monarchy as a prototype for multi-national statehood. For the atmosphere there was far from benign. Indeed, the dominant/non-dominant relationship took on a peculiar and increasingly poisoned form.

This development can be traced through the fraught evolution of the Austro-German community in the second half of the nineteenth century. Prior to this period German speakers in Austria had been as much a social as an ethnic group, formed by assimilation as well as descent. German culture in the Monarchy could thus appear as a neutral, state-forming instrument, the role Joseph II wanted for it, and which English has so far been able to play in India. But

the drawing in of Austro-Germans into the German national movement in mid-century and their defeat in 1866 destroyed this perspective. Thereafter, an imbalance existed in Dualist Austria,
whereby German liberal culture acquired perhaps even greater
symbolic significance (to cement the transition from dynastic absolutism to constitutional norms) but the German speakers themselves were a rump of declining prestige who by 1879 had slipped
from political power. This imbalance spurred Slavs to try to rectify
it by dismantling the German cultural hegemony as they had done
the political. It humiliated the Austro-Germans who engaged in
a dogged rearguard action, gradually abandoning their pretensions to an all-Austrian patriotism and seeking an uneasy identity
as German nationalists of varying shades. The envenoming of
German–Slav relations was thus the product of Austro-German
weakness rather than strength, for it made impossible the relative
stability afforded by English cultural hegemony in Canada or,
ostensibly, Hungarian in Hungary.

In these circumstances both Austro-Germans and Slavs looked to
the Reich, in respective hope and fear. A massive inferiority complex
developed, among the former particularly, *vis-à-vis* Imperial Germany. Instead of a benign convergence towards the evening up of
ethnic disadvantage, such as Bolzano had urged on German speakers
in the Pre-March years, two opposed tendencies developed. The
advance of the Slavs, whose situation inclined them on the whole to
democratic trajectories in terms of social mobilisation and ideology,
encountered a German nationalist backlash increasingly attracted to
anti-democratic aspects of contemporary Reich German culture, like
the purported 'idealism' which rejected Jewish 'materialism' and
crude democratic head-counting. This is not to put the blame for
the nationality problem primarily on the Austro-Germans – though
differences in ideological timbre are easier to relativise in hindsight.
Not for nothing did Redlich single out the power drive of the two
leading nations and the bureaucracy as obstructive of 'equal entitle-
ment'. But Slavs also had their power drive. They could have paid
more heed to the difficulties their ever-swelling demands posed for
the traditionally dominant German speakers and to the need for a
'sphere of commonality' such as any polity requires at its core. Pleas
to this effect from the Polish conservative Madeyski were unsurprisingly ignored by his fellow Slavs.[19] Thus federalism had little chance,
and the memoirs of Austria's last living minister, Alexander Spitzmüller, show the central bureaucracy's enduring unease about

wholly abandoning a German leading role in Cisleithania. Any scheme would have foundered, for example, on Czech claims to the whole of Bohemia and German Bohemians' demands for autonomy, even without Hungarian insistence on Dualism – and other tensions, like Polish opposition, shared by Madeyski, to equal status for Ruthenians. Federalism works best where relative homogeneity and goodwill already exist and is no panacea for historic differences, as the Yugoslav case also shows. If the direct cause of the Monarchy's downfall came from a decision to enter a disastrous war, the impact of seemingly endless nationality conflict in impelling that decision cannot be overlooked. The illiberal impulses which triumphed in the region after the war were rising before it, if less virulently. Their influence recalls Fritz Fischer's famous thesis of domestically rattled German elites opting for war in 1914.

The Second Reich's problems stemmed from a fraught unification movement and ill-digested modernisation. But the flaws visible in hindsight in the Reich German model were obscured for Austrian admirers by its apparent dynamism and success. The main structural weakness of the Monarchy in the Dualist period was its elite's growing dependence on Germany, diplomatically and psychologically, at a time when non-German aspirations were on the march in the Monarchy itself. The alliance of 1879 and erosion of the Monarchy's links to other powers led on to the implicit trust in German might in July 1914, when delight at German backing swept away all but Tisza in the common ministerial council of 7 July which set the course for war. The humiliating dependence on the Reich in the war years was thus more than the product of immediate military pressures. Underlying the dichotomy, repeatedly emphasised in this book, between authoritarian and reformist approaches to the empire's difficulties was this most fundamental of problems: German nationalism and Slav nationalism were set on different trajectories, which the rise of ostensibly non-nationalist socialist and Christian Social parties in pre-war years was unable to modify essentially.

Nor were the Hungarians able to escape this bind. Prussia had been their would-be ally in 1790 and 1866, and the Magyar Andrássy had negotiated the 1879 dual alliance. The strong man Tisza's failure to avert war in July 1914 shows the limits of Hungarian power. Meanwhile, their own nationalism contributed greatly to the inflammation of the south Slav question and the rigidity of the Dualist system as a whole. It is hard to see that the modernisation of the Habsburg Monarchy inaugurated by the Enlightenment could have ended without the dissolution of this multi-national community. However, the dissolution was not benign and a state which had an honourable record of achievement fell victim to a cruel and terrible war, to be followed a generation later by one more terrible still. The final collapse, as contemporaries put it, was 'an end with horror' but after the experiences of the war years this was preferable to 'horror without end'.[20]

Redlich concluded in 1920 that the Austrian problem had become a European one. This was true in a quite concrete sense in the regional tensions of the inter-war period. But in late years its relevance has grown in the more general terms of European multi-cultural community. Habsburg experience suggests that a bureaucracy with a supranational idea cannot enthuse nations for it that feel removed from the decision-making process. It shows how sensitively handled legal empowerment of people of different cultures can be fruitful and that some agreements between representatives of opposed communities can be reached. But the strongest imperative belongs to social development. Legal–constitutional prescription can do no more than create a framework, in which such development proceeds amicably enough to allow time for transition to new patterns of life, glimpsed as through a glass darkly. The Habsburg Monarchy made such a transition, from the Baroque 'court-orientated society' to the nineteenth-century *Rechtsstaat*, a unique fusion of Josephinist bureaucratism with the bourgeois spirit of the age, tinging its largely conservative masses. That this society showed few signs of developing further into a democratic federation of equal nations is neither surprising nor discreditable, because such an association still nowhere exists.

Notes

Chapter 1.   Foundations

1. R.J.W. Evans, *The Making of the Habsburg Monarchy 1550–1700* (Oxford, 1979), 174.
2. J. Van Horn Melton, 'Arbeitspläne des aufgeklärten Absolutismus', *Mitteilungen des Instituts für österreichische Geschichtsforschung (MIÖGf)* 90 (1982), 49.
3. J.G. Keysler, *Travels through Germany, Bohemia, Hungary, Switzerland, Italy and Lorraine*, tr. from the 2nd German edn, 4 vols (London, 1756–57), iv, 81–2.
4. J. Rohrer, *Abriss der westlichen Provinzen des österreichischen Staates* (Vienna, 1804), xix, 20.
5. R. Sandgruber, *Die Anfänge der Konsumgesellschaft. Konsumgüterverbrauch, Lebensstandard und Alltagskultur in Österreich im 18. und 19. Jahrhundert* (Vienna, 1982), 337.
6. G. Grüll, *Bauer, Herr und Landesfürst: Sozialrevolutionäre Bestrebungen der oberösterreichischen Bauern von 1650 bis 1848* (Linz, 1963), 432.
7. J.F. Seyfahrt, *Entwurf einer allerneusten Beschreibung des Königreichs Böhmen* (Frankfurt, 1757), 9; [J.J. Kausch], *Ausführliche Nachrichten über Böhmen* (Graz, 1794), 50.
8. Baron Riesbeck, *Travels through Germany, 3* vols (London, 1787), ii, 127; Count F. Hartig, *Genesis of the Revolution in Austria*, English translation printed as Vol. 4 of W. Coxe, *History of the House of Austria* (London, 1895), 79. Later (p. 87) the conservative Hartig argues that national tensions affected only the educated classes.
9. Gillespie Smyth, *The Romance of Diplomacy ... With a Memoir, and Selection from the Correspondence ... of Sir Robert Murray Keith*, 2 vols (London, 1861), i, 477–8.
10. B. Grünwald, *A régi Magyarország 1711–1825* (Budapest,1910*)*, 105–6.
11. A. Fortis, *Travels into Dalmatia* (London, 1778), 77–83.
12. Riesbeck, *Travels*, ii, 24–5.
13. J. Demian, *Darstellung der österreichischen Monarchie*, 4 vols (Vienna, 1804–7), ii, 49.

14. E. Bruckmüller, *Sozialgeschichte Österreichs* (Vienna, 1985), 270.
15. P. Bělina, *Česká města v 18 století a osvícenské reformy* (Prague, 1985), 48.
16. W.J. McGill, 'Kaunitz: The Personality of Political Algebra', *Topic* 34 (1980), 29–42 (35).
17. J. Haubelt, *České osvícenství* (Prague, 1986), 305.
18. F. Maass, *Der Josephinismus. Quellen zu seiner Geschichte*, 5 vols (Vienna, 1951–61), iii, 31.
19. I.N. Kiss, 'Versorgung und Preispolitik Maria Theresias im Königreich Ungarn', in R.G. Plaschka *et al.* (eds), *Österreich im Europa der Aufklärung*, 2 vols (Vienna, 1985), i, 269–85 (272).
20. P.G.M. Dickson, *Finance and Government under Maria Theresa 1740–1780* (Oxford, 1987), 325.

Chapter 2.   Joseph II and his Legacy

1. D. Beales, *Joseph II. 1. In the Shadow of Maria Theresa 1741–80* (Cambridge, 1987), 166.
2. H. Glassl, *Der österreichische Einrichtungswerk in Galizien (1772–1790)* (Wiesbaden, 1975), 214.
3. C. Tropper, 'Schicksale der Büchersammlungen niederösterreichischer Klöster nach der Aufhebung durch Joseph II und Franz II (I)', *MIÖG f* 91 (1983), 95–139 (111).
4. G. Otruba, 'Probleme von Wirtschaft und Gesellschaft in ihren Beziehungen zu Kirche und Klerus', in E. Kovács (ed.), *Katholische Aufklärung und Josephinismus* (Munich, 1979), 128–9.
5. S.K. Padover, *The Revolutionary Emperor: Joseph II of Austria*, 2nd edn (London, 1967), 175.
6. J.F. Bright, *Joseph II* (London, 1897), 133.
7. P. von Mitrofanov, *Joseph II*, 2 vols (Vienna, 1910), i, 292.
8. Beales, *Joseph II*, 406, 409.
9. Smyth, *Romance of Diplomacy*, ii, 222: Joseph's comments to the British ambassador Keith.
10. Zs. Trocsányi, *Miklós Wesselényi és világa* (Budapest, 1970), 11–12.
11. D. Beales, 'Die auswärtige Politik der Monarchie vor und nach 1780', in R. Plaschka *et al.* (eds), *Österreich im Europa der Aufklärung*, 2 vols (Vienna, 1985), i, 567–74 (570).
12. R. Rosdolsky (Rozdolski), *Die grosse Steuer- und Agrarreform Josefs II* (Warsaw, 1961), 97–102.

13. *Magyarország története 1790–1848*, chief ed. Gy. Méreir, 2 vols (Budapest, 1980), i, 46–7.
14. *Ibid.*, 199.
15. E. Wangermann, *Aufklärung und staatliche Erziehung. Gottfried van Swieten als Reformator des österreichischen Unterrichtswesens 1781–91* (Vienna, 1978), 30.
16. E. Wangermann, 'The Reaction to Joseph II's Reforms in the Pamphlet Literature', unpublished paper to the World Congress of Slavists (Harrogate, 1990), 8.
17. B. Němcová, *Granny* (Westport, 1976), 53–4.
18. M.C. Ives, *Enlightenment and National Revival . . . in Late Eighteenth Century Hungary* (London, 1979), 95.
19. H. Reinalter, 'Der Nationsbegriff der österreichischen Jakobiner', *MIÖGf* 91 (1983) 401–11 (404).
20. Ives, *Enlightenment*, 222–3.

Chapter 3.   Metternich's Austria

1. K.A. Roider, *Baron Thugut and the Austrian Response to the French Revolution* (Princeton, 1987), 260–1.
2. W.C. Langsam, *The Napoleonic Wars and German Nationalism in Austria* (New York, 1930), 17–18.
3. A. Ernstberger, *Böhmens freiwilliger Kriegseinsatz gegen Napoleon* (Munich, 1963), 68–73.
4. G. de Bertier de Sauvigny, *Metternich and his Times* (London, 1962), 54 (in 1820).
5. M. Ullrichová (ed.), *Clemens Metternich. Wilhelmine von Sagan. Ein Briefwechsel 1813–15* (Graz, 1966), 119.
6. A.G. Haas, 'Metternich and the Slavs', *Austrian History Yearbook* (1968–69), 120–49 (141).
7. Graf Stephan Széchenyi, *Über den Credit*, 2nd improved edn (Pesth, 1830), 85.
8. J. Slokar, *Geschichte der österreichischen Industrie und ihrer Förderung unter Kaiser Franz I* (Vienna, 1914), 44.
9. K. Giday, 'Hozzászolás Tolnai György: A parasztipar és tökés iparrá fejlödése Magyarországon (1842–49) c. vitacikkhez', *Századok* 91 (1957), 790–98 (794).
10. H. Freudenberger, 'Progressive Bohemian and Moravian Aristocrats', in S. Winters and J. Held (eds), *Intellectual and Social*

Developments in the Habsburg Empire (Boulder, Colorado, 1975), 115–30 (124).

11. E. Violand, *Die sociale Geschichte der Revolution in Oesterreich* (Leipzig, 1850), 47.

12. Grüll, *Bauer, Herr und Landesfürst*, 570.

13. *Ibid.*, 463.

14. J.-P. Himka, *Galician Villagers and the Ukrainian National Movement in the Nineteenth Century* (Edmonton, 1988), 23.

15. Slokar, *Österreichische Industrie*, 37, 50.

16. C. A. Macartney, *The Habsburg Empire 1790–1918* (London, 1968), 281.

Chapter 4.   Liberalism and Nationalism

1. I. Bartha, *A fiatal Kossuth* (Budapest, 1966), 17.

2. *Tagebücher des Carl Friedrich Freiherrn Kübeck von Kübau* (Vienna, 1909), 550.

3. Graf Stephan Széchenyi, *Ueber Pferde, Pferdezucht und Pferderennen* (Pesth, 1830), 71.

4. Gy. Wlassics (ed.), *Deák Ferencz munkáiból*, 2 vols (Budapest, 1906), i, 81–8.

5. K.R. Greenfield, *Economics and Liberalism in the Risorgimento*, revised ed. (Baltimore, 1965), 240.

6. E. Castle (ed.), *Sonderabdruck aus Anastasius Grün's Werken* (n.p., 1907), LXI.

7. [F. Schuselka], *Deutsche Worte eines Oesterreichers* (Hamburg, 1843), 141.

8. K. Hitchins, *The Rumanian National Movement in Transylvania, 1780–1849* (Cambridge, Mass., 1969), 164.

9. This is particularly the argument of Ernest Gellner, *Nations and Nationalism* (Oxford, 1983).

10. J.G. Herder, *Ideen zur Philosophie der Geschichte der Menschheit*, Vol. 6 of *Johann Gottfried Herder. Werke* (Frankfurt, 1989), 698–9. These words were first published in 1791.

11. A. Springer, *Aus meinem Leben* (Berlin, 1892), 1–2, 14–15.

12. I. Rudnytsky, 'The Ukrainians in Galicia under Austrian Rule', *Austrian History Yearbook* 3 (1966–67), 394–429 (397).

13. Leo Graf von Thun-Hohenstein, *Über den gegenwärtigen Stand der böhmischen Literatur* (Prague, 1842), 5.

14. E. Denis, *La Bohême depuis la Montagne-Blanche*, 2 vols (Paris, 1903), ii, 71.
15. J. Chlebowczyk, O*n Small and Young Nations in Europe* (Wrocław, 1980), 120.
16. E. Winter, *Der böhmische Vormärz in Briefen Bernard Bolzanos an F. Přihonský (1822–48)* (Berlin, 1956), 55–6.
17. A. Okáč, *Český sněm a vláda před březnem 1848* (Prague, 1947), 372.
18. M. Csáky, *Von der Aufklärung zum Liberalismus. Studien zum Frühliberalismus in Ungarn* (Vienna, 1981), 164.
19. P. Brock, *The Slovak National Awakening* (Toronto, 1976), 82.

Chapter 5. 1848–49

1. A. Sked, *The Survival of the Habsburg Empire. Radetsky, the Imperial Army and the Class War, 1848* (London, 1979), 160.
2. S. Pech, *The Czech Revolution of 1848* (Chapel Hill, 1969), 344.
3. G. Spira, *A Hungarian Count in the Revolution of 1848* (Budapest, 1974), 192.
4. A. Stein, 'Friedrich Hebbels politisch-publizistische Beteiligung an der Wiener Revolution 1848', *MIÖGf* 99 (1991), 164.
5. W. Häusler, *Von der Massenarmut zur Arbeiterbewegung. Demokratische und soziale Frage in der Wiener Revolution von 1848* (Vienna, 1979), 314.
6. R. Rosdolsky, *Die Bauernabgeordneten im konstituierenden österreichischen Reichstag 1848–49* (Vienna, 1976), 65.
7. A. Csizmadia, *A magyar választási rendszer 1848-ben* (Budapest, 1963), 326–9.
8. *Magyarország története 1848–90*, chief ed. E. Kovács, 2 vols (Budapest, 1979), i, 147–8.
9. Palacký's letter is translated in the *Slavonic and East European Review* 26 (1947–48), 303–8.
10. Haüsler, *Massenarmut*, 285.
11. K. Marx, *Revolution and Counter-Revolution in Germany* (London, 1971), 47–8. The articles were written by Engels and published under Marx's name.
12. G. Illyés, *People of the Puszta* (Budapest, 1967; first published 1936), 65–6.
13. F. Potrebica, *Požeska županija za revolucije 1848–49* (Zagreb, 1984), 118.

14. V. Krestić, *Istorija srpske štampe u Ugarskoj 1791–1914* (Novi Sad, 1980), 73.

15. J.C. Campbell, *French Influence and the Rise of Rumanian Nationalism* (New York, 1971), 346.

16. E.K. Sieber, *Ludwig von Löhner. Ein Vorkämpfer des Deutschtums in Böhmen, Mähren und Schlesien im Jahre 1848–49* (Munich, 1965), 89.

17. Cited in R.A. Kann, *The Multi-National Empire*, 2 vols (New York, 1950), ii, 32.

Chapter 6.   Eventful Transition 1849–67

1. *Metternich–Hartig. Briefwechsel des Staatskanzlers aus dem Exil 1848–51* (Vienna, 1924), 40.

2. For example, R. Austensen, 'Felix Schwarzenberg: Realpolitiker or Machiavellian? The Evidence of the Dresden Conference', *Mitteilungen des österreichischen Staatsarchivs* 30 (1977), 97–118; K.W. Rock, 'Felix Schwarzenberg, Military Diplomat', *Austrian History Yearbook* 11 (1975), 85–100, and the comments of H. Rumpler, *ibid.*, 101–5.

3. C. Wolfsgruber, *Joseph Othmar Cardinal Rauscher, Fürsterzbischof von Wien* (Freiburg, 1888), 481.

4. C. Stölzl, *Die Ära Bach in Böhmen* (Munich, 1971), 255.

5. H. Lentze, *Die Universitätsreform des Ministers Graf Leo Thun–Hohenstein* (Vienna, 1962), 135.

6. C. Czoernig, *Oesterreichs Neugestaltung 1848–58* (Stuttgart, 1858), 447.

7. J. Komlos, *The Habsburg Monarchy as a Customs Union* (Princeton, 1983), 226.

8. *Magyarország története 1848–90*, chief ed. E. Kovács, 2 vols (Budapest, 1979), i, 532.

9. I. Szabó, *A parasztság Magyarországon a kapitalizmus korában 1848–1918*, 2nd edn (Budapest, 1973), 144.

10. Komlos, *Monarchy as Customs Union*, 39–40; T. Huerta, *Economic Growth and Economic Policy in a Multi-National Setting. The Habsburg Monarchy 1841–65* (New York, 1977), ch. 2.

11. R. Sandgruber, *Ökonomie und Politik. Österreichische Wirtschaftsgeschichte* (Vienna, 1995), 238.

12. Komlos, *Monarchy as Customs Union*, 234–6.

13. H.-H. Brandt, *Der österreichische Neoabsolutismus. Staatsfinanzen und Politik 1848–60*, 2 vols (Göttingen, 1978), i, 304–14; Archduke Rainer's comments on p. 314.

14. H. von Srbik, *Deutsche Einheit*, 4 vols (Munich, 1935–42), ii, 216–31.

15. A.J.P. Taylor, *The Struggle for Mastery in Europe 1848–1918* (Oxford, 1954), 61.

16. Brandt, *Österreichischer Neoabsolutismus*, ii, 998.

17. *Magyarország története 1848–90*, i, 490.

18. R. Horvath, 'Kossuth's Views on Economics in his Lectures on National Economy at London University', *Journal of European Economic History* 2 (1973), 339–54.

19. I. Pfaff, *Česká přináležitost k Západu v letech 1815–1878* (Prague, 1996), 23; Stölzl, *Ära Bach*, 67.

20. O. Urban, *Česká společnost 1848–1918* (Prague, 1982), 126–7.

21. J. Prunk, *Slovenski narodni vzpon* (Ljubljana, 1992), 75–6.

22. F. Palacký, *Oesterreichs Staatsidee* (Prague, 1866), 13.

23. H. Rumpler, *Österreichische Geschichte 1804–1914* (Vienna, 1997), 389–90.

24. By Gerhard Ritter, in O. Pflanze (ed.), *The Unification of Germany, 1848–1871* (Hinsdale, 1968), 103.

25. A.J.P. Taylor, *The Habsburg Monarchy, 1809–1918* (London, 1948), 76.

26. J. Redlich, *Das österreichische Staats- und Reichsproblem*, 2 vols (Leipzig, 1920–6), i, 691–2, 699.

Chapter 7. Liberalism

1. A. Ara, 'Die Haltung Italiens gegenüber der Habsburgermonarchie', in vol. 6 of *Die Habsburgermonarchie 1848–1918: Im System der internationalen Beziehungen*, 2. Teilband (Vienna, 1993), 190–246 (217).

2. B. von Bruschek-Klein, 'Ernst von Pleners Weg in die Politik', *MIÖG* 89 (1981), 287–334 (322).

3. Scott W. Lackey, *The Rebirth of the Habsburg Army. Friedrich Beck and the Rise of the General Staff* (Westport, 1995), 34.

4. A. Auersperg (Anastasius Grün), *Politische Reden und Schriften* (Vienna, 1906), 150–1.

5. W. Rudolf, 'Fürst Karl Auersperg (1814–90). Ein liberaler österreichischer Staatsmann und Politiker' (Vienna D.Phil., 1975), 44.

6. E. Heinrich, 'Der Lehrkörper der Wiener Universität in den öffentlichen Vertretungskörpern Österreichs 1861–1918' (Vienna D.Phil., 1947), 62.

7. A. Wandruszka, *Geschichte einer Zeitung. Das Schicksal der 'Presse' und der 'Neuen Freien Presse' von 1848 zur zweiten Republik* (Vienna, 1958), 64.
8. W. Wadl, *Liberalismus und soziale Frage in Österreich* (Vienna, 1987), 140.
9. Heinrich, 'Lehrkörper', 107–8.
10. E. Suess, *Erinnerungen* (Leipzig, 1916), 157.
11. T. Gomperz, *Essays und Erinnerungen* (Stuttgart, 1905), 126–32 (1885 memorandum); 36 (J.S. Mill).
12. E. Stransky, 'Adolf Beer als Politiker und Historiker' (Vienna D.Phil., 1958), 55, 59.
13. F. Edelmayer, 'Das Nationalitätenproblem in der liberalen Ära am Beispiel Böhmens. Der Deutschliberalismus und das böhmische Staatsrecht 1873–79' (Vienna D.Phil., 1993), 220.
14. Wadl, *Liberalismus und soziale Frage*, 52.
15. L. von Przibram, *Erinnerungen eines alten Österreichers*, 2 vols (Stuttgart, 1910), i, 187.
16. *A Magyar Tudományos Akadémia másfél évszázada 1825–1975* (Budapest, 1975), 142.
17. T. Gottas, *Ungarn im Zeitalter des Hochliberalismus* (Vienna, 1976), 40.
18. M. Znoj *et al.* (eds), *Český liberalizmus* (Prague, 1995), 138.

Chapter 8.   Economics, 1867–1914

1. Stransky, *Beer als Politiker*, 40.
2. *Magyarország története 1848–90*, ii, 942.
3. Ibid., ii, 922.
4. P. Heumos, *Agrarische Interessen und nationale Politik in Böhmen, 1848–89* (Wiesbaden, 1979), 81–2.
5. R.L. Rudolph, *Banking and Industrialisation in Austria-Hungary* (Cambridge, 1976), 130–1.
6. S. Kieniewicz (ed.), *Galicja w dobie autonomicznej (1850–1914). Wybór tekstów* (Wrocław, 1952), 164.
7. R. Sandgruber, 'Die Agrarrevolution in Österreich', in A. Hoffmann (ed.), *Österreich-Ungarn als Agrarstaat* (Munich, 1978), 202; I. Berend and G. Ránki, *Hungary: A Century of Economic Development* (New York, 1974), 48.
8. In C. Cipolla (ed.), *The Fontana Economic History of Europe*, Vol. 3 (Glasgow, 1973), 472.

```

9. O. Jászi, *The Dissolution of the Habsburg Monarchy* (Chicago, 1929), 185–212.
10. Sandgruber, *Ökonomie und Politik*, 179 (*Zollverein*); Hoffmann, *Österreich-Ungarn als Agrarstaat*, 201 (for 1800).
11. Rudolph, *Banking*, 66, 96, 102–6.

## Chapter 9. Society and Social Movements

1. R. Musil, *The Man Without Qualities*, 3 vols (London 1953; first published in German, 1930), i, 33.
2. L. Cassels, *Clash of Generations: A Habsburg Family Drama* (Newton Abbot, 1974), 30.
3. H. Friedjung, 'Kaiser Franz Joseph I', in his *Politische Aufsätze* (Stuttgart, 1919), 504.
4. B. Hamann (ed.), *Meine liebe, gute Freundin! Die Briefe Kaiser Franz Josephs an Katharina Schratt* (Munich 1996), overpage from 177. Franz Joseph did have a sexual relationship with a railway official's wife, Anna Nahowski, from 1875 to 1889.
5. Cassels, *Clash of Generations*, 55.
6. *Memoirs of Michael Károlyi* (London, 1956), 15.
7. H. Stekl and M. Wakounig, *Windisch-Graetz. Ein Fürstenhaus im 19. und 20. Jahrhundert* (Vienna, 1992), 235.
8. Heumos, *Agrarische Interessen*, 66.
9. F. Šišić (ed.), *Korespondencija Strossmayer–Rački*, 4 vols (Zagreb, 1928–31), iv, 21.
10. V. Škutina, *Český šlechtic František Schwarzenberg* (Prague, 1990), 77.
11. W.D. Bowman, 'Religious Associations and the Formation of Political Catholicism in Vienna, 1848 to the Seventies', *Austrian History Yearbook* (1996), 65–76 (73).
12. Himka, *Galician Villagers*, 138.
13. B. Stojisavljević, *Povijest sela. Hrvatska–Slavonija–Dalmacija 1848–1918* (Zagreb, 1973), 182.
14. *Die österreichisch-ungarische Monarchie in Wort und Bild* (Vienna, 1891), Vol. 8 (Carinthia and Carniola), 409.
15. I. Karaman, *Jadranske studije* (Rijeka, 1992), 126.
16. J. Buszko, *Dzieje ruchu robotniczego w Galicji Zachodniej 1848–1918* (Cracow, 1986), 89.
17. I. Barea, *Vienna* (London, 1966), 341.
```

18. A. G. Ardelt, 'Viktor Adler vor Gericht', in K. Stadler (ed.), *Sozialistenprozesse. Politische Justiz in Österreich 1870–1936* (Vienna, 1986), 99.
19. K.M. Lienhart-Schmidlecher, 'Prozesse in der Steiermark 1875–89', in Stadler, ibid., 78.
20. H. Mommsen, *Die Sozialdemokratie und die Nationalitätenfrage im habsburgischen Vielvölkerstaat* (Vienna, 1963), 153.
21. H. Pepper, 'Die frühe österreichische Sozialdemokratie und die Anfänge der Arbeiterkultur', in W. Maderthaner (ed.), *Sozialdemokratie und Habsburgerstaat* (Vienna, 1988), 93.
22. Cassels, *Clash of Generations*, 123.
23. A. von Czedik, *Zur Geschichte der k. k. österreichischen Ministerien 1861–1916*, 4 vols (Teschen, 1917–20), i, 340.
24. Urban, *Česká společnost*, 379.
25. Heumos, *Agrarische Interessen*, 187.
26. B. Hamann (ed.), *Kronprinz Rudolf. Schriften* (Vienna, 1979), 84: unpublished article of 1883.
27. In Memorandum of July 1895, printed in W. Rauscher, *Aussenpolitik zwischen Österreich-Ungarn und dem Deutschen Reich unter besonderer Berücksichtigung der slawischen Reichsratsabgeordneten (1887–95)* (Vienna D.Phil., 1988), Appendix, 19.
28. W. Koči, 'Das Leben des kleinen Mannes im Spiegel der Annoncen der Neuen Freien Presse des Jahres 1909' (Vienna D.Phil., 1983), 2.

Chapter 10. Nationalism

1. *Památník na oslavu padesátiletého panovnického jubileu jeho veličanstva a krále Františka Josefa I* (Prague, 1898), II.
2. W. Bahner, 'Das Sprach- und Geschichtsbewusstsein in der Rumänischen Literatur von 1780–1880', *Sitzungsberichte der Deutschen Akademie der Wissenschaften zu Berlin. Klasse für Literatur und Kunst*, Jahrgang 67 (1967), 52.
3. S.Z. Pech, 'F.L. Rieger: The Road from Liberalism to Conservatism', *Journal of Central European Affairs* 17 (1957–8), 21.
4. Calculated from J. Šlebinger, *Slovenska bibliografija za let 1907–12* (Ljubljana, 1913).
5. J. Chlebowczyk, *On Small and Young Nations in Europe* (Wrocław, 1980), 38.
6. J. Pleterski, 'Die Slowenen', in A. Wandruszka and P. Urbanitsch (eds), *Die Habsburgermonarchie. Band III. Die Völker des Reiches* (Vienna, 1980), 801–38.

412   NOTES

7. F. Palacký, *Oesterreichs Staatsidee* (Prague, 1866), 16.

8. H. Kohn, *The Idea of Nationalism* (New York, 1944), 575.

9. Cited in C. Lammich, *Das deutsche Osteuropabild in der Zeit der Reichsgründung* (Boppard am Rhein, 1977), 39, 41.

10. A. Springer, *Geschichte Oesterreichs seit dem Wiener Frieden 1809*, 2 vols (Vienna, 1863–65), ii, 8.

11. J. Rak, *Bývali Čechové* (Prague, 1994), 99.

12. P. Selver, *A Century of Czech and Slovak Poetry* (Prague, n.d.), 113–15.

13. Šišić, *Korespondencija*, i, 42 (helotisation); iii, 220 (Magyars, 1886).

14. *Narodni List* (Zadar), 20 April 1889.

15. In the educational periodical *Napredak* 10 (1869), 269.

16. Himka, *Galician Villagers*, 69.

17. J. Gruchala, *Rząd austriacki i polskie stronnictwa politiczyne w Galicji wobec 'kwestii ukraińskiej' (1890–1914)* (Katowice, 1988), 48.

18. M. Artuković, *Ideologija srpsko-hrvatskih sporova (Srbobran 1884–1902)* (Zagreb, 1991), 150–62, 241–3.

19. B. Schmid-Egger, *Klerus und Politik in Böhmen um 1900* (Munich, 1974), 54.

20. K. Verdery, *Transylvanian Villagers* (Berkeley, 1983), 209.

21. Inspector Alaupović's report in Bosnian State Archives, Joint Finance Ministry records, Pr BH 705/1914.

22. B. Milanović, 'Biskup Dobrila i njegovo doba', in J. Ravlić, *Hrvatski narodni preporod u Dalmaciji i Istri* (Zadar, 1969), 351–402 (361–2).

23. Musil, *Man Without Qualities*, i, 33.

24. L. Gumplowicz, *Der Rassenkampf. Soziologische Untersuchungen* (Innsbruck, 1883), *passim*, partic. 22, 263, 345.

25. *Narodni List*, 1890, no. 89.

26. B. Garver, *The Young Czech Party 1874–1901* (New Haven, 1978), 146.

27. L. Höbelt, *Kornblume und Kaiseradler. Die deutschfreiheitlichen Parteien Altösterreichs 1882–1918* (Vienna, 1993), 161.

28. O. Bauer, *Die Nationalitätenfrage und die Sozialdemokratie* (Vienna, 1907), 452.

Chapter 11. Hungary

1. Unless otherwise stated statistics for Hungary given in this chapter do not include Croatia.

2. For Slovak towns, L. Szarka, 'Magyarosodás és magyarosítás a felsőmagyarországi szlovák regióban a kiegyezés korában', in E. Somogyi (ed.), *Polgárosodás Középeuropában* (Budapest, 1991), 36–47. Other figures are taken mainly from *Magyarország története*, vols for 1848–90 and 1890–1918.
3. A. Apponyi, 'The Hungarian Constitution', in P. Alden (ed.), *Hungary of Today* (London, 1909), 103–208 (132); J. Andrássy, *The Development of Hungarian Constitutional Liberty* (London, 1908), 165.
4. Alden, *Hungary of Today*, 140–1.
5. G. Vermes, *István Tisza* (New York, 1985), 26.
6. Gy. Szekfű, *Három nemzedék*, 5th edn (Budapest, 1938), 214–23.
7. Vermes, *Tisza*, 24.
8. *Magyarország története 1890–1918*, chief ed. P. Hanák, 2 vols (Budapest, 1988), i, 525.
9. I. Tisza, *A helyzetről* (Budapest, 1905), 8.
10. A. Gerő, *Modern Hungarian Society in the Making* (Budapest, 1993), 111, 134.
11. N. Petrović (ed.), *Svetozar Miletić i Narodna stranka. Gradja*, 2 vols (Sremski Karlovci, 1968–69), i, 593.
12. O. Jaszi, *The Dissolution of the Habsburg Monarchy* (Chicago, 1964, 1st edn, 1929), 446.
13. G. Kemény (ed.), *Iratok a nemzetiségi kérdés történetéhez Magyarországon a dualizmus korában*, Vol. 4 (Budapest, 1966), 29.
14. I. Schlett, *A szociáldemokrácia és a magyar társadalom 1914-ig* (Budapest, 1982), 5.
15. Verdery, *Transylvanian Villagers*, 263; G. Illyés, *People of the Puszta* (Budapest, 1967; first published 1936), 15.
16. Verdery, *Transylvanian Villagers*, 215.
17. A. György, 'The State and Agriculture', in Alden, *Hungary of Today*, 259–84 (272).
18. Endre Ady, *The Explosive Century. Selected Articles*, ed. G. Cushing (Budapest, 1977), 50.
19. *Dejiny Slovenska*, Vol. 4 (Bratislava, 1986), 250.

Chapter 12. Austria–Hungary in the Early Twentieth Century

1. B. Zaar, 'Frauen und Politik in Österreich, 1890–1934', in D.F. Good *et al.* (eds), *Frauen in Österreich* (Vienna, 1994), 53.
2. K. Renner, *An der Wende zweier Zeiten* (Vienna, 1946), 243 (nature), 218 ('modern heroism').

3. *Memoirs of Alexander Spitzmüller*, tr. C. de Bussy (Boulder, 1987), 137.

4. J.W. Boyer, *Cultural and Political Crisis in Vienna. Christian Socialism in Power 1897–1918* (Chicago, 1995), 318.

5. R. Wistrich, *Socialism and the Jews. Dilemmas of Assimilation in Germany and Austria-Hungary* (London, 1982), 217.

6. H. Anderson, *Utopian Feminism. Women's Movements in Fin-de-Siècle Vienna* (New Haven, 1992), 21.

7. F. Höglinger, *Ministerpräsident Heinrich Graf Clam-Martinic* (Graz, 1964), 30.

8. J.C. Allmayer-Beck, *Ministerpräsident Baron Beck* (Vienna, 1956), 163.

9. Höbelt, *Kornblume*, 359.

10. G.A. von Geyr, *Sándor Wekerle 1848–1921* (Munich, 1993), 326.

11. J. Lukacs, *Budapest 1900* (London, 1988), 200.

12. I. Banac, 'Croat–Magyar Relations, 1904–14', *Slovene Studies* (1987), 43–8; J. Bajza, *A horvát kérdés*, ed. T. László (Budapest, 1941), 65.

13. G. Schödl, *Kroatische Nationalpolitik und 'Jugoslavenstvo'* (Munich, 1990), 289.

14. F.R. Bridge, *From Sarajevo to Sadowa. The Foreign Policy of Austria-Hungary, 1866–1914* (London, 1972), 425.

15. P. Palavestra, *Književnost Mlade Bosne*, 2 vols (Sarajevo, 1965), i, 201 (bookseller); V. Dedijer, *The Road to Sarajevo* (Manchester, 1967), 211 (Princip quotation).

16. R.A. Kann, 'Count Ottokar Czernin and Archduke Francis Ferdinand', *Journal of Central European Affairs* 16 (1956–57), 117–45 (131).

Chapter 13. To World War and Collapse

1. Lukacs, *Budapest 1900*, 186.

2. S.R. Williamson, *Austria-Hungary and the Origins of the First World War* (London, 1991), 12.

3. J. Bérenger, 'Die Österreichpolitik Frankreichs von 1848 bis 1918', in Vol. 6 of *Die Habsburgermonarchie 1848–1918: Im System der internationalen Beziehungen*. 2. Teilband (Vienna, 1993), 491–538 (491).

4. E. Rutkowski, 'Gustav Graf Kálnoky von Köröspatak: österreichisch-ungarische Aussenpolitik von 1881–85' (Vienna D.Phil., 1958), 304.

5. I. Diószegi, 'Az osztrák-magyar monarchia külpolitikája', in I. Diószegi, *Hazánk és Europa* (Budapest, 1970), 246–354.
6. Rutkowski, *Kálnoky*, 551.
7. F. Hauptmann (ed.), *Dr Ludwig Thallóczy – Tagebücher, 23/6/14–31/12/1914* (Graz, 1981), 38.
8. A.J. May, *The Passing of the Habsburg Monarchy 1914–1918*, 2 vols (Philadelphia, 1966), i, 288; J. Galántai, *Hungary in the First World War* (Budapest, 1989), 65.
9. Galántai, ibid., 69.
10. H.C. Meyer, *'Mitteleuropa' in German Thought and Action, 1815–1945* (The Hague, 1955), 213.
11. Urban, *Česká spolěcnost*, 583.
12. Höglinger, *Clam-Martinic*, 187–8.
13. H.L. Rees, *The Czechs during World War I* (Boulder, 1992), 102–3.
14. Losses from I. Deák, *Beyond Nationalism. The Social and Political History of the Habsburg Officer Corps 1848–1918* (OUP, 1992), 105–6.
15. Rees, *Czechs during World War I*, 120.
16. R.J. Wegs, *Die österreichische Kriegswirtschaft 1914–1918* (Vienna, 1979), 126.
17. Musil, *Man without Qualities*, i, 32.
18. Redlich, *Staats- und Reichsproblem*, i, XIII, VI.
19. J. Radzyna, *Stanisław Madeyski 1841–1910* (Vienna, 1983), 203, 268.
20. G. Gratz and R. Schüller, *Der wirtschaftliche Zusammenbruch Österreich-Ungarns* (New Haven, 1930), 204.

Annotated Bibliography

This bibliography seeks a middle way between unwieldy compre-
hensiveness and brief nod to English-speaking students. While the
emphasis is on English-language material, the fact that English is
increasingly being used as a second language by students and scholars in the area concerned, where German has traditionally been
widely known, leads me to feel there is a place for the inclusion of
many of the German works used, where English equivalents are lacking, and occasionally of some of the books which have been of help
in other languages of the Monarchy. The hope is to suggest something of the shape and interest of the overall historiography, if rarely
the details.

The selection reflects the book's choice of themes. It does not, however, include all items referenced in footnotes. Numbers in brackets
after abbreviated items indicate the chapter bibliography where the
item is set out in full; 'General' refers to the General section below.

Abbreviations

AHR	*American Historical Review*
AHYB	*Austrian History Yearbook*
JCEA	*Journal of Central European Affairs*
JEcH	*Journal of Economic History*
JMH	*Journal of Modern History*
MIÖGf	*Mitteilungen des Instituts für Österreichische Geschichtsforschung*
MÖSA	*Mitteilungen des Österreichischen Staatsarchivs*
SEER	*Slavonic and East European Review*

General

There is no convenient bibliography of post-1945 Habsburg historiography to parallel the heavily German-language-orientated work of
M. Uhlirz (ed.), *Handbuch der Geschichte Österreichs*, 4 vols (2nd edn,

Graz, 1963). Helpful bibliographies of particular topics can be found in numbers of the American-based *Austrian History Yearbook* and in the *Historische Zeitschrift*: Sonderhefte 1 and 9 (1962, 1980) for Hungary; 3 for Slovakia and Yugoslavia (1969), 4 for the Czech lands (1970) and 5 (1973) for Poland. Periodicals in western languages like *Acta Historica* (Hungarian); *Historica* (Czech); *Acta Poloniae Historica* (Polish); *Revue Roumaine d'Histoire* (Romanian), and *Slovene Studies* are a further aid. The annual British-based *Austrian Studies* has both literary and historical themes, and books and pamphlets from 1818 are listed and evaluated in F.R. Bridge, ed. *The Habsburg Monarchy 1804–1918* (London, 1967).

General accounts of the Monarchy's latter history are surprisingly few. In English, the most knowledgeable, also bibliographically, is C.A. Macartney's *The Habsburg Empire 1790–1918* (London, 1968), rather long at nearly half a million words, the most stimulating is A.J.P. Taylor's succinct political analysis *The Habsburg Monarchy 1809–1918* and the most conceptually ambitious Oscar Jászi's sociologically-orientated *The Dissolution of the Habsburg Monarchy* (Chicago, 1929). By contrast, Robert Kann's *A History of the Habsburg Empire, 1526–1918* (Berkeley, 1974), his *The Peoples of the Eastern Habsburg Lands, 1526–1918* (Seattle, 1984) and Macartney's *The House of Austria* (Edinburgh, 1978), an abbreviation of his 1968 work, are more informative than lively. The title of A. Sked's *The Decline and Fall of the Habsburg Empire 1815–1918* (London, 1989) suggests a broader coverage than the book actually provides, though it is suggestive for foreign policy. Of two works by leading French historians available in English, I prefer the older V.-L. Tapié, *The Rise and Fall of the Habsburg Monarchy* (tr. London, 1971) to J. Bérenger's *A History of the Habsburg Empire, 1700–1918* (tr. London, 1997). N. Pelling, *The Habsburg Empire 1815–1918* (London, 1996) is a crisply-written school textbook. Books in German place a natural emphasis on the area which became the Austrian republic after 1918. Two series in German resume the state of knowledge. The magisterial *Die Habsburgermonarchie, 1848–1918*, eds. P. Urbanitsch and A. Wandruszka (Vienna, 1973–) covers the whole Monarchy, in six volumes to date, on economics, administration, nations, religions, military affairs and foreign policy; of the other, *Österreichische Geschichte*, ed. H. Wolfram, the most relevant here are those by G. Klingenstein (1998), H. Rumpler (1997) and R. Sandgruber (1995) on the periods 1699–1806, 1804–1918 and socio-economic history respectively.

Of individual countries Hungary is best served in English, with C.A. Macartney, *Hungary: A Short History* (Edinburgh, 1962) offering conciseness and E. Pamlényi (ed.), *A History of Hungary* (London, 1975) and P.F. Sugar (ed.), *A History of Hungary* (London, 1990) informed Marxist and non-Marxist approaches respectively, the latter with more political detail. In the absence of a recent full history of the Czechs in English, A. Hermann, *A History of the Czechs* (London, 1975) and the opening chapters of W.V. Wallace, *Czechoslovakia* (Boulder, 1976) may be used. The classic work of E. Denis, *La Bohême depuis la Montagne-Blanche*, 2 vols (Paris, 1903) is still useful for the Czech national movement. *Bohemia*, ed. M. Teich (Cambridge, 1998) offers fascinating new views but no overall picture. P. Wandycz, *The Lands of Partitioned Poland, 1795–1918* (Seattle, London, 1974) is helpful for the Habsburg province of Galicia, on which P.R. Magocsi, has provided *Galicia. A Historical Survey and Bibliographical Guide* (Toronto, 1983). Available for smaller nations are S.J. Kirschbaum, *A History of Slovakia* (New York, 1995); M. Tanner, *Croatia. A Nation Forged in War* (New Haven, London, 1997) and S. Goldstein, *Croatia. A History* (London, 1999). There are chapters on all the Monarchy's nations, in Volume 3 of the *Austrian History Yearbook* (3 parts, 1967) and in Volume 3 of *Die Habsburgermonarchie*, above (1980). Finally, one key disputed region has been surveyed in English by both sides: G. Barta (ed.), *History of Transylvania* (Budapest, 1994); S. Pascu, *A History of Transylvania* (Detroit, 1982).

Chapter 1.   Foundations

Habsburg Society

A concise, knowledgeable introduction is C. Ingrao, *The Habsburg Monarchy 1618–1815* (Cambridge, 1994), but P.G.M. Dickson, *Finance and Government under Maria Theresa 1740–80*, 2 vols (Oxford, 1987) is invaluable for specialists. For the concept of the 'court-orientated society', see the fine studies of E. Bruckmüller's *Sozialgeschichte Österreichs* (Vienna, 1985 – useful for the whole period of this book) and R.J.W. Evans, *The Making of the Habsburg Monarchy 1550–1700* (Oxford, 1979). H. Marczali, *Hungary in the Eighteenth Century* (Cambridge, 1910) is still useful for Hungarian constitutional details, but for a modern interpretation see L. Péter, 'Montesquieu's Paradox on Freedom and Hungary's Constitution, 1790–1990', *History of Political*

Thought, Spring 1995, 77–104. J. Bérenger and B.L. Király discuss Austria and Hungary respectively in chapters of W.D. Callahan (ed.), *Church and State in Catholic Europe of the Eighteenth Century* (Cambridge, 1977). For the army, see C. Duffy, *The Army of Maria Theresa* (London, 1977). Valuable studies of political and cultural aspects of a leading aristocratic family's life respectively are provided by R. Gates Coon, *The Landed Estates of the Esterházy Princes* (Baltimore, 1994) and M. Horányi, *The Magnificence of Esterháza* (tr. Budapest, 1962).

In a wide literature on the old social order on the land R. Rosdolsky stands out for clarity: 'The distribution of the agrarian product in feudalism', *JEcH* 2 (1951), 247–65; 'On the nature of peasant serfdom in Central and Eastern Europe', *JCEA* 12 (1952–3), 128–39. For Austrian living conditions see, besides Bruckmüller's *Sozialgeschichte* above, J. Komlos's interestingly speculative *Nutrition and Economic Development in the Eighteenth-Century Habsburg Monarchy* (Princeton, 1989) and R. Sandgruber's masterly *Die Anfänge der Konsumgesellschaft* (Vienna, 1982), covering this and the next century's consumption patterns. G.G. Grüll in *Bauer, Herr und Landesfürst: Soziale Bestrebungen der oberösterreichischen Bauern, 1650–1850* (Linz, 1963) and H. Stekl on treatment of the poor in *Österreichische Zuchts- und Arbeitshäuser 1671–1920* (Vienna, 1978) provide fascinating social history monographs. Hungarian socio-economic themes are tackled in J. Kallay 'The Management of Big Estates in Hungary, 1711–1848', *AHYB* 21 (1985), 339–62; Z. Kirilly *et al.*, 'Production et productivité agricoles en Hongrie à l'époque du feudalisme tardif (1550–1850)', *Nouvelles études historiques publiées à l'occasion du XII Congrès International des Sciences Historiques*, vol. 1 (1965), 581–638, and in D. Kosary, *Culture and Society in Eighteenth-Century Hungary* (Budapest, 1987). G. Ortutay and T. Bodrogi have edited *Europa et Hungaria* on Hungarian ethnographic themes (Budapest, 1963). For early eighteenth-century Croatia I am indebted to Catherine Simpson for the loan of her *Pavao Ritter Vitezović: defining national identity in the Baroque Age* (Cambridge D.Phil., 1991).

Enlightenment

A very readable introduction is E. Wangermann's *The Austrian Achievement 1700–1800* (London, 1973). Socio-economic reform themes are also quite well covered in English, particularly for

Bohemia: for the land by E. Link, *The Emancipation of the Austrian Peasant, 1740–98* (New York, 1949) and W.E. Wright, *Serf, Seigneur and Sovereign: Agrarian Reform in Eighteenth-Century Bohemia* (Minnesota, 1966); for manufacturing by H. Freudenberger and the Czech economic historian, A. Klima. Examples are H. Freudenberger, 'Industrialisation in Bohemia and Moravia in the eighteenth century', *JCEA* 19 (1959), 347–56, and *The Industrialisation of an East Central European City: Brno and the Fine Woollen Industry in the 18th Century* (Edington, Wiltshire, 1977); A. Klima, 'Domestic Industry, Manufactures and Early Industrialisation in Bohemia', *JEcH* (1985), 509–27; Industrial Development in Bohemia 1640–1781,' *Past and Present*, no. 11 (1956–7), 57–97. In German two collective works edited by R. Plaschka *et al.*, *Österreich im Europa der Aufklärung*, 2 vols (Vienna, 1985) and E. Zöllner (ed.), *Österreich im Zeitalter des aufgeklärten Absolutismus* (Vienna, 1983), are particularly wide-ranging.

Enlightened statecraft may be followed through F.A. Szabo, *Kaunitz and Enlightened Absolutism, 1753–1780* (Columbia UP, 1994), R.A. Kann, *Studies in Austrian Intellectual History*, part 3 (London, 1960: for Sonnenfels) and K.-H. Osterloh, *Joseph von Sonnenfels und die österreichische Reformbewegung* (Lübeck, 1970). D. Beales's *Joseph II. I. In the Shadow of Maria Theresa, 1741–1780* (Cambridge, 1987) can serve as a modern biography also for Maria Theresa, deepening E. Crankshaw's *Maria Theresa* (London, 1969). See also K.A. Roider Jr, *Austria's Eastern Question 1700–1790* (Princeton, 1982). Intriguing implications of the enlightened project can be sampled from J. Van Horn Melton, *Absolutism and Eighteenth-Century Origins of Compulsory Schooling in Prussia and Austria* (Cambridge, 1988) and H.E. Strakosch's splendid study *State Absolutism and the Rule of Law. The Struggle for the Codification of Civil Law in Austria, 1753–1811* (Sidney, 1966). But the religious theme of Enlightenment is little reflected in English. See from the extensive German literature: E. Winter, *Der Josephinismus. Die Geschichte des österreichischen Reformkatholizismus 1740–1848* (Berlin, 1962); F. Maass's documentary collection, *Der Josephinismus. Quellen zu seiner Geschichte*, 5 vols (Vienna, 1951–61), with its lengthy introductions, and H. Rieser, *Der Geist des Josephinismus* (Vienna, 1963) which provides a convenient summary of the Catholic critique of the religious reforms shared by Maass. For later perspectives: E. Kovács (ed.), *Katholische Aufklärung vor Josephinismus* (Munich, 1979) and another key theme: H. Wunder, 'Die Institutionalisierung der Invaliden-, Alters- und Hinterbliebenenversorgung der Staatsbediensteten in Österreich (1748–90)', *MIÖG* 92, (1984), 341–406.

Chapter 2.   Joseph II and his Legacy

Many works from the previous chapter remain helpful. The fullest study of Joseph II's reign is still P. Mitrofanov's *Joseph II. Seine politische und kulturelle Tätigkeit*, 2 vols (tr. Vienna, 1912; Russian edn, 1910). Stimulating biographies are F. Fejtö, *Joseph II*; S. K. Padover, *The Revolutionary Emperor. Joseph II of Austria* (2nd edn, London, 1967) and in German V. Bibl, *Kaiser Joseph II. Ein Vorkämpfer der grossdeutschen Idee* (Vienna, 1943). For convenient modern summaries see P.B. Bernard, *Joseph II* (New York, 1968); T.C W. Blanning's *Joseph II and Enlightened Despotism in Austria* (London, 1970 – concise text and documents) and D. Beales, 'Was Joseph II an Enlightened Despot?', in R. Robertson and E. Timms (eds), *The Austrian Enlightenment and its Aftermath* (Edinburgh, 1991), 1–21. Bernard criticises Joseph in *The Limits of Enlightenment. Joseph II and the Law* (Urbana, 1979); see also his *Jesuits and Jacobins. Enlightenment and Enlightened Despotism in Austria* (Urbana, 1971) and biography of police chief Pergen, *From the Enlightenment to the Police State. The Public Life of Johann Christian Pergen* (Urbana, 1991). Wangermann's analysis is in *From Joseph II to the Jacobin Trials* (Oxford, 1959). For the organisation of censorship: O. Sashegyi, *Zensur und Geistesfreiheit unter Joseph II* (Budapest, 1958). Religious aspects are well covered in C.C. O'Brien, *Ideas of Religious Toleration in the time of Joseph II* (Philadelphia, 1969) and H. Hollerweger, *Die Reform des Gottesdienstes zur Zeit des Josephinismus in Österreich* (Regensburg, 1976) – both also relevant for Maria Theresa's reign – and vol. 3 of Maass, *Josephinismus* (1). R. Rosdolsky is indispensable for the 1789 tax law: *Die grosse Steuer- und Agrarreform Josefs II* (Warsaw, 1961).

Convenient for the Turkish war are K.A. Roider Jr, 'Kaunitz, Joseph II and the Turkish War', *Slavic Review*, 54 (1976), 538–56, (which argues for Kaunitz as the more bellicose) and P.B. Bernard, 'Austria's Last Turkish War', *AHYB*, 19–20 (1983–84), 15–32. Of works on the Hungarian response to Joseph, H. Haselsteiner's concise *Joseph II und die Komitate Ungarns* (Vienna, 1983) is less concerned with Hungarian enlightenment than B. Király, *Hungary in the Late Eighteenth Century* (New York, 1969) or B.C. Ives, *Enlightenment and National Revival . . . in Late Eighteenth-Century Hungary* (London, 1979). For other responses: R. Kerner's *Bohemia in the Eighteenth Century* (New York, 1932, reprinted 1969); W.W. Davis, *Joseph II. Imperial Reformer for the Austrian Netherlands* (The Hague, 1974); K. Hitchins, *The Rumanian National Movement in Transylvania, 1780–1849* (Cambridge, Mass.,

1969); H. Glassl, *Der österreichische Einrichtungswerk in Galizien (1772–1790)* (Wiesbaden, 1975). Kerner concentrates on the noble Diet of 1790–92; for Czech speakers' response Czech is necessary: F. Kutnar, *Sociálně myšlenková tvářnost obrozenského lidu* (Prague, 1948); J. Haubelt, *České osvícenství* (Prague, 1986). The standard work on Leopold is A. Wandruszka's *Leopold II*, 2 vols (Vienna, 1963–65) but Wangermann, *From Joseph II* above can be used in English for his plans. The expert on revolutionary circles is H. Reinalter, most concisely in *Österreich und die französische Revolution* (Vienna, 1988).

Chapter 3. Metternich's Austria. Pyrrhic Victory Abroad; Social Question at Home

Issues of the French wars can be followed through: K.A. Roider Jr, *Baron Thugut and Austria's Response to the French Revolution* (Princeton, 1987); P.R. Sweet, *Friedrich von Gentz: Defender of the Old Order* (Westport, Connecticut, 1941); W.C. Langsam, *The Napoleonic Wars and German Nationalism in Austria* (New York, 1930; still the only full treatment in English); D. Kosary, *Napoléon et la Hongrie* (Budapest, 1979) and A. Ernstberger, *Böhmens freiwilliger Kriegseinsatz gegen Napoleon* (Munich, 1963). For the Archduke Karl: G.E. Rothenberg, *Napoleon's Great Adversary; the Archduke Charles and the Austrian Army* (Bloomington, 1982).

There has not been a major biography of Metternich since H. Srbik's celebrated if somewhat indulgent *Metternich: der Staatsmann und der Mensch*, 2 vols (Munich, 1925:). I have found most helpful in English: G.A. de Bertier de Sauvigny, *Metternich and his Times* (London, 1962) and A. Palmer, *Metternich* (London, 1972). Key aspects of his foreign policy are well covered in: H. Kissinger, *A World Restored. Europe after Napoleon* (New York, 1964) for the Congress system; P. Schroeder, *Metternich's Diplomacy at its Zenith 1820–23* (Austin, 1962); E. Kraehe, *Metternich and the German Question* (Princeton, 1963: up to 1814; volume 2 on 1815 is too detailed); and R.D. Billinger, *Metternich and the German Question: States' Rights and Federal Diets, 1820–34* (London, 1991). For Metternich's domestic policies, see A.J. Haas, *Metternich, Reorganisation and Nationality, 1813–18* (Wiesbaden, 1963), which somewhat overstates its case; D.E. Emerson, *Metternich and the Political Police: Society and Subversion in the Habsburg Monarchy, 1815–30* (The Hague, 1968) and R.W. Seton-Watson's lectures digested in 'Metternich and internal Austrian policy' in

SEER 17 (1938–9), 539–55, and 18 (1939–40), 129–41, which is clearer than E. Radvany, *Metternich's Proposals for Reform in Austria* (The Hague, 1971). Helpful German monographs are F.T. Hoefer, *Pressepolitik und Polizeistaat Metternichs* (Munich, 1983) and G. Seide, *Regierungspolitik und öffentliche Meinung im Kaisertum Österreich anlässlich der polnischen Novemberrevolution* (Munich, 1971).

On socio-economic themes there is no English equivalent to R. Sandgruber, *Ökonomie und Politik* (Vienna, 1995) or the detailed treatment in *Magyarország története 1790–1848*, chief ed. Gy. Mérei, 2 vols (Budapest, 1980) but Macartney (General) is informative. D.F. Good, *The Economic Rise of the Habsburg Monarchy, 1750–1914* (Berkeley, 1975) is an excellent survey. Alternative views of early industrialisation can be found in N.T Gross, 'Industrial Revolution in the Habsburg Monarchy', in C. Cipolla (ed.), *Fontana Economic History of Europe*, Vol. 4, part 1 (London, 1973) and R. Rudolph, 'The Pattern of Austrian Industrial Growth from the Eighteenth Century to the Early Twentieth Century', *AHYB* 11, 1975, 3–25. On this topic, English-language historiography tends to provides the theories, and German-language works more descriptive detail, as in F. Tremel's solid *Wirtschafts- und Sozialgeschichte Österreichs* (Vienna, 1969) or the thirty helpful concise biographies of J. Mentschl and G. Otruba, *Österreichische Industrielle und Bankiers* (Vienna, 1965). For the Czech lands, B. Michel, 'La révolution industrielle dans les pays tchèques au dix-neuvieme siècle', *Annales* 20 (1965), 984–1005, and, despite the dry title, A. Klima, 'The Beginnings of the Machine-Building Industry in the Czech Lands', JEcH 4 (1975), 49–78, are livelier reading than J. Purš, 'The industrial revolution in the Czech lands', *Historica*, 2 (1960), pp. 183–272. J. Blum, 'Transportation and Industry in Austria, 1815–48', *JMH* (1943), 24–38, fills a gap.

On rural issues J. Blum, *Noble Landowners and Agriculture in Austria, 1815–48* (Baltimore, 1948) is excellent. Fascinating case studies are provided of the Schwarzenberg and Lobkowitz families by H. Stekl in *Österreichische Aristokratie im Vormärz* (Vienna, 1973) and of a Bohemian aristocrat's world view by C. Thienen-Adlerflycht, *Graf Leo Thun im Vormärz* (Graz, 1967). For Hungary, B. Ivanyi, 'From feudalism to capitalism: the economic background of Széchenyi's reform in Hungary', *JCEA* 20–21 (1960–61), 268–88; Gy. Mérei, 'L'essor de l'agriculture capitaliste en Hongrie', *Revue d'histoire moderne et contemporaine* (1964), 51–64, and J. Varga, *Typen und Probleme des bäuerlichen Grundbesitzes in Ungarn (1767–1849)* (Budapest, 1963) give non-Hungarian readers some benefits of this richly researched field.

Czech rural life is less accessible: see F.A. Brauner's contemporary
Böhmische Bauernzustände (Vienna, 1847) and M. Michálek (ed.),
Zemědelství buditelé (Prague, 1937), on agricultural pioneers. For
Galicia, see S. Kieniewicz, *The Emancipation of the Polish Peasantry*
(Chicago, 1969) and J.-P. Himka's eloquent *Galician Villagers and
the Ukrainian National Movement in the Nineteenth Century* (Edmonton, 1988).

Cultural life is discussed in I. Barea, *Vienna. Legend and Reality*
(London, 1966), an excellent social history, and S. Musulin, *Vienna
in the Age of Metternich* (London, 1975). They illustrate censorship
issues discussed more fully in J. Marx, *Die österreichische Zensur im Vormärz* (Vienna, 1959). See also W.E. Yates's succinct biographies *Nestroy* and *Grillparzer* (Cambridge, 1972, 1974 respectively).

Chapter 4. Liberalism and Nationalism

Liberalism

For Church problems in this period, see E. Hosp, *Kirche Österreichs im
Vormärz, 1815–50* (Vienna, 1971) and B. Gordon, 'The Challenge of
Industrialisation. The Catholic Church and the Working Class in
and around Vienna, 1815–48', *AHYB* 9–10 (1973–4), 123–43.
English-language material on Austro-German liberalism is scanty.
R.J.W. Evans,' Josephinism, "Austrianness", and the Revolution of
1848', in Robertson and Timms, *Austrian Enlightenment* (2), 145–60,
gives the intellectual feel of the period. In German the study of evolving bourgeois structures and mentalities throughout the Monarchy
has been transformed by the volumes edited by E. Bruckmüller *et al.*,
Das Bürgertum in der Habsburgermonarchie (Vienna, 1990) and H. Stekl
et al., *Durch Arbeit, Besitz, Wissen und Gerechtigkeit* (Vienna, 1992).
There is also a helpful monograph on the *Leseverein*: W. Brauneder,
Leseverein und Rechtskultur (Vienna, 1992). For older intellectual history, E. Winter, *Frühliberalismus in der Donaumonarchie* (Berlin, 1968).

English material is richer elswhere, for example: G. Barany, *Stephen Széchenyi and the Awakening of Hungarian Nationalism, 1791–1841*
(Princeton, 1968); B. Király, *Ferenc Deák* (Boston, 1975); A.C.
Janos, *The Politics of Backwardness in Hungary, 1825–1945* (Princeton,
1982); K.R. Greenfield, *Economics and Liberalism in the Risorgimento;
A Study of Nationalism in Lombardy, 1815–48* (revised edn, Baltimore,
1965); B.K. Reinfeld, *Karel Havlíček (1821–56): A National Liberation*

Leader of the Czech Renascence (New York, 1982); and E. Murray Despalatović, *Ljudevit Gaj and the Illyrian Movement* (Boulder, 1975). Some important themes, however, need German, as in L. Révész on the transformation of the old feudal parliament: *Die Anfänge des ungarischen Parlamentarismus* (Munich, 1968) and M. Csáky on the emergence of a patriotic intelligentsia in *Von der Aufklärung zum Liberalismus. Studien zum Frühliberalismus in Ungarn* (Vienna, 1981). But J. Mazsu's statistically orientated *The Social History of the Hungarian Intelligentsia, 1815–1914* (Boulder, 1997) helps here.

Nationalism

Classic intellectual and sociological cases for nationalism's modernity are, respectively, E. Kedourie, *Nationalism* (4th edn, Oxford, 1993) and E. Gellner, *Nations and Nationalism* (Oxford, 1983). An influential social mobilisation approach is that of M. Hroch, *Social Preconditions of National Revival in Europe* (tr. Cambridge, 1985). P. Sugar targets eastern Europe's vogue for 'historic rights' in I. Lederer and P. Sugar (eds), *Nationalism in Eastern Europe* (Seattle, London, 1969) which has chapters on particular nations, like Vol. 3 of the *Austrian History Yearbook* mentioned above (General).

In addition to Reinfeld above, Czech national mobilisation is explored in P. Brock and G. Skilling's wide-ranging edited volume, *The Czech Renascence in the Nineteenth Century* (Toronto, 1970). For cultural-ideological issues, see V. Začek, *Palacký: The Historian as Scholar and Nationalist* (The Hague, 1970); M. Součková, *The Czech Romantics* (The Hague, 1958); R. Wellek, *Essays on Czech Literature* (The Hague, 1963) and particularly the key studies of J. Kořálka, *Tschechen im Habsburgerreich und in Europa 1815–1914* (Vienna, 1991), some of whose themes are present in H.A. Agnew, 'Noble *Natio* and the Modern Nation: the Czech case', *AHYB* 23 (1992), 50–71. Palacký's views are available in his *Gedenkblätter. Auswahl von Denkschriften, Aufsätzen und Briefen aus den letzten fünfzig Jahren* (Prague, 1874).

There is no satisfactory biography of Kossuth in English or German. Hungarian romantic nationalism can be followed through extracts from the national poet, Petőfi: B. Köpeczi (ed.), *Rebel or Revolutionary? Sándor Petőfi* (Budapest, 1973) or Gy. Illyés's biography, *Petőfi* (tr. Budapest, 1973); and L. Deme, 'Writers and Essayists and the Rise of Magyar Nationalism in the 1820's and 1830's', *Slavic Review* 43 (1984), 624–40. For other varieties of small nation nationalism rooted in romanticism, see H. Kohn, *Panslavism* (New York,

1953); D. Wilson, *The Life and Times of Vuk Stefanović Karadžić, 1787–1864* (Oxford, 1970); P. Brock, *The Slovak National Awakening* (Toronto, 1976) and K. Hitchins on the Transylvanian Romanians (2) and in *Orthodoxy and Nationality. Andreiu Şaguna and the Rumanians of Transylvania, 1846–73* (Cambridge, Mass., 1977). On the Illyrian movement Despalatović on Gaj above, and W. Vucinich, in S. Winter and J. Held (eds), *Intellectual and Social Developments in the Habsburg Empire* (Boulder, 1975), 55–113, are clearer than the rather convoluted if interesting speculations of W. Kessler, *Politik, Kultur und Gesellschaft in Kroatien und Slawonien in der ersten Hälfte des 19. Jahrhunderts* (Munich, 1981). For the leading Croat expert, see J. Šidak, 'Der Illyrismus – Ideen und Probleme' in L. Holotík (ed.), *L'udovít Štur und die slawische Wechselseitigkeit'* (Bratislava, 1969), 61–89.

Chapter 5. 1848–49

Older books are still worth starting with: P. Robertson, *Revolutions of 1848. A Social History* (Princeton, 1952) for liveliness and F. Fejtö (ed.), *The Opening of an Era – 1848* (London, 1948) for analysis. The work of Anton Springer mentioned is *Geschichte Oesterreichs seit dem Wiener Frieden 1809*, 2 vols (Leipzig, 1863–5). The major centres have standard English monographs: J.R. Rath, *The Viennese Revolution of 1848* (Austin, 1957); I. Deák, *The Lawful Revolution: Louis Kossuth and the Hungarian Revolution of 1848* (New York, 1979); S. Pech, *The Czech Revolution of 1848* (Chapel Hill, North Carolina, 1969) and P. Ginsborg, *Daniele Manin and the Venetian Revolution of 1848–49* (Cambridge, 1979). See also J.V. Polišensky's *Aristocrats and the Crowd in the Year 1848* (New York, 1980), with lively anecdotes and a Czech emphasis if less clearly focused; A. Sked on north Italy: *The Survival of the Habsburg Empire. Radetzy, the Imperial Army and Class War* (London, 1979); L. Deme, *The Hungarian Radical Left in the Hungarian Revolution of 1848* (Boulder, 1976); G. Spira, *A Hungarian Count in the Revolution of 1848* (Budapest, 1974: on Széchenyi) and the symposium on 'National Interests and Cosmopolitan Goals in the Hungarian Revolution of 1848–9', *AHYB* 12–13 (1976–7), 3–89. Despalatović, *Gaj* (3) again covers Croatia, where J. Šidak's definitive essays are in Croatian only: *Studije iz hrvatske povijesti za revolucije 1848–1849* (Zagreb, 1979).

Electoral issues are illuminatingly dealt with in P. Burian, *Die Nationalitäten in Cisleithanien und das Wahlrecht der Märzrevolution*

1848/49 (Graz, 1962); R. Rosdolsky, *Die Bauernabgeordneten im konsti-tuierenden österreichischen Reichstag 1848–1849* (Vienna, 1976), and A. Czizmadia, *A magyar választási rendszer 1848-ben* (Budapest, 1963). Major social themes are covered in W. Häusler's *Von der Massenarmut zur Arbeiterbewegung. Demokratische und soziale Frage in der Wiener Revolution von 1848* (Vienna, 1979 – a key work) and J. Varga's solid study of peasant emancipation in Hungary, *A jobbágyfelszabadítás kivívása 1848-ben* (Budapest, 1971). The central European context of the nationality problem is brought out in J. Droz's indispensable *L'Europe centrale. Evolution historique de l'idée de 'Mitteleuropa'* (Paris, 1960). R.A. Kann's *The Multi-National Empire* (New York, 1950) is the classic treatment of plans to federalise the Monarchy. For a modern treatment of the German problem, W. Siemann, *The German Revolution of 1848–49* (tr. London, 1998). Adolph Schwarzenberg covers Schwarzenberg in his *Prince Felix zu Schwarzenberg, Prime Minister of Austria 1848–52* (New York, 1946) and E. K. Sieber the beginnings of a Bohemian German backlash in *Ludwig von Löhner. Ein Vorkämpfer des Deutschtums in Bohmen, Mähren und Schlesien im Jahre 1848–1849* (Munich, 1965). Engels' journalistic articles were first published together under Karl Marx's name as *Revolution and Counter-Revolution, Germany in 1848* in Glasgow in 1896. See also R. Rosdolsky, *Engels and the 'non-historic' peoples: the national question in the revolution of 1848* (tr. Glasgow, 1986).

Chapter 6. Eventful Transition

The best treatment of Franz Joseph in these early years is still J. Redlich, *Emperor Francis Joseph of Austria* (tr. New York, 1929). Schwarzenberg's German policy is debated by K. Rock and H. Rumpler in *AHYB* 11 (1975), 85–105 and R. Austensen, 'Felix Schwarzenberg: Realpolitiker or Machiavellian? The Evidence of the Dresden Conference', *MÖSA*, 30 (1977), 97–118. For the Crimean war P.W. Schroeder's article, 'Bruck versus Buol: The Dispute over Austrian Eastern Policy, 1853–55', *JMH* 40 (1968), 193–217, is preferable to his rather dense *Austria, Great Britain and the Crimean War* (Ithaca, 1972). See also C.W. Halberg's clear *Francis Joseph and Napoleon III, 1852–64* (New York, 1955).

The domestic side of neo-absolutism is not well served in English, with the exception of economic policy: J. Komlos, *The Habsburg Monarchy as a Customs Union* (Princeton, 1983); T. Huerta, *Economic Growth*

BIBLIOGRAPHY

and Economic Policy in a Multi-National Setting. The Habsburg Monarchy, 1841–65 (New York, 1977) and Good, *Economic Development* (3). Key works are H.-H. Brandt's comprehensive *Der österreichische Neoabsolutismus. Staatsfinanzen und Politik 1848–60*, 2 vols (Göttingen, 1978); H. Lentze, *Die Universitätsreform des Ministers Graf Leo Thun-Hohenstein* (Vienna, 1962), K. Frommelt, *Die Sprachenfrage im österreichischen Unterrichtswesen, 1848–59* (Graz, 1963) and A. Schmidt-Brentano, *Die Armee in Österreich. Militär, Staat und Gesellschaft 1848–67* (Boppard am Rhein, 1975) which is less technical than *Die Bewaffnete Macht* (1987), Volume 5 of *Die Habsburgermonarchie* (General). There is no biography of Bach, but W. Heindl's 'Bachs neue Verwaltung im österreichischen Neo-Absolutismus', *Österreichische Osthefte*, 22 (1980), 231–63 is helpful. For Bohemia, O. Urban, *Česká společnost 1848–1918* (Prague, 1982: invaluable from now on, also available in German) and C. Stölzl, *Die Ära Bach in Böhmen* (Munich, 1971) offer a range not available in English, though S. Kimball, *Czech Nationalism: A Study of the Czech National Theatre Movement, 1845–83* (London, 1964) lifts the curtain on one area. For Croatia, M. Gross lucidly digests her Croatian language monographs on the 1848–80 period in *Die Anfänge des modernen Kroatien* (Vienna, 1993). There are good monographs on Hungarian socio-economic themes: J. Held, *The Modernisation of Agriculture. Rural Transformation in Hungary 1848–1975* (Boulder, 1980) and V. Sándor, *Die Hauptmerkmale der industriellen Entwicklung in Ungarn zur Zeit des Absolutismus, 1849–67* (Budapest, 1960).

For the 1860s English, lacking classics, whose conclusions are still worth consulting (L. Eisenmann, *Le compromis autriche-hongrois de 1867*, 2 vols (Paris, 1904); J. Redlich, *Das österreichische Staats- und Reichsproblem*, 2 vols (Leipzig, 1920–26)), must make do with general books and biographies (Redlich on Franz Joseph above; Király on Deák (3); Hitchins on Şaguna (4); P. Bödy, *Joseph Eötvös and the Modernisation of Hungary, 1840–70* (Philadelphia, 1972). But see also G. Szabad, *Hungarian Political Trends between Revolution and Compromise* (Budapest, 1977) and S. Pech, 'Passive resistance of the Czechs, 1863–79', *SEER* 36 (1957–8), 434–52. Haselsteiner is usefully concise on Hungarian Serbs in the 1860s: *Die Serben Ungarns und der österreichisch-ungarische Ausgleich* (Vienna, 1976). On the vast German question, E. Kraehe provides concise background in 'Austria and the Problem of Reform in the German confederation, 1851–63', *AHR* 56 (1950–51), 276–94; H. Rumpler a modern Austrian view in *Österreich 1804–1918. Eine Chance für Mitteleuropa* (Vienna, 1997), R. Bridge a mildly quizzical revisionism in 'Österreich-(Ungarn) unter den Grossmächten', in Vol. 6 of *Die Habsburgermonarchie*, Teilband I (Vienna, 1993), 196–373, and W. Carr and D. Blackbourn convenient overviews in *The Origins of the Wars of German Unification* (London, 1991) and *The Fontana History of Modern Germany, 1780–1918* (London, 1997), ch. 5 respectively.

Chapter 7.   Liberalism

In English see C. Schorske's classic essays on liberal culture and politics in his *Fin-de-siècle Vienna* (London, 1980). A.J. May's *The Habsburg Monarchy, 1867–1914* (Cambridge, Mass., 1950) is a sound introduction. For older German literature on this topic, see G. Franz, *Liberalismus. Die deutschliberale Bewegung in der habsburgischen Monarchie* (Munich, 1955) and K. Eder, *Der Liberalismus in Alt-Österreich* (Vienna, 1955: emphasis on anti-clericalism). Recent research on the bourgeoisie presented in Bruckmüller (ed.), (4) and Stekl (ed.), (4) explores social-cultural angles and the rise of national elites in non-dominant groups. An ideological picture is still best built from memoirs and biographies, for example those for Eduard Suess, Karl Auersperg, Adolf Beer and Theodor Gomperz referenced in the text of this chapter, as also A. Arneth, *Aus meinem Leben*, 2 vols (Vienna, 1891–2); C. Felder, *Erinnerungen eines Wiener Bürgermeisters* (Vienna, 1964); M. Wolf, *Ignaz von Plener* (Munich, 1975); E. von Plener, *Erinnerungen*, 3 vols (Stuttgart, 1911–21). Various aspects of Austro-German liberal experience are covered in S.C. Lackey, *The Rebirth of the Habsburg Army. Friedrich Beck and the Rise of the General Staff* (Westport, London, 1995: for Kuhn's liberal reforms); K. Paupié, *Handbuch der österreichischen Pressegeschichte, 1848–1959* (Vienna, 1960); D. Harrington-Müller, *Der Fortschrittsklub im Abgeordnetenhaus des österreichischen Reichsrates 1873–1914* (Vienna, 1972), and W. Wadl's eye-opening *Liberalismus und soziale Frage in Österreich. Deutschliberale Reaktionen und Einfluss auf die früuhe österreichische Arbeiterbewegung, 1867–79* (Vienna, 1987). K.H. Rossbacher, *Literatur und Liberalismus. Zur Kultur der Ringstrassenzeit in Wien* (Vienna, 1992) offers stimulating interpretations of literary texts.

Again English is somewhat stronger on non-German speakers. Alongside G. Barany's key analysis of the constitutional situation created by Dualism: 'Ungarns Verwaltung, 1848–1918' in volume 2 of *Die Habsburgermonarchie* (Vienna, 1975), 304–468, there is L. Péter, 'The Dualist Character of the 1867 Hungarian Settlement', in

G. Ránki (ed.), *Hungarian History-World History* (Budapest, 1984), 85–164; P. Bödy, *Joseph Eötvös and the Modernisation of Hungary, 1840–70* (Philadelphia, 1972); Király, *Deák* (3); Janos, *Politics of Backwardness* (4); and A. Vámbéry's intriguing *The Story of my Struggles*, 2 vols (London, 1904). For the Czechs there is B. Garver's immensely informative *The Young Czech Party 1874–1901* (New Haven, 1975); for socially-orientated biography not otherwise available see Z. Šolle, *Vojta Náprstek i jeho doba* (Prague, 1994). Czech readers have a feast in the compendious extracts of M. Znoj (ed.), *Český liberalizmus. Texty a osobnosti* (Prague, 1995), likewise Slovene readers in I. Prijatelj's standard work, *Slovenska kulturnopolitična in slovstvena zgodovina 1848–1895*, 6 vols (Ljubljana, 1955–85, first published 1938–40). Galician Poles are elusive, but there are good documents in Polish: S. Kieniewicz (ed.), *Galicja v dobie autonomicznej (1850–1914)*. *Wybór tekstów* (Wrocław, 1952).

For foreign policy, F.R. Bridge and I. Diószegi are the authorities: see their *From Sadowa to Sarajevo. The Foreign Policy of Austria-Hungary, 1866–1914* (London, 1972) and *Hungarians in the Ballhausplatz* (Budapest, 1983: for Andrássy) respectively, as also Bridge's *The Habsburg Monarchy among the Great Powers 1815–1918* (New York, 1990). For a leading Austrian diplomatic historian: F. Engel-Janosi, *Geschichte auf dem Ballhausplatz. Essays zur österreichischen Aussenpolitik 1830–1945* (Graz, 1963). There are many older monographs on the 'Eastern Question' in English, for example G. Rupp, *A Wavering Friendship* (Cambridge, Mass., 1941) on Austro-Russian relations in the 1875–8 crisis.

Chapter 8. Economics

English is fuller for this topic, though most widely informative is volume I of *Die Habsburgermonarchie* (General), entitled *Die wirtschaftliche Entwicklung* (1973). Alongside works mentioned under chapter 3 above, particularly Good, *Economic Development*, section 3, see H. Matis (ed.), *The Economic Development of Austria since 1870* (Aldershot, 1994); R.L. Rudolph, *Banking and Industrialisation in Austria-Hungary: the Role of Banks in the Industrialisation of the Czech Crownlands* (Cambridge 1976); I. Berend and G. Ránki, *Hungary: A Century of Economic Development* (New York, 1974); and T. Hočevar's thought-provoking *The Structure of the Slovene Economy, 1848–1953* (New York, 1965). Of German works, A. Hoffmann (ed.), *Österreich-Ungarn als Agrarstaat* (Vienna, 1978) has no English equivalent.

The interplay of economics and politics figures in I. Berend and G. Ránki's article, 'Economic factors in nationalism: the example of Hungary at the beginning of the 20th century', *AHYB*, 3 (1967), part 3, 163–86 and in B. Michel, *Banques et banquiers en Autriche au début du 20e siècle* (Paris, 1976). The works of the leading Croat economic historian of the period are not translated: see, for example, I. Karaman, *Industrijalizacija gradjanske Hrvatske (1800–1941)* (Zagreb, 1991). But G. Drage has a chapter on Croatia and much material on Galicia in his factually rich socio-economic study, *Austria-Hungary* (London, 1909). Sidney Pollard's views can be accessed in his *European Economic Integration, 1815–1970* (London, 1974), Gerschenkron's in his *Economic Backwardness in Historical Perspective* (Cambridge, Mass., 1962)

Chapter 9.   Society and Social Movements

Good recent English-language biographies of Franz Joseph are by J.-P. Bled, *Franz Joseph* (tr. Oxford, 1992) and S. Beller, *Francis Joseph* (London, 1996). The best treatment of his son is B. Hamann, *Kronprinz Rudolf* (Vienna, 1978) but English readers can learn much from L. Cassels, *Clash of Generations: A Habsburg Family Drama in the Nineteenth Century* (Newton Abbot, 1974). Hannes Stekl discusses the Austrian aristocracy in 'Österreichs Hocharistokratie vom 18. bis ins 20 Jahrhundert' in H.-U. Wehler (ed.), *Europäische Adel 1750–1950* (Göttingen, 1990), 145–65, and in case-study form in H. Stekl and M. Wakounig, *Windisch-Graetz. Ein Fürstenhaus im 19 und 20. Jahrhundert* (Vienna, 1992). For the army: G.E. Rothenberg, *The Army of Francis Joseph* (West Lafayette, 1976) and I. Deák's vivid *Beyond Nationalism. The Social and Political History of the Habsburg Officer Corps, 1848–1918* (New York, 1990), helpful not just for officers. On the Church, Volume 4 of *Die Habsburgermonarchie: Die Konfessionen* (Vienna, 1983) is rather orientated to organisational matters, but see W.D. Bowman's helpful 'Religious Associations and the Formation of Political Catholicism in Vienna, 1848 to the 1870s', *AHYB* 27 (1996), 65–76. The relation of the Church to conservative thought is a theme of J.C. Allmayer-Beck, *Der Konservatismus in Österreich* (Munich, 1959).

Bruckmüller, *Sozialgeschichte* (1), Sandgruber, *Konsumgesellschaft* (1) and Drage, *Austria-Hungary* (8) are central on ordinary people's living conditions and W. Hubbard gives an interesting monographic view in *Auf dem Weg zur Grossstadt. Eine Sozialgeschichte der Stadt Graz 1850–1914* (Vienna, 1984). For agricultural labour in Bohemia, see Kadedová, 'Die Lohnwirtschaft auf dem Grossgrundbesitz in Böhmen in der zweiten Hälfte des 19. Jahrhunderts', *Historica* 14 (1967), 123–74, and in Galicia: Kieniewicz, *Emancipation* (3); Himka, *Galician Villagers* (3), and S. Hryniuk, *Peasants with Promise: Ukrainians in Southeastern Galicia, 1880–1900* (Edmonton, 1991). Richly suggestive on peasant mobilisation in German Austria (till 1918), Bohemia and Galicia respectively are E. Bruckmüller, *Landwirtschaftliche Organisationen und gesellschaftliche Modernisierung* (Salzburg, 1977); P. Heumos, *Agrarische Interessen und nationale Politik in Böhmen, 1848–89* (Wiesbaden, 1979), and K. Stanter-Halsted on Polish peasants in patriotic celebrations in *AHYB* 25 (1994), 73–95.

G. Crossick and H.-G. Haupt's innovative collaboration is summarised in *The Petite Bourgeoisie in Europe 1780–1914* (London, New York, 1995). See, for this theme in Austria, some of Josef Ehmer's research in English in their jointly edited *Shopkeepers and Master Artisans in Nineteenth-Century Europe* (London, 1984): 'The artisan family in nineteenth-century Austria', 195–218. The politics of the conservative eighties are the subject of W. Jenks, *Austria under the Iron Ring, 1879–93* (Charlottesville, 1965) and M. Grandner, 'Conservative Social Politics in Austria, 1880–90', *AHYB* 27 (1996), pp. 77–101. J.W. Boyer's classic study of the rise of the Christian Social movement, revealing the local roots of Austrian politics, is *Political Radicalism in Late Imperial Vienna. The Origins of the Christian Social Movement, 1848–1897* (Chicago, London, 1981). Socialism is discussed in English by V.J. Knapp, *Austrian Social Democracy, 1889–1914* (Washington DC, 1988) and J.G. Polack, 'The beginnings of trade unionism among the Slavs of the Austrian Empire', *American Slavic and East European Review*, 14 (1955), pp. 239–59. In German material I have found most convenient K.R. Stadler (ed.), *Sozialistenprozesse. Politische Justiz in Österreich 1870–1936* (Vienna, 1986) for political struggles and W. Maderthaner (ed.), *Sozialdemokratie und Habsburgerstaat* (Vienna, 1988) for organisation, and in Polish the leading historian Józef Buszko's *Dzieje ruchu robotniczego w Galicji zachodniej 1848–1918* (Cracow, 1986).

There is a huge literature in English on Viennese *fin-de-siècle* culture. I recommend Schorske, *Fin-de-siècle Vienna*, A. Janik and S. Toulmin, *Wittgenstein's Vienna* (London, 1973) and S. Beller, *Vienna and the Jews 1867–1938* (CUP, 1989). W. McGrath, *Dionysian Art and Populist Politics in Austria* (New Haven, 1974) offers fascinating case studies of liberal break-up and W. Johnston, *The Austrian Mind. An Intellectual and Social History, 1848–1958* (University of California, 1972) of key intellectuals. Political transition is the theme of L. Höbelt's fine *Kornblume und Kaiseradler. Die deutschfreiheitlichen Parteien Altösterreichs 1882–1918* (Vienna, 1993) and P. Judson's suggestive articles: ' "Whether Race or Conviction Should Be the Standard." National Identity and Liberal Politics in Nineteenth-Century Austria', *AHYB* 22 (1991), 76–95, and ' "Not Another Square Foot!" German Liberalism and the Rights of National Ownership in Nineteenth-Century Austria', *AHYB* 26 (1995), 83–98. Of many recent works on Cisleithanian Jews see, apart from Beller above: R.S. Wistrich, *The Jews of Vienna in the Age of Franz Joseph* (Oxford, 1989); H.J. Kieval, *The Making of Czech Jewry* (New York, Oxford, 1988), with his convenient chapter on this theme in R.S. Wistrich (ed.), *Austrians and Jews in the Twentieth Century* (New York, 1990), and P. Wróbel, 'The Jews of Galicia, 1869–1918', *AHYB*, 25 (1994), 97–138. A general survey is W. McCagg, *A History of Habsburg Jews, 1670–1918* (Bloomington, 1989).

Chapter 10. Nationalism

See general references under chapter 4 above. There is no synthesis on Habsburg nationalism, but theoretical frameworks for east-European-style nationalism are offered by J. Chlebowczyk, *On Small and Young Nations in Europe* (Wrocław, 1980) and in M. Hroch's EUI working paper, *The Social Interpretation of Linguistic Demands in European National Movements* (Florence, 1994). The views expressed in this chapter come mainly from reading of contemporary materials. For language development: R. Lenček, *The Structure and History of the Slovene Language* (Columbia, Ohio, 1982); D. Verges, *Die Standardisierung der slowakischen Literatursprache vom 18. bis 20. Jahrhundert* (Frankfurt, 1984); Z. Vince, *Putovima hrvatskoga književnog jezika* (Zagreb, 1978); R. Hausenblas and J. Kuchař, *Čeština za školou* (Prague, 1979). Vivid case-studies of national tensions are G. Cohen, *The Politics of Ethnic Survival. Germans in Prague, 1861–1914* (Princeton, 1981); M. Glettler, *Die Wiener Tschechen um 1900* (Munich, 1972) and B. Schmid-Egger, *Klerus und Politik in Bohmen um 1900* (Munich, 1974). There is much relevant material in the eight volumes of the European Science Foundation project on *Comparative Studies on Governments and Non-Dominant Ethnic Groups in Europe, 1850–1940* (New

York, 1991–3), particularly those edited respectively by J. Tomiak, *Schooling, Educational Policy and Ethnic Identity* (1991); D.A Kerr, *Religion, State and Ethnic Groups* (1992); S. Vilfan, *Ethnic Groups and Language Rights* (1993), G. Alderman, *Governments, Ethnic Groups and Political Representation* (1993), A. Fikret, *The Formation of National Elites* (1992) and M. Engman, *Ethnic Identity in Urban Europe* (1992). Another often pertinent historiographical genre for national issues is the bi-national symposium; good examples are: K. Obermann and J. Polišenský (eds), *Aus 500 Jahren deutsch-tschechoslowakisher Geschichte* (Berlin, 1958) and W. Leitsch and S. Trawkowski (eds), *Polen im alten Österreich* (Vienna, 1993).

Suggestive on old historiographical trends is R. Plaschka, *Von Palacký bis Pekař* (Graz, 1955). Czech historians have gone furthest in trying to live down nineteenth-century stereotyping: see the witty J. Rak, *Bývali Čechové* (Prague, 1994) on Czech heroic self-images and the bravely non-partisan J. Křen, *Konfliktní společenství* (Toronto, 1989) on Czech–German relations. For an opposite approach: V. Krestić, *History of the Serbs in Croatia and Slavonia 1848–1918* (tr. Belgrade, 1997). There is a large literature on Masaryk, nearly all of whose works have been translated into English. For a respectful biography, P. Selver, *Masaryk* (London, 1940), a more astringent view, R. Szporluk, *The Political Thought of Thomas G. Masaryk* (New York, 1981) and a collective survey, R.B. Pynsent (ed.), *T.G. Masaryk*, 3 vols (London, 1989).

Most helpful on the official treatment of language in Austria are, factually, K. Hugelmann, *Das Nationalitätenrecht des alten Österreich* (Vienna, 1930) and, analytically, G. Stourzh's illuminating 'Die Gleichberechtigung der Volkstämme als Verfassungsprinzip 1848–1918' in volume 3 of *Die Habsburgermonarchie* (Vienna, 1980), 975–1206, and E. Brix's work on census classification, *Die Umgangssprachen in Altösterreich* (Vienna, 1982). The classic study of socialism and the national question is H. Mommsen, *Die Sozialdemokratie und die Nationalitätenfrage im habsburgischen Vielvölkerstaat* (Vienna, 1963) but A. Kogan, 'The Social Democrats and the Conflict of Nationalities in the Habsburg Monarchy', *JMH*, 21 (1949), pp 204–17, helps out in English. For 1897: B. Sutter, *Die Badenischen Sprachenverordnungen*, 2 vols (Graz, 1960) and for the development of extreme German nationalism, A.G. Whiteside: *The Socialism of Fools. Georg Ritter von Schönerer and Austrian Pan-Germanism* (Berkeley, 1975) and his *Austrian National Socialism before 1918* (The Hague, 1962).

Chapter 11: Hungary

There are several good analyses of general trends in Dualist Hungary: the edited volumes of Pamlényi and Sugar (General), Janos, *Politics of Backwardness* (4), and A. Gerő's lively *Modern Hungarian Society in the Making* (Budapest, London, 1995). The leading expert, Péter Hanák, appears in English in his 'Economics, Politics and Sociopolitical Thought in Hungary during the Age of Capitalism', *AHYB*, 11 (1975), 113–35, his contribution to the *AHYB* symposium, volume 3, part 1, and *The Garden and the Workshop: Essays on the Cultural History of Vienna and Budapest* (Princeton, 1998). More of his work is available in German, particularly: *Ungarn in der Donaumonarchie* (Budapest, 1984). Helpful also is L. Péter, 'The Aristocracy, the Gentry and their Political Tradition in Nineteenth-Century Hungary', *SEER*, 70 (1992), pp. 77–110. J. Lukacs, *Budapest, 1900* (London, 1989) is a splendid portait of an era. A political narrative, however, can only be constructed from Hungarian sources, particularly the double volumes apiece of *Magyarország története* covering 1848–1890 and 1890–1918 (Budapest, 1987 and 1988), strong also for socioeconomic themes. Valuable biographies are: G. Vermes, *István Tisza* (New York, 1983), M. Károlyi, *Memoirs of Michael Károlyi* (London, 1956) and G.A. Geyr, *Sándor Wekerle* (Munich, 1993: in German). T. Gottas' *Ungarn im Zeitalter des Hochliberalismus. Studien zum Tisza-Ära* (Vienna, 1976) serve for Kálmán Tisza. See also W. McCagg, *Jewish Nobles and Geniuses in Modern Hungary* (Boulder, 1972), R. Fischer, *Entwicklungsstufen des Antisemitismus in Ungarn, 1867–1939* (Munich, 1988), and J. Gergely, *A politikai katolicizmus Magyarországon (1890–1950)* (Budapest, 1977).

The above have socio-economic imformation, but Held, *Modernisation of Agriculture* (6) and Berend and Ránki, *Century of Economic Development* (8) remain relevant; see also G. Illyés's moving memoir of a farm-servant community in *People of the Puszta* (1936; tr. London, 1967). The first chapter of R. Tökés, *Béla Kun and the Hungarian Soviet Republic* (New York, 1967) and E. Kabos and A. Zsilák, *Studies on the History of the Hungarian Trade Union Movement* (Budapest, 1977) serve English readers. I have found I. Schlett, *A szociáldemokrácia és a magyar tarsadalom 1914-ig* (Budapest, 1982) concisely convenient.

R.W. Seton-Watson's Slovak-orientated *Racial Problems in Hungary* (London, 1908, reprint, 1972) and *The Southern Slav Question and the Habsburg Monarchy* (London, 1911, reprint 1969) first exposed Magyar policies to non-Magyars, the latter remaining the fullest

English account of Croatian Dualist politics. He helped provoke P. Alden (ed.), *Hungary of Today, by members of the Hungarian Government etc* (London, 1909 – revealing). Also helpful for policy to non-Magyars: M. Glettler, *Pittsburg-Wien-Budapest* (Vienna, 1980) on official attempts to oversee emigrant American Slovaks, and P. Hanák (ed.), *Die nationale Frage in der Österreichisch-Ungarischen Monarchie 1900–1918* (Budapest, 1966: concentrates on Hungary). On the 1905–06 crisis, see in English P. Sugar, 'An Underrated Event: The Hungarian Constitutional Crisis of 1905–06', *East European Quarterly*, 15 (1981), pp. 281–306; I. Dolmányos, *A koalíció az 1905–6 évi kormányzati válság idején* (Budapest, 1976) is satisfyingly full on events.

Chapter 12.   Austria-Hungary in the Early Twentieth Century

Fascinating sources for daily life in Vienna and Prague respectively are W. Koči, *Das Leben des kleinen Mannes im Spiegel der Annoncen der Neuen Freien Presse des Jahres 1909* (Vienna D.Phil., 1983) and P. Vošahlíková, *Jak se žilo za času Františka Josefa I* (Prague, 1996). For aspects of education, H. Engelbrecht, *Geschichte des österreichischen Bildungswesens*, Vol. 4 (Vienna, 1986: covers 1848–1918), of bureaucracy, K. Megner, *Beamte* (Vienna, 1986); and of feminism: H. Anderson, *Utopian Feminism. Women's Movements in Fin-de-Siècle Vienna* (New Haven, 1992); D.F. Good *et al.* (eds), *Austrian Women in the Nineteenth and Twentieth Centuries* (Providence, RI, 1996: also in German), and K. David, 'Czech Feminists and Nationalism in the late Habsburg Monarchy', *Journal of Women's History* 3 (1991), 25–45. E. Saurer, 'Women's History in Austria', *AHYB*, 27 (1996), 261–87, offers an overview. See also E. Timms, *Karl Kraus* (New Haven, 1986).

On Austrian politics A. Gerschenkron, *An Economic Spurt that Failed* (Princeton, 1977); W. Jenks, *The Austrian Electoral Reform of 1907* (New York, 1950), and J.W. Boyer's key work *Culture and Political Crisis in Vienna. Christian Socialism in Power, 1897–1918* (Chicago, London, 1995) cover much of the ground, complemented by Höbelt, *Kornblume* (9) and J.C. Allmayer-Beck, *Ministerpräsident Baron Beck* (Vienna, 1956) in German. See also Boyer's insightful articles 'The End of the Old Regime: Visions of Political Reform in Late Imperial Austria', *JMH*, 58 (1986), 159–93, and 'Religion and Political Development in Central Europe around 1900: The View from

Vienna', *AHYB*, 25 (1994), 13–57 and G. Stourzh's similarly suggestive 'The Multinational Empire Revisited: Reflections on Late Imperial Austria', *AHYB* 23 (1992), 1–22. For Czech politics: P. Vyšný, *Neo-Slavism and the Czechs. 1898–1914* (Cambridge, 1977) and S. Konirsch, 'Constitutional Struggles between Czechs and Germans in the Habsburg Monarchy' *JMH*, 27 (1955), 231–61, but further insights are available in German: J. Křen, 'Nationale Selbstbehauptung im Vielvölkerstaat', in J. Křen (ed.), *Integration oder Abgrenzung 1890–1945* (Bremen, 1986), as also Kořálka, *Tschechen im Habsburgerreich* (4). Many have written of Franz Ferdinand in German, including *Erzherzog Franz Ferdinand Studien* (Vienna, 1976) by Robert A. Kann, whose article 'Count Ottokar Czernin and Archduke Francis Ferdinand', *JCEA* 16 (1956–7), 117–45 is eye-opening. J.M. Baernreither, *Fragments of a Political Diary*, ed., J. Redlich (tr. London, 1930) and A. Spitzmüller, *Memoirs of Alexander Spitzmüller*, tr. C. de Bussy (Boulder, 1987) reveal attitudes of the Austrian mandarinate, Redlich's own political diary being available only in German. R. Löw, *Der Zerfall der 'Kleinen Internationale': Nationalitätenkonflikte in der Arbeiterbewegung des alten Österreichs (1889–1914)* (Vienna, 1984) is a helpful adjunct to Mommsen, *Sozialdemokratie und Nationalitätenfrage* (10) after 1907. For Austro-Hungarian relations, see the Introduction in E. Somogyi (ed.), *Die Protokolle des gemeinsamen Ministerrates der österreichisch-ungarischen Monarchie 1896–1907* (Budapest, 1991).

On Hungary, the references for chapter 11, with F. Pölöskei, *Kormányzati politika és parlamenti ellenzék 1910–14* (Budapest, 1970) and Z. Horvath's path-breaking *Die Jahrhundertwende in Ungarn: Geschichte der 2. Reformgeneration, 1896–1914* (Neuwied, 1966). Jászi's critique of Hungarian circumstances can be found in his *Dissolution of the Habsburg Monarchy* (General); L. Congdon reviews the extensive writings on him in 'History and Politics in Hungary: the rehabilitation of Oscar Jászi', *East European Quarterly*, 9 (1975), 315–29. On Bosnia, see S.M. Dzaja, *Bosnien-Herzegowinien in der österreichisch-ungarischen Epoche* (Munich, 1994) for the intelligentsia and V. Dedijer's vivid *The Road to Sarajevo* (London, 1967) for student terrorism; on Slovenia: C. Rogel, *The Slovenes and Yugoslavia, 1890–1914* (New York, 1977). The leading historian of Dualist Croatia, Mirjana Gross, is well represented in German, (for example, 'Erzherzog Franz Ferdinand und die kroatische Frage', *Österreichische Osthefte* 8 (1966), 277–99), less so in English, but see her 'Croatian National- Integrational Ideologies from the End of Illyrism to the Creation of Yugoslavia',

AHYB, 15–16 (1979–80), 3–33. G. Schödl, *Kroatische Politik und 'Jugoslavenstvo'* (Munich, 1990) is strongest on the 'New Course' in Dalmatia.

Chapter 13.   To World War and Collapse

Foreign policy

Can be approached through A.J.P. Taylor, *The Struggle for Mastery in Europe, 1848–1914* (London, 1954) for the European context and Bridge's standard *From Sadowa to Sarajevo* (7) for the Monarchy. Specialists have accounts of Austro-Hungarian policies and the attitudes to the Monarchy of other powers in Parts 1 and 2 respectively of Vol. 6 of *Die Habsburgermonarchie 1848–1918*. For Aehrenthal's foreign ministership, see F.R. Bridge, *Great Britain and Austria-Hungary, 1906–14* (London, 1972) and B. Molden, *Alois Graf Aehrenthal. Sechs Jahre äusserer Politik Österreichs* (Stuttgart, 1917), particularly the conclusion. Schroeder's views are in the last chapter of his Crimean war study (6) and Sked's in his *Decline and Fall* (General). S.R. Williamson, *Austria-Hungary and the Origins of the First World War* (London, 1991) is lucidly concise. For a crucial theme: S. Wank, 'Foreign Policy and the Nationality Problem in Austria-Hungary 1867–1914', *AHYB*, 3, Part 3 (1967), 37–56.

World War

Sound coverage is provided by A.J. May, *The Passing of the Habsburg Monarchy 1914–18*, 2 vols (Philadelphia, 1966); J. Galántai, *Hungary in the First World War* (Budapest, 1989) and R.A. Kann *et al.* (eds), *The Habsburg Empire in World War I* (Boulder, 1977). Military fortunes can be well traced in H. Herwig, *The First World War. Germany and the Central Powers* (London, 1997) and different aspects of the home front through H.L. Rees, *The Czechs during World War I* (Boulder, 1992); R.J. Wegs, *Die österreichische Kriegswirtschaft 1914–18* (Vienna, 1979); G. Gratz and R. Schüller, *Der wirtschaftliche Zusammenbruch Österreich-Ungarns* (Vienna, New Haven, 1930); M. Grandner, *Kooperative Gewerkschaftspolitik in der Kriegswirtschaft* (Vienna, 1992) and R.G. Plaschka *et al.*, *Innere Front*, 2 vols (Munich, 1974: military action against discontent in 1918). On Emperor Charles, G. Brook-Shepherd, *The Last Habsburg* (London, 1958).

For the foreign front, illusions are revealed in S. Burián, *Austria in Dissolution* (London, 1923: Austro-Hungarian foreign minister), G. Gratz and R. Schüller, *The Economic Policy of Austria-Hungary During the War in its External Relations* (New Haven, 1928) and R.A. Kann, *Die Sixtus-Affäre* (Munich, 1966). Of several books on British attitudes to the Monarchy, K.J. Calder, *Britain and the Origins of the New Europe 1914–18* (Cambridge, 1976) and H. and C. Seton-Watson, *The Making of a New Europe. R. W. Seton-Watson and the Last Years of Austria-Hungary* (London, 1981) are the most involved with policy making. T. Glant's lucid *Through the Prism of the Habsburg Monarchy. Hungary in American Diplomacy and Public Opinion in the First World War* (New York, 1998) replaces W. Mamatey's earlier work on the American angle. Z. Zeman, *The Break-up of the Habsburg Monarchy, 1914–18* (Oxford, 1961) is excellent for the Slav exiles but needs to be complemented by L. Valiani, *The End of Austria-Hungary* (London, 1973) on Italian and Hungarian themes. For concise and varied angles, see also M. Cornwall (ed.), *The Last Years of Austria-Hungary* (Exeter, 1990) and the still useful symposium on break-up in *AHYB* 3 (1967), part 3.

Of course, the historical imagination is often sooner stirred by literature and travel than by monographs and statistics. Available in English are the short stories of Jan Neruda and Arthur Schnitzler, the novels of Mór Jókai, the plays of Ferenc Molnár and the contrasting masterpieces of Jaroslav Hašek's *The Good Soldier Svejk* (1920–3), mordantly mocking the Monarchy, and Joseph Roth's *Radetzky March* (1932), with its tone of elegiac farewell. Hopefully, a similar pleasure can be evoked by the accounts of some of the Habsburg lands' visitors, from Sir Nathaniel Wraxall and the musical traveller Dr Charles Burney in the 1770s to John Paget and Peter Evan Turnbull in the 1830s and the historical-cultural sensitivity informing Claudio Magris' *Danube* (1986) in our own day.

Index